Stanley Gibbons
Commonwealth Stamp Catalogue

Cyprus, Gibraltar & Malta

3rd edition 2011

STANLEY GIBBONS LTD
London and Ringwood

By Appointment to Her Majesty The Queen
Stanley Gibbons Ltd, London
Philatelists

Published by Stanley Gibbons Ltd
Editorial, Publications Sales Offices
and Distribution Centre:
7 Parkside, Christchurch Road, Ringwood,
Hants BH24 3SH

British Library Cataloguing in
Publication Data.
A catalogue record for this book is available
from the British Library.

Errors and omissions excepted
the colour reproduction of stamps is only as
accurate as the printing process will allow.

ISBN-10: 0-85259-811-4
ISBN-13: 978-0-85252-811-5

Item No. R 2976-11

Printed by
Stephens & George, Wales

Contents

Stanley Gibbons Holdings Plc

Stanley Gibbons Limited, Stanley Gibbons Auctions
399 Strand, London WC2R OLX
Tel: +44 (0)207 836 8444
Fax: +44 (0)207 836 7342
E-mail: help@stanleygibbons.com
Website: www.stanleygibbons.com
for all departments, Auction and Specialist Stamp Departments.

Open Monday–Friday 9.30 a.m. to 5 p.m. Shop. Open Monday–Friday 9 a.m. to 5.30 p.m. and Saturday 9.30 a.m. to 5.30 p.m.

Stanley Gibbons Publications Gibbons Stamp Monthly and Philatelic Exporter
7 Parkside, Christchurch Road, Ringwood, Hampshire BH24 3SH.
Tel: +44 (0)1425 472363
Fax: +44 (0)1425 470247
E-mail: help@stanleygibbons.com
Publications Mail Order.
FREEPHONE 0800 611622

Monday–Friday 8.30 a.m. to 5 p.m.

Stanley Gibbons (Guernsey) Limited
18–20 Le Bordage, St Peter Port, Guernsey GY1 1DE.
Tel: +44 (0)1481 708270
Fax: +44 (0)1481 708279
E-mail: investment@stanleygibbons.com

Stanley Gibbons (Jersey) Limited
6 Vine Street, St Helier, Jersey, Channel Islands JE2 4WB.
Tel: +44 (0)1534 766711
Fax: +44 (0)1534 766177
E-mail: investment@stanleygibbons.com

Benham Collectibles Limited
Unit K, Concept Court,
Shearway Business Park
Folkestone Kent CT19 4RG
E-mail: benham@benham.com

Fraser's
(a division of Stanley Gibbons Ltd)
399 Strand, London WC2R OLX
Autographs, photographs, letters and documents
Tel: +44 (0)207 836 8444
Fax: +44 (0)207 836 7342
E-mail: sales@frasersautographs.com
Website: www.frasersautographs.com

Monday–Friday 9 a.m. to 5.30 p.m. and Saturday 10 a.m. to 4 p.m.

Stanley Gibbons Publications Overseas Representation
Stanley Gibbons Publications are represented overseas by the following

Australia ***Renniks Publications PTY LTD***
Unit 3 37-39 Green Street,
Banksmeadow, NSW 2019, Australia
Tel: +612 9695 7055
Website: www.renniks.com

Canada ***Unitrade Associates***
99 Floral Parkway, Toronto,
Ontario M6L 2C4, Canada
Tel: +1 416 242 5900
Website: www.unitradeassoc.com

Germany ***Schaubek Verlag Leipzig***
Am Glaeschen 23, D-04420
Markranstaedt, Germany
Tel: +49 34 205 67823
Website: www.schaubek.de

India ***Trustin Philatelic***
96 Richmond Road,
Bangalore 560 025, India
Tel: +9180 222 11 555/ 22 97 516
Tel: +9180500 49500
Email: trustin@vsnl.net

Italy ***Ernesto Marini S.R.L.***
V. Struppa, 300, Genova, 16165, Italy
Tel: +3901 0247-3530
Website: www.ernestomarini.it

Japan ***Japan Philatelic***
PO Box 2, Suginami-Minami,
Tokyo 168-8081, Japan
Tel: +81 3330 41641
Website: www.yushu.co.jp

Netherlands also covers Belgium Denmark, Finland & France
Uitgeverij Davo BV
PO Box 411, Ak Deventer, 7400 Netherlands
Tel: +315 7050 2700
Website: www.davo.nl

New Zealand ***House of Stamps***
PO Box 12, Paraparaumu,
New Zealand
Tel: +61 6364 8270
Website: www.houseofstamps.co.nz

New Zealand ***Philatelic Distributors***
PO Box 863
15 Mount Edgecumbe Street
New Plymouth 4615, New Zealand
Tel: +6 46 758 65 68
Website: www.stampcollecta.com

Norway ***SKANFIL A/S***
SPANAV. 52 / BOKS 2030
N-5504 HAUGESUND, Norway
Tel: +47-52703940
E-mail: magne@skanfil.no

Singapore ***C S Philatelic Agency***
Peninsula Shopping Centre #04-29
3 Coleman Street, 179804, Singapore
Tel: +65 6337-1859
Website: www.cs.com.sg

South Africa ***Peter Bale Philatelics***
P O Box 3719, Honeydew,
2040, South Africa
Tel: +27 11 462 2463
Tel: +27 82 330 3925
E-mail: balep@iafrica.com

Sweden ***Chr Winther Sorensen AB***
Box 43, S-310 20 Knaered, Sweden
Tel: +46 43050743
Website: www.ifsda.org/i/dealer.php?mid=2100&asscd=SE

USA ***Regency Superior Ltd***
229 North Euclid Avenue
Saint Louis, Missouri 63108, USA

PO Box 8277, St Louis,
MO 63156-8277, USA
Toll Free Tel: (800) 782-0066
Tel: (314) 361-5699
Website: www.RegencySuperior.com
Email: info@regencysuperior.com

General Philatelic Information and Guidelines to the Scope of Stanley Gibbons Commonwealth Catalogues

These notes reflect current practice in compiling the Stanley Gibbons Commonwealth Catalogues.

The Stanley Gibbons Stamp Catalogue has a very long history and the vast quantity of information it contains has been carefully built up by successive generations through the work of countless individuals. Philately is never static and the Catalogue has evolved and developed over the years. These notes relate to the current criteria upon which a stamp may be listed or priced. These criteria have developed over time and may have differed somewhat in the early years of this catalogue. These notes are not intended to suggest that we plan to make wholesale changes to the listing of classic issues in order to bring them into line with today's listing policy, they are designed to inform catalogue users as to the policies currently in operation.

PRICES

The prices quoted in this Catalogue are the estimated selling prices of Stanley Gibbons Ltd at the time of publication. They are, unless it is specifically stated otherwise, for examples in fine condition for the issue concerned. Superb examples are worth more; those of a lower quality considerably less.

All prices are subject to change without prior notice and Stanley Gibbons Ltd may from time to time offer stamps below catalogue price. Individual low value stamps sold at 399 Strand are liable to an additional handling charge. Purchasers of new issues should note the prices charged for them contain an element for the service rendered and so may exceed the prices shown when the stamps are subsequently catalogued. Postage and handling charges are extra.

No guarantee is given to supply all stamps priced, since it is not possible to keep every catalogued item in stock. Commemorative issues may, at times, only be available in complete sets and not as individual values.

Quotation of prices. The prices in the left-hand column are for unused stamps and those in the right-hand column are for used.

A dagger (†) denotes that the item listed does not exist in that condition and a blank, or dash, that it exists, or may exist, but we are unable to quote a price.

Prices are expressed in pounds and pence sterling. One pound comprises 100 pence (£1 = 100p).

The method of notation is as follows: pence in numerals (e.g. 10 denotes ten pence); pounds and pence, up to £100, in numerals (e.g. 4.25 denotes four pounds and twenty-five pence); prices above £100 are expressed in whole pounds with the '£' sign shown.

Unused stamps. Great Britain and Commonwealth: the prices for unused stamps of Queen Victoria to King George V are for lightly hinged examples. Unused prices for King Edward VIII, King George VI and Queen Elizabeth issues are for unmounted mint.

Some stamps from the King George VI period are often difficult to find in unmounted mint condition. In such instances we would expect that collectors would need to pay a high proportion of the price quoted to obtain mounted mint examples. Generally speaking lightly mounted mint stamps from this reign, issued before 1945, are in considerable demand.

Used stamps. The used prices are normally for stamps postally used but may be for stamps cancelled-to-order where this practice exists.

A pen-cancellation on early issues can sometimes correctly denote postal use. Instances are individually noted in the Catalogue in explanation of the used price given.

Prices quoted for bisects on cover or large piece are for those dated during the period officially authorised.

Stamps not sold unused to the public (e.g. some official stamps) are priced used only.

The use of 'unified' designs, that is stamps inscribed for both postal and fiscal purposes, results in a number of stamps of very high face value. In some instances these may not have been primarily intended for postal purposes, but if they are so inscribed we include them. We only price such items used, however, where there is evidence of normal postal usage.

Cover prices. To assist collectors, cover prices are quoted for issues up to 1945 at the beginning of each country.

The system gives a general guide in the form of a factor by which the corresponding used price of the basic loose stamp should be multiplied when found in fine average condition on cover.

Care is needed in applying the factors and they relate to a cover which bears a single of the denomination listed; if more than one denomination is present the most highly priced attracts the multiplier and the remainder are priced at the simple figure for used singles in arriving at a total.

The cover should be of non-philatelic origin; bearing the correct postal rate for the period and distance involved and cancelled with the markings normal to the offices concerned. Purely philatelic items have a cover value only slightly greater than the catalogue value for the corresponding used stamps. This applies generally to those high-value stamps used philatelically rather than in the normal course of commerce. Low-value stamps, e.g. ¼d. and ½d., are desirable when used as a single rate on cover and merit an increase in 'multiplier' value.

First day covers in the period up to 1945 are not within the scope of the system and the multiplier should not be used. As a special category of philatelic usage, with wide variations in valuation according to scarcity, they require separate treatment.

Oversized covers, difficult to accommodate on an album page, should be reckoned as worth little more than the corresponding value of the used stamps. The condition of a cover also affects its value. Except for 'wreck covers', serious damage or soiling reduce the value where the postal markings and stamps are ordinary ones. Conversely, visual appeal adds to the value and this can include freshness of appearance, important addresses, old-fashioned but legible handwriting, historic town-names, etc.

The multipliers are a base on which further value would be added to take account of the cover's postal historical importance in demonstrating such things as unusual, scarce or emergency cancels, interesting routes, significant postal markings, combination usage, the development of postal rates, and so on.

Minimum price. The minimum catalogue price quoted is 10p. For individual stamps prices between 10p. and 95p. are provided as a guide for catalogue users. The lowest price charged for individual stamps or sets purchased from Stanley Gibbons Ltd is £1

Set prices. Set prices are generally for one of each value, excluding shades and varieties, but including major colour changes. Where there are alternative shades, etc., the cheapest is usually included. The number of stamps in the set is always stated for clarity. The prices for sets containing *se-tenant* pieces are based on the prices quoted for such combinations, and not on those for the individual stamps.

Varieties. Where plate or cylinder varieties are priced in used condition the price quoted is for a fine used example with the cancellation well clear of the listed flaw.

Specimen stamps. The pricing of these items is explained under that heading.

Stamp booklets. Prices are for complete assembled booklets in fine condition with those issued before 1945 showing normal wear and tear. Incomplete booklets and those which have been 'exploded' will, in general, be worth less than the figure quoted.

Repricing. Collectors will be aware that the market factors of supply and demand directly influence the prices quoted in this Catalogue. Whatever the scarcity of a particular stamp, if there is no one in the market who wishes to buy it cannot be expected to achieve a high price. Conversely, the same item actively sought by numerous potential buyers may cause the price to rise.

All the prices in this Catalogue are examined during the preparation of each new edition by the expert staff of Stanley Gibbons and repriced as necessary. They take many factors into account, including supply and demand, and are in close touch with the international stamp market and the auction world.

Commonwealth cover prices and advice on postal history material originally provided by Edward B Proud.

GUARANTEE

All stamps are guaranteed originals in the following terms:

If not as described, and returned by the purchaser, we undertake to refund the price paid to us in the original transaction. If any stamp is certified as genuine by the Expert Committee of the Royal Philatelic Society, London, or by BPA Expertising Ltd, the purchaser shall not be entitled to make any claim against us for any error, omission or mistake in such certificate.

Consumers' statutory rights are not affected by the above guarantee.

The recognised Expert Committees in this country are those of the Royal Philatelic Society, 41 Devonshire Place, London W1G, 6JY, and BPA Expertising Ltd, PO Box 1141, Guildford, Surrey GU5 0WR. They do not undertake valuations under any circumstances and fees are payable for their services.

MARGINS ON IMPERFORATE STAMPS

Superb | Very fine | Fine | Average | Poor

GUM

Unmounted | Very lightly mounted | Lightly mounted | Mounted/ large part original gum (o.g.). | Heavily mounted small part o.g.

CENTRING

Superb | Very fine | Fine | Average | Poor

CANCELLATIONS

Superb | Very fine | Fine | Average | Poor

Superb | Very fine

Fine | Average | Poor

CONDITION GUIDE

To assist collectors in assessing the true value of items they are considering buying or in reviewing stamps already in their collections, we now offer a more detailed guide to the condition of stamps on which this catalogue's prices are based.

For a stamp to be described as 'Fine', it should be sound in all respects, without creases, bends, wrinkles, pin holes, thins or tears. If perforated, all perforation 'teeth' should be intact, it should not suffer from fading, rubbing or toning and it should be of clean, fresh appearance.

Margins on imperforate stamps: These should be even on all sides and should be at least as wide as half the distance between that stamp and the next. To have one or more margins of less than this width, would normally preclude a stamp from being described as 'Fine'. Some early stamps were positioned very close together on the printing plate and in such cases 'Fine' margins would necessarily be narrow. On the other hand, some plates were laid down to give a substantial gap between individual stamps and in such cases margins would be expected to be much wider.

An 'average' four-margin example would have a narrower margin on one or more sides and should be priced accordingly, while a stamp with wider, yet even, margins than 'Fine' would merit the description 'Very Fine' or 'Superb' and, if available, would command a price in excess of that quoted in the catalogue.

Gum: Since the prices for stamps of King Edward VIII, King George VI and Queen Elizabeth are for 'unmounted' or 'never hinged' mint, even stamps from these reigns which have been very lightly mounted should be available at a discount from catalogue price, the more obvious the hinge marks, the greater the discount.

Catalogue prices for stamps issued prior to King Edward VIII's reign are for mounted mint, so unmounted examples would be worth a premium. Hinge marks on 20th century stamps should not be too obtrusive, and should be at least in the lightly mounted category. For 19th century stamps more obvious hinging would be acceptable, but stamps should still carry a large part of their original gum—'Large part o.g.'—in order to be described as 'Fine'.

Centring: Ideally, the stamp's image should appear in the exact centre of the perforated area, giving equal margins on all sides. 'Fine' centring would be close to this ideal with any deviation having an effect on the value of the stamp. As in the case of the margins on imperforate stamps, it should be borne in mind that the space between some early stamps was very narrow, so it was very difficult to achieve accurate perforation, especially when the technology was in its infancy. Thus, poor centring would have a less damaging effect on the value of a 19th century stamp than on a 20th century example, but the premium put on a perfectly centred specimen would be greater.

Cancellations: Early cancellation devices were designed to 'obliterate' the stamp in order to prevent it being reused and this is still an important objective for today's postal administrations. Stamp collectors, on the other hand, prefer postmarks to be lightly applied, clear, and to leave as much as possible of the design visible. Dated, circular cancellations have long been 'the postmark of choice', but the definition of a 'Fine' cancellation will depend upon the types of cancellation in use at the time a stamp was current—it is clearly illogical to seek a circular datestamp on a Penny Black.

'Fine', by definition, will be superior to 'Average', so, in terms of cancellation quality, if one begins by identifying what 'Average' looks like, then one will be half way to identifying 'Fine'. The illustrations will give some guidance on mid-19th century and mid-20th century cancellations of Great Britain, but types of cancellation in general use in each country and in each period will determine the appearance of 'Fine'.

As for the factors discussed above, anything less than 'Fine' will result in a downgrading of the stamp concerned, while a very fine or superb cancellation will be worth a premium.

Combining the factors: To merit the description 'Fine', a stamp should be fine in every respect, but a small deficiency in one area might be made up for in another by a factor meriting an 'Extremely Fine' description.

Some early issues are so seldom found in what would normally be considered to be 'Fine' condition, the catalogue prices are for a slightly lower grade, with 'Fine' examples being worth a premium. In such cases a note to this effect is given in the catalogue, while elsewhere premiums are given for well-centred, lightly cancelled examples.

Stamps graded at less than fine remain collectable and, in the case of more highly priced stamps, will continue to hold a value. Nevertheless, buyers should always bear condition in mind.

ACKNOWLEDGEMENTS

We are grateful to individual collectors, members of the philatelic trade and specialist societies and study circles for their assistance in improving and extending the Stanley Gibbons range of catalogues. The addresses of societies and study circles relevant to this volume are:

Cyprus Study Circle
Membershop Secretary — Mr. J. Wigmore
19 Riversmeet, Appledore, Bideford,
North Devon EX39 1RE

Gibraltar Study Circle
Membership Secretary — Mr. E.D. Holmes
29 Highgate Road, Woodley, Reading RG5 3ND

Malta Study Circle
Honorary Secretary — Mr. D. Crookes
9a Church Street, Durham DH1 3DG

The Catalogue in General

Contents. The Catalogue is confined to adhesive postage stamps, including miniature sheets. For particular categories the rules are:

(a) Revenue (fiscal) stamps or telegraph stamps are listed only where they have been expressly authorised for postal duty.

(b) Stamps issued only precancelled are included, but normally issued stamps available additionally with precancel have no separate precancel listing unless the face value is changed.

(c) Stamps prepared for use but not issued, hitherto accorded full listing, are nowadays foot-noted with a price (where possible).

(d) Bisects (trisects, etc.) are only listed where such usage was officially authorised.

(e) Stamps issued only on first day covers or in presentation packs and not available separately are not listed but may be priced in a footnote.

(f) New printings are only included in this Catalogue where they show a major philatelic variety, such as a change in shade, watermark or paper. Stamps which exist with or without imprint dates are listed separately; changes in imprint dates are mentioned in footnotes.

(g) Official and unofficial reprints are dealt with by footnote.

(h) Stamps from imperforate printings of modern issues which occur perforated are covered by footnotes, but are listed where widely available for postal use.

Exclusions. The following are excluded:

(a) non-postal revenue or fiscal stamps;

(b) postage stamps used fiscally (although prices are now given for some fiscally used high values);

(c) local carriage labels and private local issues;

(d) bogus or phantom stamps;

(e) railway or airline letter fee stamps, bus or road transport company labels or the stamps of private postal companies operating under licence from the national authority;

(f) cut-outs;

(g) all types of non-postal labels and souvenirs;

(h) documentary labels for the postal service, e.g. registration, recorded delivery, air-mail etiquettes, etc.;

(i) privately applied embellishments to official issues and privately commissioned items generally;

(j) stamps for training postal officers.

(k) Telegraph stamps

Full listing. 'Full listing' confers our recognition and implies allotting a catalogue number and (wherever possible) a price quotation.

In judging status for inclusion in the catalogue broad considerations are applied to stamps. They must be issued by a legitimate postal authority, recognised by the government concerned, and must be adhesives valid for proper postal use in the class of service for which they are inscribed. Stamps, with the exception of such categories as postage dues and officials, must be available to the general public, at face value, in reasonable quantities without any artificial restrictions being imposed on their distribution.

For errors and varieties the criterion is legitimate (albeit inadvertent) sale through a postal administration in the normal course of business. Details of provenance are always important; printers' waste and deliberately manufactured material are excluded.

Certificates. In assessing unlisted items due weight is given to Certificates from recognised Expert Committees and, where appropriate, we will usually ask to see them.

Date of issue. Where local issue dates differ from dates of release by agencies, 'date of issue' is the local date. Fortuitous stray usage before the officially intended date is disregarded in listing.

Catalogue numbers. Stamps of each country are catalogued chronologically by date of issue. Subsidiary classes are placed at the end of the country, as separate lists, with a distinguishing letter prefix to the catalogue number, e.g. D for postage due, O for official and E for express delivery stamps.

The catalogue number appears in the extreme left-column. The boldface Type numbers in the next column are merely cross-references to illustrations.

Once published in the Catalogue, numbers are changed as little as possible; really serious renumbering is reserved for the occasions when a complete country or an entire issue is being rewritten. The edition first affected includes cross-reference tables of old and new numbers.

Our catalogue numbers are universally recognised in specifying stamps and as a hallmark of status.

Illustrations. Stamps are illustrated at three-quarters linear size. Stamps not illustrated are the same size and format as the value shown, unless otherwise indicated. Stamps issued only as miniature sheets have the stamp alone illustrated but sheet size is also quoted. Overprints, surcharges, watermarks and postmarks are normally actual size. Illustrations of varieties are often enlarged to show the detail. Stamp booklet covers are illustrated half-size, unless otherwise indicated.

Designers. Designers' names are quoted where known, though space precludes naming every individual concerned in the production of a set. In particular, photographers supplying material are usually named only where they also make an active contribution in the design stage; posed photographs of reigning monarchs are, however, an exception to this rule.

CONTACTING THE CATALOGUE EDITOR

The editor is always interested in hearing from people who have new information which will improve or correct the Catalogue. As a general rule he must see and examine the actual stamps before they can be considered for listing; photographs or photocopies are insufficient evidence.

Submissions should be made in writing to the Catalogue Editor, Stanley Gibbons Publications at the Ringwood office. The cost of return postage for items submitted is appreciated, and this should include the registration fee if required.

Where information is solicited purely for the benefit of the enquirer, the editor cannot undertake to reply if the answer is already contained in these published notes or if return postage is omitted. Written communications are greatly preferred to enquiries by telephone or e-mail and the editor regrets that he or his staff cannot see personal callers without a prior appointment being made. Correspondence may be subject to delay during the production period of each new edition.

The editor welcomes close contact with study circles and is interested, too, in finding reliable local correspondents who will verify and supplement official information in countries where this is deficient.

We regret we do not give opinions as to the genuineness of stamps, nor do we identify stamps or number them by our Catalogue.

TECHNICAL MATTERS

The meanings of the technical terms used in the catalogue will be found in our *Philatelic Terms Illustrated.*

References below to (more specialised) listings are to be taken to indicate, as appropriate, the Stanley Gibbons *Great Britain Specialised Catalogue* in five volumes or the *Great Britain Concise Catalogue*.

1. Printing

Printing errors. Errors in printing are of major interest to the Catalogue. Authenticated items meriting consideration would include: background, centre or frame inverted or omitted; centre or subject transposed; error of colour; error or omission of value; double prints and impressions; printed both sides; and so on. Designs *tête-bêche*, whether intentionally or by accident, are listable. *Se-tenant* arrangements of stamps are recognised in the listings or footnotes. Gutter pairs (a pair of stamps separated by blank margin) are not included in this volume. Colours only partially omitted are not listed. Stamps with embossing omitted are reserved for our more specialised listings.

Printing varieties. Listing is accorded to major changes in the printing base which lead to completely new types. In recess-printing this could be a design re-engraved; in photogravure or photolithography a screen altered in whole or in part. It can also encompass flat-bed and rotary printing if the results are readily distinguishable.

To be considered at all, varieties must be constant.

Early stamps, produced by primitive methods, were prone to numerous imperfections; the lists reflect this, recognising re-entries, retouches, broken frames, misshapen letters, and so on. Printing technology has, however, radically improved over the years, during which time photogravure and lithography have become predominant. Varieties nowadays are more in the nature of flaws and these, being too specialised for this general catalogue, are almost always outside the scope.

In no catalogue, however, do we list such items as: dry prints, kiss prints, doctor-blade flaws, colour shifts or registration flaws (unless they lead to the complete omission of a colour from an individual stamp), lithographic ring flaws, and so on. Neither do we recognise fortuitous happenings like paper creases or confetti flaws.

Overprints (and surcharges). Overprints of different types qualify for separate listing. These include overprints in different colours; overprints from different printing processes such as litho and typo; overprints in totally different typefaces, etc. Major errors in machine-printed overprints are important and listable. They include: overprint inverted or omitted; overprint double (treble, etc.); overprint diagonal; overprint double, one inverted; pairs with one overprint omitted, e.g. from a radical shift to an adjoining stamp; error of colour; error of type fount; letters inverted or omitted, etc. If the overprint is handstamped, few of these would qualify and a distinction is drawn. We continue, however, to list pairs of stamps where one has a handstamped overprint and the other has not.

Varieties occurring in overprints will often take the form of broken letters, slight differences in spacing, rising spaces, etc. Only the most important would be considered for listing or footnote mention.

Sheet positions. If space permits we quote sheet positions of listed varieties and authenticated data is solicited for this purpose.

De La Rue plates. The Catalogue classifies the general plates used by De La Rue for printing British Colonial stamps as follows:

VICTORIAN KEY TYPE

Die I

1. The ball of decoration on the second point of the crown appears as a dark mass of lines.
2. Dark vertical shading separates the front hair from the bun.
3. The vertical line of colour outlining the front of the throat stops at the sixth line of shading on the neck.
4. The white space in the coil of the hair above the curl is roughly the shape of a pin's head.

Die II

1. There are very few lines of colour in the ball and it appears almost white.
2. A white vertical strand of hair appears in place of the dark shading.

3. The line stops at the eighth line of shading.
4. The white space is oblong, with a line of colour partially dividing it at the left end.

Plates numbered 1 and 2 are both Die I. Plates 3 and 4 are Die II.

GEORGIAN KEY TYPE

Die I

A. The second (thick) line below the name of the country is cut slanting, conforming roughly to the shape of the crown on each side.
B. The labels of solid colour bearing the words "POSTAGE" and "& REVENUE" are square at the inner top corners.
C. There is a projecting "bud" on the outer spiral of the ornament in each of the lower corners.

Die I

A. The second line is cut vertically on each side of the crown.
B. The labels curve inwards at the top.
C. There is no "bud" in this position.

Unless otherwise stated in the lists, all stamps with watermark Multiple Crown CA (w **8**) are Die I while those with watermark Multiple Crown Script CA (w **9**) are Die II. The Georgian Die II was introduced in April 1921 and was used for Plates 10 to 22 and 26 to 28. Plates 23 to 25 were made from Die I by mistake.

2. Paper

All stamps listed are deemed to be on (ordinary) paper of the wove type and white in colour; only departures from this are normally mentioned.

Types. Where classification so requires we distinguish such other types of paper as, for example, vertically and horizontally laid; wove and laid bâtonné; card(board); carton; cartridge; glazed; granite; native; pelure; porous; quadrillé; ribbed; rice; and silk thread.

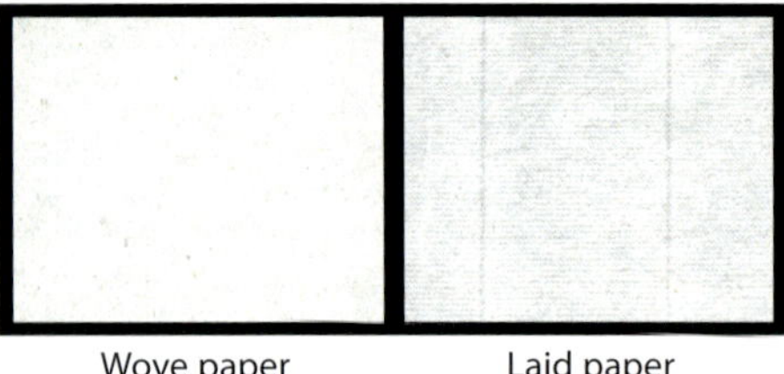

Wove paper　　Laid paper

Granite paper　　Quadrillé paper

Burelé band

The various makeshifts for normal paper are listed as appropriate. The varieties of double paper and joined paper are recognised. The security device of a printed burelé band on the back of a stamp, as in early Queensland, qualifies for listing.

Descriptive terms. The fact that a paper is handmade (and thus probably of uneven thickness) is mentioned where necessary. Such descriptive terms as "hard" and "soft"; "smooth" and "rough"; "thick", "medium" and "thin" are applied where there is philatelic merit in classifying papers.

Coloured, very white and toned papers. A coloured paper is one that is coloured right through (front and back of the stamp). In the Catalogue the colour of the paper is given in italics, thus:

black/*rose* = black design on rose paper.

Papers have been made specially white in recent years by, for example, a very heavy coating of chalk. We do not classify shades of whiteness of paper as distinct varieties. There does exist, however, a type of paper from early days called toned. This is off-white, often brownish or buffish, but it cannot be assigned any definite colour. A toning effect brought on by climate, incorrect storage or gum staining is disregarded here, as this was not the state of the paper when issued.

"Ordinary" and "Chalk-surfaced" papers. The availability of many postage stamps for revenue purposes made necessary some safeguard against the illegitimate re-use of stamps with removable cancellations. This was at first secured by using fugitive inks and later by printing on paper surfaced by coatings containing either chalk or china clay, both of which made it difficult to remove any form of obliteration without damaging the stamp design.

This catalogue lists these chalk-surfaced paper varieties from their introduction in 1905. Where no indication is given, the paper is "ordinary".

The "traditional" method of indentifying chalk-surfaced papers has been that, when touched with a silver wire, a black mark is left on the paper, and the listings in this catalogue are based on that test. However, the test itself is now largely discredited, for, although the mark can be removed by a soft rubber, some damage to the stamp will result from its use.

The difference between chalk-surfaced and pre-war ordinary papers is fairly clear: chalk-surfaced papers being smoother to the touch and showing a characteristic sheen when light is reflected off their surface. Under good magnification tiny bubbles or pock marks can be seen on the surface of the stamp and at the tips of the perforations the surfacing appears "broken". Traces of paper fibres are evident on the surface of ordinary paper and the ink shows a degree of absorption into it.

Initial chalk-surfaced paper printings by De La Rue had a thinner coating than subsequently became the norm. The characteristics described above are less pronounced in these printings.

During and after the Second World War, substitute papers replaced the chalk-surfaced papers, these do not react to the silver test and are therefore classed as "ordinary", although differentiating them without recourse to it is more difficult, for, although the characteristics of the chalk-surfaced paper remained the same, some of the ordinary papers appear much smoother than earlier papers and many do not show the watermark clearly. Experience is the only solution to identifying these, and comparison with stamps whose paper type is without question will be of great help.

Another type of paper, known as "thin striated" was used only for the Bahamas 1s. and 5s. (Nos. 155a, 156a, 171 and 174) and for several stamps of the Malayan states. Hitherto these have been described as "chalk-surfaced" since they gave some reaction to the silver test, but they are much thinner than usual chalk-surfaced papers, with the watermark showing clearly. Stamps on this paper show a slightly 'ribbed' effect when the stamp is held up to the light. Again, comparison with a known striated paper stamp, such as the 1941 Straits Settlements Die II 2c. orange (No. 294) will prove invaluable in separating these papers.

Glazed paper. In 1969 the Crown Agents introduced a new general-purpose paper for use in conjunction with all current printing processes. It generally has a marked glossy surface but the degree varies according to the process used, being more marked in recess-printing stamps. As it does not respond to the silver test this presents a further test where previous printings were on chalky paper. A change of paper to the glazed variety merits separate listing.

Green and yellow papers. Issues of the First World War and immediate postwar period occur on green and yellow papers and these are given separate Catalogue listing. The original coloured papers (coloured throughout) gave way to surface-coloured papers, the stamps having "white backs"; other stamps show one colour on the front and a different one at the back. Because of the numerous variations a grouping of colours is adopted as follows:

Yellow papers

(1) The original *yellow* paper (throughout), usually bright in colour. The gum is often sparse, of harsh consistency and dull-looking. Used 1912–1920.

(2) The *white-backs*. Used 1913–1914.

(3) A bright lemon paper. The colour must have a pronounced greenish tinge, different from the "yellow" in (1). As a rule, the gum on stamps using this lemon paper is plentiful, smooth and shiny, and the watermark shows distinctly. Care is needed with stamps printed in green on yellow paper (1) as it may appear that the paper is this lemon. Used 1914–1916.

(4) An experimental *orange-buff* paper. The colour must have a distinct brownish tinge. It is not to be confused with a muddy yellow (1) nor the misleading appearance (on the surface) of stamps printed in red on yellow paper where an engraved plate has been insufficiently wiped. Used 1918–1921.

(5) An experimental *buff* paper. This lacks the brownish tinge of (4) and the brightness of the yellow shades. The gum is shiny when compared with the matt type used on (4). Used 1919–1920.

(6) A *pale yellow* paper that has a creamy tone to the yellow. Used from 1920 onwards.

Green papers

(7) The original "green" paper, varying considerably through shades of blue-green and yellow-green, the front and back sometimes differing. Used 1912–1916.

(8) The *white backs*. Used 1913–1914.

(9) A paper blue-green on the surface with *pale olive* back. The back must be markedly paler than the front and this and the pronounced olive tinge to the back distinguish it from (7). Used 1916–1920.

(10) Paper with a vivid green surface, commonly called *emerald-green*; it has the olive back of (9). Used 1920.

(11) Paper with *emerald-green* both back and front. Used from 1920 onwards.

3. Perforation and Rouletting

Perforation gauge. The gauge of a perforation is the number of holes in a length of 2 cm. For correct classification the size of the holes (large or small) may need to be distinguished; in a few cases the actual number of holes on each edge of the stamp needs to be quoted.

Measurement. The Gibbons *Instanta* gauge is the standard for measuring perforations. The stamp is viewed against a dark background with the transparent gauge put on top of it. Though the gauge measures to decimal accuracy, perforations read from it are generally quoted in the Catalogue to the nearest half. For example:

Just over perf 12¾ to just under 13¼	= perf 13
Perf 13¼ exactly, rounded up	= perf 13½
Just over perf 13¼ to just under 13¾	= perf 13½
Perf 13¾ exactly, rounded up	= perf 14

However, where classification depends on it, actual quarter-perforations are quoted.

Notation. Where no perforation is quoted for an issue it is imperforate. Perforations are usually abbreviated (and spoken) as follows, though sometimes they may be spelled out for clarity. This notation for rectangular stamps (the majority) applies to diamond shapes if "top" is read as the edge to the top right.

P 14: perforated alike on all sides (read: "perf 14").

P 14×15: the first figure refers to top and bottom, the second to left and right sides (read: "perf 14 by 15"). This is a compound perforation. For an upright triangular stamp the first figure refers to the two sloping sides and second to the base. In inverted triangulars the base is first and the second figure to the sloping sides.

P 14–15: perforation measuring anything between 14 and 15: the holes are irregularly spaced, thus the gauge may vary along a single line or even along a single edge of the stamp (read: "perf 14 to 15").

P 14 *irregular*: perforated 14 from a worn perforator, giving badly aligned holes irregularly spaced (read: "irregular perf 14").

P *comp(ound)* 14×15: two gauges in use but not necessarily on opposite sides of the stamp. It could be one side in one gauge and three in the other; or two adjacent sides with the same gauge. (Read: "perf compound of 14 and 15".) For three gauges or more, abbreviated as "P 12, 14½, 15 *or compound*" for example.

P 14, 14½: perforated approximately 14¼ (read: "perf 14 or 14½"). It does *not* mean two stamps, one perf 14 and the other perf 14½. This obsolescent notation is gradually being replaced in the Catalogue.

Imperf: imperforate (not perforated)

Imperf×P 14: imperforate at top ad bottom and perf 14 at sides.

P 14×*imperf*: perf 14 at top and bottom and imperforate at sides.

Such headings as "P 13×14 (*vert*) and P 14×13 (*horiz*)" indicate which perforations apply to which stamp format—vertical or horizontal.

Some stamps are additionally perforated so that a label or tab is detachable; others have been perforated for use as two halves. Listings are normally for whole stamps, unless stated otherwise.

Imperf×perf

Other terms. Perforation almost always gives circular holes; where other shapes have been used they are specified, e.g. square holes; lozenge perf. Interrupted perfs are brought about by the omission of pins at regular intervals. Perforations merely simulated by being printed as part of the design are of course ignored. With few exceptions, privately applied perforations are not listed.

In the 19th century perforations are often described as clean cut (clean, sharply incised holes), intermediate or rough (rough holes, imperfectly cut, often the result of blunt pins).

Perforation errors and varieties. Authenticated errors, where a stamp normally perforated is accidentally issued imperforate, are listed provided no traces of perforation (blind holes or indentations) remain. They must be provided as pairs, both stamps wholly imperforate, and are only priced in that form.

Stamps imperforate between stamp and sheet margin are not listed in this catalogue, but such errors on Great Britain stamps will be found in the *Great Britain Specialised Catalogue*.

Pairs described as "imperforate between" have the line of perforations between the two stamps omitted.

Imperf between (horiz pair): a horizontal pair of stamps with perfs all around the edges but none between the stamps.

Imperf between (vert pair): a vertical pair of stamps with perfs all around the edges but none between the stamps.

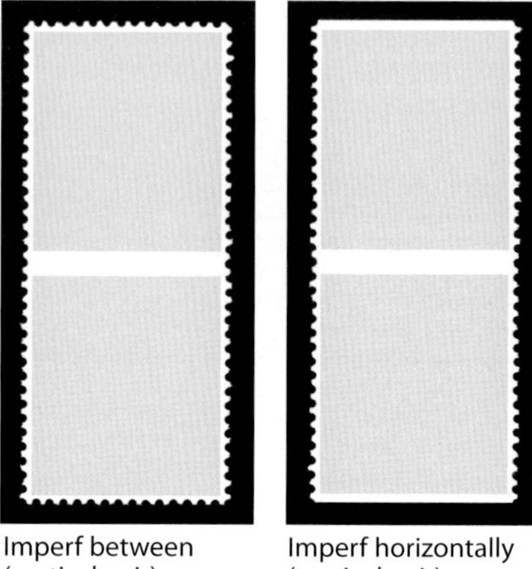
Imperf between (vertical pair) | Imperf horizontally (vertical pair)

Where several of the rows have escaped perforation the resulting varieties are listable. Thus:

Imperf vert (horiz pair): a horizontal pair of stamps perforated top and bottom; all three vertical directions are imperf—the two outer edges and between the stamps.

Imperf horiz (vert pair): a vertical pair perforated at left and right edges; all three horizontal directions are imperf—the top, bottom and between the stamps.

Straight edges. Large sheets cut up before issue to post offices can cause stamps with straight edges, i.e. imperf on one side or on two sides at right angles. They are not usually listable in this condition and are worth less than corresponding stamps properly perforated all round. This does not, however, apply to certain stamps, mainly from coils and booklets, where straight edges on various sides are the manufacturing norm affecting every stamp. The listings and notes make clear which sides are correctly imperf.

Malfunction. Varieties of double, misplaced or partial perforation caused by error or machine malfunction are not listable, neither are freaks, such as perforations placed diagonally from paper folds, nor missing holes caused by broken pins.

Types of perforating. Where necessary for classification, perforation types are distinguished.
These include:

Line perforation from one line of pins punching single rows of holes at a time.

Comb perforation from pins disposed across the sheet in comb formation, punching out holes at three sides of the stamp a row at a time.

Harrow perforation applied to a whole pane or sheet at one stroke.

Rotary perforation from toothed wheels operating across a sheet, then crosswise.

Sewing machine perforation. The resultant condition,

clean-cut or rough, is distinguished where required.

Pin-perforation is the commonly applied term for pin-roulette in which, instead of being punched out, round holes are pricked by sharp-pointed pins and no paper is removed.

Mixed perforation occurs when stamps with defective perforations are re-perforated in a different gauge.

Punctured stamps. Perforation holes can be punched into the face of the stamp. Patterns of small holes, often in the shape of initial letters, are privately applied devices against pilferage. These (perfins) are outside the scope except for Australia, Canada, Cape of Good Hope, Papua and Sudan where they were used as official stamps by the national administration. Identification devices, when officially inspired, are listed or noted; they can be shapes, or letters or words formed from holes, sometimes converting one class of stamp into another.

Rouletting. In rouletting the paper is cut, for ease of separation, but none is removed. The gauge is measured, when needed, as for perforations. Traditional French terms descriptive of the type of cut are often used and types include:

Arc roulette (percé en arc). Cuts are minute, spaced arcs, each roughly a semicircle.

Cross roulette (percé en croix). Cuts are tiny diagonal crosses.

Line roulette (percé en ligne or *en ligne droite).* Short straight cuts parallel to the frame of the stamp. The commonest basic roulette. Where not further described, "roulette" means this type.

Rouletted in colour or coloured roulette (percé en lignes colorées or *en lignes de coleur).* Cuts with coloured edges, arising from notched rule inked simultaneously with the printing plate.

Saw-tooth roulette (percé en scie). Cuts applied zigzag fashion to resemble the teeth of a saw.

Serpentine roulette (percé en serpentin). Cuts as sharply wavy lines.

Zigzag roulette (percé en zigzags). Short straight cuts at angles in alternate directions, producing sharp points on separation. US usage favours "serrate(d) roulette" for this type.

Pin-roulette (originally *percé en points* and now *perforés trous d'epingle*) is commonly called pin-perforation in English.

4. Gum

All stamps listed are assumed to have gum of some kind; if they were issued without gum this is stated. Original gum (o.g.) means that which was present on the stamp as issued to the public. Deleterious climates and the presence of certain chemicals can cause gum to crack and, with early stamps, even make the paper deteriorate. Unscrupulous fakers are adept in removing it and regumming the stamp to meet the unreasoning demand often made for "full o.g." in cases where such a thing is virtually impossible.

The gum normally used on stamps has been gum ararbic until the late 1960s when synthetic adhesives were introduced. Harrison and Sons Ltd for instance use *polyvinyl alcohol,* known to philatelists as PVA. This is almost invisible except for a slight yellowish tinge which was incorporated to make it possible to see that the stamps have been gummed. It has advantages in hot countries, as stamps do not curl and sheets are less likely to stick together. Gum arabic and PVA are not distinguished in the lists except that where a stamp exists with both forms this is indicated in footnotes. Our more specialised catalogues provide separate listing of gums for Great Britain.

Self-adhesive stamps are issued on backing paper, from which they are peeled before affixing to mail. Unused examples are priced as for backing paper intact, in which condition they are recommended to be kept. Used examples are best collected on cover or on piece.

5. Watermarks

Stamps are on unwatermarked paper except where the heading to the set says otherwise.

Detection. Watermarks are detected for Catalogue description by one of four methods: (1) holding stamps to the light; (2) laying stamps face down on a dark background; (3) adding a few drops of petroleum ether 40/60 to the stamp laid face down in a watermark tray; (4) by use of the Stanley Gibbons Detectamark, or other equipment, which work by revealing the thinning of the paper at the watermark. (Note that petroleum ether is highly inflammable in use and can damage photogravure stamps.)

Listable types. Stamps occurring on both watermarked and unwatermarked papers are different types and both receive full listing.

Single watermarks (devices occurring once on every stamp) can be modified in size and shape as between different issues; the types are noted but not usually separately listed. Fortuitous absence of watermark from a single stamp or its gross displacement would not be listable.

To overcome registration difficulties the device may be repeated at close intervals *(a multiple watermark),* single stamps thus showing parts of several devices. Similarly, a *large sheet watermark* (or *all-over watermark*) covering numerous stamps can be used. We give informative notes and illustrations for them. The designs may be such that numbers of stamps in the sheet automatically lack watermark: this is not a listable variety. Multiple and all-over watermarks sometimes undergo modifications, but if the various types are difficult to distinguish from single stamps notes are given but not separate listings.

Papermakers' watermarks are noted where known but not listed separately, since most stamps in the sheet will lack them. Sheet watermarks which are nothing more than officially adopted papermakers' watermarks are, however, given normal listing.

Marginal watermarks, falling outside the pane of stamps, are ignored except where misplacement caused the adjoining row to be affected, in which case they may be footnoted.

Watermark errors and varieties. Watermark errors are recognised as of major importance. They comprise stamps intended to be on unwatermarked paper but issued watermarked by mistake, or stamps printed on paper with the wrong watermark. Varieties showing letters omitted from the watermark are also included, but broken or deformed bits on the dandy roll are not listed unless they represent repairs.

Watermark positions. The diagram shows how watermark position is described in the Catalogue. Paper has a side intended for printing and watermarks are usually impressed so that they read normally when looked through from that printed side. However, since philatelists customarily detect watermarks by looking at the back of the stamp the watermark diagram also makes clear what is actually seen.

Illustrations in the Catalogue are of watermarks in normal positions (from the front of the stamps) and are actual size where possible.

Differences in watermark position are collectable varieties. This Catalogue now lists inverted, sideways inverted and reversed watermark varieties on Commonwealth stamps from the 1860s onwards except where the watermark position is completely haphazard.

Great Britain inverted and sideways inverted watermarks can be found in the *Great Britain Specialised Catalogue* and the *Great Britain Concise Catalogue*.

Where a watermark comes indiscriminately in various positions our policy is to cover this by a general note: we do not give separate listings because the watermark position in these circumstances has no particular philatelic importance.

AS DESCRIBED (Read through front of stamp)		AS SEEN DURING WATERMARK DETECTION (Stamp face down and back examined)
GvR	Normal	GvR
GvR	Inverted	GvR
GvR	Reversed	GvR
GvR	Reversed and Inverted	GvR
GvR	Sideways	GvR
GvR	Sideways Inverted	GvR

Standard types of watermark. Some watermarks have been used generally for various British possessions rather than exclusively for a single colony. To avoid repetition the Catalogue classifies 11 general types, as under, with references in the headings throughout the listings being given either in words or in the form ("W w **9**") (meaning "watermark type w **9**"). In those cases where watermark illustrations appear in the listings themselves, the respective reference reads, for example, W **153**, thus indicating that the watermark will be found in the normal sequence of illustrations as (type) **153**.

The general types are as follows, with an example of each quoted.

W	*Description*	*Example*
w **1**	Large Star	St. Helena No. 1
w **2**	Small Star	Turks Is. No. 4
w **3**	Broad (pointed) Star	Grenada No. 24
w **4**	Crown (over) CC, small stamp	Antigua No. 13
w **5**	Crown (over) CC, large stamp	Antigua No. 31
w **6**	Crown (over) CA, small stamp	Antigua No. 21
w **7**	Crown CA (CA over Crown), large stamp	Sierra Leone No. 54
w **8**	Multiple Crown CA	Antigua No. 41
w **9**	Multiple Script CA	Seychelles No. 158
w **9***a*	do. Error	Seychelles No. 158a
w **9***b*	do. Error	Seychelles No. 158b
w **10**	V over Crown	N.S.W. No. 327
w **11**	Crown over A	N.S.W. No. 347

CC in these watermarks is an abbreviation for "Crown Colonies" and CA for "Crown Agents". Watermarks w **1**, w **2** and w **3** are on stamps printed by Perkins, Bacon; w **4** onwards on stamps from De La Rue and other printers.

w **1**
Large Star

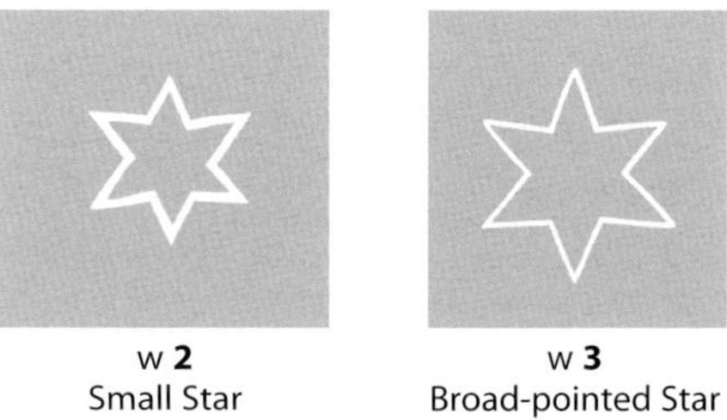

w **2**
Small Star

w **3**
Broad-pointed Star

Watermark w **1**, *Large Star*, measures 15 to 16 mm across the star from point to point and about 27 mm from centre to centre vertically between stars in the sheet. It was made for long stamps like Ceylon 1857 and St. Helena 1856.

Watermark w **2**, *Small Star* is of similar design but measures 12 to 13½ mm from point to point and 24 mm from centre to centre vertically. It was for use with ordinary-size stamps such as Grenada 1863–71.

When the Large Star watermark was used with the smaller stamps it only occasionally comes in the centre of the paper. It is frequently so misplaced as to show portions of two stars above and below and this eccentricity will very often help in determining the watermark.

Watermark w **3**, *Broad-pointed Star*, resembles w **1** but the points are broader.

w **4**
Crown (over) CC

w **5**
Crown (over) CC

Two *Crown (over) CC* watermarks were used: w **4** was for stamps of ordinary size and w **5** for those of larger size.

w **6**
Crown (over) CA

w **7**
CA over Crown

Two watermarks of *Crown CA* type were used, w **6** being for stamps of ordinary size. The other, w **7**, is properly described as *CA over Crown*. It was specially made for paper on which it was intended to print long fiscal stamps: that some were used postally accounts for the appearance of w **7** in the Catalogue. The watermark occupies twice the space of the ordinary Crown CA watermark, w **6**. Stamps of normal size printed on paper with w **7** watermark show it *sideways*; it takes a horizontal pair of stamps to show the entire watermark.

w **8**
Multiple Crown CA

w **9**
Multiple Script CA

Multiple watermarks began in 1904 with w **8**, *Multiple Crown CA,* changed from 1921 to w **9**, *Multiple Script CA*. On stamps of ordinary size portions of two or three watermarks appear and on the large-sized stamps a greater number can be observed. The change to letters in script character with w **9** was accompanied by a Crown of distinctly different shape.

It seems likely that there were at least two dandy rolls for each Crown Agents watermark in use at any one time with a reserve roll being employed when the normal one was withdrawn for maintenance or repair.

Both the Mult Crown CA and the Mult Script CA types exist with one or other of the letters omitted from individual impressions. It is possible that most of these occur from the reserve rolls as they have only been found on certain issues. The MCA watermark experienced such problems during the early 1920s and the Script over a longer period from the early 1940s until 1951.

During the 1920s damage must also have occurred on one of the Crowns as a substituted Crown has been found on certain issues. This is smaller than the normal and consists of an oval base joined to two upright ovals with a circle positioned between their upper ends. The upper line of the Crown's base is omitted, as are the left and right-hand circles at the top and also the cross over the centre circle.

Substituted Crown

The *Multiple Script CA* watermark, w **9**, is known with two errors, recurring among the 1950–52 printings of several territories. In the first a crown has fallen away from the dandy-roll that impresses the watermark into the paper pulp. It gives w **9a**, *Crown missing*, but this omission has been found in both "Crown only" (*illustrated*) and "Crown CA" rows. The resulting faulty paper was used for Bahamas, Johore, Seychelles and the postage due stamps of nine colonies

w **9a**: Error, Crown missing

w **9b**: Error, St. Edward's Crown

When the omission was noticed a second mishap occurred, which was to insert a wrong crown in the space, giving w **9b**, St. Edward's Crown. This produced varieties in Bahamas, Perlis, St. Kitts-Nevis and Singapore and the incorrect crown likewise occurs in (Crown only) and (Crown CA) rows.

w **10**
V over Crown

w **11**
Crown over A

Resuming the general types, two watermarks found in issues of several Australian States are: w **10**, *V over Crown*, and w **11**, *Crown over A*.

w **12**
Multiple St. Edward's Crown Block CA

w **13**
Multiple PTM

The *Multiple St. Edward's Crown Block CA* watermark, w **12**, was introduced in 1957 and besides the change in the Crown (from that used in Multiple Crown Script CA, w **9**) the letters reverted to block capitals. The new watermark began to appear sideways in 1966 and these stamps are generally listed as separate sets.

The watermark w **13**, *Multiple PTM*, was introduced for new Malaysian issues in November 1961.

w **14**
Multiple Crown CA Diagonal

By 1974 the two dandy-rolls (the "upright" and the "sideways") for w **12** were wearing out; the Crown Agents therefore discontinued using the sideways watermark one and retained the other only as a stand-by. A new dandy-roll with the pattern of w **14.** *Multiple Crown CA Diagonal,* was introduced and first saw use with some Churchill Centenary issues.

The new watermark had the design arranged in gradually spiralling rows. It is improved in design to allow smooth passage over the paper (the gaps between letters and rows had caused jolts in previous dandy-rolls) and the sharp corners and angles, where fibres used to accumulate, have been eliminated by rounding.

This watermark had no "normal" sideways position amongst the different printers using it. To avoid confusion our more specialised listings do not rely on such terms as "sideways inverted" but describe the direction in which the watermark points.

w **15**
Multiple POST OFFICE

During 1981 w **15.** *Multiple POST OFFICE* was introduced for certain issues prepared by Philatelists Ltd, acting for various countries in the Indian Ocean, Pacific and West Indies.

w **16**
Multiple Crown Script CA Diagonal

A new Crown Agents watermark was introduced during 1985, w **16**, *Multiple Crown Script CA Diagonal.* This was very similar to the previous w **14**, but showed "CA" in script rather than block letters. It was first used on the omnibus series of stamps commemorating the Life and Times of Queen Elizabeth the Queen Mother.

6. Colours

Stamps in two or three colours have these named in order of appearance, from the centre moving outwards. Four colours or more are usually listed as multicoloured.

In compound colour names the second is the predominant one, thus:

orange-red = a red tending towards orange;
red-orange = an orange containing more red than usual.

Standard colours used. The 200 colours most used for stamp identification are given in the Stanley Gibbons Stamp Colour Key. The Catalogue has used the Stamp Colour Key as standard for describing new issues for some years. The names are also introduced as lists are rewritten, though exceptions are made for those early issues where traditional names have become universally established.

Determining colours. When comparing actual stamps with colour samples in the Stamp Colour Key, view in a good north daylight (or its best substitute; fluorescent "colour matching" light). Sunshine is not recommended. Choose a solid portion of the stamp design; if available, marginal markings such as solid bars of colour or colour check dots are helpful. Shading lines in the design can be misleading as they appear lighter than solid colour. Postmarked portions of a stamp appear darker than normal. If more than one colour is present, mask off the extraneous ones as the eye tends to mix them.

Errors of colour. Major colour errors in stamps or overprints which qualify for listing are: wrong colours; one colour inverted in relation to the rest; albinos (colourless impressions), where these have Expert Committee certificates; colours completely omitted, but only on unused stamps (if found on used stamps the information is footnoted) and with good credentials, missing colours being frequently faked.

Colours only partially omitted are not recognised, Colour shifts, however spectacular, are not listed.

Shades. Shades in philately refer to variations in the intensity of a colour or the presence of differing amounts of other colours. They are particularly significant when they can be linked to specific printings. In general, shades need to be quite marked to fall within the scope of this Catalogue; it does not favour nowadays listing the often numerous shades of a stamp, but chooses a single applicable colour name which will indicate particular groups of outstanding shades. Furthermore, the listings refer to colours as issued; they may deteriorate into something different through the passage of time.

Modern colour printing by lithography is prone to marked differences of shade, even within a single run, and variations can occur within the same sheet. Such shades are not listed.

Aniline colours. An aniline colour meant originally one derived from coal-tar; it now refers more widely to colour of a particular brightness suffused on the surface of a stamp and showing through clearly on the back.

Colours of overprints and surcharges. All overprints and surcharges are in black unless stated otherwise in the heading or after the description of the stamp.

7. Specimen Stamps

Originally, stamps overprinted SPECIMEN were circulated to postmasters or kept in official records, but after the establishment of the Universal Postal Union supplies were sent to Berne for distribution to the postal administrations of member countries.

During the period 1884 to 1928 most of the stamps of British Crown Colonies required for this purpose were overprinted SPECIMEN in various shapes and sizes by their printers from typeset formes. Some locally produced provisionals were handstamped locally, as were sets prepared for presentation. From 1928 stamps were punched with holes forming the word SPECIMEN, each firm of printers using a different machine or machines. From 1948 the stamps supplied for UPU distribution were no longer punctured.

Stamps of some other Commonwealth territories were overprinted or handstamped locally, while stamps of Great Britain and those overprinted for use in overseas postal agencies (mostly of the higher denominations) bore SPECIMEN overprints and handstamps applied by the Inland Revenue or the Post Office.

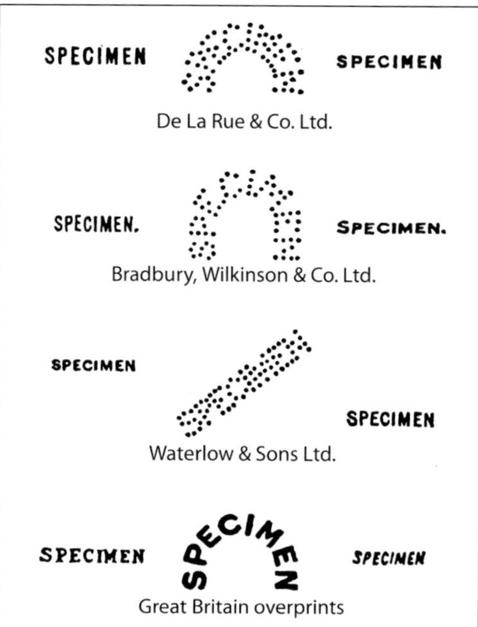

Some of the commoner types of overprints or punctures are illustrated here. Collectors are warned that dangerous forgeries of the punctured type exist.

The *Stanley Gibbons Commonwealth Catalogues* record those Specimen overprints or perforations intended for distribution by the UPU to member countries. In addition the Specimen overprints of Australia and its dependent territories, which were sold to collectors by the Post Office, are also included.

Various Perkins Bacon issues exist obliterated with a "CANCELLED" within an oval of bars handstamp.

Perkins Bacon "CANCELLED" Handstamp

This was applied to six examples of those issues available in 1861 which were then given to members of Sir Rowland Hill's family. 75 different stamps (including four from Chile) are recorded with this handstamp although others may possibly exist. The unauthorised gift of these "CANCELLED" stamps to the Hill family was a major factor in the loss of the Agent General for the Crown Colonies (the forerunner of the Crown Agents) contracts by Perkins Bacon in the following year. Where examples of these scarce items are known to be in private hands the catalogue provides a price.

For full details of these stamps see *CANCELLED by Perkins Bacon* by Peter Jaffé (published by Spink in 1998).

All other Specimens are outside the scope of this volume.

Specimens are not quoted in Great Britain as they are fully listed in the Stanley Gibbons *Great Britain Specialised Catalogue*.

In specifying type of specimen for individual high-value stamps, "H/S" means handstamped, "Optd" is overprinted and "Perf" is punctured. Some sets occur mixed, e.g. "Optd/Perf". If unspecified, the type is apparent from the date or it is the same as for the lower values quoted as a set.

Prices. Prices for stamps up to £1 are quoted in sets; higher values are priced singly. Where specimens exist in more than one type the price quoted is for the cheapest. Specimen stamps have rarely survived even as pairs; these and strips of three, four or five are worth considerably more than singles.

8. Luminescence

Machines which sort mail electronically have been introduced in recent years. In consequence some countries have issued stamps on flourescent or phosphorescent papers, while others have marked their stamps with phosphor bands.

The various papers can only be distinguished by ultraviolet lamps emitting particular wavelengths. They are separately listed only when the stamps have some other means of distinguishing them, visible without the use of these lamps. Where this is not so, the papers are recorded in footnotes or headings.

For this catalogue we do not consider it appropriate that collectors be compelled to have the use of an ultraviolet lamp before being able to identify stamps by our listings. Some experience will also be found necessary in interpreting the results given by ultraviolet. Collectors using the lamps, nevertheless, should exercise great care in their use as exposure to their light is potentially dangerous to the eyes.

Phosphor bands are listable, since they are visible to the naked eye (by holding stamps at an angle to the light and looking along them, the bands appear dark). Stamps existing with or without phosphor bands or with differing numbers of bands are given separate listings. Varieties such as double bands, bands omitted, misplaced or printed on the back are not listed.

Detailed descriptions appear at appropriate places in the listings in explanation of luminescent papers; see, for example, Australia above No.363, Canada above Nos. 472 and 611, Cook Is. above 249, etc.

For Great Britain, where since 1959 phosphors have played a prominent and intricate part in stamp issues, the main notes above Nos. 599 and 723 should be studied, as well as the footnotes to individual listings where appropriate. In general the classification is as follows.

Stamps with phosphor bands are those where a separate cylinder applies the phosphor after the stamps are printed. Issues with "all-over" phosphor have the "band" covering the entire stamp. Parts of the stamp covered by phosphor bands, or the entire surface for "all-over" phosphor versions, appear matt. Stamps on phosphorised paper have the phosphor added to the paper coating before the stamps are printed. Issues on this paper have a completely shiny surface.

Further particularisation of phosphor – their methods of printing and the colours they exhibit under ultraviolet – is outside the scope. The more specialised listings should be consulted for this information.

9. Coil Stamps

Stamps issued only in coil form are given full listing. If stamps are issued in both sheets and coils the coil stamps are listed separately only where there is some feature (e.g. perforation or watermark sideways) by which singles can be distinguished. Coil stamps containing different stamps *se-tenant* are also listed.

Coil join pairs are too random and too easily faked to permit of listing; similarly ignored are coil stamps which have accidentally suffered an extra row of perforations from the claw mechanism in a malfunctioning vending machine.

10. Stamp Booklets

Stamp booklets are now listed in this catalogue.

Single stamps from booklets are listed if they are distinguishable in some way (such as watermark or perforation) from similar sheet stamps.

Booklet panes are listed where they contain stamps of different denominations *se-tenant*, where stamp-size labels are included, or where such panes are otherwise identifiable. Booklet panes are placed in the listing under the lowest denomination present.

Particular perforations (straight edges) are covered by appropriate notes.

11. Miniature Sheets and Sheetlets

We distinguish between "miniature sheets" and "sheetlets" and this affects the catalogue numbering. An item in sheet form that is postally valid, containing a single stamp, pair, block or set of stamps, with wide, inscribed and/or decorative margins, is a miniature sheet if it is sold at post offices as an indivisable entity. As such the Catalogue allots a single MS number and describes what stamps make it up. The sheetlet or small sheet differs in that the individual stamps are intended to be purchased separately for postal purposes. For sheetlets, all the component postage stamps are numbered individually and the composition explained in a footnote. Note that the definitions refer to post office sale—not how items may be subsequently offered by stamp dealers.

12. Forgeries and Fakes

Forgeries. Where space permits, notes are considered if they can give a concise description that will permit unequivocal detection of a forgery. Generalised warnings, lacking detail, are not nowadays inserted, since their value to the collector is problematic.

Forged cancellations have also been applied to genuine stamps. This catalogue includes notes regarding those manufactured by "Madame Joseph", together with the cancellation dates known to exist. It should be remembered that these dates also exist as genuine cancellations.

For full details of these see *Madame Joseph Forged Postmarks* by Derek Worboys (published by the Royal Philatelic Society London and the British Philatelic Trust in 1994) or *Madame Joseph Revisited* by Brian Cartwright (published by the Royal Philatelic Society London in 2005).

Fakes. Unwitting fakes are numerous, particularly "new shades" which are colour changelings brought about by exposure to sunlight, soaking in water contaminated with dyes from adherent paper, contact with oil and dirt from a pocketbook, and so on. Fraudulent operators, in addition, can offer to arrange: removal of hinge marks; repairs of thins on white or coloured papers; replacement of missing margins or perforations; reperforating in true or false gauges; removal of fiscal cancellations; rejoining of severed pairs, strips and blocks; and (a major hazard) regumming. Collectors can only be urged to purchase from reputable sources and to insist upon Expert Committee certification where there is any kind of doubt.

The Catalogue can consider footnotes about fakes where these are specific enough to assist in detection.

Abbreviations

Printers

A.B.N. Co.	American Bank Note Co, New York.
B.A.B.N.	British American Bank Note Co. Ottawa
B.D.T.	B.D.T. International Security Printing Ltd, Dublin, Ireland
B.W.	Bradbury Wilkinson & Co, Ltd.
Cartor	Cartor S.A., La Loupe, France
C.B.N.	Canadian Bank Note Co, Ottawa.
Continental	Continental Bank Note Co. B.N. Co.
Courvoisier	Imprimerie Courvoisier S.A., La-Chaux-de-Fonds, Switzerland.
D.L.R.	De La Rue & Co, Ltd, London.
Enschedé	Joh. Enschedé en Zonen, Haarlem, Netherlands.
Format	Format International Security Printers Ltd., London
Harrison	Harrison & Sons, Ltd. London
J.W.	John Waddington Security Print Ltd., Leeds
P.B.	Perkins Bacon Ltd, London.
Questa	Questa Colour Security Printers Ltd, London
Walsall	Walsall Security Printers Ltd
Waterlow	Waterlow & Sons, Ltd, London.

General Abbreviations

Alph	Alphabet
Anniv	Anniversary
Comp	Compound (perforation)
Des	Designer; designed
Diag	Diagonal; diagonally
Eng	Engraver; engraved
F.C.	Fiscal Cancellation
H/S	Handstamped
Horiz	Horizontal; horizontally
Imp, Imperf	Imperforate
Inscr	Inscribed
L	Left
Litho	Lithographed
mm	Millimetres
MS	Miniature sheet
N.Y.	New York
Opt(d)	Overprint(ed)
P or P-c	Pen-cancelled
P, Pf or Perf	Perforated
Photo	Photogravure
Pl	Plate
Pr	Pair
Ptd	Printed
Ptg	Printing
R	Right
R.	Row
Recess	Recess-printed
Roto	Rotogravure
Roul	Rouletted
S	Specimen (overprint)
Surch	Surcharge(d)
T.C.	Telegraph Cancellation
T	Type
Typo	Typographed
Un	Unused
Us	Used
Vert	Vertical; vertically
W or wmk	Watermark
Wmk s	Watermark sideways

(†) = Does not exist

(–) (or blank price column) = Exists, or may exist, but no market price is known.

/ between colours means "on" and the colour following is that of the paper on which the stamp is printed.

Colours of Stamps

Bl (blue); blk (black); brn (brown); car, carm (carmine); choc (chocolate); clar (claret); emer (emerald); grn (green); ind (indigo); mag (magenta); mar (maroon); mult (multicoloured); mve (mauve); ol (olive); orge (orange); pk (pink); pur (purple); scar (scarlet); sep (sepia); turq (turquoise); ultram (ultramarine); verm (vermilion); vio (violet); yell (yellow).

Colour of Overprints and Surcharges

(B.) = blue, (Blk.) = black, (Br.) = brown, (C.) = carmine, (G.) = green, (Mag.) = magenta, (Mve.) = mauve, (Ol.) = olive, (O.) = orange, (P.) = purple, (Pk.) = pink, (R.) = red, (Sil.) = silver, (V.) = violet, (Vm.) or (Verm.) = vermilion, (W.) = white, (Y.) = yellow.

Arabic Numerals

As in the case of European figures, the details of the Arabic numerals vary in different stamp designs, but they should be readily recognised with the aid of this illustration.

0 1 2 3 4 5 6 7 8 9

Features Listing

An at-a-glance guide to what's in the Stanley Gibbons catalogues

Area	Feature	Collect British Stamps	Stamps of the World	Thematic Catalogues	Comprehensive Catalogue, Parts 1-22 (including Commonwealth and British Empire Stamps and country catalogues)	Great Britain Concise	Specialised catalogues
General	SG number	√	√	√	√	√	√
General	Specialised Catalogue number						√
General	Year of issue of first stamp in design	√	√	√	√	√	√
General	Exact date of issue of each design				√	√	√
General	Face value information	√	√	√	√	√	√
General	Historical and geographical information	√	√	√	√	√	√
General	General currency information, including dates used	√	√	√	√	√	√
General	Country name	√	√	√	√	√	√
General	Booklet panes				√	√	√
General	Coil stamps				√		√
General	First Day Covers	√				√	√
General	Brief footnotes on key areas of note	√	√	√	√	√	√
General	Detailed footnotes on key areas of note				√	√	√
General	Extra background information				√	√	√
General	Miniature sheet information (including size in mm)	√	√	√	√	√	√
General	Sheetlets				√		
General	Stamp booklets				√	√	√
General	Perkins Bacon "Cancelled"				√		
General	PHQ Cards	√				√	√
General	Post Office Label Sheets					√	
General	Post Office Yearbooks	√				√	√
General	Presentation and Souvenir Packs	√				√	√
General	*Se-tenant* pairs	√			√	√	√
General	Watermark details - errors, varieties, positions				√	√	√
General	Watermark illustrations	√			√	√	√
General	Watermark types	√			√	√	√
General	Forgeries noted				√		√
General	Surcharges and overprint information	√	√	√	√	√	√
Design and Description	Colour description, simplified		√	√			
Design and Description	Colour description, extended	√			√	√	√
Design and Description	Set design summary information	√	√	√	√	√	√
Design and Description	Designer name				√	√	√
Design and Description	Short design description	√	√	√	√	√	√

Area	Feature	Collect British Stamps	Stamps of the World	Thematic Catalogues	Comprehensive Catalogue, Parts 1-22 (including Commonwealth and British Empire Stamps and country catalogues)	Great Britain Concise	Specialised catalogues
Design and Description	Shade varieties				√	√	√
Design and Description	Type number	√	√		√	√	√
Illustrations	Multiple stamps from set illustrated	√			√	√	√
Illustrations	A Stamp from each set illustrated in full colour (where possible, otherwise mono)	√	√	√	√	√	√
Price	Catalogue used price	√	√	√	√	√	√
Price	Catalogue unused price	√	√	√	√	√	√
Price	Price - booklet panes				√	√	√
Price	Price - shade varieties				√	√	√
Price	On cover and on piece price				√	√	√
Price	Detailed GB pricing breakdown	√			√	√	√
Print and Paper	Basic printing process information	√	√	√	√	√	√
Print and Paper	Detailed printing process information, e.g. Mill sheets				√		√
Print and Paper	Paper information				√		√
Print and Paper	Detailed perforation information	√			√	√	√
Print and Paper	Details of research findings relating to printing processes and history						√
Print and Paper	Paper colour	√	√		√	√	√
Print and Paper	Paper description to aid identification				√	√	√
Print and Paper	Paper type				√	√	√
Print and Paper	Ordinary or chalk-surfaced paper				√	√	√
Print and Paper	Embossing omitted note						√
Print and Paper	Essays, Die Proofs, Plate Descriptions and Proofs, Colour Trials information						√
Print and Paper	Glazed paper				√	√	√
Print and Paper	Gum details				√		√
Print and Paper	Luminescence/Phosphor bands - general coverage	√			√	√	√
Print and Paper	Luminescence/Phosphor bands - specialised coverage						√
Print and Paper	Overprints and surcharges - including colour information	√	√	√	√	√	√
Print and Paper	Perforation/Imperforate information	√	√		√	√	√
Print and Paper	Perforation errors and varieties				√	√	√
Print and Paper	Print quantities				√		√
Print and Paper	Printing errors				√	√	√
Print and Paper	Printing flaws						√
Print and Paper	Printing varieties				√	√	√
Print and Paper	Punctured stamps - where official				√		
Print and Paper	Sheet positions				√	√	√
Print and Paper	Specialised plate number information						√
Print and Paper	Specimen overprints (only for Commonwealth & GB)				√	√	√
Print and Paper	Underprints					√	√
Print and Paper	Visible Plate numbers	√			√	√	√
Print and Paper	Yellow and Green paper listings				√		√
Index	Design index	√			√	√	

International Philatelic Glossary

English	French	German	Spanish	Italian
Agate	Agate	Achat	Agata	Agata
Air stamp	Timbre de la poste aérienne	Flugpostmarke	Sello de correo aéreo	Francobollo per posta aerea
Apple Green	Vert-pomme	Apfelgrün	Verde manzana	Verde mela
Barred	Annulé par barres	Balkenentwertung	Anulado con barras	Sbarrato
Bisected	Timbre coupé	Halbiert	Partido en dos	Frazionato
Bistre	Bistre	Bister	Bistre	Bistro
Bistre-brown	Brun-bistre	Bisterbraun	Castaño bistre	Bruno-bistro
Black	Noir	Schwarz	Negro	Nero
Blackish Brown	Brun-noir	Schwärzlichbraun	Castaño negruzco	Bruno nerastro
Blackish Green	Vert foncé	Schwärzlichgrün	Verde negruzco	Verde nerastro
Blackish Olive	Olive foncé	Schwärzlicholiv	Oliva negruzco	Oliva nerastro
Block of four	Bloc de quatre	Viererblock	Bloque de cuatro	Bloco di quattro
Blue	Bleu	Blau	Azul	Azzurro
Blue-green	Vert-bleu	Blaugrün	Verde azul	Verde azzuro
Bluish Violet	Violet bleuâtre	Bläulichviolett	Violeta azulado	Violtto azzurrastro
Booklet	Carnet	Heft	Cuadernillo	Libretto
Bright Blue	Bleu vif	Lebhaftblau	Azul vivo	Azzurro vivo
Bright Green	Vert vif	Lebhaftgrün	Verde vivo	Verde vivo
Bright Purple	Mauve vif	Lebhaftpurpur	Púrpura vivo	Porpora vivo
Bronze Green	Vert-bronze	Bronzegrün	Verde bronce	Verde bronzo
Brown	Brun	Braun	Castaño	Bruno
Brown-lake	Carmin-brun	Braunlack	Laca castaño	Lacca bruno
Brown-purple	Pourpre-brun	Braunpurpur	Púrpura castaño	Porpora bruno
Brown-red	Rouge-brun	Braunrot	Rojo castaño	Rosso bruno
Buff	Chamois	Sämisch	Anteado	Camoscio
Cancellation	Oblitération	Entwertung	Cancelación	Annullamento
Cancelled	Annulé	Gestempelt	Cancelado	Annullato
Carmine	Carmin	Karmin	Carmín	Carminio
Carmine-red	Rouge-carmin	Karminrot	Rojo carmín	Rosso carminio
Centred	Centré	Zentriert	Centrado	Centrato
Cerise	Rouge-cerise	Kirschrot	Color de ceresa	Color Ciliegia
Chalk-surfaced paper	Papier couché	Kreidepapier	Papel estucado	Carta gessata
Chalky Blue	Bleu terne	Kreideblau	Azul turbio	Azzurro smorto
Charity stamp	Timbre de bienfaisance	Wohltätigkeitsmarke	Sello de beneficenza	Francobollo di beneficenza
Chestnut	Marron	Kastanienbraun	Castaño rojo	Marrone
Chocolate	Chocolat	Schokolade	Chocolate	Cioccolato
Cinnamon	Cannelle	Zimtbraun	Canela	Cannella
Claret	Grenat	Weinrot	Rojo vinoso	Vinaccia
Cobalt	Cobalt	Kobalt	Cobalto	Cobalto
Colour	Couleur	Farbe	Color	Colore
Comb-perforation	Dentelure en peigne	Kammzähnung, Reihenzähnung	Dentado de peine	Dentellatura e pettine
Commemorative stamp	Timbre commémoratif	Gedenkmarke	Sello conmemorativo	Francobollo commemorativo
Crimson	Cramoisi	Karmesin	Carmesí	Cremisi
Deep Blue	Blue foncé	Dunkelblau	Azul oscuro	Azzurro scuro
Deep bluish Green	Vert-bleu foncé	Dunkelbläulichgrün	Verde azulado oscuro	Verde azzurro scuro

English	French	German	Spanish	Italian
Design	Dessin	Markenbild	Diseño	Disegno
Die	Matrice	Urstempel. Type, Platte	Cuño	Conio, Matrice
Double	Double	Doppelt	Doble	Doppio
Drab	Olive terne	Trüboliv	Oliva turbio	Oliva smorto
Dull Green	Vert terne	Trübgrün	Verde turbio	Verde smorto
Dull purple	Mauve terne	Trübpurpur	Púrpura turbio	Porpora smorto
Embossing	Impression en relief	Prägedruck	Impresión en relieve	Impressione a relievo
Emerald	Vert-eméraude	Smaragdgrün	Esmeralda	Smeraldo
Engraved	Gravé	Graviert	Grabado	Inciso
Error	Erreur	Fehler, Fehldruck	Error	Errore
Essay	Essai	Probedruck	Ensayo	Saggio
Express letter stamp	Timbre pour lettres par exprès	Eilmarke	Sello de urgencia	Francobollo per espresso
Fiscal stamp	Timbre fiscal	Stempelmarke	Sello fiscal	Francobollo fiscale
Flesh	Chair	Fleischfarben	Carne	Carnicino
Forgery	Faux, Falsification	Fälschung	Falsificación	Falso, Falsificazione
Frame	Cadre	Rahmen	Marco	Cornice
Granite paper	Papier avec fragments de fils de soie	Faserpapier	Papel con filamentos	Carto con fili di seta
Green	Vert	Grün	Verde	Verde
Greenish Blue	Bleu verdâtre	Grünlichblau	Azul verdoso	Azzurro verdastro
Greenish Yellow	Jaune-vert	Grünlichgelb	Amarillo verdoso	Giallo verdastro
Grey	Gris	Grau	Gris	Grigio
Grey-blue	Bleu-gris	Graublau	Azul gris	Azzurro grigio
Grey-green	Vert gris	Graugrün	Verde gris	Verde grigio
Gum	Gomme	Gummi	Goma	Gomma
Gutter	Interpanneau	Zwischensteg	Espacio blanco entre dos grupos	Ponte
Imperforate	Non-dentelé	Geschnitten	Sin dentar	Non dentellato
Indigo	Indigo	Indigo	Azul indigo	Indaco
Inscription	Inscription	Inschrift	Inscripción	Dicitura
Inverted	Renversé	Kopfstehend	Invertido	Capovolto
Issue	Émission	Ausgabe	Emisión	Emissione
Laid	Vergé	Gestreift	Listado	Vergato
Lake	Lie de vin	Lackfarbe	Laca	Lacca
Lake-brown	Brun-carmin	Lackbraun	Castaño laca	Bruno lacca
Lavender	Bleu-lavande	Lavendel	Color de alhucema	Lavanda
Lemon	Jaune-citron	Zitrongelb	Limón	Limone
Light Blue	Bleu clair	Hellblau	Azul claro	Azzurro chiaro
Lilac	Lilas	Lila	Lila	Lilla
Line perforation	Dentelure en lignes	Linienzähnung	Dentado en linea	Dentellatura lineare
Lithography	Lithographie	Steindruck	Litografía	Litografia
Local	Timbre de poste locale	Lokalpostmarke	Emisión local	Emissione locale
Lozenge roulette	Percé en losanges	Rautenförmiger Durchstich	Picadura en rombos	Perforazione a losanghe
Magenta	Magenta	Magentarot	Magenta	Magenta
Margin	Marge	Rand	Borde	Margine
Maroon	Marron pourpré	Dunkelrotpurpur	Púrpura rojo oscuro	Marrone rossastro
Mauve	Mauve	Malvenfarbe	Malva	Malva
Multicoloured	Polychrome	Mehrfarbig	Multicolores	Policromo
Myrtle Green	Vert myrte	Myrtengrün	Verde mirto	Verde mirto
New Blue	Bleu ciel vif	Neublau	Azul nuevo	Azzurro nuovo
Newspaper stamp	Timbre pour journaux	Zeitungsmarke	Sello para periódicos	Francobollo per giornali

English	*French*	*German*	*Spanish*	*Italian*
Obliteration	Oblitération	Abstempelung	Matasello	Annullamento
Obsolete	Hors (de) cours	Ausser Kurs	Fuera de curso	Fuori corso
Ochre	Ocre	Ocker	Ocre	Ocra
Official stamp	Timbre de service	Dienstmarke	Sello de servicio	Francobollo di
Olive-brown	Brun-olive	Olivbraun	Castaño oliva	Bruno oliva
Olive-green	Vert-olive	Olivgrün	Verde oliva	Verde oliva
Olive-grey	Gris-olive	Olivgrau	Gris oliva	Grigio oliva
Olive-yellow	Jaune-olive	Olivgelb	Amarillo oliva	Giallo oliva
Orange	Orange	Orange	Naranja	Arancio
Orange-brown	Brun-orange	Orangebraun	Castaño naranja	Bruno arancio
Orange-red	Rouge-orange	Orangerot	Rojo naranja	Rosso arancio
Orange-yellow	Jaune-orange	Orangegelb	Amarillo naranja	Giallo arancio
Overprint	Surcharge	Aufdruck	Sobrecarga	Soprastampa
Pair	Paire	Paar	Pareja	Coppia
Pale	Pâle	Blass	Pálido	Pallido
Pane	Panneau	Gruppe	Grupo	Gruppo
Paper	Papier	Papier	Papel	Carta
Parcel post stamp	Timbre pour colis postaux	Paketmarke	Sello para paquete postal	Francobollo per pacchi postali
Pen-cancelled	Oblitéré à plume	Federzugentwertung	Cancelado a pluma	Annullato a penna
Percé en arc	Percé en arc	Bogenförmiger Durchstich	Picadura en forma de arco	Perforazione ad arco
Percé en scie	Percé en scie	Bogenförmiger Durchstich	Picado en sierra	Foratura a sega
Perforated	Dentelé	Gezähnt	Dentado	Dentellato
Perforation	Dentelure	Zähnung	Dentar	Dentellatura
Photogravure	Photogravure, Heliogravure	Rastertiefdruck	Fotograbado	Rotocalco
Pin perforation	Percé en points	In Punkten durchstochen	Horadado con alfileres	Perforato a punti
Plate	Planche	Platte	Plancha	Lastra, Tavola
Plum	Prune	Pflaumenfarbe	Color de ciruela	Prugna
Postage Due stamp	Timbre-taxe	Portomarke	Sello de tasa	Segnatasse
Postage stamp	Timbre-poste	Briefmarke, Freimarke, Postmarke	Sello de correos	Francobollo postale
Postal fiscal stamp	Timbre fiscal-postal	Stempelmarke als Postmarke verwendet	Sello fiscal-postal	Fiscale postale
Postmark	Oblitération postale	Poststempel	Matasello	Bollo
Printing	Impression, Tirage	Druck	Impresión	Stampa, Tiratura
Proof	Épreuve	Druckprobe	Prueba de impresión	Prova
Provisionals	Timbres provisoires	Provisorische Marken. Provisorien	Provisionales	Provvisori
Prussian Blue	Bleu de Prusse	Preussischblau	Azul de Prusia	Azzurro di Prussia
Purple	Pourpre	Purpur	Púrpura	Porpora
Purple-brown	Brun-pourpre	Purpurbraun	Castaño púrpura	Bruno porpora
Recess-printing	Impression en taille douce	Tiefdruck	Grabado	Incisione
Red	Rouge	Rot	Rojo	Rosso
Red-brown	Brun-rouge	Rotbraun	Castaño rojizo	Bruno rosso
Reddish Lilac	Lilas rougeâtre	Rötlichlila	Lila rojizo	Lilla rossastro
Reddish Purple	Poupre-rouge	Rötlichpurpur	Púrpura rojizo	Porpora rossastro
Reddish Violet	Violet rougeâtre	Rötlichviolett	Violeta rojizo	Violetto rossastro
Red-orange	Orange rougeâtre	Rotorange	Naranja rojizo	Arancio rosso
Registration stamp	Timbre pour lettre chargée (recommandée)	Einschreibemarke	Sello de certificado lettere	Francobollo per raccomandate
Reprint	Réimpression	Neudruck	Reimpresión	Ristampa
Reversed	Retourné	Umgekehrt	Invertido	Rovesciato

English	French	German	Spanish	Italian
Rose	Rose	Rosa	Rosa	Rosa
Rose-red	Rouge rosé	Rosarot	Rojo rosado	Rosso rosa
Rosine	Rose vif	Lebhaftrosa	Rosa vivo	Rosa vivo
Roulette	Percage	Durchstich	Picadura	Foratura
Rouletted	Percé	Durchstochen	Picado	Forato
Royal Blue	Bleu-roi	Königblau	Azul real	Azzurro reale
Sage green	Vert-sauge	Salbeigrün	Verde salvia	Verde salvia
Salmon	Saumon	Lachs	Salmón	Salmone
Scarlet	Écarlate	Scharlach	Escarlata	Scarlatto
Sepia	Sépia	Sepia	Sepia	Seppia
Serpentine roulette	Percé en serpentin	Schlangenliniger Durchstich	Picado a serpentina	Perforazione a serpentina
Shade	Nuance	Tönung	Tono	Gradazione de colore
Sheet	Feuille	Bogen	Hoja	Foglio
Slate	Ardoise	Schiefer	Pizarra	Ardesia
Slate-blue	Bleu-ardoise	Schieferblau	Azul pizarra	Azzurro ardesia
Slate-green	Vert-ardoise	Schiefergrün	Verde pizarra	Verde ardesia
Slate-lilac	Lilas-gris	Schierferlila	Lila pizarra	Lilla ardesia
Slate-purple	Mauve-gris	Schieferpurpur	Púrpura pizarra	Porpora ardesia
Slate-violet	Violet-gris	Schieferviolett	Violeta pizarra	Violetto ardesia
Special delivery stamp	Timbre pour exprès	Eilmarke	Sello de urgencia	Francobollo per espressi
Specimen	Spécimen	Muster	Muestra	Saggio
Steel Blue	Bleu acier	Stahlblau	Azul acero	Azzurro acciaio
Strip	Bande	Streifen	Tira	Striscia
Surcharge	Surcharge	Aufdruck	Sobrecarga	Soprastampa
Tête-bêche	Tête-bêche	Kehrdruck	Tête-bêche	Tête-bêche
Tinted paper	Papier teinté	Getöntes Papier	Papel coloreado	Carta tinta
Too-late stamp	Timbre pour lettres en retard	Verspätungsmarke	Sello para cartas retardadas	Francobollo per le lettere in ritardo
Turquoise-blue	Bleu-turquoise	Türkisblau	Azul turquesa	Azzurro turchese
Turquoise-green	Vert-turquoise	Türkisgrün	Verde turquesa	Verde turchese
Typography	Typographie	Buchdruck	Tipografia	Tipografia
Ultramarine	Outremer	Ultramarin	Ultramar	Oltremare
Unused	Neuf	Ungebraucht	Nuevo	Nuovo
Used	Oblitéré, Usé	Gebraucht	Usado	Usato
Venetian Red	Rouge-brun terne	Venezianischrot	Rojo veneciano	Rosso veneziano
Vermilion	Vermillon	Zinnober	Cinabrio	Vermiglione
Violet	Violet	Violett	Violeta	Violetto
Violet-blue	Bleu-violet	Violettblau	Azul violeta	Azzurro violetto
Watermark	Filigrane	Wasserzeichen	Filigrana	Filigrana
Watermark sideways	Filigrane couché liegend	Wasserzeichen	Filigrana acostado	Filigrana coricata
Wove paper	Papier ordinaire, Papier uni	Einfaches Papier	Papel avitelado	Carta unita
Yellow	Jaune	Gelb	Amarillo	Giallo
Yellow-brown	Brun-jaune	Gelbbraun	Castaño amarillo	Bruno giallo
Yellow-green	Vert-jaune	Gelbgrün	Verde amarillo	Verde giallo
Yellow-olive	Olive-jaunâtre	Gelboliv	Oliva amarillo	Oliva giallastro
Yellow-orange	Orange jaunâtre	Gelborange	Naranja amarillo	Arancio giallastro
Zig-zag roulette	Percé en zigzag	Sägezahnartiger Durchstich	Picado en zigzag	Perforazione a zigzag

Guide to Entries

A **Country of Issue** – When a country changes its name, the catalogue listing changes to reflect the name change, for example Namibia was formerly known as South West Africa, the stamps in Southern Africa are all listed under Namibia, but split into South West Africa and then Namibia.

B **Country Information** – Brief geographical and historical details for the issuing country.

C **Currency** – Details of the currency, and dates of earliest use where applicable, on the face value of the stamps.

D **Illustration** – Generally, the first stamp in the set. Stamp illustrations are reduced to 75%, with overprints and surcharges shown actual size.

E **Illustration or Type Number** – These numbers are used to help identify stamps, either in the listing, type column, design line or footnote, usually the first value in a set. These type numbers are in a bold type face – **123**; when bracketed (**123**) an overprint or a surcharge is indicated. Some type numbers include a lower-case letter – **123a**, this indicates they have been added to an existing set.

F **Date of issue** – This is the date that the stamp/set of stamps was issued by the post office and was available for purchase. When a set of definitive stamps has been issued over several years the Year Date given is for the earliest issue. Commemorative sets are listed in chronological order. Stamps of the same design, or issue are usually grouped together, for example some of the New Zealand landscapes definitive series were first issued in 2003 but the set includes stamps issued to May 2007.

G **Number Prefix** – Stamps other than definitives and commemoratives have a prefix letter before the catalogue number.
Their use is explained in the text: some examples are A for airmail, D for postage due and O for official stamps.

H **Footnote** – Further information on background or key facts on issues.

I **Stanley Gibbons Catalogue number** – This is a unique number for each stamp to help the collector identify stamps in the listing. The Stanley Gibbons numbering system is universally recognized as definitive.

Where insufficient numbers have been left to provide for additional stamps to a listing, some stamps will have a suffix letter after the catalogue number (for example 214a). If numbers have been left for additions to a set and not used they will be left vacant.

The separate type numbers (in bold) refer to illustrations (see **E**).

J **Colour** – If a stamp is printed in three or fewer colours then the colours are listed, working from the centre of the stamp outwards (see **R**).

K **Design line** – Further details on design variations

L **Key Type** – Indicates a design type on which the stamp is based. These are the bold figures found below each illustration, for example listed in Cameroon, in the West Africa catalogue, is the Key type A and B showing the ex-Kaiser's yacht *Hohenzollern*. The type numbers are also given in bold in the second column of figures alongside the stamp description to indicate the design of each stamp. Where an issue comprises stamps of similar design, the corresponding type number should be taken as indicating the general design. Where there are blanks in the type number column it means that the type of the corresponding stamp is that shown by the number in the type column of the same issue. A dash (–) in the type column means that the stamp is not illustrated. Where type numbers refer to stamps of another country, e.g. where stamps of one country are overprinted for use in another, this is always made clear in the text.

M **Coloured Papers** – Stamps printed on coloured paper are shown – e.g. "brown/*yellow*" indicates brown printed on yellow paper.

N **Surcharges and Overprints** – Usually described in the headings. Any actual wordings are shown in bold type. Descriptions clarify words and figures used in the overprint. Stamps with the same overprints in different colours are not listed separately. Numbers in brackets after the descriptions are the catalogue numbers of the non-overprinted stamps. The words "inscribed" or "inscription" refer to the wording incorporated in the design of a stamp and not surcharges or overprints.

O **Face value** – This refers to the value of each stamp and is the price it was sold for at the Post Office when issued. Some modern stamps do not have their values in figures but instead it is shown as a letter, for example Great Britain use 1st or 2nd on their stamps as opposed to the actual value.

P **Catalogue Value** – Mint/Unused. Prices quoted for Queen Victoria to King George V stamps are for lightly hinged examples.

Q **Catalogue Value** – Used. Prices generally refer to fine postally used examples. For certain issues they are for cancelled-to-order.

Prices
Prices are given in pence and pounds. Stamps worth £100 and over are shown in whole pounds:

Shown in Catalogue as	Explanation
10	10 pence
1.75	£1.75
15.00	£15
£150	£150
£2300	£2300

Prices assume stamps are in 'fine condition'; we may ask more for superb and less for those of lower quality. The minimum catalogue price quoted is 10p and is intended as a guide for catalogue users. The lowest price for individual stamps purchased from Stanley Gibbons is £1.

Prices quoted are for the cheapest variety of that particular stamp. Differences of watermark, perforation, or other details, often increase the value. Prices quoted for mint issues are for single examples, unless otherwise stated. Those in *se-tenant* pairs, strips, blocks or sheets may be worth more. Where no prices are listed it is either because the stamps are not known to exist (usually shown by a †) in that particular condition, or, more usually, because there is no reliable information on which to base their value.

All prices are subject to change without prior notice and we cannot guarantee to supply all stamps as priced. Prices quoted in advertisements are also subject to change without prior notice.

R **Multicoloured** – Nearly all modern stamps are multicoloured (more than three colours); this is indicated in the heading, with a description of the stamp given in the listing.

S **Perforations** – Please see page xi for a detailed explanation of perforations.

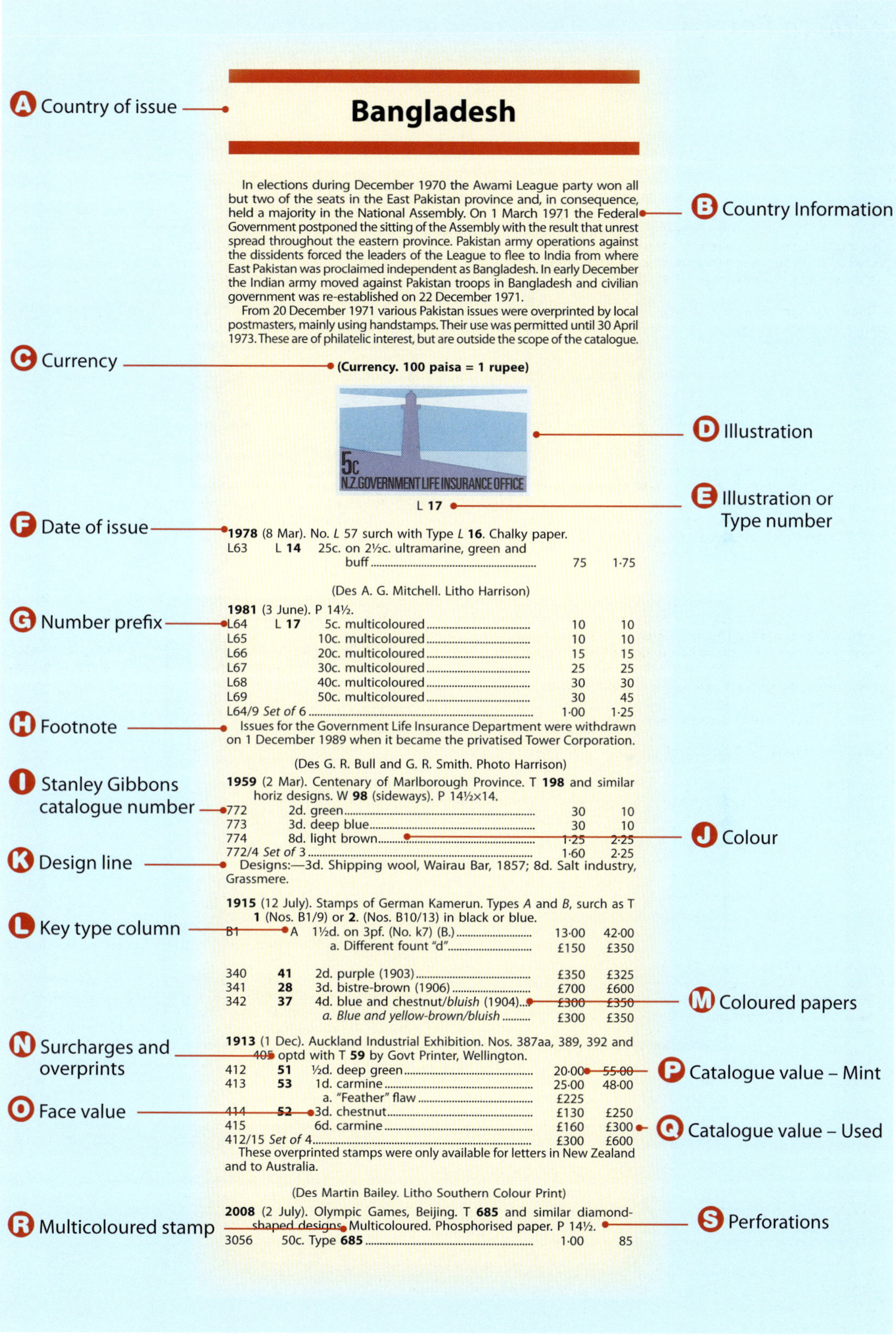
A Country of issue
Bangladesh
In elections during December 1970 the Awami League party won all but two of the seats in the East Pakistan province and, in consequence, held a majority in the National Assembly. On 1 March 1971 the Federal Government postponed the sitting of the Assembly with the result that unrest spread throughout the eastern province. Pakistan army operations against the dissidents forced the leaders of the League to flee to India from where East Pakistan was proclaimed independent as Bangladesh. In early December the Indian army moved against Pakistan troops in Bangladesh and civilian government was re-established on 22 December 1971.
From 20 December 1971 various Pakistan issues were overprinted by local postmasters, mainly using handstamps. Their use was permitted until 30 April 1973. These are of philatelic interest, but are outside the scope of the catalogue.
B Country Information
C Currency
(Currency. 100 paisa = 1 rupee)
5c
N.Z.GOVERNMENT LIFE INSURANCE OFFICE
D Illustration
L 17
E Illustration or Type number
F Date of issue
1978 (8 Mar). No. L 57 surch with Type L 16. Chalky paper.
L63 L 14 25c. on 2½c. ultramarine, green and buff 75 1·75
(Des A. G. Mitchell. Litho Harrison)
G Number prefix
1981 (3 June). P 14½.
L64 L 17 5c. multicoloured 10 10
L65 10c. multicoloured 10 10
L66 20c. multicoloured 15 15
L67 30c. multicoloured 25 25
L68 40c. multicoloured 30 30
L69 50c. multicoloured 30 45
L64/9 Set of 6 1·00 1·25
H Footnote
Issues for the Government Life Insurance Department were withdrawn on 1 December 1989 when it became the privatised Tower Corporation.
(Des G. R. Bull and G. R. Smith. Photo Harrison)
I Stanley Gibbons catalogue number
1959 (2 Mar). Centenary of Marlborough Province. T 198 and similar horiz designs. W 98 (sideways). P 14½×14.
772 2d. green 30 10
773 3d. deep blue 30 10
774 8d. light brown 1·25 2·25
772/4 Set of 3 1·60 2·25
J Colour
K Design line
Designs:—3d. Shipping wool, Wairau Bar, 1857; 8d. Salt industry, Grassmere.
1915 (12 July). Stamps of German Kamerun. Types A and B, surch as T 1 (Nos. B1/9) or 2. (Nos. B10/13) in black or blue.
L Key type column
B1 A 1½d. on 3pf. (No. k7) (B.) 13·00 42·00
a. Different fount "d" £150 £350
340 41 2d. purple (1903) £350 £325
341 28 3d. bistre-brown (1906) £700 £600
342 37 4d. blue and chestnut/bluish (1904) £300 £350
a. Blue and yellow-brown/bluish £300 £350
M Coloured papers
N Surcharges and overprints
1913 (1 Dec). Auckland Industrial Exhibition. Nos. 387aa, 389, 392 and 405 optd with T 59 by Govt Printer, Wellington.
412 51 ½d. deep green 20·00 55·00
413 53 1d. carmine 25·00 48·00
a. "Feather" flaw £225
414 52 3d. chestnut £130 £250
415 6d. carmine £160 £300
412/15 Set of 4 £300 £600
These overprinted stamps were only available for letters in New Zealand and to Australia.
O Face value
P Catalogue value – Mint
Q Catalogue value – Used
(Des Martin Bailey. Litho Southern Colour Print)
2008 (2 July). Olympic Games, Beijing. T 685 and similar diamond-shaped designs. Multicoloured. Phosphorised paper. P 14½.
3056 50c. Type 685 1·00 85
R Multicoloured stamp
S Perforations

British P.Os in Crete

BRITISH ADMINISTRATION OF CANDIA PROVINCE (HERAKLEION)

Crete, formerly part of the Turkish Empire, was made autonomous, under Turkish suzerainty, in November 1898 with British, French, Italian and Russian troops stationed in separate zones to keep the peace.

Overseas mail franked with Nos. B1/5 was forwarded through the Austrian post office at Canea, being additionally franked with stamps of the Austro-Hungarian Post Offices in the Turkish Empire.

(Currency. 40 paras = 1 piastre)

PRICES FOR STAMPS ON COVER	
No. B1	*from* × 8
Nos. B2/5	—

B **1**

B **2**

1898 (25 Nov). Handstruck locally. Imperf.

B1	B **1**	20pa. bright violet	£425	£225

1898 (3 Dec). Litho by M. Grundmann, Athens. P 11½.

B2	B **2**	10pa. blue	9·00	22·00
		a. Imperf (pair)	£250	
B3		20pa. green	17·00	20·00
		a. Imperf (pair)	£250	

1899. P 11½.

B4	B **2**	10pa. brown	11·00	29·00
		a. Imperf (pair)	£250	
B5		20pa. rose	20·00	17·00
		a. Imperf (pair)	£250	

The British postal service closed at the end of 1899.

Cyprus

Cyprus was part of the Turkish Ottoman Empire from 1571.

The first records of an organised postal service date from 1871 when a post office was opened at Nicosia (Lefkosa) under the jurisdiction of the Damascus Head Post Office. Various stamps of Turkey from the 1868 issue onwards are known used from this office, cancelled "KIBRIS", in Arabic, within a double-lined oblong. Manuscript cancellations have also been reported. The records report the opening of a further office at Larnaca (Tuzla) in 1873, but no cancellation for this office has been identified.

To provide an overseas postal service the Austrian Empire opened a post office in Larnaca during 1845. Stamps of the Austrian Post Offices in the Turkish Empire were placed on sale there from 1 June 1864 and were cancelled with an unframed straight-line mark or circular date stamp. This Austrian post office closed on 6 August 1878.

BRITISH ADMINISTRATION

Following the convention with Turkey, Great Britain assumed the administration of Cyprus on 11 July 1878 and the first post office, as part of the British G.P.O. system, was opened at Larnaca on 27 July 1878. Further offices at Famagusta, Kyrenia, Limassol, Nicosia and Paphos followed in September 1878.

The stamps of Great Britain were supplied to the various offices as they opened and continued to be used until the Cyprus Administration assumed responsibility for the postal service on 1 April 1880. With the exception of "969" (Nicosia) similar numeral cancellations had previously been used at offices in Great Britain.

Numeral postmarks for Headquarters Camp, Nicosia ("D48") and Polymedia (Polemidhia) Camp, Limassol ("D47") were supplied by the G.P.O. in London during January 1881. These cancellations had three bars above and three bars below the numeral. Similar marks, but with four bars above and below, had previously been used in London on newspapers and bulk mail.

Although both three bar cancellations subsequently occur on Cyprus issues only, isolated examples have been found on loose Great Britain stamps and there are no known covers or pieces which confirm such usage in Cyprus.

(**9**)

FAMAGUSTA

Stamps of GREAT BRITAIN cancelled "982" as Type **9**.

1878–80.

Z1	½d. rose-red (1870–79) (Plate Nos. 11, 13)		£700
Z2	1d. rose-red (1864–79)		£500
	Plate Nos. 145, 174, 181, 193, 202, 204, 206, 215, 217.		
Z3	2d. blue (1858–69) (Plate Nos. 13, 14, 15)		£1000
Z4	2½d. rosy mauve (1876) (Plate Nos. 13, 16)		£1100
Z5	6d. grey (1874–80) (Plate No. 15)		£2000
Z6	1s. green (1873–77) (Plate No. 12)		£2750

KYRENIA

Stamps of GREAT BRITAIN cancelled "974" as Type **9**.

1878–80.

Z8	½d. rose-red (1870–79) (Plate No. 13)		£1000
Z9	1d. rose-red (1864–79)	*From*	£650
	Plate Nos. 168, 171, 193, 196, 206, 207, 209, 220.		
Z10	2d. blue (1858–69) (Plate Nos. 13, 15)	*From*	£1100
Z11	2½d. rosy mauve (1876–79) (Plate Nos. 12, 13, 14, 15)	*From*	£1100
Z12	4d. sage-green (1877) (Plate No. 16)		
Z13	6d. grey (1874–80) (Plate No. 16)		

LARNACA

Stamps of GREAT BRITAIN cancelled "942" as Type **9**.

1878–80.

Z14	½d. rose-red (1870–79)	*From*	£250
	Plate Nos. 11, 12, 13, 14, 15, 19, 20.		

Z15 1d. rose-red (1864–79) *From* £180
Plate Nos. 129, 131, 146, 154, 170, 171, 174, 175, 176, 177, 178, 179, 181, 182, 183, 184, 187, 188, 190, 191, 192, 193, 194, 195, 196, 197, 198, 199, 200, 201, 202, 203, 204, 205, 206, 207, 208, 209, 210, 212, 213, 214, 215, 216, 217, 218, 220, 221, 222, 225.
Z16 1½d. lake-red (1870) (Plate No. 3) £2000
Z17 2d. blue (1858–69) (Plate Nos. 9, 13, 14, 15) £300
Z18 2½d. rosy mauve (1876–79) *From* 75·00
Plate Nos. 4, 5, 6, 8, 9, 10, 11, 12, 13, 14, 15, 16, 17.
Z19 2½d. blue (1880) (Plate Nos. 17, 18) £500
Z21 4d. sage-green (1877) (Plate Nos. 15, 16) £550
Z22 6d. grey (1874–76) (Plate Nos. 15, 16, 17) £550
Z23 6d. pale buff (1872–73) (Plate No. 11) £2750
Z24 8d. orange (1876) £6000
Z25 1s. green (1873–77) (Plate Nos. 12, 13) £1000
Z27 5s. rose (1874) (Plate No. 2) £6000

LIMASSOL

Stamps of GREAT BRITAIN cancelled "975" as Type **9**.

1878–80.
Z28 ½d. rose-red (1870–79) (Plate Nos. 11, 13, 15, 19) £450
Z29 1d. rose-red (1864–79) *From* £275
Plate Nos. 159, 160, 171, 173, 174, 177, 179, 184, 187, 190, 193, 195, 196, 197, 198, 200, 202, 206, 207, 208, 209, 210, 213, 215, 216, 218, 220, 221, 222, 225.
Z30 1½d. lake-red (1870–74) (Plate No. 3) £2500
Z31 2d. blue (1858–69) (Plate Nos. 14, 15) *From* £550
Z32 2½d. rosy-mauve (1876–80) *From* £250
Plate Nos. 11, 12, 13, 14, 15, 16.
Z33 2½d. blue (1880) (Plate No. 17) £1200
Z34 4d. sage-green (Plate No. 16) £900

NICOSIA

Stamps of GREAT BRITAIN cancelled "969" as Type **9**.

1878–80.
Z35 ½d. rose-red (1870–79) £475
Plate Nos. 12, 13, 14, 15, 20.
Z36 1d. rose-red (1864–79) *From* £275
Plate Nos. 170, 171, 174, 189, 190, 192, 193, 195, 196, 198, 200, 202, 203, 205, 206, 207, 210, 212, 214, 215, 218, 221, 222, 225.
Z36*a* 1½d. lake red (1870) (Plate No. 3) £3250
Z37 2d. blue (1858–69) (Plate Nos. 14, 15) £550
Z38 2½d. rosy mauve (1876–79) *From* £200
Plate Nos. 10, 11, 12, 13, 14, 15, 16.
Z39 2½d. blue (1880) (Plate No. 17) £800
Z42 4d. sage-green (1877) (Plate No. 16) £850
Z43 6d. grey (1873) (Plate No. 16) £1000

PAPHOS

Stamps of GREAT BRITAIN cancelled "981" as Type **9**.

1878–80.
Z44 ½d. rose-red (1870–79) (Plate Nos. 13, 15)
Z45 1d. rose-red (1864–79) *From* £650
Plate Nos. 196, 201, 202, 204, 206, 213, 217.
Z46 2d. blue (1858–69) (Plate No. 15) £1100
Z47 2½d. rosy mauve (1876–79) *From* £600
Plate Nos. 13, 14, 15, 16.

PRICES FOR STAMPS ON COVER TO 1945

Nos.	1/4	*from* × 50
Nos.	5/6	—
Nos.	7/10	*from* × 100
Nos.	11/15	*from* × 12
No.	16	—
Nos.	16*a*/22	*from* × 20
Nos.	23/5	*from* × 100
No.	26	—
No.	27	*from* × 25
No.	28	—
No.	29	*from* × 200
Nos.	31/5*a*	*from* × 10
Nos.	36/7	—
Nos.	40/9	*from* × 8
Nos.	50/71	*from* × 5
Nos.	74/99	*from* × 4
Nos.	100/2	—
Nos.	103/17	*from* × 4
No.	117*a*	—
Nos.	118/31	*from* × 8
No.	132	—
Nos.	133/43	*from* × 5
Nos.	144/7	*from* × 6
Nos.	148/63	*from* × 5

PERFORATION. Nos. 1/122 are perf 14.

Stamps of Great Britain overprinted

CYPRUS (**1**) **CYPRUS** (**2**)

(Optd by D.L.R.)

1880 (1 April).
1 **1** ½d. rose £120 £110
a. Opt double (Plate 15) † £42000

Plate No.	*Un.*	*Used.*	*Plate No.*	*Un.*	*Used*
12.	£225	£250	19.	£5000	£700
15.	£120	£100			

2 **2** 1d. red 17·00 38·00
a. Opt double (Plate 208) £26000 †
aa. Opt double (Plate 218) £4250 †
b. Vert pair, top stamp without opt (Plate 208) £26000 †

Plate No.	*Un.*	*Used.*	*Plate No.*	*Un.*	*Used*
174.	£1400	£1400	208.	£130	55·00
181.	£500	£190	215.	17·00	55·00
184.	£20000	£3000	216.	18·00	38·00
193.	£800	†	217.	18·00	60·00
196.	£700	†	218.	25·00	60·00
201.	20·00	55·00	220.	£350	£375
205.	85·00	55·00			

3 **2** 2½d. rosy mauve 4·00 13·00
a. Large thin "C" (Plate 14) (BK, JK) 90·00 £325
b. Large thin "C" (Plate 15) (BK, JK) £150 £750
w. Wmk inverted (Plate 15) £500

Plate No.	*Un.*	*Used.*	*Plate No.*	*Un.*	*Used*
14.	4·00	13·00	15.	5·50	35·00

4 **2** 4d. sage-green (Plate 16) £140 £225
5 6d. grey (Plate 16) £500 £650
6 1s. green (Plate 13) £850 £475

HALF-PENNY (**3**) 18 mm **HALF-PENNY** (**4**) 16 or 16½ mm

HALF-PENNY (**5**) 13 mm **30 PARAS** (**6**)

(Optd by Govt Ptg Office, Nicosia)

1881 (Feb–June). No. 2 surch.
7 **3** ½d. on 1d. red (Feb) 75·00 85·00
a. "HALFPENN" (BG, LG) (*all plates*) *From* £3000 £2750
b. Surch double (Plate 220) £2500

Plate No.	*Un.*	*Used.*	*Plate No.*	*Un.*	*Used*
174.	£200	£375	215.	£800	£950
181.	£200	£250	216.	75·00	85·00
201.	£110	£130	217.	£900	£850
205.	80·00	85·00	218.	£500	£650
208.	£200	£350	220.	£300	£400

8 **4** ½d. on 1d. red (Apr) £120 £160
a. Surch double (Plates 201 and 216) £3500 £2500

Plate No.	*Un.*	*Used.*	*Plate No.*	*Un.*	*Used*
201.	£120	£160	218.	—	£15000
216.	£350	£425			

9 **5** ½d. on 1d. red (1 June) 45·00 65·00
aa. Surch double (Plate 205) £800
ab. Surch double (Plate 215) £450 £650
b. Surch treble (Plate 205) £4500
ba. Surch treble (Plate 215) £800
bc. Surch treble (Plate 218) £4500
c. Surch quadruple (Plate 205) £7000
ca. Surch quadruple (Plate 215) £7000

Plate No.	*Un.*	*Used.*	*Plate No.*	*Un.*	*Used*
205.	£400	—	217.	£160	£100
215.	45·00	65·00	218.	85·00	£120

The surcharge on No. 8 was handstamped; the others were applied by lithography.

(New Currency: 40 paras = 1 piastre, 180 piastres = £1)

1881 (June). No. 2 surch with T **6** by lithography.
10 **6** 30 paras on 1d. red £140 85·00
a. Surch double, one invtd (Plate 216) £7000
aa. Surch double, one invtd (Plate 220) £1900 £1400

Plate No.	*Un.*	*Used.*	*Plate No.*	*Un.*	*Used*
201.	£170	£100	217.	£200	£200
216.	£140	85·00	220.	£170	£180

7

"US" damaged at foot (R. 5/5 of both panes)

(Typo D.L.R)

1881 (1 July). Die I. Wmk Crown CC.

11	**7**	½pi. emerald-green	£180	45·00
		w. Wmk inverted	£900	£500
12		1pi. rose	£375	32·00
13		2pi. blue	£450	35·00
		w. Wmk inverted	—	£1400
14		4pi. pale olive-green	£950	£275
15		6pi. olive-grey	£1700	£475

Stamps of Queen Victoria initialled "J.A.B." or overprinted "POSTAL SURCHARGE" with or without the same initials were employed for accounting purposes between the Chief Post Office and sub-offices, the initials are those of the then Postmaster, Mr. J. A. Bulmer.

1882 (May)–**86**. Die I*. Wmk Crown CA.

16	**7**	½pi. emerald-green (5.82)	£5000	£500
		a. Dull green (4.83)	22·00	3·00
		ab. Top left triangle detached	£1100	£275
17		30pa. pale mauve (7.6.82)	80·00	26·00
		a. Top left triangle detached	£1700	£850
		b. Damaged "US"	£1100	£500
18		1pi. rose (3.83)	£100	3·75
		a. Top left triangle detached	—	£325
19		2pi. blue (4.83)	£160	3·75
		a. Top left triangle detached	—	£375
20		4pi. deep olive-green (10.83)	£550	45·00
		a. Pale olive-green	£350	32·00
		ab. Top left triangle detached	£4500	£950
21		6pi. olive-grey (7.82)	65·00	17·00
		a. Top left triangle detached	—	£1000
22		12pi. orange-brown (1886)	£200	42·00
		s. Optd "SPECIMEN"	£1600	
16*a*/22 *Set of 7*			£900	£110

*For description and illustrations of Dies I and II see Introduction.

For illustration of "top left triangle detached" variety see above No. 21 of Antigua.

No. 21 with manuscript "Specimen" endorsement is known with "CYPRUS" and value double.

See also Nos. 31/7.

½ (8) ½ 30 PARAS (9)

Spur on "1" (position 3 in setting)

(Surch litho by Govt Ptg Office, Nicosia)

1882. Surch with T **8/9**.

		(a) Wmk Crown CC		
23		½ on ½pi. emerald-green (6.82)	£700	75·00
		c. Spur on "1"	£1400	£140
		w. Wmk inverted		
24		30pa. on 1pi. rose (22.5.82)	£1600	£110
		(b) Wmk Crown CA		
25	**7**	½ on ½pi. emerald-green (22.5.82)	£170	7·00
		a. Surch double	†	£2750
		b. "½" inserted by hand	†	£5000
		c. Spur on "1"	£300	14·00

Nos. 23 and 25 were surcharged by a setting of 6 arranged as a horizontal row.

No. 25b shows an additional handstamped "½" applied to examples on which the surcharge was so misplaced as to almost omit one of the original "½"s.

1/2 1/2
(**10**)

11

Varieties of numerals:

1 Normal 1 Large 1 Small

2 Normal 2 Large

1886 (Apr). Surch with T **10** (fractions approx 6 mm apart) in typography.

		(a) Wmk Crown CC		
26	**7**	½ on ½pi. emerald-green	£22000	†
		(b) Wmk Crown CA		
27	**7**	½ on ½pi. emerald-green	£300	70·00
		a. Large "2" at right	£3000	£750

No. 27a occured at R. 10/1 and another unknown position in the setting of 60.

1886 (27 May–June). Surch with T **10** (fractions approx 8 mm apart) in typography.

		(a) Wmk Crown CC		
28	**7**	½ on ½pi. emerald-green	£8000	£425
		a. Large "1" at left	—	£1900
		b. Small "1" at right	£15000	£2250
		c. Large "2" at left	—	£2250
		d. Large "2" at right	†	£2250
		(b) Wmk Crown CA		
29	**7**	½ on ½pi. emerald-green (June)	£500	15·00
		a. Large "1" at left	£4000	£250
		b. Small "1" at right	£3500	£275
		c. Large "2" at left	£4000	£325
		d. Large "2" at right	£4000	£325

Nos. 28/9 were surcharged in a setting of 60. The large "1" at left and large "2" at right both occur in the fourth vertical row, the large "2" at left in the fifth vertical row and the small "1" at right in the top horizontal row.

A third type of this surcharge is known with the fractions spaced approximately 10 mm apart on CA paper with postmarks from August 1886. This may be due to the shifting of type.

1892–**94**. Die II. Wmk Crown CA.

31	**7**	½pi. dull green	10·00	2·00
		w. Wmk inverted		
32		30pa. mauve	8·00	11·00
		a. Damaged "US"	£300	£325
33		1pi. carmine	15·00	6·50
34		2pi. ultramarine	14·00	1·75
35		4pi. olive-green	50·00	40·00
		a. Pale olive-green	18·00	32·00
36		6pi. olive-grey (1894)	£250	£750
37		12pi. orange brown (1893)	£180	£425
31/7 *Set of 7*			£450	£1100

Large "S" in "PIASTRE"

1894 (14 Aug)–**96**. Colours changed and new values. Die II. Wmk Crown CA.

40	**7**	½pi. green and carmine (1896)	4·25	1·25
		a. Large "S" in "PIASTRE"	£120	65·00
		w. Wmk inverted	†	£2250
41		30pa. bright mauve and green (1896)	2·75	3·00
		a. Damaged "US"	£170	£170
42		1pi. carmine and blue (1896)	8·00	1·25
43		2pi. blue and purple (1896)	11·00	1·25
44		4pi. sage-green and purple (1896)	17·00	11·00
45		6pi. sepia and green (1896)	18·00	32·00
46		9pi. brown and carmine	22·00	26·00
47		12pi. orange-brown and black (1896)	22·00	65·00
48		18pi. greyish slate and brown	50·00	55·00
49		45pi. grey-purple and blue	£100	£160
40/9 *Set of 10*			£225	£325
40s/9s Optd "SPECIMEN" *Set of 10*			£350	

The large "S" in "PIASTRE" was a retouch to correct a damaged letter (R. 1/4, both panes). It was corrected when a new duty plate (120-set) was introduced in 1905.

LIMASSOL FLOOD HANDSTAMP. Following a flood on 14 November 1894, which destroyed the local stamp stocks, the postmaster of Limassol produced a temporary handstamp showing "½C.P." which was applied to local letters with the usual c.d.s.

(Typo D.L.R.)

1902–**04**. Wmk Crown CA.

50	**11**	½pi. green and carmine (12.02)	9·00	1·25
		a. Large "S" in "PIASTRE"	£130	55·00
		w. Wmk inverted	£130	80·00

51		30pa. violet and green (2.03)	19·00	4·00
		a. Mauve and green	25·00	9·00
		b. Damaged "US"	£375	£150
52		1pi. carmine and blue (9.03)	28·00	4·75
53		2pi. blue and purple (2.03)	85·00	17·00
54		4pi. olive-green and purple (9.03)	45·00	22·00
55		6pi. sepia and green (9.03)	50·00	£140
56		9pi. brown and carmine (5.04)	£120	£250
57		12pi. chestnut and black (4.03)	20·00	75·00
58		18pi. black and brown (5.04)	90·00	£160
59		45pi. dull purple and ultramarine (10.03)	£200	£500
50/9 *Set of* 10			£600	£1100
50sw/9s Optd "SPECIMEN" *Set of* 10			£450	

The ½pi "SPECIMEN" is only known with watermark inverted.

Broken top left triangle
(Left pane R. 7/5)

1904–10. Wmk Mult Crown CA.

60	**11**	5pa. bistre and black (14.1.08)	1·00	2·00
		a. Broken top left triangle	85·00	£110
		w. Wmk inverted	£1800	
61		10pa. orange and green (12.06)	5·50	1·75
		aw. Wmk inverted	—	£130
		b. Orange-yellow and green	45·00	5·50
		bw. Wmk inverted	—	£150
		c. Broken top left triangle	£140	70·00
62		½pi. green and carmine (1.7.04)	8·50	1·50
		a. Broken top left triangle	£180	55·00
		b. Large "S" in "PIASTRE"	£150	60·00
		w. Wmk inverted	£170	£120
		y. Wmk inverted and reversed	†	£1500
63		30pa. purple and green (1.7.04)	18·00	2·50
		a. Violet and green (1910)	22·00	2·50
		b. Broken top left triangle	£350	£100
		c. Damaged "US"	£275	80·00
		w. Wmk inverted	†	£1600
64		1pi. carmine and blue (11.04)	9·00	1·00
		a. Broken top left triangle	£170	80·00
65		2pi. blue and purple (11.04)	14·00	1·75
		a. Broken top left triangle	£250	£100
66		4pi. olive-green and purple (2.05)	21·00	13·00
		a. Broken top left triangle	£350	£275
67		6pi. sepia and green (17.7.04)	22·00	15·00
		a. Broken top left triangle	£375	£375
68		9pi. brown and carmine (30.5.04)	50·00	8·50
		a. Yellow-brown and carmine	55·00	23·00
		aw. Wmk inverted	£225	£120
		b. Broken top left triangle	£550	£325
69		12pi. chestnut and black (4.06)	35·00	55·00
		a. Broken top left triangle	£600	£700
70		18pi. black and brown (16.6.04)	45·00	14·00
		a. Broken top left triangle	£650	£375
71		45pi. dull purple & ultram (15.6.04)	£110	£150
		a. Broken top left triangle	£1600	
60/71 *Set of* 12			£300	£225
60s/1s Optd "SPECIMEN" *Set of* 2			£130	

12

13

Broken bottom left triangle
(Right pane R. 10/6)

(Typo D.L.R.)

1912 (July)–**15**. Wmk Mult Crown CA.

74	**12**	10pa. orange and green (11.12)	5·00	2·50
		a. Wmk sideways	†	£3500
		b. Orange-yellow & brt green (8.15)	2·25	1·25
		ba. Broken bottom left triangle	£110	60·00
75		½pi. green and carmine	2·75	30
		a. Yellow-green and carmine	7·50	1·90
		ab. Broken bottom left triangle	£140	70·00
		w. Wmk inverted	†	£2000
76		30pa. violet and green (3.13)	3·00	2·25
		a. Broken bottom left triangle	£120	70·00
		w. Wmk inverted		
77		1pi. rose-red and blue (9.12)	5·50	1·75
		a. Broken bottom left triangle	£160	70·00
		b. Carmine and blue (1.15?)	13·00	4·25
		ba. Broken bottom left triangle	£275	95·00
78		2pi. blue and purple (7.13)	6·50	2·00
		a. Broken bottom left triangle	£180	75·00
79		4pi. olive-green and purple	4·25	5·00
		a. Broken bottom left triangle	£150	£160
80		6pi. sepia and green	5·50	11·00
		a. Broken bottom left triangle	£170	£275
81		9pi. brown and carmine (3.15)	38·00	26·00
		a. Yellow-brown and carmine	42·00	30·00
		b. Broken bottom left triangle	£550	£550
82		12pi. chestnut and black (7.13)	23·00	55·00
		b. Broken bottom left triangle	£375	£550
83		18pi. black and brown (3.15)	40·00	45·00
		a. Broken bottom left triangle	£550	£600
84		45pi. dull purple and ultramarine (3.15)	£120	£160
		a. Broken bottom left triangle	£1500	
74/84 *Set of* 11			£225	£275
74s/84s Optd "SPECIMEN" *Set of* 11			£500	

1921–23.

(a) Wmk Mult Script CA

85	**12**	10pa. orange and green	15·00	13·00
		a. Broken bottom left triangle	£225	£225
		w. Wmk inverted	£3250	£3250
86		10pa. grey and yellow (1923)	15·00	9·00
		a. Broken bottom left triangle	£225	£170
87		30pa. violet and green	2·50	2·00
		a. Broken bottom left triangle	£120	70·00
		w. Wmk inverted	£3000	£3000
		y. Wmk inverted and reversed	†	£2500
88		30pa. green (1923)	7·50	1·75
		a. Broken bottom left triangle	£190	65·00
		w. Wmk inverted	†	£2500
89		1pi. carmine and blue	25·00	42·00
		a. Broken bottom left triangle	£325	
90		1pi. violet and red (1922)	3·50	4·00
		a. Broken bottom left triangle	£140	£150
91		1½pi. yellow and black (1922)	12·00	7·00
		a. Broken bottom left triangle	£200	£160
92		2pi. blue and purple	32·00	24·00
		a. Broken bottom left triangle	£425	£325
93		2pi. carmine and blue (1922)	15·00	27·00
		a. Broken bottom left triangle	£300	£500
94		2¾pi. blue and purple (1922)	10·00	9·00
		a. Broken bottom left triangle	£225	£250
95		4pi. olive-green and purple	18·00	25·00
		a. Broken bottom left triangle	£300	£375
		w. Wmk inverted	†	£2500
96		6pi. sepia and green (1923)	28·00	85·00
		a. Broken bottom left triangle	£375	
97		9pi. brown and carmine (1922)	40·00	90·00
		a. Yellow-brown and carmine	£120	£160
		b. Broken bottom left triangle	£500	£800
98		18pi. black and brown (1923)	80·00	£160
		a. Broken bottom left triangle	£800	
99		45pi. dull purple & ultramarine (1923)	£250	£275
		a. Broken bottom left triangle	£2000	£2250
85/99 *Set of* 15			£500	£700
85s/99s Optd "SPECIMEN" *Set of* 15			£650	

A ½pi. black was prepared for use but not issued. One example exists, opt "SPECIMEN".

(b) Wmk Mult Crown CA (1923)

100	**12**	10s. green and red/*pale yellow*	£375	£800
		a. Broken bottom left triangle	£4000	
101		£1 purple and black/*red*	£1300	£2750
		a. Broken bottom left triangle	£6500	£10000
100s/1s Optd "SPECIMEN" *Set of* 2			£600	

Examples of Nos. 96/101 are known showing a forged Limassol postmark dated "14 MR 25".

1924–28. Chalk-surfaced paper.

(a) Wmk Mult Crown CA

102	**13**	£1 purple and black/*red*	£300	£850

(b) Wmk Mult Script CA

103	**13**	¼pi. grey and chestnut	2·00	50
		w. Wmk inverted	†	£2500
104		½pi. brownish black and black	6·00	14·00
105		¾pi. green	4·00	1·00

106		1pi. purple and chestnut	2·25	2·00
107		1½pi. orange and black	3·25	14·00
108		2pi. carmine and green	4·00	20·00
109		2¾pi. bright blue and purple	3·25	4·75
110		4pi. sage-green and purple	5·00	5·00
111		4½pi. black and orange/*emerald*	3·50	5·00
112		6pi. olive-brown and green	5·00	8·50
113		9pi. brown and purple	8·50	5·50
114		12pi. chestnut and black	14·00	60·00
115		18pi. black and orange	24·00	5·00
116		45pi. purple and blue	55·00	38·00
117		90pi. green and red/*yellow*	£120	£250
117*a*		£5 black/*yellow* (1928) (F.C. £275)	£3250	£7500
		as. Optd "SPECIMEN"	£1000	

Examples of No. 102 are known showing a forged Limassol postmark dated "14 MR 25" and of No. 117*a* showing a forged Registered Nicosia postmark dated "6 MAY 35".

CROWN COLONY

1925. Wmk Mult Script CA. Chalk-surfaced paper (½, ¾ and 2pi.).

118	**13**	½pi. green	2·25	1·00
119		¾pi. brownish black and black	4·25	1·00
120		1½pi. scarlet	5·00	1·50
121		2pi. yellow and black	14·00	3·25
122		2½pi. bright blue	5·00	1·75
102/22 (*ex* £5) *Set of* 21			£500	£1200
102s/22s (*ex* £5) Optd "SPECIMEN" *Set of* 21			£1000	

In the above set the fraction bar in the value is horizontal. In Nos. 91, 94, 107 and 109 it is diagonal.

14 Silver Coin of Amathus, 6th-cent B.C.

15 Zeno (philosopher)

16 Map of Cyprus

17 Discovery of body of St. Barnabas

18 Cloister, Abbey of Bella Paise

19 Badge of Cyprus

20 Tekke of Umm Haram

21 Statue of Richard I, Westminster

22 St. Nicholas Cathedral (now Lala Mustafa Pasha Mosque), Famagusta

23 King George V

(Recess B.W.)

1928 (1 Feb). 50th Anniv of British Rule. T **14/23**. Wmk Mult Script CA. P 12.

123	**14**	¾pi. deep dull purple	3·50	1·50
124	**15**	1pi. black and greenish blue	3·50	1·50
125	**16**	1½pi. scarlet	5·50	2·00
126	**17**	2½pi. light blue	3·75	2·25
127	**18**	4pi. deep brown	9·00	9·00
128	**19**	6pi. blue	12·00	28·00
129	**20**	9pi. maroon	9·50	15·00
130	**21**	18pi. black and brown	28·00	32·00
131	**22**	45pi. violet and blue	42·00	50·00
132	**23**	£1 blue and bistre-brown	£225	£300
123/32 *Set of* 10			£300	£400
123s/32s Optd "SPECIMEN" *Set of* 10			£700	

24 Ruins of Vouni Palace

25 Small Marble Forum, Salamis

26 Church of St. Barnabas and St. Hilarion, Peristerona

27 Roman theatre, Soli

28 Kyrenia Harbour

29 Kolossi Castle

30 St. Sophia Cathedral, Nicosia (now Selimiye Mosque)

31 Bayraktar Mosque, Nicosia

32 Queen's window, St. Hilarion Castle

33 Buyuk Khan, Nicosia

34 Forest scene, Troodos

(Recess Waterlow)

1934 (1 Dec). T **24/34**. Wmk Mult Script CA (sideways on ½pi., 1½pi., 2½pi., 4½pi., 6pi., 9pi. and 18pi.). P 12½.

No.	Type	Description	Unused	Used
133	**24**	¼pi. ultramarine and orange-brown	1·25	1·00
		a. Imperf between (vert pair)	£50000	£32000
134	**25**	½pi. green	1·75	1·00
		a. Imperf between (vert pair)	£17000	£19000
135	**26**	¾pi. black and violet	3·25	40
		a. Imperf between (vert pair)	£50000	
136	**27**	1pi. black and red-brown	2·75	2·25
		a. Imperf between (vert pair)	£25000	£25000
		b. Imperf between (horiz pair)	£18000	
137	**28**	1½pi. carmine	3·75	2·00
138	**29**	2½pi. ultramarine	5·00	1·75
139	**30**	4½pi. black and crimson	5·00	4·75
140	**31**	6pi. black and blue	12·00	19·00
141	**32**	9pi. sepia and violet	14·00	8·00
142	**33**	18pi. black and olive-green	50·00	45·00
143	**34**	45pi. green and black	£100	80·00
133/43 *Set of* 11			£180	£150
133s/43s Perf "SPECIMEN" *Set of* 11			£550	

34a Windsor Castle

Kite and horizontal log (Plate "2B" R. 10/6)

(Recess Waterlow & Sons)

1935 (6 May). Silver Jubilee. Wmk Mult Script CA. P11×12.

No.	Type	Description	Unused	Used
144	**34a**	¾pi. ultramarine and grey	4·00	1·50
145		1½pi. deep blue and scarlet	6·00	2·75
		l. Kite and horizontal log	£425	£350
146		2½pi. brown and deep blue	5·00	1·75
147		9pi. slate and purple	23·00	27·00
144/7 *Set of* 4			35·00	30·00
144s/7s Perf "SPECIMEN" *Set of* 4			£190	

34b King George VI and Queen Elizabeth

(Des D.L.R. Recess B.W.)

1937 (12 May). Coronation. Wmk Mult Script CA. P 11×11½.

No.	Type	Description	Unused	Used
148	**34b**	¾pi. grey	2·00	1·00
149		1½pi. carmine	2·50	2·50
150		2½pi. blue	3·00	3·00
148/50 *Set of* 3			6·75	6·00
148s/50s Perf "SPECIMEN" *Set of* 3			£190	

35 Vouni Palace

36 Map of Cyprus

37 Othello's Tower, Famagusta

38 King George VI

(Recess Waterlow)

1938 (12 May)–**51**. T **35** to **38** and other designs as 1934, but with portrait of King George VI. Wmk Mult Script CA. P 12½.

No.	Type	Description	Unused	Used
151	**35**	¼pi. ultramarine and orange-brown	1·75	60
152	**25**	½pi. green	2·25	50
152*a*		½pi. violet (2.7.51)	3·00	75
153	**26**	¾pi. black and violet	21·00	1·75
154	**27**	1pi. orange	2·50	40
		a. Perf 13½×12½ (4.44)	£550	27·00
155	**28**	1½pi. carmine	6·00	1·50
155*a*		1½pi. violet (15.3.43)	2·50	75
155*ab*		1½pi. green (2.7.51)	6·00	1·25
155*b*	**26**	2pi. black and carmine (2.2.42)	2·75	40
		c. Perf 12½×13½ (10.44)	3·00	12·00
156	**29**	2½pi. ultramarine	42·00	2·50
156*a*		3pi. ultramarine (2.2.42)	3·25	60
156*b*		4pi. ultramarine (2.7.51)	4·50	1·25
157	**36**	4½pi. grey	2·50	40
158	**31**	6pi. black and blue	3·50	1·00
159	**37**	9pi. black and purple	2·75	75
160	**33**	18pi. black and olive-green	14·00	1·75
		a. Black and sage-green (19.8.47)	20·00	2·50
161	**34**	45pi. green and black	45·00	4·75
162	**38**	90pi. mauve and black	35·00	8·00
163		£1 scarlet and indigo	65·00	30·00
151/63 *Set of* 19			£250	50·00
151s/63s Perf "SPECIMEN" *Set of* 16			£700	

38a Houses of Parliament, London

Dot between "1" and "½" in right-hand value tablet (Pl B1 R. 7/1)

1946 (21 Oct). Victory. Wmk Mult Script CA. P 13½×14.

No.	Type	Description	Unused	Used
164	**38a**	1½pi. deep violet	50	10
		a. Dot between "1" and "½"	48·00	
165		3pi. blue	50	40
164s/5s Perf "SPECIMEN" *Set of* 2			£180	

38b King George VI and Queen Elizabeth

38c

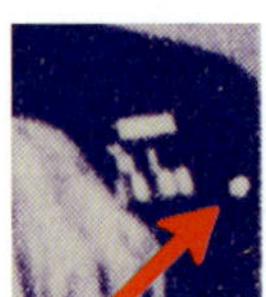

Extra decoration (R. 3/5)

(Des and photo Waterlow (T **38b**). Design recess, name typo B.W. (T **38c**))

1948 (20 Dec). Royal Silver Wedding. Wmk Mult Script CA.

166	**38b**	1½pi. violet (P 14×15)	1·00	50
		a. Extra decoration	50·00	55·00
167	**38c**	£1 indigo (P 11½×11)	55·00	75·00

38d Hermes, Globe and Forms of Transport

38e Hemispheres, Jet powered Vickers Viking Airliner, Steamer

38f Hermes and Globe

38g U.P.U. Monument

Recess Waterlow (T **38d**, **38g**) or B.W. (T **38e**, **38f**)

1949 (10 Oct). 75th Anniv of Universal Postal Union. Wmk Mult Script CA.

168	**38d**	1½pi. violet (P 13½–14)	60	1·50
169	**38e**	2pi. carmine-red (P 11×11½)	1·50	1·50
170	**38f**	3pi. deep blue (P 11×11½)	1·00	1·00
171	**38g**	9pi. purple (P 13½–14)	1·00	3·75
168/71		*Set of* 4	3·50	7·00

38h Queen Elizabeth II

(Des and eng B.W. Recess D.L.R.)

1953 (2 June). Coronation. Wmk Mult Script CA. P 13½×13.

172	**38h**	1½pi. black and emerald	2·00	10

(New Currency = 1000 mils = £1)

39 Carobs

40 Grapes

41 Oranges

42 Mavrovouni Copper Pyrites Mine

43 Troodos Forest

44 Beach of Aphrodite

45 5th-century B.C. coin of Paphos

46 Kyrenia

47 Harvest in Mesaoria

48 Famagusta Harbour

49 St. Hilarion Castle

50 Hala Sultan Tekke

51 Kanakaria Church

52 Coins of Salamis, Paphos, Citium and Idalium

53 Arms of Byzantium, Lusignan, Ottoman Empire and Venice

1955 (1 Aug)–**60**. T **39**/**53**. Wmk Mult Script CA. P 13½ (Nos. 183/5) or 11½ (others).

173	**39**	2m. blackish brown	1·00	40
174	**40**	3m. blue-violet	65	15
175	**41**	5m. brown-orange	2·50	10
		a. Orange-brown (17.9.58)	9·00	60
176	**42**	10m. deep brown and deep green	2·75	10
177	**43**	15m. olive-green and indigo	4·50	45
		aa. Yellow-olive and indigo (17.9.58)	35·00	4·75
		a. Bistre and indigo (14.6.60)	32·00	11·00
178	**44**	20m. brown and deep bright blue	1·50	15
179	**45**	25m. deep turquoise-blue	4·00	60
		a. Greenish blue (17.9.58)	25·00	5·50
180	**46**	30m. black and carmine-lake	3·75	10
181	**47**	35m. orange-brown and deep turquoise-blue	3·25	40
182	**48**	40m. deep green and sepia	3·25	60
183	**49**	50m. turquoise-blue and reddish brown	3·25	30
184	**50**	100m. mauve and bluish green	13·00	60
185	**51**	250m. deep grey-blue and brown	16·00	13·00
186	**52**	500m. slate and purple	38·00	15·00
187	**53**	£1 brown-lake and slate	30·00	55·00
173/87		*Set of* 15	£110	75·00

ΚΥΠΡΙΑΚΗ
ΔΗΜΟΚΡΑΤΙΑ
KIBRIS
CUMHURIYETI

(**54** "Cyprus Republic")

55 Map of Cyprus

(Recess B.W.)

1960 (16 Aug)–**61**. Nos. 173/87 optd as T **54** in blue by B.W. Opt larger on Nos. 191/7 and in two lines on Nos 198/202.

188	2m. blackish brown	20	75
189	3m. blue-violet	20	15
190	5m. brown-orange	1·50	10
	a. Orange-brown (15.8.61)	8·50	70
191	10m. deep brown and deep green	1·00	10
192	15m. yellow-bistre and indigo	2·25	40
	a. Olive-green and indigo	£160	75·00
	b. Brownish bistre and deep indigo (10.10.61)	11·00	4·50
193	20m. brown and deep bright blue	1·75	1·50
	a. Opt double	†	£12000
194	25m. deep turquoise-blue	1·75	1·75
	a. Greenish blue (7.2.61)	38·00	14·00
195	30m. black and carmine-lake	1·75	30
	a. Opt double	†	£42000
196	35m. orange-brown and deep turquoise-blue	1·75	70
197	40m. deep green and sepia	2·00	2·50
198	50m. turquoise-blue and reddish brown	2·00	60
199	100m. mauve and bluish green	9·00	2·50
200	250m. deep grey-blue and brown	30·00	5·50
201	500m. slate and purple	45·00	27·00
202	£1 brown-lake and slate	48·00	60·00
188/202 *Set of 15*		£130	90·00

Only two used examples of No. 195a are known.

(Recess B.W.)

1960 (16 Aug). Constitution of Republic. W w **12**. P 11½.

203	**55** 10m. sepia and deep green	30	10
204	30m. ultramarine and deep brown	65	10
205	100m. purple and deep slate	2·00	2·00
203/5 *Set of 3*		2·75	2·00

PRINTERS. All the following stamps were designed by A. Tassos and lithographed by Aspioti-Elka, Athens, unless otherwise stated.

56 Doves

(Des T. Kurpershoek)

1962 (19 Mar). Europa. P 14×13.

206	**56** 10m. purple and mauve	10	10
207	40m. ultramarine and cobalt	20	15
208	100m. emerald and pale green	20	20
206/8 *Set of 3*		45	40

57 Campaign Emblem

1962 (14 May). Malaria. Eradication. P 14×13½.

209	**57** 10m. black and olive-green	15	15
210	30m. black and brown	30	15

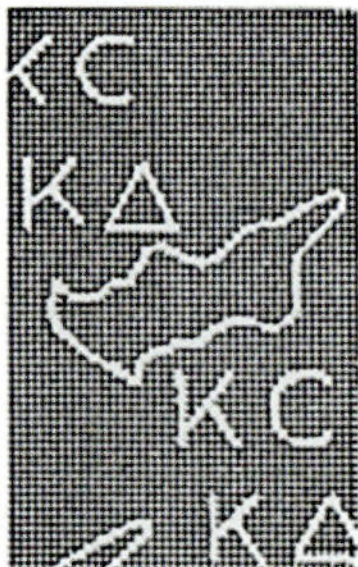

58 Mult K C K Δ and Map

WATERMARK VARIETIES. The issues printed by Aspioti-Elka with W **58** are known with the vertical stamps having the watermark normal or inverted and the horizontal stamps with the watermark reading upwards or downwards. Such varieties are not given separate listing.

62 Selimiye Mosque, Nicosia

63 St. Barnabas's Church

1962 (17 Sept). T **62/3** and similar designs. W **58** (sideways) on 25, 30, 40, 50, 250m., £1). P 13½×14 (vert) or 14×13½ (horiz).

211	3m. deep brown and orange-brown	10	30
212	5m. purple and grey-green	10	10
213	10m. black and yellow-green	15	10
214	15m. black and reddish purple	50	15
215	25m. deep brown and chestnut	60	20
216	30m. deep blue and light blue	20	10
217	35m. light green and blue	35	10
218	40m. black and violet-blue	1·25	1·75
219	50m. bronze-green and bistre	50	10
220	100m. deep brown and yellow-brown	3·50	30
221	250m. black and cinnamon	15·00	2·25
222	500m. deep brown and light green	19·00	10·00
223	£1 bronze-green and grey	17·00	30·00
211/23 *Set of 13*		50·00	40·00

Designs: *Vert*—3m. Iron Age jug; 5m. Grapes; 10m. Bronze head of Apollo; 35m. Head of Aphrodite; 100m. Hala Sultan Tekke; 500m. Mouflon. *Horiz*—30m. Temple of Apollo Hylates; 40m. Skiing, Troodos; 50m. Salamis Gymnasium; 250m. Bella Paise Abbey; £1 St. Hilarion Castle.

72 Europa "Tree"

(Des L. Weyer)

1963 (28 Jan). Europa. W **58** (sideways). P 14×13½.

224	**72** 10m. bright blue and black	1·75	20
225	40m. carmine-red and black	6·50	2·00
226	150m. emerald-green and black	20·00	6·00
224/6 *Set of 3*		25·00	7·25

73 Harvester

75 Wolf Cub in Camp

1963 (21 Mar). Freedom from Hunger. T **73** and similar vert design. W **58**. P 13½×14.

227	25m. ochre, sepia and bright blue	30	25
228	75m. grey, black and lake	1·75	1·00

Design:—75m. Demeter, Goddess of Corn.

1963 (21 Aug). 50th Anniv of Cyprus Scout Movement and Third Commonwealth Scout Conference, Platres. T **75** and similar vert designs. Multicoloured. W **58**. P 13½×14.

229	3m. Type **75**	10	20
230	20m. Sea Scout	35	10
231	150m. Scout with Mouflon	1·00	2·50
229/31 *Set of 3*		1·25	2·50
MS231*a* 110×90 mm. Nos. 229/31 (*sold at 250m.*). Imperf		£110	£180

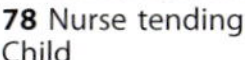
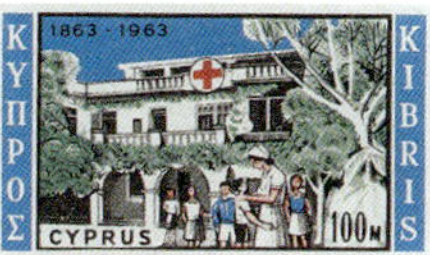

78 Nurse tending Child **79** Children's Centre, Kyrenia

1963 (9 Sept). Centenary of Red Cross. W **58** (sideways on 100m.). P 13½×14 (10m.) or 14×13½ (100m.).

232	**78**	10m. red, blue, grey-blue, chestnut and black	50	15
233	**79**	100m. red, green, black and blue	2·75	3·50

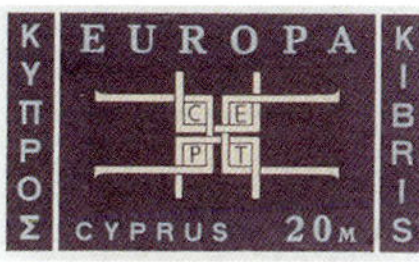

80 "Co-operation" (emblem) (**81**)

(Des A. Holm)

1963 (4 Nov). Europa. W **58** (sideways). P 14×13½.

234	**80**	20m. buff, blue and violet	1·75	40
235		30m. grey, yellow and blue	1·75	40
236		150m. buff, blue and orange-brown	21·00	9·00
234/6 *Set of 3*			22·00	9·00

1964 (5 May). U.N. Security Council's Cyprus Resolutions, March, 1964. Nos. 213, 216, 218/20 optd with T **81** in blue by Govt Printing Office, Nicosia.

237	10m. black and yellow-green	15	10
238	30m. deep blue and light blue	20	10
239	40m. black and violet-blue	25	30
240	50m. bronze-green and bistre	25	10
241	100m. deep brown and yellow-brown	25	50
237/41 *Set of 5*		1·00	1·00

82 Soli Theatre

1964 (15 June). 400th Birth Anniv of Shakespeare. T **82** and similar horiz designs. Multicoloured. W **58**. P 13½×13.

242	15m. Type **82**	80	15
243	35m. Curium Theatre	80	15
244	50m. Salamis Theatre	80	15
245	100m. Othello Tower and scene from *Othello*	1·25	2·25
242/5 *Set of 4*		3·25	2·50

86 Running **89** Europa "Flower"

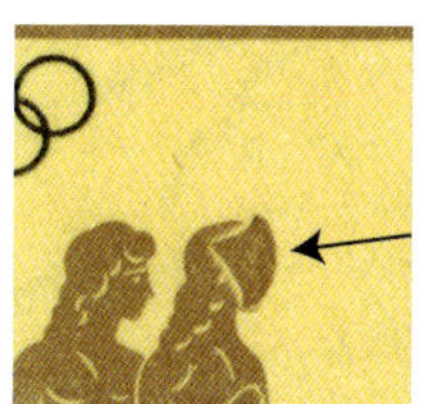

10m. Brown flaw covering face of right-hand runner gives the appearance of a mask (R. 9/2).

As these stamps were printed in sheets of 400, divided into four post office sheets of 100, the variety was only constant on one sheet in four. Moreover, it was quickly discovered and many were removed from the sheets by post office clerks.

1964 (6 July). Olympic Games, Tokyo. T **86** and similar designs. W **58** (sideways, 25m., 75m.). P 13½×14 (10m.) or 14×13½ (others).

246	10m. brown, black and yellow	10	10
	a. Blind runner	£550	
247	25m. brown, blue and blue-grey	20	10
248	75m. brown, black and orange-red	35	65
246/8 *Set of 3*		60	75
MS248*a* 110×90 mm. Nos. 246/8 (*sold at 250m.*). Imperf		6·00	15·00

Designs: *Horiz*—25m. Boxing; 75m. Charioteers.

(Des G. Bétemps)

1964 (14 Sept). Europa. W **58**. P 13½×14.

249	**89**	20m. chestnut and light ochre	1·25	10
250		30m. ultramarine and light blue	1·25	10
251		150m. olive and light blue-green	11·00	5·50
249/51 *Set of 3*			12·00	5·50

90 Dionysus and Acme **91** Silenus (satyr)

1964 (26 Oct). Cyprus Wines. T **90/1** and similar multicoloured designs. W **58** (sideways, 10m. or 100m.). P 14×13½ (horiz) or 13½×14 (vert).

252	10m. Type **90**	30	10
253	40m. Type **91**	65	1·25
254	50m. Commandaria Wine (*vert*)	65	10
255	100m. Wine factory (*horiz*)	1·50	2·00
252/5 *Set of 4*		2·75	3·00

94 President Kennedy

1965 (16 Feb). President Kennedy Commemoration. W **58** (sideways). P 14×13½.

256	**94**	10m. ultramarine	10	10
257		40m. green	25	35
258		100m. carmine-lake	30	35
256/8 *Set of 3*			60	70
MS258*a* 110×90 mm. Nos. 256/8 (*sold at 250m.*). Imperf			3·25	8·00

95 "Old Age" **96** "Maternity"

1965 (12 Apr). Introduction of Social Insurance Law. T **95/6** and similar design. W **58**. P 13½×12 (75m.) or 13½×14 (others).

No.	Type	Description	Unused	Used
259		30m. drab and dull green	15	10
260		45m. light grey-green, blue and deep ultramarine	20	10
261		75m. red-brown and flesh	1·25	2·50
259/61 *Set of 3*			1·40	2·50

Design: *Vert as T* **95**—45m. "Accident".

98 I.T.U. Emblem and Symbols

1965 (17 May). I.T.U. Centenary. W **58** (sideways). P 14×13½.

No.	Type	Description	Unused	Used
262	**98**	15m. black, brown and yellow	75	20
263		60m. black, green and light green	7·50	3·25
264		75m. black, indigo and light blue	8·50	4·75
262/4 *Set of 3*			15·00	7·25

99 I.C.Y. Emblem

1965 (17 May). International Co-operation Year. W **58** (sideways). P 14×13½.

No.	Type	Description	Unused	Used
265	**99**	50m. brown, deep green and light yellow-brown	75	10
266		100m. purple, deep green and light purple	1·25	50

100 Europa "Sprig"

U. N.
Resolution
on Cyprus
18 Dec. 1965

(**101**)

(Des H. Karlsson)

1965 (27 Sept). Europa. W **58** (sideways). P 14×13½.

No.	Type	Description	Unused	Used
267	**100**	5m. black, orange-brown and orange	50	10
268		45m. black, orange-brown and light emerald	4·00	2·00
269		150m. black, orange-brown and light grey	9·00	4·50
267/9 *Set of 3*			12·00	6·00

1966 (31 Jan). U.N. General Assembly's Cyprus Resolution, 18 December 1965. Nos. 211, 213, 216 and 221 optd with T **101** in blue by Govt Printing Office, Nicosia.

No.	Type	Description	Unused	Used
270		3m. deep brown and orange-brown	10	50
271		10m. black and yellow-green	10	10
272		30m. deep blue and light blue	15	15
273		250m. black and cinnamon	80	2·25
270/3 *Set of 4*			1·00	2·75

102 Discovery of St. Barnabas's Body

104 St. Barnabas (icon)

103 St. Barnabas's Chapel

105 "Privileges of Cyprus Church" (*Actual size 102×82 mm*)

1966 (25 Apr). 1900th Death Anniv of St. Barnabas. W **58** (sideways on 15m., 100m., 250m). P 14×13 (25m) or 13×14 (others).

No.	Type	Description	Unused	Used
274	**102**	15m. multicoloured	10	10
275	**103**	25m. drab, black and blue	15	10
276	**104**	100m. multicoloured	45	2·00
274/6 *Set of 3*			60	2·00
MS277		110×91 mm. **105** 250m. mult. Imperf	3·50	13·00

(**106**)

107 General K. S. Thimayya and U.N. Emblem

1966 (30 May). No. 211 surch with T **106** by Govt Printing Office, Nicosia.

No.	Type	Description	Unused	Used
278		5m. on 3m. deep brown and orange-brown	10	10

1966 (6 June). General Thimayya Commemoration. W **58** (sideways). P 14×13.

No.	Type	Description	Unused	Used
279	**107**	50m. black and light orange-brown	30	10

108 Europa "Ship"

(Des G. and J. Bender)

1966 (26 Sept). Europa. W **58**. P 13½×14.

No.	Type	Description	Unused	Used
280	**108**	20m. green and blue	40	10
281		30m. bright purple and blue	40	10
282		150m. bistre and blue	3·25	3·00
280/2 *Set of 3*			3·50	3·00

110 Church of St. James, Trikomo

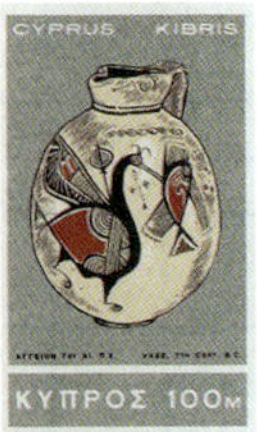

119 Vase of 7th Century B.C.

120 Bronze Ingot-stand

1966 (21 Nov)–**69**. T **110**, **119/20** and similar designs. W **58** (sideways on 3, 15, 25, 50, 250, 500m., £1. P 12×13 (3m.), 13×12 (5, 10m.), 14×13½ (15, 25, 50m.), 13½×14 (20, 30, 35, 40, 100m.) or 13×14 (others).

283	3m. grey-green, buff, black and light blue	40	10
284	5m. bistre, black and steel-blue	10	10
	a. Brownish bistre, black and steel-blue (18.4.69)	75	20
285	10m. black and bistre	15	10
286	15m. black, chestnut and light orange-brown	15	10
287	20m. black, slate and brown	1·25	1·00
288	25m. black, drab and lake-brown	30	10
289	30m. black, yellow-ochre and turquoise	50	20
290	35m. yellow, black and carmine-red	50	30
291	40m. black, grey and new blue	70	30
	a. Grey (background) omitted		
292	50m. black, slate and brown	90	10
293	100m. black, red, pale buff and grey	4·00	15
294	250m. olive-green, black and light yellow-ochre	1·00	40
295	500m. multicoloured	2·75	70
296	£1 black, drab and slate	2·25	6·50
283/96	*Set of* 14	13·00	8·50

Designs: *Horiz* (*as T* **110**)—3m. Stavrovouni Monastery. (*As T* **119**)—15m. Minoan wine ship of 700 B.C. (painting); 25m. Sleeping Eros (marble statue); 50m. Silver coin of Alexander the Great. *Vert* (*as T* **110**)—10m. Zeno of Cibium (marble bust). (*As T* **119**)—20m. Silver coin of Evagoras I; 30m. St. Nicholas Cathedral, Famagusta; 35m. Gold sceptre from Curium; 40m. Silver dish from 7th century. (*As T* **120**)—500m. "The Rape of Ganymede" (mosaic); £1 Aphrodite (marble statue).

123 Power Station, Limassol

124 Cogwheels

1967 (10 Apr). First Development Programme. T **123** and similar designs but horiz. Multicoloured. W **58** (sideways on 15 to 100m.). P 13½×14 (10m.) or 14×13½ (others).

297	10m. Type **123**	10	10
298	15m. Arghaka-Maghounda Dam	15	10
299	35m. Troodos Highway	20	10
300	50m. Hilton Hotel, Nicosia	20	10
301	100m. Famagusta Harbour	20	1·10
297/301	*Set of* 5	75	1·25

(Des O. Bonnevalle)

1967 (2 May). Europa. W **58**. P 13½×14.

302	**124**	20m. olive-green, green and pale yellow-green	30	10
303		30m. reddish violet, lilac and pale lilac	30	10
304		150m. brown, light reddish brown and pale yellow-brown	2·25	2·25
302/4		*Set of* 3	2·50	2·25

125 Throwing the Javelin

126 Running (amphora) and Map of Eastern Mediterranean (*Actual size 97×77 mm*)

1967 (4 Sept). Athletic Games, Nicosia. T **125** and similar designs and T **126**. Multicoloured. W **58**. P 13½×13.

305	15m. Type **125**	20	10
306	35m. Running	20	35
307	100m. High jumping	30	1·00
305/7	*Set of* 3	60	1·25
MS308	110×90 mm. 250m. Type **126** (wmk sideways). Imperf	1·25	6·50

127 Ancient Monuments

128 St. Andrew Mosaic

1967 (16 Oct). International Tourist Year. T **127** and similar horiz designs. Multicoloured. W **58**. P 13×13½.

309	10m. Type **127**	10	10
310	40m. Famagusta Beach	15	90
311	50m. Hawker Siddeley Comet 4 at Nicosia Airport	15	10
312	100m. Skier and youth hostel	20	95
309/12	*Set of* 4	55	1·75

1967 (8 Nov). Centenary of St. Andrew's Monastery. W **58** (sideways). P 13×13½.

313	**128**	25m. multicoloured	10	10

129 "The Crucifixion" (icon)

130 The Three Magi

(Photo French Govt Ptg Wks, Paris)

1967 (8 Nov). Cyprus Art Exhibition, Paris. P 12½×13½.

314	**129**	50m. multicoloured	10	10

1967 (8 Nov). 20th Anniv of U.N.E.S.C.O. W **58** (sideways). P 13×13½.

315	**130**	75m. multicoloured	20	20

131 Human Rights Emblem over Stars

132 Human Rights and U.N. Emblems

133 Scroll of Declaration (*Actual size* 95×75½ *mm*)

1968 (18 Mar). Human Rights Year. W **58**. P 13×14.

316	**131**	50m. multicoloured	10	10
317	**132**	90m. multicoloured	30	70
MS318		95×75½ mm. **133** 250m. multicoloured. W **58** (sideways). Imperf	60	4·75

134 Europa "Key"

(Des H. Schwarzenbach)

1968 (29 Apr). Europa. W **58** (sideways). P 14×13.

319	**134**	20m. multicoloured	25	10
320		30m. multicoloured	25	10
321		150m. multicoloured	1·00	2·25
319/21		*Set of* 3	1·40	2·25

135 U.N. Children's Fund Symbol and Boy drinking Milk

137 Throwing the Discus

136 Aesculapius

1968 (2 Sept). 21st Anniv of U.N.I.C.E.F. W **58** (sideways). P 14×13.

322	**135**	35m. yellow-brown, carmine-red and black	10	10

1968 (2 Sept). 20th Anniv of W.H.O. W **58**. P 13×14.

323	**136**	50m. black, green and light olive	10	10

138 I.L.O. Emblem

1968 (24 Oct). Olympic Games, Mexico. T **137** and similar designs. Multicoloured. W **58** (sideways on 100m.). P 14×13 (100m.) or 13×14 (others).

324	10m. Type **137**	10	10
325	25m. Sprint finish	10	10
326	100m. Olympic Stadium (*horiz*)	20	1·25
324/6	*Set of* 3	35	1·25

1969 (3 Mar). 50th Anniv of International Labour Organization. W **58**. P 12×13½.

327	**138**	50m. yellow-brown, blue and light blue	15	10
328		90m. yellow-brown, black and pale grey	15	55

139 Mercator's Map of Cyprus, 1554

140 Blaeu's Map of Cyprus, 1635

1969 (7 Apr). First International Congress of Cypriot Studies. W **58** (sideways). P 14×14½.

329	**139**	35m. multicoloured	20	30
330	**140**	50m. multicoloured	20	10
		a. Wmk upright	—	2·75
		ab. Grey (shading on boats and cartouche) omitted	£450	

141 Europa Emblem

142 European Roller

(Des L. Gasbarra and G. Belli)

1969 (28 Apr). Europa. W **58** (sideways). P 14×13½.

331	**141**	20m. multicoloured	30	10
332		30m. multicoloured	30	10
333		150m. multicoloured	1·00	2·00
331/3		*Set of* 3	1·40	2·00

1969 (7 July). Birds of Cyprus. T **142** and similar designs. Multicoloured. W **58** (sideways on horiz designs). P 13½×12 (horiz designs) or 12×13½ (vert designs).

334	5m. Type **142**	40	15
335	15m. Audouin's Gull	50	15
336	20m. Cyprus Warbler	50	15
337	30m. Jay (*vert*)	50	15
338	40m. Hoopoe (*vert*)	55	30
339	90m. Eleanora's Falcon (*vert*)	1·25	4·50
334/9	*Set of* 6	3·25	4·75

The above were printed on glazed Samuel Jones paper with very faint watermark.

143 "The Nativity" (12th-century Wall Painting)

145 "Virgin and Child between Archangels Michael and Gabriel" (6th–7th-century Mosaic) (*Actual size* 102×81 *mm*)

1969 (24 Nov). Christmas. T **143** and similar horiz design, and T **145**. Multicoloured. W **58** (sideways). P 13½×13.

340	20m. Type **143**	15	10
341	45m. "The Nativity" (14th-century wall painting)	15	20
MS342	110×90 mm. 250m. Type **145**. Imperf	3·00	12·00
	a. Grey and light brown omitted	£3250	

146 Mahatma Gandhi

1970 (26 Jan). Birth Centenary of Mahatma Gandhi. W **58** (sideways). P 14×13½.

343	**146**	25m. ultramarine, drab and black	50	10
344		75m. yellow-brown, drab and black	75	65

147 "Flaming Sun"

148 Gladioli

(Des L. le Brocquy)

1970 (4 May). Europa. W **58** (sideways). P 14×13.

345	**147**	20m. brown, greenish yellow and orange	30	10
346		30m. new blue, greenish yellow and orange	30	10
347		150m. bright purple, greenish yellow and orange	1·00	2·50
345/7		*Set of* 3	1·40	2·50

1970 (3 Aug). European Conservation Year. T **148** and similar vert designs. Multicoloured. W **58**. P 13×13½.

348	10m. Type **148**	10	10
349	50m. Poppies	15	10
350	90m. Giant fennel	50	1·40
348/50	*Set of* 3	65	1·40

149 I.E.Y. Emblem

150 Mosaic

151 Globe, Dove and U.N. Emblem

(Des G. Simonis (75m.))

1970 (7 Sept). Anniversaries and Events. W **58** (sideways on horiz designs). P 13×14 (5m.) or 14×13 (others).

351	**149**	5m. black, red-brown and light yellow-brown	10	10
352	**150**	15m. multicoloured	10	10
353	**151**	75m. multicoloured	15	75
351/3		*Set of* 3	30	85

Events:—5m. International Education Year; 15m. 50th General Assembly of International Vine and Wine Office; 75m. 25th anniv of United Nations.

152 Virgin and Child

153 Cotton Napkin

(Photo Harrison)

1970 (23 Nov). Christmas. Wall-painting from Church of Panayia Podhythou, Galata. T **152** and similar multicoloured designs. P 14×14½.

354	25m. Archangel (facing right)	15	20
	a. Horiz strip of 3. Nos. 354/6	40	55
355	25m. Type **152**	15	20
356	25m. Archangel (facing left)	15	20
357	75m. Virgin and Child between Archangels	15	30
354/7	*Set of* 4	55	80

The 75m. is horiz, size 42×30 mm, and the 25m. values are vert, size as T **152**.

Nos. 354/6 were issued in *se-tenant* strips of three, throughout the sheet. The triptych thus formed is depicted in its entirety on the 75m. value.

1971 (22 Feb). Multicoloured designs as T **153**. W **58** (sideways on horiz designs).

(a) Vert designs 23×33 mm. P 12×13½

358	3m. Type **153**	30	35
359	5m. St. George and Dragon (19th-cent bas-relief)	10	10

(b) Vert (10, 20, 25, 40, 50, 75m.) or horiz (15, 30, 90m.) designs, each 24×37 or 37×24 mm. P 13×14 (15, 30, 90m.) or 14×13 (others)

360	10m. Woman in festival costume	15	50
361	15m. Archaic Bichrome Kylix (cup)	20	10
	a. Vert laid paper	1·00	
362	20m. A pair of donors (St. Mamas Church)	35	65
363	25m. "The Creation" (6th-cent mosaic)	30	10
364	30m. Athena and horse-drawn chariot (4th-cent B.C. terracotta)	30	10
365	40m. Shepherd playing pipe (14th-cent fresco)	1·00	1·00
366	50m. Hellenistic head (3rd cent B.C.)	80	10
367	75m. "Angel" (mosaic detail), Kanakaria Church	2·00	1·00
368	90m. Mycenaean silver bowl	2·00	2·25

(c) Horiz (250, 500m.) or vert (£1) designs, each 41×28 or 28×41 mm. P 13½×13 (250, 500m or 13×13½ (£1)

369	250m. Moufflon (detail of 3rd-cent mosaic) (*shades*)	1·50	30
370	500m. Ladies and sacred tree (detail, 6th-cent amphora)	1·00	30
371	£1 Horned god from Enkomi (12th-cent bronze statue)	1·75	45
358/71	*Set of* 14	10·00	5·50

154 Europa Chain

155 Archbishop Kyprianos

(Des H. Haflidason)

1971 (3 May). Europa. W **58** (sideways). P 14 ×13.

372 **154** 20m. pale blue, ultramarine and black 25 10
373 30m. apple green, myrtle-green and black 25 10
374 150m. lemon, bright green and black .... 1·10 3·00
372/4 *Set of 3* .... 1·40 3·00

The above were printed on glazed paper with very faint watermark.

1971 (9 July). 150th Anniv of Greek War of Independence. T **155** and similar multicoloured designs. W **58** (sideways on 30m.). P 13½×12½ (30m or 12½×13½ (others).

375 15m. Type **155** 10 10
376 30m. "Taking the Oath" (*horiz*) 10 10
377 100m. Bishop Germanos, flag and freedom fighters 20 50
375/7 *Set of 3* 30 55

156 Kyrenia Castle

157 Madonna and Child in Stable

1971 (20 Sept). Tourism. T **156** and similar multicoloured designs. W **58** (sideways on 15 and 100m.). P 13½×13 (15m., 100m.) or 13×13½ (others).

378 15m. Type **156** 10 10
379 25m. Gourd on sunny beach (*vert*) 10 10
380 60m. Mountain scenery (*vert*) 20 60
381 100m. Church of St. Evlalios, Lambousa 20 65
378/81 *Set of 4* .... 45 1·25

1971 (22 Nov). Christmas. T **157** and similar vert designs. Multicoloured. W **58**. P 13×14.

382 10m. Type **157** 10 10
a. Horiz strip of 3. Nos. 382/4 .... 35 70
383 50m. The Three Wise Men 15 35
384 100m. The Shepherds 20 35
382/4 *Set of 3* 35 70

The 10m. was issued in sheets of 100, and all three values were printed horizontally *se-tenant* in sheets of 36, the order being 50, 10 and 100m.

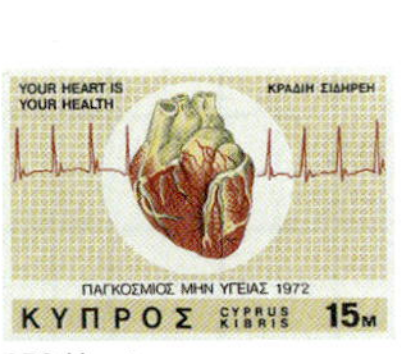

158 Heart

159 "Communications"

1972 (11 Apr). World Heart Month. W **58** (sideways). P 13½×12.

385 **158** 15m. multicoloured 10 10
386 50m. multicoloured 20 45

(Des P. Huovinen)

1972 (22 May). Europa. W **58**. P 12½×13½.

387 **159** 20m. yellow-orange, sepia and pale grey-brown 40 15
388 30m. yellow-orange, bright deep ultramarine and cobalt 40 15
389 150m. yellow-orange, myrtle-green and pale turquoise-green .... 2·50 4·50
387/9 *Set of 3* .... 3·00 4·50

160 Archery

1972 (24 July). Olympic Games, Munich. T **160** and similar horiz designs. Multicoloured. W **58** (sideways). P 14×13.

390 10m. Type **160** 25 10
391 40m. Wrestling 35 15
392 100m. Football .... 75 1·75
390/2 *Set of 3* .... 1·25 1·75

161 Stater of Marion

162 Bathing the Child Jesus

1972 (25 Sept). Ancient Coins of Cyprus (1st series), T **161** and similar horiz designs. W **58** (sideways). P 14×13.

393 20m. pale turquoise-blue, black and silver 20 10
394 30m. pale violet-blue, black and silver 20 10
395 40m. brownish stone, black and silver 20 20
396 100m. light salmon-pink, black and silver .... 60 1·00
393/6 *Set of 4* .... 1·10 1·25

Coins:—30m. Stater of Paphos; 40m. Stater of Lapithos; 100m. Stater of Idalion.

See also Nos. 486/9.

1972 (20 Nov). Christmas. T **162** and similar vert designs showing portions of a mural in the Church of the Holy Cross of Agiasmati. Multicoloured. W **58** (sideways on **MS**400). P 13×14.

397 10m. Type **162** 10 10
398 20m. The Magi 10 10
399 100m. The Nativity 15 30
397/9 *Set of 3* 30 35

MS400 100×90 mm. 250m. Showing the mural in full. Imperf .... 1·10 4·50

163 Mount Olympus, Troodos

1973 (13 Mar). 29th International Ski Federation Congress. T **163** and similar horiz design. Multicoloured. W **58** (sideways). P 14×13.

401 20m. Type **163** 10 10
402 100m. Congress emblem 25 35

164 Europa "Posthorn"

(Des I. Anisdahl)

1973 (7 May). Europa. W **58** (sideways). P 14×13.

403 **164** 20m. multicoloured 25 10
404 30m. multicoloured 25 10
405 150m. multicoloured .... 1·50 3·50
403/5 *Set of 3* .... 1·75 3·50

165 Archbishop's Palace, Nicosia

20M

(166)

1973 (23 July). Traditional Architecture. T **165** and similar multicoloured designs. W **58** (sideways on 20 and 100m.). P 14×13 (20 and 100m.) or 13×14 (others).

406	20m. Type **165**	10	10
407	30m. House of Hajigeorgajis Cornessios, Nicosia (*vert*)	10	10
408	50m. House at Gourri, 1850 (*vert*)	15	10
409	100m. House at Rizokarpaso, 1772	40	85
406/9	*Set of* 4	65	1·00

1973 (24 Sept). No. 361 surch with T **166**.

410	20m. on 15m. Archaic Bichrome Kylix (cup)	15	15
	a. Vert laid paper	1·00	
	b. Surch inverted		

167 Scout Emblem

168 Archangel Gabriel

1973 (24 Sept). Anniversaries and Events. T **167** and similar designs. W **58** (sideways on 25 and 35m.). P 13×14 (10, 50 and 100m.) or 14×13 (others).

411	10m. yellow-olive and deep brown	20	10
412	25m. deep blue and slate-lilac	20	10
413	35m. light brown-olive, stone and sage-green	20	25
414	50m. dull blue and indigo	20	10
415	100m. brown and sepia	50	80
411/15	*Set of* 5	1·10	1·10

Designs and Events: *Vert*—10m. Type **167** (60th anniv of Cyprus Boy Scouts); 50m. Airline emblem (25th anniv of Cyprus Airways); 100m. Interpol emblem (50th anniv of Interpol). *Horiz*—25m. Outline of Cyprus and E.E.C. nations (Association of Cyprus with the E.E.C); 35m. F.A.O. emblem (Tenth anniv of F.A.O.).

1973 (26 Nov). Christmas. Murals from Araka Church. T **168** and similar multicoloured designs. W **58** (sideways on 100m.). P 14×13 (100m.) or 13×14 (others).

416	10m. Type **168**	10	10
417	20m. Madonna and Child	10	10
418	100m. Araka Church (*horiz*)	40	75
416/18	*Set of* 3	45	75

169 Grapes

170 "The Rape of Europa" (Silver Stater of Marion)

1974 (18 Mar). Products of Cyprus. T **169** and similar vert designs. Multicoloured. W **58**. P 13×14.

419	25m. Type **169**	10	15
420	50m. Grapefruit	20	70
	a. Horiz strip of 3. Nos. 420/2	55	2·00
421	50m. Oranges	20	70
422	50m. Lemons	20	70
419/22	*Set of* 4	65	2·00

Nos. 420/2 were printed together, horizontally *se-tenant* throughout the sheet.

1974 (29 Apr). Europa. W **58**. P 13½×14.

423	**170** 10m. multicoloured	15	10
424	40m. multicoloured	40	30
425	150m. multicoloured	1·40	2·75
423/5	*Set of* 3	1·75	2·75

171 Title Page of A. Kyprianos' "History of Cyprus" (1788)

REFUGEE
FUND
ΤΑΜΕΙΟΝ
ΠΡΟΣΦΥΓΩΝ
GÖÇMENLER
FONU

10M

(172)

1974 (22 July*). Second International Congress of Cypriot Studies. T **171** and similar multicoloured designs. W **58** (sideways on 25m. and **MS**429). P 14×13½ (25m.) or 13½×14 (others).

426	10m. Type **171**	10	10
427	25m. Solon (philosopher) in mosaic (*horiz*)	15	10
428	100m. "St. Neophytos" (wall painting)	60	75
426/8	*Set of* 3	70	80
MS429	111×90 mm. 250m. Ortelius' map of Cyprus and Greek Islands, 1584. Imperf	1·25	5·00

*Although this is the date appearing on first day covers the stamps were not put on sale until the 24th.

1974 (1 Oct). Obligatory Tax. Refugee Fund. No. 359 surch with T **172**.

430	10m. on 5m. St. George and Dragon	10	10

SECURITY
COUNCIL
RESOLUTION
353
20 JULY 1974

(173)

174 "Refugees"

1974 (14 Oct). U.N. Security Council Resolution 353. Nos. 360, 365, 366 and 369 optd as T **173**.

431	10m. Woman in festival costume	20	10
432	40m. Shepherd playing pipe	25	60
433	50m. Hellenistic head	25	10
434	250m. Moufflon (*shades*)	60	3·00
431/4	*Set of* 4	1·10	3·50

1974 (2 Dec). Obligatory Tax. Refugee Fund. W **58** (sideways). P 12×12½.

435	**174** 10m. black and light grey	10	10

175 "Virgin and Child between Two Angels", Stavros Church

1974 (2 Dec). Christmas. T **175** and similar multicoloured designs showing wall-paintings. W **58** (sideways on10m. and 100m.). P 13×14 (50m.) or 14×13 (others).

436	10m. Type **175**	10	10
437	50m. "Adoration of the Magi", Ayios Neophytos Monastery (*vert*)	20	10
438	100m. "Flight into Egypt", Ayios Neophytos Monastery	25	45
436/8	*Set of* 3	45	50

176 Larnaca–Nicosia Mail-coach, 1878

177 "The Distaff" (M. Kashalos)

(Photo Harrison)

1975 (17 Feb). Anniversaries and Events. T **176** and similar designs. No wmk. P 14.

439	**176**	20m. multicoloured	25	10
440	–	30m. ultramarine, slate-black and dull orange	25	60
441	**176**	50m. multicoloured	25	10
442	–	100m. multicoloured	40	1·40
439/42		*Set of* 4	1·00	2·00

Designs and Events: 20m., 50m. Type **176** (Centenary of Universal Postal Union). *Vert* 30m. "Disabled Persons" (Eighth European Meeting of International Society for the Rehabilitation of Disabled Persons); 100m. Council flag (25th anniv of Council of Europe).

(Photo Harrison)

1975 (28 Apr). Europa. T **177** and similar vert designs. Multicoloured. P 13½×14½.

443	20m. Type **177**	25	40
	a. Horiz strip of 3. Nos. 443/5	80	1·50
444	30m. "Nature Morte" (C. Savva)	25	50
445	150m. "Virgin and Child of Liopetri" (G. P. Georghiou)	40	80
443/5	*Set of* 3	80	1·50

Nos. 443/5 were printed horizontally *se-tenant* throughout the sheet.

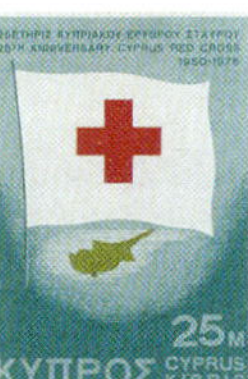

178 Red Cross Flag over Map

179 Submarine Cable Links

1975 (4 Aug). Anniversaries and Events. T **178** and similar horiz designs. P 12½×13½ (25m.) or 13½×12½ (others).

446	25m. multicoloured	20	10
447	30m. turquoise-green and greenish blue	20	10
448	75m. red-brown, orange-brown and pale blue-grey	20	90
446/8	*Set of* 3	55	1·00

Designs and Events: *Vert*—25m. Type **178** (25th anniversary of Cyprus Red Cross). *Horiz*—30m. Nurse and lamp (International Nurses' Day); 75m. Woman's Steatite Idol (International Women's Year).

1975 (13 Oct). Telecommunications Achievements. T **179** and similar design. W **58** (sideways on 100m.). P 12×13½ (50m.) or 13½×12 (100m).

449	50m. multicoloured	30	10
450	100m. orange-yellow, dull violet and lilac	35	90

Design: *Horiz*—100m. International subscriber dialling.

10M

(**180**)

181 Human-figured Vessel, 19th-Century

1976 (5 Jan). No. 358 surch with T **180**.

451	10m. on 3m. Cotton napkin	20	1·00

1976 (3 May). Europa. Ceramics. T **181** and similar vert designs. Multicoloured. W **58**. P 13×14.

452	20m. Type **181**	20	10
453	60m. Composite vessel, 2100–2000 B.C	50	80
454	100m. Byzantine goblet	90	1·75
452/4	*Set of* 3	1·40	2·40

182 Self-help Housing

183 Terracotta Statue of Youth

1976 (3 May). Economic Reactivation. T **182** and similar horiz designs. Multicoloured. W **58** (sideways). P 14×13.

455	10m. Type **182**	10	10
456	25m. Handicrafts	15	20
457	30m. Reafforestation	15	20
458	60m. Air Communications	30	55
455/58	*Set of* 4	55	90

1976 (7 June). Cypriot Treasures. T **183** and similar designs. W **58** (sideways on horiz designs, upright on vert designs). *Ordinary cream paper*. P 12×13½ (5, 10m.), 13×14 (20 25, 30m.), 14×13 (40, 50, 60m.), 13½×12 (100m.) or 13×13½ (250m. to £1).

459	5m. multicoloured	10	80
460	10m. multicoloured	10	60
461	20m. red, yellow and black	20	60
462	25m. multicoloured	20	10
463	30m. multicoloured	20	10
464	40m. grey-green, light olive-bistre and black	30	55
465	50m. buff, brown and black	30	10
466	60m. multicoloured	30	20
467	100m. multicoloured	40	50
468	250m. deep dull blue, grey and black	50	1·75
469	500m. black, stone and deep blue-green	60	2·00
470	£1 multicoloured	1·00	2·25
459/70	*Set of* 12	3·75	8·25

Sizes:—23×34 mm, 5m., 10m.; 34×23 mm, 100m.; 24×37 mm, 20, 25, 30m.; 37×24 mm, 40, 50, 60m.; 28×41 mm, others.

Designs:—10m. Limestone head; 20m. Gold necklace from Lambousa; 25m. Terracotta warrior; 30m. Statue of a priest of Aphrodite; 40m. Bronze tablet; 50m. Mycenaean crater; 60m. Limestone sarcophagus; 100m. Gold bracelet from Lambousa; 250m. Silver dish from Lambousa; 500m. Bronze stand; £1 Statue of Artemis.

184 Olympic Symbol

185 "George Washington" (G. Stuart)

(Litho Harrison)

1976 (5 July). Olympic Games, Montreal. T **184** and similar designs. P 14.

471	20m. carmine-red, black and yellow	10	10
472	60m. multicoloured	20	30
473	100m. multicoloured	30	35
471/3	*Set of* 3	55	65

Designs: *Horiz*—60, 100m. Olympic symbols (*different*).

1976 (5 July). Bicentenary of American Revolution. W **58**. P 13×13½.

474	**185**	100m. multicoloured	40	30

186 Children in Library **187** Archangel Michael

1976 (27 Sept). Anniversaries and Events. T **186** and similar vert designs. W **58**. P 13½×12½ (50m.) or 13½ (others).

475	40m. multicoloured	15	15
476	50m. yellow-brown and black	15	10
477	80m. multicoloured	30	60
475/7	*Set of 3*	55	75

Designs and Events:—40m. Type **186** (Promotion of Children's Books); 50m. Low-cost housing (HABITAT Conference, Vancouver); 80m. Eye protected by hands (World Health Day).

(Litho Harrison)

1976 (15 Nov). Christmas. T **187** and similar vert designs showing icons from Ayios Neophytis Monastery. Multicoloured. P 12½.

478	10m. Type **187**	10	10
479	15m. Archangel Gabriel	10	10
480	150m. The Nativity	45	80
478/80	*Set of 3*	60	80

188 "Cyprus 74" (wood-engraving by A. Taesos) **189** "View of Prodhromos" (A. Diamantis)

1977 (10 Jan*)–**82**. Obligatory Tax. Refugee Fund. W **58**. Ordinary cream paper. P 13×12½.

481	**188** 10m. grey-black	20	10
	a. Chalk-surfaced cream paper		

*Earliest known date of use.

For 1c. value, see Nos. 634/b, 729 and 747.

1977 (2 May). Europa. Paintings. T **189** and similar horiz designs. Multicoloured. No wmk. P 13½×13.

482	20m. Type **189**	20	10
483	60m. "Springtime at Monagroulli" (T. Kanthos)	30	55
484	120m. "Old Port, Limassol" (V. Ioannides)	60	2·40
482/4	*Set of 3*	1·00	2·75

190 Overprinted 500m. Stamp of 1960 **191** Bronze Coin of Emperor Trajan

1977 (13 June). Silver Jubilee. W **58**. P 13×13½.

485	**190** 120m. multicoloured	30	30

(Litho Harrison)

1977 (13 June). Ancient Coins of Cyprus (2nd series). T **191** and similar horiz designs. P 14.

486	10m. brownish black, gold and ultramarine	15	10
487	40m. brownish black, silver and pale blue	30	30
488	60m. brownish black, silver and dull orange	35	35
489	100m. brownish black, gold and blue-green	50	95
486/9	*Set of 4*	1·10	1·50

Designs:—110m. Silver tetradrachm of Demetrios Poliorcetes; 60m. Silver tetradrachm of Ptolemy VIII; 100m. Gold Octadrachm of Arsinoe II.

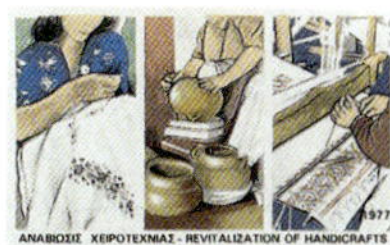

192 Archbishop Makarios in Ceremonial Robes **193** Embroidery, Pottery and Weaving

1977 (10 Sept). Death of Archbishop Makarios. T **192** and similar vert designs. Multicoloured. P 13×13½.

490	20m. Type **192**	15	10
491	60m. Archbishop and doorway	20	10
492	250m. Head and shoulders portrait	50	1·10
490/2	*Set of 3*	75	1·10

1977 (17 Oct). Anniversaries and Events. T **193** and similar horiz designs. Multicoloured. W **58** (sideways). P 13½×13.

493	20m. Type **193**	10	10
494	40m. Map of Mediterranean	15	20
495	60m. Gold medals	20	20
496	80m. "Sputnik"	20	85
493/6	*Set of 4*	60	1·25

Events:—20m. Revitalisation of handicrafts; 40m. "Man and the Biosphere" Programme in the Mediterranean region; 60m. Gold medals won by Cypriot students in the Orleans Gymnasiade; 80m. 60th anniv of Russian October Revolution.

194 "Nativity"

(Litho Harrison)

1977 (21 Nov). Christmas. T **194** and similar horiz designs showing children's paintings. Multicoloured. P 14×13½.

497	10m. Type **194**	10	10
498	40m. "The Three Kings"	10	10
499	150m. "Flight into Egypt"	25	80
497/9	*Set of 3*	35	90

195 Demetrios Libertis **196** Chrysorrhogiatissa Monastery Courtyard

(Des A. Ioannides)

1978 (6 Mar). Cypriot Poets. T **195** and similar horiz design. W **58** (sideways). P 14×13.

500	40m. dull brown and olive-bistre	10	10
501	150m. grey, grey-black and light red	30	80

Design:—150m. Vasilis Michaelides.

(Litho Harrison)

1978 (24 Apr). Europa. Architecture. T **196** and similar horiz designs. Multicoloured. P 14×13½.

502	25m. Type **196**	15	10
503	75m. Kolossi Castle	25	35
504	125m. Municipal Library, Paphos	45	1·50
502/4	*Set of 3*	75	1·75

197 Archbishop of Cyprus, 1950–77

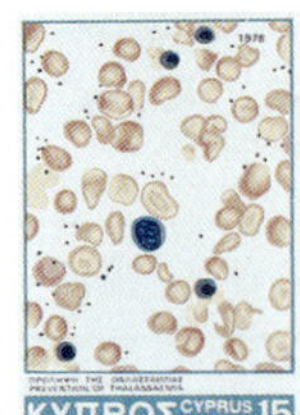

198 Affected Blood Corpuscles (Prevention of Thalassaemia)

(Des A. Ioannides (300m.). Photo Harrison)

1978 (3 Aug). Archbishop Makarios Commemoration. T **197** and similar vert designs. Multicoloured. P 14×15.

505 15m. Type **197** 15 20
a. Silver (inscr and emblem) omitted ....
b. Horiz strip of 5. Nos. 505/9 85
ba. Imperf (horiz strip of 5) £1000
bb. Silver omitted (horiz strip of 5) £1000
506 25m. Exiled in Seychelles, 9 March 1956–28 March 1957 .... 15 20
507 50m. President of the Republic, 1960–77 .... 20 25
508 75m. "Soldier of Christ" 20 30
509 100m. "Fighter for Freedom" 25 35
a. Silver (inscr and emblem) omitted ....
505/9 *Set of 5* .... 85 1·10
MS510 110×80 mm. 300m. "The Great Leader". Imperf. 1·00 2·50

Nos. 505/9 were printed together, *se-tenant*, in horizontal strips of 5 throughout the sheet.

Sheets of this issue are known with the silver omitted completely or only from the first or last vertical rows.

(Des A. Ioannides)

1978 (23 Oct). Anniversaries and Events. T **198** and similar designs. P 13½×14 (15, 35m.) or 14×13½ (others).

511 15m. multicoloured 10 10
512 35m. multicoloured 15 10
513 75m. black and grey 20 30
514 125m. multicoloured 35 80
511/14 *Set of 4* .... 70 1·10

Designs and Events. *Vert*—35m. Aristotle (sculpture) (2300th death anniversary). *Horiz*—75m. "Heads" (Human Rights); 125m. Wright brothers and *Wright Flyer I* (75th anniversary of powered flight).

199 Icon Stand

200 Aphrodite (statue from Soli)

(Litho Harrison)

1978 (4 Dec). Christmas. T **199** and similar vert designs showing icon stands. P 14×14½.

515 15m. multicoloured 10 10
516 35m. multicoloured 15 10
517 150m. multicoloured 40 60
515/17 *Set of 3* 60 65

(Des G. Simonis. Litho Harrison)

1979 (12 Mar). Aphrodite (Greek goddess of love and beauty) Commemoration (1st issue). T **200** and similar horiz design showing Aphrodite emerging from the sea at Paphos (legendary birthplace). Multicoloured. P 14×13½.

518 75m. Type **200** 25 10
519 125m. Aphrodite on a shell (detail from "Birth of Venus" by Botticelli) 35 25

See also Nos. 584/5.

201 Van, Larnaca–Nicosia Post van and Envelope

202 Peacock Wrasse (*Thalassoma pavo*)

(Des G. Simonis)

1979 (30 Apr). Europa. Communications. T **201** and similar horiz designs. Multicoloured. W **58** (sideways). P 14×13.

520 25m. Type **201** 20 10
521 75m. Radar, satellite and early telephone 30 20
522 125m. Aircraft, ship and envelopes .... 85 1·50
520/2 *Set of 3* .... 1·25 1·60

1979 (25 June). Flora and Fauna. T **202** and similar multicoloured designs. W **58** (sideways on 25 and 125m.). P 13½×12 (25, 125m.) or 12×13½ (others).

523 25m. Type **202** 15 10
524 50m. Black Partridge (*Francolinus francolintus*) (*vert*) 70 60
525 75m. Cedar (*Cedar brevifolia*) (*vert*) 45 30
526 125m. Mule (*Equus mulus*) .... 50 1·25
523/6 *Set of 4* .... 1·60 2·00

203 I.B.E. and U.N.E.S.C.O. Emblems

204 "Jesus" (from Church of the Virgin Mary of Arakas, Lagoudhera)

(Des Mrs. A. Kalathia (25m.), A. Ioannides (others). Litho Harrison)

1979 (1 Oct). Anniversaries and Events. T **203** and similar designs in black, yellow-brown arid yellow-ochre (50m.) or multicoloured (others). P 12½.

527 15m. Type **203** 10 10
528 25m. Graphic design of dove and stamp album (*horiz*) 10 10
529 50m. Lord Kitchener and map of Cyprus (*horiz*) 20 15
530 75m. Child's face (*horiz*) 25 10
531 100m. Graphic design of footballers (*horiz*) 30 20
532 125m. Rotary International emblem and "75" 30 75
527/32 *Set of 6* .... 1·10 1·25

Events:—15m. 50th anniversary of International Bureau of Education; 25m. 20th anniversary of Cyprus Philatelic Society; 50m. Centenary of Cyprus Survey; 75m. International Year of the Child; 100m. 25th anniversary of U.E.F.A. (European Football Association); 125m. 75th anniversary of Rotary International.

1979 (5 Nov). Christmas. Icons. T **204** and similar vert designs. Multicoloured. W **58**. P 13½×13 (35m.) or 13½×14 (others).

533 15m. Type **204** 10 10
534 35m. "Nativity" (from the Iconostasis of the Church of St. Nicholas, Famagusta District) (29×41 mm) 10 10
535 150m. "Holy Mary" (from Church of the Virgin Mary of Arakas, Lagoudhera) 25 45
533/5 *Set of 3* 35 55

205 1880 ½d. Stamp with "969" (Nicosia) Postmark

206 St. Barnabas (Patron Saint of Cyprus)

1980 (17 Mar). Cyprus Stamp Centenary. T **205** and similar horiz designs. Multicoloured. W **58** (sideways). P 13½×13.

No.	Description	Unused	Used
536	40m. Type **205**	10	10
537	125m. 1880 2½d. stamp with "974" (Kyrenia) postmark	15	20
538	175m. 1880 1s. stamp with "942" (Larnaca) postmark	15	25
536/8	*Set of 3*	30	45
MS539	105×85 mm. 500m. 1880 1d., ½d., 2½d., 4d., 6d. and 1s. stamps (90×75 mm). Imperf	70	85

(Photo Harrison)

1980 (28 Apr). Europa. Personalities. T **206** and similar vert design. Multicoloured. P 12½.

No.	Description	Unused	Used
540	40m. Type **206**	15	10
541	125m. Zeno of Citium (founder of the Stoic philosophy)	30	20
	a. Pale Venetian red omitted	£130	

The pale Venetian red colour on No. 541 appears as an overlay on the bust. On No. 541a the bust is pure grey.

207 Sailing

208 Gold Necklace, Arsos (7th-century B.C.)

(Des A. Ioannides)

1980 (23 June). Olympic Games, Moscow. T **207** and similar horiz designs. Multicoloured. W **58** (sideways). P 13½×13.

No.	Description	Unused	Used
542	40m. Type **207**	10	10
543	125m. Swimming	20	20
544	200m. Gymnastics	25	25
542/4	*Set of 3*	50	50

1980 (15 Sept). Archaeological Treasures. Multicoloured designs as T **208**. W **58** (sideways on 15, 40, 150 and 500m.). *Chalk-surfaced cream paper*. P 14×13 (15, 40, 150 and 500m.) or 13×14 (others).

No.	Description	Unused	Used
545	10m. Type **208**	30	1·00
546	15m. Bronze cow, Vouni Palace (5th-century B.C.) (*horiz*)	30	1·00
547	25m. Amphora, Salamis (6th-century B.C.)	30	30
548	40m. Gold finger-ring, Enkomi (13th-century B.C.) (*horiz*)	40	75
549	50m. Bronze cauldron, Salamis (8th-century B.C.)	40	10
550	75m. Funerary stele, Marion (5th-century B.C.)	1·25	1·50
551	100m. Jug (15–14th-century B.C.)	65	15
552	125m. Warrior (Terracotta) (6–5th-century B.C.)	65	1·00
553	150m. Lions attacking bull (bronze relief), Vouni Palace (5th-century B.C.) (*horiz*)	75	15
554	175m. Faience rhyton, Kition (13th-century B.C.)	75	1·25
555	200m. Bronze statue of Ingot God, Enkomi (12th-century B.C.)	75	30
556	500m. Stone bowl, Khirokitia (6th-millennium B.C.) (*horiz*)	75	1·50
557	£1 Ivory plaque, Salamis (7th-century B.C.)	1·00	1·25
558	£2 "Leda and the Swan" (mosaic), Kouklia (3rd-century A.D.)	1·75	2·00
545/58	*Set of 14*	9·00	11·00

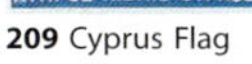

209 Cyprus Flag

210 Peace Dove and Head Silhouettes

1980 (1 Oct). 20th Anniv of Republic. T **209** and similar multicoloured designs. P 13½×13 (125m.) or 13×14 (others).

No.	Description	Unused	Used
559	40m. Type **209**	20	10
560	125m. Signing Treaty of Establishment (41×29 mm)	25	15
561	175m. Archbishop Makarios	35	25
559/61	*Set of 3*	70	45

(Des A. Ioannides)

1980 (29 Nov). International Palestinian Solidarity Day. T **210** and similar horiz design showing Peace Dove and head silhouettes. W **58** (sideways). P 13½×13.

No.	Description	Unused	Used
562	40m. grey and black	20	20
	a. Horiz pair. Nos. 562/3	55	55
563	125m. grey and black	35	35

Nos. 562/3 were printed together, *se-tenant*, in horizontal pairs throughout the sheet.

211 Pulpit, Tripiotis Church, Nicosia

212 Folk-dancing

1980 (29 Nov). Christmas. T **211** and similar vert designs. Multicoloured. W **58**. P 13×14.

No.	Description	Unused	Used
564	25m. Type **211**	10	10
565	100m. Holy Doors, Panayia Church, Paralimni (24×37 mm)	15	20
566	125m. Pulpit, Ayios Lazaros Church, Larnaca	15	20
564/6	*Set of 3*	30	40

(Litho Harrison)

1981 (4 May). Europa. Folklore. T **212** and similar vert design showing folk-dancing from paintings by T. Photiades. P 14.

No.	Description	Unused	Used
567	40m. multicoloured	30	10
568	175m. multicoloured	60	50

213 Self-portrait

214 *Ophrys kotschyi*

1981 (15 June). 500th Anniv of Leonardo da Vinci's Visit. T **213** and similar multicoloured designs. W **58** (sideways on 125m.). P 12×14 (125m.) or 13½×14 (others).

No.	Description	Unused	Used
569	50m. Type **213**	40	10
570	125m. "The Last Supper" (50×25 mm)	70	40
571	175m. Cyprus lace and Milan Cathedral	95	60
569/71	*Set of 3*	1·90	1·00

(Des A. Tassos)

1981 (6 July). Cypriot Wild Orchids. T **214** and similar vert designs. Multicoloured. W **58**. P 13½×14.

No.	Description	Unused	Used
572	25m. Type **214**	40	60
	a. Block of 4. Nos. 572/5	1·90	2·75
573	50m. *Orchis punctulata*	50	70
574	75m. *Ophrys argolica elegans*	55	80
575	150m. *Epipactis veratrifolia*	65	90
572/5	*Set of 4*	1·90	2·75

Nos. 572/5 were printed together, *se-tenant*, in blocks of 4 throughout the sheet.

215 Heinrich von Stephan

216 "The Lady of the Angels" (from Church of the Transfiguration of Christ, Palekhori)

(Des A. Tassos (200m.), A. Ioannides (others))

1981 (28 Sept). Anniversaries and Events. T **215** and similar horiz designs. W **58** (sideways). P 13½×13.

576 25m. brown-olive, deep yellow-green & bright blue 15 10
577 40m. multicoloured 15 10
578 125m. black, vermilion and deep yellow-green 30 25
579 150m. multicoloured 35 30
580 200m. multicoloured 70 80
576/80 *Set of 5* .... 1·50 1·40

Designs and Events:—25m. Type **215** (150th birth anniversary of Heinrich von Stephan (founder of U.P.U.); 40m. Stylized man holding dish of food (World Food Day); 125m. Stylized hands (International Year for Disabled Persons); 150m. Stylized building and flower (European Campaign for Urban Renaissance); 200m. Prince Charles, Lady Diana Spencer and St. Paul's Cathedral (Royal Wedding).

1981 (16 Nov). Christmas. Murals from Nicosia District Churches. T **216** and similar multicoloured designs. W **58** (sideways on 25 and 125m.). P 12½.

581 25m. Type **216** 20 10
582 100m. "Christ Pantokrator" (from Church of Madonna of Arakas, Lagoudera) (*vert*) 60 20
583 125m. "Baptism of Christ" (from Church of Our Lady of Assinou, Nikitari) 70 30
581/3 *Set of 3* .... 1·25 50

217 "Louomene" (statue of Aphrodite bathing, 250 B.C.)

218 Naval Battle with GreekFire, 985 A.D.

1982 (12 Apr). Aphrodite (Greek goddess of love and beauty) Commemoration (2nd issue). T **217** and similar vert design. Multicoloured. W **58**. P 13½×14.

584 125m. Type **217** 55 45
585 175m. "Anadyomene" (Aphrodite emerging from the waters) (Titian) 70 65

(Des G. Simonis. Photo Harrison)

1982 (3 May). Europa. Historical Events. T **218** and similar horiz design. Multicoloured. P 12½.

586 40m. Type **218** 60 10
587 175m. Conversion of Roman Proconsul Sergius Paulus to Christianity, Paphos, 45 A.D..... 80 2·00

219 Monogram of Christ (mosaic)

100 =

(**220**)

1982 (5 July). World Cultural Heritage. T **219** and similar multicoloured designs. W **58** (sideways on 50 and 225m.). P 13½×14 (125m.) or 12½ (others).

588 50m. Type **219** 20 10
589 125m. Head of priest-king of Paphos (sculpture) (24×37 mm) 40 25
590 225m. Theseus (Greek god) (mosaic) 60 95
588/90 *Set of 3* .... 1·10 1·10

1982 (6 Sept). No. 550 surch with T **220** by Govt Ptg Office, Nicosia.

591 100m. on 75m. Funerary stele, Marion (5th-century B.C.) 50 50

221 Cyprus and Stylized "75"

222 Holy Communion—The Bread

1982 (8 Nov). 75th Anniv of Boy Scout Movement. T **221** and similar multicoloured designs. W **58** (sideways on 100m. and 175m.). P 12½×13½ (125m.) or 13½×12½ (others).

592 100m. Type **221** 35 20
593 125m. Lord Baden-Powell (*vert*) 40 40
594 175m. Camp-site 40 90
592/4 *Set of 3* .... 1·00 1·40

1982 (6 Dec). Christmas. T **222** and similar designs. W **58** (sideways on 25 and 250m.). P 12½×12 (25 and 250m.) or 13½×14 (100m.).

595 25m. multicoloured 10 10
596 100m. gold and black 30 15
597 250m. multicoloured .... 70 1·50
595/7 *Set of 3* .... 1·00 1·60

Designs: *Vert*—100m. Holy Chalice. *Horiz*—250m. Holy Communion—The Wine.

223 Cyprus Forest Industries' Sawmill

1983 (14 Mar). Commonwealth Day. T **223** and similar horiz designs. Multicoloured. W **58** (sideways). P 14×13½.

598 50m. Type **223** 10 10
599 125m. "Ikarios and the Discovery of Wine" (3rd-cent mosaic) 20 25
600 150m. Folk-dancers, Commonwealth Film and Television Festival, 1980 .... 25 35
601 175m. Royal Exhibition Building, Melbourne (Commonwealth Heads of Government Meeting, 1981) 25 40
598/601 *Set of 4* .... 70 1·00

224 Cyprosyllabic Inscription (6th-cent B.C.)

225 *Pararge aegeria*

(Des G. Simonis. Photo Harrison)

1983 (3 May). Europa. T **224** and similar horiz design. Multicoloured. P 14½×14.

602 50m. Type **224** 30 10
603 200m. Copper ore, ingot (Enkomi 1400–1250 B.C.) and bronze jug (2nd-cent A.D.) .... 80 2·00

1983 (28 June). Butterflies. T **225** and similar horiz designs. Multicoloured. W w **58**. P 12½.

604 60m. Type **225** 25 20
605 130m. *Aricia agestis* 45 25
606 250m. *Glaucopsyche melanops* .... 85 2·50
604/6 *Set of 3* .... 1·40 2·75

(New Currency: 100 cents = £1 (Cyprus))

1c

=

(**226**)

227 View of Power Station

1983 (3 Oct). Nos. 545/56 surch as T **226** by Govt Printing Office, Nicosia.

607	1c. on 10m. Type **208**	35	1·00
608	2c. on 15m. Bronze cow, Vouni Palace (5th-century B.C.)	35	1·25
609	3c. on 25m. Amphora, Salamis (6th-century B.C.)	35	1·00
610	4c. on 40m. Gold finger-ring, Enkomi (13th-century B.C.)	40	1·00
611	5c. on 50m. Bronze cauldron, Salamis (8th-century B.C.)	50	50
612	6c. on 75m. Funerary stele, Marion (5th-century B.C.)	50	1·00
613	10c. on 100m. Jug (15–14th-century B.C.)	50	40
614	13c. on 125m. Warrior (Terracotta) (6–5th-century B.C.)	50	50
615	15c. on 150m. Lions attacking bull (bronze relief), Vouni Palace (5th-century B.C.)	50	55
616	20c. on 200m. Bronze statue of Ingot God, Enkomi (12th-century B.C.)	50	65
617	25c. on 175m. Faience rhyton, Kition (13th-century B.C.)	55	1·10
618	50c. on 500m. Stone bowl, Khirokitia (6th-millennium B.C.)	75	2·00
607/18 *Set of* 12		5·25	9·75

1983 (27 Oct). Anniversaries and Events. T **227** and similar vert designs. Multicoloured. W **58**. P 13×14.

619	3c. Type **227**	10	20
620	6c. W.C.Y. logo	15	15
621	13c. *Sol Olympia* (liner) and *Polys* (tanker)	30	35
622	15c. Human Rights emblem and map of Europe	20	25
623	20c. Nicos Kazantzakis (poet)	20	75
624	25c. Archbishop Makarios in church	25	75
619/24 *Set of* 6		1·00	2·25

Events:—3c. 30th anniv of the Cyprus Electricity Authority; 6c. World Communications Year; 13c. 25th anniv of International Maritime Organization; 15c. 35th anniv of Universal Declaration of Human Rights; 20c. Birth centenary; 25c. 70th birth anniv.

228 St. Lazarus Church, Larnaca

229 Waterside Cafe, Larnaca

1983 (12 Dec). Christmas. Church Towers. T **228** and similar vert designs. Multicoloured. W **58**. P 12 ×13½.

625	4c. Type **228**	15	10
626	13c. St. Varvara Church, Kaimakli, Nicosia	40	35
627	20c. St. Ioannis Church, Larnaca	70	1·50
625/7 *Set of* 3		1·10	1·75

(Litho Harrison)

1984 (6 Mar). Old Engravings. T **229** and similar horiz designs. Each pale stone and black. P 14½×14 (6c.) or 14 (others).

628	6c. Type **229**	15	15
629	20c. Bazaar at Larnaca (30×25 mm)	40	85
630	30c. Famagusta Gate, Nicosia (30×25 mm)	65	1·50
628/30 *Set of* 3		1·10	2·25
MS631 110×85 mm. 75c. "The Confession" (St. Lazarus Church, Larnaca)		1·50	2·00

230 C.E.P.T. 25th Anniversary Logo

(Des J. Larrivière. Litho Harrison)

1984 (30 Apr). Europa. W **58**. P 12½.

632	**230**	6c. apple-green, deep blue-green & black	40	10
633		15c. light blue, dull ultramarine & black	70	2·00

ΤΑΜΕΙΟΝ ΠΡΟΣΦΥΓΩΝ
REFUGEE FUND GOÇMENLER FONU

A. Waddington ptgs (Nos. 634/a)

ΤΑΜΕΙΟΝ ΠΡΟΣΦΥΓΩΝ
REFUGEE FUND GÖÇMENLER FONU

B. Aspioti-Elka ptg (No. 634*b*)

(Des A. Tassos)

1984 (18 June)–**87**. Obligatory Tax. Refugee Fund. Design as T **188** but new value and "1984" date. P 13×12½.

(a) Litho J.W. W **58**. *Chalk-surfaced cream paper*

634	1c. grey-black (A)	10	10
	a. Wmk sideways. Ordinary paper (21.2.87)*	70	70

(b) Litho Aspioti-Elka. W **58**. *Chalk-surfaced cream paper*

634*b*	1c. grey-black (B) (3.11.87)*	75	65

*Earliest known date of use.

In addition to the redrawn inscriptions there are other minor differences between the work of the two printers.

For a further version of this design, showing "1974" at top right, see Nos. 729, 747, 807 and 892.

231 Running

(Des. K. Haine. Litho Harrison)

1984 (18 June). Olympic Games, Los Angeles. T **231** and similar horiz designs. Multicoloured. W **58** (sideways). P 14.

635	3c. Type **231**	15	10
636	4c. Olympic column	15	20
637	13c. Swimming	35	75
638	20c. Gymnastics	45	1·50
635/8 *Set of* 4		1·00	2·25

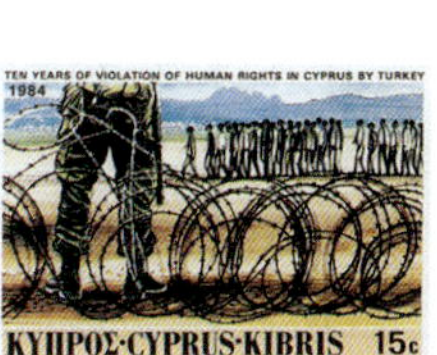

232 Prisoners-of-War

233 Open Stamp Album (25th Anniv of Cyprus Philatelic Society)

1984 (20 July). 10th Anniv of Turkish Landings in Cyprus. T **232** and similar horiz design. Multicoloured. P 14×13½.

639	15c. Type **232**	40	45
640	20c. Map and burning buildings	50	55

(Des P. St. Antoniades (6c.), A. Ioannides (10c.), Harrison (others). Litho Harrison)

1984 (15 Oct). Anniversaries and Events. T **233** and similar multicoloured designs. W **58** (sideways on horiz designs). P 12½.

641	6c. Type **233**	30	20
642	10c. Football in motion (*horiz*) (50th anniv of Cyprus Football Association)	45	30

643	15c. "Dr. George Papanicolaou" (medical scientist–birth cent)	75	50
644	25c. Antique map of Cyprus and ikon (*horiz*) (International Symposia on Cartography and Medieval Paleography)	1·10	2·00
641/4 *Set of 4*		2·40	2·75

234 St. Mark (miniature from 11th-century Gospel)

235 Autumn at Platania, Troodos Mountains

(Des and litho Harrison)

1984 (26 Nov). Christmas. Illuminated Gospels. T **234** and similar vert designs. Multicoloured. W **58**. P 12½.

645	4c. Type **234**	25	10
646	13c. Beginning of St. Mark's Gospel	45	50
647	20c. St. Luke (miniature from 11th-century Gospel)	70	2·00
645/7 *Set of 3*		1·25	2·40

(Des and litho Harrison)

1985 (18 Mar). Cyprus Scenes and Landscapes. T **235** and similar multicoloured designs. Ordinary white paper. P 14×15 (6c., 20c., 25c., £1, £5 or 15×14 others).

648	1c. Type **235**	20	60
649	2c. Ayia Napa Monastery	20	60
650	3c. Phini Village—panoramic view	20	60
651	4c. Kykko Monastery	20	30
652	5c. Beach at Makronissos, Ayia Napa	20	20
653	6c. Village street, Omodhos (*vert*)	30	20
654	10c. Panoramic sea view	45	30
655	13c. Windsurfing	55	25
656	15c. Beach at Protaras	75	25
657	20c. Forestry for development (*vert*)	1·00	50
658	25c. Sunrise at Protaras (*vert*)	1·25	1·00
659	30c. Village house, Pera	1·50	1·25
660	50c. Apollo Hylates Sanctuary, Curium	2·50	1·75
661	£1 Snow on Troodos Mountains (*vert*)	4·00	3·00
662	£5 Personification of Autumn, House of Dionyssos, Paphos (*vert*)	14·00	15·00
648/62 *Set of 15*		24·00	23·00

236 Clay Idols of Musicians (7/6th Century B.C.)

237 Cyprus Coat of Arms (25th Anniv of Republic)

(Des and litho Harrison)

1985 (6 May). Europa. European Music Year. T **236** and similar horiz design. Multicoloured. W **58** (sideways). P 12½.

663	6c. Type **236**	50	35
664	15c. Violin, lute, flute and score from the "Cyprus Suite"	90	2·25

(Des G. Simonis (4c., 13c.), Harrison (others). Litho Harrison)

1985 (23 Sept). Anniversaries and Events. T **237** and similar designs. P 14½ (4, 20c.) or 14×13½ (others).

665	4c. multicoloured	15	15
666	6c. multicoloured	15	15
667	13c. multicoloured	25	1·00
668	15c. black, olive-black and yellow-orange	1·00	1·25

669	20c. multicoloured	30	1·75
665/9 *Set of 5*		1·60	3·75

Designs and Events: *Horiz* (43×30 mm)—6c. "Barn of Liopetri" (detail) (Pol. Georghiou) (30th anniv of EOKA Campaign); 13c. Three profiles (International Youth Year); 15c. Solon Michaelides (composer and conductor) (European Music Year). *Vert* (*as T* **237**)—20c. U.N. Building, New York, and flags (40th anniv of United Nations Organization).

238 "The Visit of the Madonna to Elizabeth" (Lambadistis Monastery, Kalopanayiotis)

239 Figure from Hellenistic Spoon Handle

(Des and litho Harrison)

1985 (18 Nov). Christmas. Frescoes from Cypriot Churches. T **238** and similar vert designs. Multicoloured. P 12½.

670	4c. Type **238**	20	10
671	13c. "The Nativity" (Lambadistis Monastery, Kalopanayiotis)	50	65
672	20c. "Candlemas-day" (Asinou Church)	70	2·00
670/2 *Set of 3*		1·25	2·50

(Des A. Ioannides. Litho Harrison)

1986 (17 Feb). New Archaeological Museum Fund. T **239** and similar horiz designs. Multicoloured. P 15×14.

673	15c. Type **239**	45	45
674	20c. Pattern from early Ionian helmet and foot from statue	60	75
675	25c. Roman statue of Eros and Psyche	65	95
676	30c. Head of statue	75	1·10
673/6 *Set of 4*		2·25	3·00
MS677 111×90 mm. Nos. 673/6 (sold at £1)		13·00	17·00

Two-thirds of the amount received from sales of Nos. 673/7 was devoted to the construction of a new Archaeological Museum, Nicosia.

No. 676 also commemorates the 50th anniversary of the Department of Antiquities.

240 Cyprus Mouffion and Cedars

(Des G. Simonis)

1986 (28 Apr). Europa. Protection of Nature and the Environment. T **240** and similar horiz design. Multicoloured. W **58** (sideways). P 14×13.

678	7c. Type **240**	35	30
679	17c. Greater Flamingos at Larnaca Salt Lake	1·40	2·75

241 Cat's-paw Scallop (*Manupecten pesfelis*)

7c

(242)

(Des T. Katsoulides)

1986 (1 July). Sea Shells. T **241** and similar horiz designs. Multicoloured. W **58** (sideways). P 14×13½.

680	5c. Type **241**	30	15
681	7c. Atlantic Trumpet Triton (*Charonia variegata*)	35	15

682	18c. Purple Dye Murex (*Murex brandaris*)	60	70
683	25c. Yellow Cowrie (*Cypraea spurca*)	1·00	2·00
680/3	*Set of* 4	2·00	2·75

1986 (13 Oct). Nos. 653 and 655 surch as T **242**.

684	7c. on 6c. Village street, Omodhos (*vert*)	40	30
685	18c. on 13c. Windsurfing	1·10	70

For 15c. on 4c. see No. 730.

243 Globe, Outline Map of Cyprus and Barn Swallows (Overseas Cypriots' Year)

(Des T. Katsoulides)

1986 (13 Oct). Anniversaries and Events. T **243** and similar horiz designs. Multicoloured. W **58** (sideways). P 13½×13.

686	15c. Type **243**	1·00	45
687	18c. Halley's Comet over Cyprus beach (40×23 mm)	1·25	2·00
	a. Horiz pair. Nos. 687/8	2·50	4·00
688	18c. Comet's tail over sea and Edmond Halley (40×23 mm)	1·25	2·00
686/8	*Set of* 3	3·25	4·00

Nos. 687/8 were printed together, *se-tenant*, in horizontal pairs throughout the sheet, each pair forming a composite design.

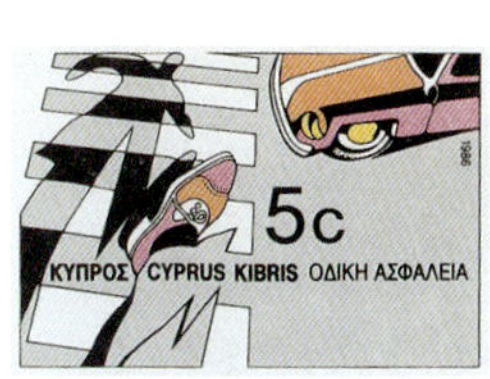

244 Pedestrian Crossing

245 "The Nativity" (Church of Panayia tou Araka)

(Des A. Ioannides)

1986 (10 Nov). Road Safety Campaign. T **244** and similar horiz designs. Multicoloured. W **58** (sideways). P 14×13.

689	5c. Type **244**	65	30
690	7c. Motor cycle crash helmet	70	30
691	18c. Hands fastening car seat belt	1·50	3·00
689/91	*Set of* 3	2·50	3·25

(Des G. Simonis)

1986 (24 Nov). Christmas. International Peace Year. T **245** and similar vert designs showing details of Nativity frescoes from Cypriot churches. Multicoloured. W **58** (inverted). P 13½×14.

692	5c. Type **245**	30	15
693	15c. Church of Panayia tou Moutoulla	75	30
694	17c. Church of St. Nicholas tis Steyis	90	2·00
692/4	*Set of* 3	1·75	2·25

246 Church of Virgin Mary, Asinou

(Des and photo Harrison)

1987 (22 Apr). Troodos Churches on the World Heritage List. T **246** and similar horiz designs. Multicoloured. P 12½.

695	15c. Type **246**	70	1·10
	a. Sheetlet. Nos. 695/703	5·50	9·00
696	15c. Fresco of Virgin Mary, Moutoulla's Church	70	1·10
697	15c. Church of Virgin Mary, Podithou	70	1·10
698	15c. Fresco of Three Apostles, St. Ioannis Lampadistis Monastery	70	1·10
699	15c. Annunciation fresco, Church of the Holy Cross, Pelentriou	70	1·10
700	15c. Fresco of Saints, Church of the Cross, Ayiasmati	70	1·10
701	15c. Fresco of Archangel Michael and Donor, Pedoula's Church of St. Michael	70	1·10
702	15c. Church of St. Nicolaos, Steyis	70	1·10
703	15c. Fresco of Prophets, Church of Virgin Mary, Araka	70	1·10
695/703	*Set of* 9	5·50	9·00

Nos. 695/703 were printed together, *se-tenant*, in sheetlets of nine.

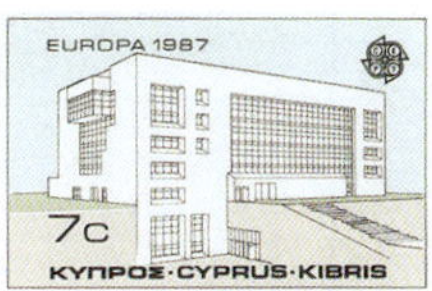

247 Proposed Central Bank of Cyprus Building

(Des G. Simonis)

1987 (11 May). Europa. Modern Architecture. T **247** and similar horiz design. W **58** (sideways). P 14×13½.

704	7c. multicoloured	40	30
705	18c. black, brownish grey and sage-green	85	2·00

Design:—18c. Headquarters complex, Cyprus Tele-communications Authority.

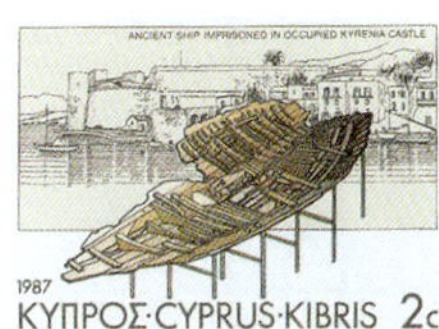

248 Remains of Ancient Ship and Kyrenia Castle

(Des Y. Pantsopoulos)

1987 (3 Oct). Voyage of "Kyrenia II" (replica of ancient ship). T **248** and similar horiz designs. Multicoloured. W **58** (sideways). P 14×13½.

706	2c. Type **248**	35	20
707	3c. *Kyrenia II* under construction, 1982–5	45	90
708	5c. *Kyrenia II* at Paphos, 1986	75	20
709	17c. *Kyrenia II* at New York, 1986	1·75	90
706/9	*Set of* 4	3·00	2·00

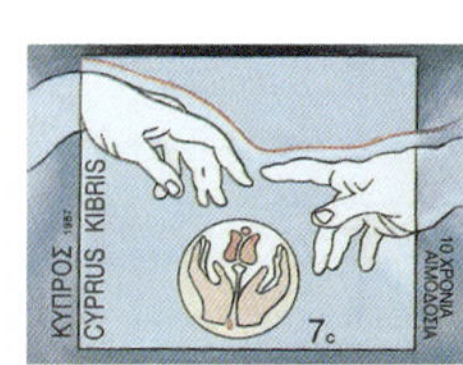

249 Hands (from Michelangelo's *Creation*) and Emblem (10th anniv of Blood Donation Coordinating Committee)

250 Nativity Crib

(Des A. Ioannides)

1987 (2 Nov). Anniversaries and Events. T **249** and similar horiz designs. Multicoloured. W **58** (sideways). P 14×13½.

710	7c. Type **249**	50	25
711	15c. Snail with flowered shell and countryside (European Countryside Campaign)	1·10	40
712	20c. Symbols of ocean bed and Earth's crust ("Troodos '87" Ophiolites and Oceanic Lithosphere Symposium)	1·40	3·00
710/12	*Set of* 3	2·75	3·25

(Des A. Ioannides)

1987 (30 Nov). Christmas. Traditional Customs. T **250** and similar square designs. Multicoloured. W **58** (sideways). P 14.

713	5c. Type **250**	35	15
714	15c. Door knocker decorated with foliage	1·10	35
715	17c. Bowl of fruit and nuts	1·25	2·00
713/15	*Set of* 3	2·40	2·25

251 Flags of Cyprus and E.E.C.

(Des G. Simonis. Litho Alexandros Matsoukis, Athens)

1988 (11 Jan). Cypriot–E.E.C. Customs Union. T **251** and similar horiz design. Multicoloured. W **58**. P 13×13½.

716	15c. Type **251**	90	1·50
717	18c. Outline maps of Cyprus and E.E.C. countries	90	80

252 Intelpost Telefax Terminal

(Des A. Ioannides. Litho Alexandros Matsoukis, Athens)

1988 (9 May). Europa. Transport and Communications. T **252** and similar horiz designs. Multicoloured. W **58**. P 14×14½.

718	7c. Type **252**	75	1·25
	a. Horiz pair. Nos. 718/19	1·50	2·50
719	7c. Car driver using mobile telephone	75	1·25
720	18c. Nose of Cyprus Airways airliner and Greater Flamingos	2·50	3·00
	a. Horiz pair. Nos. 720/1	5·00	6·00
721	18c. Boeing airliner in flight and Greater Flamingos	2·50	3·00
718/21 *Set of* 4		6·00	7·50

The two designs of each value were printed together, *se-tenant*, in horizontal pairs throughout the sheet of ten.

253 Sailing

254 Conference Emblem

(Des A. Ioannides. Photo Courvoisier)

1988 (27 June). Olympic Games, Seoul. T **253** and similar vert designs. Multicoloured. Granite paper. P 12.

722	5c. Type **253**	30	20
723	7c. Athletes at start	35	40
724	10c. Shooting	40	70
725	20c. Judo	90	1·50
722/5 *Set of* 4		1·75	2·50

(Des A. Ioannides. Litho M. A. Moatsos, Athens)

1988 (5 Sept). Non-Aligned Foreign Ministers' Conference, Nicosia. T **254** and similar horiz designs. W **58** (sideways). P 14×13½.

726	1c. black, pale blue and emerald	10	10
727	10c. multicoloured	45	70
728	50c. multicoloured	3·50	2·50
726/8 *Set of* 3		3·50	3·00

Designs:—10c. Emblem of Republic of Cyprus; 50c. Nehru, Tito, Nasser and Makarios.

255 "Cyprus 74" (wood-engraving by A. Tassos)

(Des A. Tassos. Litho M. A. Moatsos, Athens)

1988 (12 Sept). Obligatory Tax. Refugee Fund. Design as Nos. 634/b, but with upper and lower inscriptions redrawn and "1974" added as in T **255**. W **58**. *Ordinary paper*. P 13×12½.

729	**255**	1c. brownish black and brownish grey	10	10

For this design printed in photogravure and perforated 11½ see No. 747, in lithography perforated 13 see No. 807 and in lithography perforated 14½×13½ see No. 892.

1988 (3 Oct). No. 651 surch as T **242**.

730	15c. on 4c. Kykko Monastery	1·75	1·25

256 "Presentation of Christ at the Temple" (Church of Holy Cross tou Agiasmati)

(Des G. Simonis. Litho M. A. Montana, Athens)

1988 (28 Nov). Christmas. T **256** and similar vert designs showing frescoes from Cypriot churches. Multicoloured. W **58**. P 13½×14.

731	5c. Type **256**	25	20
732	15c. "Virgin and Child" (St. John Lampadistis Monastery)	55	25
733	17c. "Adoration of the Magi" (St. John Lampadistis Monastery)	80	1·75
731/3 *Set of* 3		1·40	2·00

257 Human Rights Logo

258 Basketball

(Des G. Simonis. Litho M. A. Moatsos, Athens)

1988 (10 Dec). 40th Anniv of Universal Declaration of Human Rights. W **58** (inverted). P 13½×14.

734	**257**	25c. azure, dull violet-blue and cobalt	1·00	1·25

(Des A. Ioannides. Litho Alexandros Matsoukis, Athens)

1989 (10 Apr). Third Small European States' Games, Nicosia. T **258** and similar horiz designs. Multicoloured. P 13½.

735	1c. Type **258**	30	15
736	5c. Javelin	30	15
737	15c. Wrestling	65	20
738	18c. Athletics	85	1·00
735/8 *Set of* 4		1·90	1·40
MS739 109×80 mm. £1 Angel and laurel wreath (99×73 mm). Imperf		6·00	6·50

259 Lingri Stick Game

(Des S. Michael. Litho Alexandros Matsoukis, Athens)

1989 (8 May). Europa. Children's Games. T **259** and similar horiz designs. Multicoloured. P 13×13½.

740	7c. Type **259**	1·10	1·50
	a. Horiz pair. Nos. 740/1	2·10	3·00
741	7c. Ziziros	1·10	1·50
742	18c. Sitsia	1·25	1·60
	a. Horiz pair. Nos. 742/3	2·50	3·00
743	18c. Leapfrog	1·25	1·60
740/3 *Set of* 4		4·25	5·50

Nos. 740/1 and 742/3 were each printed together, *se-tenant*, in horizontal pairs throughout the sheets.

260 "Universal Man"

261 Stylized Human Figures

(Des A. Ioannides. Photo Courvoisier)

1989 (7 July). Bicentenary of the French Revolution. Granite paper. P 11½.

744	**260**	18c. multicoloured	1·00	60

(Des A. Ioannides. Litho Alexandros Matsoukis, Athens)

1989 (4 Sept). Centenary of Interparliamentary Union (15c.) and 9th Non-Aligned Summit Conference, Belgrade (30c.). T **261** and similar vert design. Multicoloured. P 13½.

745	15c. Type **261**	65	40
746	30c. Conference logo	1·10	1·10

(Photo Courvoisier)

1989 (4 Sept). Obligatory Tax. Refugee Fund. As T **255**, but reduced in size and inscr "1989" or "1990". Chalk-surfaced. P 11½.

747	**255**	1c. brownish black and brownish grey	60	50

262 Worker Bees tending Larvae

263 Outstretched Hand and Profile (aid for Armenian earthquake victims)

(Litho Alexandros Matsoukis, Athens)

1989 (16 Oct). Bee-keeping. T **262** and similar vert designs. Multicoloured. P 13½.

748	3c. Type **262**	30	25
749	10c. Bee on Rock-rose flower	70	50
750	15c. Bee on Lemon flower	95	50
751	18c. Queen and worker bees	1·10	1·75
748/51	*Set of 4*	2·75	2·75

(Des A. Ioannides. Litho Alexandros Matsoukis, Athens)

1989 (13 Nov). Anniversaries and Events. T **263** and similar vert designs. Multicoloured. P 13½.

752	3c. Type **263**	30	1·25
753	5c. Airmail envelope (Cyprus Philatelic Society F.I.P. membership)	45	10
754	7c. Crab symbol and daisy (European Cancer Year)	75	1·40
755	17c. Vegetables and fish (World Food Day)	1·10	1·40
752/5	*Set of 4*	2·40	3·75

264 Winter (detail from "Four Seasons")

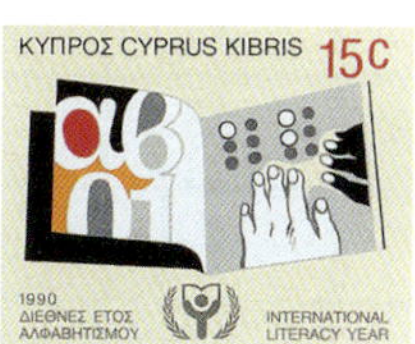

265 Hands and Open Book (International Literacy Year)

(Litho Alexandros Matsoukis, Athens)

1989 (29 Dec). Roman Mosaics from Paphos. T **264** and similar multicoloured designs showing details. P 13 (1, 5, 7, 15c.), 13×13½ (2, 4, 18, 40c.), 13½×13 (3, 10, 20, 25c.) or 14 (50c., £1, £3).

756	1c. Type **264**	35	1·50
757	2c. Personification of Crete (32×24 mm)	45	1·50
758	3c. Centaur and Maenad (24×32 mm)	55	1·50
759	4c. Poseidon and Amymone (32×24 mm)	80	1·60
760	5c. Leda	80	20
761	7c. Apollon	90	25
762	10c. Hermes and Dionysos (24×32 mm)	1·25	30
763	15c. Cassiopeia	2·00	45
764	18c. Orpheus (32×24 mm)	2·00	50
765	20c. Nymphs (24×32 mm)	2·25	75
766	25c. Amazon (24×32 mm)	2·25	80
767	40c. Doris (32×24 mm)	3·50	1·75
768	50c. Heracles and the Lion (39×27 mm)	3·50	1·75
769	£1 Apollon and Daphne (39×27 mm)	6·00	3·25
770	£3 Cupid (39×27 mm)	12·00	14·00
756/70	*Set of 15*	35·00	27·00

(Des A. Ioannides. Litho Alexandros Matsoukis, Athens)

1990 (3 Apr). Anniversaries and Events. T **265** and similar horiz designs. Multicoloured. P 13½.

771	15c. Type **265**	55	50
772	17c. Dove and profiles (83rd Inter-Parliamentary Conference, Nicosia)	65	90
773	18c. Lions International emblem (Lions Europa Forum, Limassol)	75	90
771/3	*Set of 3*	1·75	2·10

266 District Post Office, Paphos

(Des A. Ioannides. Litho Alexandros Matsoukis, Athens)

1990 (10 May). Europa. Post Office Buildings. T **266** and similar horiz design. Multicoloured. P 13×13½.

774	7c. Type **266**	1·10	25
775	18c. City Centre Post Office, Limassol	1·40	3·00

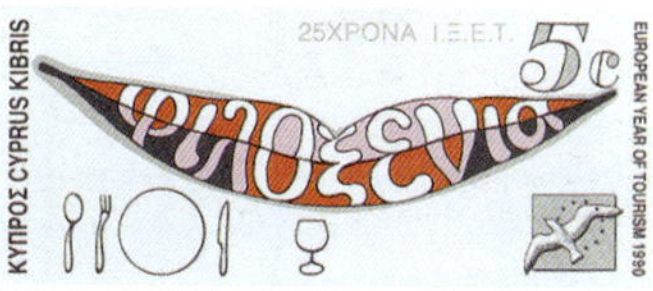

267 Symbolic Lips (25th anniv of Hotel and Catering Institute)

(Des A.Ioannides. Litho Alexandros Matsoukis, Athens)

1990 (9 July). European Tourism Year. T **267** and similar horiz designs. Multicoloured. P 14.

776	5c. Type **267**	25	25
777	7c. Bell tower, St. Lazarus Church (1100th anniv)	30	25
778	15c. Butterflies and woman	2·25	45
779	18c. Birds and man	2·50	4·25
776/9	*Set of 4*	4·75	4·75

268 Sun (wood carving)

269 *Chionodoxa lochiae*

(Des A. Ioannides. Photo Courvoisier)

1990 (29 Sept). 30th Anniv of Republic. T **268** and similar square designs. Multicoloured. Granite paper. P 11½.

780	15c. Type **268**	65	45
781	17c. Bulls (pottery design)	75	60
782	18c. Fishes (pottery design)	85	70
783	40c. Tree and birds (woodcarving)	2·50	5·50
780/3	*Set of 4*	4·25	6·50
MS784	89×89 mm. £1 30th Anniversary emblem. Imperf	3·75	6·50

(Litho Alexandros Matsoukis, Athens)

1990 (5 Nov). Endangered Wild Flowers. T **269** and similar vert designs taken from book illustrations by Elektra Megaw. Multicoloured. P 13½×13.

785	2c. Type **269**	60	1·60

786	3c. *Pancratium maritimum*	60	1·60
787	5c. *Paeonia mascula*	85	20
788	7c. *Cyclamen cyprium*	90	25
789	15c. *Tulipa cypria*	1·75	30
790	18c. *Crocus cyprius*	1·90	3·75
785/90 *Set of 6*		6·00	7·00

270 "Nativity"

271 Archangel

(Litho Alexandros Matsoukis, Athens)

1990 (3 Dec). Christmas. 16th-century Icons. T **270** and similar vert designs. Multicoloured. P 13½.

791	5c. Type **270**	50	20
792	15c. "Virgin Hodegetria"	1·40	30
793	17c. "Nativity" (*different*)	1·60	3·50
791/3 *Set of 3*		3·25	3·50

(Des A. Ioannides. Photo Courvoisier)

1991 (28 Mar). 6th-century Mosaics from Kanakaria Church. T **271** and similar vert designs. Multicoloured. Granite paper. P 12.

794	5c. Type **271**	20	15
795	15c. Christ Child	75	20
796	17c. St. James	1·50	1·75
797	18c. St. Matthew	1·75	2·25
794/7 *Set of 4*		3·75	4·00

272 *Ulysses* Spacecraft

273 Young Cyprus Wheatear

(Des G. Simonis. Litho Alexandros Matsoukis, Athens)

1991 (6 May). Europa. Europe in Space. T **272** and similar horiz design. Multicoloured. P 13×13½.

798	7c. Type **272**	90	20
799	18c. *Giotto* and Halley's Comet	1·60	2·50

(Des A. Ioannides. Litho Alexandros Matsoukis, Athens)

1991 (4 July). Cyprus Wheatear. T **273** and similar horiz designs. Multicoloured. P 13½.

800	5c. Type **273**	1·00	40
801	7c. Adult bird in autumn plumage	1·10	40
802	15c. Adult male in breeding plumage	1·50	50
803	30c. Adult female in breeding plumage	2·00	4·00
800/3 *Set of 4*		5·00	4·75

274 Mother and Child with Tents

275 The Nativity

(Des A. Ioannides. Litho Alexandros Matsoukis, Athens)

1991 (7 Oct). 40th Anniv of U.N. Commission for Refugees. T **274** and similar horiz designs, each brown, orange-brown and silver. P 13½.

804	5c. Type **274**	25	15
805	15c. Three pairs of legs	90	65
806	18c. Three children	1·10	2·50
804/6 *Set of 3*		2·00	3·00

(Litho Gieseche & Devrient Matsoukis (No. 807a) or Alexandros Matsoukis, Athens) (others)

1991 (7 Oct)–**2007**. Obligatory Tax. Refugee Fund. As T **255**, but inscr "1991", "1992", "1993", "1994", "2002", "2003", "2004", "2005", "2006" or "2007" (No. 807a only). Chalk-surfaced paper. P 13.

807	**255**	1c. brownish black and olive-grey (shades)	20	20
		a. perf 13½×14 (15.3.07)	20	20

(Des Revd. D. Demosthenous. Litho Alexandros Matsoukis, Athens)

1991 (25 Nov). Christmas. T **275** and similar vert designs. Multicoloured. P 13½.

808	5c. Type **275**	40	15
	a. Sheetlet of 9. Nos. 808/10×3	5·50	
809	15c. Saint Basil	80	40
810	17c. Baptism of Jesus	1·10	2·00
808/10 *Set of 3*		2·10	2·25

Nos. 808/10 were issued in separate sheets of 20 and in *se-tenant* sheetlets of 9.

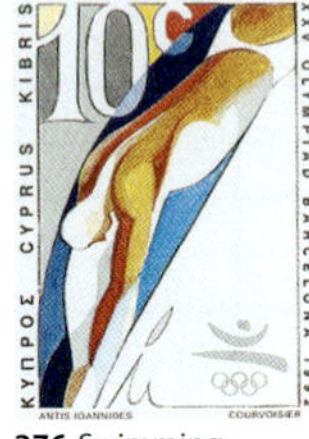
276 Swimming

277 World Map and Emblem ("EXPO '92" Worlds Fair, Seville)

(Des A. Ioannides. Photo Courvoisier)

1992 (3 Apr). Olympic Games, Barcelona. T **276** and similar vert designs. Multicoloured. Granite paper. P 12.

811	10c. Type **276**	60	35
812	20c. Long jump	1·00	70
813	30c. Running	1·40	1·40
814	35c. Discus	1·60	2·50
811/14 *Set of 4*		4·25	4·50

(Des S. Karamallakis. Litho Alexandros Matsoukis, Athens)

1992 (20 Apr). Anniversaries and Events. T **277** and similar horiz designs. Multicoloured. P 14.

815	20c. Type **277**	1·60	80
816	25c. European map and football (10th Under-16 European Football Championship)	1·75	1·10
817	30c. Symbols of Learning (inauguration of University of Cyprus)	1·75	3·00
815/17 *Set of 3*		4·50	4·50

278 Compass Rose and Map of Voyage

279 *Chamaeleo chamaeleon*

(Des G. Simonis. Litho Alexandros Matsoukis, Athens)

1992 (29 May). Europa. 500th Anniv of Discovery of America by Columbus. T **278** and similar horiz designs. Multicoloured. P 13×13½.

818	10c. Type **278**	1·10	1·40
	a. Horiz pair. Nos. 818/19	2·10	2·75
819	10c. "Departure from Palos" (R. Balaga)	1·10	1·40
820	30c. Fleet of Columbus	1·50	2·00
	a. Horiz pair. Nos. 820/1	3·00	4·00
821	30c. Christopher Columbus	1·50	2·00
818/21 *Set of 4*		4·75	6·00

Nos. 818/19 and 820/1 were printed together, *se-tenant*, in separate sheets, each horizontal pair forming a composite design.

(Litho Alexandros Matsoukis, Athens)

1992 (14 Sept). Reptiles. T **279** and similar horiz designs. Multicoloured. P 13½.

822	7c. Type **279**	75	30
823	10c. *Lacerta laevis troodica* (lizard)	95	45
824	15c. *Mauremys caspica* (turtle)	1·40	80
825	20c. *Coluber cypriensis* (snake)	1·60	2·75
822/5 *Set of 4*		4·25	3·75

280 Minoan Wine Ship of 7th-century B.C.

281 "Visitation of the Virgin Mary to Elizabeth", Church of the Holy Cross, Pelendri

(Des S. Vasiliou. Litho Alexandros Matsoukis, Athens)

1992 (9 Nov). 7th International Maritime and Shipping Conference, Nicosia. P 14.

826	**280**	50c. multicoloured	3·00	3·00

(Litho Alexandros Mataoukis, Athens)

1992 (9 Nov). Christmas. Church Fresco Paintings. T **281** and similar vert designs. Muitlcoloured. P 13½.

827	7c. Type **281**	50	15
828	15c. "Virgin and Child Enthroned", Church of Panayia tou Araka	85	45
829	20c. "Virgin and Child", Ayios Nicolaos tis Stegis Church	1·25	2·50
827/9	*Set of 3*	2·40	2·75

282 School Building and Laurel Wreath

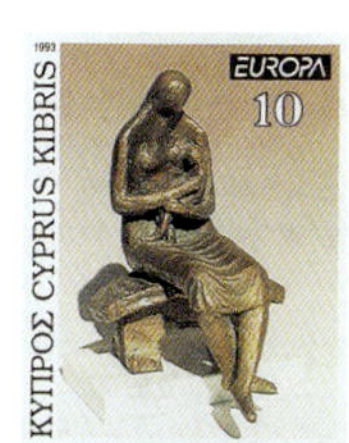

283 "Motherhood" (bronze sculpture, Nicos Dymiotis)

(Des A. Ladommates. Litho Alexandros Matsoukis, Athens)

1993 (15 Feb). Centenary of Pancyprian Gymnasium (secondary school). P 14.

830	**282**	10c. multicoloured	75	60

(Litho Alexandros Matsoukis, Athens)

1993 (5 Apr). Europa. Contemporary Art. T **283** and similar multicoloured design. P 13½.

831	10c. Type **283**	75	50
832	30c. "Motherhood" (painting, Christoforos Savva) (*horiz*)	1·50	2·25

284 Women Athletes (13th European Cup for Women)

285 Red Squirrelfish

Two types of 20c.:

I. Incorrectly inscribed "MUFFLON ENCOURAGEMENT CUP"

II. Inscription corrected to "MOUFFLON ENCOURAGEMENT CUP"

(Des Maria Trillidou (10c.), G. Simonis (25c.), M. Christou (others). Litho Alexandras Matsoukis, Athens)

1993 (24 May–24 June). Anniversaries and Events. T **284** and similar multicoloured designs. P 14.

833	7c. Type **284**	40	30
834	10c. Scout symbols (80th anniv of Scouting in Cyprus) (*vert*)	55	40
835	20c. Water-skier, dolphin and gull (Moufflon Encouragement Cup) (I)	11·00	11·00
	a. Type II (24 June)	95	95
836	25c. Archbishop Makarios III and monastery (80th birth anniv)	1·40	2·00
833/6	*Set of 4*	3·00	3·25

No. 835 was withdrawn on 2 June 1993, after the spelling error had been spotted. No. 835a, with the spelling corrected, was placed on sale from 24 June.

(Des A. Ioannides. Litho Alexandros Matsoukis, Athens)

1993 (6 Sept). Fish. T **285** and similar horiz designs. Multicoloured. P 13½.

837	7c. Type **285**	50	25
838	15c. Red Scorpionfish	75	55
839	20c. Painted Comber	85	85
840	30c. Grey Triggerfish	1·60	2·50
837/40	*Set of 4*	3·25	3·75

286 Conference Emblem

(Des A. Ioannides. Litho Alexandros Matsoukis, Athens)

1993 (4 Oct). 12th Commonwealth Summit Conference. P 13½.

841	**286**	35c. orange-brown and pale ochre	1·60	1·90
842		40c. bistre-brown and ochre	1·90	2·40

287 Ancient Sailing Ship and Modern Coaster

288 Cross from Stavrovouni Monastery

(Des G. Simonis. Litho Alexandros Matsoukis, Athens)

1993 (4 Oct). "Maritime Cyprus '93" International Shipping Conference, Nicosia. P 13½×14.

843	**287**	25c. multicoloured	1·40	1·40

(Litho Alexandros Matsoukis, Athens)

1993 (22 Nov). Christmas. Church Crosses. T **288** and similar multicoloured designs. P 13½.

844	7c. Type **288**	40	15
845	20c. Cross from Lefkara	1·00	60
846	25c. Cross from Pedoulas (*horiz*)	1·25	2·50
844/6	*Set of 3*	2·40	3·00

289 Copper Smelting

290 Symbols of Disability (Persons with Special Needs Campaign)

(Des G. Simonis. Litho Alexandros Matsoukis, Athens)

1994 (1 Mar). Europa. Discoveries. Ancient Copper Industry. T **289** and similar horiz design. Multicoloured. P 13×13½.

847	10c. Type **289**	50	35
848	30c. Ingot, ancient ship and map of Cyprus	1·25	2·00

(Des E. Hadjimichael (7c., 25c.), S. Karamallakis (others). Litho Alexandros Matsoukis, Athens)

1994 (9 May). Anniversaries and Events. T **290** and similar vert designs. Multicoloured. P 13½.

849	7c. Type **290**	50	25
850	15c. Olympic rings in flame (Centenary of International Olympic Committee)	75	55
851	20c. Peace Doves (World Gymnasiade, Nicosia)	90	80

852 25c. Adults and unborn baby in tulip (International Year of the Family) 1·25 2·25
849/52 *Set of 4* 3·00 3·50

291 Houses, Soldier and Family

292 Black Pine

(Des A. Ioannides. Litho Alexandros Matsoukis, Athens)

1994 (27 June). 20th Anniv of Turkish Landings in Cyprus. T **291** and similar horiz design. Multicoloured. P 14.
853 10c. Type **291** 50 40
854 50c. Soldier and ancient columns 2·00 3·25

(Des A. Ioannides. Litho Alexandros Matsoukis, Athens)

1994 (10 Oct). Trees. T **292** and similar vert designs. Multicoloured. P 13½×14.
855 7c. Type **292** 50 25
856 15c. Cyprus Cedar 75 55
857 20c. Golden Oak 90 80
858 30c. Strawberry Tree 1·40 2·50
855/8 *Set of 4* 3·25 3·75

293 Airliner, Route Map and Emblem

294 "Virgin Mary" (detail) (Philip Goul)

(Des G. Simonis. Litho Alexandros Matsoukis, Athens)

1994 (21 Nov). 50th Anniv of International Civil Aviation Organization. P 14.
859 **293** 30c. multicoloured 2·00 2·00

(Litho Alexandros Matsoukis, Athens)

1994 (21 Nov). Christmas. Church Paintings. T **294** and similar horiz designs. Multicoloured. P 13½.
860 7c. Type **294** 60 15
861 20c. "The Nativity" (detail) (Byzantine) 1·40 60
862 25c. "Archangel Michael" (detail) (Goul) 1·60 2·75
860/2 *Set of 3* 3·25 3·25

295 Woman from Paphos wearing Foustani

296 "Hearth Room" Excavation, Alassa and Frieze

(Des A. Ioannides. Litho Alexandros Matsoukis, Athens)

1994 (27 Dec). Traditional Costumes. T **295** and similar vert designs. Multicoloured. Cream paper. With "1994" imprint date. P 13½×13.
863 1c. Type **295** 50 1·50
864 2c. Bride from Karpass 65 1·50
865 3c. Woman from Paphos wearing sayia 70 1·50
866 5c. Woman from Messaoria wearing foustani 80 1·50
867 7c. Bridegroom 85 20
868 10c. Shepherd from Messaoria 1·10 40
869 15c. Woman from Nicosia in festive costume 2·00 40
870 20c. Woman from Karpass wearing festive sayia 2·00 50
871 25c. Woman from Pitsillia 2·25 60
872 30c. Woman from Karpass wearing festive doupletti 2·25 70
873 35c. Countryman 2·25 1·50
874 40c. Man from Messaoria in festive costume 2·50 2·00
875 50c. Townsman 2·50 2·50
876 £1 Townswoman wearing festive sarka 4·00 4·50
863/76 *Set of 14* 22·00 17·00

For £1 on white paper and perforated 14 see No. 958.

(Des Andreas. Ladommatos. Litho Alexandros Matsoukis, Athens)

1995 (27 Feb). 3rd International Congress of Cypriot Studies, Nicosia. T **296** and similar multicoloured designs. P 14.
877 20c. Type **296** 75 75
878 30c. Hypostyle hall, Kalavasos, and Mycenaean amphora 1·00 1·75
MS879 110×80 mm. £1 Old Archbishop's Palace, Nicosia (107×71 mm). Imperf 3·50 5·00

297 Statue of Liberty, Nicosia (left detail)

298 Nazi Heads on Peace Dove over Map of Europe

(Des George Simonis. Litho Alexandros Matsoukis, Athens)

1995 (31 Mar). 40th Anniv of Start of E.O.K.A. Campaign. T **297** and similar vert designs showing different details of the statue. Multicoloured. P 13×13½.
880 20c. Type **297** 1·10 1·40
a. Horiz strip of 3. Nos. 880/2 3·00 3·75
881 20c. Centre detail (face value at top right) 1·10 1·40
882 20c. Right detail (face value at bottom right) 1·10 1·40
880/2 *Set of 3* 3·00 3·75

Nos. 880/2 were printed together, *se-tenant*, in horizontal strips of 3 forming a composite design.

(Des Toulla Paphitis. Litho Alexandros Matsoukis, Athens)

1995 (8 May). Europa. Peace and Freedom. T **298** and similar vert design. Multicoloured. P 13½.
883 10c. Type **298** 1·00 50
884 30c. Concentration camp prisoner and peace dove 2·25 3·25

299 Symbolic Figure holding Healthy Food

300 European Union Flag and European Culture Month Logo

(Des Liza Petridou-Mala. Litho Alexandros Matsoukis, Athens)

1995 (26 June). Healthy Living. T **299** and similar multicoloured designs. P 13½.
885 7c. Type **299** 30 25
886 10c. "AIDS" and patients (*horiz*) 70 60
887 15c. Drug addict (*horiz*) 75 60
888 20c. Smoker and barbed wire 95 1·50
885/8 *Set of 4* 2·40 2·75

(Des George Simonis (Nos. 889/90), Nicos Rangos (No. **MS**891). Litho Oriental Press, Bahrain (Nos. 889/90) or Alexandros Matsoukis, Athens (No. **MS**891))

1995 (18 Sept). European Culture Month and "Europhilex '95" International Stamp Exhibition, Nicosia. T **300** and similar horiz designs. Royal blue, orange-yellow and pale stone (No. **MS***891*) or multicoloured (others). P 13×13½.
889 20c. Type **300** 55 60
890 25c. Map of Europe and Cypriot church 70 1·25
MS891 95×86 mm. 50c. Peace dove (42×30 mm); 50c. European Cultural Month symbol (42×30 mm). P 14 6·00 7·00

A limited quantity of No. **MS**891 was surcharged "£5" on each stamp and sold at "Europhilex '95" on 27 and 28 October 1995.

(Litho Oriental Press, Bahrain)

1995 (24 Oct). Obligatory Tax. Refugee Fund. As T **255**, but reduced in size and inscr "1995", "1996", "1997", "1998", "1999", "2000" or "2001". Chalk-surfaced paper. P 14½×13½.

892	**255**	1c. brownish black and olive-grey (*shades*)	10	10

301 Peace Dove with Flags of Cyprus and United Nations

302 Reliquary from Kykko Monastery

(Des Soteris Hadjimichael (10, 25c.), Stelios Karamallakis (15c.), Ermis Georgiades (20c.). Litho Oriental Press, Bahrain)

1995 (24 Oct). Anniversaries and Events. T **301** and similar multicoloured designs. P 13×13½ (horiz) or 13½×13 (vert).

893	10c. Type **301** (50th anniv of United Nations)	50	35
894	15c. Hand pushing ball over net (Centenary of volleyball) (*vert*)	95	50
895	20c. Safety pin on leaf (European Nature Conservation Year) (*vert*)	1·10	80
896	25c. Clay pigeon contestant (World Clay Target Shooting Championship)	1·25	2·25
893/6	*Set of* 4	3·50	3·50

(Des Stelios Karamallakis. Litho Oriental Press, Bahrain)

1995 (27 Nov). Christmas. T **302** and similar vert designs showing different reliquaries of Virgin and Child from Kykko Monastery. P 13½×13.

897	7c. multicoloured	40	15
898	20c. multicoloured	90	45
899	25c. multicoloured	1·40	2·25
897/9	*Set of* 3	2·40	2·50

303 Family (25th anniv of Pancyprian Organisation of Large Families)

304 Maria Synglitiki

(Des Liza Petridou-Mala. Litho Oriental Press, Bahrain)

1996 (4 Jan). Anniversaries and Events. T **303** and similar vert designs. Multicoloured. P 13½×13.

900	10c. Type **303**	50	35
901	20c. Film camera (Centenary of cinema)	1·25	70
902	35c. Silhouette of parent and child in globe (50th anniv of U.N.I.C.E.F.)	1·75	1·75
903	40c. "13" and Commonwealth emblem (13th Conference of Commonwealth Speakers and Presiding Officers)	1·75	2·75
900/3	*Set of* 4	4·75	5·00

(Des George Simonis. Litho Oriental Press, Bahrain)

1996 (8 Apr). Europa. Famous Women. T **304** and similar vert design. Multicoloured. P 14.

904	10c. Type **304**	1·00	30
905	30c. Queen Caterina Cornaro	2·00	2·75

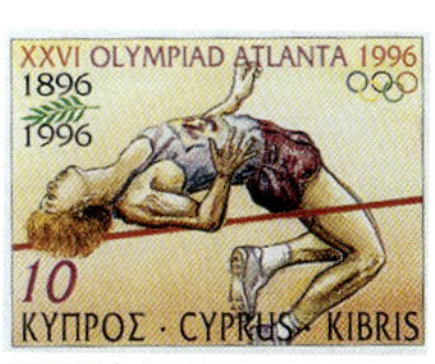

305 High Jump

306 Watermill

(Des Maximos Christou. Litho Oriental Press, Bahrain)

1996 (10 June). Centennial Olympic Games, Atlanta. T **305** and similar horiz designs. Multicoloured. P 13×13½.

906	10c. Type **305**	75	30
907	20c. Javelin	1·25	65
908	25c. Wrestling	1·40	1·10
909	30c. Swimming	1·60	2·50
906/9	*Set of* 4	4·50	4·00

(Des Ermis Georgiades. Litho Oriental Press, Bahrain)

1996 (23 Sept). Mills. T **306** and similar vert designs. Multicoloured. P 13½×13.

910	10c. Type **306**	70	40
911	15c. Olivemill	85	50
912	20c. Windmill	1·00	90
913	25c. Handmill	1·10	2·00
910/13	*Set of* 4	3·25	3·50

307 Icon of Our Lady of Iberia, Moscow

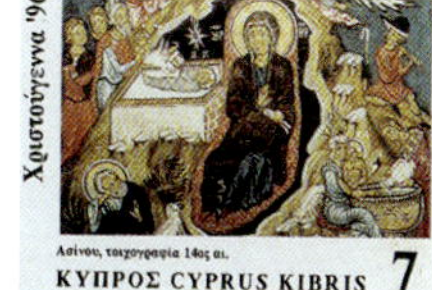

308 "The Nativity" (detail)

(Des Demetry Komissarov (Nos. 914, 917), George Simonis (Nos. 915/16). Litho State Ptg Wks, Moscow)

1996 (13 Nov). Cyprus–Russia Joint Issue. Orthodox Religion. T **307** and similar square designs. Multicoloured. P 11½.

914	30c. Type **307**	1·75	2·00
	a. Block of 4. Nos. 914/17	6·00	7·00
915	30c. Stravrovouni Monastery, Cyprus	1·75	2·00
916	30c. Icon of St. Nicholas, Cyprus	1·75	2·00
917	30c. Voskresenskie Gate, Moscow	1·75	2·00
914/17	*Set of* 4	6·00	7·00

Nos. 914/17 were printed together, *se-tenant*, in blocks of 4 throughout the sheet.

Stamps in similar designs were also issued by Russia.

(Des George Koumouros. Litho Oriental Press, Bahrain)

1996 (2 Dec). Christmas. Religious Murals from Church of the Virgin of Asinou. T **308** and similar multicoloured designs. P 13½×13 (25c.) or 13×13½ (others).

918	7c. Type **308**	60	15
919	20c. "Virgin Mary between the Archangels Gabriel and Michael"	1·50	45
920	25c. "Christ bestowing Blessing" (*vert*)	1·90	2·75
918/20	*Set of* 3	3·50	3·00

309 Basketball

310 "The Last Supper"

(Des Stelios Karamallakis. Litho Oriental Press, Bahrain)

1997 (24 Mar). Final of European Basketball Cup. P 13½×13.

921	**309**	30c. multicoloured	2·25	2·00

(Des George Koumouros. Litho Oriental Press, Bahrain)

1997 (24 Mar). Easter. Religious Frescoes from Monastery of St. John Lambadestis. T **310** and similar horiz design. Multicoloured. P 13×13½.

922	15c. Type **310**	1·00	50
923	25c. "The Crucifixion"	1·25	1·50

311 Kori Kourelleni and Prince

312 *Oedipoda miniata* (grasshopper)

(Des Liza Petridou-Mala. Litho Oriental Press, Bahrain)

1997 (5 May). Europa. Tales and Legends. T **311** and similar vert design. Multicoloured. P 13½×13.

924	15c. Type **311**	1·00	40
925	30c. Digenis and Charon	1·75	2·50

(Des Andreas Ladommatos. Litho Oriental Press, Bahrain)

1997 (30 June). Insects. T **312** and similar horiz designs. Multicoloured. P 13×13½.

926	10c. Type **312**	65	30
927	15c. *Acherontia atropos* (hawk moth)	95	40
928	25c. *Daphnis nerii* (hawk moth)	1·60	1·25
929	35c. *Ascalaphus macaronius* (owl-fly)	1·75	2·50
926/9 *Set of 4*		4·50	4·00

313 Archbishop Makarios III and Chapel

314 The Nativity

(Des Chairs. Sophocleous Litho Oriental Press, Bahrain)

1997 (1 Aug). 20th Death Anniv of Archbishop Makarios III. P 13×13½.

930	**313**	15c. multicoloured	1·25	50

(Des George Koumouros. Litho Oriental Press, Bahrain)

1997 (17 Nov). Christmas. Byzantine Frescos from the Monastery of St. John Lambadestis. T **314** and similar vert designs. Multicoloured. P 13½×13.

931	10c. Type **314**	60	15
932	25c. Three Kings following the star	1·75	60
933	30c. Flight into Egypt	1·90	2·75
931/3 *Set of 3*		3·75	3·25

315 Green Jasper

316 Players competing for Ball

(Des Andreas Ladommatos. Litho Oriental Press, Bahrain)

1998 (9 Mar). Minerals. T **315** and similar horiz designs. Multicoloured. P 13.

934	10c. Type **315**	70	30
935	15c. Iron Pyrite	95	45
936	25c. Gypsum	1·40	1·25
937	30c. Chalcedony	1·50	2·50
934/7 *Set of 4*		4·00	4·00

(Des Charis Sophocleous. Litho Oriental Press, Bahrain)

1998 (4 May). World Cup Football Championship, France. P 14.

938	**316**	35c. multicoloured	1·75	1·40

317 Cataclysmos Festival, Larnaca

318 Mouflon Family Group

(Des Sotiris Vassiliou (15c.), Andreas Ladommatos (30c.). Litho Oriental Press, Bahrain)

1998 (4 May). Europa. Festivals. T **317** and similar horiz design. Multicoloured. P 14.

939	15c. Type **317**	1·25	40
940	30c. House of Representatives, Nicosia (Declaration of Independence)	1·75	2·50

(Des Sotiris Hadjimichael. Litho Oriental Press, Bahrain)

1998 (22 June). Endangered Species. Cyprus Mouflon. T **318** and similar horiz designs. Multicoloured. P 13×13½.

941	25c. Type **318**	1·25	1·40
	a. Block of 4. Nos. 941/4	4·50	5·00
942	25c. Mouflon herd	1·25	1·40
943	25c. Head of ram	1·25	1·40
944	25c. Ram on guard	1·25	1·40
941/4 *Set of 4*		4·50	5·00

Nos. 941/4 were printed together, *se-tenant*, in blocks of 4 throughout the sheet.

(Litho Oriental Press, Bahrain)

1998 (22 June). As No. 876, but different printer. White paper. With imprint date ("1998"). P 14.

958	£1 Townswoman wearing festive sarka	5·00	4·00

319 Flames and Globe Emblem

320 World "Stamp" and Magnifying Glass

(Des Sakis Vassiliou. Litho Oriental Press, Bahrain)

1998 (9 Oct). 50th Anniv of Universal Declaration of Human Rights. P 14.

959	**319**	50c. multicoloured	1·25	1·60

(Des Theodoros Kakoullis. Litho Oriental Press, Bahrain)

1998 (9 Oct). World Stamp Day. P 14.

960	**320**	30c. multicoloured	1·60	1·60
		a. Booklet pane of 8	13·00	

No. 960a has the horizontal edges of the pane imperforate and margins at left and right.

321 "The Annunciation"

322 *Pleurotus eryngii*

(Des Theodoros Kakoullis. Litho Oriental Press, Bahrain)

1998 (16 Nov). Christmas. T **321** and similar vert designs showing religious murals. Multicoloured. P 14.

961	10c. Type **321**	60	20
962	25c. "The Nativity"	1·40	65
963	30c. "The Baptism of Christ"	1·40	2·50
961/3 *Set of 3*		3·00	3·00
MS964 102×75 mm. Nos. 961/3		3·00	3·50

(Des Sakis. Vassiliou. Litho Oriental Press, Bahrain)

1999 (4 Mar). Mushrooms of Cyprus. T **322** and similar vert designs. Multicoloured. P 13½×13.

965	10c. Type **322**	50	30
966	15c. *Lactarius deliciosus*	80	40
967	25c. *Sparassis crispa*	1·10	90
968	30c. *Morchella elata*	1·40	2·25
965/8 *Set of 4*		3·50	3·50

323 Pair of Moufflons at Tripylos Reserve

324 Council of Europe Building, Emblem and Flags

(Des Eleni Lambrou. Litho Oriental Press, Bahrain)

1999 (6 May). Europa. Parks and Gardens. T **323** and similar horiz design. Multicoloured. P 14.

969	15c. Type **323**	1·00	50
	a. Booklet pane. Nos. 969/70, each × 4, with margins all round	10·00	
970	30c. Turtles on beach at Lara Reserve	1·75	2·25

(Des Stella Symeonidou. Litho Oriental Press, Bahrain)

1999 (6 May). 50th Anniv of Council of Europe. P 14.

971	**324**	30c. multicoloured	1·50	1·75

325 Temple of Hylates Apollo, Kourion

(Des Andreas. Ladommatos. Litho Alexandros Matsoukis, Athens)

1999 (28 June). Cyprus–Greece Joint Issue. 4000 Years of Greek Culture. T **325** and similar vert designs. Multicoloured. P 13½×13.

972	25c. Type **325**	1·40	1·75
	a. Block of 4. Nos. 972/5	5·00	6·00
973	25c. Mycenaean pot depicting warriors	1·40	1·75
974	25c. Mycenaean crater depicting horse	1·40	1·75
975	25c. Temple of Apollo, Delphi	1·40	1·75
972/5 *Set of 4*		5·00	6·00

Nos. 972/5 were printed together, *se-tenant*, in blocks of 4 throughout the sheet.

326 Paper Aeroplane Letters and U.P.U. Emblem

327 Container Ship and Cypriot Flag

(Des Sakis Vassiliou. Litho Oriental Press, Bahrain)

1999 (4 Oct). 125th Anniv of Universal Postal Union. T **326** and similar horiz design. Multicoloured. P 14.

976	15c. Type **326**	1·00	50
977	35c. "125" and U.P.U. emblem	1·50	2·00

(Des Thompson Communications. Litho Oriental Press, Bahrain)

1999 (4 Oct). "Maritime Cyprus '99" Conference. Sheet 103×80 mm, containing T **327** and similar horiz designs. Multicoloured. P 14*.

MS978 25c. Type **327**; 25c. Binoculars and chart; 25c. Stern of container ship; 25c. Tanker	3·50	4·00

*On No. **MS**978 the row of perforations across the foot of the lower pair gauges 13.

328 Cypriot Refugee Fund Stamps and Barbed Wire (*Illustration reduced. Actual size 110×75 mm*)

(Des Glafkos Theofylactou. Litho Oriental Press, Bahrain)

1999 (11 Nov). 25th Anniv of Turkish Landings in Cyprus. Sheet 110×75 mm. Imperf.

MS979 **328** 30c. multicoloured	1·50	2·25

329 Angel

330 Woman's Silhouette with Stars and Globe

(Des Glafkos Theofylactou. Litho Oriental Press, Bahrain)

1999 (11 Nov). Christmas. T **329** and similar vert designs. Multicoloured. P 14.

980	10c. Type **329**	60	10
981	25c. The Three Kings	1·40	70
982	30c. Madonna and Child	1·50	2·50
980/2 *Set of 3*		3·25	3·00

(Des Glafkos Theophylaktou. Litho Oriental Press, Bahrain)

2000 (2 Mar). Miss Universe Beauty Contest. Cyprus. Sheet 80×65 mm containing T **330** and similar vert design. Multicoloured. P 13½×13.

MS983 15c. Type **330**; 35c. Statue of Aphrodite and apple	2·75	2·75

331 Necklace, 4500–4000 B.C.

332 "Building Europa"

(Des A. Koutas. Litho Oriental Press, Bahrain)

2000 (30 Mar). Jewellery. T **331** and similar multicoloured designs. P 14.

984	10c. Type **331**	45	30
985	15c. Gold earrings, 3rd-cent B.C.	65	40
986	20c. Gold earring from Lampousa, 6th–7th-cent	75	50
987	25c. Brooch, 19th-cent	75	60
988	30c. Gold cross, 6th–7th-cent	95	75
989	35c. Necklace, 18th–19th-cent	1·00	85
990	40c. Gold earring, 19th-cent	1·50	95
991	50c. Spiral hair ring, 5th–4th-cent B.C	1·60	1·25
992	75c. Gold-plated silver plaques from Gialia, 700–600 B.C. (*horiz*)	2·25	2·50
993	£1 Gold frontlet from Egkomi, 14th–13th-cent B.C. (*horiz*)	4·25	3·25
994	£2 Gold necklace from Egkomi, 13th-cent B.C. (*horiz*)	7·50	7·50
995	£3 Buckles, 19th-cent (*horiz*)	11·00	12·00
984/95 *Set of 12*		29·00	28·00

(Des Jean Paul Cousin. Litho Oriental Press, Bahrain)

2000 (9 May). Europa. P 14.

996	**332**	30c. multicoloured	1·75	1·75

333 "50", Cross and Map of Cyprus

334 Flame, Map of Cyprus and Broken Chain

(Des Liza Petridou. Litho Oriental Press, Bahrain)

2000 (9 May). 50th Anniv of Red Cross in Cyprus. P 13×13½.

997 **333** 15c. multicoloured .... 1·75 1·00

(Des Andreas Ladommatos. Litho Oriental Press, Bahrain)

2000 (9 May). 45th Anniv of Struggle for Independence. P 13½×13.

998 **334** 15c. multicoloured .... 1·75 1·00

335 Weather Balloon, Map and Satellite

336 Monastery of Antifontis, Kalograia

(Des Liza Petridou. Litho Oriental Press, Bahrain)

2000 (9 May). 50th Anniv of World Meteorological Organization. P 14.

999 **335** 30c. multicoloured .... 2·25 2·25

(Des Andreas Koutas. Litho Oriental Press, Bahrain)

2000 (29 June). Greek Orthodox Churches in Northern Cyprus. T **336** and similar designs. P 13½×13 (10c. and 15c.) or 13×13½ (25c. and 30c.).

1000 10c. red-brown and carmine 70 25
1001 15c. deep bluish green and bottle green .... 1·00 45
1002 25c. deep slate-violet and reddish violet .... 1·40 1·10
1003 30c. carmine-red and grey .... 1·50 2·50
1000/3 *Set of 4* .... 4·25 3·75

Designs: *Vert*—15c. Church of St. Themonianos, Lysi. *Horiz*—25c. Church of Panagia Kanakaria, Lytrhagkomi; 30c. Church of Avgasida Monastery, Milia.

337 Council of Europe Emblem

338 Archery

(Des Stella Symeonidou. Litho Oriental Press, Bahrain)

2000 (29 June). 50th Anniv of European Convention of Human Rights. P 13×13½.

1004 **337** 30c. multicoloured .... 2·00 2·00

(Des Maximos Christou. Litho Oriental Press, Bahrain)

2000 (14 Sept). Olympic Games, Sydney. T **338** and similar horiz designs. Multicoloured. P 13×13½.

1005 10c. Type **338** 70 25
1006 15c. Gymnastics 90 40
1007 25c. Diving .... 1·40 1·00
1008 35c. Trampolining .... 1·60 2·50
1005/8 *Set of 4* .... 4·25 3·75

339 "The Annunciation"

(Des Nicolas Ladommatos. Litho Oriental Press, Bahrain)

2000 (2 Nov). Christmas. Gold Gospel Covers. T **339** and similar vert designs. Multicoloured. P 13½×13.

1009 10c. Type **339** 75 25
1010 25c. "The Nativity" .... 1·75 70
1011 30c. "The Baptism of Christ" .... 1·75 2·00
1009/11 *Set of 3* .... 3·75 2·75

340 "25" and Commonwealth Symbol

(Des George Simonis. Litho Oriental Press, Bahrain)

2001 (12 Mar). 25th Anniv of Commonwealth Day. P 13.

1012 **340** 30c. multicoloured .... 1·75 2·00

341 Silhouette, Dove and Barbed Wire

342 Pavlos Liasides

(Des Stella Symeonidou. Litho Oriental Press, Bahrain)

2001 (12 Mar). 50th Anniv of United Nations High Commissioner for Refugees. P 13.

1013 **341** 30c. multicoloured .... 1·75 2·00

(Des Andreas Ladommatos. Litho Oriental Press, Bahrain)

2001 (12 Mar). Birth Centenary of Pavlos Liasides (poet). P 13.

1014 **342** 13c. chocolate, ochre and yellow-brown .... 1·25 60

343 Bridge over River Diarizos

344 Parthenope massena

(Des Georgia Koulendrou. Litho Oriental Press, Bahrain)

2001 (3 May). Europa. Cypriot Rivers. T **343** and similar horiz design. Multicoloured. P 13×13½.

1015 20c. Type **343** .... 1·00 50
a. Booklet pane. Nos. 1015/16, each ×4, with margins all round .... 9·00
1016 30c. Mountain torrent, River Akaki .... 1·75 2·25

(Des Sakis Vassiliou. Litho Oriental Press, Bahrain)

2001 (7 June). Crabs. T **344** and similar horiz designs. Multicoloured. P 13×13½.

1017 13c. Type **344** 75 20
1018 20c. Calappa granulate .... 1·25 85
1019 25c. Ocypode cursor .... 1·50 1·25
1020 30c. Pagurus bernhardus .... 1·75 2·25
1017/20 *Set of 4* .... 4·75 4·00

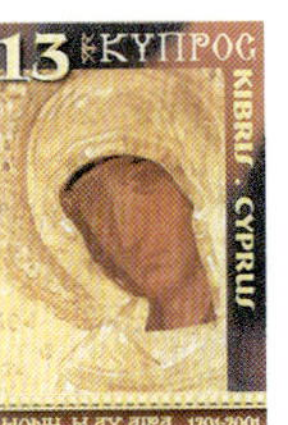

345 Icon of Virgin Mary

346 Loukis Akritas

(Des Glafkos Theofylactou. Litho Alexandros Matsoukis, Athens)

2001 (25 Oct). Christmas. 800th Anniv of Macheras Monastery. T **345** and similar vert designs. Multicoloured. P 13½×13.

1021 13c. Type **345** ... 55 20
1022 25c. Macheras Monastery ... 1·50 65
1023 30c. Ornate gold crucifix ... 1·75 2·25
1021/3 *Set of 3* ... 3·50 2·75

(Des Andreas Ladommatos. Litho Alexandros Matsoukis, Athens)

2001 (25 Oct). Loukis Akritas (writer). Commemoration. P 13½ ×13.

1024 **346** 20c. brown-olive and olive-bistre ... 1·50 1·00

347 Tortoiseshell and White Cat

348 Acrobat on Horseback

(Des Andreas Koutas. Litho Alexandros Matsoukis, Athens)

2002 (21 Mar). Cats. T **347** and similar horiz designs. Multicoloured. P 13×13½.

1025 20c. Type **347** ... 1·40 1·75
a. Pair. Nos. 1025/6 ... 2·75 3·50
1026 20c. British blue ... 1·40 1·75
1027 25c. Tortoiseshell and white ... 1·40 1·75
a. Pair. Nos. 1027/8 ... 2·75 3·50
1028 25c. Red and silver tabby ... 1·40 1·75
1025/8 *Set of 4* ... 5·00 6·25

Nos. 1025/6 and 1027/8 were each printed together, *se-tenant*, as horizontal and vertical pairs throughout the sheets of 16.

(Des Glafkos Theofylactou. Litho Alexandros Matsoukis, Athens)

2002 (9 May). Europa. Circus. T **348** and similar vert design. Multicoloured. P 13½ ×13.

1029 20c. Type **348** ... 1·00 50
a. Booklet pane. Nos. 1029/30, each ×4 with margins all round ... 9·00
1030 30c. Clown on high wire ... 1·75 2·25

349 *Myrtus communis*

350 Mother Teresa

(Des Maria Trillidou. Litho Alexandros Matsoukis, Athens)

2002 (13 June). Medicinal Plants. T **349** and similar horiz designs. Multicoloured. P 13×13½.

1031 13c. Type **349** ... 75 30
1032 20c. *Lavandula stoechas* ... 1·25 85
1033 25c. *Capparis spinosa* ... 1·50 1·25
1034 30c. *Ocimum basilicum* ... 1·75 2·25
1031/4 *Set of 4* ... 4·75 4·25

(Des Toula Paphitou. Litho A. Matsoukis, Athens)

2002 (12 Sept). Mother Teresa (founder of Missionaries of Charity) Commemoration. P 13½×13.

1035 **350** 40c. multicoloured ... 2·75 2·50

351 Blackboard on Easel

352 Agate Seal-stone (5th century B.C.)

(Des Katia Georgiadou. Litho A. Matsoukis, Athens)

2002 (12 Sept). International Teachers' Day. T **351** and similar horiz design. Multicoloured. P 13×13½.

1036 13c. Type **351** ... 1·50 1·50
a. Horiz pair. Nos. 1036/7 ... 3·75 4·00
1037 30c. Computer ... 2·25 2·50

Nos. 1036/7 were printed together, *se-tenant*, as horizontal pairs throughout sheets of 20.

(Des Glafkos Theofylaktou and Nicos Rangos (No. **MS**1044) or Glafkos Theofylaktou (others). Litho A. Matsoukis, Athens)

2002 (22 Oct). "Cyprus - Europhilex '02", Stamp Exhibition, Nicosia. Cypriot Antiquities showing Europa. T **352** and similar horiz designs. Multicoloured. P 13×13½.

1038 20c. Type **352** ... 1·10 1·25
a. Horiz strip of 3. Nos. 1038/40 ... 3·00 3·25
1039 20c. Silver coin of Timochares (5th–4th century BC) ... 1·10 1·25
1040 20c. Silver coin of Stasioikos (5th century BC) ... 1·10 1·25
1041 30c. Clay lamp (green backgound) (2nd century AD) ... 1·50 1·75
a. Horiz strip of 3. Nos. 1041/3 ... 4·00 4·75
1042 30c. Statuette of Europa on the Bull (7th–6th century BC) ... 1·50 1·75
1043 30c. Clay lamp (purple backgound) (1st century BC) ... 1·50 1·75
1038/43 *Set of 6* ... 7·00 8·00
MS1044 105×71 mm. 50c. Statue of Aphrodite with maps of Crete and Cyprus; 50c. "Europa on the Bull" (painting by Francesco di Giogio) ... 6·50 7·50

Nos. 1038/40 and 1041/3 were each printed together, *se-tenant*, as horizontal strips of 3 throughout sheets of 12.

353 "Nativity"

(Des Andreas Koutas. Litho A. Matsoukis, Athens)

2002 (21 Nov). Christmas. Details from "Birth of Christ" (wall painting), Church of Metamorphosis Sotiros, Palechori. T **353** and similar multicoloured designs. P 13½ (30c.) or 13×13½ (others).

1045 13c. Type **353** ... 80 20
1046 25c. "Three Wise Men" ... 1·50 75
1047 30c. "Birth of Christ" (complete painting) (38×38 mm) ... 2·25 2·50
1045/7 *Set of 3* ... 4·00 3·00

354 Triumph Roadster 1800, 1946

355 "POSTER IS ART"

(Des Glafkos Theofylaktou. Litho A. Matsoukis, Athens)

2003 (20 Mar). International Historic Car Rally. T **354** and similar horiz designs. Multicoloured. P 13.

1048 20c. Type **354** ... 1·60 1·75
a. Vert strip of 3. Nos. 1048/50 ... 4·25 4·75
1049 25c. Ford model T, 1917 ... 1·60 1·75
1050 30c. Baby Ford Y 8hp, 1932 ... 1·60 1·75
1048/50 *Set of 3* ... 4·25 4·75

Nos. 1048/50 were printed together, *se-tenant*, in vertical strips of 3 throughout the sheet.

(Des Sakis Vassiliou. Litho A. Matsoukis, Athens)

2003 (5 May). Europa. Poster Art. P 13½×13.

1051 **355** 20c. multicoloured ... 80 50
a. Perf 13½ ... 90 1·25
b. Booklet pane. Nos. 1051/2, each ×4 ... 8·00
1052 – 30c. multicoloured ... 1·40 1·75
a. Perf 13½ ... 1·25 1·50

Nos. 1051a and 1052a were only issued in £2 booklets, No. SB5.

Booklet pane No. 1051b has the horizontal edges of the pane imperforate and margins at left and right.

356 Bat in Flight

357 Stylized Owl

(Des Owen Bell. Litho A. Matsoukis, Athens)

2003 (12 June). Endangered Species. Mediterranean Horseshoe Bat. T **356** and similar horiz designs. Multicoloured. P 13×13½.

1053	25c. Type **356**	1·50	1·75
	a. Block of 4. Nos. 1053/6	5·50	6·25
1054	25c. Head of bat (facing forwards)	1·50	1·75
1055	25c. Bats roosting	1·50	1·75
1056	25c. Head of bat (facing sideways, mouth open)	1·50	1·75
1053/6 *Set of 4*		5·50	6·25

Nos. 1053/6 were printed together, *se-tenant*, in blocks of four throughout sheets of 16.

(Des Sakis Vassiliou. Litho A. Matsoukis, Athens)

2003 (12 June). 7th Conference of European Ministers of Education, Nicosia. P 13½×13.

1057	**357**	30c. multicoloured	1·75	2·00

358 Eleonora's Falcon

359 Constantinos Spyridakis (historian, author and Minister of Education 1965–70)

(Des Glafkos Theofylaktou. Litho A. Matsoukis, Athens)

2003 (25 Sept). Birds of Prey. T **358** and similar triangular designs. Multicoloured. P 14.

1058	20c. Type **358**	1·50	1·75
	a. Horiz pair. Nos. 1058/9	3·00	3·50
1059	20c. Eleonora's Falcon in flight	1·50	1·75
1060	25c. Imperial Eagle	1·50	1·75
	a. Horiz pair. Nos. 1060/1	3·00	3·50
1061	25c. Imperial Eagle in flight	1·50	1·75
1062	30c. Little Owl	1·50	1·75
	a. Horiz pair. Nos. 1062/3	3·00	3·50
1063	30c. Little Owl in flight and eggs in nest	1·50	1·75
1058/63 *Set of 6*		8·00	9·50

Nos. 1058/9, 1060/1 and 1062/3 were each printed together, *se-tenant*, in horizontal pairs in sheets of 12.

(Des Stella Symeonidou. Litho A. Matsoukis, Athens)

2003 (13 Nov). Birth Centenaries. T **359** and similar design. P 13×13½ (No. 1064) or 13½×13 (No. 1065).

1064	5c. black and drab	50	65
1065	5c. blackish olive and grey-olive	50	65

Design: 23×31 mm.—No. 1065, Tefkros Anthias (poet).

360 Three Angels

361 Stylised Footballer

(Des Pana Kazazi El-Alwani and Melanie Efstathiadou. Litho A. Matsoukis, Athens)

2003 (13 Nov). Christmas. T **360** and similar multicoloured designs. P 13 (13, 30c.) or 14 (40c.).

1066	13c. Type **360**	80	20
1067	30c. Three Wise Men	1·50	85
1068	40c. Nativity (37×59 mm)	2·25	2·75
1066/8 *Set of 3*		4·00	3·50

Nos. 1066/7 show details from icon of Nativity in Church of Virgin Mary, Kourdali. No. 1068 shows the complete painting.

(Des Elena Eliadou. Litho A. Matsoukis, Athens)

2004 (11 Mar). Centenary of FIFA (Fédération Internationale de Football Association). P 13½.

1069	**361**	30c. multicoloured	1·75	2·00

362 Stylised Footballer

363 Flags of New Member Countries

(Des Kakia Katselli. Litho A. Matsoukis, Athens)

2004 (11 Mar). 50th Anniv of UEFA (Union of European Football Associations). P 13½×13.

1070	**362**	30c. multicoloured	1·75	2·00

(Des Jean Pierre. Mizzi. Litho A. Matsoukis, Athens)

2004 (1 May). Enlargement of the European Union. P 14.

1071	**363**	30c. multicoloured	1·75	2·00

364 Yiannos Kranidiotis and EU Emblem

365 Sailing Boat and Ancient Amphitheatre

(Des Nicolas. Ladommatos. Litho A. Matsoukis, Athens)

2004 (1 May). Fifth Death Anniv of Yiannos Kranidiotis (politician). P 13×13½.

1072	**364**	20c. multicoloured	1·25	80

(Des Melanie Efstathiadou. Litho A. Matsoukis, Athens)

2004 (1 May). Europa. Holidays. T **365** and similar horiz design. Multicoloured. P 13½.

1073	20c. Type **365**	75	50
	a. Booklet pane. Nos. 1073/4, each ×4	7·00	
1074	30c. Family at seaside and statue	1·50	1·75

The exact gauge of the perforations on the sheet stamps is 13.7×13.3, but stamps from the booklet pane measure 13.7 all round.

Booklet pane No. 1073a has the horizontal edges of the pane imperforate and margins at left and right.

366 Horse Racing

(Des Glafkos. Theofylaktou. Litho Alexandros Matsoukis)

2004 (10 June). Olympic Games, Athens. T **366** and similar horiz designs showing ancient Olympic sports. Multicoloured. P 13×13½.

1075	13c. Type **366**	65	35
1076	20c. Running	1·00	50
1077	30c. Diving	1·50	1·10
1078	40c. Discus	1·75	2·50
1075/8 *Set of 4*		4·50	4·00

367 Dolphin

(Des Antonia Hadjigeorgiou. Litho Alexandros Matsoukis)

2004 (9 Sept). Mammals. T **367** and similar horiz designs. Multicoloured. P 13½.

1079	20c. Type **367**	1·25	1·25
1080	20c. Dolphin (blue background)	1·25	1·25
1081	30c. Fox (white background)	1·60	1·60
1082	30c. Fox (green background)	1·60	1·60
1083	40c. Hare (white background)	1·75	1·75
1084	40c. Hare (yellow background)	1·75	1·75
1079/84	*Set of 6*	8·25	8·25

368 Choir of Angels

(Des Liza Petridou-Mala. Litho Alexandros Matsoukis)

2004 (11 Nov). Christmas. T **368** and similar multicoloured designs. P 14×13½ (13c, 30c) or 14 (40c, £1).

1085	13c. Type **368**	85	20
1086	30c. Three Wise Men	1·75	85
1087	40c. Annunciation to the Shepherds (37×60 mm)	2·25	2·50
1085/7	*Set of 3*	4·25	3·25
MS1088	63×84 mm. £1 Virgin and Child (38×38 mm)	5·50	6·00

The stamp in No. **MS**1088 was printed along the bottom edge of the sheet and was imperforate at foot.

369 Georgios Philippou Pierides

370 Carolina Pelendritou and Medal

(Des Liza Petridou-Mala. Litho Alexandros Matsoukis)

2004 (11 Nov). Intellectual Personalities. T **369** and similar vert design. Multicoloured. P 13½×13.

1089	5c. Type **369**	65	75
1090	5c. Emilios Chourmouzios (wearing tie)	65	75

Nos. 1091/2 were relisted. See No. 807.

(Des Antonia Hadjigeorgiou. Litho A. Matsoukis, Athens)

2005 (3 Mar). Carolina Pelendritou's Gold Medal for 100 Metres Swimming at Paralympic Games, Athens (2004). P 13½×14.

1093 **370** 20c. multicoloured ... 1·00 70

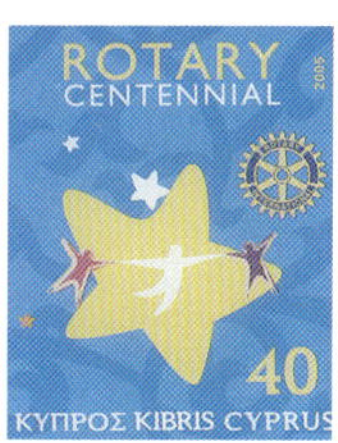
371 Emblem

372 "The Entrance" (Kyriacos Koulli)

(Des Antonia Hadjigeorgiou. Litho A. Matsoukis, Athens)

2005 (3 Mar). Centenary of Rotary International. P 13½×14.

1094 **371** 40c. multicoloured ... 1·25 1·60

(Des Antonia Hadjigeorgiou. Litho A. Matsoukis, Athens)

2005 (3 Mar). 50th Anniv of EOKA Struggle. P 13½×14.

1095 **372** 50c. multicoloured ... 2·00 2·50

373 Table with Fish, Casserole, Wine, Garlic, Tomato and Bread

374 German Shepherd Dog and Police Dog with Handler

(Des Glafkos Theofylactou. Litho Alexandros Matsoukis)

2005 (5 May). Europa. Gastronomy. T **373** and similar vert design. Multicoloured. P 13½×13.

1096	20c. Type **373**	75	50
	a. Perf 13½×14	75	80
	ab. Booklet pane. Nos. 1096a/7a, each ×4	8·00	
1097	30c. Table with coffee, cheese, cocktail and desserts	1·25	1·50
	a. Perf 13½×14	1·25	1·60

No. 1096a has no white margins at left and No. 1097a has no white margins at right.

Nos. 1096a and 1097a were only issued in horizontal pairs, each pair forming a composite design, from booklet pane No. 1096ab from £2 booklets, No. SB7.

Booklet pane No. 1096ab has the horizontal edges imperforate and margins at left and right.

(Des Nicolas Ladommatos. Litho Alexandros Matsoukis)

2005 (16 June). Dogs in Man's Life. T **374** and similar square designs. Multicoloured. P 13½.

1098	13c. Type **374**	85	30
	a. Booklet pane. Nos. 1098/1101 with margins all round	5·25	
1099	20c. Hungarian Vizsla and hunter with dog	1·25	85
1100	30c. Labrador and man with guide dog	1·75	1·40
1101	40c. Dalmatian and boy with pet dog	2·00	2·50
1098/101	*Set of 4*	5·25	4·50

375 Angel appearing to Shepherds

376 1964 30c. Flower Stamp

(Des Melanie Efstathiadou. Litho Alexandros Matsoukis)

2005 (10 Nov). Christmas. T **375** and similar multicoloured designs. P 13½ (13, 30c.) or 14 (40c.).

1102	13c. Type **375**	80	20
1103	30c. Holy Family and shepherds	1·60	90
1104	40c. Virgin Mary and Jesus Christ (37×59 mm)	1·90	2·50
1102/4	*Set of 3*	3·75	3·25

Nos. 1102/3 show details from icon "Birth of Christ" and No. 1104 shows icon of the "Virgin Mary Karmiotissa".

(Des Melanie Efstathiadou. Litho Alexandros Matsoukis)

2006 (23 Feb). 50th Anniv of First Europa Stamp. T **376** and similar square designs showing Cyprus Europa stamps. Multicoloured. P 14.

MS1105 94×84 mm. 30c. Type **376**; 30c. 1962 40m. doves stamp; 30c. 1963 40m. tree stamp; 30c. 1963 150m. CEPT stamp ... 4·75 5·50

The stamps within No. **MS**1105 have composite background designs.

377 "25" and Hand Stamp

(Des Melanie Efstathiadou. Litho Alexandros Matsoukis)

2006 (30 Mar). 25th Anniv of the Postal Museum, Nicosia. P 14×13½.
1106 **377** 25c. multicoloured .... 1·00 1·00

378 Self-portrait and "The Anatomy Lesson of Dr. Nicolaes Tulp"

379 Footballer kicking Ball

(Des Melanie Efstathiadou. Litho Alexandros Matsoukis)

2006 (30 Mar). 400th Birth Anniv of Rembrandt (artist). P 14×13½.
1107 **378** 40c. multicoloured .... 2·50 2·50

(Des Liza Petridou. Litho Alexandros Matsoukis)

2006 (30 Mar). World Cup Football Championship, Germany. P 13½×14.
1108 **379** 50c. multicoloured .... 2·00 2·25

380 Stamna or Kouza (Pitcher) Dance, Cyprus

381 Stylized Hand and Swallow

(Des Glafkos Theofylactou. Litho Alexandros Matsoukis, Athens)

2006 (12 Apr). Folk Dances. Sheet 100×70 mm containing T **380** and similar horiz design. Multicoloured. P 13×13½.
MS1109 40c. Type **380**; 40c. Nati dance, Himachal Pradesh, India .... 3·50 4·50

Stamps in similar designs were issued by India.

(Des Sakis Vasiliou. Litho Alexandros Matsoukis, Athens)

2006 (4 May). Europa. Integration. Multicoloured, background colour given. P 13½×13.
1110 **381** 30c. bright green .... 1·25 50
a. Perf 13½×14 .... 1·40 1·50
ab. Booklet pane. Nos. 1110a/11a, each ×4 .... 11·00
1111 40c. bright cerise-pink .... 1·50 2·00
a. Perf 13½×14 .... 1·50 2·00

Nos. 1110a and 1111a were only issued in £2.80 booklets, No. SB9.

Booklet pane No. 1110ab has the horizontal edges of the pane imperforate and margins at left and right.

382 *Elaeagnus angustifolia* (olive)

383 Flowers and Silhouettes

(Des Costas Panayi. Litho Alexandros Matsoukis)

2006 (15 June). Cyprus Fruits. T **382** and similar multicoloured designs. P 13½×14 (vert) or 14×13½ (horiz).
1112 20c. Type **382** .... 1·00 50
1113 25c. *Mespilus germanica* (medlar) (horiz) .... 1·00 55
1114 60c. *Opuntia ficus barbarica* (prickly pear) .... 2·75 4·00
1112/14 *Set of 3* .... 4·25 4·50

(Des Melanie Efstathiadou. Litho Alexandros Matsoukis)

2006 (15 June). Transplants. P 13.
1115 **383** 13c. multicoloured 75 60

384 Bedford Water Carrier, 1997

385 Nicos Nicolaides

(Des Antonia Hadjigeorgiou. Litho Alexandros Matsoukis)

2006 (14 Sept). Fire Engines. T **384** and similar horiz designs. Multicoloured. P 14×13½.
1116 13c. Type **384** .... 1·00 30
1117 20c. Hino fire engine, 1994 .... 1·25 80
1118 50c. Bedford fire engine with turntable ladder, 1959 .... 2·75 3·25
1116/18 *Set of 3* .... 4·50 4·00

(Des Liza Petridou. Litho Alexandros Matsoukis)

2006 (16 Nov). 50th Death Anniv of Nicos Nicolaides (writer). P 13½×13.
1119 **385** 5c. multicoloured 45 35

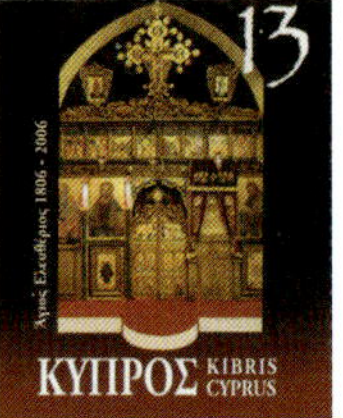

386 Wood-carved Iconostasis (Arsenios), 1868

387 *Antedon mediterranea* (feather star)

(Des Sophia Malekou. Litho Alexandros Matsoukis)

2006 (16 Nov). Christmas. T **386** and similar vert designs showing carvings from Agiou Eleftheriou Church, Nicosia. Multicoloured. P 13½×14.
1120 13c. Type **386** 70 25
1121 30c. Christ on the Cross from top of iconostasis .... 1·40 1·25
1122 40c. Stone bas-relief showing cross, spear and sponge .... 1·60 2·00
1120/2 *Set of 3* .... 3·25 3·25

(Des Ioanna Kalli. Litho Alexandros Matsoukis)

2007 (8 Feb). Echinodermata of Cyprus. T **387** and similar horiz designs. Multicoloured. P 14×13½.
1123 25c. Type **387** .... 1·50 1·50
a. Horiz strip of 4. Nos. 1123/6 .... 5·50 5·50
1124 25c. *Centrostephanus longispinus* (sea urchin) .... 1·50 1·50
1125 25c. *Astropecten jonstoni* (starfish) .... 1·50 1·50
1126 25c. *Ophioderma longicaudum* (brittle star) .... 1·50 1·50
1123/6 *Set of 4* .... 5·50 5·50

Nos. 1123/6 were printed together, *se-tenant*, in sheetlets of eight stamps containing two horizontal strips of four.

388 St. Zenon the Postman

(Des Sophia Malekou. Litho Alexandros Matsoukis)

2007 (8 Feb). St. Zenon the Postman. Sheet 75 ×65 mm. Imperf.
MS1127 **388** £1 multicoloured ..... 7·00 8·00

389 Triumph Daytona T100R, 1972

390 Emblem

(Des Xenia Christodoulou. Litho Alexandros Matsoukis)

2007 (15 Mar). Old Motorcycles. T **389** and similar horiz designs. Multicoloured. P 14×13½.

1128 13c. Type **389** 80 30
1129 20c. Matchless G3L, 1941 ..... 1·40 70
1130 40c. BSAWM20, 1940 ..... 2·00 1·50
1131 60c. Ariel Red Hunter NH 359, 1939 ..... 2·25 3·00
1128/31 *Set of* 4 ..... 5·75 5·00

(Des Melanie Efstathiadou. Litho Alexandros Matsoukis)

2007 (3 May). 50th Anniv of the Treaty of Rome. P 13½×14.
1132 **390** 30c. multicoloured ..... 1·10 1·25

391 Ear of Wheat and Scout Badge

392 "50" and Stylized Figures

(Des Melanie Efstathiadou. Litho and embossed Alexandros Matsoukis)

2007 (3 May). Europa. Centenary of Scouting. P 13½×14.
1133 **391** 30c. multicoloured ..... 1·25 1·40
a. Booklet pane. Nos. 1133/4, each ×4 ..... 11·00
1134 40c. multicoloured ..... 1·50 1·60

Booklet pane 1133a has the horizontal edges imperforate and margins at left and right.

(Des Sakis Vassiliou. Litho Alexandros Matsoukis)

2007 (14 June). 50th Anniv of Social Insurance. T **392** and similar horiz design. Multicoloured. P 13×13½.
1135 40c. Type **392** (inscr in Greek) ..... 1·50 1·75
a. Horiz pair. Nos. 1135/6 ..... 3·00 3·50
1136 40c. Stylized figures (at left) and '50' (inscr "50 YEARS OF SOCIAL INSURANCE" in English) ..... 1·50 1·75

Nos. 1135/6 were printed together, *se-tenant*, as horizontal pairs in sheets of 16 stamps, each pair forming a composite design.

393 Pygmy Hippopotamus, 10000 BC

(Des Melanie Efstathiadou, Glafkos Theofylactou and Liza Petridou. Litho Giesecke & Devrient Matsoukis, Greece)

2007 (2 Oct). Cyprus through the Ages (1st series). T **393** and similar square designs. Multicoloured. P 14.
1137 25c. Type **393** ..... 1·10 1·25
a. Sheetlet. Nos. 1137/44 ..... 8·00 9·00
1138 25c. Stone vessel, 7000 BC ..... 1·10 1·25
1139 25c. Ruins of Choirokoitia settlement of 7000 BC ..... 1·10 1·25
1140 25c. Figurine of a woman, 3000 BC ..... 1·10 1·25
1141 25c. Terracotta vessel, 2000 BC ..... 1·10 1·25
1142 25c. Greek inscription on a bronze skewer, 1000 BC ..... 1·10 1·25
1143 25c. Bird-shaped vessel, 800 BC ..... 1·10 1·25
1144 25c. Map of 1718 showing the ancient Kingdoms of Cyprus in the first millennium BC ..... 1·10 1·25
1137/44 *Set of* 8 ..... 8·00 9·00

Nos. 1137/44 were printed together, *se-tenant*, in sheetlets of eight stamps.

394 Limassol District Administration Building

395 Virgin Mary and Christ Child

(Des Antonis Farmakas and Melanie Efstathiadou. Litho Alexandros Matsoukis)

2007 (2 Oct). Neoclassical Buildings of Cyprus. T **394** and similar horiz designs. Multicoloured. P 14×13½.
1145 13c. Type **394** 80 75
1146 15c. National Bank of Greece Building, Nicosia 90 80
1147 20c. Archaeological Research Unit's Building, Nicosia ..... 1·10 95
1148 30c. National Art Gallery Building, Nicosia ..... 1·25 1·00
1149 40c. Paphos Municipal Library Building ..... 1·40 1·40
1150 50c. Office Building of A. G. Leventis Foundation, Nicosia ..... 1·75 2·00
1151 £1 Limassol Municipal Library Building ..... 3·75 4·00
1152 £3 Phaneromeni Gymnasium Building, Nicosia ..... 8·50 11·00
1145/52 *Set of* 8 ..... 18·00 20·00

(Des Costas Panayi. Litho Giesecke & Devrient Matsoukis, Greece)

2007 (15 Nov). Christmas. T **395** and similar vert designs showing murals taken from Chapel of St. Themonianus, Lysi. Multicoloured. P 14.
1153 13c. Type **395** 65 20
1154 30c. Archangel Gabriel ..... 1·40 1·10
1155 40c. Christ Pantocrater (34×44 mm) ..... 1·75 2·00
1153/5 *Set of* 3 ..... 3·50 3·00

(New Currency: 100 cents = 1 euro)

396 "Aphrodite" (statue)

397 "Cyprus 74" (wood-engraving by A. Tassos)

(Litho Giesecke & Devrient Matsoukis, Greece)

2008 (1 Jan). Adoption of the Euro Currency. Sheet 100×62 mm containing T **396** and similar square design. Multicoloured. P 14.
MS1156 €1 Type **396**; €1 "Sleeping Lady" Statuette of Malta ..... 6·50 7·50

No. **MS**1156 was denominated in both euros and Cyprus pounds. A similar miniature sheet was issued by Malta.

(Litho Giesecke & Devrient Matsoukis, Greece)

2008 (1 Jan). Obigatory Tax. Refugee Fund. Design as T **255** but denominated in cents and euros as T **397**. Inscr "2008". Chalk-surfaced paper. P 13½×14.
1157 **255** 2c. brownish black and brownish grey 15 15

Nos. 1158/69 were denominated in both euros and Cyprus pounds.

398 Pink Anemone

399 "CYPRUS" on Letters

(Des Stelios Karamallakis. Litho Giesecke & Devrient Matsoukis, Greece)

2008 (6 Mar). *Anemone coronaria*. T **398** and similar vert designs. Multicoloured. P 13½×14.

1158 26c. Type **398** ... 80 70
1159 34c. White anemone ... 1·00 90
1160 51c. Red anemone ... 1·60 1·60
1161 68c. Mauve anemone ... 1·90 2·75
1158/61 *Set of* 4 ... 4·75 5·50

(Des Glafkos Theofylaktou. Litho Giesecke & Devrient Matsoukis)

2008 (2 May). Europa. The Letter. T **399** and similar vert design. Multicoloured. P 13½×14.

1162 51c. Type **399** ... 1·40 1·40
a. Booklet pane. Nos. 1162/3, each ×4 ... 11·00
1163 68c. "CYPRUS" on ballot boxes ... 1·60 1·75

Booklet pane No. 1162a has the horizontal edges imperforate and margins at left and right.

400 Ancient Pottery Vase and Silver Vase

402 Emblem

401 Windsurfing

(Des Sophia Malekou. Litho Giesecke & Devrient Matsoukis)

2008 (2 May). 4th International Congress of Cypriot Studies, Nicosia. Sheet 75×65 mm. P 14×imperf (at foot).

MS1164 **400** 85c. multicoloured ... 3·00 3·00

(Des Theodoros Kakoulis. Litho Giesecke & Devrient Matsoukis)

2008 (5 June). Olympic Games, Beijing. T **401** and similar horiz designs. Multicoloured. P 13×13½.

1165 22c. Type **401** ... 55 55
1166 34c. High jump ... 90 90
1167 43c. Volleyball ... 1·40 1·50
1168 51c. Shooting ... 1·50 1·75
1165/8 *Set of* 4 ... 4·00 4·25

(Des Sakis Vassiliou. Litho Giesecke & Devrient Matsoukis)

2008 (5 June). 12th Francophone Summit, Quebec. P 14.

1169 **402** 85c. multicoloured ... 2·25 2·50

403 Coin, Archaic Period (750–480 BC)

404 Archangel Gabriel

(Des Liza Petridou and Melanie Efstathiadou. Litho Giesecke & Devrient Matsoukis)

2008 (2 Oct). Cyprus through the Ages (2nd series). T **403** and similar square designs. Multicoloured. P 14.

1170 43c. Type **403** ... 1·25 1·25
a. Sheetlet. Nos. 1170/7 ... 9·00 9·00
1171 43c. Ancient ship, Archaic period (750–780 BC) ... 1·25 1·25
1172 43c. Statue of Athenian General Kimon and sailing galley, Classical period (480–310 BC) ... 1·25 1·25
1173 43c. Tombs of the Kings, Hellenistic period (310–30 BC) ... 1·25 1·25
1174 43c. Coin, Hellenistic period (310–30 BC) ... 1·25 1·25
1175 43c. St. Paul (missionary to Cyprus, 45 AD) ... 1·25 1·25
1176 43c. Bronze statue of Roman Emperor Septimus Severus, Roman period (30 BC–324 AD) ... 1·25 1·25
1177 43c. Granting of privileges to Church of Cyprus, Byzantine period (324–481 AD). 1·25 1·25
1170/7 *Set of* 8 ... 9·00 9·00

Nos. 1170/7 were printed together, *se-tenant*, in sheetlets of eight stamps.

(Des Antonia Hadjigeorgiou. Litho Geisecke & Devrient Matsoukis)

2008 (13 Nov). Christmas. T **404** and similar vert designs showing icons from Panagia Catholic Church, Pelendri. Multicoloured. P 13½×13.

1178 22c. Type **404** ... 65 65
1179 51c. Archangel Michael ... 1·50 1·40
1180 68c. Virgin Mary and Christ Child ... 2·25 2·50
1178/80 *Set of* 3 ... 4·00 4·00

(Litho Giesecke & Devrient Matsoukis)

2009 (12 Mar). Obligatory Tax. Refugee Fund. Inscr '2009'. Chalk-surfaced paper. P 13½×14.

1181 **397** 2c. black and grey-lilac ... 20 20

405 Stylized Euro Coin

406 Centenary Emblem

(Des Nicolas Ladommatos. Litho Giesecke & Devrient Matsoukis)

2009 (12 Mar). Tenth Anniv of the Euro. T **405** and similar square design. Multicoloured. P 13½.

1182 51c. Type **405** ... 1·50 1·50
1183 68c. Euro coin showing map of Europe ... 2·25 2·25

(Des Elena Eliadou. Litho Geisecke & Devrient Matsoukis)

2009 (12 Mar). Anniversaries. T **406** and similar square design. Multicoloured. P 13½.

1184 26c. Type **406** (Centenary of the Cyprus Co-operative Movement) ... 75 55
1185 68c. Louis Braille (birth bicentenary) ... 2·10 2·10

No. 1185 has the face value in Braille.

407 Satellite Image of the Americas

408 Cassiopeia

(Des Constantinos Panayi. Litho Giesecke & Devrient Matsoukis)

2009 (4 May). International Year of Planet Earth (2008). T **407** and similar horiz design. Multicoloured. P 13.

1186 51c. Type **407** ... 1·50 1·50
a. Horiz pair. Nos. 1186/7 ... 3·00 3·00
1187 51c. Satellite image of Europe, Asia and North Africa ... 1·50 1·50

Nos. 1186/7 were printed together, *se-tenant*, as horizontal pairs in sheetlets of eight stamps (4×2), each pair forming a composite design showing the Earth's continents enclosed in a heart.

(Des Christina Vasiliadou. Litho Giesecke & Devrient Matsoukis)

2009 (4 May). Europa. Astronomy. T **408** and similar vert design showing constellations. Multicoloured. P 13×13½.

1188	51c. Type **408**	1·75	2·00
	a. Booklet pane. Nos. 1188/9, each ×4	12·00	
1189	68c. Andromeda	1·75	2·00

Booklet pane No. 1188a has the horizontal edges imperforate and margins at left and right.

409 Letters forming Player with Racket

410 Map of Cyprus on Stamp on Globe

(Des Andria Talli. Litho Giesecke & Devrient Matsoukis)

2009 (1 June). 13th Games of the Small States of Europe, Nicosia and Limassol. T **409** and similar vert designs. Multicoloured. P 13×13½.

1190	22c. Type **409**	60	60
1191	34c. Letters forming sailor and yacht	1·00	1·00
1192	43c. Letters forming cyclist	1·75	1·75
1190/2	*Set of 3*	3·00	3·00

(Des Yiota Tsiaklidou. Litho and embossed Giesecke & Devrient Matsoukis)

2009 (1 June). 50th Anniv of Cyprus Philatelic Society. Sheet 67×67 mm. P 13½.

MS1193	**410** 85c. multicoloured	2·75	3·00

411 Pigeon

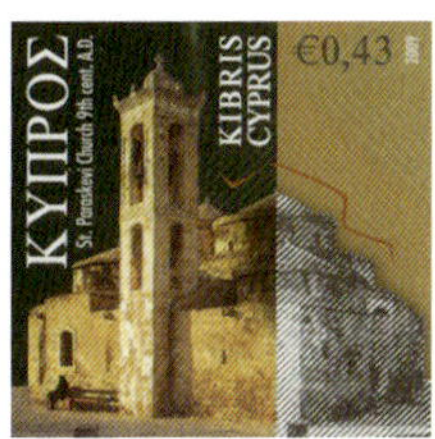

412 St. Paraskevi Church (9th century)

(Des Theodoros Kakoulis. Litho Giesecke & Devrient Matsoukis)

2009 (10 Sept). Domestic Fowl. T **411** and similar horiz designs. Multicoloured. P 13½.

1194	22c. Type **411**	65	65
1195	34c. Turkey	1·25	1·25
1196	43c. Cockerel	1·40	1·40
1197	51c. Duck	1·60	1·60
1194/7	*Set of 4*	4·50	4·50

(Des Melanie Efstathiadou, Liza Petridou-Mala and Glafkos Theofylaktou. Litho Giesecke & Devrient Matsoukis)

2009 (10 Sept). Cyprus through the Ages (3rd series). T **412** and similar square designs. Multicoloured. P 13½.

1198	43c. Type **412**	1·40	1·40
	a. Sheetlet. Nos. 1198/205	10·00	10·00
1199	43c. Monastery of St. Chrysostomos (1090–1100)	1·40	1·40
1200	43c. Lusignan coat of arms (1192–1489)	1·40	1·40
1201	43c. Chronicle of Machairas (early 15th century)	1·40	1·40
1202	43c. Queen Cornaro passes crown to Venice	1·40	1·40
1203	43c. Nicosia's Venetian walls (1567–1570)	1·40	1·40
1204	43c. Ottoman siege of Nicosia (1570)	1·40	1·40
1205	43c. Larnaca aqueduct (18th century)	1·40	1·40
1198/1205	*Set of 8*	10·00	10·00

Nos. 1198/1205 were printed together, *se-tenant*, in sheetlets of eight stamps.

413 European Court of Human Rights, Strasbourg

(Des R. Rogers and C. Bucher. Litho Giesecke & Devrient Matsoukis)

2009 (12 Nov). 50th Anniv of European Court of Human Rights, Strasbourg. P 13.

1206	**413** 51c. multicoloured	1·50	1·50

414 Birth of Christ (16th-century fresco), Church of Archangel Michael, Vyzakia

415 Mauve Star within Silver Star

(Des Xenia Christadoulou. Litho (Nos. 1208/9 also recess) Giesecke & Devrient Matsoukis)

2009 (12 Nov). Christmas. Multicoloured.

(a) P 13×13½

1207	22c. Type **414**	60	30

(b) As T **415**. *P 13½*

1208	51c. Type **415**	1·50	1·40
1209	68c. Silver star	2·50	3·00
1207/9	*Set of 3*	4·25	4·25

416 Arms of Cyprus

417 Pig

(Des Marianna Iacovu. Litho Giesecke & Devrient Matsoukis)

2010 (27 Jan). 50th Anniv of the Republic of Cyprus. P 13½.

1210	**416** 68c. multicoloured	2·25	2·25
1211	85c. multicoloured	2·75	2·75

(Des Theodoros Kakoullis. Litho Giesecke & Devrient Matsoukis)

2010 (17 Mar). Farm Animals. T **417** and similar horiz designs. Multicoloured. P 13½.

1212	22c. Type **417**	60	60
1213	26c. Sheep	75	75
1214	34c. Goat	1·10	1·10
1215	43c. Cow	1·25	1·25
1216	€1.71 Rabbit	7·25	7·25
1212/16	*Set of 5*	9·75	9·75

418 Emblem and 'Better City Better Life'

(Des Ioanna Kalli. Litho Giesecke & Devrient Matsoukis)

2010 (17 Mar). Expo 2010, Shanghai, China. P 13.

1217	**418** 51c. multicoloured	1·50	1·50

419 Football

420 Stack of Books and Flowering Tree

(Des Antonia Hadjigeorgiou. Litho Giesecke & Devrient Matsoukis)

2010 (17 Mar). World Cup Football Championship, South Africa. P 13½.
1218 **419** €1.71 multicoloured .... 7·25 7·25

(Litho Giesecke & Devrient Matsoukis)

2010 (5 May). Obligatory Tax. Refugee Fund. Inscr '2010'. Chalk-surfaced paper. P 13½×14.
1218*a* **397** 2c. black and cinnamon 20 20

(Des Christina Vasiliadou. Litho Giesecke & Devrient Matsoukis)

2010 (5 May). Europa. Children's Books. T **420** and similar vert designs. Multicoloured. P 13×13½.
1219 51c. Type **420** .... 1·50 1·50
a. Horiz pair. Nos. 1219/20 .... 3·00 3·00
b. Booklet pane. Nos. 1219/20, each ×4 .... 11·00
1220 51c. Stack of books (at left) .... 1·50 1·50

Nos. 1219/20 were printed, *se-tenant*, as horizontal pairs in sheetlets of 16, each pair forming a composite design of a stack of books.

Booklet pane 1219a has the horizontal edges imperforate and margins at left and right.

421 Pope Benedict XVI, Ayia Kyriaki Church and Ancient Temple Pillars, Paphos

(Des Melanie Efstathiadou. Litho Giesecke & Devrient Matsoukis)

2010 (4 June). Visit of Pope Benedict XVI to Cyprus. P 13½×14.
1221 **421** 51c. multicoloured .... 1·40 1·40

422 Steam Locomotive

(Des Andreas Mavrogenis. Litho Giesecke & Devrient Matsoukis)

2010 (4 June). The Cyprus Railway 1905–51. T **422** and similar horiz design. Multicoloured. P 13½×13.
1222 43c. Type **422** .... 1·25 1·25
a. Pair. Nos. 1222/3 .... 2·50 2·50
1223 43c. Steam locomotive (seen from front) .... 1·25 1·25
MS1224 70×70 mm. 85c. Steam train and map of railway .... 3·00 3·25

Nos. 1222/3 were printed together, *se-tenant*, in horizontal and vertical pairs in sheetlets of eight stamps (4×2).

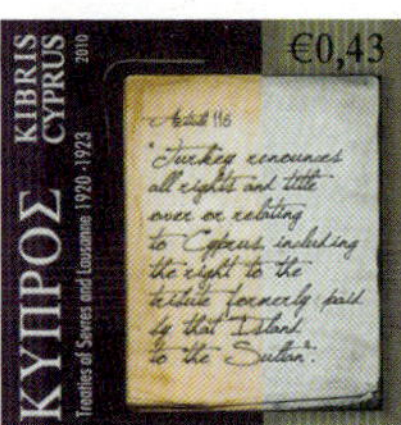

423 Treaties of Sevres, 1920, and Lausanne, 1923

(Des Melanie Efstathiadou, Liza Petridou-Mala and Glafkos Theofylaktou. Litho Giesecke & Devrient Matsoukis)

2010 (1 Oct). Cyprus through the Ages (4th series). T **423** and similar square designs. Multicoloured. P 13½.
1225 43c. Type **423** .... 1·25 1·25
a. Sheetlet. Nos. 1225/32 .... 10·00
1226 43c. Burnt Government House , 1931 .... 1·25 1·25
1227 43c. 'Imprisoned Graves' of EOKA fighters, Central Prisons, 1955–9 .... 1·25 1·25
1228 43c. Statue of Gregoris Afxentiou (EOKA second in command), 1957 .... 1·25 1·25
1229 43c. Presidential Palace, 1960 .... 1·25 1·25
1230 43c. *The Black Summer of 1974* (Telemachos Kanthos) .... 1·25 1·25
1231 43c. Pres. Tassos Papadopoulos signing EU Treaty of Accession, 16 April 2003 .... 1·25 1·25
1232 43c. National flag of Republic of Cyprus .... 1·25 1·25
1225/32 *Set of 8* .... 10·00 10·00

Nos. 1225/32 were printed together, *se-tenant*, in sheetlets of eight stamps.

424 Birth of Christ (16th-century icon), Church of Agios Nicolas, Klonari

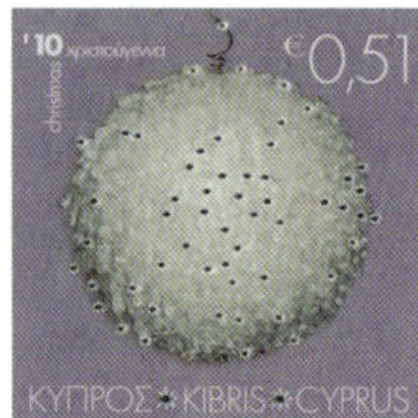

425 White Bauble

(Des Xenia Christodoulou. Litho (Nos. 1234/5 also recess) Giesecke & Devrient Matsoukis)

2010 (10 Nov). Christmas. Multicoloured designs as T **424/5**. P 13½.
1233 22c. Type **424** 65 65
1234 51c. Type **425** .... 1·40 1·40
1235 68c. Filigree bauble .... 2·00 2·00
1233/5 *Set of 3* .... 3·75 3·75

426 Wine Barrels

(Des Melanie Efstathiadou. Litho Giesecke & Devrient Matsoukis)

2010 (10 Nov). Viticulture. Sheet 80×60 mm containing T **426** and similar horiz design. Multicoloured. P 13½×14.
MS1236 **426** 51c. Type **426**; 51c. Grapes and decorated ceramic wine jug .... 3·00 3·00

Stamps in similar designs were issued by Romania.

427 Emblem

(Des Rodoula Nicolaou. Litho Giesecke & Devrient Matsoukis)

2011 (28 Jan). Centenary of Anorthosis Ammochostos (football and volleyball club). P 13½.
1237 **427** 34c. multicoloured .... 1·10 1·10

428 Johann Sebastian Bach

(Des Theodoros Kakoullis. Litho Giesecke & Devrient Matsoukis)

2011 (28 Jan). Famous 18th-century Composers. T **428** and similar horiz designs. Multicoloured. P 14.
1238 51c. Type **428** .... 1·40 1·40
a. Horiz strip of 3. Nos. 1238/40 .... 4·00 4·00

1239 51c. Wolfgang Amadeus Mozart .... 1·40 1·40
1240 51c. Ludwig van Beethoven .... 1·40 1·40
1238/40 *Set of 3* .... 4·00 4·00

Nos. 1238/40 were printed together, *se-tenant*, as horizontal strips of three stamps in sheetlets of six.

429 Embroidery

(Des Konstantinos Panagi. Litho Giesecke & Devrient Matsoukis)

2011 (23 Mar). Cyprus Embroidery. T **429** and similar horiz design. Multicoloured. P 13½×14.
1241 26c. Type **429** 75 55
1242 43c. Embroidery (pattern of diamonds) .... 1·25 1·25

Nos. 1241/2 were printed in separate sheetlets of eight stamps.

430 Roses

(Des Elena Eliadou. Litho Giesecke & Devrient Matsoukis)

2011 (23 Mar). Aromatic Flowers – Roses. T **430** and similar square design. Multicoloured. P 13½.
1243 34c. Type **430** .... 1·00 1·00
MS1244 75×75 mm. 85c. Roses and rosebuds .... 2·75 3·00

Nos. 1243/**MS**1244 have a rose scent.

(Litho Giesecke and Devrient Matsoukis)

2011 (4 May). Obligatory Tax. Refugee Fund. Inscr '2011'. Chalk-surfaced paper. P 13½×14.
1245 **397** 2c. black and pale green 15 15

431 Forest at Dusk with Fox and Owl

(Des Stelios Karamallakis. Litho Giesecke and Devrient Matsoukis)

2011 (4 May). Europa. Forests. T **431** and similar horiz design. Multicoloured. P 14.
1246 51c. Type **431** .... 1·75 1·75
1247 68c. Forest in daytime with moufflon and bird .... 2·25 2·25

432 Pafos Lighthouse

(Des Melanie Efstathiadou. Litho Giesecke and Devrient Matsoukis)

2011 (4 May). Lighthouses. T **432** and similar vert designs. Multicoloured. P 13½×13 (**MS**1250) or 14 (others).
1248 34c. Type **432** .... 1·00 1·00
1249 43c. Cape Greco Lighthouse .... 1·25 1·25
MS1250 70×65 mm. €1.71 Cape Kiti Lighthouse .... 5·50 6·00

MACHINE LABELS

From 29 May 1989 gummed labels in the above design, ranging in value from 1c. to £99.99, were available from machines at Eleftheria Square P.O., Nicosia ("001") (until 1991), District Post Office, Nicosia ("001") (1991 to January 1992) and District P.O., Limassol ("002") (until January 1999).

Machines issuing labels in a revised design (above) were gradually introduced from 12 May 1999 onwards. The multicoloured labels exist with or without machine number indicator and were initially available with face values of 11, 16, 21, 26, 31, 41 and 75 cents. Subsequent rate changes added further values.

From 2 January 2002 labels in five different designs depicting wild flowers of Cyprus with face values of 14c., 21c., 26c., 31c., 41c. and £1 were available from machines at Nicosia and Limassol District Post Offices and Agia Napa and Kato Paphos Post Offices. From May 2002 they were also available from Larnaca and Famagusta.

From 3 March 2005 labels in two different designs showing apricot blossom and poppies with face values of 14c. 21c., 26c., 31c., 41c. and £1 were available from machines at Nicosia, Famagusta, Limassol, Paphos and Larnaca.

STAMP BOOKLETS

Stamp-vending machines were introduced by the Cyprus Post Office in 1962. These were originally fitted to provide stamps to the value of 50m., but in 1979 some were converted to accept 100m. coins and, a year later, others were altered to supply 150, 200 or 300m. worth of stamps.

The stamps contained in these booklets were a haphazard selection of low values to the required amount, attached by their sheet margins to the cardboard covers. From 1968 these covers carried commercial advertising and details of postage rates.

Following the change of currency in 1983 the machines were converted to supply 5, 10, 20 or 30c. booklets.

B **1** World "Stamp" and Magnifying Glass

1998 (9 Oct). World Stamp Day. Multicoloured cover, 98×60 mm, as Type B **1**. Pane attached by selvedge.
SB1 £2.40 booklet containing pane of 8 30c. (No. 960a) .... 13·00

B **2** Turtles on Beach at Lara Reserve

1999 (6 May). Europa. Parks and Gardens. Multicoloured cover, 100×95 mm, as Type B **2**. Pane attached by selvedge.
SB2 £1.80 booklet containing *se-tenant* pane of 8 (No. 969a) (4×2) .... 10·00

B **3** River Diarizos

2001 (3 May). Europa. Cypriot Rivers. Multicoloured cover, 100×95 mm, as Type B **3**. Pane attached by selvedge.
SB3 £2 booklet containing *se-tenant* pane of 8 (No. 1015a) .... 9·00

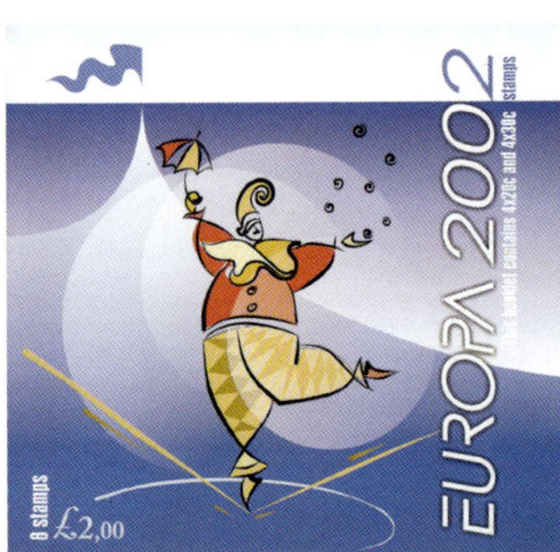

B **4** Clown on High Wire

2002 (9 May). Europa. Circus. Multicoloured cover, 101×96 mm, as Type B **4**. Pane attached by selvedge.
SB4 £2 booklet containing *se-tenant* pane of 8 (No. 1029a) .... 9·00

B **5**

2003 (8 May). Europa. Poster Art. Multicoloured cover, 101×94 mm, as Type B **5**. Pane attached by selvedge.
SB5 £2 booklet containing *se-tenant* pane of 8 (No. 1051b) .... 8·00

B **6** Family at Seaside and Statue

2004 (1 May). Europa. Holidays. Multicoloured cover, 100×75 mm, as Type B **6**. Pane attached by selvedge.
SB6 £2 booklet containing *se-tenant* pane of 8 (No. 1073a) .... 7·00

B **7** Table with Coffee, Cheese, Cocktail and Desserts

2005 (5 May). Europa. Gastronomy. Multicoloured cover, 95×90 mm, as Type B **7**. Pane attached by selvedge.
SB7 £2 booklet containing *se-tenant* pane of 8 (No. 1096ab) .... 8·00

B **8** Hunter with Hungarian Vizsla and Man with Labrador Guide Dog

2005 (16 June). Dogs in Man's Life. Black and grey cover, 95×75 mm, as Type B **8**. Pane attached by selvedge.
SB8 £1.03 booklet containing *se-tenant* pane of 4 (No. 1098a) .... 5·25

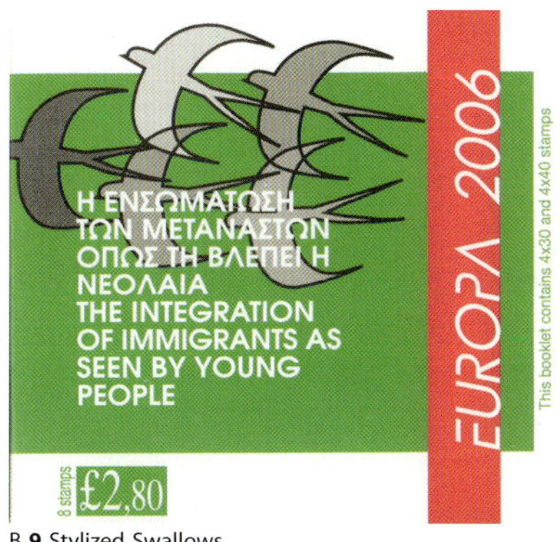

B **9** Stylized Swallows

2006 (4 May). Europa. Integration. Multicoloured cover, 99×95 mm, as Type B **9**. Pane attached by selvedge.

SB9 £2.80 booklet containing *se-tenant* pane of 8 (No. 1110ab) .... 11·00

B **10** Scout Badge and Stylized Figure

2007 (3 May). Europa. Centenary of Scouting. Multicoloured cover, 86×92 mm, as Type B **10**. Pane attached by selvedge.

SB10 £2.80 booklet containing *se-tenant* pane of eight (No. 1133a) .... 11·00

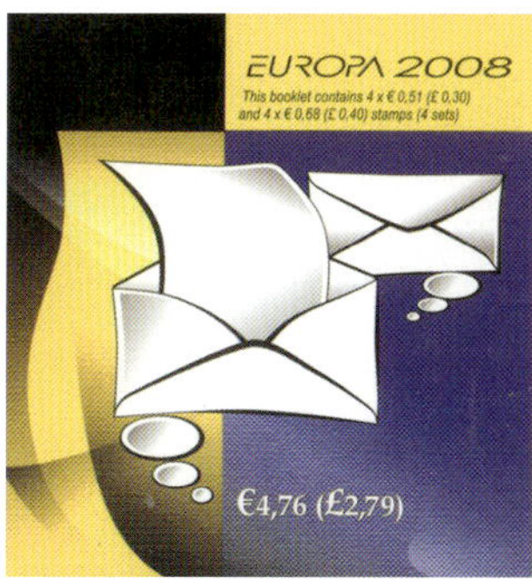

B **11** Letters

2008 (2 May). Europa. The Letter. Multicoloured cover, 85×90 mm, as Type B **11**. Pane attached by selvedge.

SB11 €4.76 booklet containing *se-tenant* pane of eight (No. 1162a) .... 11·00

B **12** Telescopes on Earth and Starry Sky

2009 (4 May). Europa. Astronomy. Multicoloured cover, 85×90 mm, as Type B **12**. Pane attached by selvedge.

SB12 €4.76 booklet containing *se-tenant* pane of eight (No. 1188a) .... 12·00

B **13** Flowering Tree, Tulip and Sun

2010 (5 May). Europa. Children's Books. Multicoloured cover, 85×91 mm, as Type B **13**. Pane attached by selvedge.

SB13 €4.08 booklet containing *se-tenant* pane of eight (No. 1219b) .... 11·00

B **14** Forest

2011 (4 May). Europa. Forests. Multicoloured cover, 105×70 mm, as Type B **14**. Stamps attached by selvedge.

SB14 €4.76 booklet containing *se-tenant* pane of eight (No. 1246b) .... 12·00

Turkish Cypriot Posts

After the inter-communal clashes during December 1963, a separate postal service was established on 6 January 1964 between some of the Turkish Cypriot areas, using handstamps inscribed "KIBRIS TURK POSTALARI". During 1964, however, an agreement was reached between representatives of the two communities for the restoration of postal services. This agreement, to which the United Nations representatives were a party, was ratified in November 1966 by the Republic's Council of Ministers. Under the scheme postal services were provided for the Turkish Cypriot communities in Famagusta, Larnaca, Limassol, Lefka, Nicosia and Paphos staffed by Turkish Cypriot employees of the Cypriot Department of Posts.

On 8 April 1970 5m. and 15m. locally-produced labels, originally designated "Social Aid Stamps", were issued by the Turkish Cypriot community and these can be found on commercial covers. These local stamps are outside the scope of this catalogue.

On 29 October 1973 Nos. 1/7 were placed on sale, but were used only on mail between the Turkish Cypriot areas.

Following the intervention by the Republic of Turkey on 20 July 1974 these stamps replaced issues of the Republic of Cyprus in that part of the island, north and east of the Attila Line, controlled by the Autonomous Turkish Cypriot Administration.

(Currency. 1000 mils = £1)

1 50th Anniversary Emblem

KIBRIS
TÜRK
FEDERE
DEVLETI
13.2.1975

30M

(2)

(Des F. Direkoglu Miss E. Ata and G. Pir. Litho Darbhane, Istanbul)

1974 (27 July*). 50th Anniv of Republic of Turkey. T **1** and similar designs in vermilion and black (15m.) or multicoloured (others). P 12×11½ (vert) or 11½×12 (horiz).

1	3m. Woman sentry (*vert*)	30·00	30·00
2	5m. Military Parade, Nicosia	60	40
3	10m. Man and woman with Turkish flags (*vert*)	50	20
4	15m. Type **1**	2·50	1·50
5	20m. Atatürk statue, Kyrenia Gate, Nicosia (*vert*)	70	20
6	50m. "The Fallen" (*vert*)	2·00	1·50
7	70m. Turkish flag and map of Cyprus	16·00	16·00
1/7	*Set of 7*	48·00	48·00

*This is the date on which Nos. 1/7 became valid for international mail.

On 13 February 1975 a Turkish Cypriot Federated State was proclaimed in that part of Cyprus under Turkish occupation and later 9,000 Turkish Cypriots were transferred from the South to the North of the island.

1975 (3 Mar). Proclamation of the Turkish Federated State of Cyprus. Nos. 3 and 5 surch as T **2** by Halkin Sesi, Nicosia.

8	30m. on 20m. Atatürk statue, Kyrenia Gate, Nicosia	75	1·00
9	100m. on 10m. Man and woman with Turkish flags	1·25	2·00

On No. 9 the surcharge appears at the top of the stamp and the inscription at the bottom.

3 Namik Kemal's Bust, Famagusta

4 Map of Cyprus

(Des I. Özisik. Litho Güzel Sanatlar Matbaasi, Ankara)

1975 (21 Apr). Multicoloured designs as T **3**. Imprint at foot with date "1975". P 13.

10	3m. Type **3**	15	40
11	10m. Atatürk Statue, Nicosia	25	10
12	15m. St. Hilarion Castle	35	20
13	20m. Atatürk Square, Nicosia	45	20
14	25m. Famagusta Beach	45	30
15	30m. Kyrenia Harbour	55	10
16	50m. Lala Mustafa Pasha Mosque, Famagusta (*vert*)	60	10
17	100m. Interior, Kyrenia Castle	80	90
18	250m. Castle walls, Kyrenia	1·00	2·25
19	500m. Othello Tower, Famagusta (*vert*)	1·50	4·50
10/19	*Set of 10*	5·50	8·00

See also Nos. 37/8.

(Des B. Erkmen (30m.), S. Tuga (50m.), N. Cünes (160m). Litho Ajans-Türk Matbaasi, Ankara)

1975 (20 July). "Peace in Cyprus". T **4** and similar multicoloured designs. P 13.

20	30m. Type **4**	20	15
21	50m. Map, laurel and broken chain	25	20
22	150m. Map and laurel-sprig on globe (*vert*)	65	1·40
20/2	*Set of 3*	1·00	1·60

5 "Pomegranates" (I. V. Guney)

(Litho Güzel Sanatlar Matbaasi, Ankara)

1975 (29 Dec). Europa. Paintings. T **5** and similar horiz design. Multicoloured. P 13.

23	90m. Type **5**	1·40	1·75
24	100m. "Harvest Time" (F. Direkoglu)	1·40	1·75

10 M

(6)

7 "Expectation"

1976 (28 Apr). Nos. 16/17 surch as T **6** at Govt Printing House, Nicosia in horizontal clichés of 10.

25	10m. on 50m. Lala Mustafa Pasha Mosque, Famagusta	35	70
26	30m. on 100m. Interior, Kyrenia Castle	35	80

(Litho Ajans-Türk Matbaasi, Ankara)

1976 (3 May). Europa. T **7** and similar vert design showing ceramic statuette. Multicoloured. P 13.

27	60m. Type **7**	60	80
28	120m. "Man in Meditation"	80	1·75

8 Carob

9 Olympic Symbol "Flower"

(Des S. Atlihan. Litho Güzel Sanatlar Matbaasi, Ankara)

1976 (28 June). Export Products—Fruits. T **8** and similar horiz designs. Multicoloured. P 13.

29	10m. Type **8**	15	10
30	25m. Mandarin	20	10
31	40m. Strawberry	25	25
32	60m. Orange	35	65
33	80m. Lemon	40	2·00
29/33	*Set of 5*	1·25	2·75

(Des C. Mutver (60m.), A. B. Kocamanoglu (100m.). Litho Güzel Sanatlar Matbaasi, Ankara)

1976 (17 July). Olympic Games, Montreal. T **9** and similar horiz design. Multicoloured. P 13.

34 60m. Type **9** ... 25 20
35 100m. Olympic symbol and doves ... 35 25

10 Kyrenia Harbour

11 Liberation Monument, Karaeglanoolu (Ay. Georghios)

(Des I. Özisik. Litho Ajans-Türk Matbaasi, Ankara)

1976 (2 Aug). New design (5m.) or as Nos. 12/13 but redrawn with lettering altered and new imprint at foot with date "1976". P 13.

36 5m. Type **10** ... 40 15
37 15m. St. Hilarion Castle ... 40 15
38 20m. Atatürk Square, Nicosia ... 40 15
36/8 *Set of* 3 ... 1·10 40

Nos. 39/46 are vacant.

(Des D. Erimez and C. Gizer. Litho Ajans-Türk Matbaasi, Ankara)

1976 (1 Nov). Liberation Monument. T **11** and similar vert design. P 13.

47 **11** 30m. light turquoise-blue, light flesh and black ... 15 20
48 – 150m. light verm, light flesh & blk ... 35 80

No. 48 shows a different view of the Monument.

12 Hotel, Salamis Bay

(Litho Türk Tarih Kurumu Basimevi, Ankara)

1977 (2 May). Europa. T **12** and similar horiz design. Multicoloured. P 13.

49 80m. Type **12** ... 65 95
50 100m. Kyrenia Port ... 75 95

13 Pottery

14 Arap Ahmet Pasha Mosque, Nicosia

(Litho Güzel Sanatlar Matbaasi, Ankara)

1977 (27 June). Handicrafts. T **13** and similar designs. Multicoloured. P 13.

51 15m. Type **13** ... 10 10
52 30m. Decorated gourds (*vert*) ... 10 10
53 125m. Basketware ... 30 50
51/3 *Set of* 3 ... 40 65

(Litho APA Ofset Baeimevi, Istanbul)

1977 (2 Dec). Turkish Buildings in Cyprus. T **14** and similar horiz designs. Multicoloured. P 13.

54 20m. Type **14** ... 10 10
55 40m. Paphos Castle ... 10 10
56 70m. Bekir Pasha aqueduct ... 15 20
57 80m. Sultan Mahmut library ... 15 25
54/7 *Set of* 4 ... 45 60

15 Namik Kemal (bust) and House, Famagusta

16 Old Man and Woman

(Des B. Ozak. Litho Ticaret Matbaacilik TAS, Izmir)

1977 (21 Dec). Namik Kemal (patriotic poet). T **15** and similar multicoloured design. P 12½×13 (30m.) or 13×12½ (140m.).

58 30m. Type **15** ... 15 15
59 140m. Namik Kemal (portrait) (*vert*) ... 35 60

(New Currency. 100 kurus = 1 lira)

(Des G. Pir. Litho Ajans-Türk Matbaasi, Ankara)

1978 (17 Apr). Social Security. T **16** and similar vert designs. P 13×13½.

60 150k. black, yellow and blue ... 10 10
61 275k. black, red-orange and green ... 15 15
62 375k. black, blue and red-orange ... 25 20
60/2 *Set of* 3 ... 45 40

Designs:—275k. Injured man with crutch; 375k. Woman with family.

17 Oratory in Büyük Han, Nicosia

18 Motorway Junction

(Des I. Özisik. Litho APA Ofset Basimevi, Istanbul)

1978 (2 May). Europa. T **17** and similar horiz design. Multicoloured. P 13.

63 225k. Type **17** ... 85 50
64 450k. Cistern in Selimiye Mosque, Nicosia ... 1·25 1·50

(Litho APA Ofset Basimevi, Istanbul)

1978 (10 July). Communications. T **18** and similar horiz designs. Multicoloured. P 13.

65 75k. Type **18** ... 15 10
66 100k. Hydrofoil ... 15 10
67 650k. Boeing 720 at Ercan Airport ... 50 60
65/7 *Set of* 3 ... 70 70

19 Dove with Laurel Branch

20 Kemal Atatürk

(Des E. Kaya (725k.), C. Kirkbesoglu (others). Litho APA Ofset Basimevi, Istanbul)

1978 (13 Sept). National Oath. T **19** and similar designs. P 13.

68 150k. orange-yellow, violet and black ... 10 10
69 225k. black, Indian red and orange-yellow ... 10 10
70 725k. black, cobalt and orange-yellow ... 20 20
68/70 *Set of* 3 ... 35 35

Designs: *Vert*—225k. "Taking the Oath". *Horiz*—725k. Symbolic dove.

(Des C. Mutver. Litho Türk Tarih Kurumu Basimevi, Ankara)

1978 (10 Nov). Kemal Ataturk Commemoration. P 13.

71 **20** 75k. pale turquoise-grn & turq-grn ... 10 10
72 450k. pale flesh and light brown ... 15 15
73 650k. pale blue and light blue ... 20 25
71/3 *Set of* 3 ... 40 40

50 Krs.

(**21**)

22 Gun Barrel with Olive Branch and Map of Cyprus

1979 (4 June). Nos. 30/3 surch as T **21**, by Govt Printing Office, Lefkosa.

74	50k. on 25m. Mandarin	10	10
75	1l. on 40m. Strawberry	15	10
76	3l. on 60m. Orange	15	10
77	5l. on 80m. Lemon	35	15
74/7	*Set of* 4	65	30

(Des N. Dündar. Litho Ajans-Türk Matbaasi, Ankara)

1979 (20 July). 5th Anniv of Turkish Peace Operation in Cyprus. Sheet 72×52 mm. Imperf.

MS78 **22** 15l. black, deep turquoise-blue and pale green .... 80 1·25

23 Postage Stamp and Map of Cyprus

24 Symbolised Microwave Antenna

(Des S. Mumcu. Litho Ajana-Türk Matbaasi, Ankara)

1979 (20 Aug). Europa. Communications. T **23** and similar horiz designs. Multicoloured. P 13.

79	2l. Type **23**	20	10
80	3l. Postage stamps, building and map	20	10
81	8l. Telephones, Earth and satellite	70	30
79/81	*Set of* 3	1·00	45

(Litho Ticaret Matbaacilik TAS, Izmir)

1979 (24 Sept). 50th Anniv of International Consultative Radio Committee. P 13×12½.

82	**24**	2l. multicoloured	20	10
83		5l. multicoloured	20	10
84		6l. multicoloured	25	15
82/4		*Set of* 3	60	30

25 School Children

26 Lala Mustafa Pasha Mosque, Magusa

(Des H. Hastürk (1½l.) G. Akansel (4½l.), P. Yalyali (6l.). Litho APA Ofset Basimevi, Istanbul)

1979 (29 Oct). International Year of the Child. Children's Drawings. T **25** and similar multicoloured designs. P 13.

85	1½l. Type **25**	25	20
86	4½l. Children and globe (*horiz*)	40	45
87	6l. College children	60	45
85/7	*Set of* 3	1·10	1·00

(Des S. Mumcu (20l.), I. Özisik (others). Litho Ajans-Türk Matbaasi, Ankara)

1980 (23 Mar). Islamic Commemorations. T **26** and similar vert designs. Multicoloured. P 13.

88	2½l. Type **26**	10	10
89	10l. Arap Ahmet Pasha Mosque, Lefkosa	30	15
90	20l. Mecca and Medina	50	20
88/90	*Set of* 3	80	40

Commemorations:—2½l. Ist Islamic Conference in Turkish Cyprus; 10l. General Assembly of World Islam Congress; 20l. Moslem Year 1400AH.

27 Ebu-Su'ud Efendi (philosopher)

28 Omer's Shrine, Kyrenia

(Litho Ajans-Türk Matbaasi, Ankara)

1980 (23 May). Europa. Personalities. T **27** and similar vert design. Multicoloured. P 13.

91	5l. Type **27**	20	10
92	30l. Sultan Selim II	80	40

(Litho Guzel Sanatlar Matbaasi, Ankara)

1980 (25 June). Ancient Monuments, T **28** and similar horiz designs. P 13.

93	2½l. new blue and stone	10	10
94	3½l. grey-green and pale rose-pink	10	10
95	5l. lake and pale blue-green	15	10
96	10l. deep mauve and pale green	20	10
97	20l. dull ultramarine & pale greenish yellow	35	25
93/7	*Set of* 5	70	45

Designs:—3½l. Entrance gate, Famagusta; 5l. Funerary monuments (16th-century), Famagusta; 10l. Bella Poise Abbey, Kyrenia; 20l. Selimiye Mosque, Nicosia.

29 Cyprus 1880 6d.

30 Dome of the Rock

31 Extract from World Muslim Congress Statement in Turkish

(Des S. Mumcu. Litho Ajans-Türk Matbaasi, Ankara)

1980 (16 Aug). Cyprus Stamp Centenary. T **29** and similar designs showing stamps. P 14.

98	7½l. black, drab and grey-olive	20	10
99	15l. brown, grey-blue and blue	25	10
100	50l. black, rose and grey	65	60
98/100	*Set of* 3	1·00	70

Designs: *Horiz*:—15l. Cyprus 1960 Constitution of the Republic 30m. commemorative. *Vert*—50l. Social Aid local, 1970.

(Litho Guzel Sanatlar Matbaasi, Ankara)

1980 (16 Oct). Palestinian Solidarity. T **30** and similar multicoloured design. P 13.

101	15l. Type **30**	30	15
102	35l. Dome of the Rock (*horiz*)	70	30

(Des S. Mumcu. Litho Turk Tarih Kurumu Basimevi, Ankara)

1981 (24 Mar). Solidarity with Islamic Countries Day. T **31** and similar vert design showing extract from World Muslim Congress statement. P 13.

103	1l. rosine, stone and olive-sepia	15	75
104	35l. black, pale blue-green and myrtle-green	55	1·00

Design:—35l. Extract in English.

32 "Atatürk" (F. Duran)

33 Folk-dancing

(Litho Ajans-Türk Matbaasi, Ankara)

1981 (19 May). Atatürk Stamp Exhibition, Lefkosa. P 13.

105 **32** 20l. multicoloured 25 35

No. 105 was printed in sheets of 100, including 50 *se-tenant* stamp-size labels.

(Litho Ticaret Matbaacilik TAS, Izmir)

1981 (29 June). Europa, Folklore. T **33** and similar horiz design showing folk-dancing. P 12½×13.

106 10l. multicoloured 40 25
107 30l. multicoloured .... 60 1·00

34 "Kemal Atatürk" (I. Calli)

35 Wild Convolvulus

(Litho Basim Ofset, Ankara)

1981 (23 July). Birth Centenary of Kemal Atatürk. Sheet 70×96 mm. Imperf.

MS108 **34** 150l. multicoloured .... 1·10 1·25

(Litho Turk Tarih Kurumu Basimevi, Ankara)

1981 (28 Sept)–**82**. Flowers, Multicoloured designs as T **36**. P 13.

109 1l. Type **35** 10 10
110 5l. Persian Cyclamen (*horiz*) (22.1.82) 10 10
111 10l. Spring Mandrake (*horiz*) 10 15
112 25l. Corn Poppy 15 20
113 30l. Wild Arum (22.1.82) 15 10
114 50l. Sage-leaved Rock Rose (*horiz*) (22.1.82). 20 20
115 100l. *Cistus salviaefolius L.* (22.1.82) 30 30
116 150l. Giant Fennel (*horiz*) .... 50 1·00
109/16 *Set of* 8 .... 1·40 1·75

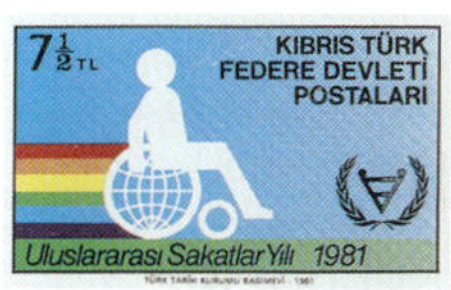

36 Stylized Disabled Person in Wheelchair

37 Turkish and Palestinian Flags

(Des H. Ulucam (7½l.), N. Kozal (others). Litho Türk Tarih Kurumu Basimevi, Ankara)

1981 (16 Oct). Commemorations. T **36** and similar multicoloured designs. P 13.

117 7½l. Type **36** 25 35
118 10l. Heads of people of different races, peace dove and barbed wire (*vert*) 35 55
119 20l. People of different races reaching out from globe, with dishes (*vert*) 50 85
117/19 *Set of* 3 .... 1·00 1·60

Commemorations:—7½l. International Year for Disabled Persons; 10l. Anti-apartheid Publicity; 20l. World Food Day.

(Des H. Ulucam. Litho Türk Tarih Kurumu Basimevi, Ankara)

1981 (29 Nov). Palestinian Solidarity. P 13.

120 **37** 10l. multicoloured 45 60

38 Prince Charles and Lady Diana Spencer

39 Charter issued by Sultan Abdul Aziz to Archbishop Sophronios

(Des H. Ulucam. Litho Türk Tarih Kurumu Basimevi, Ankara)

1981 (30 Nov). Royal Wedding. P 13.

121 **38** 50l. multicoloured .... 1·00 85

(Des H. Ulucam, Litho Tezel Ofset, Lefkosa)

1982 (30 July). Europa (CEPT). Sheet 83×124 mm containing T **39** and similar vert design. Multicoloured. P 12½×13.

MS122 30l.×2. Type **39**; 70l.×2, Turkish forces landing at Tuzla, 1571 .... 4·50 5·00

40 Buffavento Castle

41 "Wedding" (A. Örek)

(Des H. Ulucam (Nos. 123/5). Litho Tezel Ofset, Lefkosa)

1982 (20 Aug). Tourism. T **40** and similar multicoloured designs. P 12.

123 5l. Type **40** 10 10
124 10l. Windsurfing (*horiz*) 15 10
125 15l. Kantara Castle (*horiz*) 25 15
126 30l. Shipwreck (300 B.C.) (*horiz*) 60 40
123/6 *Set of* 4 .... 1·00 65

(Litho Ajans-Türk Matbaasi, Ankara)

1982 (3 Dec). Art (1st series). T **41** and similar multicoloured design. P 13.

127 30l. Type **41** 15 30
128 50l. "Carob Pickers" (Naxim Selenge) (*vert*) 30 70

See also Nos. 132/3, 157/8, 176/7, 185/6, 208/9, 225/7, 248/50, 284/5, 315/16, 328/9, 369/70, 436/7, 567/8, 629/30 and 654/5.

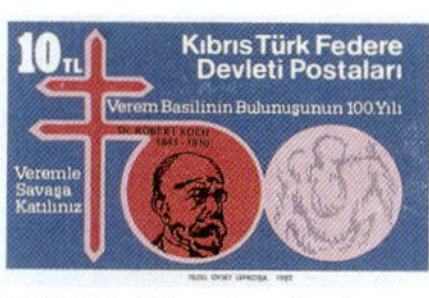

42 Cross of Lorraine, Koch and Bacillus (Cent of Koch's Discovery of Tubercle Bacillus)

43 "Calloused Hands" (Salih Oral)

(Des H. Ulucam. Litho Tezel Ofset, Lefkosa)

1982 (15 Dec). Anniversaries and Events. T **42** and similar multicoloured designs. P 12.

129 10l. Type **42** .... 1·00 40
130 30l. Spectrum on football pitch (World Cup Football Championships, Spain) .... 1·75 1·10
131 70l. "75" and Lord Baden-Powell (75th anniv of Boy Scout movement and 125th birth anniv) (*vert*) .... 2·25 4·00
129/31 *Set of* 3 .... 4·50 5·00

(Litho Ajans-Türk Matbaasi, Ankara)

1983 (16 May). Art (2nd series). T **43** and similar vert design. Multicoloured. P 13.

132	30l. Type **43**	75	1·40
133	35l. "Malya—Limassol Bus" (Emin Cizenel)	75	1·40

44 Old Map of Cyprus by Piri Reis

45 First Turkish Cypriot 10 m. Stamp

(Litho Türk Tarih Kurumu Basimevi, Ankara)

1983 (30 June). Europa. Sheet 82×78 mm, containing T **44** and similar horiz design. Multicoloured. P 13.

MS134	100l. Type **44**; 100l. Cyprus as seen from "Skylab"	30·00	15·00

(Des E. Ata (15l.), A. Hasan (20l.), G. Pir (25l.), H. Ulucam (others). Litho Ajans-Türk Matbaasi, Ankara)

1983 (1 Aug). Anniversaries and Events. T **45** and similar multicoloured designs commemorating World Communications Year (30, 50l.) or 25th Anniv. of T.M.T. (Turkish Cypriot Resistance Organization). P 13.

135	15l. Type **45**	90	50
136	20l. "Turkish Achievements in Cyprus" (*horiz*)	90	60
137	25l. "Liberation Fighters"	1·00	80
138	30l. Dish aerial and telegraph pole (*horiz*)	1·25	1·50
139	50l. Dove and envelopes (*horiz*)	2·75	3·75
135/9 *Set of 5*		6·25	6·50

46 European Bee Eater

Kuzey Kıbrıs
Türk Cumhuriyeti
15.11.1983
15

(**47**)

(Des E. Cizenel. Litho Ajans-Türk Matbaasi, Ankara)

1983 (10 Oct). Birds of Cyprus. T **46** and similar horiz designs. Multicoloured. P 13.

140	10l. Type **46**	80	1·25
	a. Block of 4. Nos. 140/3	4·00	5·00
141	15l. Eurasian Goldfinch	1·00	1·25
142	50l. European Robin	1·25	1·50
143	65l. Golden Oriole	1·40	1·50
140/3 *Set of 4*		4·00	5·00

Nos. 140/3 were printed together, *se-tenant*, in blocks of 4 throughout the sheet.

1983 (7 Dec). Establishment of the Republic. Nos. 109, 111/2 and 116 surch as T **47** (No. 145) or optd only.

144	10l. Spring Mandrake	20	15
145	15l. on 1l. Type **35**	30	15
	a. Surch inverted	80·00	
146	25l. Corn Poppy	40	25
147	150l. Giant Fennel	2·25	3·25
144/7 *Set of 4*		2·75	3·50

48 C.E.P.T. 25th Anniversary Logo.

49 Olympic Flame

(Des J. Larrivière. Litho Tezel Ofset, Lefkosa)

1984 (30 May). Europa. P 12×12½.

148	**48**	50l. lemon, chestnut and black	2·25	3·00
		a. Pair. Nos. 148/9	4·50	6·00
149		100l. pale blue, bright blue and black	2·25	3·00

Nos. 148/9 were printed together, *se-tenant*, in horizontal and vertical pairs throughout the sheet.

(Des H. Ulucam. Litho Tezel Ofset, Lefkosa)

1984 (19 June). Olympic Games, Los Angeles. T **49** and similar multicoloured designs. P 12½×12 (10l.) or 12×12½ (*others*).

150	10l. Type **49**	15	10
151	20l. Olympic events within rings (*horiz*)	35	25
152	70l. Martial arts event (*horiz*)	60	1·75
150/2 *Set of 3*		1·00	1·90

50 Atatürk Cultural Centre

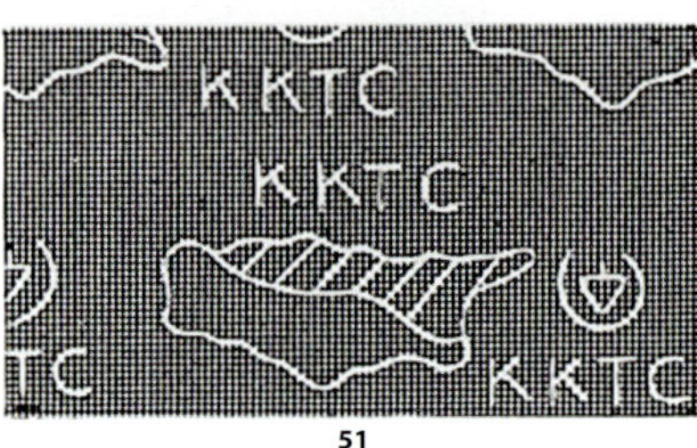

51

(Des H. Ulucam. Litho Tezel Ofset, Lefkosa)

1984 (20 July). Opening of Atatürk Cultural Centre, Lefkosa. W **51**. P 12×12½.

153	**50**	120l. stone, black and chestnut	1·25	1·75

52 Turkish Cypriot Flag and Map

(Des C. Guzeloglu (20l.), M. Gozbebek (70l.). Litho Tezel Ofset Lefkosa)

1984 (20 July). 10th Anniv of Turkish Landings in Cyprus. T **52** and similar horiz design. Multicoloured. W **51**. P 12×12½.

154	20l. Type **52**	50	25
155	70l. Turkish Cypriot flag within book	1·00	2·00

53 Burnt and Replanted Forests

(Des H. Ulucam. Litho Tezel Ofset, Lefkosa)

1984 (20 Aug). World Forestry Resources. W **51**. P 12×12½.

156	**53**	90l. multicoloured	1·25	1·75

54 "Old Turkish Houses, Nicosia" (Cevdet Cagdas)

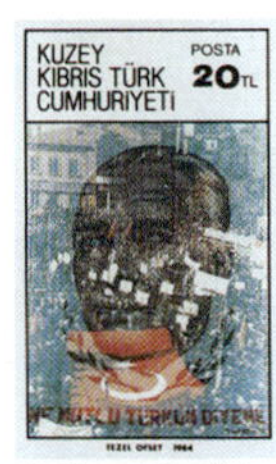

55 Kemal Atatürk, Flag and Crown

(Litho Tezel Ofset, Lefkosa)

1984 (21 Sept). Art (3rd series). T **54** and similar horiz design. Multicoloured. W **51**. P 13×12½.

157	20l. Type **54**	50	40
158	70l. "Scenery" (Olga Rauf)	1·10	2·00

See also Nos. 176/7, 185/6, 208/9, 225/7, 248/50, 284/5, 315/16 and 328/9.

(Des H. Ulucam (20l.), F. Isiman 70l.). Litho Tezel Ofset, Lefkosa)

1984 (15 Nov). 1st Anniv of Turkish Republic of Northern Cyprus. T **55** and similar multicoloured design. W **51** (sideways on 20 l., inverted on 70 l.). P 12½.

159	20l. Type **55**	50	40
160	70l. Legislative Assembly voting for Republic (*horiz*)	1·10	2·00

56 Taekwondo Bout

57 "Le Regard" (Saulo Mercader)

(Des H. Ulucam. Litho Tezel Ofset, Lefkosa)

1984 (10 Dec). International Taekwondo Championship, Girne. T **56** and similar horiz design. W **51** (sideways on 10l.). P 12½.

161	10l. black, pale cinnamon and grey-black	40	25
162	70l. multicoloured	1·60	2·50

Design:—70l. Emblem and flags of competing nations.

(Litho Tezel Ofset, Lefkosa)

1984 (10 Dec). Exhibition by Saulo Mercader (artist). T **57** and similar multicoloured design. W **51** (sideways on 20l.). P 12½×13 (20l.) or 13 ×12½ (70l.).

163	20l. Type **57**	30	25
164	70l. "L'equilibre de L'esprit" (*horiz*)	1·10	2·25

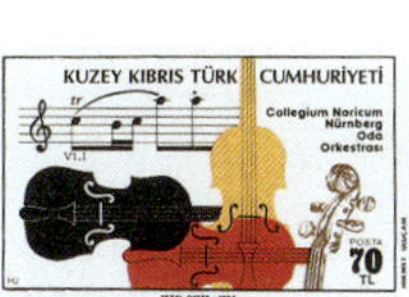

58 Musical Instruments and Music

59 Dr. Fazil Kucuk (politician)

(Des H. Ulucam. Litho Tezel Ofset, Lefkosa)

1984 (10 Dec). Visit of Nurnberg Chamber Orchestra. W **51** (sideways). P 12½.

165	**58**	70l. multicoloured	1·50	2·25

(Des Y. Calli (20l.), E. Cizenel (70l.). Litho Tezel Ofset, Lefkosa)

1985 (15 Jan). 1st Death Anniv of Dr. Fazil Kucuk (politician). T **59** and similar vert design. Multicoloured. W **51** (inverted on 70l.). P 12½×12.

166	20l. Type **59**	30	30
167	70l. Dr. Fazil Kucuk reading newspaper	95	2·00

60 Goat

61 George Frederick Handel

(Des E. Cizenel. Litho Tezel Ofset, Lefkosa)

1985 (29 May). Domestic Animals. T **60** and similar horiz designs. Multicoloured. W **51**. P 12×12½.

168	100l. Type **60**	55	30
169	200l. Cow and calf	90	80
170	300l. Ram	1·25	2·00
171	500l. Donkey	2·00	3·25
168/71	*Set of 4*	4·25	5·75

(Litho Tezel Ofset, Lefkosa)

1985 (26 June). Europa. Composers. T **61** and similar vert designs. W **51** (sideways). P 12½×12.

172	20l. brown-purple, myrtle-green and pale green	2·00	2·50
	a. Block of 4. Nos. 172/5	8·00	10·00
173	20l. brown-purple, lake-brown and pale pink	2·00	2·50
174	100l. brown-purple, steel blue and pale grey-bl	2·50	3·00
175	100l. brown-purple, bistre-brown and pale cinnamon	2·50	3·00
172/5	*Set of 4*	8·00	10·00

Designs:—No. 172, Type **61**; 173, Guiseppe Domenico Scarlatti; 174, Johann Sebastian Bach; 175, Buhurizade Mustafa Itri Efendi.

Nos. 172/5 were printed together, *se-tenant*, in blocks of four throughout the sheet.

(Litho Tezel Ofset, Lefkosa)

1985 (15 Aug). Art (4th series). Vert designs as T **54**. Multicoloured. W **51**. P 12½×13.

176	20l. "Village Life" (Ali Atakan)	60	50
177	50l. "Woman carrying Water" (Ismet V. Güney)	1·40	2·50

62 Heads of Three Youths

63 Parachutist (Aviation League)

(Des H. Uluçam. Litho Tezel Ofset, Letkosa)

1985 (29 Oct). International Youth Year. T **62** and similar horiz design. Multicoloured. W **51** (sideways). P 12×12½.

178	20l. Type **62**	75	40
179	100l. Dove and globe	4·00	4·50

(Des H. Uluçam. Litho Tezel Ofset. Lefkosa)

1985 (29 Nov). Anniversaries and Events. T **63** and similar designs. W **51** (inverted on Nos, 181/2, sideways on Nos. 1834. P 12×12½ (Nos. 1834) or 12½×12 (others).

180	20l. multicoloured	1·75	45
181	50l. grey-black. light brown and dull ultramarine	2·00	1·25
182	100l. light brown	1·75	2·75
183	100l. multicoloured	1·75	2·75
184	100l. multicoloured	2·25	2·75
180/4	*Set of 5*	8·50	9·00

Designs: *Vert*—No. 181, Louis Pasteur (Centenary of Discovery of Rabies vaccine); 182 İsmet Inönü (Turkish statesman) (birth centenary (1984)(. *Horiz*—183, "40" in figures and symbolic flower (40th anniv of United Nations Organizations: 184, Patient receiving blood transfusion (Prevention of Thalassaemia).

(Litho Tezel Ofset, Lefkosa)

1986 (20 June). Art (5th series). Horiz designs as T **54**. Multicoloured. W **51** (sideways). P 13×12½.

185	20l. "House with Arches" (Gönen Atakol)	50	30
186	100l. "Atatürk Square" (Yalkin Muhtaroglu)	1·75	1·75

64 Griffin Vulture

65 Karagöz Show Puppets

(Des E. Çizenel (100l.), H. Uluçam (200l.). Litho Tezel Ofset, Lefkosa)

1986 (20 June). Europa. Protection of Nature and the Environment. Sheet *82×76* mm. containing T **64** and similar horiz design. Multicoloured. W **51** (sideways). P 12×12½.
MS187 100l. Type **64**; 200l. Litter on Cyprus landscape 10·00 7·50

(Des Y. Yazgin. Litho Tezel Ofset, Lefkosa)

1986 (25 July). Karagöz Folk Puppets. W **51** (inverted). P 12½×13.
188 **65** 100l. multicoloured 2·25 2·50

66 Old Bronze Age Composite Pottery

67 Soldiers, Defence Force Badge and Atatürk (10th anniv of Defence Forces)

(Litho Tezel Ofset, Lefkosa)

1886 (15 Sept). Archaeological Artifacts. Cultural Links with Anatolia. T **66** and similar multicoloured designs. W **51** (sideways on 10, 50l., inverted on 20, 100l.). P 12×12½ (10, 50l.) or 12½×12 (20, 100l.).

189	10l. Type **66**	55	20
190	20l. Late Bronze Age bird jug (*vert*)	95	30
191	50l. Neolithic earthenware pot	1·75	2·00
192	100l. Roman statue of Artemis (*vert*)	2·25	3·50
189/92 *Set of 4*		5·00	5·50

(Des. H. Uluçam (No. 196). Litho Tezel Ofset, Lefkosa)

1986 (13 Oct). Anniversaries and Events. T **67** and similar multicoloured designs. W **51** (inverted on 20, 50l., sideways on others). P 12½×12 (vert) or 12×12½ (horiz).

193	20l. Type **67**	1·25	30
194	50l. Woman and two children (40th anniv of Food and Agriculture Organization)	1·40	1·40
195	100l. Football and world map (World Cup Football Championship, Mexico) (*horiz*).	3·75	4·25
196	100l. Orbit of Halley's Comet and Giotto spacecraft (*horiz*)	3·75	4·25
193/6 *Set of 4*		9·25	9·25

68 Güzelyurt Dam and Power Station

69 Prince Andrew and Miss Sarah Ferguson

(Litho Tezel Ofset, Letkoea)

1986 (17 Nov). Modern Development (1st series). T **68** and similar horiz designs. Multicoloured. W **51** (sideways). P 12×12½.

197	20l. Type **68**	1·25	30
198	50l. Low cost housing project, Lefkosa	1·40	1·40
199	100l. Kyrenia Airport	3·25	4·25
197/9 *Set of 3*		5·50	5·50

See also Nos. 223/4 and 258/63.

(Litho Tezel Ofset, Lefkosa)

1986 (20 Nov). 60th Birthday of Queen Elizabeth II and Royal Wedding. T **69** and similar vert design. Multicoloured. P 12½×13. W **51** (inverted).

200	100l. Type **69**	2·25	3·00
	a. Pair. Nos. 200/1	4·50	6·00
201	100l. Queen Elizabeth II	2·25	3·00

Nos. 200/1 were printed together, *se-tenant*, in horizontal and vertical pairs throughout the sheet.

70 Locomotive No. 11 and Trakhoni Station

(Des H. Uluçam (50l.). Litho Tezel Ofset, Lefkosa)

1986 (31 Dec). Cyprus Railway. T **70** and similar horiz design. Multicoloured. W **61** (sideways). P 12×12½.

202	50l. Type **70**	3·75	2·75
203	100l. Locomotive No. 1	4·25	4·75

Kuzey Kıbrıs Türk Cumhuriyeti

(**71**)

1987 (18 May). Nos. *94, 86/7* and *113* optd as T **71** or surch also.

204	10l. deep mauve and pale green	50	80
205	15l. on 3½l. grey-green and pale rose-pink	50	80
206	20l. dull ultramarine and pale greenish yellow	55	85
207	30l. multicoloured	70	1·25
204/7 *Set of 4*		2·00	3·25

(Litho Tezel Ofset, Letkosa)

1987 (27 May). Art (6th series). Vert designs as T **54**. Multicoloured. W **61** (inverted). P 12½×13.

208	50l. "Shepherd" (Feridun Isiman)	1·25	1·25
209	125l. "Pear Woman" (Mehmet Uluhan)	1·75	3·00

72 Modern House (architect A. Vural Behaeddin)

73 Kneeling Folk Dancer

(Des H. Uluçam (60l.). Litho Tezel Ofset, Lefkosa)

1987 (30 June). Europa. Modern Architecture. T **72** and similar horiz design. Multicoloured. W **51** (sideways). P 12×12½.

210	50l. Type **72**	1·00	30
	a. Perf 12×imperf	2·25	3·25
	ab. Booklet pane. Nos. 210a/11a, each×2	9·00	
211	200l. Modern house (architect Necdet Turgay)	1·75	3·25
	a. Perf 12×imperf	2·25	3·25

Nos. 210a and 211a come from 500l. stamp booklets containing *se-tenant* pane No. 210ab.

(Des B. Ruhi. Litho Tezel Ofset, Lefkosa)

1987 (20 Aug). Folk Dancers. T **73** and similar vert designs. Multicoloured. W **51** (inverted). P 12½×12.

212	20l. Type **73**	80	20
213	50l. Standing male dancer	90	40
214	200l. Standing female dancer	2·00	1·75
215	1000l. Woman's headdress	4·75	6·50
212/15	*Set of 4*	7·75	8·00

74 Regimental Colour (1st Anniv of Infantry Regiment)

75 Ahmet Belig Pasha (Egyptian judge)

(Des H. Uluçam. Litho Tezel Ofset, Lefkosa)

1987 (30 Sept). Anniversaries and Events. T **74** and similar multicoloured designs. W **51** (inverted on vert designs, sideways on horiz). P 12½×12 (vert) or 12×12½ (horiz).

216	50l. Type **74**	1·75	1·00
217	50l. Pres. Denktash and Turgut Özal (1st anniv. of Turkish Prime Minister's visit) (*horiz*) (2.11)	1·75	1·00
218	200l. Emblem and Crescent (5th Islamic Summit Conference, Kuwait)	3·00	4·25
219	200l. Emblem and laurel leaves (Membership of Pharmaceutical Federation) (*horiz*)	3·00	4·25
216/19	*Set of 4*	8·50	9·50

(Des H. Uluçam. Litho Tezel Ofset, Lefkosa)

1987 (22 Oct). Turkish Cypriot Personalities. T **75** and similar vert designs. W **51** (inverted). P 12½×12.

220	**75**	50l. brown and greenish yellow	65	40
221	–	50l. multicoloured	65	40
222	–	125l. multicoloured	1·50	3·00
220/2		*Set of 3*	2·50	3·50

Designs:—50l. (No. 221) Mehmet Emin Pasha (Ottoman Grand Vizier); 125l. Mehmet Kâmil Pasha (Ottoman Grand Vizier).

76 Tourist Hotel, Girne

77 *Piyale Pasha* (tug)

(Des A. Erduran. Litho Tezel Ofset, Lefkosa)

1987 (20 Nov). Modern Development (2nd series). T **76** and similar horiz design. Multicoloured. W **51** (sideways). P 12×12½.

223	150l. Type **76**	1·50	1·50
224	200l. Dogu Akdeniz University	1·75	2·25

(Litho Tezel Ofset, Lefkosa)

1988 (2 May). Art (7th series). Multicoloured designs as T **54**. W **51** (inverted on 20, 150l. sideways on 50l.). P 12½×13 (20, 150l.) or 13×12½ (50l.).

225	20l. "Woman making Pastry" (Ayhan Mentes) (*vert*)	50	30
226	50l. "Chair Weaver" (Osman Güvenir)	75	75
227	150l. "Woman weaving a Rug" (Zekäi Yesiladali) (*vert*)	1·75	4·00
225/7	*Set of 3*	2·75	4·50

(Des H. Uluçam. Litho Tezel Ofset, Lefkosa)

1988 (31 May). Europa. Transport and Communications. T **77** and similar multicoloured design. W **51** (sideways on 200l., inverted on 500l. P 12×12½ (200l.) or 12½×12 (500l.).

228	200l. Type **77**	2·50	75
229	500l. Dish aerial and antenna tower, Selvilitepe (*vert*)	3·25	5·00

No. 229 also commemorates the 25th anniversary of Bayrak Radio and Television Corporation.

78 Lefkosa

79 Bülent Ecevit

(Litho Tezel Ofset, Lefkosa)

1988 (17 June). Tourism. T **78** and similar horiz designs. Multicoloured. W **51** (sideways). P 12×12½.

230	150l. Type **78**	80	80
231	200l. Gazi-Magusa	90	1·00
232	300l. Girne	1·50	2·00
230/2	*Set of 3*	2·75	3·50

(Litho Tezel Ofset, Lefkosa)

1988 (20 July). Turkish Prime Ministers. T **79** and similar vert designs. Multicoloured. W **51**. P 12½×12.

233	50l. Type **79**	60	85
234	50l. Bülent Ulusu	60	85
235	50l. Turgut Ozal	60	85
233/5	*Set of 3*	1·60	2·25

80 Red Crescent Members on Exercise

81 Hodori the Tiger (Games mascot) and Fireworks

(Des N. Kozel. Litho Tezel Ofset, Lefkosa)

1988 (8 Aug). Civil Defence. W **51** (sideways). P 12×12½.

236	**80**	150l. multicoloured	1·75	2·00

(Des E. Cizenel (200l.), N. Kozal (250l.), H. Uluçam (400l.). Litho Tezel Ofset, Lefkosa)

1988 (17 Sept). Olympic Games, Seoul. T **81** and similar horiz designs. Multicoloured. W **51** (sideways). P 12×12½.

237	200l. Type **81**	1·40	1·00
	a. Imperf (pair)	90·00	
238	250l. Athletics	1·60	1·25
239	400l. Shot and running track with letters spelling "SEOUL"	2·25	2·00
237/9	*Set of 3*	4·75	3·75

82 Sedat Simavi (journalist)

83 "Kemal Atatürk" (I. Calli)

(Des H. Uluçam (Nos. 241/3). Litho Tezel Ofset, Lefkosa)

1988 (17 Oct). Anniversaries and Events. T **82** and similar designs. W **51** (inverted on Nos. 240, 243 and 245, sideways on Nos. 241 and 244). P 12½×12 (vert) or 12×12½ (horiz).

240	50l. olive-green	25	25
241	100l. multicoloured	75	45
242	300l. multicoloured	80	1·00
243	400l. multicoloured	2·00	2·00
244	400l. multicoloured	1·25	2·00
245	600l. multicoloured	2·75	2·75
240/5	*Set of 6*	7·00	7·75

Designs: *Horiz*—No. 241, Stylised figures around table and flags of participating countries (International Girne Conferences); 244, Presidents Gorbachev and Reagan signing treaty (Summit Meeting). *Vert*—No. 242, Cogwheels as flowers (North Cyprus Industrial Fair); 243, Globe (125th anniv of International Red Cross); 245, "Medical Services" (40th anniv of W.H.O.).

(Litho Tezel Ofset, Lefkosa)

1988 (10 Nov). 50th Death Anniv of Kemal Atatürk. Sheet 72×102 mm containing T **83** and similar vert designs. Multicoloured. W **51** (inverted). P 12½×12.

MS246 250l. Type **83**; 250l. "Kemal Atatürk" (N. Ismail); 250l. in army uniform; 250l. In profile .... 3·25 3·25

84 Abstract Design

(Des E. Cizenel. Litho Tezel Ofset, Lefkosa)

1988 (15 Nov). 5th Anniv of Turkish Republic of Northern Cyprus. Sheet *98×76* mm. Imperf. W **51** (sideways).

MS247 **84** 500l. multicoloured .... 2·25 2·25

(Litho Tezel Ofset, Lefkosa)

1989 (28 Apr). Art (8th series). Multicoloured designs as T **54**. W **51** (sideways on 150, 400l., inverted on 600l.). P 12½×13 (600l.) or 13×12½ (others).

248	150l. "Dervis Pass Mansion, Lefkosa" (Inci Kansu)	90	60
249	400l. "Gamblers' Inn, Lefkosa" (Osman Güvenir)	1·75	2·25
250	600l. "Mosque, Paphos" (Hikmet Ulucam) (*vert*)	2·50	3·00
248/50	*Set of 3*	4·75	5·25

85 Girl with Doll

86 Meeting of Presidents Vassiliou and Denktas

(Des N. Kozal. Litho Tezel Ofset, Lefkosa)

1989 (31 May). Europa. Children's Games. T **85** and similar vert design. Multicoloured. W **51**. P 12½×12.

251	600l. Type **85**	2·25	1·25
	a. Imperf×p 12	2·50	3·75
	ab. Booklet pane. Nos. 251a/2a, each×2	9·00	
252	1000l. Boy with kite	2·50	3·75
	a. Imperf×p 12	2·50	3·75

Nos. 251a and 252a come from 3200l. stamp booklets containing *se-tenant* pane No. 251ab.

(Litho Tezel Ofset, Lefkosa)

1989 (30 June). Cyprus Peace Summit, Geneva, 1988. W **51** (sideways). P 12×12½.

253 **86** 500l dawn rose-red and black .... 1·25 1·25

87 Chukar Partridge

88 Road Construction

(Des E. Cizenel. Litho Tezel Ofset, Lefkosa)

1989 (31 July). Wildlife. T **87** and similar horiz designs. Multicoloured. W **51** (sideways). P 12×12½.

254	100l. Type **87**	65	25
255	200l. Cyprus Hare	70	35
256	700l. Black Partridge	2·50	2·00
257	2000l. Red Fox	3·00	4·00
254/7	*Set of 4*	6·00	6·00

(Litho Tezel Ofset, Leprosy)

1989 (29 Sept). Modern Development (3rd series). T **88** and similar multicoloured designs. W **61** (sideways on 100, 700l.). P 12×12½ (100, 700l.) or 12½×12 (others).

258	100l. Type **88**	25	15
259	150l. Laying water pipeline (*vert*)	30	20
260	200l. Seedling trees (*vert*)	40	30
261	450l. Modern telephone exchange (*vert*)	1·00	1·00
262	650l. Steam turbine power station (*vert*)	1·25	1·75
263	700l. Irrigation reservoir	1·50	1·75
258/63	*Set of 6*	4·25	4·50

89 Unloading *Polly Pioneer* (freighter) at Quayside (15th anniv of Gazi Magusa Free Port)

90 Erdal Inonu

(Des E. Çizenel (450, 600l.), Ö. Özünalp (500l.), S. Oral (1000l.). Litho Tezel Ofset, Lefkosa)

1989 (17 Nov). Anniversaries. T **89** and similar designs. W **51** (inverted on 450l., sideways on others). P 12½×13 (450l.) or 12×12½ (others).

264	100l. multicoloured	70	20
265	450l. black, dull ultramarine and scarlet-vermilion	80	80
266	500l. black, yellow-ochre and olive-grey	80	80
267	600l. black, vermilion and new blue	2·25	2·25
268	1000l. multicoloured	3·50	4·50
264/8	*Set of 5*	7·25	7·75

Designs: *Vert* (26×47 mm)—450l. Airmail letter and stylized bird (25th same of Turkish Cypriot postal service). *Horiz* (*as T* **89**)—500l. Newspaper and printing press (centenary of *Saded* newspaper) 600l. Statue of Aphrodite, lifebelt and seabird (30th anniv of International Maritime Organization) 1000l. Soldiers (25th anniv of Turkish Cypriot resistance).

(Litho Tezel Ofset, Lefkosa)

1989 (15 Dec). Visit of Professor Erdal Inonu (Turkish politician). W **51** (inverted). P 12½×12.

269 **90** 700l. multicoloured .... 80 1·00

91 Mule-drawn Plough

92 Smoking Ashtray and Drinks

(Des N. Kozal. Litho Tezel Ofset, Lefkosa)

1989 (25 Dec). Traditional Agricultural Implements. T **91** and similar multicoloured designs. W **51** (sideways on 150, 450l.). P 12½×12 (550l.) or 12×12½ (others).

270	150l. Type **91**	30	25
271	450l. Ox-drawn threshing sledge	75	85
272	650l. Olive press (*vert*)	90	1·25
270/2	*Set of 3*	1·75	2·10

(Des O. Ozünalp (200l.), H. Ulucam (700l). Litho Tezel Ofset, Lefkosa)

1990 (19 Apr). World Health Day. T **92** and similar horiz design. Multicoloured. W **51** (sideways) P 12×12½.

273	200l. Type **92**	1·25	40
274	700l. Smoking cigarette and heart	2·50	3·25

93 Yenierenköy Post Office

94 Song Thrush

(Des H. Billur. Litho Tezel Ofset, Lefkosa)

1990 (31 May). Europa. Post Office Buildings. T **93** and similar horiz design. Multicoloured. W **61** (sideways). P 12×12½.

275	1000l. Type **93**	2·00	75
276	1500l. Atatürk Meydani Post Office	2·75	3·75
MS277	105×72 mm. Nos. 275/6, each×2	7·50	8·50

(Des H. Billur. Litho Tezel Ofset, Lefkosa)

1990 (5 June). World Environment Day. T **94** and similar vert designs showing birds. Multicoloured. W **51** (inverted). P 12½×12.

278	150l. Type **94**	2·75	65
279	300l. Blackcap	3·50	1·00
280	900l. Black Redstart	5·50	4·50
281	1000l. Chiff-chaff	5·50	4·50
278/81	*Set of 4*	15·00	9·50

95 Two Football Teams

96 Amphitheatre, Soli

(Des H. Billur (1000l.). Litho Tezel Ofset, Lefkosa)

1990 (8 June). World Cup Football Championship, Italy. T **95** and similar horiz design. Multicoloured. W **51** (sideways). P 12×12½.

282	300l. Type **95**	75	50
283	1000l. Championship symbol, globe and ball	2·50	3·50

(Litho Tezel Ofset, Lefkosa)

1990 (31 July). Art (9th series). Multicoloured designs as T **54**. W **51** (sideways on 300l.). P 13×12½ (300l.) or 12½×13 (1000l.).

284	300l. "Abstract" (Filiz Ankaçç)	40	25
285	1000l. Wooden sculpture (S. Tekman) (*vert*)	1·25	1·50

(Litho Tezel Ofset, Lefkosa)

1990 (24 Aug). Tourism. T **96** and similar vert design. Multicoloured. W **51**. P 12½.

286	150l. Type **96**	40	20
287	1000l. Swan mosaic, Soli	1·75	2·50

97 Kenan Evren and Rauf Denktas

98 Road Signs and Heart wearing Seat Belt

(Litho Tezel Ofset, Lefkosa)

1990 (19 Sept). Visit of President Kenan Evren of Turkey. W **51** (sideways). P 12½.

288	**97**	500l. multicoloured	1·00	1·00

(Des H. Billur. Litho Tezel Ofset, Lefkosa)

1990 (21 Sept). Traffic Safety Campaign. T **98** and similar horiz designs. Multicoloured. W **61** (sideways). P 12½.

289	150l. Type **98**	1·25	30
290	300l. Road signs, speeding car and spots of blood	1·50	50
291	1000l. Traffic lights and road signs	3·75	4·50
289/91	*Set of 3*	6·00	4·75

99 Yildirim Akbulut

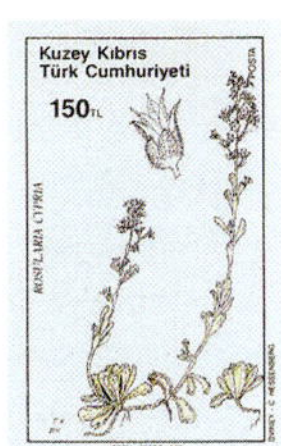

100 *Rosularia cypria*

(Litho Tezel Ofset, Lefkosa)

1990 (1 Oct). Visit of Turkish Prime Minister Yildrim Akbulat. (*inverted*). W **51** P 12½.

292	**99**	1000l. multicoloured	1·10	1·10

(Des D. Viney and P. Jacobs 1200, 1500l.), D. Viney and C. Hessenberg (others). Litho Tezel Ofset, Lefkosa)

1990 (31 Oct). Plants. T **100** and similar Vert designs. Multicoloured. W **51**. P 12½.

293	150l. Type **100**	70	20
294	200l. *Silene fraudratrix*	80	30
295	300l. *Scutellaria sibthorpii*	90	35
296	600l. *Sedum lampusae*	1·40	85
297	1000l. *Onosma caespitosum*	1·50	2·25
298	1500l. *Arabis cypria*	2·25	4·00
293/8	*Set of 6*	6·75	7·25

101 Kemal Atatürk at Easel (wood carving)

250 TL

(**102**)

(Des M. Uzel (300l.), H. Billur (750l.). Litho Tezel Ofset, Letkosa)

1990 (24 Nov). International Literacy Year. T **101** and similar horiz design. Multicoloured. W **51** (sideways). P 12½.

299	300l. Type **101**	1·25	35
300	750l. Globe, letters and books	2·50	3·25

1991 (3 June). Nos. 189, 212 and 293 surch as T **102**.

301	250l. on 10l. Type **66**	1·50	1·50
302	250l. on 20l. Type **73**	1·50	1·50
303	500l. on 150l. Type **100**	2·00	2·50
	a. Surch inverted	55·00	
301/3	*Set of 3*	4·50	5·00

PRINTER. Issues from Nos. 304/5 onwards were printed in lithography by the State Printing Works, Lefkosa, *unless otherwise stated.*

103 *Ophrys lapethica*

104 *Hermes* (projected shuttle)

1991 (8 July). Orchids (1st series). T **103** and similar vert design. Multicoloured. W **51** (inverted). P 14.

304	250l. Type **103**	1·25	60
305	500l. *Ophrys kotschyi*	2·25	2·75

See also Nos. 311/14.

1991 (29 July). Europa. Europe in Space. Sheet 78×82 mm containing T **104** and similar vert design. Multicoloured. W **51**. P 12½.

MS306	2000l. Type **104**; 2000l. *Ulysses* (satellite)	9·00	10·00

105 Kucuk Medrese Fountain, Lefkosa

106 Symbolic Roots (Year of Love to Yunus Emre)

(Des H. Billur)

1991 (9 Sept). Fountains T **105** and similar horiz designs. Multicoloured. W **51** (sideways). P 12½.

307	250l. Type **105**	55	15
308	500l. Cafer Pasa Fountains, Magusa	75	30
309	1500l. Sarayönü Mosque Fountains, Lefkosa	1·50	1·60
310	5000l. Arabahmet Mosque Fountains, Lefkosa	3·75	6·00
307/10 *Set of* 4		6·00	7·25

1991 (10 Oct). Orchids (2nd series). Vert design as T **103** Mutlicoloured. W **51** (sideways). P 14.

311	100l. *Serapias Levantina*	85	20
312	500l. *Dactylorhiza romana*	2·50	50
313	2000l. *Orchis simia*	4·25	4·50
314	3000l. *Orchis sancta*	4·75	6·00
311/14 *Set of* 4		11·00	10·00

1991 (5 Nov). Art (10th series). Multicoloured designs as T **54**. W **51**. P 12½×13.

315	250l. "Hindiler" (S. Çizel) (*vert*)	2·00	50
316	500l. "Düsme" (A. Mene) (*vert*)	2·50	2·50

(Des K. Sarikavak (250l.) H Billur (500, 1500l.)

1991 (20 Nov). Anniversaries and Events T **106** and similar designs. W **51** (sideways on 1500l. inverted on others). P 12×12½ (1500l.) or 12½×12 (others).

317	250l. greenish yellow, black and bright magenta	25	25
318	500l. multicoloured	45	60
319	500l. multicoloured	45	60
320	1500l. multicoloured	5·50	5·50
317/20 *Set of* 4		6·00	6·25

Designs: *Vert*—No. 318 Mustafa Cagatay commemoration; No. 319, University building (5th anniv of Eastern Mediterranean University). *Horiz*—No. 320, Mozart (death bicent).

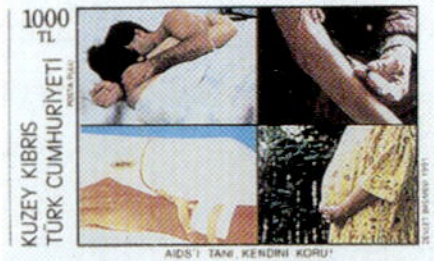

107 Four Sources of Infection

108 Lighthouse, Gazimagusa

1991 (13 Dec). AIDS Day. W **51** (sideways). P 12×12½.

321	**107** 1000l. multicoloured	2·50	2·00

(Des H. Billur)

1991 (16 Dec). Lighthouses. T **108** and similar horiz designs. Multicoloured. W **51** (sideways). P 12×12½.

322	250l. Type **108**	2·50	65
323	500l. Ancient lighthouses, Girne harbour	3·25	1·25
324	1500l. Modern lighthouse, Girne harbour	5·50	6·50
322/4 *Set of* 3		10·00	7·50

109 Elephant and Hippopotamus Fossils, Karaoglanoglu

1991 (27 Dec). Tourism (1st series). T **109** and similar horiz designs. Multicoloured. W **51** (sideways). P 12.

325	250l. Type **109**	2·00	55
326	500l. Roman fish ponds, Lambusa	2·25	80
327	1500l. Roman remains, Lambusa	3·50	5·00
325/7 *Set of* 3		7·00	5·75

See also Nos. 330/3 and 351/2.

1992 (31 Mar). Art (11th series). Multicoloured designs as T **54**, but 31×49 mm. W **51** (sideways). P 14.

328	500l. "Ebru" (A. Kandulu)	1·00	25
329	3600l. "Street in Lefkosa" (I. Tatar)	4·00	5·50

1992 (21 Apr). Tourism (2nd series). Multicoloured designs as T **109**. W **51** (sideways). P 14×13½ (1500l.) or 13½×14 (others).

330	500l. Bugday Camii, Gazimagusa	80	80
331	500l. Clay pigeon shooting	80	80
332	1000l. Salamis Bay Hotel, Gazimagusa	1·50	1·50
333	1500l. Casino, Girne (*vert*)	2·50	3·50
330/3 *Set of* 4		5·00	6·00

110 Fleet of Columbus and Early Map

(Des H. Billur)

1992 (29 May). Europa. 500th Anniv of Discovery of America by Columbus. Sheet, 80×76 mm, containing T **110** and similar horiz design. Multicoloured. W **51** (sideways). P 13½×14.

MS334 1500l. Type **110**; 3500l. Christopher Columbus and signature	4·00	4·25

111 Green Turtle

112 Gymnastics

(Des H. Billur)

1992 (30 June). World Environment Day. Sea Turtles. Sheet, 105×75 mm, containing T **111** and similar horiz design. W **51** (sideways). P 13½×14.

MS335 1000l.×2, Type **111**; 1500l.×2, Loggerhead Turtle	6·50	7·00

(Des H. Billur)

1992 (25 July). Olympic Games, Barcelona. T **112** and similar multicoloured designs. W **51** (inverted on 500l., sideways on 1000, 1500l.). P 14×13½ (500l.) or 13½×14 (others).

336	500l. Type **112**	80	90
	a. Horiz pair. Nos. 336/7	1·60	1·75
337	500l. Tennis	80	90
338	1000l. High jumping (*horiz*)	1·00	1·25
339	1500l. Cycling (*horiz*)	4·50	4·50
336/9 *Set of* 4		6·25	6·75

Nos. 336/7 were printed together, *se-tenant*, in horizontal pairs throughout the sheet.

113 New Generating Station, Girne

(Des H. Billur (Nos. 341/2), Therese Coustry (No. 343))

1992 (30 Sept). Anniversaries and Events (1st series). T **113** and similar horiz designs. Multicoloured. W **51** (sideways). P 14.

340	500l. Type **113**	50	50
341	500l. Symbol of Housing Association (15th anniv)	50	50
342	1500l. Domestic animals and birds (30th anniv of Veterinary Service)	3·75	4·00
343	1500l. Cat (International Federation of Cat Societies Conference)	3·75	4·00
340/3 *Set of* 4		7·75	8·00

114 Airliner over Runway

(Des H. Billur)

1992 (20 Nov). Anniversaries and Events (2nd series). T **114** and similar horiz designs. Multicoloured. W **51** (sideways). P 13×14.

344	1000l. Type **114** (17th anniv of civil aviation)	2·50	2·50

345 1000l. Meteorological instruments and weather (18th anniv of Meteorological Service) ..... 2·50 2·50
346 1200l. Surveying equipment and map (14th anniv of Survey Department) ..... 3·25 3·50
344/6 *Set of 3* ..... 7·50 7·75

115 Zübiye

116 Painting by Turksal Ince

(Des A. Erduran)

1992 (14 Dec). International Conference on Nutrition, Rome. Turkish Cypriot Cuisine. T **115** and similar horiz designs. W **51** (sideways). P 13½×14.
347 2000l. Type **115** ..... 1·50 1·50
348 2500l. Çiçek Dolmasi ..... 1·75 1·75
349 3000l. Tatar Böregi ..... 2·00 2·25
350 4000l. Seftali Kebabi ..... 2·25 2·50
347/50 *Set of 4* ..... 6·75 7·25

1993 (1 Apr). Tourism (3rd series). Horiz designs as T **109**. Multicoloured. W **61** (sideways). P 13½×14.
351 500l. Saint Barnabas Church and Monastery, Salamis 50 15
352 10000l. Ancient pot ..... 5·50 6·50

(Des T. Ince and I. Onsoy)

1993 (5 May). Europa. Contemporary Art. Sheet 79×69 mm containing T **116** and similar vert design. Multicoloured. W **51**. P 14.
MS353 2000l. Type **116**; 3000l. Painting by Ilkay Onsoy ..... 1·75 2·50

117 Olive Tree, Girne

118 Traditional Houses

1993 (11 June). Ancient Trees. T **117** and similar vert designs. Multicoloured. W **51** (inverted). P 14.
354 500l. Type **117** 45 15
355 1000l. River red gum, Kyrenia Gate, Lefkosa 80 40
356 3000l. Oriental plane, Lapta ..... 1·75 2·00
357 4000l. Calabrian pine, Cinarli ..... 2·00 2·25
354/7 *Set of 4* ..... 4·50 4·25

(Des H. Billur)

1993 (20 Sept). Arabahmet District Conservation Project, Lefkosa. T **118** and similar horiz design. Multicoloured. W **51** (sideways). P 13½×14.
358 1000l. Type **118** ..... 1·00 40
359 3000l. Arabahmet street ..... 2·50 3·25

119 National Flags turning into Doves

120 Kemal Atatürk

(Des H. Ulucam (5000l.), H. Billur (others))

1993 (15 Nov). 10th Anniv of Proclamation of Turkish Republic of Northern Cyprus. T **119** and similar designs. W **51** (sideways on Nos. 361/3). P 14×13½ (No. 360) or 13½×14 (others).
360 500l. carmine-red, black and new blue 30 30
361 500l. rosine and new blue 30 30
362 1000l. carmine-red, black and new blue 40 30
363 5000l. multicoloured ..... 1·75 3·00
360/3 *Set of 4* ..... 2·50 3·50
Designs: *Horiz*—No. 361, National flag forming figure "10"; No. 362, Dove carrying national flag; No. 363, Map of Cyprus and figure "10" wreath.

(Des H. Billur (Nos. 366/8))

1993 (27 Dec). Anniversaries. T **120** and similar multicoloured designs. W **51** (inverted on No. 364 or sideways on others). P 14×13½ (No. 384) or 13½×14 (others).
364 500l. Type **120** (55th death anniv) 30 30
365 500l. Stage and emblem (30th anniv of Turkish Cypriot theatre) (*horiz*) 30 30
366 1500l. Branch badges (35th anniv of T.M.T. organization) (*horiz*) 30 50
367 2000l. World map and computer (20th anniv of Turkish Cypriot news agency) (*horiz*) . 1·75 1·75
368 5000l. Ballet dancers and Caykovski'nin (Death centenary) (*horiz*) ..... 5·50 5·50
364/8 *Set of 5* ..... 7·50 7·50

121 "Söyle Falci" (Göral Ozkan)

1994 (31 Mar). Art (12th series). T **121** and similar vert design. Multicoloured. W **51**. P 14.
369 1000l. Type **121** 30 20
370 6500l. "IV. Hareket" (sculpture) (Senol Ozdevrim) ..... 1·50 2·25
See also Nos. 436/7.

122 Dr. Kucuk and Memorial

1994 (1 Apr). 10th Death Anniv of Dr. Fazil Kucuk (politician). W **51** (sideways). P 14.
371 **122** 1500l. multicoloured 70 85

123 Neolithic Village, Girne

(Des H. Billur)

1994 (16 May). Europa. Archaeological Discoveries. Sheet 73×79 mm containing T **123** and similar horiz design. Multicoloured. W **61** (sideways). P 13½×14.
MS372 8500l. Type **123**; 8500l. Neolithic man and implements ..... 6·50 7·00

124 Peace Doves and Letters over Pillar Box

125 World Cup Trophy

(Des H. Billur)

1994 (30 June). 30th Anniv of Turkish Cypriot Postal Service. W **51** (sideways). P 13½×14.

373	**124** 50000l. multicoloured	3·00	4·50

(Des H. Billur)

1994 (30 June). World Cup Football Championship, U.S.A. T **125** and similar multicoloured design. W **51** (sideways on 10000l.). P 14×13½ (2500l.) or 13½×14 (10000l.).

374	2500l. Type **125**	50	25
375	10000l. Footballs on map of U.S.A. (*horiz*)	2·00	2·75

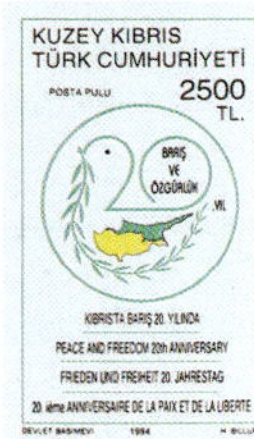

126 Peace Emblem

127 Cyprus 1934 4½ pi. Stamp and Karpas Postmark

(Des H. Billur (2500, 8500l.))

1994 (20 July). 20th Anniv of Turkish Landings in Cyprus. T **126** and similar designs. W **51** (sideways on horiz designs). P 14×13½ (2600l.) or 13½×14 (others).

376	2500l. greenish yellow, emerald and black	40	30
377	5000l. multicoloured	60	60
378	7000l. multicoloured	80	1·00
379	8500l. multicoloured	1·10	1·50
376/9	*Set of* 4	2·50	3·00

Designs: *Horiz*—5000l. Memorial; 7000l. Sculpture; 8500l. Peace doves forming map of Cyprus and flame.

1994 (15 Aug). Postal Centenary. T **127** and similar horiz designs. Multicoloured. W **61** (sideways). P 13½×14.

380	1500l. Type **127**	20	20
381	2500l. Turkish Cypriot Posts 1979 Europa 2l. and Gazimagusa postmark	40	30
382	5000l. Cyprus 1938 6pi. and Bey Keuy postmark	70	90
383	7000l. Cyprus 1955 100m. and Aloa postmark	1·00	1·50
384	8500l. Cyprus 1938 18pi. and Pyla postmark	1·25	2·00
380/4	*Set of* 5	3·25	4·50

128 Trumpet Triton (*Charonia tritonis*)

1500TL

(**129**)

***

1994 (15 Nov). Sea Shells. T **128** and similar horiz designs. Multicoloured. W **51** (sideways). P 13½×14.

385	2500l. Type **128**	45	30
386	12500l. Mole Cowrie (*Cypraea talpa*)	1·25	1·75
387	12500l. Giant Tun (*Tonna galea*)	1·25	1·75
385/7	*Set of* 3	2·75	3·50

1994 (12 Dec)–**95**. Nos. 280, 295, 315 and 317 surch as T **129**.

388	1500l. on 25ol. Type **106**	20	10
389	2000l. on 90ol. Black Redstart (21.4.95)	3·00	90
390	2500l. on 25ol. "Hindiler" (S. Cizel)	40	30
391	3500l. on 30ol. *Scutellaria sibthorpii* (21.4.95)	2·75	3·00
388/91	*Set of* 4	5·75	3·75

Nos. 389/90 show the surcharge value horizontally.

130 Donkeys on Mountain

131 Peace Dove and Globe

1995 (10 Feb). European Conservation Year. T **130** and similar horiz designs. W **51** (sideways). P 13½×14.

392	2000l. Type **130**	30	20
393	3500l. Coastline	30	30
394	15000l. Donkeys in field	1·50	2·50
392/4	*Set of* 3	1·90	2·75

(Des Hüseyin Billur)

1995 (20 Apr). Europa. Peace and Freedom. Sheet 72×78 mm containing T **131** and similar horiz design. W **51** (sideways). P 13½×14.

MS395	Type **131** 15000l. Peace doves over map of Europe	3·75	4·00

132 Sini Katmeri

133 *Papilio machaon*

1995 (29 May). Turkish Cypriot Cuisine. T **132** and similar horiz designs. Multicoloured. W **51** (sideways). P 13¾×14.

396	3500l. Type **132**	20	20
397	10000l. Kolokas musakka and bullez kizartma	55	65
398	14000l. Enginar dolmasi	90	1·60
396/8	*Set of* 3	1·50	2·25

(Des Hüseyin Billur)

1995 (30 June). Butterflies. T **133** and similar horiz designs. Multicoloured. W **51** (sideways). P 13½×14.

399	3500l. Type **133**	30	15
400	4500l. *Charaxes jasius*	35	20
401	15000l. *Cynthia cardui*	1·00	1·40
402	30000l. *Vanessa atalanta*	1·75	2·50
399/402	*Set of* 4	3·00	3·75

134 Forest

135 Beach, Girne

1995 (7 Aug). Obligatory Tax. Forest Regeneration Fund. P 14×13½.

403	**134** 1000l. emerald and black	3·75	40

No. 403 was for compulsory use on all mail, in addition to the normal postage, between 7 August and 6 February 1996. It was intended to provide funds for the replanting of those forests destroyed by fire in June 1995. A similar 50000l. stamp was issued for fiscal use only.

1995 (21 Aug). Tourism. T **135** and similar multicoloured designs. W **51** (sideways on horiz designs). P 13½×14 (horiz) or 14×13½ (vert).

404	3500l. Type **135**	30	20
405	7500l. Sail boards	50	45
406	15000l. Ruins of Salamis (*vert*)	1·00	1·25
407	20000l. St. George's Cathedral, Gazimagusa (*vert*)	1·00	1·25
401/7	*Set of* 4	2·50	2·75

136 Süleyman Demirel and Rauf Denktas

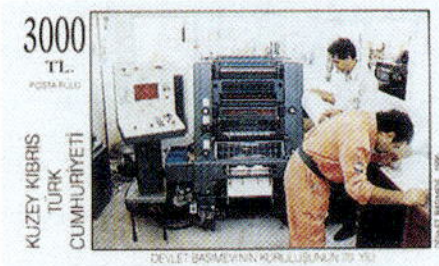

137 Stamp Printing Press

1995 (21 Aug). Visit of President Süleyman Demirel of Turkey. W **51** (sidesways). P 14.

408	**136** 5000l. multicoloured	60	60

(Des H. Billur (Nos. 410/14))

1995 (7 Nov). Anniversaries. T **137** and similar designs. W **51** (sideways on horiz designs). P 14×13½ (No. 414) or 13½×14 (others).

409	3000l. multicoloured	40	40
410	3000l. multicoloured	40	40
411	5000l. multicoloured	70	70
412	22000l. dull ultramarine, new blue and black	1·00	1·75
413	30000l. multicoloured	1·40	2·25
414	30000l. multicoloured	1·40	2·25
409/14	*Set of* 6	4·75	7·00

Designs: *Horiz*—No. 409, 137 (20th anniv od State Printing Works); No. 410, Map of Turkey (75th anniv of Turkish National Assembly); No. 411, Louis Pasteur (chemist) and microscope (Death centenary); No. 412, United Nations anniversary emblem (50th anniv); No. 413, Guglielmo Marconi (radio pioneer) and dial (Centenary of first radio transmissions). *Vert*—No. 414, Stars and reel of film (Centenary of cinema).

138 Kültegin Epitaph and Sculpture

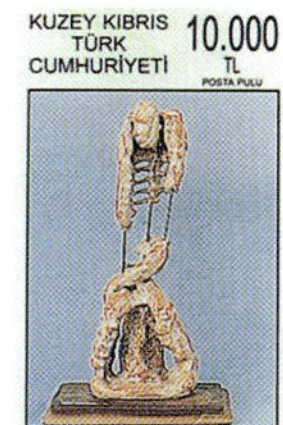

139 "Bosnia" (sculpture)

(Des Hüseyin Billur)

1995 (28 Dec). Centenary of Deciphering of Orhon Epitaphs. T **138** and similar vert design. W **51**. P 14.

415	5000l. Type **138**	1·00	50
416	10000l. Epitaph and tombstone	1·75	2·25

(Des S. Özdevrim)

1996 (31 Jan). Support for Moslems in Bosnia and Herzegovina. W **51** (inverted). P 14×13½.

417	**139** 10000l. multicoloured	1·75	2·00

140 Striped Red Mullet

141 Palm Trees

(Des Hüseyin Billur)

1996 (29 Mar). Fish. T **140** and similar horiz designs. Multicoloured. W **51** (sideways). P 13½×14.

418	6000l. Type **140**	1·00	30
419	10000l. Peacock Wrasse	1·25	45
420	28000l. Common Two-banded Seabream	2·25	2·50
421	40000l. Dusky Grouper	2·75	3·50
418/21	*Set of* 4	6·50	6·00

1996 (26 Apr). Tourism. T **141** and similar multicoloured designs. W **51** (sideways on horiz designs). P 14×13½ (perf) or 13½×14 (horiz).

422	100000l. Type **141**	1·25	45
423	150000l. Pomegranate	1·75	1·00
424	250000l. Ruins of Bella Paise Abbey (*horiz*)	2·25	2·75
425	500000l. Traditional dancers (*horiz*)	4·75	6·00
422/5	*Set of* 4	9·00	9·25

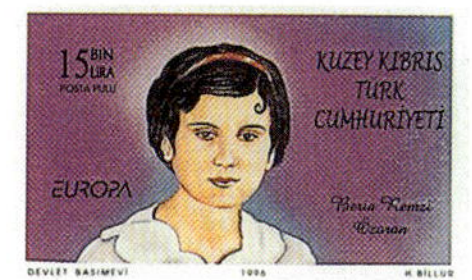

142 Beria Remzi Ozoran

143 Established Forest

(Des Hüseyin Billur)

1996 (31 May). Europa. Famous Women. T **142** and similar horiz design. Multicoloured. W **51** (sideways). P 13½×14.

426	15000l. Type **142**	1·00	25
427	50000l. Kadriye Hulusi Hacibulgur	2·25	3·50

1996 (28 June). World Environment Day. Sheet 72×78 mm containing T **143** and similar horiz design. Multicoloured. W **51** (sideways). P 13½×14.

MS428	50000l. Type **143**; 50000l. Conifer plantation	8·00	8·00

144 Basketball

145 Symbolic Footballs

(Des Hüseyin Billur)

1996 (31 July). Olympic Games, Atlanta. Sheet 105×74 mm containing T **144** and similar horiz designs. Multicoloured. W **51** (sideways). P 13½×14.

MS429	15000l. Type **144**; 15000l. Discus throwing; 5000l. Javelin throwing; 50000l. Volleyball	3·50	4·25

(Des Hüseyin Billur)

1996 (31 Oct). European Football Championship, England. T **145** and similar horiz design. Multicoloured. W **51** (sideways). P 13½×14.

430	15000l. Type **145**	1·25	65
	a. Pair. Nos. 430/1	3·50	3·50
431	35000l. Football and flags of participating nations	2·25	3·25

In addition to separate sheets Nos. 430/1 were also available in pairs, *se-tenant* horizontally and vertically.

146 Houses on Fire (Auxiliary Fire Service)

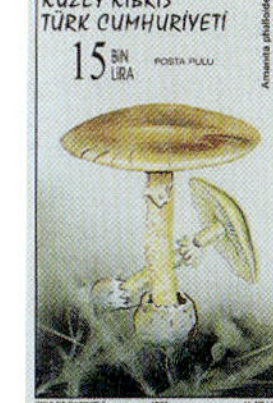

147 *Amanita phalloides*

(Des Özer Oker (10000l.), Hüseyin Billur (50000, 75000l.))

1996 (23 Dec). Anniversaries and Events. T **146** and similar multicoloured designs. W **51** (inverted on 20000l., sideways on others). P 14×13½ (20000l.) or 13½×14 (others).

432	10000l. Type **146**	1·00	40
433	20000l. Colour party (20th anniv of Defence Forces) (*vert*)	1·10	55
434	50000l. Children by lake (Nasreddin-Hoca Year)	1·40	1·60
435	75000l. Flowers (Children's Rights)	1·75	3·00
432/5	*Set of* 4	4·75	5·00

1997 (31 Jan). Art (13th series). Multicoloured designs as T **121**. W **51** (sideways). P 14.

436	25000l. "City" (Lebibe Sonuç) (*horiz*)	1·25	50
437	70000l. "Woman opening Letter" (Ruzen Atakan) (*horiz*)	2·50	3·25

(Des Hüseyin Billur)

1997 (31 Mar). Fungi. T **147** and similar vert designs. Multicoloured. W **51** (inverted). P 14×13½.

438	15000l. Type **147**	1·00	30
439	25000l. *Morchella esculenta*	1·25	1·50
440	25000l. *Pleurotus eryngii*	1·25	1·50
441	70000l. *Amanita muscaria*	2·50	3·50
438/41	*Set of* 4	5·50	6·00

148 Flag on Hillside

149 Mother and Children playing Leapfrog

(Des Hüseyin Billur)

1997 (23 Apr). Besparmak Mountains Flag Sculpture. W **51** (inverted). P 14×13½.

442 **148** 60000l. multicoloured .... 2·00 2·25

(Des Hüseyin Billur)

1997 (30 May). Europa. Tales and Legends. T **149** and similar horiz design. Multicoloured. W **51** (sideways). P 13½×14.

443 25000l. Type **149** .... 1·50 30
444 70000l. Apple tree and well .... 3·00 3·50

150 Prime Minister Necmettin Erbakan of Turkey

151 Golden Eagle

1997 (20 June). Visit of the President and the Prime Minister of Turkey. T **150** and similar multicoloured design. W **51** (sideways on 80000l.). P 14×13½ (vert) or 13½×14 (horiz).

445 15000l. Type **150** 50 30
446 80000l. President Suleyman Demirel of Turkey (*horiz*) .... 2·25 3·25

(Des Hüseyi. Billur)

1997 (31 July). Birds of Prey. T **151** and similar vert designs. Multicoloured. W **51**. P 14×13½.

447 40000l. Type **151** .... 1·75 1·75
448 40000l. Eleonora's Falcon .... 1·75 1·75
449 75000l. Common Kestrel .... 2·50 2·75
450 100000l. Western Honey Buzzard .... 2·75 3·00
447/50 *Set of 4* .... 8·00 8·25

152 Coin of Sultan Abdulaziz, 1861–76

153 Open Book and Emblem

1997 (28 Oct). Rare Coins. T **152** and similar vert designs. Multicoloured. W **51**. P 14×13½.

451 25000l. Type **152** 60 20
452 40000l. Coin of Sultan Mahmud II, 1808–39 .... 80 45
453 75000l. Coin of Sultan Selim II, 1566–74 .... 1·50 1·75
454 100000l. Coin of Sultan Mehmed V, 1909–18 .... 1·75 2·50
451/4 *Set of 4* .... 4·25 4·50

(Des Hüseyin Billur)

1997 (22 Dec). Anniversaries. T **153** and similar designs. W **51** (sideways on horiz designs). P 13½×14 (horiz) or 14×13½ (vert).

455 25000l. multicoloured 75 20
456 40000l. multicoloured .... 1·10 30
457 100000l. black, bright scarlet and yellow ochre .... 2·75 2·50
458 150000l. multicoloured .... 3·50 4·00
455/8 *Set of 4* .... 7·25 6·25

Designs: *Horiz*—25000l. Type **153** (Centenary of Turkish Cypriot Scouts); 40000l. Guides working in field (90th anniv of Turkish Cypriot Guides); 150000l. Rudolf Diesel and diesel motor (Centenary of the diesel engine). *Vert*—100000l. Couple and symbols (AIDS prevention campaign).

154 Ahmet and Ismet Sevki

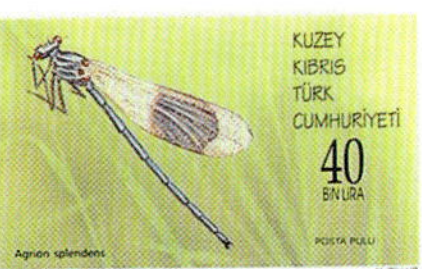

155 *Agrion spleondens* (dragonfly)

1998 (28 Jan). Ahmet and Ismet Sevki (photographers) Commemoration. T **154** and similar multicoloured design. W **61** (sideways on 40000l.). P 13½×14 (horiz) or 14×13½ (vert).

459 40000l. Type **154** 75 25
460 106000l. Ahmet Sevki (*vert*) .... 2·00 3·00

(Des Hüseyin Billur)

1998 (30 Mar). Useful Insects. T **155** and similar horiz designs. Multicoloured. W **51** (sideways). P 13½×14.

461 40000l. Type **155** 80 25
462 65000l. *Ascalaphus macaronius* (owl-fly) .... 1·40 40
463 125000l. *Podalonia hirsuta* .... 2·25 2·75
464 150000l. *Rhyssa persuasoria* .... 2·50 3·25
461/4 *Set of 4* .... 6·25 6·00

156 Wooden Double Door

157 Legislative Assembly Building (Republic Establishment Festival)

(Des Hüseyin Billur)

1998 (30 Apr). Old Doors. T **156** and similar vert design showing different door. W **51**. P 14×13½.

465 115000l. multicoloured .... 2·25 2·50
466 140000l. multicoloured .... 2·25 2·50

(Des Hüseyin Billur)

1998 (30 May). Europa. Festivals. T **157** and similar multicoloured design. W **51** (sideways on 40000l., inverted on 160000l.) P 13½×14 (horiz) or 14×13½ (vert).

467 40000l. Type **157** 75 25
468 150000l. Globe, flags and map (Int Children's Folk Dance Festival) (vert) .... 4·25 4·50

158 Marine Life

159 Prime Minister Mesut Yilmaz of Turkey

(Des Hüseyin Billur)

1998 (30 June). International Year of the Ocean. T **158** and similar horiz design showing different underwater scene. W **51** (sideways). P 13½×14.

469 40000l. multicoloured .... 1·00 40
470 90000l. multicoloured .... 2·00 2·50

1998 (20 July). Prime Minister Yilmaz's Visit to Northern Cyprus. W **51** (sideways). P 13½×14.

471 **159** 75000l. multicoloured .... 1·75 2·00

160 Pres. Suleyman Demirel of Turkey

161 Victorious French Team

1998 (25 July). President Demirel's "Water for Peace" Project. T **160** and similar multicoloured design. W **51** (inverted on 75000l., sideways on 175000l.). P 14×13½ (vert) or 13½×14 (horiz).

472 75000l. Type **160** .... 1·25 50
473 175000l. Turkish and Turkish Cypriot leaders with inflatable water tank (*horiz*) .... 2·50 3·50

1998 (31 July). World Cup Football Championship, France. T **161** and similar multicoloured design. W **51** (sideways on 75000l., inverted on 175000l.). P 13½×14 (horiz) or 14×13½ (vert).

474 75000l. Type **161** .... 1·25 50
475 175000l. World Cup trophy (*vert*) .... 2·50 3·50

162 Deputy Prime Minister Bulent Ecevit

163 Itinerant Tinsmiths

1998 (5 Sept). Visit of the Deputy Prime Minister of Turkey. W **51** (inverted). P 14×13½.

476 **162** 200000l. multicoloured .... 2·00 2·25

(Des Hüseyin Billur)

1998 (26 Oct). Local Crafts. T **163** and similar multicoloured designs. W **51** (sideways on horiz designs, inverted on vert). P 13½×14 (horiz designs) or 14×13½ (others).

477 50000l. Type **163** 45 25
478 75000l. Basket weaver (*vert*) 65 35
479 130000l. Grinder sharpening knife (*vert*) .... 1·25 1·40
480 400000l. Wood carver .... 3·50 5·00
477/80 *Set of* 4 .... 5·25 6·25

164 Stylized Satellite Dish

165 Dr. Fazil Kucuk

(Des Hüseyin Billur and Hikmet Ulucam)

1998 (15 Nov). Anniversaries. T **164** and similar multicoloured designs (except No. 483). W **51** (inverted on 175000l. sideways on others). P 14×13½ (175000l). or 13½×14 (others).

481 50000l. Type **164** 80 30
482 75000l. Stylised birds and "15" .... 1·25 1·40
483 75000l. "75" and Turkish flag (rosine, black and dull orange) .... 1·25 1·40
484 175000l. Scroll, "50" and quill pen (*vert*) .... 2·00 3·50
481/4 *Set of* 4 .... 4·75 6·00
MS485 72×78 mm. 75000l. As No. 452; 75000l. Map of Northern Cyprus .... 2·50 3·00

Anniversaries—No. 481, 35th anniv of Bayrak Radio and Television; Nos. 482, **MS**485, 15th anniv of Turkish Republic of Northern Cyprus; No. 483, 75th anniv of Turkish Republic; No. 484, 50th anniv of Universal Declaration of Human Rights.

1999 (15 Jan). 15th Death Anniv of Dr. Fazil Kucuk (politician). W **51** (inverted). P 14×13½.

486 **165** 75000l. multicoloured .... 1·50 1·50

166 Otello

167 *Malpolon monspessulanus insignitus* (Montepellier)

1999 (30 Jan). Performance of Verdi's Opera *Otello* in Cyprus. Sheet, 78×74 mm, containing T **166** and similar vert design. Multicoloured. W **51** (inverted). P 14×13½.

MS487 200000l. Type **166**; 200000l. Desdemona dead in front of fireplace .... 6·00 6·00

1999 (26 Mar). Snakes. T **167** and similar horiz designs. Multicoloured. W **51** (sideways). P 13½×14.

488 50000l. Type **167** 85 30
489 75000l. *Hierophis jugularis* .... 1·10 45
490 195000l. *Vipera lebetina lebetina* (Levantine Viper) .... 2·00 2·50
491 220000l. *Natrix natrix* (Grass Snake) .... 2·00 2·50
488/91 *Set of* 4 .... 5·50 5·25

168 Entrance to Cave

1999 (17 May). Europa. Parks and Gardens. Incirli Cave. T **168** and similar multicoloured design. W **51** (sideways on 75000l., inverted on 200000l.). P 13½×14 (horiz) or 14×13½ (vert).

492 75000l. Type **168** .... 1·25 25
493 200000l. Limestone rocks inside cave (*vert*) .... 2·50 3·25

169 Peace Dove and Map

170 Air Mail Envelope and of Cyprus Labels (35th anniv of Turkish Cypriot Posts)

(Des Hüseyin Billur)

1999 (20 July). 25th Anniv of Turkish Landings in Cyprus. T **169** and similar horiz designs. Multicoloured. W **51** (sideways). P 13½×14.

494 150000l. Type **169** .... 2·00 1·50
495 250000l. Peace dove, map of Cyprus and Sun ... 2·50 3·00

(Des Hüseyin Billur)

1999 (12 Nov). Anniversaries and Events. T **170** and similar horiz designs. Multicoloured. W **51** (sideways). P 13½×14.

496 75000l. Type **170** 65 25
497 225000l. "125" and U.P.U. emblem (125th anniv of U.P.U) .... 1·50 1·75
498 250000l. Total eclipse of the Sun, August 1999. 2·00 2·25
496/8 *Set of* 3 .... 3·75 3·75

171 Turkish Gateway, Limassol

172 Mobile Phone

1999 (3 Dec). Destruction of Turkish Buildings in Southern Cyprus. T **171** and similar grey-brown and orange-brown designs. W **51** (sideways on horiz designs). P 14×13½ (No. 502) or 13½×14 (others).

499 75000l. Type **171** 60 25
500 150000l. Mosque, Evdim 85 40
501 210000l. Bayraktar Mosque, Lefkosa .... 1·10 75
502 1000000l. Kebir Mosque, Baf (*vert*) .... 5·00 7·00
499/502 *Set of* 4 .... 6·75 7·50

(Des H. Billur)

2000 (2 Mar). New Millennium. Technology. T **172** and similar horiz designs. W **51** (sideways). P 14.

503 75000l. black, emerald and new blue 70 20
504 150000l. black and new blue 90 35
505 275000l. multicoloured .... 1·60 2·25
506 300000l. multicoloured .... 2·00 2·75
503/6 *Set of* 4 .... 4·75 5·00

Designs—150000l. "Hosgeldin 2000"; 275000l. Computer and "internet" in squares; 300000l. Satellite over Earth.

173 Beach Scene

174 "Building Europe"

(Des H. Biller and A. Tosun)

2000 (29 Apr). Holidays. T **173** and similar horiz design. Multicoloured. W **51** (sideways). P 13½×14.

507	300000l. Type **173**	1·75	2·00
508	340000l. Deck-chair on sea-shore	1·75	2·00

(Des J.-P. Cousin and H. Billur)

2000 (31 May). Europa. Sheet, 77×68 mm containing T **174** and similar vert design. Multicoloured. W **51** (inverted). P 14.

MS509 300000l. Type **174**; 300000l. Map of Europe with flower creating Council of Europe emblem and map of Cyprus ... 3·50 4·25

175 Bellapais Abbey

176 Pres. Ahmet Sezer of Turkey

(Des A. Tosun and H. Billur)

2000 (21 June). 4th International Bellapais Music Festival. T **175** and similar multicoloured design. W **51** (sideways on No. 510). P 13½×14 (No. 510) or 14×13½ (No. 511).

510	150000l. Type **175**	1·00	60
511	350000l. Emblem (*vert*)	2·25	3·00

2000 (22 June). Visit of President Ahmet Sezer of Turkey. W **51** (inverted). P 14×13½.

512	**176** 150000l. multicoloured	1·50	1·50

177 Olympic Torch and Rings

(178)

(Des Alev B. Tosun (125000l.), Hüseyin Billur (200000l.)

2000 (25 July). Olympic Games, Sydney. T **177** and similar multicoloured design. W **51** (inverted on 125000l., sideways on 200000l.) P 14×13½ (125000l.) or 13½×14 (200000l.).

513	125000l. Type **177**	1·25	50
514	200000l. Runner (*horiz*)	2·00	2·50

2000 (28 Sept). No. 418 surch with T **178**.

515	50000l. on 6000l. Type **140**	2·50	1·00

179 Grasshopper on Cactus

180 Traditional Kerchief

(Des Gazi Yüksel)

2000 (16 Oct). Nature. Insects and Flowers. T **179** and similar vert designs. Multicoloured. W **51**. P 13½×14.

516	125000l. Type **179**	80	25
517	200000l. Butterfly on flower	1·40	45
518	275000l. Bee on flower	1·50	1·25
519	600000l. Snail on flower	3·00	4·50
516/19	*Set of 4*	6·00	5·75

(Des Gazi Yüksel)

2000 (28 Nov). Traditional Handicrafts. Kerchiefs. T **180** and similar horiz designs showing different kerchiefs. W **51** (sideways). P 14.

520	125000l. multicoloured	70	30
521	200000l. multicoloured	1·10	60
522	265000l. multicoloured	1·40	1·60
523	350000l. multicoloured	2·00	3·00
520/3	*Set of 4*	4·75	5·00

181 Lusignan House, Lefkosa

(Des Hüseyin Billur)

2001 (28 Mar). Restoration of Historic Buildings. T **181** and similar horiz design. Multicoloured. W **51** (sideways). P 13½×14.

524	125000l. Type **181**	1·25	50
525	200000l. The Eaved House, Lefkosa	2·00	2·50

182 "Cuprum Kuprum Bakir Madeni" (Inci Kansu)

183 Degirmenlik Reservoir

2001 (30 Mar). Modern Art. T **182** and similar multicoloured designs. W **51** (sideways on horiz designs). P 14×13½ (350000l) or 13½×14 (others).

526	125000l. Type **182**	1·00	30
527	200000l. "Varolus" (Emel Samioglu)	1·60	45
528	350000l. "Ask Kuslara Ucar" (Ozden Selenge) (*vert*)	2·25	3·00
529	400000l. "Suyun Yolculugu" (Ayhatun Atesin)	2·25	3·00
526/9	*Set of 4*	6·25	6·00

2001 (31 May). Europa. Water Resources. T **183** and similar vert design. Multicoloured. W **51**. P 14×13½.

530	200000l. Type **183**	1·25	30
531	500000l. The Waters of Sinar	2·00	2·75

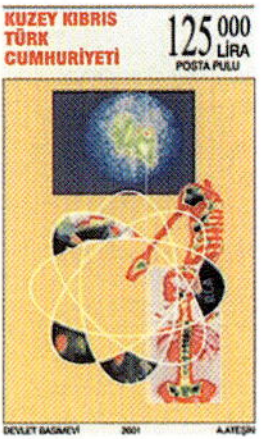

184 Atomic Symbol and X-ray

185 Ottoman Policeman, 1885

(Des Ayhatun Atesin)

2001 (22 June). World Environment Day. Radiation. T **184** and similar vert design. Multicoloured. W **51**. P 14.

532	125000l. Type **184**	75	20
533	450000l. Radiation symbol and x-ray of hand	2·25	3·00

(Des Hüseyin Billur)

2001 (24 Aug). Turkish Cypriot Police Uniforms. T **185** and similar vert designs. Multicoloured. W **51**. P 14.

534	125000l. Type **185**	1·25	50
535	200000l. Colonial policeman, 1933	2·00	80

536 500000l. Mounted policeman, 1934 .... 3·00 2·75
537 750000l. Policewoman, 1983 .... 4·00 5·00
534/7 *Set of 4* .... 9·25 8·00

186 MG TF Sports Car, 1954

187 Graduate at Top of Steps and College Names

(Des Hüseyin Billur)

2001 (21 Nov). Classic Cars. T **186** and similar horiz designs. Multicoloured. W **51** (sideways). P 14.

538 175000l. Type **186** .... 1·00 30
539 300000l. Vauxhall 14, 1948 .... 1·75 75
540 475000l. Bentley, 1922 .... 2·25 2·50
541 600000l. Jaguar XK 120, 1955 .... 2·50 3·25
538/41 *Set of 4* .... 6·75 6·00

2001 (24 Dec). Anniversaries. T **187** and similar design. W **51** (sideways on No. 542). P 13½×14 (horiz) or 14×13½ (vert).

542 200000l. multicoloured .... 1·60 1·60
543 200000l. black, magenta and yellow-brown .... 1·60 1·60

Designs: *Horiz*—No. 542, Type **187** (Centenary of Higher Education). *Vert*—No. 543, Book cover of *The Genocide Files* by Harry Scott Gibbons (Anniversary of publication).

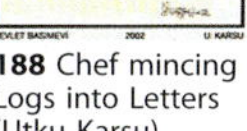

188 Chef mincing Logs into Letters (Utku Karsu)

189 Turtle

2002 (28 Feb). Caricatures. T **188** and similar multicoloured designs. W **51** (sideways on horiz design). P 13½×14 (No. 545) or 14×13½ (others).

544 250000l. Type **188** .... 1·25 40
545 300000l. Overfed people drinking from inflated cow, and starving children (Musa Kayra) (*horiz*) .... 1·40 55
546 475000l. Can of cola parachuting down to pregnant African woman (Serhan Gazi) .... 1·75 2·00
547 850000l. Artist painting trees in city (Mustafa Tozaki) .... 2·75 4·50
544/7 *Set of 4* .... 6·25 6·75

2002 (27 Mar). Tourism. Underwater Scenes. T **189** and similar horiz designs. Multicoloured. W **51** (sideways). P 13½×14.

548 250000l. Type **189** .... 1·25 45
549 300000l. Starfish on rock .... 1·40 60
550 500000l. Fish in rocks .... 1·90 1·90
551 750000l. Part of wreck .... 2·75 4·25
548/51 *Set of 4* .... 6·50 6·50

190 Stilt-walker

191 Turkish Football Team

(Des Hüseyin Billur)

2002 (27 May). Europa. Circus. Sheet, 79×72 mm, containing T **190** and similar vert design. Multicoloured. W **51** (inverted). P 13½.

MS552 600000l. Type **190**; 600000l. Child on high wire 4·25 5·00

2002 (24 June). World Cup Football Championship, Japan and Korea (2002). T **191** and similar horiz design. Multicoloured. W **51** (sideways). P 13½×14.

553 300000l. Type **191** .... 1·25 30
554 1000000l. Football Stadium, World Cup Trophy and footballer .... 3·25 3·75

192 Woman in White Tunic and Trousers

193 "Accident by Bridge" (Mehmet Ali Alpdogan)

(Des Hüseyin Billur)

2002 (8 Aug). Traditional Costumes. T 192 and similar vert designs. Multicoloured. W **51**. P 14×13½.

555 250000l. Type **192** .... 1·25 35
556 300000l. Man wearing grey jacket .... 1·40 55
557 425000l. Man in blue jacket and trousers .... 2·00 2·00
558 700000l. Woman in yellow tunic .... 3·50 4·50
555/8 *Set of 4* .... 7·25 6·75

2002 (30 Sept). Children's Paintings. T **193** and similar multicoloured designs. W w **51** (sideways on 300000l.). P 13½.

559 300000l. Type **193** .... 1·25 60
560 600000l. "Burning House" (Sercan avci) (*vert*) .... 2·50 3·50

194 Sureyya Ayhan (athlete)

195 Oguz Karayel (footballer) (70th birth anniv)

2002 (28 Oct). Sporting Celebrities. T **194** and similar vert design. Multicoloured. W **51** (inverted). P 14×13½.

561 300000l. Type **194** .... 1·00 40
562 1000000l. Grand Master Park Jung-tae (taekwon-do) .... 2·50 3·75

(Des Hüseyin Billur)

2002 (3 Dec). Celebrities' Anniversaries. T **195** and similar multicoloured designs. W **51** (sideways on No. 566, inverted on others). P 13½×14 (No. 566) or 13½×14 (others).

563 100000l. Type **195** 55 15
564 175000l. Mete Adanir (footballer) (40th birth anniv) 85 40
565 300000l. M. Necati Ozkan (30th death anniv) .... 1·50 90
566 575000l. Osman Turkay (astronomer) (1st death anniv) (*horiz*) .... 2·75 4·50
563/6 *Set of 4* .... 5·00 5·50

196 Untitled Painting by Salih Bayraktar

197 Tree containing Meadow and Forest in Polluted Industrial Landscape

2003 (21 Feb). Art (14th series). T **196** and similar vert design. Multicoloured. W **51**. P 14×13½.

567	250000l. Type **196**	1·25	50
568	1000000l. Untitled painting of woman's head (Feryal Sükan)	3·00	4·00

(Des Hüseyin Billur)

2003 (8 May). Europa. Poster Art. Sheet, 78×72 mm, containing T **197** and similar vert design. Multicoloured. W **51**. P 14×13½.

MS569	600000l. Type **197**; 600000l. Question mark containing wildlife in polluted Landscape	2·75	3·50

198 Cyprus Wheatear

199 Carved Wooden Chest

(Des Hüseyin Billur)

2003 (30 June). World Environment Day. Birds. T **198** and similar multicoloured designs. W **51** (sideways on horiz designs). P 13½×14 (horiz) or 14×13½ (vert).

570	100000l. Type **198**	90	55
571	300000l. Cyprus Warbler	1·75	85
572	500000l. Pygmy Cormorant (*vert*)	2·50	3·00
573	600000l. Greater Flamingo (*vert*)	2·50	3·00
570/3	*Set of 4*	7·00	6·75

2003 (25 July). Wooden Chests. T **199** and similar horiz designs. Multicoloured. W **51** (sideways). P 13½×14.

574	250000l. Type **199**	50	25
575	300000l. Chest carved with circular designs	60	30
576	525000l. Chest carved with turquoise-blue figures	1·00	1·25
577	1000000l. Chest carved with flower heads and white birds	1·75	3·00
574/7	*Set of 4*	3·50	4·25

200 *Gladiolus triphyllus*

201 Kemal Atatürk and Flag of Turkish Republic of Northern Cyprus

(Des Hüseyin Billur)

2003 (21 Oct). Flowers. T **200** and similar vert designs. Multicoloured. W **51**. P 14×13½.

578	150000l. Type **200**	40	20
579	175000l. *Tulipa cypria*	60	45
580	500000l. *Ranunculus asiaticus*	1·25	1·75
581	525000l. *Narcissus tazetta*	1·25	1·75
578/81	*Set of 4*	3·25	3·75

(Des Hüseyin Billur)

2003 (14 Nov). Political Anniversaries. T **201** and similar horiz design. Multicoloured. W **51** (sideways). P 13½×14.

582	3000000l. Type **201** (20th anniv of proclamation of Turkish Republic of Northern Cyprus)	3·25	4·00
	a. Pair. Nos. 582/3	6·50	8·00
583	3000000l. Kemal Atatürk and Turkish flag (80th anniv of Republic of Turkey)	3·25	4·00

Nos. 582/3 were printed together, *se-tenant*, in horizontal and vertical pairs in sheets of 40.

202 Horse-drawn Plough and Modern Farm Machinery

2003 (12 Dec). Anniversaries. T **202** and similar horiz design. Multicoloured. W **51** (sideways). P 13½×14.

584	300000l. Type **202** (60th anniv of International Federation of Agricultural Producers)	75	40
585	500000l. Emblem (40th anniv of Lions Clubs in Cyprus)	1·25	1·60

203 Post Office and Pillar Box

(Des Hüseyin Billur)

2004 (30 Apr). 40th Anniv of Turkish Cyprus Postal Services. T **203** and similar horiz design. Multicoloured. W **51** (sideways). P 13½×14.

586	250000l. Type **203**	40	25
587	1500000l. Globe and winged envelopes	2·00	2·75

204 Beach and Harbour Scenes

2004 (25 May). Europa. Holidays. Sheet 72×75 mm containing T **204** and similar horiz design. Multicoloured. Perf and Imperf. W **51** (sideways). P 13½×14.

MS588	600000l. Type **204**; 600000l. Seated woman with drink and beachside café	3·25	3·75

205 Pack Animals and Caravanserai

206 *Salvia veneris*

2004 (7 June). Silk Road. W **51** (sideways). P 13½×14.

589	**205** 300000l. multicoloured	1·00	70

(Des Hüseyin Billur)

2004 (9 July). Plants. T **206** and similar vert designs. Multicoloured. W **51** (inverted on 250000l.). P 14×13½.

590	250000l. Type **206**	40	25
591	300000l. *Phlomis cypria*	50	30
592	500000l. *Pimpinella cypria*	90	1·00
593	600000l. *Rosularia cypria*	1·10	1·60
590/3	*Set of 4*	2·50	2·75

207 Inside Stadium

208 Footballer

2004 (28 Aug). 50th Anniv of UEFA (Union of European Football Associations). T **207** and similar horiz design. Multicoloured. W **51** (sideways). P 14.

594	300000l. Type **207**	60	30
595	1000000l. View from top of stadium	1·90	2·50

(Des Gamze Anil)

2004 (24 Sept). Olympic Games, Athens. T **208** and similar vert designs. Multicoloured. W **51** (inverted). P 14.

596	300000l. Type **208**	65	75
	a. Horiz pair. Nos. 596/7	1·25	1·50
597	300000l. Boxing and horse riding	65	75
598	500000l. Weight lifting and gymnastics	1·00	1·40
	a. Horiz pair. No. 598/9	2·00	2·75
599	500000l. Pole vaulting and tennis	1·00	1·40
596/9 *Set of 4*		3·00	4·00

Nos. 596/7 and 598/9, respectively, were each printed together, *se-tenant*, in horizontal pairs with the backgrounds forming composite designs.

(New Currency. 100 yeni kurus = 1 yeni lira)

209 Students Celebrating

(Des Gamze Anil (15, 30ykr), Serkan Saçildi (50ykr))

2005 (15 Feb). Anniversaries. T **209** and similar horiz designs. Multicoloured. W **51** (sideways). P 14.

600	15ykr. Type **209** (25th anniv of Eastern Mediterranean University, Gazimagusa)	35	30
601	30ykr. Eye and outlines of stamps (25th anniv of Cyprus Turkish Philatelic Association)	65	65
602	50ykr. Turtle emblem and outline map (www.studyinnorthcyprus.org)	95	1·25
600/2 *Set of 3*		1·75	2·00

210 Stylized Dinghy

211 Boy and Girl in Orchard (Elmaziye Demirci)

(Des Görel Korol Sönmezer)

2005 (9 Mar). Tourism. T **210** and similar horiz design. Multicoloured. W **51** (sideways). P 14.

603	10ykr. Type **210**	20	20
604	1ytl. Temple ruins, setting sun and windsurfer	1·50	2·00

2005 (22 Apr). Children's Paintings. T **211** and similar vert design. Multicoloured. W **51** (inverted). P 14.

605	25ykr. Type **211**	55	45
606	50ykr. Couple (Elçim Öztemiz)	1·10	1·40

212 Brick Oven and Table laden with Food

213 *Dianthus cyprius*

(Des Hüseyin Billur)

2005 (30 May). Europa. Gastronomy. T **212** and similar horiz designs. Multicoloured. W **51** (sideways). P 14.

607	60ykr. Type **212**	80	1·00
	a. Pair. Nos. 607/8	1·60	2·00
608	60ykr. Table laden with food and wine	80	1·00
MS609	113×77 mm. Nos. 607/8, each ×2	2·75	3·50

Nos. 607/8 were printed together, *se-tenant*, in horizontal and vertical pairs in sheets of 40.

(Des Hüseyin Billur)

2005 (8 July). Endemic and Medicinal Plants. T **213** and similar vert designs. Multicoloured. W **51** (inverted on 15, 25ykr.). P 14.

610	15ykr. Type **213**	35	25
611	25ykr. *Delphinium caseyi*	50	35
612	30ykr. *Brassica hilarionis*	55	50
613	50ykr. *Limonium albidum ssp. cyprium*	95	1·40
610/13 *Set of 4*		2·10	2·25

214 Olive Branches and Sun Umbrellas

215 Ercan Airport

(Des Görel Korol Sönmezer)

2005 (9 Sept). Cultural and Art Activities. T **214** and similar horiz designs. Multicoloured. W **51** (sideways). P 14.

614	10ykr. Type **214** (International Olive Festival, Girne)	20	20
615	25ykr. Lala Mustafa Pasa Mosque and musical notes (International Culture and Art Festival, Gazimagusa)	50	35
616	50ykr. Folk dancers and Kyrenia Gate (International Folk Dances Festival, Lefkosa)	85	1·10
617	1ytl. Masks and stage (International Cyprus Theatre Festival)	1·50	2·00
614/17 *Set of 4*		2·75	3·25

(Des Özge Luricinali)

2005 (23 Nov). Developments. T **215** and similar multicoloured designs. W **51** (inverted on 50ykr, sideways on 1ytl.). P 14.

618	50ykr. Type **215**	95	1·10
619	1ytl. Emblem and Middle East Technical University Northern Cyprus Campus, Güzelyurt (horiz)	1·50	2·00

216 Outline Map of Cyprus

217 *Helianthemum obtusifolium*

2006 (6 Jan). 50th Anniv of First Europa Stamp. T **216** and similar horiz design. Multicoloured. W **51** (sideways). P 13½×14.

620	1ytl40 Type **216**	2·00	2·50
621	1ytl40 View of Cyprus from satellite orbiting Earth	2·00	2·50
MS622	83×78 mm. Nos. 620/1	4·25	5·00

MS622 also exists imperforate.

(Des Hüseyin Billur)

2006 (28 Feb). Wild Flowers. T **217** and similar multicoloured designs. W **51** (sideways on horiz designs). P 14.

623	15ykr. Type **217**	35	25
624	25ykr. *Iris sisyrhinchium* (horiz)	50	35
625	40ykr. *Ranunculus asiaticus* (horiz)	80	1·10
626	50ykr. *Crocus veneris* (horiz)	95	1·25
627	60ykr. *Anemone coronaria* (horiz)	1·00	1·40
628	70ykr. *Cyclamen persicum*	1·10	1·60
623/8 *Set of 6*		4·25	5·50

218 "Adaption of a Woman's Figure to an Amphora" (ceramic by Semral Oztan)

219 Birds (Selma Gürani)

2006 (7 Apr). Art (15th series). T **218** and similar vert design. Multicoloured. W **51** (inverted). P 14.

629	55ykr. Type **218**	1·00	1·40
630	60ykr. "Female Figures" (Mustafa Hastürk)	1·00	1·40

2006 (18 May). Europa. Integration. T **219** and similar vert design showing winning entries in thematic drawing competition for high school students. Multicoloured. W **51**. P 14.

631	70ykr. Type **219**	1·25	1·50
632	70ykr. Pregnant woman and flags of many nations (Suzan Özcan)	1·25	1·50
MS633	78×72 mm. Nos. 631/2	2·50	3·00

No. **MS**633 was also available imperforate.

220 Dr. Fazil Küçük

221 Mustafa Kemal Atatürk

2006 (18 May). Birth Centenary of Dr. Fazil Küçük (Deputy President (1959–73) of Republic of Cyprus). W **51**. P 14.

634	**220** 40ykr. multicoloured	1·25	1·00

2006 (18 May). 125th Birth Anniv of Mustafa Kemal Atatürk (first President (1923–38) of Turkey). W **51**. P 14.

635	**221** 1ytl. multicoloured	2·00	2·25

222 World Cup Trophy and Map of Germany

223 Lapwing

(Des Görel Korol Sönmezer)

2006 (7 July). World Cup Football Championship, Germany. T **222** and similar vert design. Multicoloured. W **51** (inverted). P 14.

636	50ykr. Type **222**	75	1·25
	a. Pair. Nos. 636/7	2·25	3·00
637	1ytl. Football, player and Brandenburg Gate, Berlin	1·50	1·75

Nos. 636/7 were printed together, *se-tenant*, in horizontal and vertical pairs in sheets of 16 stamps.

(Des Hüseyin Billur)

2006 (22 Sept). Birds. T **223** and similar vert designs. Multicoloured. W **51** (inverted on 40ykr., 1ytl.). P 14.

638	40ykr. Type **223**	1·25	80
639	50ykr. Mallard	1·40	1·00
640	60ykr. Kingfisher	1·75	1·60
641	1ytl. Black-winged stilt	2·75	3·25
638/41	*Set of 4*	6·50	6·00

224 Trees ("Protect our Forests against Fire")

225 Naci Talat

(Des Görel Korol Sönmezer)

2006 (10 Nov). Anniversaries and Events. T **224** and similar diamond-shaped design. Multicoloured. W **51** (inverted on 1ytl.50). P 14.

642	50ykr. Type **224**	1·00	75
643	1ytl.50 Yachts (Eastern Mediterranean Yacht Rally)	2·25	3·00

2006 (10 Nov). 15th Death Anniv of Naci Talat (former General Secretary of Turkish Cypriot Republican Turkish Party). W **51**. P 14.

644	**225** 70ykr. multicoloured	1·00	1·00

226 Skeletal Leaf

227 Ewer

(Des Görel Korol Sönmezer)

2007 (19 Feb). International Conference on Environment: Survival and Sustainability, Lefkosa. T **226** and similar vert design. Multicoloured. W **51**. P 14.

645	50ykr. Type **226**	1·00	75
646	80ykr. Red globe and parched ground	1·40	1·75

(Des Görel Korol Sönmezer)

2007 (6 Apr). Antique Household Utensils. T **227** and similar multicoloured designs. W **51** (sideways on horiz designs; inverted on vert). P 13½×14 (horiz) or 14×13½ (vert).

647	70ykr. Type **227**	1·00	1·00
648	80ykr. Coal iron	1·40	1·50
649	1ytl.50 Oil lamp (vert)	2·25	2·75
650	2ytl. Coffee pot on stove (vert)	3·50	4·00
647/50	*Set of 4*	7·25	8·25

228 Scout and Camp in Countryside

229 Painting by Osman Keten

(Des Hüseyin Billur)

2007 (4 May). Europa. Centenary of Scouting. T **228** and similar vert design. Multicoloured. W **51**. P 14×13½.

651	80ykr. Type **228**	2·25	2·25
652	80ykr. Three scouts playing music	2·25	2·25
MS653	79×73 mm. Nos. 651/2. Wmk inverted. Imperf	4·50	4·50

2007 (12 July). Art (16th series). T **229** and similar multicoloured design. W **51** (sideways on horiz design). P 14.

654	50ykl. Type **229**	1·00	80
655	70ykl. 'FRAGMENT CITY INTEGRI CITY' (Senih Çavuşoğlu) (horiz)	1·25	1·25

230 Chair-caner

231 Post Pigeon and Pigeon carrying Letter

(Des Hüseyin Billur)

2007 (14 Sept). Crafts. T **230** and similar horiz designs. Multicoloured. W **51** (sideways). P 13½×14.

656 40ykr. Type **230** 70 70
657 65ykr. Barrow man .... 90 1·25
658 70ykr. Cobbler .... 1·00 1·25
659 1ytl. Shoeshine man .... 1·75 2·00
656/9 *Set of 4* .... 4·00 4·75

(Des Görel Korol Sönmezer. Litho State Ptg Wks, Lefkosa)

2007 (16 Nov). Post Office Past and Present. T **231** and similar multicoloured designs. W **51** (inverted on 50ykr., sideways on horiz designs). P 14.

660 50ykr. Type **231** .... 1·00 80
661 60ykr. Mounted postman and early motor vehicles .... 1·25 1·00
662 1ytl. Postman on bicycle and wall letterbox (horiz) .... 2·00 2·50
663 1ytl.25 Modern postman on moped and postbox (horiz) .... 2·25 3·00
660/3 *Set of 4* .... 6·00 6·50

232 *Asphodelus aestivus*

233 Woman writing Letter

(Des Görel Korol Sönmezer (25, 60, 80ykr., 2ytl.20, 5ytl.) or Hüseyin Billur (others))

2008 (20 Mar). Wild Flowers. T **232** and similar vert designs. Multicoloured. W **51**. P 14.

664 25ykr. Type **232** 50 40
665 50ykr. *Ophrys fusca* ssp. *iricolor* .... 1·00 80
666 60ykr. *Bellis perennis* .... 1·50 90
667 70ykr. *Ophrys sphegodes* .... 1·50 1·25
668 80ykr. *Dianthus strictus* .... 1·75 1·75
669 1ytl.60 *Ophrys argolica* ssp. *elegans* .... 2·50 2·25
670 2ytl.20 *Crocus cyprius* .... 4·00 3·50
671 3ytl. *Limodorum abortivum* .... 6·00 6·00
672 5ytl. *Carlina pygmaea* .... 9·00 9·50
673 10ytl. *Ophrys kotschyi* .... 18·00 20·00
664/73 *Set of 10* .... 42·00 42·00

(Des Görel Korol Sönmezer)

2008 (8 May). Europa. The Letter. T **233** and similar vert design. Multicoloured. W **51** (inverted). P 14×13½.

674 80ykr. Type **233** .... 1·75 2·00
675 80ykr. World map and fragments of printed paper .... 1·75 2·00

234 Diver

(Des Görel Korol Sönmezer. Litho State Ptg Works, Lefkosa)

2008 (24 July). Olympic Games, Beijing. Sheet 78×73 mm containing T **234** and similar vert design. Multicoloured. W **51** (inverted). P 14.

MS676 65ykr. Type **234**; 65ykr. Gymnast .... 4·25 4·25

No. **MS**676 also exists imperforate.

235 Anniversary Emblem

(Des Görel Korol Sönmezer. Litho State Ptg Works, Lefkosa)

2008 (1 Aug). 50th Anniv of Türk Mukavemet Teskîlati'nin (Turkish resistance organization). Sheet containing T **235** and similar horiz design. Multicoloured. W **51** (sideways). Imperf.

MS677 1ytl. Type **235**; 1ytl. Monument .... 6·25 6·25

236 Council Buildings

(Des Görel Korol Sönmezer (55, 80ykr., 1ytl.50). Litho State Ptg Works, Lefkosa)

2008 (18 Sept). Anniversaries and Events. T **236** and similar multicoloured designs. W **51** (sideways on 1ytl.). P 14×13½ (vert) or 13½×14 (horiz).

678 55ykr. Type **236** (50th anniv of Lefkosa Turkish Municipality) .... 1·40 1·10
679 80ykr. Gateway and emblems (Inner Wheel) .... 2·50 2·00
680 1ytl. Airliner (35th anniv of Cyprus Turkish Airlines) (horiz) .... 2·75 2·75
681 1ytl.50 Landing of Turkish forces, 1974 (32nd anniv of Turkish Federated State of Northern Cyprus) .... 3·50 3·50
678/81 *Set of 4* .... 9·00 8·50

237 Coin

(Des Görel Korol Sönmezer. Litho State Ptg Wks, Lefkosa)

2008 (15 Nov). 25th Anniv of the Establishment of the Turkish Republic of Northern Cyprus. W **51**. P 14.

682 **237** 1ytl. multicoloured .... 2·75 2·75

238 Halit Karabina (upholsterer)

(Des Hüseyin Billur. Litho State Ptg Wks, Lefkosa)

2008 (20 Nov). The Masters and the Craftsmen. T **238** and similar horiz designs. Multicoloured. W **51** (sideways). P 13½×14.

683 60ykr. Type **238** .... 1·50 1·25

684 70ykr. Burhan Bardak (oil miller) .... 1·75 1·75
685 80ykr. Kemal Köse (bicycle repairer) .... 2·00 2·00
686 2ytl. Kemal Sah (circumciser) .... 5·00 6·00
683/6 *Set of 4* .... 9·25 10·00

239 Gold Brooch

(Des Görel Korol Sönmezer. Litho State Ptg Wks, Lefkosa)

2009 (23 Mar). The Golden Leaves of Soli Exhibition, Museum of Archaeology and Nature, Güzelyurt. T **239** and similar horiz design. Multicoloured. W **51** (sideways). P 13½.

687 60ykr. Type **239** .... 1·50 1·10
688 2ytl. Golden leaves .... 5·50 6·00

240 Galaxy and Comet

(Des Hüseyin Bíllur. Litho State Ptg Wks, Lefkosa)

2009 (5 May). Europa. Astronomy. T **240** and similar horiz design. Multicoloured. W **51** (sideways). P 13½.

689 80ykr. Type **240** .... 2·25 2·25
a. Horiz pair. Nos. 689/90 .... 4·50 4·50
690 80ykr. Solar system .... 2·25 2·25

Nos. 689/90 were printed together, *se-tenant*, as horizontal and vertical pairs in sheets of 40.

241 *Cistus creticus*

(Des Hüseyin Billur. Litho State Ptg Wks, Lefkosa)

2009 (9 July). Medicinal Plants. T **241** and similar vert designs. Multicoloured. W **51**. P 13½.

691 50ykr. Type **241** .... 1·50 1·00
692 60ykr. *Capparis spinosa* .... 1·60 1·25
693 70ykr. *Pancratium maritimum* .... 1·90 1·75
694 1ytl. *Passiflora caerulea* .... 3·00 3·50
691/4 *Set of 4* .... 7·25 6·75

242 *Agama stellio*

(Des Görel Korol Sönmezer. Litho State Ptg Wks, Lefkosa)

2009 (14 Sept). Fauna. T **242** and similar triangular design. Multicoloured. W **51** (sideways). P 13.

695 80ykr. Type **242** .... 2·75 2·75
696 1ytl.50 *Bufo viridis* (toad) .... 4·75 5·00

243 Control Tower and Aircraft

(Des Görel Korol Sönmezer. Litho State Ptg Wks, Lefkosa)

2009 (12 Nov). 'Our Institutions and Foundations'. T **243** and similar multicoloured designs. W **51** (sideways on 65ykr.). P 13½×14 (horiz) or 14×13½ (vert).

697 65ykr. Type **243** (CTATCA Cyprus Turkish Air Traffic Controllers) .... 2·00 1·50
698 1ytl. Open door leading to globe and ktto emblems (Turkish Cypriot Chamber of Commerce) (*vert*) .... 3·00 3·00
699 1ytl.50 Ziya Rizki (Ziya Rizki Vakfi) (*vert*) .... 4·50 4·50
697/9 *Set of 3* .... 8·50 8·00

244 Islamic Architecture, Emblem, Flag and Outline Map

(Des Görel Korol Sönmezer. Litho State Ptg Wks, Lefkosa)

2010 (17 Mar). 34th Anniv of Representation of Turkish Cyprus at Organization of Islamic Conference. T **244** and similar vert design. Multicoloured. W **51**. P 14×13½.

700 70ykr. Type **244** .... 2·25 2·25
701 1ytl. Arch, emblem and minaret .... 3·00 3·00

245 Girls reading (Nadide Keles)

(Litho State Ptg Wks, Lefkosa)

2010 (28 May). Europa. Children's Books. T **245** and similar horiz design showing children's paintings. Multicoloured. W **51** (sideways). P 13½×14.

702 80ykr. Type **245** .... 2·25 2·25
a. Pair. Nos. 702/3 .... 4·50 4·50
703 80ykr. Girl reading with book characters at her shoulders (Afet Deniz) .... 2·25 2·25

Nos. 702/3 were printed together, *se-tenant*, as horizontal and vertical pairs in sheetlets of 16.

Nos. 702/3 were also issued in vertical panes of 4 containing two vertical pairs of Nos. 702/3, attached by the selvedge to an illustrated card and sold for 4ytl., a premium of 80ykr. over the face value. Stamps from these panes have imperforate vertical edges.

246 *Larus audouinii*

(Des Hüseyin Billur. Litho State Ptg Wks, Lefkosa)

2010 (4 June). Endangered Species. Seagulls. T **246** and similar horiz designs. Multicoloured. W **51** (sideways). P 14.

704 25ykr. Type **246** .... 1·00 70
705 25ykr. *Larus melanocephalus* .... 1·00 70
706 30ykr. *Larus ridibundus* .... 1·25 1·00
707 30ykr. *Larus genei* .... 1·25 1·00
704/7 *Set of 4* .... 4·00 3·00

247 World Cup Trophy and Crowd

(Des Görel Korol Sönmezer. Litho State Ptg Wks, Lefkosa)

2010 (8 July). World Cup Football Championship, South Africa. T **247** and similar vert design. Multicoloured. W 51 (inverted). P 14×13½.

708	50ykr. Type **247**	1·50	1·00
709	2ytl. Footballer, South African flag, elephants and mascot	6·00	6·00

247a Kemal Asik

2010 (1 Sept). Journalists. T **247a** and similar vert designs. Multicoloured. Litho. W **51** (inverted on 70, 80ykr., 1ytl.). P 14.

709*a*	60ykr. Type **247a**	1·50	1·25
709*b*	70ykr. Abdi Ipekçi	1·75	1·75
709*c*	80ykr. Adem Yavuz	2·50	2·00
709*d*	1ytl. Sedat Simavi	2·75	2·75
709*a/d* *Set of 4*		8·50	7·75

248 *Bozcaada* (ferry) and Temple Ruins

(Des Görel Korol Sönmezer. Litho State Ptg Wks, Lefkosa)

2010 (20 Oct). Passenger Ships which Sail to Cyprus. T **248** and similar horiz design. Multicoloured. W **51** (sideways). P 13½×14.

710	1ytl.50 Type **248**	4·50	4·50
711	2ytl. *Yesilada* (ferry)	6·00	6·00

249 Özdemir Sennaroglu

(Des Görel Korol Sönmezer. Litho State Ptg Wks, Lefkosa)

2010 (24 Dec). Personalities. T **249** and similar vert designs. Multicoloured. W **51** (sideways). P 14×13½.

712	50ykr. Type **249**	1·75	1·25
713	60ykr. Osman Örek	2·25	2·25
714	70ykr. Salih Miroglu	2·50	2·50
715	80ykr. Özker Özgür	2·75	2·75
712/15 *Set of 4*		9·25	8·75

250 University Building and Arms

(Des Görel Korol Sönmezer. Litho State Ptg Wks, Lefkosa)

2010 (24 Dec). 25th Anniv of Girne American University. W **51** (sideways). P 13½×14.

716	**250**	1ytl. multicoloured	3·00	3·00

251 Dr. Niyazi Manyera

(Des Hüseyin Billur. Litho State Ptg Wks, Lefkosa)

2011 (9 Mar). Turkish Cypriot Vice President and Government Ministers. T **251** and similar vert designs. Multicoloured. W **51**. P 14×13½.

717	80ykr. Type **251** (Minister of Health 1963–74).	2·25	2·25
718	1ytl.10 Mustafa Fazil Plümer (Agriculture Minister, Republic of Cyprus, 1960–3)	3·25	3·50
719	2ytl. Osman Örek (Prime Minister of Northern Cyprus 1978)	5·50	6·00
720	2ytl.20 Dr. Fazil Küçük (Vice President, Republic of Cyprus, 1960–3)	6·50	6·75
717/20 *Set of 4*		17·00	18·00

252 Ayios Philon Church

(Des Görel Korol Sönmezer. Litho State Ptg Wks, Lefkosa)

2011 (18 Apr). Tourism. T **252** and similar multicoloured designs. W **51** (sideways on horiz designs). P 13½×14 (horiz) or 14×13½ (vert).

721	50ykr. Type **252**	1·75	1·25
722	80ykr. Ruins of Salamis (vert)	2·75	2·75
723	1ytl.10 Ruins	3·00	3·00
724	2ytl. Apostolos Andreas Monastery and Karpaz Peninsula (vert)	6·75	6·75
721/4 *Set of 4*		12·00	12·00

253 Log and Forest

(Des Görel Korol Sönmezer. Litho State Press Office, Lefkosa)

2011 (16 May). Europa. Forests. T **253** and similar vert design. Multicoloured. W **51** (inverted). P 14×13½.

725	1ytl.50 Type **253**	5·25	5·25
726	1ytl.50 Pine cone and forest	5·25	5·25
MS727 77×72 mm. Nos. 725/6		10·00	10·00

254 Prince William and Miss Catherine Middleton

(Litho State Ptg Wks, Lefkosa)

2011 (27 May). Royal Wedding. W **51** (inverted). P 14×13½.

728	**254**	1ytl. multicoloured	3·00	3·00

STAMP BOOKLETS

Following the inauguration of the Turkish Cypriot postal service in 1974 several postmasters continued to use the covers previously supplied by the Cyprus Post Office in conjunction with Turkish Cypriot Posts issues.

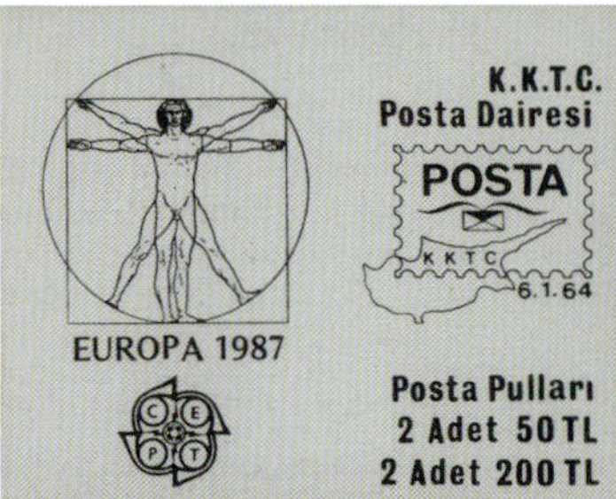

B **1**

1987 (30 June). Europa. Modern. Architecture. Black on bluish grey cover, 61×50 mm, showing Europa symbols. Pane attached by selvedge.

SB1	500l. booklet containing *se-tenant* pane of 4 (No. 210ab)	9·00

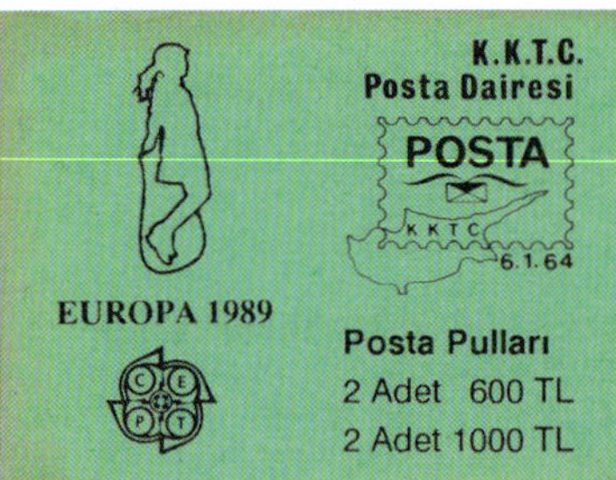

B **2**

1989 (31 May). Europa. Children's Games. Black on pale blue-green cover, 62×48 mm, showing Europa symbols. Pane attached by selvedge.

SB2	3200l. booklet containing *se-tenant* pane of 4 (No. 251ab)	9·00

Gibraltar

CROWN COLONY

Early details of postal arrangements in Gibraltar are hard to establish, although it is known that postal facilities were provided by the Civil Secretary's Office from 1749. Gibraltar became a packet port in July 1806, although the Civil Secretary's office continued to be responsible for other mail. The two services were amalgamated on 1 January 1857 as a Branch Office of the British G.P.O., the control of the postal services not reverting to Gibraltar until 1 January 1886.

Spanish stamps could be used at Gibraltar from their introduction in 1850 and, indeed, such franking was required on letters weighing over ½ oz. sent to Spain after 1 July 1854. From 1 July 1856 until 1 January 1876 all mail to Spain required postage to be prepaid by Spanish stamps and these issues were supplied by the Gibraltar postal authorities, acting as a Spanish Postal Agent. The mail forwarded under this system was cancelled at San Roque with a horizontal barred oval, later replaced by a cartwheel type mark showing numeral 63. From 1857 combination covers showing the 2d. ship mail fee paid in British stamps and the inland postage by Spanish issues exist.

Stamps of Great Britain were issued for use in Gibraltar from 3 September 1857 (earliest recorded cover is dated 7 September 1857) to the end of 1885.

The initial supply contained 1d., 4d. and 6d. values. No supplies of the 2d. or 1s. were sent until the consignment of October 1857. No other values were supplied until early 1862.

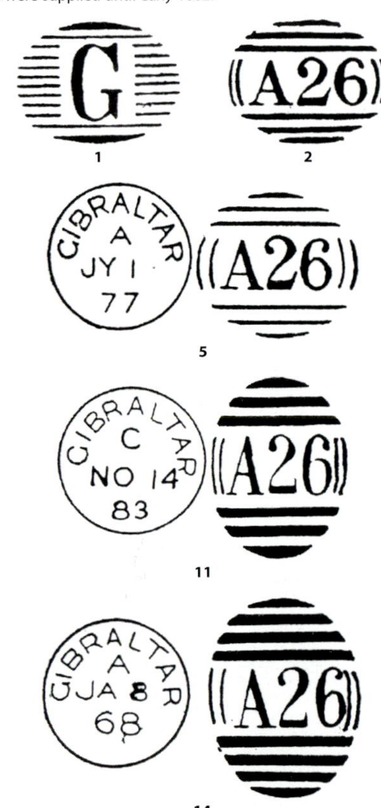

1 2 5 11 14

Stamps of GREAT BRITAIN cancelled "G" as Type **1** (3 Sept 1857 to 19 Feb 1859).

Z1	1d. red-brown (1854) Die I, *wmk* Small Crown, *perf* 16	£425
Z2	1d. red-brown (1855), Die II, *wmk* Small Crown, *perf* 16	£750
Z3	1d. red-brown (1855), Die II, *wmk* Small Crown *perf* 14	£375
Z4	1d. red-brown (1855), Die II, *wmk* Large Crown, *perf* 14	95·00
Z5	1d. rose-red (1857), Die II, *wmk* Large Crown, *perf* 14	25·00
Z6	2d. blue (1855), *wmk* Small Crown, *perf* 14	£475

Z7	2d. blue (1855–58), *wmk* Large Crown, *perf* 16	£400
Z8	2d. blue (1855), *wmk* Large Crown, *perf* 14 *From*	75·00
	Plate Nos. 5, 6.	
Z9	2d. blue (1858) (Plate No. 7)	£350
Z10	4d. rose (1857)	60·00
	a. Thick glazed paper	
Z11	6d. lilac (1856)	42·00
Z12	6d. lilac (1856) (blued *paper*)	£850
Z13	1s. green (1856)	£120
	a. Thick paper	
Z14	1s. green (1856) (blued *paper*)	£1500

Stamps of GREAT BRITAIN cancelled "A 26" as in Types **2**, **5**, **11** or **14** (20 Feb 1859 to 31 Dec 1885).

Z15	½d. rose-red (1870–79) *From*	38·00
	Plate Nos. 4, 5, 6, 8, 10, 11, 12, 13, 14, 15, 19, 20.	
Z16	1d. red-brown (1841), *imperf*	£2000
Z17	1d. red-brown (1855), *wmk* Large Crown, *perf* 14	£250
Z18	1d. rose-red (1857), *wmk* Large Crown, *perf* 14	14·00
Z19	1d. rose-red (1864–79) *From*	23·00
	Plate Nos. 71, 72, 73, 74 ,76, 78, 79, 80, 81, 82, 83, 84, 85, 86, 87, 88, 89, 90, 91, 92, 93, 94, 95, 96, 97, 98, 99, 100, 101, 102, 103, 104, 105, 106, 107, 108, 109, 110, 111, 112, 113, 114, 115, 116, 117, 118, 119, 120, 121, 122, 123, 124, 125, 127, 129, 130, 131, 132, 133, 134, 135, 136, 137, 138, 139, 140, 141, 142, 143, 144, 145, 146, 147, 148, 149, 150, 151, 152, 153, 154, 155, 156, 157, 158, 159, 160, 161, 162, 163, 164, 165, 166, 167, 168, 169, 170, 171, 172, 173, 174, 175, 176, 177, 178, 179, 180, 181, 182, 183, 184, 185, 186, 187, 188, 189, 190, 191, 192, 193, 194, 195, 196, 197, 198, 199, 200, 201, 202, 203, 204, 205, 206, 207, 208, 209, 210, 211, 212, 213, 214, 215, 216, 217, 218, 219, 220, 221, 222, 223, 224, 225.	
Z20	1½d. lake-red (1870) (Plate No. 3)	£700
Z21	2d. blue (1855), *wmk* Large Crown, *perf* 14	£160
	Plate No. 6.	
Z22	2d. blue (1858–69) *From*	23·00
	Plate Nos. 7, 8, 9, 12, 13, 14, 15.	
Z23	2½d. rosy mauve (1875) (blued *paper*) *From*	£100
	Plate Nos. 1, 2, 3.	
Z24	2½d. rosy mauve (1875–76) *From*	30·00
	Plate Nos. 1, 2, 3.	
Z25	2½d. rosy mauve (*Error of Lettering*)	£2500
Z26	2½d. rosy mauve (1876–79) *From*	21·00
	Plate Nos. 3, 4, 5, 6, 7, 8, 9, 10, 11, 12, 13, 14, 15, 16, 17.	
Z27	2½d. blue (1880–81) *From*	13·00
	Plate Nos. 17, 18, 19, 20.	
Z28	2½d. blue (1881) (Plate Nos. 21, 22, 23) *From*	10·00
Z29	3d. carmine-rose (1862)	£300
Z30	3d. rose (1865) (Plate No. 4)	80·00
Z31	3d. rose (1867–73) *From*	55·00
	Plate Nos. 4, 5, 6, 7, 8, 9, 10.	
Z32	3d. rose (1873–76) *From*	75·00
	Plate Nos. 11, 12, 14, 15, 16, 17, 18, 19, 20.	
Z33	3d. rose (1881) (Plate Nos. 20, 21)	
Z34	3d. lilac (1883) (3d. *on* 3d.)	£180
Z35	4d. rose (1857)	95·00
Z36	4d. red (1862) (Plate Nos. 3, 4) *From*	48·00
Z37	4d. vermilion (1865–73) *From*	30·00
	Plate Nos. 7, 8, 9, 10, 11, 12, 13, 14.	
Z38	4d. vermilion (1876) (Plate No. 15)	£300
Z39	4d. sage-green (1877) (Plate Nos. 15, 16)	£130
Z40	4d. grey-brown (1880) *wmk* Large Garter	£375
	Plate No. 17.	
Z41	4d. grey-brown (1880) *wmk* Crown *From*	70·00
	Plate Nos. 17, 18.	
Z42	6d. lilac (1856)	42·00
Z43	6d. lilac (1862) (Plate Nos. 3, 4) *From*	40·00
Z44	6d. lilac (1865–67) (Plate Nos. 5, 6) *From*	35·00
Z45	6d. lilac (1867) (Plate No. 6)	48·00
Z46	6d. violet (1867–70) (Plate Nos. 6, 8, 9) *From*	32·00
Z47	6d. buff (1872–73) (Plate Nos. 11, 12) *From*	£150
Z48	6d. chestnut (1872) (Plate No. 11)	35·00
Z49	6d. grey (1873) (Plate No. 12)	95·00
Z50	6d. grey (1874–80) *From*	38·00
	Plate Nos. 13, 14, 15, 16, 17.	
Z51	6d. grey (1881) (Plate Nos. 17, 18)	£350
Z52	6d. lilac (1883) (6d. *on* 6d.)	£120
Z53	8d. orange (1876)	£700
Z54	9d. bistre (1862)	£400
Z55	9d. straw (1862)	£850
Z56	9d. straw (1865)	£800
Z57	9d. straw (1867)	£275
Z58	10d. red-brown (1867)	£150
Z59	1s. green (1856)	£110
Z60	1s. green (1862)	70·00
Z61	1s. green (1862) ("K" *variety*)	£2250
Z62	1s. green (1865) (Plate No. 4)	60·00
Z63	1s. green (1867–73) (Plate Nos. 4, 5, 6, 7) *From*	35·00
Z64	1s. green (1873–77) *From*	85·00
	Plate Nos. 8, 9, 10, 11, 12, 13.	
Z65	1s. orange-brown (1880) (Plate No. 13)	£450
Z66	1s. orange-brown (1881) *From*	£120
	Plate Nos. 13, 14.	
Z67	2s. blue (1867)	£300
Z68	5s. rose (1867) (Plate No. 1)	£1000

1880.

Z69	½d. deep green	29·00
Z70	½d. pale green	29·00
Z71	1d. Venetian red	28·00
Z72	1½d. Venetian red	£350
Z73	2d. pale rose	75·00
Z74	2d. deep rose	75·00
Z75	5d. indigo	£160

1881.

Z76	1d. lilac (14 *dots*)	38·00
Z77	1d. lilac (16 *dots*)	11·00

1884.

Z78	½d. slate-blue	29·00
Z79	2d. lilac	£120
Z80	2½d. lilac	19·00
Z81	3d. lilac	
Z82	4d. dull green	£200
Z83	6d. dull green	

POSTAL FISCAL

Z83*a*	1d. purple (Die 4) (1878) *wmk* Small Anchor	£700
Z84	1d. purple (1881), *wmk* Orb	£1100

PRICES FOR STAMPS ON COVER TO 1945

Nos.	1/2	*from* × 25
No.	3	*from* × 10
No.	4	*from* × 25
Nos.	5/6	*from* × 8
Nos.	7/33	*from* × 6
Nos.	39/45	*from* × 5
Nos.	46/109	*from* × 3
Nos.	110/13	*from* × 4
Nos.	114/17	*from* × 3
Nos.	118/20	*from* × 5
Nos.	121/31	*from* × 3

GIBRALTAR

(**1**)

1886 (1 Jan). Contemporary types of Bermuda optd with T **1** by D.L.R. Wmk Crown CA. P 14.

1	**9**	½d. dull green	18·00	9·50
2	**1**	1d. rose-red	80·00	4·50
3	**2**	2d. purple-brown	£140	80·00
		w. Wmk inverted		
4	**11**	2½d. ultramarine	£180	3·25
		a. Optd in blue-black	£500	£150
		w. Wmk inverted	—	£500
5	**10**	4d. orange-brown	£180	£100
6	**4**	6d. deep lilac	£300	£225
7	**5**	1s. yellow-brown	£450	£375
1/7 *Set of 7*			£1200	£700
1s/3s, 4as/7s Optd "SPECIMEN" *Set of 7*			£4000	

PRINTER. All Gibraltar stamps to No. 109 were typographed by De La Rue & Co, Ltd.

2 3

4 5

1886 (Nov)–**87**. Wmk Crown CA. P 14.

8	**2**	½d. dull green (1.87)	14·00	4·25
		w. Wmk inverted	†	£800
9	**3**	1d. rose (2.87)	50·00	4·75

10	4	2d. brown-purple (12.86)	30·00	27·00
		w. Wmk inverted	£700	
11	5	2½d. blue	80·00	3·00
		w. Wmk inverted	£325	75·00
12	4	4d. orange-brown (16.4.87)	85·00	80·00
13		6d. lilac (16.4.87)	£140	£130
14		1s. bistre (2.87)	£250	£200
		w. Wmk inverted		
8/14 *Set of 7*			£600	£400
8s/14s Optd "SPECIMEN" *Set of 7*			£500	

Examples of Nos. 3, 6/7 and 14 are known showing a forged Gibraltar postmark dated "JU-13 87".

See also Nos. 39/45.

5 CENTIMOS (6)

5 "5" with short foot (all stamps in 1st, 5th and 6th vertical columns (5c. on ½d.) or all stamps in 2nd vertical column (25c. on 2d., 25c. on 2½d., 50c. on 6d. and 75c. on 1s.)

1889 (1 Aug). Surch as T **6**.

15	2	5c. on ½d. green	8·00	29·00
		a. "5" with short foot	8·00	29·00
16	3	10c. on 1d. rose	13·00	16·00
17	4	25c. on 2d. brown-purple	4·75	11·00
		a. "5" with short foot	10·00	21·00
		ab. Small "I" (R. 6/2)	£100	£170
		b. Broken "N" (R. 10/5)	£100	£170
18	5	25c. on 2½d. bright blue	24·00	2·25
		a. "5" with short foot	42·00	5·00
		ab. Small "I" (R. 6/2)	£325	£100
		b. Broken "N" (R. 10/5)	£325	£100
19	4	40c. on 4d. orange-brown	55·00	75·00
20		50c. on 6d. bright lilac	55·00	75·00
		a. "5" with short foot	£130	£160
21		75c. on 1s. bistre	55·00	65·00
		a. "5" with short foot	£140	£160
15/21 *Set of 7*			£190	£225
15s/21s Optd "SPECIMEN" *Set of 7*			£375	

10c., 40c. and 50c. values from this issue and that of 1889–96 are known bisected and used for half their value from various post offices in Morocco (*price on cover from* £500). These bisects were never authorised by the Gibraltar Post Office.

Broken "M" (Pls 1 & 2 R. 4/5)

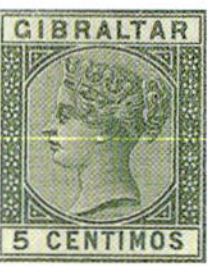

7

Flat top to "C" (Pl 2 R. 4/4)

1889 (8 Oct*)–**96**. Issue in Spanish currency. Wmk Crown CA. P 14.

22	7	5c. green	5·50	80
		a. Broken "M"	£180	80·00
		w. Wmk inverted	£275	£225
23		10c. carmine	4·50	50
		b. Value omitted	£6500	
24		20c. olive-green and brown (2.1.96)	45·00	23·00
		w. Wmk inverted	—	£600
25		20c. olive-green (8.7.96)	15·00	£100
		a. Flat top to "C"	£325	
26		25c. ultramarine	23·00	70
		a. Deep ultramarine	35·00	1·00
27		40c. orange-brown	3·75	4·00
28		50c. bright lilac (1890)	3·25	2·00
29		75c. olive-green (1890)	32·00	32·00
30		1p. bistre (11.89)	75·00	20·00
31		1p. bistre and ultramarine (6.95)	4·75	8·00
32		2p. black and carmine (2.1.96)	11·00	30·00
33		5p. slate-grey (12.89)	42·00	£100
22/33 *Set of 12*			£225	£300
22s/4s, 26s/33s Optd "SPECIMEN" *Set of 11*			£425	

*Earliest recorded postmark date.

1898 (1 Oct). Reissue in Sterling currency. Wmk Crown CA. P 14.

39	2	½d. grey-green	11·00	1·75
		w. Wmk inverted		
40	3	1d. carmine	11·00	50
		w. Wmk inverted	†	£1400
41	4	2d. brown-purple and ultramarine	24·00	1·75
42	5	2½d. bright ultramarine	35·00	50
		w. Wmk inverted	£300	80·00
43	4	4d. orange-brown and green	18·00	4·75
		a. "FOUR PENCE" trimmed at top (Pl 2 R. 6/4 and 5, R. 8/4-6)	£500	
44		6d. violet and red	42·00	24·00
45		1s. bistre and carmine	38·00	11·00
		w. Wmk inverted		
39/45 *Set of 7*			£160	40·00
39s/45s Optd "SPECIMEN" *Set of 7*			£275	

No. 39 is greyer than No. 8, No. 40 brighter and deeper than No. 9 and No. 42 much brighter than No. 11.

The degree of "trimming" on No. 43a varies, but is most prominent on R. 6/4 and 5.

8

9

½ Normal — ½ Large "2"

2½d.

This occurs on R. 10/1 in each pane of 60. The diagonal stroke is also longer.

1903 (1 May). Wmk Crown CA. P 14.

46	8	½d. grey-green and green	10·00	9·50
47		1d. dull purple/*red*	32·00	60
48		2d. grey-green and carmine	24·00	32·00
49		2½d. dull purple and black/*blue*	7·50	60
		a. Large "2" in "½"	£325	£130
50		6d. dull purple and violet	30·00	21·00
51		1s. black and carmine	28·00	38·00
52	9	2s. green and blue	£170	£275
53		4s. dull purple and green	£120	£200
54		8s. dull purple and black/*blue*	£160	£180
55		£1 dull purple and black/*red*	£550	£700
46/55 *Set of 10*			£1000	£1300
46s/55s Optd "SPECIMEN" *Set of 10*			£550	

1904–08. Wmk Mult Crown CA. Ordinary paper (½d. to 2d. and 6d. to 2s.) or chalk-surfaced paper (others). P 14.

56	8	½d. dull and bright green (4.4.04*)	16·00	3·00
		a. Chalk-surfaced paper (10.05)	14·00	8·00
57		1d. dull purple/*red* (6.9.04*)	23·00	50
		a. Bisected (½d.) (on card or cover)	†	£1800
		bw. Wmk inverted	†	£850
		c. Chalk-surfaced paper (16.9.05)	8·00	85
58		2d. grey-green and carmine (9.1.05)	23·00	10·00
		a. Chalk-surfaced paper (2.07)	10·00	11·00
59		2½d. purple and black/*blue* (4.5.07)	35·00	90·00
		a. Large "2" in "½"	£600	£1000
60		6d. dull purple and violet (19.4.06)	50·00	30·00
		a. Chalk-surfaced paper (4.08)	32·00	18·00
61		1s. black and carmine (13.10.05)	65·00	20·00
		a. Chalk-surfaced paper (4.06)	55·00	20·00
62	9	2s. green and blue (2.2.05)	£100	£130
		a. Chalk-surfaced paper (10.07)	95·00	£120
63		4s. deep purple and green (6.08)	£325	£400
64		£1 deep purple and black/*red* (15.3.08)	£550	£650
56/64 *Set of 9*			£1000	£1200

*Earliest known date of use.

1906 (Oct)–**12**. Colours changed. Wmk Mult Crown CA. Chalk-surfaced paper (6d. to 8s.). P 14.

66	8	½d. blue-green (1907)	10·00	1·75
		x. Wmk reversed	†	£1700
67		1d. carmine	5·50	60
		a. Wmk sideways	£3750	£3500
		w. Wmk inverted	†	£550
68		2d. greyish slate (5.10)	8·50	11·00
69		2½d. ultramarine (6.07)	6·00	1·60
		a. Large "2" in "½"	£250	£120
70		6d. dull and bright purple (18.3.12)	£140	£375
71		1s. black/*green* (1910)	23·00	21·00
72	9	2s. purple and bright blue/*blue* (4.10)	50·00	48·00
73		4s. black and carmine (4.10)	£150	£170
		x. Wmk reversed	£1800	£2000
74		8s. purple and green (1911)	£225	£225
66/74 *Set of 9*			£550	£750
67s/74s Optd "SPECIMEN" *Set of 8*			£600	

Examples of Nos. 54, 55, 64 and 73/4 are known showing a forged oval registered postmark dated "6 OC 10".

10

11

1912 (17 July)–**24**. Wmk Mult Crown CA. Ordinary paper (½d. to 2½d) or chalk-surfaced paper (others). P 14.

76	**10**	½d. blue-green	3·25	70
		a. Yellow-green (4.17)	6·00	2·00
		w. Wmk inverted	†	£1200
		x. Wmk reversed	†	£1700
77		1d. carmine-red	3·50	75
		a. Scarlet (6.16)	5·00	1·25
		ay. Wmk inverted and reversed		
78		2d. greyish slate	15·00	1·50
79		2½d. deep bright blue	10·00	2·00
		a. Large "2" in "½"	£275	£150
		b. Pale ultramarine (1917)	8·50	2·00
		ba. Large "2" in "½"	£275	£150
80		6d. dull purple and mauve	9·00	17·00
81		1s. black/*green*	12·00	3·25
		a. Ordinary paper (8.18)	£850	
		b. On blue-green, olive back (1919)	21·00	26·00
		c. On emerald surface (12.23)	27·00	70·00
		d. On emerald back (3.24)	24·00	£110
		ds. Optd "SPECIMEN"	75·00	
82	**11**	2s. dull purple and blue/*blue* (*shades*)	26·00	3·50
83		4s. black and carmine	35·00	55·00
84		8s. dull purple and green	85·00	£120
85		£1 dull purple and black/*red*	£140	£225
76/85 *Set of* 10			£300	£375
76s/85s Optd "SPECIMEN" *Set of* 10			£500	

WAR TAX

(**12**)

1918 (15 Apr). Optd with T **12** by Beanland, Malin & Co, Gibraltar.

86	**10**	½d. green	1·00	1·75
		a. Opt double	£900	
		w. Wmk inverted	£650	
		y. Wmk inverted and reversed	£500	

Two printings of this overprint exist, the second being in slightly heavier type on a deeper shade of green.

3 PENCE (I) **THREE PENCE** (II)

1921–**27**. Wmk Mult Script CA. Chalk-surfaced paper (6d. to 8s.). P 14.

89	**10**	½d. green (25.4.27)	1·50	1·50
90		1d. carmine-red (2.21)	1·75	1·00
91		1½d. chestnut (1.12.22)	2·00	55
		a. Pale chestnut (7.24)	2·00	30
		w. Wmk inverted	†	£1100
93		2d. grey (17.2.21)	1·25	1·25
94		2½d. bright blue (2.21)	20·00	55·00
		a. Large "2" in "½"	£550	£750
95		3d. bright blue (I) (1.1.22)	3·50	4·50
		a. Ultramarine	2·50	1·50
97		6d. dull purple and mauve (1.23)	6·00	5·00
		a. Bright purple & magenta (22.7.26)	1·60	3·50
98		1s. black/*emerald* (20.6.24)	10·00	23·00
99	**11**	2s. grey-purple and blue/*blue* (20.6.24)	19·00	75·00
		a. Reddish purple and blue/blue (1925)	7·00	45·00
100		4s. black and carmine (20.6.24)	70·00	£130
101		8s. dull purple and green (20.6.24)	£275	£475
89/101 *Set of* 11			£350	£650
89s/101s Optd "SPECIMEN" *Set of* 11			£600	

The ½d. exists in coils, constructed from normal sheets, first issued in 1937.

1925 (15 Oct)–**32**. New values and colours changed. Wmk Mult Script CA. Chalk-surfaced paper. P 14.

102	**10**	1s. sage-green and black (8.1.29)	14·00	30·00
		a. Olive and black (1932)	14·00	18·00
103	**11**	2s. red-brown and black (8.1.29)	10·00	38·00
104		2s.6d. green and black	10·00	25·00
105		5s. carmine and black	16·00	75·00
106		10s. deep ultramarine and black	32·00	80·00
107		£1 red-orange and black (16.11.27)	£180	£275
108		£5 violet and black	£1500	£5500
		s. Optd "SPECIMEN"	£750	
102/7 *Set of* 6			£225	£450
102s/7s Optd or Perf (1s., 2s.) "SPECIMEN" *Set of* 6			£425	

Examples of Nos. 83/5, 99/101 and 102/8 are known showing forged oval registered postmarks dated "24 JA 25" or "6 MY 35".

1930 (11 Apr). T **10** inscribed "THREE PENCE". Wmk Mult Script CA. P 14.

109		3d. ultramarine (II)	7·50	2·00
		s. Perf "SPECIMEN"	75·00	

13 The Rock of Gibraltar

(Des Capt. H. St. C. Garrood. Recess D.L.R.)

1931–**33**. Wmk Mult Script CA. P 14.

110	**13**	1d. scarlet (1.7.31)	2·50	2·50
		a. Perf 13½×14	16·00	7·00
111		1½d. red-brown (1.7.31)	1·75	2·25
		a. Perf 13½×14	13·00	4·00
112		2d. pale grey (1.11.32)	6·50	1·75
		a. Perf 13½×14	18·00	3·75
113		3d. blue (1.6.33)	6·00	3·00
		a. Perf 13½×14	30·00	40·00
110/13 *Set of* 4			15·00	8·50
110a/13a *Set of* 4			70·00	50·00
110s, 111as/3s Perf "SPECIMEN" *Set of* 4			£190	

Figures of value take the place of both corner ornaments at the base of the 2d. and 3d.

Extra flagstaff (Plate "1" R. 9/1)

Short extra flagstaff (Plate "2" R. 2/1)

Lightning conductor (Plate "3" R. 2/5)

Flagstaff on right-hand turret (Plate "5" R. 7/1)

Double flagstaff (Plate "6" R. 5/2)

1935 (6 May). Silver Jubilee. As Nos. 144/7 of Cyprus but ptd by B.W. P 11×12.

114		2d. ultramarine and grey-black	1·60	2·50
		a. Extra flagstaff	75·00	£100
		b. Short extra flagstaff	£160	£180
		c. Lightning conductor	95·00	£130
		d. Flagstaff on right-hand turret	£325	£350
		e. Double flagstaff	£325	£350

115	3d. brown and deep blue	3·75	5·00
	a. Extra flagstaff	£325	£375
	b. Short extra flagstaff	£300	£350
	c. Lightning conductor	£350	£400
116	6d. green and indigo	13·00	19·00
	a. Extra flagstaff	£275	£325
	b. Short extra flagstaff	£500	£550
	c. Lightning conductor	£275	£325
117	1s. slate and purple	15·00	19·00
	a. Extra flagstaff	£225	£275
	b. Short extra flagstaff	£550	£550
	c. Lightning conductor	£275	£300
114/17 *Set of 4*		30·00	40·00
114s/17s Perf "SPECIMEN" *Set of 4*		£200	

For illustrations of plate varieties see Omnibus section following Zanzibar.

1937 (12 May). Coronation. As Nos. 148/50 of Cyprus. P 11×11½.

118	½d. green	25	50
119	2d. grey-black	2·00	3·25
120	3d. blue	2·75	3·25
118/20 *Set of 3*		4·50	6·25
118s/20s Perf "SPECIMEN" *Set of 3*		£180	

14 King George VI

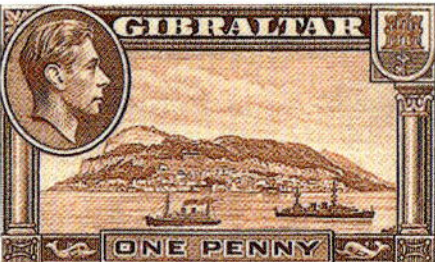

15 Rock of Gibraltar

16 The Rock (North Side)

17 Europa Point

18 Moorish Castle

19 Southport Gate

20 Eliott Memorial

21 Government House

22 Catalan Bay

Ape on rock (R. 1/5)

Bird on memorial (R. 9/3)

Broken second "R" in "GIBRALTAR" (Frame Pl 2 R. 9/4)

(Des Captain H. St. C. Garrood. Recess D.L.R.)

1938 (25 Feb)–**51**. T **14/22**. Mult Script CA.

121	**14**	½d. deep green (P 13½×14)	10	40
122	**15**	1d. yellow-brown (P 14)	26·00	2·25
		a. Perf 13½ (1940)	27·00	2·25
		ab. Perf 13½. Wmk sideways (1940)	6·50	7·00
		b. Perf 13. Wmk sideways. *Red-brown* (1942)	50	60
		c. Perf 13. Wmk sideways. *Deep brown* (1944)	2·25	3·50
		d. Perf 13. *Red-brown* (1949)	4·25	1·50
123		1½d. carmine (P 14)	35·00	1·00
		a. Perf 13½	£275	22·00
123*b*		1½d. slate-violet (P 13) (1.1.43)	50	1·50
124	**16**	2d. grey (P 14)	32·00	40
		aa. Ape on rock	£450	70·00
		a. Perf 13½ (1940)	5·00	35
		ab. Perf 13½. Wmk sideways (1940)	£750	45·00
		b. Perf 13. Wmk sideways (1943)	2·00	2·50
		ba. "A" of "CA" missing from wmk	£1500	
124*c*		2d. carm (P 13) (*wmk sideways*) (15.7.44)	50	60
125	**17**	3d. light blue (P 13½)	30·00	1·00
		a. Perf 14	£130	5·50
		b. Perf 13 (1942)	1·75	30
		ba. Greenish blue (2.51)	5·50	1·50
125*c*		5d. red-orange (P 13) (1.10.47)	1·25	1·25
126	**18**	6d. carm & grey-violet (P 13½) (16.3.38)	48·00	3·00
		a. Perf 14	£120	1·25
		b. Perf 13 (1942)	7·50	1·75
		c. Perf 13. *Scarlet and grey-violet* (1945)	8·50	3·75
127	**19**	1s. black and green (P 14) (16.3.38)	45·00	27·00
		a. Perf 13½	75·00	6·00
		b. Perf 13 (1942)	3·25	4·25
		ba. Broken "R"	£550	
128	**20**	2s. black and brown (P 14) (16.3.38)	65·00	22·00
		a. Perf 13½	£130	42·00
		b. Perf 13 (1942)	7·50	6·50
		ba. Broken "R"	£650	
		bb. Bird on memorial	£450	£475
129	**21**	5s. black and carmine (P 14) (16.3.38)	£100	£170
		a. Perf 13½	48·00	14·00
		b. Perf 13 (1944)	30·00	17·00
		ba. Broken "R"	£1200	
130	**22**	10s. black and blue (P 14) (16.3.38)	70·00	£130
		a. Perf 13 (1943)	40·00	25·00
		ab. Broken "R"	£1500	£1200
131	**14**	£1 orange (P 13½×14) (16.3.38)	40·00	48·00
121/31 Set of 14			£150	90·00
121s/31s Perf "SPECIMEN" *Set of 14*			£800	

The ½d., 1d. and both colours of the 2d. exist in coils constructed from normal sheets. These were originally joined vertically, but, because of technical problems, the 1d. and 2d. grey were subsequently issued in horizontal coils. The 2d. carmine only exists in the horizontal version.

Examples of Nos. 129/31 are known showing forged oval registered postmarks dated "6 OC 43", "18 OC 43", "3 MR 44" and "4 AU 44".

1946 (12 Oct). Victory. As Nos. 164/5 of Cyprus.

132	½d. green	10	1·50
133	3d. ultramarine	50	1·25
132s/3s Perf "SPECIMEN" *Set of 2*		£140	

1948 (1 Dec). Royal Silver Wedding. As Nos. 166/7 of Cyprus.

134	½d. green	1·50	3·00
135	£1 brown-orange	60·00	75·00

1949 (10 Oct). 75th Anniv of Universal Postal Union. As Nos. 168/71 of Cyprus but country name typo on Nos. 137/8.

136	2d. carmine	1·00	1·25
137	3d. deep blue	2·00	1·50
138	6d. purple	1·25	2·00
139	1s. blue-green	1·00	3·50
136/9 *Set of 4*		4·75	7·50

NEW
CONSTITUTION
1950
(**23**)

1950 (1 Aug). Inauguration of Legislative Council. Nos. 124*c*, 125*ba*, 126b and 127b optd as T **23**.

140	**16**	2d. carmine	30	1·50
141	–	3d. greenish blue	65	1·00

142	–	6d. carmine and grey-violet	75	2·00
		a. Opt double	£1000	£1300
143	–	1s. black and green (R.)	75	2·00
		a. Broken "R"	£130	
140/3 *Set of 4*			2·25	6·00

Four sheets of No. 142 received double overprints. On some examples the two impressions are almost coincident.

Stop before "2" in "½" in right-hand value tablet (Pl. 1A–5A, R. 4/4)

1953 (2 June). Coronation. As No. 172 of Cyprus.

144	½d. black and bronze-green	60	1·75
	a. Stop before "2" in "½"	8·00	

24 Cargo and Passenger Wharves

25 South View from Straits

26 Gibraltar Fish Canneries

27 Southport Gate

28 Sailing in the Bay

29 *Saturnia* (liner)

30 Coaling wharf

31 Airport

32 Europa Point

33 Straits from Buena Vista

34 Rosia Bay and Straits

35 Main Entrance, Government House

36 Tower of Homage, Moorish Castle

37 Arms of Gibraltar

Major re-entry causing doubling of "ALTA" in "GIBRALTAR" (R. 4/6)

(Des N. Cummings. Recess (except £1, centre litho) De La Rue)

1953 (19 Oct)–**59**. T **24**/**37**. Wmk Mult Script CA. P 13.

145	**24**	½d. indigo and grey-green	15	30
146	**25**	1d. bluish green	1·50	1·00
		a. Deep bluish green (31.12.57)	3·75	1·50
147	**26**	1½d. black	1·00	2·25
148	**27**	2d. deep olive-brown	2·00	1·00
		a. Sepia (18.6.58)	3·75	1·25
149	**28**	2½d. carmine	4·75	1·25
		a. Deep carmine (11.9.56)	6·50	1·50
		aw. Wmk inverted	£500	
150	**29**	3d. light blue	4·75	10
		a. Deep greenish blue (8.6.55)	9·50	45
		b. Greenish blue (18.6.58)	22·00	2·25
151	**30**	4d. ultramarine	6·50	3·50
		a. Blue (17.6.59)	24·00	10·00
152	**31**	5d. maroon	1·75	1·25
		a. Major re-entry	50·00	
		b. Deep maroon (31.12.57)	3·25	2·50
		ba. Major re-entry	65·00	
153	**32**	6d. black and pale blue	4·00	1·75
		a. Black and blue (24.4.57)	7·00	2·50
		b. Black and grey-blue (17.6.59)	12·00	7·00
154	**33**	1s. pale blue and red-brown	85	1·50
		a. Pale blue and deep red-brown (27.3.56)	70	1·75
155	**34**	2s. orange and reddish violet	42·00	12·00
		a. Orange and violet (17.6.59)	28·00	7·00
156	**35**	5s. deep brown	40·00	16·00
157	**36**	10s. reddish brown and ultramarine	45·00	42·00
158	**37**	£1 scarlet and orange-yellow	50·00	50·00
145/58 *Set of 14*			£170	£110

Nos. 145/6, 148 and 150 exist in coils, constructed from normal sheets.

1954 (10 May). Royal Visit. As No. 150 but inscr "ROYAL VISIT 1954" at top.

159	3d. greenish blue	50	20

38 Gibraltar Candytuft

39 Moorish Castle

40 St. George's Hall

41 The Keys

42 The Rock by moonlight

43 Catalan Bay

44 Map of Gibraltar

45 Air terminal

46 American War Memorial

47 Barbary Ape

48 Barbary Partridge

49 Blue Rock Thrush

50 Rock lily (*Narcissus niveus*)

51 Rock and Badge of Gibraltar Regiment

1d. Retouch right of flag appears as an extra flag (Pl. 1B, R. 5/5)

1d. Jagged brown flaw in wall to right of gate appears as a crack (Pl. 1B, R. 2/5)

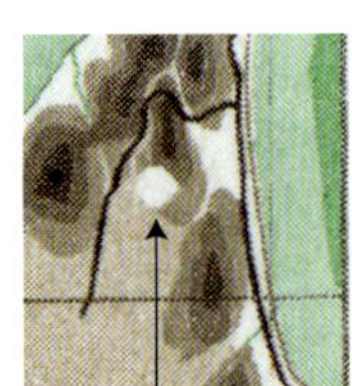

6d. Large white spot on map S.W. of "CEUTA" (Pl. 1B, R. 4/5)

(Des J. Celecia (½d. 2d., 2½d., 2s., 10s.), N. A. Langdon 1d. 3d., 6d. 7d. 9d., 1s.), M. Bonilla (4d.), L. V. Gomez (5s.), Sgt. T. A. Griffths (£1). Recess (£1) or photo (others) D.L.R.)

1960 (29 Oct)–**62**. Designs as T **38**/**51**. W w **12** (upright). P 14 (£1) or 13 (others).

160	½d. bright purple and emerald-green	15	50
161	1d. black and yellow-green	20	10
	a. Crack in wall	7·50	
	b. "Phantom flag"	7·50	
162	2d. indigo and orange-brown	1·00	20
163	2½d. black and blue	1·25	80
	a. Black and grey-blue (16.10.62)	1·25	30
164	3d. deep blue and red-orange	1·00	10
165	4d. deep red-brown and turquoise	2·75	70
166	6d. sepia and emerald	1·00	70
	a. White spot on map	17·00	
167	7d. indigo and carmine-red	2·50	1·75
168	9d. grey-blue and greenish blue	1·00	1·00
169	1s. sepia and bluish green	1·50	70
170	2s. chocolate and ultramarine	19·00	3·25
171	5s. turquoise-blue and olive-brown	8·00	7·50
172	10s. yellow and blue	25·00	20·00
173	£1 black and brown-orange	20·00	20·00
160/73	*Set of* 14	75·00	50·00

Vignette cylinders 2A and 2B, used for printings of the 9d. from 13 March 1962 onwards, had a finer screen (250 dots per inch instead of the 200 of the original printing) (*Price* £1.50 *un* or *us*).

Nos. 160/2, 164 and 166 exist in coils, constructed from normal sheets.

See also No. 199.

The 1d. imperforate comes from stolen printer's waste.

51a Protein foods

(Des M. Goaman. Photo Harrison)

1963 (4 June). Freedom from Hunger. W w **12**. P 14×14½.

174	**51a**	9d. sepia	3·00	1·50

51b Red Cross Emblem

(Des V. Whiteley. Litho B.W.)

1963 (2 Sept). Red Cross Centenary. W w **12**. P 13½

175	**51b**	1d. red and black	1·00	2·00
176		9d. red and blue	2·50	4·50

51c Shakespeare and Memorial Theatre, Stratford-upon-Avon

(Des R. Granger Barrett. Photo Harrison)

1964 (23 Apr). 400th Birth Anniv of William Shakespeare. W w **12**. P 11×11½.

177 **51c** 7d. bistre-brown 60 20

NEW CONSTITUTION 1964.
(**52**)

1964 (16 Oct). New Constitution. Nos. 164 and 166 optd with T **52**.

178 3d. deep blue and red-orange 20 10
179 6d. sepia and emerald 20 60
a. No stop after "1964" (R. 2/5) .... 17·00 38·00
b. White spot on map .... 16·00 35·00

52a I.T.U. Emblem

(Des M. Goaman. Litho Enschedé)

1965 (17 May). I.T.U. Centenary. W w **12**. P 11×11½.

180 **52a** 4d. light emerald and yellow .... 2·00 50
w. Wmk inverted .... 32·00
181 2s. apple-green and deep blue .... 5·50 3·25

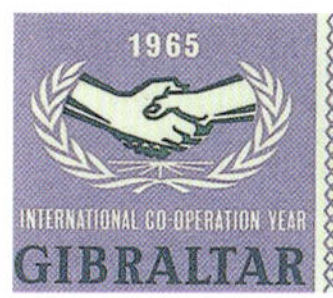

52b I.C.Y. Emblem

(Des V. Whiteley. Litho Harrison)

1965 (25 Oct). International Co-operation Year. W w **12**. P 14½.

182 **52b** ½d. deep bluish green and lavender .... 20 2·75
183 4d. reddish purple and turquoise-green 80 50

The value of the ½d. stamp is shown as "1/2".

52c Sir Winston Churchill and St. Paul's Cathedral in Wartime

(Des Jennifer Toombs. Photo Harrison)

1966 (24 Jan). Churchill Commemoration. Printed in black, cerise and gold and with background in colours stated. W w **12**. P 14.

184 **52c** ½d. new blue .... 20 2·25
w. Wmk inverted .... 60·00
185 1d. deep green 30 10
186 4d. brown .... 1·25 10
187 9d. bluish violet .... 1·25 2·50
184/7 *Set of 4* .... 2·75 4·50

52d Footballer's legs, ball and Jules Rimet cup

(Des V. Whiteley. Litho Harrison)

1966 (1 July). World Cup Football Championship. W w **12** (sideways). P 14.

188 **52d** 2½d. violet, yellow-green, lake and yellow and brown .... 75 1·00
189 6d. chocolate, blue-green, lake and yellow and brown .... 1·00 50

PRINTERS. All stamps from here to No. 239 were printed in photogravure by Harrison and Sons Ltd, London, unless otherwise stated.

53 Red Seabream

4d. Break at top right corner of "d" of value (R. 9/3).

(Des A. Ryman)

1966 (27 Aug). European Sea Angling Championships, Gibraltar. T **53** and similar designs. W w **12** (sideways on 1s.). P 13½×14(1s.) or 14×13½ (others)

190 4d. rosine, bright blue and black 30 10
a. Broken "d" .... 4·50
191 7d. rosine, deep olive-green and black 60 70
a. Black (value and inscr) omitted £1600
w. Wmk inverted .... 3·00
192 1s. lake-brown, emerald and black 50 30
190/2 *Set of 3* .... 1·25 1·00

Designs: *Horiz*—7d. Red Scorpionfish. *Vert*—1s. Stone Bass.

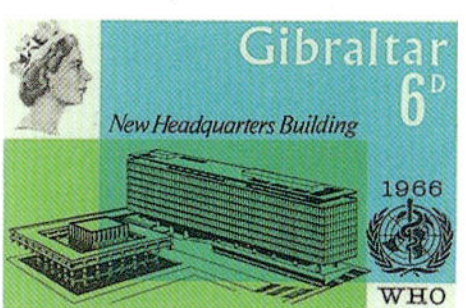

54 W.H.O. Building

(Des M. Goaman. Litho Harrison)

1966 (20 Sept). Inauguration of W.H.O. Headquarters, Geneva. W w **12** (sideways). P 14.

193 **54** 6d. black, yellow-green and light blue. 3·00 1·75
194 9d. black, light purple and yellow-brown .... 3·50 3·00

56 "Our Lady of Europa"

(Des A. Ryman)

1966 (15 Nov). Centenary of Re-enthronement of "Our Lady of Europa". W w **12**. P 14×14½.

195 **56** 2s. bright blue and black 30 80

56a "Education"

56b "Science"

56c "Culture"

(Des Jennifer Toombs. Litho Harrison)

1966 (1 Dec). 20th Anniv of U.N.E.S.C.O. W w **12** (sideways). P 14.

196	**56a**	2d. slate-violet, red, yellow and orange	60	10
197	**56b**	7d. orange-yellow, violet and deep olive	2·25	10
198	**56c**	5s. black, bright purple and orange	4·50	3·00
196/8 *Set of* 3			6·50	3·00

1966 (23 Dec). As No. 165 but wmk w **12** sideways.

199	4d. deep red-brown and turquoise	30	2·50

57 H.M.S. *Victory*

½d. Gash in shape of boomerang in topsail (Pl. 1A, R. 8/4).

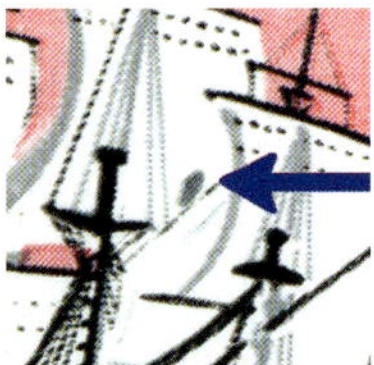

½d. Grey mark in topsail resembling a stain (Pl. 1A, R. 8/6).

7d. Bold shading on sail appearing as patch (Pl. 1A, R. 10/5).

(Des A. Ryman)

1967 (3 Apr)–**69**. Horiz designs as T **57**. Multicoloured. W w **12**. P 14×14½.

200	½d. Type **57**	10	20
	a. Grey (sails, etc) omitted	£700	
	b. Gash in sail	1·50	
	c. Stained sail	1·50	
201	1d. *Arab* (early steamer)	10	10
	w. Wmk inverted	3·25	3·50
202	2d. H.M.S. *Carmania* (merchant cruiser)	15	10
	a. Grey-blue (hull) omitted	£7000	
203	2½d. *Mons Calpe* (ferry)	40	30
204	3d. *Canberra* (liner)	20	10
	w. Wmk inverted	30·00	8·00
205	4d. H.M.S. *Hood* (battle cruiser)	30	10
	w. Wmk inverted		
205*a*	5d. *Mirror* (cable ship) (7.7.69)	2·00	55
	aw. Wmk inverted		
206	6d. *Xebec* (sailing vessel)	30	50
207	7d. *Amerigo Vespucci* (Italian cadet ship)	30	1·00
	a. Patched sail	13·00	
	w. Wmk inverted	17·00	
208	9d. *Raffaello* (liner)	30	1·75
209	1s. *Royal Katherine* (galleon)	30	35
210	2s. H.M.S. *Ark Royal* (aircraft carrier), 1937	4·00	2·50
211	5s. H.M.S. *Dreadnought* (nuclear submarine)	3·50	7·00
212	10s. *Neuralia* (liner)	14·00	23·00
213	£1 *Mary Celeste* (sailing vessel)	14·00	24·00
200/13 *Set of* 15		35·00	55·00

No. 202a results from the misaligning of the grey-blue cylinder. The bottom horizontal row of the sheet involved has this colour completely omitted except for the example above the cylinder numbers which shows the grey-blue "1A" towards the top of the stamp.

The ½d., 1d., 2d. 3d. 6d. 2s. 5s. and £1 exist with PVA gum as well as gum arabic, but the 5d. exists with PVA gum only.

Nos. 201/2, 204/5 and 206 exist in coils constructed from normal sheets.

58 Aerial Ropeway

(Des A. Ryman)

1967 (15 June). International Tourist Year. T **58** and similar designs but horiz. Multicoloured. W w **12** (sideways on 7d.). P 14½×14 (7d.) or 14×14½ (others).

214	7d. Type **58**	15	10
215	9d. Shark fishing	15	10
216	1s. Skin-diving	20	15
214/16 *Set of* 3		45	30

59 Mary, Joseph and Child Jesus

60 Church Window

1967 (1 Nov). Christmas. W w **12** (sideways* on 6d.). P 14.

217	**59**	2d. multicoloured	15	10
		w. Wmk inverted	1·25	
218	**60**	6d. multicoloured	15	10
		w. Wmk Crown to right of CA	£325	

*The normal sideways watermark shows Crown to left of CA, *as seen from the back of the stamp*.

61 Gen. Eliott and Route Map

62 Eliott directing Rescue Operations

(Des A. Ryman)

1967 (11 Dec). 250th Birth Anniv of General Eliott. Multicoloured designs as T **61** (4d. to 1s.) or T **62**. W w **12** (sideways on horiz designs). P 14×15 (1s.) or 15×14 (others).

219	4d. Type **61**	15	10
220	9d. Heathfield Tower and Monument, Sussex (38×22 mm)	15	10
221	1s. General Eliott (22×38 mm)	15	10
222	2s. Type **62**	25	50
219/22 *Set of* 4		65	70

65 Lord Baden-Powell

(Des A. Ryman)

1968 (27 Mar). 60th Anniv of Gibraltar Scout Association. T **65** and similar horiz designs. W w **12**. P 14×14½.

223		4d. buff and bluish violet	15	10
224		7d. ochre and blue-green	15	20
225		9d. bright blue, yellow-orange and black	15	30
226		1s. greenish yellow and emerald	15	30
223/6 *Set of 4*			55	75

Designs:—7d. Scout Flag over the Rock; 9d. Tent, scouts and salute; 1s. Scout badges.

66 Nurse and W.H.O. Emblem

68 King John signing Magna Carta

(Des A. Ryman)

1968 (1 July). 20th Anniv of World Health Organization. T **66** and similar horiz design. W w **12**. P 14×14½.

227		2d. ultramarine, black and yellow	10	15
228		4d. slate, black and pink	10	10

Design:—4d. Doctor and W.H.O. emblem.

(Des A. Ryman)

1968 (26 Aug). Human Rights Year. T **68** and similar vert design. W w **12** (sideways). P 13½×14.

229		1s. yellow-orange, brown and gold	15	10
230		2s. myrtle and gold	15	20

Design:—2s. "Freedom" and Rock of Gibraltar.

70 Shepherd, Lamb and Star

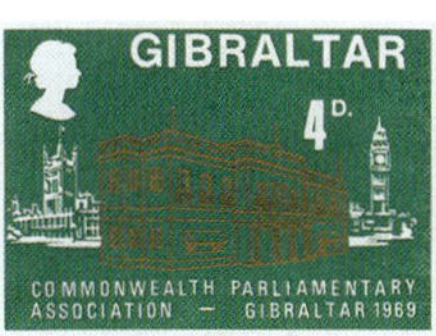

72 Parliament Houses

(Des A. Ryman)

1968 (1 Nov). Christmas. T **70** and similar vert design. Multicoloured. W w **12**. P 14½×13½.

231		4d. Type **70**	10	10
		a. Gold (star) omitted	£850	£850
232		9d. Mary holding Holy Child	15	20

(Des A. Ryman)

1969 (26 May). Commonwealth Parliamentary Association Conference. T **72** and similar designs. W w **12** (sideways on 2s.). P 14×14½ (2s.) or 14½×14 (others).

233		4d. green and gold	10	10
234		9d. bluish violet and gold	10	10
235		2s. multicoloured	15	20
233/5 *Set of 3*			30	30

Designs: *Horiz*—9d. Parliamentary emblem and outline of "The Rock". *Vert*—2s. Clock Tower, Westminster (Big Ben) and arms of Gibraltar.

75 Silhouette of Rock, and Queen Elizabeth II

77 Soldier and Cap Badge, Royal Anglian Regiment, 1969

(Des A. Ryman)

1969 (30 July). New Constitution. W w **12**. P 14×13½ (in addition, the outline of the Rock is perforated).

236	**75**	½d. gold and orange	10	10
237		5d. silver and bright green	20	10
		a. Portrait and inscr in gold and silver*		
238		7d. silver and bright purple	20	10
239		5s. gold and ultramarine	65	1·10
236/9 *Set of 4*			1·00	1·25

*No. 237a was first printed with the head and inscription in gold and then in silver but displaced slightly to lower left.

(Des A. Ryman. Photo D.L.R.)

1969 (6 Nov). Military Uniforms (1st series). T **77** and similar vert designs. Multicoloured. W w **12**. P 14.

240		1d. Royal Artillery officer, 1758 and modern cap badge	15	10
241		6d. Type **77**	20	15
242		9d. Royal Engineers' Artificer, 1786 and modern cap badge	30	15
243		2s. Private, Fox's Marines, 1704 and modern Royal Marines cap badge	75	70
240/3 *Set of 4*			1·25	1·00

Nos. 240/3 have a short history of the Regiment printed on the reverse side over the gum, therefore, once the gum is moistened the history disappears.

See also Nos. 248/51.

80 "Madonna of the Chair" (detail, Raphael)

83 Europa Point

(Des A. Ryman. Photo Enschedé)

1969 (1 Dec). Christmas. T **80** and similar vert designs. Multicoloured. W w **12** (sideways). P 14 × Roulette 9.

244		5d. Type **80**	10	35
		a. Strip of 3. Nos. 244/6	45	1·00
245		7d. "Virgin and Child" (detail, Morales)	20	35
246		1s. "The Virgin of the Rocks" (detail, Leonardo da Vinci)	20	40
244/6 *Set of 3*			45	1·00

Nos. 244/6 were issued together in *se-tenant* strips of three throughout the sheet.

(Des A. Ryman. Photo Enschedé)

1970 (8 June). Europa Point. W w **12**. P 13½.

247	**83**	2s. multicoloured	45	50
		w. Wmk inverted	2·00	2·00

(Des A. Ryman. Photo D.L.R.)

1970 (28 Aug). Military Uniforms (2nd series). Vert designs as T **77**. Multicoloured. W w **12**. P 14.

248		2d. Royal Scots officer, 1839 and cap badge	25	10
249		5d. South Wales Borderers private, 1763 and cap badge	35	10
250		7d. Queens Royal Regiment private, 1742 and cap badge	35	10
251		2s. Royal Irish Rangers piper, 1969 and cap badge	1·00	90
248/51 Set of 4			1·75	1·00

Nos. 248/51 have a short history of the Regiment printed on the reverse side under the gum.

88 No. 191a and Rock of Gibraltar

(Des A. Ryman. Litho D.L.R.)

1970 (18 Sept). "Philympia 1970" Stamp Exhibition, London. T **88** and similar horiz design. W w **12** (sideways). P 13.

252 1s. vermilion and bronze-green 15 10
253 2s. bright blue and magenta 25 65

Design:—2s. Victorian stamp (No. 23b) and Moorish Castle.

The stamps shown in the designs are well-known varieties with values omitted.

90 "The Virgin Mary" (stained-glass window by Gabriel Loire)

(Photo Enschedé)

1970 (1 Dec). Christmas. W w **12**. P 13×14.

254 **90** 2s. multicoloured 30 80

(New Currency: 100 pence = £1)

91 Saluting Battery, Rosia

92 Saluting Battery, Rosia, Modern View

(Des A. Ryman. Litho Questa)

1971 (15 Feb). Decimal Currency. Designs as T **91/2**. W w **12** (sideways* on horiz designs). P 14.

255 ½p. multicoloured 20 30
a. Pair. Nos. 255/6 40 60
256 ½p. multicoloured 20 30
257 1p. multicoloured 80 30
a. Pair. Nos. 257/8 1·60 60
258 1p. multicoloured 80 30
259 1½p. multicoloured 20 70
a. Pair. Nos. 259/60 40 1·40
260 1½p. multicoloured 20 70
261 2p. multicoloured 1·25 2·25
a. Pair. Nos. 261/2 2·50 4·50
262 2p. multicoloured 1·25 2·25
263 2½p. multicoloured 20 70
a. Pair. Nos. 263/4 40 1·40
264 2½p. multicoloured 20 70
265 3p. multicoloured 20 20
a. Pair. Nos. 265/6 40 40
266 3p. multicoloured 20 20
267 4p. multicoloured 1·40 2·50
a. Pair. Nos. 267/8 2·75 5·00
268 4p. multicoloured 1·40 2·50
269 5p. multicoloured 35 65
a. Pair. Nos. 269/70 70 1·25
270 5p. multicoloured 35 65
271 7p. multicoloured 65 65
aw. Wmk Crown to right of CA 85·00
b. Pair. Nos. 271/2 1·25 1·25
bw. Pair. Nos. 271aw/2aw £170
272 7p. multicoloured 65 65
aw. Wmk Crown to right of CA 85·00
273 8p. multicoloured 70 80
a. Pair. Nos. 273/4 1·40 1·60
274 8p. multicoloured 70 80
275 9p. multicoloured 70 80
a. Pair. Nos. 275/6 1·40 1·60
276 9p. multicoloured 70 80
277 10p. multicoloured 80 80
aw. Wmk Crown to right of CA £130
b. Pair. Nos. 277/8 1·60 1·60
bw. Pair. Nos. 277aw/8aw £260
278 10p. multicoloured 80 80
aw. Wmk Crown to right of CA £130
279 12½p. multicoloured 1·00 1·75
a. Pair. Nos. 279/80 2·00 3·50
280 12½p. multicoloured 1·00 1·75
281 25p. multicoloured 1·10 1·75
a. Pair. Nos. 281/2 2·10 3·50
282 25p. multicoloured 1·10 1·75
283 50p. multicoloured 1·50 2·75
a. Pair. Nos. 283/4 3·00 5·50
284 50p. multicoloured 1·50 2·75
285 £1 multicoloured 2·25 4·25
a. Pair. Nos. 285/6 4·50 8·50
286 £1 multicoloured 2·25 4·25
255/86 *Set of 32* 24·00 38·00

Designs (the two versions of each value show the same Gibraltar view taken from an early 19th-century print (first design) or modern photograph (second design): *Horiz*—1p. Prince George of Cambridge Quarters and Trinity Church; 1½p. The Wellington Bust, Alameda Gardens; 2p. Gibraltar from the North Bastion 2½p. Catalan Bay; 3p. Convent Garden; 4p The Exchange and Spanish Chapel; 5p Commercial Square and Library; 7p. South Barracks and Rosia Magazine; 8p. Moorish Mosque and Castle; 9p. Europa Pass Road; 10p. South Barracks from Rosia Bay; 12½p. Southport Gates; 25p. Trooping the Colour, The Alameda. *Vert*—50p. Europa Pass Gorge; £1 Prince Edward's Gate.

The two designs of each value were printed together, *se-tenant*, in horizontal and vertical pairs throughout. Prices are for horizontal pairs, vertical pairs are worth less.

*The normal sideways watermark shows Crown to left of CA, *as seen from the back of the stamp.*

See also Nos. 317/20 and 344/5.

93

94 Regimental Arms

(Des A. Ryman. Photo Harrison)

1971 (15 Feb). Coil Stamps. W w **12**. P 14½×14.

287 **93** ½p. red-orange 15 30
a. Coil strip (287 × 2, 288 × 2 and 289 *se-tenant*) 1·00 1·50
288 1p. blue 15 30
289 2p. bright green 50 1·10
287/9 *Set of 3* 70 1·50

(Des A. Ryman. Litho Questa)

1971 (6 Sept). Military Uniforms (3rd series). Multicoloured designs as T **77**, showing uniform and cap badge. W w **12**. P 14.

290 1p. The Black Watch (1845) 35 30
291 2p. Royal Regt of Fusiliers (1971) 55 30
w. Wmk inverted £100
292 4p. King's Own Royal Border Regt (1704) 75 50
293 10p. Devonshire and Dorset Regt (1801) 2·75 3·00
w. Wmk inverted 4·50 6·50
290/3 *Set of 4* 4·00 3·50

Nos. 290/3 have a short history of the regiment printed on the reverse side under the gum.

(Des A. Ryman. Litho Harrison)

1971 (25 Sept). Presentation of Colours to the Gibraltar Regiment. W w **12** (sideways). P 12½×12.

294 **94** 3p. black, gold and red 55 30

95 Nativity Scene

96 Soldier Artificer, 1773

(Des A. Ryman. Photo Enschedé)

1971 (1 Dec). Christmas. T **95** and similar horiz design. Multicoloured. W w **12**. P 13×13½.

295		3p. Type **95**	40	60
296		5p. Mary and Joseph going to Bethlehem	40	65

(Des A. Ryman. Litho Questa)

1972 (6 Mar). Bicentenary of Royal Engineers in Gibraltar. T **96** and similar multicoloured designs. W w **12** (sideways on 1 and 3p.). P 13½×14 (5p.) or 14×13½ (others).

297		1p. Type **96**	50	60
298		3p. Modern tunneller	60	80
299		5p. Old and new uniforms and badge (*horiz*)	70	90
297/9 *Set of 3*			1·60	2·10

(Des A. Ryman. Litho Questa)

1972 (19 July). Military Uniforms (4th series). Multicoloured designs as T **77**. W w **12** (sideways). P 14.

300		1p. Duke of Cornwall's Light Infantry, 1704	50	20
301		3p. King's Royal Rifle Corps, 1830	1·25	40
302		7p. Officer, 37th North Hampshire, 1825	2·00	70
303		10p. Royal Navy, 1972	2·25	1·50
300/3 *Set of 4*			5·50	2·50

Nos. 300/303 have a short history of the Regiment printed on the reverse side under the gum.

97 "Our Lady of Europa"

98 Keys of Gibraltar and *Narcissus niveus*

(Des A. Ryman. Litho Harrison)

1972 (4 Oct). Christmas. W w **12** (sideways*). P 14½×14.

304	**97**	3p. multicoloured	10	20
		w. Wmk Crown to right of CA	14·00	
305		5p. multicoloured	10	35
		w. Wmk Crown to right of CA	1·00	

*The normal sideways watermark shows Crown to left of CA, *as seen from the back of the stamp.*

These stamps have an inscription printed on the reverse side.

(Des (from photograph by D. Groves) and photo Harrison)

1972 (20 Nov). Royal Silver Wedding. Multicoloured; background colour given. W w **12**. P 14×14½.

306	**98**	5p. carmine-red	25	20
		w. Wmk inverted	70·00	
307		7p. deep grey-green	25	20
		w. Wmk inverted	£500	

99 Flags of Member Nations and E.E.C. Symbol

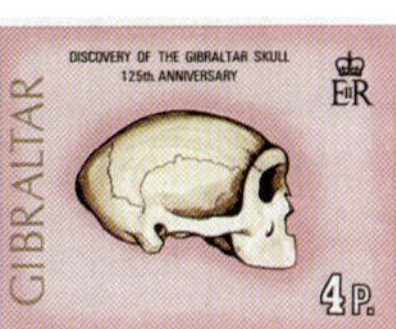

100 Skull

(Des A. Ryman. Litho Questa)

1973 (22 Feb). Britain's Entry into E.E.C. W w **12** (sideways). P 14½×14.

308	**99**	5p. multicoloured	40	50
309		10p. multicoloured	60	1·00

(Des A. Ryman. Litho B.W.)

1973 (22 May). 125th Anniv of Gibraltar Skull Discovery. T **100** and similar horiz designs. Multicoloured. W w **12**. P 13 (10p.) or 13½ (others).

310		4p. Type **100**	1·25	60
		a. Gold ("GIBRALTAR") omitted	£6000	
311		6p. Prehistoric man	1·50	1·25
312		10p. Prehistoric family (40×26 mm)	2·00	2·50
310/12 *Set of 3*			4·25	4·00

Several mint examples of No. 310a have been found in presentation packs.

(Des A. Ryman. Litho Questa)

1973 (22 Aug). Military Uniforms (5th series). Multicoloured designs as T **77**. W w **12** (sideways). P 14.

313		1p. King's Own Scottish Borderers, 1770	50	50
314		4p. Royal Welch Fusiliers, 1800	1·25	80
315		6p. Royal Northumberland Fusiliers, 1736	1·75	1·75
316		10p. Grenadier Guards, 1898	2·50	4·00
313/16 *Set of 4*			5·50	6·25

Nos. 313/16 have a short history of the Regiment printed on the reverse side under the gum.

1973 (12 Sept). As Nos. 261/2 and 267/8 but W w **12** upright.

317		2p. multicoloured	1·25	2·50
		aw. Wmk inverted	†	—
		b. Pair. Nos. 317/18	2·50	5·00
		bw. Pair nos. 317aw/8aw	†	—
318		2p. multicoloured	1·25	2·50
		aw. Wmk inverted	†	—
319		4p. multicoloured	1·40	2·75
		a. Pair. Nos. 319/20	2·75	5·50
320		4p. multicoloured	1·40	2·75
317/20 *Set of 4*			4·75	9·50

Prices are for horizontal pairs, vertical pairs are worth less.

101 "Nativity" (Danckerts)

(Des and litho Enschedé)

1973 (17 Oct). Christmas. W w **12**. P 12½×12.

321	**101**	4p. violet and Venetian red	30	15
322		6p. magenta and turquoise-blue	40	1·10

101a Princess Anne and Captain Mark Phillips

102 Victorian Pillar-box

1973 (14 Nov). Royal Wedding. Centre multicoloured. W w **12** (sideways). P 13½.

323	**101a**	6p. turquoise	10	10
324		14p. yellow-green	20	20

(Des A. Ryman. Litho Walsall)

1974 (2 May). Centenary of Universal Postal Union. T **102** and similar vert designs. Multicoloured.

(a) W w **12** *(sideways). P 14½*

325		2p. Type **102**	15	30
326		6p. Pillar-box of George VI	20	35
327		14p. Pillar-box of Elizabeth II	30	80
325/7 *Set of 3*			60	1·25

(b) No wmk. Imperf × roul 5. Self-adhesive (from booklets)*

328		2p. Type **102**	25	1·00
		a. Booklet pane Nos. 328/30 *se-tenant*	7·00	

	b. Booklet pane Nos. 328 × 3 and 329 × 3.	1·40	
329	6p. As No. 326	25	1·00
330	14p. As No. 327	7·00	8·50
328/30 *Set of 3*		7·00	9·50

*Nos. 328/30 were separated by various combinations of rotary knife (giving a straight edge) and roulette.

(Des A. Ryman. Litho Questa)

1974 (21 Aug). Military Uniforms (6th series). Multicoloured designs as T **77**. W w **12** (sideways). P 14.

331	4p. East Lancashire Regt, 1742	50	50
332	6p. Somerset Light Infantry, 1833	70	70
333	10p. Royal Sussex Regt, 1790	1·00	1·40
334	16p. R.A.F. officer, 1974	2·25	4·00
	w. Wmk Crown to right of CA	£180	
331/4 *Set of 4*		4·00	6·00

*The normal sideways watermark shows Crown to left of CA, *as seen from the back of the stamp.*

Nos. 331/4 have a short history of the regiment printed on the reverse side under the gum.

103 "Madonna with the Green Cushion" (Solario)

104 Churchill and Houses of Parliament

(Des A. Ryman and M. Infante. Litho Questa)

1974 (5 Nov). Christmas. T **103** and similar vert design. Multicoloured. W w **14**. P 14.

335	4p. Type **103**	40	30
336	6p. "Madonna of the Meadow" (Bellini)	60	95

(Des L. Curtis. Litho Harrison)

1974 (30 Nov). Birth Centenary of Sir Winston Churchill. T **104** and similar horiz design. W w **12**. P 14×14½.

337	6p. black, reddish purple and light lavender	25	15
338	20p. brownish black, lake-brown and light orange-red	35	45
MS339	114×93 mm. Nos. 337/8. W w **12** (sideways*). P 14	4·50	6·50
	w. Wmk Crown to right of CA	£500	

Design:—20p. Churchill and *King George V* (battleship).

*The normal sideways watermark shows Crown to left of CA, *as seen from the back of the stamp.*

(Des A. Ryman. Litho Questa)

1975 (14 Mar). Military Uniforms (7th series). Multicoloured designs as T **77**. W w **14**. P 14.

340	4p. East Surrey Regt, 1846	35	20
341	6p. Highland Light Infantry, 1777	50	40
342	10p. Coldstream Guards, 1704	70	70
343	20p. Gibraltar Regt, 1974	1·25	2·50
340/3 *Set of 4*		2·50	3·50

Nos. 340/3 have a short history of each regiment printed on the reverse side under the gum.

1975 (9 July). As Nos. 257/8 but W w **14** (sideways).

344	1p. multicoloured	1·60	2·25
	a. Pair. Nos. 344/5	3·00	4·50
345	1p. multicoloured	1·60	2·25

See note below No. 320.

105 Girl Guides' Badge

106 Child at Prayer

(Des A. Ryman. Litho Harrison)

1975 (10 Oct). 50th Anniv of Gibraltar Girl Guides. W w **12**. P 13×13½.

346	**105**	5p. gold, light blue and dull violet	25	55
		a. *Tête-bêche* (pair)	65	1·25
		w. Wmk inverted	40	70
347		7p. gold, sepia and light lake-brown	35	60
		a. *Tête-bêche* (pair)	90	1·40
		w. Wmk inverted	55	80
348	–	15p. silver, brownish black and yellow and brown	50	1·25
		a. *Tête-bêche* (pair)	1·25	2·75
		b. Silver omitted	£2500	
		w. Wmk inverted	80	1·50
346/8 *Set of 3*			1·00	2·25

No. 348 is as T **105** but shows a different badge.

Nos. 346/8 were each issued in sheets of 25 (5×5) with each horizontal row containing three upright stamps and two inverted.

(Des A. Ryman. Litho Walsall)

1975 (26 Nov). Christmas. T **106** and similar vert designs. Multicoloured. W w **14** (sideways*). P 14.

349	6p. Type **106**	40	60
	aw. Wmk Crown to right of CA	8·50	
	b. Sheetlet. Nos. 349/54	2·10	3·25
	bw. Sheetlet. Nos. 349aw/54aw	45·00	
350	6p. Angel with lute	40	60
	aw. Wmk Crown to right of CA	8·50	
351	6p. Child singing carols	40	60
	aw. Wmk Crown to right of CA	8·50	
352	6p. Three children	40	60
	aw. Wmk Crown to right of CA	8·50	
353	6p. Girl at prayer	40	60
	aw. Wmk Crown to right of CA	8·50	
354	6p. Boy and lamb	40	60
	aw. Wmk Crown to right of CA	8·50	
349/54 *Set of 6*		2·10	3·25

*The normal sideways watermark shows Crown to left of CA, *as seen from the back of the stamp.*

Nos. 349/54 were issued together *se-tenant* in sheetlets of 6 (3×2).

107 Bruges Madonna

108 Bicentennial Emblem and Arms of Gibraltar

(Des Jennifer Toombs. Litho Walsall)

1975 (17 Dec). 500th Birth Anniv of Michelangelo. T **107** and similar vert designs. Multicoloured.

(a) W w **14** (sideways*). P 14

355	6p. Type **107**	20	25
356	9p. Taddei Madonna	20	40
357	15p. Pieta	30	1·10
	w. Wmk Crown to right of CA	£150	
355/7 *Set of 3*		65	1·60

(b) No wmk. Imperf × roul 5†. Self-adhesive (from booklets)

358	6p. Type **107**	35	45
	a. Booklet pane. Nos. 358/60 *se-tenant*	1·50	
	b. Booklet pane. Nos. 358 × 2, 359 × 2 and 360 × 2	3·00	
359	9p. As No. 356	55	75
360	15p. As No. 357	80	1·25
358/60 *Set of 3*		1·50	2·25

*The normal sideways watermark shows Crown to left of CA, *as seen from the back of the stamp.*

†Nos. 358/60 were separated by various combinations of rotary knife (giving a straight edge) and roulette.

(Des A. Ryman. Litho Walsall)

1976 (28 May). Bicentenary of American Revolution. W w **14** (inverted). P 14.

361	**108**	25p. multicoloured	50	50
MS362		85×133 mm. No. 361×4	2·75	4·50

The edges of **MS**362 are rouletted.

(Des A. Ryman. Litho Walsall)

1976 (21 July). Military Uniforms (8th series). Multicoloured designs as T **77**. W w **14** (inverted). P 14.

363	1p. Suffolk Regt, 1795	20	20
364	6p. Northamptonshire Regt, 1779	40	30
365	12p. Lancashire Fusiliers, 1793	50	60
366	25p. Ordnance Corps, 1896	60	1·40
363/6 *Set of 4*		1·50	2·25

Nos. 363/6 have a short history of each regiment printed on the reverse side under the gum.

109 The Holy Family

110 Queen Elizabeth II, Royal Arms and Gibraltar Arms

(Des A. Ryman. Litho Questa)

1976 (3 Nov). Christmas. T **109** and similar vert designs showing stained glass windows in St. Joseph's Church, Gibraltar. Multicoloured. W w **14**. P 14.

367	6p. Type **109**	25	15
368	9p. Madonna and Child	35	25
369	12p. St. Bernard	50	60
370	20p. Archangel Michael	85	1·40
367/70 *Set of 4*		1·75	2·25

(Des A. Ryman. Litho J.W.)

1977 (7 Feb). Silver Jubilee. W w **14**. P 13½.

371 **110**	6p. multicoloured	15	20
372	£1 multicoloured	1·10	2·00
MS373 124×115 mm. Nos. 371/2. P 13		1·25	1·50

The outer edges of the miniature sheet are either guillotined or rouletted.

111 Toothed Orchid (*Orchis tridentata*)

(Des A. Ryman. Litho Questa)

1977 (1 Apr)–**82**. Multicoloured designs as T **111**. W w **14** (sideways* on horiz designs; inverted on £5). *Chalk surfaced paper (15p , £5). Imprint date at foot.* P 14.

374	½p. Type **111**	60	2·50
	a. Chalk-surfaced paper (22.2.82)	5·50	4·50
375	1p. Red Mullet (*Mullus surmuletus*) (*horiz*)	15	70
	w. Wmk Crown to right of CA	6·50	7·00
376	2p. *Maculinea arion* (butterfly) (*horiz*)	30	1·75
377	2½p. Sardinian Warbler (*Sylvia melanocephala*)	1·75	2·75
378	3p. Grant Squill (*Scilla peruviana*)	20	10
379	4p. Grey Wrasse (*Crenilabrus cinereus*) (*horiz*)	30	10
	b. Chalk-surfaced paper (21.4.81)	55	70
380	5p. *Vanessa atalanta* (butterfly) (*horiz*)	50	1·00
381	6p. Black Kite (*Milvus migrans*)	2·25	55
	w. Wmk inverted	£160	
382	9p. Shrubby Scorpion-vetch (*Coronilla valentina*)	70	70
383	10p. John Dory (fish) (*Zeus faber*) (*horiz*)	40	20
	a. Chalk-surfaced paper (21.4.81)	1·00	1·50
384	12p. *Colias crocea* (butterfly) (*horiz*)	1·00	35
	a. Chalk-surfaced paper (21.4.81)	4·25	4·50
384*b*	15p. Winged Asparagus Pea (*Tetragonolobus purpureus*) (12.11.80)	1·50	55
	bw. Wmk inverted	£160	
385	20p. Audouin's Gull (*Larus audouinii*)	2·00	3·25
386	25p. Barbary Nut (iris) (*Iris sisyrinchium*)	1·25	2·00
	a. Chalk-surfaced paper (21.4.81)	5·00	5·50
387	50p. Swordfish (*Xiphias gladius*) (*horiz*)	2·00	2·50
	a. Chalk-surfaced paper (21.4.81)	6·50	7·00
388	£1 *Papilio machaon* (butterfly) (*horiz*)	4·25	5·00
389	£2 Hoopoe (*Upupa epops*)	9·00	12·00
389*a*	£5 Arms of Gibraltar (16.5.79)	10·00	12·00
374/89a *Set of 18*		32·00	42·00

The ½p. to £2 values have a descriptive text printed on the reverse, beneath the gum. Examples are known with this text omitted.

*The normal sideways watermark shows Crown to left of CA, *as seen from the back of the stamp*.

Imprint dates: "1977" Nos. 374/84, 385/9; "1978", No. 382; "1979", No. 389a; "1980" No. 384b; "1981", Nos. 379b, 383a, 384a, 386a, 387a; "1982", No. 374a.

112 "Our Lady of Europa" Stamp

(Des J. Cooter. Litho Questa)

1977 (27 May). "Amphilex 77" Stamp Exhibition, Amsterdam. T **112** and similar vert designs. Multicoloured. W w **14** (sideways on 6p.; inverted on 12p.). P 13½.

390	6p. Type **112**	10	20
391	12p. "Europe Point" stamp	15	30
	w. Wmk upright	28·00	
392	25p. "E.E.C. Entry" stamp	20	50
	w. Wmk inverted	2·25	
390/2 *Set of 3*		40	90

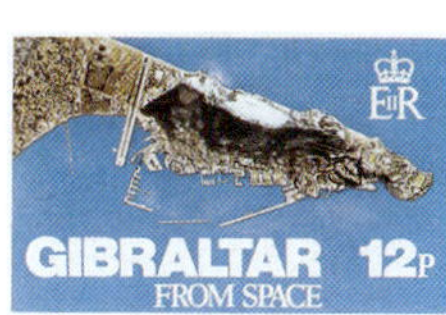

113 "The Annunciation" (Rubens)

114 Aerial View of Gibraltar

(Des A. Ryman. Litho Enschedé)

1977 (2 Nov). Christmas and Rubens' 400th Birth Anniv. T **113** and similar multicoloured designs. W w **14** (sideways on 12p.). P 13½.

393	3p. Type **113**	10	10
394	9p. "The Adoration of the Magi"	25	25
395	12p. "The Adoration of the Magi" (*horiz*)	30	50
396	15p. "The Holy Family under the Apple Tree"	30	55
393/6 *Set of 4*		85	1·25
MS397 110×200 mm. Nos. 393/6 (wmk upright)		2·75	4·00

(Des A. Ryman. Litho Enschedé)

1978 (3 May). Gibraltar from Space. P 13½.

398 **114**	12p. multicoloured	25	50
	a. Horiz pair imperf 3 sides	£7500	
MS399 148×108 mm. 25p. multicoloured		80	80

Design:—25p. Aerial view of Straits of Gibraltar.

No. 398a occurs on the bottom pair from at least three sheets of 10 (2×5) and shows the stamps perforated at top only.

115 Holyroodhouse

(Des and litho Walsall)

1978 (12 June). 25th Anniv of Coronation. T **115** and similar horiz designs. Multicoloured.

(a) From sheets. P 13½×14

400	6p. Type **115**	20	15
401	9p. St. James's Palace	25	15
402	12p. Sandringham	30	30

403		18p. Balmoral	40	85
400/3 *Set of 4*			1·00	1·25

(b) From booklets. Imperf × roul 5. Self-adhesive*

404		12p. As No. 402	25	90
		a. Booklet pane. Nos. 404/5, each × 3	1·25	
405		18p. As No. 403	25	90
406		25p. Windsor Castle	1·00	2·00
		a. Booklet pane of 1	1·00	
404/6 *Set of 3*			1·40	3·50

*Nos. 404/5 were separated by various combinations of rotary knife (giving a straight edge) and roulette. No. 406 exists only with straight edges.

116 Short S.25 Sunderland, 1938–58

117 "Madonna with Animals"

(Des A. Theobald. Litho Harrison)

1978 (6 Sept). 60th Anniv of Royal Air Force. T **116** and similar horiz designs. Multicoloured. W w **14** (sideways). P 14.

407		3p. Type **116**	15	10
408		9p. Caudron G-3, 1918	35	40
409		12p. Awn Shackleton M.R.2, 1953–66	40	55
410		16p. Hawker Hunter F.6, 1954–77	45	1·00
411		18p. Hawker Siddeley H.S.801 Nimrod M.R.1, 1969-78	50	1·10
407/11 *Set of 5*			1·75	2·75

(Des A. Ryman. Litho Questa)

1978 (1 Nov). Christmas. Paintings by Dürer. T **117** and similar vert designs. Multicoloured. W w **14**. P 14.

412		5p. Type **117**	20	10
413		9p. "The Nativity"	25	15
414		12p. "Madonna of the Goldfinch"	30	40
415		15p. "Adoration of the Magi"	35	1·00
412/15 *Set of 4*			1·00	1·50

118 Sir Rowland Hill and 1d. Stamp of 1886

(Des A. Ryman. Litho Format)

1979 (7 Feb). Death Centenary of Sir Rowland Hill. T **118** and similar horiz designs. W w **14** (sideways*). P 13½×14.

416		3p. multicoloured	10	10
417		9p. multicoloured	15	15
418		12p. multicoloured	15	20
		w. Wmk Crown to right of CA	£110	
419		25p. black, dull claret and yellow	25	50
416/19 *Set of 4*			55	80

Designs:—9p. Sir Rowland Hill and 1p. coil stamp of 1971; 12p Sir Rowland Hill and Post Office Regulations document, 1840 25p. Sir Rowland Hill and "G" cancellation.

*The normal sideways watermark shows Crown to left of CA, *as seen from the back of the stamp*.

119 Posthorn, Dish Antenna and Early Telephone

120 African Child

(Des A. Hyman. Litho Format)

1979 (16 May). Europa. Communications. W w **14** (sideways). P 13½.

420	**119**	3p. green and pale green	15	10
421		9p. lake-brown and ochre	30	90
422		12p. ultramarine and dull violet-blue	35	1·25
420/2 *Set of 3*			70	2·00

(Des G. Hutchins. Litho Walsall)

1979 (14 Nov). Christmas. International Year of the Child. T **120** and similar vert designs. Multicoloured. W w **14** (sideways). P 14.

423		12p. Type **120**	25	30
		a. Block of 6. Nos. 423/8	1·40	1·60
424		12p. Asian child	25	30
425		12p. Polynesian child	25	30
426		12p. American Indian child	25	30
427		12p. Children of different races and Nativity scene	25	30
428		12p. European child	25	30
423/8 *Set of 6*			1·40	1·60

Nos. 423/8 were printed together, *se-tenant*, in blocks of 6, with margin separating the two blocks in each sheet.

121 Early Policemen

122 Peter Amigo (Archbishop)

(Des C. Abbott. Litho Questa)

1980 (5 Feb). 150th Anniv of Gibraltar Police Force. T **121** and similar horiz designs. Multicoloured. W w **14** (sideways). P 14.

429		3p. Type **121**	20	10
430		6p. Policemen of 1895, early 1900s and 1980	20	15
431		12p. Policeman and police ambulance	25	20
432		37p. Policewoman and police motor-cyclist	55	1·25
429/32 *Set of 4*			1·10	1·50

(Des A. Hyman. Litho Questa)

1980 (6 May). Europa. Personalities. T **122** and similar Vert designs. Multicoloured. W w **14** (inverted on No. 434). P 14½×14.

433		12p. Type **122**	20	30
434		12p. Gustavo Bacarisas (artist)	20	30
435		12p. John Mackintosh (philanthropist)	20	30
433/5 *Set of 3*			55	80

123 Queen Elizabeth the Queen Mother

124 "Horatio Nelson" (J. F. Rigaud)

(Des Harrison. Litho Questa)

1980 (4 Aug). 80th Birthday of Queen Elizabeth the Queen Mother. W w **14** (sideways). P 14.

436	**123**	15p. multicoloured	30	30

(Des BG Studio. Litho Questa)

1980 (20 Aug). 175th Death Anniv of Nelson. Paintings. T **124** and similar multicoloured designs. W w **14** (sideways on 9 and 40p.). P 14.

437		3p. Type **124**	15	10
438		9p. "H.M.S. *Victory*" (*horiz*)	25	25
439		15p. "Horatio Nelson" (Sir William Beechey)	35	35
440		40p. "H.M.S. *Victory* being towed into Gibraltar" (Clarkson Stanfield) (*horiz*)	80	1·00
437/40 *Set of 4*			1·40	1·50
MS441		159×99 mm. No. 439	1·00	1·50

Examples of the 3p. value showing Nelson facing left in error were prepared, but not issued by the Gibraltar Post Office.

125 Three Kings

126 Hercules creating Mediterranean Sea

(Des A. Hyman. Litho Questa)

1980 (12 Nov). Christmas. T **125** and similar horiz design, each in deep brown and orange-yellow. W w **14** (sideways). P 14½.

442	15p. Type **125**	25	35
	a. Horiz pair. Nos. 442/3	50	70
443	15p. Nativity scene	25	35

Nos. 442/3 were printed together, *se-tenant*, in horizontal pairs throughout the sheet.

(Des G. Vasarhelyi. Litho Enschedé)

1981 (24 Feb). Europa. Folklore. T **126** and similar Vert design. Multicoloured. W w **14**. P 13½×13.

444	9p. Type **126**	20	15
445	15p. Hercules and Pillars of Hercules (Straits of Gibraltar)	25	35

127 Dining-room

128 Prince Charles and Lady Diana Spencer

(Des A. Hyman. Litho Harrison)

1981 (22 May). 450th Anniv of The Convent (Governor's Residence). T **127** and similar square designs. Multicoloured. W w **14** (sideways). P 14½×14.

446	4p. Type **127**	10	10
447	14p. King's Chapel	15	15
448	15p. The Convent	15	15
449	55p. Cloister	60	80
446/9 *Set of 4*		85	1·00

(Des A. Hyman. Litho Questa)

1981 (27 July). Royal Wedding. W w **14** (sideways). P 14½.

450	**128** £1 multicoloured	1·25	1·25

129

130 Paper Aeroplane

(Des A. Hyman. Litho Questa)

1981 (2 Sept). W w **14**. P 13½×14.

451	**129** 1p. black	50	60
	a. Booklet pane. Nos. 451/2 and 453×3 plus printed label	1·75	
	b. Booklet pane. Nos. 451/2×2 and 453×6 plus two printed labels	3·25	
452	4p. Prussian blue	50	50
453	15p. light green	30	40
451/3 *Set of 3*		1·10	1·40

Nos. 451/3 were only issued in 50p. and £1 stamp booklets.

(Des A. Hyman. Litho Walsall)

1981 (29 Sept*). 50th Anniv of Gibraltar Airmail Service. T **130** and similar horiz designs. Multicoloured. W w **14** (sideways). P 14½×14.

454	14p. Type **130**	15	15
455	15p. Airmail letters, post box and aircraft tail fin	15	15
456	55p. Jet airliner circling globe	60	80
454/6 *Set of 3*		80	1·00

*This is the local release date. The Crown Agents released the stamps on 21 September.

131 Carol Singers

132 I.Y.D.P. Emblem and Stylised Faces

(Des Clive Torres (15p.); Peter Parody (55p.); adapted G. Vasarhelyi. Litho Questa)

1981 (19 Nov). Christmas. Children's Drawings. T **131** and similar multicoloured design. W w **14** (sideways on 15p.). P 14.

457	15p. Type **131**	30	15
458	55p. Postbox (*Vert*)	1·00	85

(Des A. Hyman. Litho Questa)

1981 (19 Nov). International Year Far Disabled Persons. W w **14** (sideways). P 14×14½.

459	**132** 14p. multicoloured	30	30

133 Douglas DC-3

134 Crest, H.M.S. *Opossum*

(Des A. Theobald. Litho J.W.)

1982 (10 Feb). Aircraft. Horiz designs as T **133**. Multicoloured. W w **14**. Imprint date at foot. P 14.

460	1p. Type **133**	25	2·00
461	2p. Vickers Viking 1B	30	2·00
462	3p. Airspeed A.S.57 Ambassador	30	1·75
463	4p. Vickers Viscount 800	40	20
464	5p. Boeing 727-100	90	60
465	10p. Vickers 953 Vanguard	1·75	50
466	14p. Short S.45A Solent 2	1·75	4·00
467	15p. Fokker F.27 Friendship	2·75	4·00
468	17p. Boeing 737	1·00	75
469	20p. B.A.C. One Eleven	1·00	65
470	25p. Lockheed Constellation	4·00	5·00
471	50p. Hawker Siddeley Comet 4B	4·00	2·25
472	£1 Saro A.21 Windhover	5·50	2·25
473	£2 Hawker Siddeley Trident 2E	6·50	5·00
474	£5 De Havilland D.H.89A Dragon Rapide	8·00	14·00
460/74 *Set of 15*		35·00	40·00

Imprint dates: "1982", Nos. 460/74; "1985", No. 469.

For 2p. and 5p. values watermarked w **16** see Nos. 549 and 552.

(Des A. Hyman. Litho Questa)

1982 (14 Apr). Naval Crests (1st series). T **134** and similar Vert designs. Multicoloured. W w **14**. P 14.

475	½p. Type **134**	10	30
476	15½p. H.M.S. *Norfolk*	40	55
477	17p. H.M.S. *Fearless*	40	60
478	60p. H.M.S. *Rooke*	85	2·75
	w. Wmk inverted	45·00	
475/8 *Set of 4*		1·50	3·75

See also Nos. 493/6, 510/13, 522/5, 541/4, 565/8, 592/5, 616/19, 638/41 and 651/4.

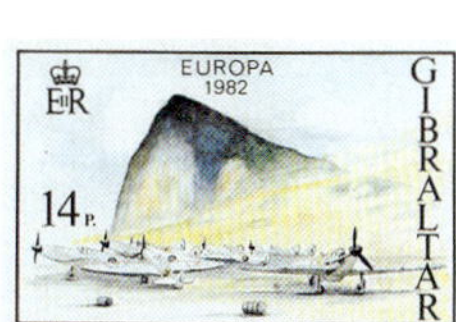

135 Hawker Hurricane Mk 1 and Supermarine Spitfires at Gibraltar

136 Gibraltar Chamber of Commerce Centenary

(Des A. Hyman. Litho Questa)

1982 (11 June). Europa. Operation Torch. T **135** and similar horiz design. Multicoloured. W w **14** (sideways). P 14.

479	14p. Type **135**	25	70
480	17p. General Giraud, General Eisenhower and Gibraltar	35	80

(Des A. Hyman. Litho Questa)

1982 (22 Sept). Anniversaries. T **136** and similar vert designs. Multicoloured. W w **14** (sideways). P 14½.

481	½p. Type **136**	10	65
482	15½p. British Forces Postal Service centenary	45	30
483	60p. 75th anniv of Gibraltar Scout Association	1·25	2·00
481/3 *Set of* 3		1·50	2·75

137 Printed Circuit forming Map of World

(Des A. Hyman. Litho Harrison)

1982 (1 Oct). International Direct Dialling. W w **14** (sideways). P 14½.

484 **137**	17p. black, pale blue and bright orange	35	35

138 Gibraltar illuminated at Night and Holly

(Des A. Ryman. Litho Questa)

1982 (18 Nov). Christmas. T **138** and similar horiz design. Multicoloured. W w **14** (sideways). P 14×14½.

485	14p. Type **138**	50	30
486	17p. Gibraltar illuminated at night and Mistletoe	50	35

139 Yacht Marina

(Des Olympia Reyes. Litho Questa)

1983 (14 Mar). Commonwealth Day. T **139** and similar multicoloured designs. W w **14** (sideways on 4, 14p.). P 14.

487	4p. Type **139**	10	10
488	14p. Scouts and Guides Commonwealth Day Parade	20	15
489	17p. Flag of Gibraltar (*vert*)	25	20
490	60p. Queen Elizabeth II (from photo by Tim Graham) (*vert*)	70	1·00
487/90 *Set of* 4		1·00	1·25

140 St George's Hall Gallery

(Des A. Ryman. Litho Harrison)

1983 (21 May). Europa. T **140** and similar horiz design. W w **14** (sideways). P 13½×13.

491	16p. black and brown-ochre	35	50
492	19p. black and pale blue	40	75

Design:—19p. Water catchment slope.

(Des A. Ryman. Litho Questa)

1983 (1 July). Naval Crests (2nd series). Vert designs as T **134**. Multicoloured. W w **14**. P 14.

493	4p. H.M.S. *Faulknor*	30	10
494	14p. H.M.S. *Renown*	70	35
495	17p. H.M.S. *Ark Royal*	75	40
496	60p. H.M.S. *Sheffield*	1·75	1·50
	w. Wmk inverted	40·00	
493/6 *Set of* 4		3·25	2·10

141 Landport Gate, 1729

(Des Olympia Reyes. Lithe Enschedé)

1983 (13 Sept). Fortress Gibraltar in the 18th Century. T **141** and similar horiz designs. Multicoloured. W w **14** (sideways*). P 13×13½.

497	4p. Type **141**	15	10
498	17p. Koehler Gun, 1782	35	30
499	77p. King's Bastion, 1779	1·00	1·25
497/9 *Set of* 3		1·40	1·50
MS500 97×145 mm. Nos. 497/9		2·25	1·50

*The normal sideways watermark shows Crown to right of CA on Nos. 497/9 and Crown to left on No. **MS**500, *all as seen from the back of the stamp*. Examples of No. 498 are also known from sheets with the Crown to left.

142 "Adoration of the Magi" (Raphael)

143 1932 2d. Stamp and Globe

(Des A. Ryman. Litho Questa)

1983 (17 Nov). Christmas. 500th Birth Anniv of Raphael. T **142** and similar multicoloured designs. W w **14** (sideways on 4p.). P 14.

501	4p. Type **142**	25	10
502	17p. "Madonna of Foligno" (*vert*)	70	35
503	60p. "Sistine Madonna" (*vert*)	1·75	1·40
501/3 *Set of* 3		2·40	1·60

(Des E. Field. Litho Walsall)

1984 (6 Mar). Europa. Posts and Telecommunications. T **143** and similar vert design. Multicoloured. W w **14**. P 14½×14.

504	17p. Type **143**	45	50
505	23p. Circuit board and globe	55	1·00
	w. Wmk inverted	£100	

144 Hockey

145 Mississippi River Boat Float

(Des A. Ryman. Litho Walsall)

1984 (25 May). Sports. T **144** and similar horiz designs. Multicoloured. W w **14** (sideways). P 14×14½.

506	20p. Type **144**	70	80
507	21p. Basketball	70	80
508	26p. Rowing	70	1·25
509	29p. Football	70	1·50
506/9 *Set of* 4		2·50	4·00

(Des A. Ryman. Litho Walsall)

1984 (21 Sept). Naval Crests (3rd series). Vert designs as T **134**. Multicoloured. W w **14**. P 13½×13.

510	20p. H.M.S. *Active*	1·75	2·25

511	21p. H.M.S. *Foxhound*	1·75	2·50
512	26p. H.M.S. *Valiant*	2·00	2·50
513	29p. H.M.S. *Hood*	2·50	2·75
	w. Wmk inverted	20·00	
510/13 *Set of 4*		7·25	9·00

(Des A. Ryman. Litho Questa)

1984 (7 Nov). Christmas. Epiphany Floats. T **145** and similar horiz design. Multicoloured. W w **14** (sideways). P 14×14½.

514	20p. Type **145**	30	30
515	80p. Roman Temple float	1·40	2·75

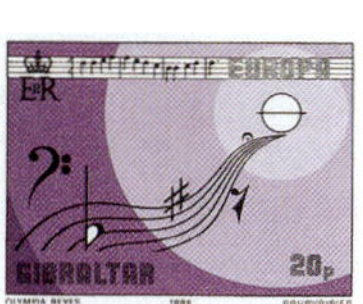

146 Musical Symbols, and Score from Beethoven's 9th (Choral) Symphony

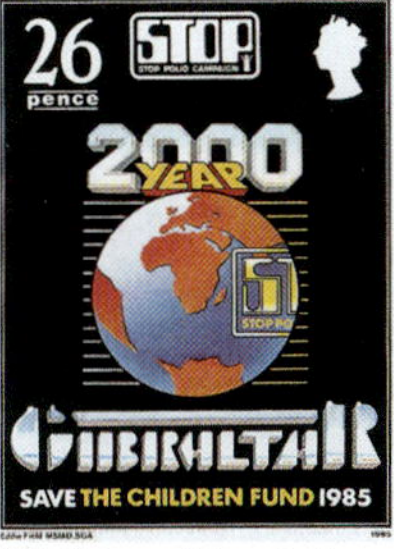

147 Globe and Stop Polio Campaign Logo

(Des Olympia Reyes. Photo Courvoisier)

1985 (26 Feb). Europa. European Music Year. T **146** and similar horiz design. Multicoloured. Granite paper. P 12½.

516	**146**	20p. multicoloured	30	30
517	–	29p. multicoloured	40	1·50

The 29p. is as T **146** but shows different symbols.

(Des E. Field. Litho J.W.)

1985 (3 May). Stop Polio Campaign. Vert designs as T **147**. Multicoloured. W w **14** (inverted). P 13×13½.

518	26p. multicoloured (Type **147**)	90	1·40
	a. Horiz strip of 4. Nos. 518/21	3·25	5·00
519	26p. multicoloured ("ST" visible)	90	1·40
520	26p. multicoloured ("STO" visible)	90	1·40
521	26p. multicoloured ("STOP" visible)	90	1·40
518/21 *Set of 4*		3·25	5·00

Nos 518/21 were printed in horizontal *se-tenant* strips of four within the sheet. Each design differs in the position of the logo across the centre of the globe. On the left hand stamp in the strip only the letter "S" is visible, on the next "ST", on the next "STO" and on the last "STOP".

Other features of the design also differ, so that the word "Year" moves towards the top of the stamp and on No. 521 the upper logo is omitted.

(Des A. Ryman. Litho Questa)

1985 (3 July). Naval Crests (4th series). Vert designs as T **134**. Multicoloured. W w **16**. P 14.

522	4p. H.M.S. *Duncan*	70	10
523	9p. H.M.S. *Fury*	1·25	50
524	21p. H.M.S. *Firedrake*	2·50	2·00
525	80p. H.M.S. *Malaya*	4·50	6·00
522/5 *Set of 4*		8·00	7·75

148 I.Y.Y. Logo

149 St. Joseph

(Des Olympia Reyes. Litho Walsall)

1985 (6 Sept). International Youth Year. T **148** and similar horiz designs. Multicoloured. W w **14** (sideways). P 14×14½.

526	4p. Type **148**	35	10
527	20p. Hands passing diamond	1·40	1·10
528	80p. 75th anniv logo of Girl Guide Movement	3·25	3·75
526/8 *Set of 3*		4·50	4·50

(Des A. Ryman (4p.), Olympia Reyes (80p.). Litho Cartor)

1985 (25 Oct). Christmas. Centenary of St. Joseph's Parish Church. T **149** and similar vert designs. Multicoloured. W w **16**. P 13½*.

529	4p. Type **149**	65	1·00
	a. Vert pair. Nos. 529/30	1·25	2·00
530	4p. St. Joseph's Parish Church	65	1·00
531	80p. Nativity crib	4·50	5·50
529/31 *Set of 3*		5·25	6·75

*Nos. 529/30 were printed together in panes of 25; No. 529 on rows 1, 3 and 5, and No. 530 on rows 2 and 4. *Se-tenant* vertical pairs from rows 1/2 and 3/4, forming composite designs, have the stamps separated by a line of roulettes instead of perforations. Examples of No. 529 from row 5 have perforations on all four sides.

150 *Papilio machaon* (butterfly) and The Convent

151 1887 Queen Victoria 6d. Stamp

(Des E. Field. Litho Walsall)

1986 (10 Feb). Europa. Nature and the Environment. T **150** and similar horiz design. Multicoloured. W w **16** (sideways). P 13×13½.

532	22p. Type **150**	1·00	50
533	29p. Herring Gull and Europa Point	1·50	4·25

(Des A. Ryman. Litho Walsall)

1986 (26 Mar). Centenary of First Gibraltar Postage Stamps. T **151** and similar vert designs showing stamps. Multicoloured. W w **16**. P 14×13½ (44p.) or 13½×13 (others).

534	4p. Type **151**	30	10
535	22p. 1903 Edward VII 2½d.	1·00	1·00
536	32p. 1912 George V 1d.	1·50	2·00
537	36p. 1938 George VI £1	1·60	2·50
538	44p. 1953 Coronation ½d. (29×46 mm)	2·00	3·00
534/8 *Set of 5*		5·75	7·75
MS539 102×73 mm. 29p. 1886 "GIBRALTAR" overprint on Bermuda 1d.		3·25	3·75
	w. Wmk inverted		

152 Queen Elizabeth II in Robes of Order of the Bath

153 Prince Andrew and Miss Sarah Ferguson

(Des A. Ryman. Litho Walsall)

1986 (22 May). 60th Birthday of Queen Elizabeth II. W w **16**. P 14×13½.

540	**152**	£1 multicoloured	1·75	3·00

(Des A. Ryman. Litho Questa)

1986 (28 Aug). Naval Crests (5th series). Vert designs as T **134**. Multicoloured. W w **16**. P 14.

541	22p. H.M.S. *Lightning*	1·75	1·00
542	29p. H.M.S. *Hermione*	2·00	1·75
543	32p. H.M.S. *Laforey*	2·25	3·25
544	44p. H.M.S. *Nelson*	2·75	5·50
541/4 *Set of 4*		8·00	10·50

(Des A. Ryman. Litho Questa)

1986 (28 Aug). Royal Wedding. Sheet 115×85 mm. W w **16**. P 14½.

MS545	**153** 44p. multicoloured	1·40	2·25

154 Three Kings and Cathedral of St. Mary the Crowned

155 Neptune House

(Des M. Infante. Litho Walsall)

1986 (14 Oct). Christmas. International Peace Year. T **154** and similar vert design. Multicoloured. W w **16**. P 14.

546	18p. Type **154**	1·00	50
547	32p. St. Andrew's Church	1·50	3·00

(Litho Questa)

1986 (12 Dec)–**87**. As Nos. 461 and 464, but W w **16** (sideways). With "1986" imprint date. P 14.

549	2p. Vickers Viking 1B	2·00	3·50
552	5p. Boeing 727-100 (2.1.87)	2·00	3·50

(Des M. Infante. Litho Questa)

1987 (17 Feb). Europa. Architecture. T **155** and similar horiz design. Multicoloured. W w **16**. P 14½.

563	22p. Type **155**	1·25	50
564	29p. Ocean Heights	2·00	4·25

(Des A. Ryman. Litho Walsall)

1987 (15 Apr). Naval Crests (6th series). Vert designs as T **134**. Multicoloured. W w **16**. P 13½×13.

565	18p. H.M.S. *Wishart* (destroyer)	1·60	75
566	22p. H.M.S. *Charybdis* (cruiser)	1·75	1·10
567	32p. H.M.S. *Antelope* (destroyer)	2·50	3·50
568	44p. H.M.S. *Eagle* (aircraft carrier)	3·00	4·50
565/8 *Set of 4*		8·00	9·00

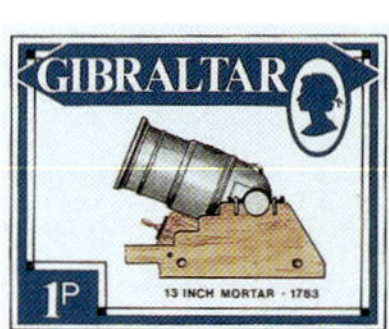

156 13-inch Mortar, 1783

157 Victoria Stadium

(Des A. Ryman. Litho Format)

1987 (1 June). Guns. T **156** and similar horiz designs. Multicoloured. W w **14**. P 12½.

569	1p. Type **156**	20	70
570	2p. 6-inch coastal gun, 1909	30	70
571	3p. 8-inch howitzer, 1783	40	1·00
572	4p. Bofors "L40/70" AA gun, 1951	40	10
573	5p. 100 ton rifled muzzle-loader, 1882	40	70
	w. Wmk inverted	†	—
574	10p. 5.25-inch heavy AA gun, 1953	40	70
575	18p. 25-pounder gun-how, 1943	65	1·00
576	19p. 64-pounder rifled muzzle-loader, 1873	70	1·25
577	22p. 12-pounder gun, 1758	70	50
578	50p. 10-inch rifled muzzle-loader, 1870	1·40	3·00
579	£1 Russian 24-pounder gun, 1854	2·50	2·50
580	£3 9.2-inch "MK. 10" coastal gun, 1935	3·00	12·00
581	£5 24-pounder gun, 1779	5·00	14·00
569/81 *Set of 13*		14·50	35·00

One sheet of the £5 value is known showing "12-pounder gum, 1758" (the vignette used for the 22p. stamp). The provenance of this item is unknown.

(Des A. Ryman. Litho Walsall)

1987 (16 Sept). Bicentenary of Royal Engineers' Royal Warrant. T **157** and similar vert designs. Multicoloured. W w **14**. P 14½.

582	18p. Type **157**	1·25	65
583	32p. Freedom of Gibraltar scroll and casket	1·75	3·25
584	44p. Royal Engineers' badge	2·50	4·50
582/4 *Set of 3*		5·00	7·50

158 The Three Kings

(Des Olympia Reyes. Litho Walsall)

1987 (12 Nov). Christmas. T **158** and similar horiz designs. Multicoloured. W w **16** (sideways). P 14½.

585	4p. Type **158**	20	10
586	22p. The Holy Family	1·00	1·00
587	44p. The Shepherds	1·90	3·50
585/7 *Set of 3*		2·75	4·00

159 *Canberra* (liner) passing Gibraltar

160 European Bee Eater

(Des Olympia Reyes. Litho Format)

1988 (16 Feb). Europa. Transport and Communications. T **159** and similar horiz designs. Multicoloured. W w **14**. P 14½×14×roul between *se-tenant* pairs.

588	22p. Type **159**	1·50	2·25
	a. Horiz pair. Nos. 588/9	3·00	4·50
589	22p. *Gibline I* (ferry), dish aerial and Boeing 737	1·50	2·25
590	32p. Horse-drawn carriage and modern coach	2·00	2·75
	a. Horiz pair. Nos. 590/1	4·00	5·50
591	32p. Rover SD1 saloon (1976), telephone and Rock of Gibraltar	2·00	2·75
588/91 *Set of 4*		6·25	9·00

The two designs for each value were printed in sheets, of ten, each containing five horizontal *se-tenant* pairs in which the stamps were rouletted between vertically.

(Des A. Ryman. Litho Walsall)

1988 (7 Apr). Naval Crests (7th series). Vert designs as T **134**. W w **16**. P 13½×13.

592	18p. multicoloured	1·50	65
593	22p. black, brownish black and gold	2·00	1·25
594	32p. multicoloured	2·25	3·50
595	44p. multicoloured	3·00	4·75
592/5 *Set of 4*		8·00	9·25

Designs:—18p. H.M.S. *Clyde*; 22p. H.M.S. *Foresight*; 32p. H.M.S. *Severn*; 44p. H.M.S. *Rodney*.

(Des Olympia Reyes. Litho B.D.T.)

1988 (15 June). Birds. T **160** and similar horiz designs. Multicoloured. W w **14** (sideways). P 13½.

596	4p. Type **160**	75	20
597	22p. Atlantic Puffin	1·75	90
598	32p. Honey Buzzard	2·25	2·50
599	44p. Blue Rock Thrush	2·75	4·00
596/9 *Set of 4*		6·75	7·00

161 *Zebu* (brigantine)

162 "Snowman" (Rebecca Falero)

(Des A. Ryman. Litho B.D.T.)

1988 (14 Sept). Operation Raleigh. T **161** and similar horiz designs. Multicoloured. W w **14**. P 13.

600	19p. Type **161**	65	60
601	22p. Miniature of Sir Walter Raleigh and logo	75	70
602	32p. *Sir Walter Raleigh* (expedition ship) and world map	1·10	2·00
600/2 *Set of 3*		2·25	3·00
MS603	135×86 mm. 22p As No. 601; 44p. *Sir Walter Raleigh* (expedition ship) passing Gibraltar	4·50	5·50

(Des A. Ryman. Litho Questa)

1988 (2 Nov). Christmas. Children's Paintings. T **162** and similar multicoloured designs. W w **16** (sideways). P 14½ (44p.) or 14 (others).

604	4p. Type **162**	15	10
605	22p. "The Nativity" (Dennis Penalver)	55	60
606	44p. "Father Christmas" (Gavin Key) (23×31 mm)	1·00	2·40
604/6 *Set of* 3		1·50	2·75

163 Soft Toys and Toy Train

164 Port Sergeant with Keys

(Des Olympia Reyes. Litho Walsall)

1989 (15 Feb). Europa. Children's Toys. T **163** and similar horiz design. Multicoloured. W w **16** (sideways). P 13×13½.

607	25p. Type **163**	1·25	75
608	32p. Soft toys, toy boat and doll's house	1·75	2·75

(Des A. Ryman. Litho Walsall)

1989 (28 Apr). 50th Anniv of Gibraltar Regiment. T **164** and similar vert designs. Multicoloured. W w **14**. P 13½×13.

609	4p. Type **164**	50	10
610	22p. Regimental badge and colours	1·40	1·10
611	32p. Drum major	1·90	3·50
609/11 *Set of* 3		3·50	4·25
MS612 124×83 mm. 22p. As No. 610; 44p. Former Gibraltar Defence Force badge		4·75	5·50

165 Nurse and Baby

166 One Penny Coin

(Des E. Field. Litho Questa)

1989 (7 July). 125th Anniv of International Red Cross. T **165** and similar vert designs. W w **16**. P 15×14½.

613	25p. black, bright scarlet and grey-brown	1·00	60
614	32p. black, bright scarlet and grey-brown	1·25	1·75
615	44p. black, bright scarlet and grey-brown	1·50	3·50
613/15 *Set of* 3		3·25	5·25

Designs:—32p. Famine victims; 44p. Accident victims.

(Des A. Ryman. Litho B.D.T.)

1989 (7 Sept). Naval Crests (8th series). Vert designs as T **134**. W w **16**. P 14×13½.

616	22p. multicoloured	1·50	75
617	25p. black and gold	1·50	1·50
618	32p. gold, black and bright scarlet	2·00	3·25
619	44p. multicoloured	3·00	5·50
616/19 *Set of* 4		7·25	10·00

Designs:—22p. H.M.S. *Blankney*; 25p. H.M.S. *Deptford*; 32p. H.M.S. *Exmoor*; 44p. H.M.S. *Stork*.

(Des A. Ryman. Litho Questa)

1989 (11 Oct). New Coinage. T **166** and similar vert designs in two miniature sheets. W w **16** (sideways). P 14½.

MS620 72×94 mm. 4p. bronze, black & dull verm (Type **166**); 4p. bronze, blk & dp brn (two pence); 4p. silver, blk & greenish yellow (ten pence); 4p. silver, black and emerald (five pence)	1·25	2·25
MS621 100×95 mm. 22p. silver, black & reddish orge (fifty pence); 22p. gold, black & ultram (five pounds); 22p gold, blk & orge-brn (two pounds); 22p gold, blk & brt emer (one pound); 22p gold, blk & brt reddish vio (obverse of coin series); 22p. silver, black and pale violet-blue (twenty pence)	5·50	7·50

167 Father Christmas in Sleigh

168 General Post Office Entrance

(Des M. Infante. Litho Questa)

1989 (11 Oct). Christmas. T **167** and similar horiz designs. Multicoloured. W w **16** (sideways). P 14½.

622	4p. Type **167**	20	10
623	22p. Shepherds and sheep	90	70
624	32p. The Nativity	1·40	1·75
625	44p. The Three Wise Men	2·25	4·00
622/5 *Set of* 4		4·25	6·00

(Des Olympia Reyes. Litho Questa)

1990 (6 Mar). Europa. Post Office Buildings. T **168** and similar vert designs. Multicoloured. P 14½×roul between *se-tenant* pairs.

626	22p. Type **168**	1·25	1·75
	a. Horiz pair. Nos. 626/7	2·50	3·50
627	22p. Interior of General Post Office	1·25	1·75
628	32p. Interior of South District Post Office	1·50	2·50
	a. Horiz pair. Nos. 628/9	3·00	5·00
629	32p. South District Post Office	1·50	2·50
626/9 *Set of* 4		5·00	7·75

Nos. 626/7 and 628/9 were printed in *se-tenant* horizontal pairs within separate sheets of eight, the stamps in each pair being divided by a line of roulettes.

169 19th-century Firemen

170 Henry Corbould (artist) and Penny Black

(Des D. Gonzalez. Litho Questa)

1990 (2 Apr). 125th Anniv of Gibraltar Fire Service. T **169** and similar multicoloured designs. P 14½×14 (vert) or 14×14½ (horiz).

630	4p. Type **169**	1·00	15
631	20p. Early fire engine (*horiz*)	2·50	1·10
632	42p. Modern fire engine (*horiz*)	3·00	3·75
633	44p. Fireman in breathing apparatus	3·00	3·75
630/3 *Set of* 4		8·50	8·00

(Des A. Ryman. Litho Questa)

1990 (3 May). 150th Anniv of the Penny Black. T **170** and similar vert designs. Multicoloured. P 13½×14.

634	19p. Type **170**	1·10	1·00
635	22p. Bath Royal Mail coach	1·25	1·00
636	32p. Sir Rowland Hill and Penny Black	2·50	4·50
634/6 *Set of* 3		4·25	6·00
MS637 145×95 mm. 44p. Penny Black with Maltese Cross cancellation. P 14½×14		4·75	6·00

(Des A. Ryman. Litho Questa)

1990 (10 July). Naval Crests (9th series). Vert designs as T **134**. Multicoloured. P 14.

638	22p. H.M.S. *Calpe*	1·75	70
639	25p. H.M.S. *Gallant*	1·90	1·75
640	32p. H.M.S. *Wrestler*	2·50	3·25
641	44p. H.M.S. *Greyhound*	3·00	6·50
638/41 *Set of* 4		8·25	11·00

171 Model of Europort Development

172 Candle and Holly

(Des A. Ryman. Litho Questa)

1990 (10 Oct). Development Projects. T **171** and similar horiz designs. Multicoloured. P 14½.

642 22p. Type **171** ... 75 80
643 23p. Construction of building material factory ... 75 1·50
644 25p. Land reclamation ... 95 1·50
642/4 *Set of 3* ... 2·25 3·50

(Des D. Gonzalez. Litho B.D.T.)

1990 (10 Oct). Christmas. T **172** and similar vert designs. Multicoloured. P 13½.

645 4p. Type **172** ... 15 10
646 22p. Father Christmas ... 75 65
647 42p. Christmas Tree ... 1·50 2·50
648 44p. Nativity crib ... 1·50 2·50
645/8 *Set of 4* ... 3·50 5·25

173 Space Laboratory and Spaceplane (Colombus Development Programme)

174 Shag

(Des D. Gonzalez. Litho B.D.T.)

1991 (26 Feb). Europa. Europe in Space. T **173** and similar horiz design. Multicoloured. P 13½×13.

649 25p. Type **173** ... 75 75
650 32p. "ERS-1" earth resources remote sensing satellite ... 1·00 2·25

(Des A. Ryman. Litho Walsall)

1991 (9 Apr). Naval Crests (10th series). Vert designs as T **134**. P 13½×13.

651 4p. black, new blue and gold ... 60 10
652 21p. multicoloured ... 1·75 1·25
653 22p. multicoloured ... 1·75 1·25
654 62p. multicoloured ... 3·75 7·00
651/4 *Set of 4* ... 7·00 8·75

Designs:—4p. H.M.S. *Hesperus*; 21p. H.M.S. *Forester*; 22p. H.M.S. *Furious*; 62p. H.M.S. *Scylla*.

(Des Olympia Reyes. Litho B.D.T.)

1991 (30 May). Endangered Species. Birds. T **174** and similar horiz designs. Multicoloured. P 13½.

655 13p. Type **174** ... 1·40 1·60
a. Block of 4. Nos. 655/8 ... 5·00 5·75
656 13p. Barbary Partridge ... 1·40 1·60
657 13p. Egyptian Vulture ... 1·40 1·60
658 13p. Black Stork ... 1·40 1·60
655/8 *Set of 4* ... 5·00 5·75

Nos. 655/8 were printed together, *se-tenant*, in differently arranged blocks of 4 throughout the sheet of 16.

£1.05

(**175**)

176 "North View of Gibraltar" (Gustavo Bacarisas)

1991 (30 May). No. 580 surch with T **175**.

659 £1.05 on £3 9.2-inch "Mk.10" coastal gun, 1935 ... 3·50 1·60

(Des A. Ryman. Litho B.D.T.)

1991 (10 Sept). Local Paintings. T **176** and similar multicoloured designs. P 14×15 (42p.) or 15×14 (others).

660 22p. Type **176** ... 85 50
661 26p. "Parsons Lodge" (Elena Mifsud) ... 1·00 1·00
662 32p. "Governor's Parade" (Jacobo Azagury) ... 1·50 2·25
663 42p. "Waterport Wharf" (Rudesindo Mannia) (*vert*) ... 2·25 4·50
660/3 *Set of 4* ... 5·00 7·50

177 "Once in Royal David's City"

178 *Donnaus chrysippus*

(Des D. Gonzalez. Litho Questa)

1991 (15 Oct). Christmas. Carols. T **177** and similar horiz designs. Multicoloured. P 14×14½.

664 4p. Type **177** ... 40 10
665 24p. "Silent Night" ... 1·75 70
666 25p. "Angels We have Heard on High" ... 1·75 1·25
667 49p. "O Come All Ye Faithful" ... 2·50 6·00
664/7 *Set of 4* ... 5·75 7·25

(Des A. Ryman. Litho Questa)

1991 (15 Nov). "Phila Nippon '91" International Stamp Exhibition, Tokyo. Sheet 116×91 mm. P 14½.

MS668 **178** £1.05 multicoloured ... 3·25 4·50

179 Columbus and *Santa Maria*

(Des Olympia Reyes. Litho Walsall)

1992 (6 Feb). Europa. 500th Anniv of Discovery of America by Columbus. T **179** and similar horiz designs. Multicoloured. P 14½.

669 24p. Type **179** ... 1·25 2·00
a. Horiz pair. Nos. 669/70 ... 2·50 4·00
670 24p. Map of Old World and *Nina* ... 1·25 2·00
671 34p. Map of New World and *Pinta* ... 1·50 2·50
a. Horiz pair. Nos. 671/2 ... 3·00 5·00
672 34p. Map of Old World and look-out ... 1·50 2·50
669/72 *Set of 4* ... 5·00 8·00

The two designs of each value were printed together, *se-tenant*, in sheets of eight, the background to each horizontal pair forming a composite design.

179a Gibraltar from North

180 Compass Rose, Sail and Atlantic Map

(Des D. Miller. Litho Questa (54p), B.D.T. (others))

1992 (6 Feb). 40th Anniv of Queen Elizabeth II's Accession. Horiz designs as T **179a**. Multicoloured. W w **14** (sideways). P 14.

673 4p. Type T **179a** ... 15 10
674 20p. H.M.S. *Arrow* (frigate) and Gibraltar from South ... 60 60
675 24p. Southport Gates ... 75 80
676 44p. Three portraits of Queen Elizabeth ... 1·25 1·60
677 54p. Queen Elizabeth II ... 1·60 1·90
673/7 *Set of 5* ... 4·00 4·50

(Des E. Field. Litho B.D.T.)

1992 (15 Apr). Round the World Yacht Rally. T **180** and similar multicoloured designs, each incorporating compass rose and sail. P 13½.

678 21p. Type **180** ... 75 80

679	24p. Map of Indonesian Archipelago (*horiz*)	95	1·40
680	25p. Map of Indian Ocean (*horiz*)	95	1·75
678/80 *Set of 3*		2·40	3·50

MS681 108×72 mm. 21p Type **180**; 49p. Map of Mediterranean and Red Sea .... 2·50 3·50

181 Holy Trinity Cathedral

182 Sacred Heart of Jesus Church

(Des M. Infante. Litho Questa)

1992 (21 Aug). 150th Anniv of Anglican Diocese of Gibraltar in Europe. T **181** and similar multicoloured designs. P 14.

682	4p. Type **181**	20	10
683	24p. Diocesan crest and map (*horiz*)	1·00	65
684	44p. Construction of Cathedral and Sir George Don (*horiz*)	1·75	3·00
685	54p. Bishop Tomlinson	2·00	3·50
682/5 *Set of 4*		4·50	6·50

(Des W. Stagnetto. Litho B.D.T.)

1992 (10 Nov). Christmas. Churches. T **182** and similar vert designs. Multicoloured. P 14×13½.

686	4p. Type **182**	35	10
687	24p. Cathedral of St. Mary the Crowned	1·50	55
688	34p. St. Andrew's Church of Scotland	2·00	2·50
689	49p. St. Joseph's Church	2·50	5·50
686/9 *Set of 4*		5·75	7·75

183 "Drama and Music"

184 H.M.S. *Hood* (battle cruiser)

(Des E. Field. Litho Questa)

1993 (2 Mar). Europa. Contemporary Art. T **183** and similar vert designs. Multicoloured. P 14½×14.

690	24p. Type **183**	1·50	2·00
	a. Horiz pair. Nos. 690/1	3·00	4·00
691	24p. "Sculpture, Art and Pottery"	1·50	2·00
692	34p. "Architecture"	2·00	2·75
	a. Horiz pair. Nos. 692/3	4·00	5·50
693	34p. "Printing and Photography"	2·00	2·75
690/3 *Set of 4*		6·25	8·50

Nos. 690/1 and 692/3 were printed together, *se-tenant*, as horizontal pairs in sheetlets of 8 with decorative margins.

(Des D. Miller. Litho B.D.T.)

1993 (27 Apr). Second World War Warships (1st series). Sheet 120×79 mm containing T **184** and similar horiz designs. Multicoloured. P 14.

MS694 24p. Type **184**; 24p. H.M.S. *Ark Royal* (aircraft carrier, 1937); 24p. H.M.A.S. *Waterhen* (destroyer); 24p. U.S.S. *Gleaves* (destroyer) .... 11·00 11·00

See also Nos. **MS**724, **MS**748, **MS**779 and **MS**809.

185 Landport Gate

186 £sd and Decimal British Coins (25th anniv of Decimal Currency)

(Des Olympia Reyes. Litho and thermography Cartor (£5), litho Cartor (6, 7, 8, 9, 20, 30, 40p. and £2) or B.D.T. (others))

1993 (28 June)–**95**. Architectural Heritage. T **185** and similar multicoloured designs. P 13.

695	1p. Type **185**	30	1·25
696	2p. St. Mary the Crowned Church (*horiz*)	50	1·25
697	3p. Parsons Lodge Battery (*horiz*)	50	1·50
698	4p. Moorish Castle (*horiz*)	65	1·25
699	5p. General Post Office	65	30
699*a*	6p. House of Assembly (1.9.95)	2·00	1·25
699*b*	7p. Bleak House (*horiz*) (1.9.95)	2·00	1·25
699*c*	8p. General Eliott Memorial (1.9.95)	2·00	1·25
699*d*	9p. Supreme Court Building (*horiz*) (1.9.95)	2·00	1·25
700	10p. South Barracks (*horiz*)	50	60
700*a*	20p. The Convent (*horiz*) (1.9.95)	3·00	1·25
701	21p. American War Memorial	1·00	80
702	24p. Garrison Library (*horiz*)	1·10	80
703	25p. Southport Gates	1·10	80
704	26p. Casemates Gate (*horiz*)	1·10	80
704*a*	30p. St. Bernard's Hospital (1.9.95)	4·00	1·25
704*b*	40p. City Hall (*horiz*) (1.9.95)	4·00	2·00
705	50p. Central Police Station (*horiz*)	2·50	2·25
706	£1 Prince Edward's Gate	2·25	2·75
706*a*	£2 Church of the Sacred Heart of Jesus (1.9.95)	8·50	8·00
707	£3 Lighthouse, Europa Point	11·00	11·00
708	£5 Coat of arms and Fortress keys (6.6.94)	10·00	15·00
695/708 *Set of 22*		55·00	50·00

(Des W. Stagnetto. Litho Cartor)

1993 (21 Sept). Anniversaries. T **186** and similar horiz designs. Multicoloured. P 13.

709	21p. Type **186**	1·00	65
710	24p. R.A.F. crest with Handley Page 0/400 biplane and Panavia Tornado F Mk 3 fighter (75th anniv)	1·75	75
711	34p. Garrison Library badge and building (Bicent)	1·60	2·25
712	49p. Sir Winston Churchill and air raid (50th anniv of visit)	4·00	5·00
709/12 *Set of 4*		7·50	7·75

187 Mice decorating Christmas Tree

(Des Josie Evans. Litho Cartor)

1993 (16 Nov). Christmas. T **187** and similar horiz designs. Multicoloured. P 13½.

713	5p. Type **187**	25	10
714	24p. Mice pulling cracker	1·10	70
715	44p. Mice singing carols	2·25	3·00
716	49p. Mice building snowman	2·75	3·75
713/16 *Set of 4*		5·75	6·75

188 Exploding Atom (Lord Penney)

(Des M. Braunewell. Litho Cartor)

1994 (1 Mar). Europa. Scientific Discoveries. T **188** and similar horiz designs. Multicoloured. P 13½.

717	24p. Type **188**	1·00	1·50
	a. Horiz pair. Nos. 717/18	2·00	3·00
718	24p. Polonium and radium experiment (Marie Curie)	1·00	1·50
719	34p. First oil engine (Rudolph Diesel)	1·25	2·00
	a. Horiz pair. Nos. 719/20	2·50	4·00
720	34p. Early telescope (Galileo)	1·25	2·00
717/20 *Set of 4*		4·00	6·25

Nos. 717/18 and 719/20 were each printed together, *se-tenant*, in horizontal pairs in sheetlets of 8 with decorative margins.

189 World Cup and Map of U.S.A.

(Des M. Braunewell. Litho Cartor)

1994 (19 Apr). World Cup Football Championship, U.S.A. T **189** and similar multicoloured designs. P 13½.

721	26p. Type **189**	80	55
722	39p. Players and pitch in shape of U.S.A.	1·25	2·00
723	49p. Player's legs (*vert*)	1·60	2·75
721/3 *Set of* 3		3·25	4·75

(Des D. Miller. Litho Cartor)

1994 (6 June). Second World War Warships (2nd series). Sheet 112×72 mm containing horiz designs as T **184**. Multicoloured. P 13.

MS724 5p H.M.S. *Penelope* (cruiser); 25p. H.M.S. *Warspite* (battleship); 44p. U.S.S. *McLanahan* (destroyer); 49p. *Isaac Sweers* (Dutch destroyer) ..... 10·00 11·00

190 Pekingese

191 Golden Star Coral

(Des M. Braunewell. Litho B.D.T.)

1994 (16 Aug). "Philakorea '94" International Stamp Exhibiton, Seoul. Sheet *102×76* mm. P 13.

MS725 **190** £1.05 multicoloured ..... 2·50 4·00

(Des M. Whyte. Litho Walsall)

1994 (27 Sept). Marine Life. T **191** and similar square designs. Multicoloured. P 14½×14.

726	21p. Type **191**	75	45
727	24p. Star Fish	90	55
728	34p. Gorgonian Sea-fan	1·50	2·25
729	49p. Peacock Wrasse ("Turkish Wrasse")	2·00	3·50
726/9 *Set of* 4		4·75	6·00

192 Throwing the Discus and Centenary Emblem

193 Great Tit

(Des S. Perera. Litho Walsall)

1994 (22 Nov). Centenary of International Olympic Committee. T **192** and similar horiz design. Multicoloured. P 14.

730	49p. Type **192**	1·75	2·25
731	54p. Javelin throwing and emblem	1·75	2·50

(Des W. Stagnetto. Litho B.D.T.)

1994 (22 Nov). Christmas. Songbirds. T **193** and similar multicoloured designs. P 14×13½ (vert) or 13½×14 (horiz).

732	5p. Type **193**	80	10
733	24p. European Robin (*horiz*)	2·25	70
734	34p. Blue Tit (*horiz*)	2·50	1·50
735	54p. Goldfinch	3·25	5·50
732/5 *Set of* 4		8·00	7·00

194 Austrian Flag, Hand and Star

(Des R. Ollington. Litho Questa)

1995 (3 Jan). Expansion of European Union. T **194** and similar horiz designs. Multicoloured. P 14.

736	24p. Type **194**	60	55
737	26p. Finnish flag, hand and star	60	60
738	34p. Swedish flag, hand and star	90	1·50
739	49p. Flags of new members and European Union emblem	1·60	3·25
736/9 *Set of* 4		3·25	5·50

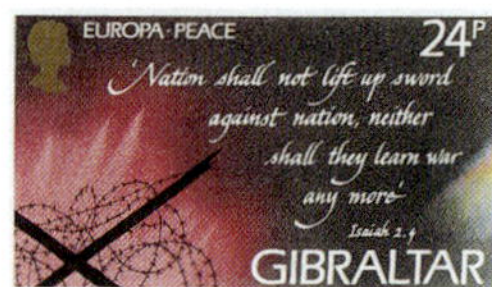

195 Barbed Wire and Quote from Isaiah Ch 2.4

(Des Jennifer Toombs. Litho B.D.T.)

1995 (28 Feb). Europa. Peace and Freedom. T **195** and similar horiz designs. Multicoloured. P 13½.

740	24p. Type **195**	1·40	1·60
	a. Horiz pair. Nos. 740/1	2·75	3·00
741	24p. Rainbow and hands releasing peace dove	1·40	1·60
742	34p. Shackles on wall and quote from Isaiah ch 61.1	1·60	2·25
	a. Horiz pair. Nos. 742/3	3·00	4·50
743	34p. Hands and Mediterranean Gulls	1·60	2·25
740/3 *Set of* 4		5·50	7·00

Nos. 740/1 and 742/3 were each printed together, *se-tenant*, as horizontal pairs in sheetlets of 8 with decorative margins.

196 Fairey Swordfish, I Class Destroyer and Rock of Gibraltar

(Des A. Theobald. Litho B.D.T.)

1995 (8 May). 50th Anniv of End of Second World War. Sheet 101×66 mm. P 13½.

MS744 **196** £1.05 multicoloured ..... 3·25 4·25

197 Yachting

198 Bee Orchid

(Des Stephen Perera. Litho B.D.T.)

1995 (8 May). Island Games '95. T **197** and similar vert designs. Multicoloured. P 14×13½.

745	24p. Type **197**	70	60
	a. Booklet pane. No. 745×3, with margins all round	1·90	
	b. Booklet pane. Nos. 745/7, with margins all round	3·50	
746	44p. Athlete on starting blocks	1·60	2·50
	a. Booklet pane. No. 746×3, with margins all round	4·25	
747	49p. Swimmer at start of race	1·60	2·50
	a. Booklet pane. No. 747×3, with margins all round	4·25	
745/7 *Set of* 3		3·50	5·00

(Des D. Miller. Litho Questa)

1995 (6 June). Second World War Warships (3rd series). Sheet 133×85 mm containing horiz designs as T **184**. Multicoloured. P 13½×14.

MS748 5p. H.M.S. *Calpe* (destroyer); 24p. H.M.S. *Victorious* (aircraft carrier); 44p. U.S.S. *Weehawken* (attack transport); 49p. *Savorgan de Brazza* (French destroyer) ..... 10·00 11·00

(Des Roger Gorringe. Litho B.D.T.)

1995 (1 Sept). "Singapore '95" International Stamp Exhibition. Orchids. T **198** and similar vert designs. Multicoloured. P 14×14½.

749	22p. Type **198**	1·40	1·60
	a. Horiz strip of 5. Nos. 749/53	6·25	7·25
750	23p. Brown Bee Orchid	1·40	1·60
751	24p. Pyramidal Orchid	1·40	1·60
752	25p. Mirror Orchid	1·40	1·60
753	26p. Sawfly Orchid	1·40	1·60
749/53 *Set of 5*		6·25	7·25

Nos. 749/53 were printed together, *se-tenant*, in horizontal strips of 5.

199 Handshake and United Nations Emblem

(Des Stephen Perera. Litho B.D.T.)

1995 (24 Oct). 50th Anniv of United Nations. T **199** and similar horiz design. Multicoloured. P 13½.

754	34p. Type **199**	1·50	1·10
755	49p. Peace dove and U.N. emblem	1·75	3·00

200 Marilyn Monroe

201 Father Christmas

(Des Mark Whyte. Litho Questa)

1995 (13 Nov). Centenary of Cinema. T **200** and similar horiz designs showing film stars. Multicoloured. P 14½×14.

MS756 Two sheets each 116×80 mm. (a) 5p. Type **200**; 25p. Romy Schneider; 28p. Yves Montand; 38p. Audrey Hepburn. (b) 24p Ingrid Bergman; 24p. Vittorio de Sica; 24p. Marlene Dietrich; 24p. Laurence Olivier *Set of 2 sheets* 4·50 5·50

(Des Mark Whyte. Litho B.D.T.)

1995 (27 Nov). Christmas. T **201** and similar square designs. Multicoloured. P 14.

757	5p. Type **201**	40	10
758	24p. Toys in sack	1·25	55
759	34p. Reindeer	1·75	1·25
760	54p. Sleigh over houses	3·00	4·50
757/60 *Set of 4*		5·75	5·75

202 Shih Tzu

(Des Doreen McGuinness. Litho B.D.T.)

1996 (24 Jan). Puppies. T **202** and similar horiz designs. Multicoloured. P 14.

761	5p. Type **202**	40	85
	a. Sheetlet. Nos. 761/6	4·00	6·00
762	21p. Dalmatians	75	95
763	24p. Cocker Spaniels	80	1·10
764	25p. West Highland White Terriers	80	1·10
765	34p. Labrador	90	1·25
766	35p. Boxer	90	1·25
761/6 *Set of 6*		4·00	6·00

Nos. 761/6 were printed together, *se-tenant*, in sheetlets of 6.
No. 762 is inscr "Dalmation" in error.

203 Princess Anne

204 West German Player, 1980

(Des Robin Ollington. Litho B.D.T.)

1996 (9 Feb). Europe. Famous Women. T **203** and similar horiz designs. P 13½.

767	**203**	24p. black and yellow	1·60	1·60
768	–	24p. black and deep turquoise-green	1·60	1·60
769	–	34p. black and vermilion	2·00	2·25
770	–	34p. black and purple	2·00	2·25
767/70 *Set of 4*			6·50	7·00

Details:—No. 768, Princess Diana; No. 769, Queen Elizabeth II; No. 770 Queen Elizabeth the Queen Mother.

Nos. 767/70 were each printed in sheets of 10 with inscribed margins all round.

(Des Steven Noon. Litho Walsall)

1996 (2 Apr). European Football Championship, England. T **204** and similar vert designs showing players from previous winning teams. Multicoloured. P 13.

771	21p. Type **204**	55	45
772	24p. French player, 1984	65	55
773	34p. Dutch player, 1988	95	1·10
774	£1.20 Danish player, 1992	2·50	4·75
771/4 *Set of 4*		4·25	6·25
MS775 135×91 mm. As Nos. 771/4. P 13×13½		5·50	7·50

205 Ancient Greek Athletes

206 Asian Children

(Des Keith Bassford. Litho Walsall)

1996 (2 May). Centenary of Modern Olympic Games. T **205** and similar horiz designs. P 13½.

776	34p. black, deep reddish purple and bright orange	95	90
777	49p. black and grey-brown	1·40	1·75
778	£1.05 multicoloured	3·00	4·50
776/8 *Set of 3*		4·75	6·50

Designs:—49p. Start of early race; £1.05 Start of modern face.

(Des Derek Miller. Litho Walsall)

1996 (8 June). Second World War Warships (4th series). Sheet, 118×84 mm containing horiz designs as T **184**. Multicoloured. P 14.

MS779 5p. H.M.S. *Starling* (sloop); 25p. H.M.S. *Royalist* (cruiser); 49p U.S.S. *Philadelphia* (cruiser); 54p. H.M.C.S. *Prescott* (corvette) 7·50 8·50

(Des Steven Noon. Litho Walsall)

1996 (8 June). 50th Anniv of U.N.I.C.E.F. T **206** and similar horiz designs showing children from different continents. P 13½×13.

780	21p. multicoloured	60	80
	a. Horiz strip of 4. Nos. 780/3	3·50	5·50
781	24p. multicoloured	70	90
782	49p. multicoloured	1·25	2·00
783	54p. multicoloured	1·40	2·25
780/3 *Set of 4*		3·50	5·50

Nos. 780/3 were printed together, *se-tenant*, in horizontal strips of 4 throughout the sheet.

207 Red Kites in Flight

(Des Roger Gorringe. Litho Walsall)

1996 (30 Sept). Endangered Species. Red Kite. T **207** and similar horiz designs. Multicoloured. P 14½.

784 34p. Type **207** ... 1·60 1·90
a. Block of 4. Nos. 784/7 ... 5·75 7·00
785 34p. Red Kite on ground ... 1·60 1·90
786 34p. On rock ... 1·60 1·90
787 34p. Pair at nest ... 1·60 1·90
784/7 *Set of 4* ... 5·75 7·00

Nos. 784/7 were printed together, *se-tenant*, in blocks of four throughout the sheet.

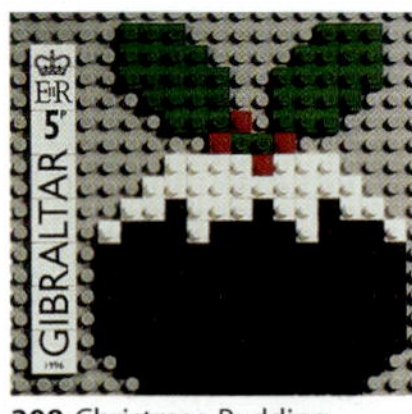

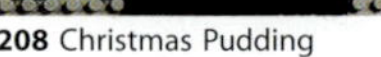

208 Christmas Pudding

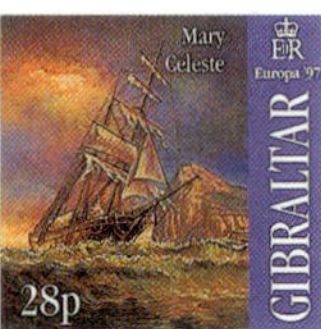

209 *Mary Celeste* passing Gibraltar

(Des Keith Bassford. Litho Questa)

1996 (27 Nov). Christmas. T **208** and similar horiz designs created from "Lego" blocks. Multicoloured. P 14×14½.

788 5p. Type **208** ... 15 15
789 21p. Snowman face ... 70 45
790 24p. Present ... 80 55
791 34p. Father Christmas face ... 1·10 1·25
792 54p. Candle ... 1·50 2·75
788/92 *Set of 5* ... 3·75 4·75

(Des S. Tarabay. Litho Questa)

1997 (12 Feb). Europe. Tales and Legends. The *Mary Celeste*. T **209** and similar square designs. Multicoloured. P 14.

793 28p. Type **209** ... 1·40 1·40
794 28p. Boarding the *Mary Celeste* ... 1·40 1·40
795 30p. Crew leaving *Mary Celeste* ... 1·40 1·60
796 30p. *Mary Celeste* found by *Dei Gratis* ... 1·40 1·60
793/6 *Set of 4* ... 5·00 5·50

210 American Shorthair Silver Tabby

211 *Anthocharis belia euphenoides*

(Des Colleen Corlett. Litho B.D.T.)

1997 (12 Feb). Kittens. T **210** and similar horiz designs. Multicoloured. P 13½×14.

797 5p. Type **210** ... 40 1·00
a. Booklet pane. Nos. 797, 799 and 801 with margins all round ... 1·75
b. Booklet pane. Nos. 797/8 and 801/2 with margins all round ... 2·50
798 24p. Rumpy Manx Red Tabby ... 75 1·25
a. Booklet pane. Nos. 798/800 with margins all round ... 2·00
799 26p. Blue Point Birmans ... 75 1·25
a. Booklet pane. Nos. 799/802 with margins all round ... 3·00
800 28p. Red Self Longhair ... 80 1·25
801 30p. British Shorthair Tortoiseshell and White ... 80 1·25
802 35p. British Bicolour Shorthairs ... 90 1·40
797/802 *Set of 6* ... 4·00 6·75
MS803 132×80 mm. Nos. 797/802 with "HONG KONG '97" International Stamp Exhibition logo at bottom left ... 5·50 8·00
a. Booklet pane. As No. **MS**803, but without "HONG KONG '97" logo and with additional line of roulettes at left ... 7·00 8·00

Nos. 797/802 were only issued in £5 stamp booklets or miniature sheet No. **MS**803.

(Des Roger Gorringe. Litho Enschedé)

1997 (7 Apr). Butterflies. T **211** and similar vert designs. Multicoloured. P 14×13½.

804 23p. Type **211** ... 70 50
805 26p. *Charaxes jasius* ... 85 60
806 30p. *Vanessa cardui* ... 95 90
807 £1.20 *Iphiclides podalirius* ... 3·25 5·00
804/7 *Set of 4* ... 5·25 6·25
MS808 135×90 mm. Nos. 804/7 ... 5·25 6·50

(Des Derek Miller. Litho Cartor)

1997 (9 June). Second World War Warships (5th series). Sheet, 117×82 mm, containing horiz designs as T **184**. Multicoloured. P 13½.

MS809 24p. H.M.S. *Enterprise* (cruiser); 26p. H.M.S. *Cleopatra* (cruiser); 38p. U.S.S. *Iowa* (battleship); 50p. *Orkan* (Polish destroyer) ... 4·00 5·00

212 Queen Elizabeth and Prince Philip at Carriage-driving Trials

(Des Clive Abbott. Litho Questa)

1997 (10 July). Golden Wedding of Queen Elizabeth and Prince Philip. T **212** and similar horiz design. Multicoloured. P 13½.

810 £1.20 Type **212** ... 4·75 5·50
a. Horiz pair. Nos. 810/11 ... 9·50 11·00
811 £1.40 Queen Elizabeth in Trooping the Colour uniform ... 4·75 5·50

Nos. 810/11 were printed together, *se-tenant*, in horizontal pairs throughout the sheet.

213 Christian Dior Evening Dress

214 "Our Lady and St. Bernard" (St. Joseph's Parish Church)

(Des M. Whyte. Litho B.D.T.)

1997 (24 Oct). Christian Dior Spring/Summer '97 Collection designed by John Galliano. T **213** and similar vert designs. Multicoloured. P 13½.

812 30p. Type **213** ... 80 1·25
a. Horiz pair. Nos. 812 and 814 ... 1·75 3·00
813 35p. Tunic top and skirt ... 1·00 1·60
a. Horiz pair. Nos. 813 and 815 ... 2·25 3·50
814 50p. Ballgown ... 1·00 1·75
815 62p. Two-piece suit ... 1·25 2·25
812/15 *Set of 4* ... 4·00 6·50
MS816 110×90 mm. £1.20 Ballgown (different) ... 2·25 3·50

Nos. 812 with 814 and 813 with 815 were each printed together, *se-tenant*, in sheets of 8 with enlarged illustrated right-hand margin.

(Des Stephen Perera. Litho Cartor)

1997 (18 Nov). Christmas. Stained Glass Windows. T **214** and similar vert designs. Multicoloured. P 13½.

817 5p. Type **214** ... 25 10
818 26p. "The Epiphany" (Our Lady of Sorrows Church) ... 1·00 60
819 38p. "St. Joseph" (Our Lady of Sorrows Church) ... 1·25 95
820 50p. "The Holy Family" (St. Joseph's Parish Church) ... 1·50 2·25
821 62p. "The Miraculous Medal" (St. Joseph's Parish Church) ... 1·75 3·25
817/21 *Set of 5* ... 5·25 6·50

215 Sir Joshua Hassan

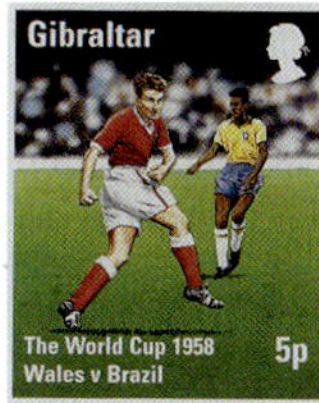

216 Wales v Brazil (1958)

(Des Stephen Perera. Litho Cartor)

1997 (15 Dec). Sir Joshua Hassan (former Chief Minister) Commemoration. P 13.

822	**215**	26p. black	1·50	75

(Des Lee Montgomery. Litho Cartor)

1998 (23 Jan). World Football Championship, France (1998). T **216** and similar vert designs. Multicoloured. P 13.

823	5p. Type **216**	25	10
824	26p. Northern Ireland v France (1958)	1·00	60
825	38p. Scotland v Holland (1978)	1·25	90
826	£1.20 England v West Germany (1966)	2·25	4·75
823/6 *Set of 4*		4·25	6·00
MS827 153×96 mm. Nos. 823/6		4·25	6·00

216a Princess Diana wearing Jacket with White Fur Collar, 1988

216b Saro London (flying boat)

(Des Derek Miller. Litho Questa)

1998 (31 Mar). Diana, Princess of Wales Commemoration. Sheet, 145×70 mm, containing vert designs as T **216a**. Multicoloured. P 14½×14.

MS828 26p. Wearing jacket with white fur collar, 1988; 26p. Wearing pink checked suit and hat; 38p. Wearing black jacket, 1995; 38p. Wearing blue jacket with gold embroidery, 1987 (sold at £1.28 + 20p. *charity premium*) 2·25 3·75

(Des A. Theobald. Litho B.D.T.)

1998 (1 Apr). 80th Anniv of Royal Air Force. Horiz designs as T **216b**. Multicoloured. P 14.

829	24p. Type **216b**	70	55
830	26p. Fairey Fox	75	60
831	38p. Handley Page Halifax GR.VI	95	1·25
832	50p. Hawker Siddeley Buccaneer S.2B	1·25	2·50
829/32 *Set of 4*		3·25	4·50
MS833 110×77 mm. 24p. Sopwith 1½ Strutter; 26p. Bristol M.1B; 38p. Supermarine Spitfire XII; 50p. Avro York		3·50	4·50

217 Miss Gibraltar saluting

218 Striped Dolphin

(Des Stephen Perera. Litho Cartor)

1998 (22 May). Europa. Festivals. National Day. T **217** and similar vert designs showing Miss Gibraltar in various costumes. Multicoloured. P 13½×13.

834	26p. Type **217**	1·10	1·25
835	26p. In black bodice and long red skirt	1·10	1·25
836	38p. In black bodice and short red skirt, with Gibraltar flag	1·40	1·60
837	38p. In Genoese-style costume	1·40	1·60
834/7 *Set of 4*		4·50	5·25

Nos. 834/7 were each printed in sheets of 10 with enlarged illustrated right-hand margins.

(Des Lee Montgomery. Litho Questa)

1998 (22 May). International Year of the Ocean. Sheet, *155×64* mm, containing T **218** and similar multicoloured designs. P 14.

MS838 5p. Type **218**; 5p Common Dolphin (*vert*); 26p. Killer Whale (*vert*); £1.20 Blue Whale 5·50 6·50

219 Nileus (dog) with Hat and Telescope

220 "Love comforts like Sunshine after Rain" (William Shakespeare)

(Des Martin Hargreaves. Litho Cartor)

1998 (1 Aug). Bicentenary of Battle of the Nile. T **219** and similar multicoloured designs. P 13½.

839	12p. Type **219**	1·00	1·25
	a. Booklet pane. Nos. 839/41 with margins all round	3·25	
	b. Booklet pane. Nos. 839/43 with margins all round	6·50	
840	26p. Rear-Admiral Sir Horatio Nelson	1·00	80
	a. Booklet pane. No. 840 with margins all round	1·00	
	b. Booklet pane. Nos. 840×2 and 842/3 with margins all round	5·00	
	c. Booklet pane. Nos. 840 and 842/3 with margins all round	4·00	
841	28p. Frances Nisbet, Lady Nelson	1·75	2·00
842	35p. H.M.S. *Vanguard* (ship of the line)	1·75	2·25
843	50p. Battle of the Nile (47×29 mm)	1·75	3·25
839/43 *Set of 5*		6·50	8·50

(Des Mark Whyte. Litho Questa)

1998 (6 Oct). Famous Quotations. T **220** and similar horiz designs. Multicoloured. P 14½.

844	26p. Type **220**	90	1·00
845	26p. "The price of greatness is responsibility" (Sir Winston Churchill)	90	1·00
846	38p. "Hate the sin, love the sinner" (Mahatma Gandhi)	1·10	1·50
847	38p. "Imagination is more important than knowledge" (Albert Einstein)	1·10	1·50
844/7 *Set of 4*		3·50	4·50

Nos. 844/7 were each issued in sheets of 6 stamps and 6 half stamp-size labels showing the quotations in different languages.

221 The Nativity

222 Barbary Macaque

(Des Petula Stone. Litho Walsall)

1998 (10 Nov). Christmas. T **221** and similar vert designs. Multicoloured. P 13½.

848	5p. Type **221**	35	10
849	26p. Star and stable	1·25	70
850	30p. King with gold	1·40	75
851	35p. King with myrrh	1·40	1·25
852	50p. King with frankincense	1·75	3·25
848/52 *Set of 5*		5·50	5·50

(Des Roger Gorringe. Litho Cartor)

1999 (4 Mar). Europa. Parks and Gardens. Upper Rock Nature Reserve. T **222** and similar vert designs. Multicoloured. P 13½×13.

853	30p. Type **222**	1·75	1·50
854	30p. Dartford Warbler	2·00	1·50
855	42p. Dusky Grouper	2·00	2·50
856	42p. River Kingfisher	2·25	2·50
853/6 *Set of 4*		7·25	7·25

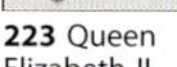

223 Queen Elizabeth II

224 Roman Marine and Galley

(Des Stephen Perera. Litho B.D.T.)

1999 (4 Mar)–**2001**.

(a) P 14 (50p., £1, £1.20, £1.40, £3) or 13½×13 (others)

No.	Type	Description	Unused	Used
857	**223**	1p. reddish purple	10	70
858		2p. olive-sepia	10	70
859		4p. light greenish blue	20	60
860		5p. emerald	20	30
861		10p. orange	40	30
862		12p. rosine	45	40
863		20p. turquoise-green	1·00	45
864		28p. magenta	1·25	60
865		30p. reddish orange	1·50	65
866		40p. deep olive-grey	2·00	85
867		42p. deep grey-green	2·00	90
868		50p. bistre	2·00	1·25
869		£1 brownish black	3·50	2·75
869*a*		£1.20 bright carmine (1.6.01)	4·50	4·00
869*b*		£1.40 bright blue (1.6.01)	4·50	4·25
870		£3 bright blue	8·50	11·00

(b) Self-adhesive. P 9½

No.	Type	Description	Unused	Used
871	**223**	(1st) reddish orange	1·00	60
857/71		*Set of 15*	30·00	28·00

Nos. 868/71 are larger, 25×30 mm.

No. 871 was printed in rolls of 100, on which the surplus self adhesive paper around each stamp was retained, and was initially sold at 26p.

(Des Simon Williams. Litho Cartor)

1999 (19 Mar). Maritime Heritage. T **224** and similar square designs. Multicoloured. P 12½.

No.	Description	Unused	Used
872	5p. Type **224**	25	10
873	30p. Arab sailor, medieval galley house and dhow	95	65
874	42p. Marine officer and British ship of the line (1779–83)	1·50	1·50
875	£1.20 Naval rating, Queen Alexandra Dry Dock and H.M.S. *Berwick* (cruiser) (1904)	3·25	4·25
872/5	*Set of 4*	5·50	6·00
MS876	116×76 mm. Nos. 872/5	6·00	7·00

No. **MS**876 includes the "Australia '99" International Stamp Exhibition, Melbourne, emblem on the sheet margin.

225 John Lennon (musician)

226 Postal Van at Dockside, 1930s

(Des Stephen Perera. Litho Cartor)

1999 (20 Mar). 30th Wedding Anniv of John Lennon and Yoko Ono. T **225** and similar vert designs showing John Lennon. P 13½×13.

No.	Description	Unused	Used
877	20p. multicoloured	1·00	55
878	30p. black and pale turquoise-blue	1·25	90
879	40p. multicoloured	1·50	1·90
877/9	*Set of 3*	3·25	3·00
MS880	Two sheets, each 62×100 mm. (a) £1 black and deep slate-blue. (b) £1 multicoloured *Set of 2 sheets*	8·50	8·50

Designs: 20p. With flower over left eye; 40p. Wearing orange glasses; £1 (No. **MS**880a), Holding marriage certificate; £1 (No. **MS**880*b*), Standing on aircraft steps.

Nos. 877/9 were each printed in small sheets of 10 with enlarged illustrated right margins.

(Des N. Walton. Litho Cartor)

1999 (20 Mar). 125th Anniv of Universal Postal Union. T **226** and similar square design. Multicoloured. P 12½.

No.	Description	Unused	Used
881	5p. Type **226**	25	25
882	30p. Space shuttle and station	75	1·25

227 EF-2000 Eurofighter

228 Prince Edward and Sophie Rhys-Jones

(Des Stephen Perera (30p.), Mike Atkinson (42p.). Litho Cartor)

1999 (17 June). "Wings of Prey" (1st series). Birds of Prey and R.A.F. Fighter Aircraft. T **227** and similar horiz designs. Multicoloured. P 13×13½.

No.	Description	Unused	Used
883	30p. Type **227**	1·25	1·40
	a. Horiz pair. Nos. 883 and 886	2·50	3·00
884	30p. Panavia Tornado F3	1·25	1·40
	a. Horiz pair. Nos. 884 and 887	2·50	3·00
885	30p. BAe Harrier II GR7	1·25	1·40
	a. Horiz pair. Nos. 885 and 888	2·50	3·00
886	42p. Lesser Kestrel	1·40	1·60
887	42p. Peregrine Falcon	1·40	1·60
888	42p. Common Kestrel	1·40	1·60
883/8	*Set of 6*	7·00	8·00
MS889	Two sheets, each 105×86 mm. (a) Nos. 883/5. (b) Nos. 886/8 *Set of 2 sheets*	8·00	8·50

Nos. 883 with 886, 884 with 887 and 885 with 888 were each printed together, *se-tenant*, as horizontal pairs in sheets of 10 with enlarged illustrated margins at right and foot.

See also Nos. 913/8 and 982/**MS**988.

(Des Stephen Perera. Litho Cartor)

1999 (19 June). Royal Wedding. T **228** and similar multicoloured designs. P 13×13½ (horiz) or 13½×13 (vert).

No.	Description	Unused	Used
890	30p. Type **228**	1·25	65
891	42p. Prince Edward and Sophie Rhys-Jones holding hands (*vert*)	1·60	1·00
892	54p. In carriage on wedding day (11 Oct)	2·00	2·50
893	66p. On Chapel steps after wedding (vert) (11 Oct)	2·50	3·00
890/3	*Set of 4*	6·50	6·50

Nos. 890/3 were printed in sheets with illustrated gutter margins.

229 Football

230 "Seasons Greetings"

(Des Jon Sayer. Litho Cartor)

1999 (2 July). Local Sporting Centenaries. T **229** and similar vert designs. Multicoloured. P 13½×13.

No.	Description	Unused	Used
894	30p. Type **229**	75	65
895	42p. Rowing	1·00	90
896	£1.20 Cricket	3·25	4·25
894/6	*Set of 3*	4·50	5·25

(Des Simon Williams. Litho B.D.T.)

1999 (11 Nov). Christmas. T **230** and similar square designs. Multicoloured. P 14.

No.	Description	Unused	Used
897	5p. Type **230**	15	10
898	5p. "Happy Christmas"	15	10
899	30p. "Happy Millennium"	80	80
900	30p. "Happy Christmas" and Santa with reindeer	80	80
901	42p. Santa Claus in chimney	1·25	1·75
902	54p. Santa Claus leaving presents	1·40	2·50
897/902	*Set of 6*	4·00	5·50

231 "People travelling with Environmentally-friendly Jet-packs" (Colin Grech)

232 Dutch Football Player and Flag, 1988

(Litho Questa)

2000 (28 Jan). "Stampin' the Future" (children's stamp design competition). T **231** and similar horiz designs. Multicoloured. P 14½×14.

903	30p. Type **231**	1·50	1·60
	a. Strip of 4. Nos. 903/6	5·50	5·75
904	42p. "Robotic Postman" (Kim Barea)	1·50	1·60
905	54p. "Living on the Moon" (Stephan Williamson-Fa)	1·50	1·60
906	66p. "Jet-powered Cars" (Michael Podesta)	1·50	1·60
903/6 *Set of 4*		5·50	5·75

Nos. 903/6 were printed together, *se-tenant*, as vertical or horizontal strips of 4 in sheets of 16.

(Des Lee Montgomery and Anselmo Torres. Litho Cartor)

2000 (17 Apr). European Football Championship, Netherlands. T **232** and similar square designs. Multicoloured. P 12½.

907	30p. Type **232**	85	90
908	30p. French player and flag, 1984	85	90
909	42p. German player scoring and flag, 1996	1·10	1·40
910	42p. Danish player and flag, 1992	1·10	1·40
907/10 *Set of 4*		3·50	4·25
MS911	Two sheets, each 115×85 mm. (a) 54p. ×4, English player and flag. (b) Nos. 907/10 *Set of 2 sheets*	11·00	12·00

Nos. 907/10 were each printed in sheets of 10 (5×2) with enlarged illustrated right margins showing national newspapers reports of football matches.

233 Fountain of Stars

234 3000 Metre Waterfall between Gibraltar and North African Coast, 5 Million B.C.

(Des Jon Sayer. Litho Cartor)

2000 (17 Apr). Europa. T **233** and similar vert designs. Multicoloured. P 13½×13.

912	30p. Type **233**	1·00	80
913	40p. Exchanging star	1·25	1·40
914	42p. Stars and airplane	1·25	1·40
915	54p. Stars and end of rainbow	1·75	2·75
912/15 *Set of 4*		4·75	5·75

Nos. 912/15 were each printed in sheets of 10 (5×2) with enlarged illustrated right margins.

(Des Christian Hook and Stephen Perera. Litho Questa)

2000 (9 May). New Millennium. History of Gibraltar. T **234** and similar square designs. Multicoloured (except Nos. 926/30). P 14.

916	5p. Type **234**	30	50
	a. Sheetlet. Nos. 916/31	9·50	12·50
	b. Booklet pane. No. 916×2	60	
917	5p. Sabre-tooth Tiger, 2 million B.C.	30	50
	b. Booklet pane. No. 917×2	60	
918	5p. Neanderthal hunting goat, and skull, 30,000 B.C.	30	50
	b. Booklet pane. No. 918×2	60	
919	5p. Phoenician traders and galley, 700 B.C.	30	50
	b. Booklet pane. No. 919×2	60	
920	5p. Roman warship, 100 B.C.	30	50
	b. Booklet pane. No. 920×2	60	
921	5p. Tarik-ibn-Zayad, ape and Moorish Castle, 711 A.D.	30	50
	b. Booklet pane. No. 921×2	60	
922	5p. Coat of arms, 1502	30	50
	b. Booklet pane. No. 922×2	60	
923	5p. Admiral George Rooke and Union Jack 1704	30	50
	b. Booklet pane. No. 923×2	60	
924	30p. General Eliott at The Great Siege, 1779–83	1·00	1·25
	b. Booklet pane. No. 924×2	2·00	
925	30p. H.M.S. *Victory*, 1805	1·00	1·25
	b. Booklet pane. No. 925×2	2·00	
926	30p. Queen Alexandra in horse-drawn carriage, 1903 (reddish brown, silver and black)	1·00	1·25
	b. Booklet pane. No. 926×3	2·75	
927	30p. 100 ton gun, 1870s (olive-grey, silver and black)	1·00	1·25
	b. Booklet pane. No. 927×3	2·75	
928	30p. Evacuees, 1940 (deep dull purple, silver and black)	1·00	1·25
	b. Booklet pane. No. 928×3	2·75	
929	30p. Tank and anti-aircraft gun 1940s (bistre-brown, silver and black)	1·00	1·25
	b. Booklet pane. No. 929×3	2·75	
930	30p. Queen Elizabeth II in Gibraltar, 1954 (violet-grey, silver and black)	1·00	1·25
	b. Booklet pane. No. 930×3	2·75	
931	30p. Aerial view of office district, 2000	1·00	1·25
	b. Booklet pane. No. 931×3	2·75	
916/31 *Set of 16*		9·50	12·50

Nos. 916/31 were printed together, *se-tenant*, in sheetlets of 16.

The booklet panes contain two or three stamps within larger illustrations. Some of the 30p. stamps from the booklet differ slightly in shade from those in the sheetlet.

235 Princess Diana holding Prince William, 1982

236 Lady Elizabeth Bowes-Lyon signing Book

(Des Anselmo Torres. Litho Cartor)

2000 (21 June). 18th Birthday of Prince William. T **235** and similar square designs. Multicoloured. P 12½.

932	30p. Type **235**	90	65
933	42p. Prince William as a toddler	1·25	90
934	54p. Prince William with Prince Charles	1·50	2·00
935	66p. Prince William at 18	1·75	2·75
932/5 *Set of 4*		4·75	5·50
MS936	115×75 mm. Nos. 932/5	5·00	6·00

Nos. 932/5 were each printed in sheets of 80 containing two panes separated by a large vertical gutter, showing further photographs extending to the height of two vertical rows.

(Des Stephen Perera. Litho Cartor)

2000 (4 Aug). Queen Elizabeth the Queen Mother's 100th Birthday. T **236** and similar square designs. P 12½.

937	30p. black and Prussian blue	90	65
938	42p. black and sepia	1·25	90
939	54p. multicoloured	1·50	2·00
940	66p. multicoloured	1·75	2·75
937/40 *Set of 4*		4·75	5·50
MS941	115×75 mm. Nos. 937/40	4·75	6·00

Designs:—42p. Duke and Duchess of York; 54p. Queen Mother with bouquet; 66p. Queen Mother in orange coat and hat.

Nos. 937/40 were printed in similar sheet format to Nos. 932/5.

237 Moorish Castle

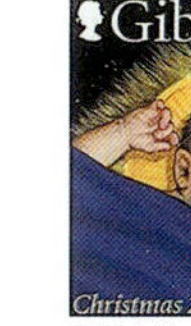

238 Infant Jesus

(Eng Czelaw Slania. Recess and photo Stamp Printing Office, Belgium)

2000 (15 Sept). P 11½.

942	**237**	£5 black, silver and gold†	13·00	14·00

†The Queen's head on this stamp is printed in optically variable ink which changes colour from gold to green when viewed from different angles.

(Des Stephen Perera (30p.), Roger Gorringe (42p.). Litho Questa)

2000 (15 Sept). "Wings of Prey" (2nd series). Birds of Prey and R.A.F. Second World War Aircraft. Horiz designs as T **227**. Multicoloured. P 14½×14.

943	30p. Supermarine Spitfire MkIIA *Gibraltar*	1·75	1·75
	a. Horiz pair. Nos. 943 and 946	3·75	3·75
944	30p. Hawker Hurricane MkIIC	1·75	1·75
	a. Horiz pair. Nos. 944 and 947	3·75	3·75
945	30p. Avro Lancaster BI-III *City of Lincoln*	1·75	1·75
	a. Horiz pair. Nos. 945 and 948	3·75	3·75
946	42p. Merlin (male)	2·00	2·00
947	42p. Merlin (female)	2·00	2·00
948	42p. Bonelli's Eagle	2·00	2·00
943/8 *Set of 6*		10·00	10·00

MS949 Two sheets, each 105×85 mm. (a) Nos. 943/5. (b) Nos. 946/8 *Set of 2 sheets* .... 10·00 10·00
ab. Lower stamp (No. 944) imperf on three sides £1500
ba. Lower stamp (No. 947) imperf on three sides £1500

Nos. 943/8 were printed in a similar *se-tenant* format as Nos. 883/8.

(Des Christian Hook. Litho Questa)

2000 (13 Nov). Christmas. T **238** and similar square designs. Multicoloured. P 14.

950	5p. Type **238**	25	15
951	30p. Virgin Mary with infant Jesus	85	65
952	30p. Journey to Bethlehem	85	65
953	40p. Mary and Joseph with innkeeper	1·10	1·00
954	42p. The Nativity	1·10	1·25
955	54p. Visit of the Wise Men	1·60	2·25
950/5 *Set of 6*		5·25	5·50

239 Wedding of Queen Victoria and Prince Albert

240 Grass Snake

(Des Anselmo Torres. Litho Cartor)

2001 (22 Jan). Death Centenary of Queen Victoria. T **239** and similar square designs. P 12½.

956	30p. deep violet-blue, deep violet and black	1·00	65
957	42p. myrtle-green, blackish green and black.	1·40	1·00
958	54p. blackish purple, scarlet and black	2·00	2·50
959	66p. olive-brown, god and black	2·25	3·25
956/9 *Set of 4*		6·00	6·75

Designs:—42p. Victoria as Empress of India; 54p. Queen Victoria in carriage; 66p. Queen Victoria standing by chair.

Nos. 956/9 were printed in similar sheet format to Nos. 932/5.

(Des Roger Gorringe and Anselmo Torres. Litho Questa)

2001 (1 Feb). Snakes. T **240** and similar multicoloured designs. P 14.

960	5p. Type **240**	25	40
961	5p. Ladder Snake	25	40
962	5p. Montpellier Snake	25	40
963	30p. Viperine Snake	85	1·00
964	30p. Southern Smooth Snake	85	1·00
965	30p. False Smooth Snake	85	1·00
966	66p. Horseshoe Whip Snake (30×62 mm)	1·75	2·50
960/6 *Set of 7*		4·50	6·00
MS967 155×87 mm. Nos. 960/6		7·00	7·50

No. **MS**967 also commemorates the Chinese New Year "Year of the Snake".

Nos. 962 and **MS**967 are inscribed "MONTPELIER" in error.

241 Long-snouted Seahorse

(Des Anselmo Torres. Litho Cartor)

2001 (1 Feb). Europa. Water and Nature. T **241** and similar vert designs. Multicoloured. P 13.

968	30p. Type **241**	1·75	80
969	40p. Snapdragon	2·25	1·25
970	42p. Herring Gull	3·25	1·75
971	54p. Goldfish	2·75	5·00
968/71 *Set of 4*		9·00	8·00

Nos. 967/71 were each printed in sheets of 10 with enlarged illustrated and inscribed right margins. The margin of the 54p. sheet includes the "Hong Kong 2001" Stamp Exhibition logo.

242 Queen Elizabeth II as a Baby

(Des Stephen Perera. Litho Questa)

2001 (20 Apr). 75th Birthday of Queen Elizabeth II. T **242** and similar designs. P 14.

972	30p. brownish black and magenta	85	75
973	30p. brownish black and bluish violet	85	75
974	42p. brownish black and vermilion	1·25	1·50
975	42p. brownish black and reddish violet	1·25	1·50
976	54p. multicoloured	1·60	2·25
972/6 *Set of 5*		5·25	6·00
MS977 101×89 mm. £2 multicoloured. P 13½		5·50	6·50

Designs: *Square*—No. 972, Type **242**; No. 973, Queen Elizabeth as teenager; No. 974, On wedding day, 1947; No. 975, After Coronation, 1953; No. 976, Queen Elizabeth in blue hat. Vert (35×49 mm)—No. **MS**977, Queen Elizabeth II, 2001 (photo by Fiona Hanson).

Nos. 972/6 were printed in a similar sheet format to Nos. 932/5.

No. **MS**977 marks a successful attempt on the record for the fastest produced stamp issue. The miniature sheet was on sale in Gibraltar 10 hours and 24 minutes after the artwork was approved at Buckingham Palace.

243 Battle of Trafalgar, 1805

244 Snoopy as Father Christmas with Woodstock

(Des Stephen Perera. Litho Questa)

2001 (21 May). Bicentenary of *The Gibraltar Chronicle* (newspaper). T **243** and similar vert designs. Each black. P 14×14½.

978	30p. Type **243**	1·50	65
979	42p. Invention of the Telephone, 1876	1·25	90
980	54p. Winston Churchill (Victory in Second World War, 1945)	2·50	2·50
981	66p. Footprint on Moon (Moon landing, 1969)	2·50	3·75
978/81 *Set of 4*		7·00	7·00

(Des Stephen Perera (Nos. 982, 984, 986). Mike Atkinson (others). Litho Questa)

2001 (3 Sept). "Wings of Prey" (3rd series). Birds of Prey and Modern Military Aircraft. Horiz designs as T **227**. Multicoloured. P 14½×14.

982	40p. Royal Navy Sea Harrier FA MK.2	1·25	1·50
	a. Horiz pair. Nos. 982/3	2·50	3·00
983	40p. Western Marsh Harrier	1·25	1·50
984	40p. RAF Hawk T MK1	1·25	1·50
	a. Horiz pair. Nos. 984/5	2·50	3·00
985	40p. Northern Sparrow Hawk	1·25	1·50
986	40p. RAF Jaguar GR1B	1·25	1·50
	a. Horiz pair. Nos. 986/7	2·50	3·00
987	40p. Northern Hobby	1·25	1·50
982/7 *Set of 6*		6·75	8·00
MS988 Two sheets, each 103×84 mm. (a) Nos. 982, 984 and 986. (b) Nos. 983, 985 and 987		6·50	7·00

Nos. 982/7 were printed in a similar, *se-tenant* format to Nos. 883/8.

(Des Anselmo Torres. Litho Questa)

2001 (12 Nov). Christmas. Peanuts (cartoon characters by Charles Schulz). T **244** and similar square designs. Multicoloured. P 14.

989	5p. Type **244**	25	15
990	30p. Charlie Brown and Snoopy with Christmas tree	85	65
991	40p. Snoopy asleep in wreath	1·10	1·00
992	42p. Snoopy with plate of biscuits	1·25	1·25
993	54p. Snoopy asleep on kennel	1·75	2·50
989/93 *Set of 5*		4·75	5·00
MS994 140×85 mm. Nos. 989/93		4·75	5·50

245 One Cent Coin

246 Joshua Grimaldi

245a Princess Elizabeth and Princess Margaret making Radio Broadcast, 1940

(Des Anselmo Torres. Litho and thermography Cartor)

2002 (1 Jan). Introduction of Euro Currency by European Union. Coins. Sheet, 165×105 mm, containing T **245** and similar square designs showing coins. Multicoloured. P 13.

MS995 5p. Type **245**; 12p. 2 cents; 30p. 5 cents; 35p. 10 cents; 40p. 20 cents; 42p. (50 cents); 54p. 1 Euro; 66p. 2 Euros .... 7·00 7·50

(Des Andrew Robinson. Litho Questa)

2002 (6 Feb). Golden Jubilee. T **245a** and similar designs. W w **14** (sideways Nos. 996/9). P 13½ (75p.) or 14½ (others).

996	30p. brownish black, rosine and gold	1·25	1·40
997	30p. agate, rosine and gold	1·25	1·40
998	30p. multicoloured	1·25	1·40
999	30p. multicoloured	1·25	1·40
1000	75p. multicoloured	2·25	3·00
996/1000 *Set of 5*		6·50	7·75
MS1001 162×95 mm. Nos. 996/1000. Wmk sideways		7·00	8·00

Designs: *Horiz* (as Type **245a**)—No. 997, Princess Elizabeth in Girl Guide uniform, 1942; No. 998, Queen Elizabeth in evening dress, 1961; No. 999, Queen Elizabeth in Chelsea, 1993. *Vert* (38×51 mm)—No. 1000, Queen Elizabeth after Annigoni.

Nos. 996/1000 were each printed together, in sheets of 80, the two panes (each 4×10), separated by a gutter showing further photographs extending to a height of two horizontal rows.

(Des Anselmo Torres. Litho Cartor)

2002 (4 Mar). Europa. Circus. Famous Clowns. T **246** and similar vert designs. Multicoloured. P 13½×13.

1002	30p. Type **246**	90	65
1003	40p. Karl Wettach ("Grock")	1·25	1·25
1004	42p. Nicolai Polakovs ("Coco")	1·25	1·25
1005	54p. Charlie Cairoli	1·75	2·50
1002/5 *Set of 4*		4·75	5·00

Nos. 1002/5 were each printed in sheets of 10 with enlarged illustrated and inscribed right margins.

247 Bobby Moore holding Jules Rimet Trophy, 1966

248 Barbary Macaque

(Des Anselmo Torres. Litho Cartor)

2002 (29 Apr). World Cup Football Championship, Japan and Korea (2002). England's Victory, 1966. T **247** and similar vert designs. Multicoloured. P 13½×13.

1006	30p. Type **247**	80	65
1007	42p. Kissing Trophy	1·25	90
1008	54p. Bobby Moore with Queen Elizabeth II	1·50	2·00
1009	66p. Bobby Moore in action	1·75	2·75
1006/9 *Set of 4*		4·75	4·75
MS1010 135×90 mm. Nos. 1006/9		5·50	6·00

Nos. 1006/9 were each printed in sheets of 8 with enlarged illustrated and inscribed right margins.

(Des Roger Gorringe and Anselmo Torres. Litho B.D.T.)

2002 (6 June). Wildlife. T **248** and similar multicoloured designs. P 14.

1011	30p. Type **248**	90	80
1012	30p. Red Fox (horiz)	90	80
1013	40p. White-toothed Shrew (horiz)	1·25	85
1014	£1 Rabbit	2·75	3·50
1011/14 *Set of 4*		5·25	5·50
MS1015 125×100 mm. Nos. 1011/14		6·00	7·00

249 Gibraltar from the North

250 Princess Diana holding Prince Harry

(Des Anselmo Torres. Litho and themography Cartor)

2002 (15 Sept). Views of the Rock of Gibraltar. T **249** and similar multicoloured designs. P 13½×13.

1016	30p. Type **249**	1·25	1·25
	a. Horiz strip of 4. Nos. 1016/19	7·25	8·50
1017	30p. View from the south	1·25	1·25
1018	£1 View from the east (50×40 mm)	2·75	3·50
1019	£1 View from the west (50×40 mm)	2·75	3·50
1016/19 *Set of 4*		7·25	8·50

Nos. 1016/19 were printed together, horizontally se-tenant, in sheets of 24 (2 panes, 4×3) with powdered particles of the Rock sintered to their surface using thermography.

(Des Anselmo Torres. Litho Cartor)

2002 (31 Oct). 18th Birthday of Prince Harry. T **250** and similar square designs. Multicoloured. P 12½.

1020	30p. Type **250**	90	65
1021	42p. Prince Harry waving	1·25	90
1022	54p. Prince Harry skiing	1·50	1·60
1023	66p. Wearing dark suit	1·90	2·75
1020/3 *Set of 4*		5·00	5·25
MS1024 115×75 mm. Nos. 1120/3		5·50	6·50

Nos. 1020/3 were each printed in sheets of 80, the two panes (each 4×10) separated by a gutter showing further photographs extending to the height of two vertical rows.

251 Crib, Cathedral of St. Mary the Crowned

(Des Anselmo Torres. Litho B.D.T.)

2002 (13 Nov). Christmas. Cribs from Gibraltar Cathedrals and Churches. T **251** and similar horiz designs. Multicoloured. P 13½×13.

1025	5p. Type **251**	35	10
1026	30p. St. Joseph's Parish Church	1·25	65
1027	40p. St. Theresa's Parish Church	1·50	85
1028	42p. Our Lady of Sorrows Church	1·50	90
1029	52p. St. Bernard's Church	1·75	2·50
1030	54p. Cathedral of the Holy Trinity	1·75	2·50
1025/30 *Set of 6*		7·25	6·75

Nos. 1025/30 were each printed in sheets of 40 containing two panes separated by a horizontal gutter showing the featured cathedral or church.

252 Archbishop of Canterbury crowning Queen Elizabeth II

253 Young Prince William with Princess Diana

(Des Stephen Perera. Litho Cartor)

2003 (20 Feb). 50th Anniv of the Coronation. T **252** and similar square designs, each black, grey and brown-purple. P 12½.

1031	30p. Type **252**	90	85
1032	30p. Queen Elizabeth II in Coronation robes	90	85
1033	40p. Queen Elizabeth holding the Orb and Sceptre	1·40	85
1034	£1 Queen Elizabeth in Coronation Coach	3·00	3·50
1031/4 *Set of 4*		5·50	5·50
MS1035 116×76 mm. Nos. 1131/4		5·50	6·50

Nos. 1031/4 were each printed in sheets of 80, the two panes of 40 (4×10) separated by a gutter showing further photographs extending to the height of two horizontal rows.

(Des Stephen Perera. Litho Cartor)

2003 (20 Feb). 21st Birthday of Prince William of Wales. T **253** and similar square designs. Each black, grey and bluish violet. P 12½.

1036	30p. Type **253**	1·50	1·00
1037	30p. Prince William at Eton College	1·50	1·00
1038	40p. Prince William	2·00	1·00
1039	£1 Prince William in Operation Raleigh sweatshirt	3·75	4·50
1036/9 *Set of 4*		8·00	6·75
MS1040 115×75 mm. Nos. 1136/9		7·00	7·50

254 Drama Festival Poster

255 Wright Brothers' *Flyer I*, 1903

(Des Stephen Perera. Litho De La Rue)

2003 (3 Mar). Europa. Poster Art. T **254** and similar vert designs. Multicoloured. P 14×14½.

1041	30p. Type **254**	80	65
1042	40p. Spring Festival poster	1·00	1·00
1043	42p. Art Festival poster	1·00	1·00
1044	54p. Dance festival poster	1·50	2·50
1041/4 *Set of 4*		4·00	4·75

Nos. 1041/4 were each printed in sheets of ten with enlarged, illustrated right margins.

(Des Anselmo Torres. Litho Cartor)

2003 (31 Mar). Centenary of Powered Flight. T **255** and similar designs showing aircraft. P 13.

1045	30p. multicoloured	90	65
1046	40p. black and agate	1·25	1·25
1047	40p. black and dull blue	1·25	1·25
1048	42p. black and greenish blue	1·25	1·25
1049	44p. multicoloured	1·40	1·40
1050	66p. multicoloured	2·00	3·25
1045/50 *Set of 6*		7·00	8·00
MS1051 140×110 mm. Nos. 1140/5. P 12½		7·75	8·25

Designs: *Horiz* (37×28 mm)—30p. Type 255; 40p. (No. 1046) Charles Lindbergh and *Spirit of St. Louis* (first Transatlantic solo flight, 1927); 40p. (No. 1047) Boeing 314 *Yankee Clipper* flying boat (first Transatlantic scheduled air service, 1939). (77×28 mm)—42p. Saunders Roe Saro A 21 Windhover amphibian (first scheduled air service between Gibraltar and Tangier, 1931); 44p. British Airways Concorde (first supersonic airliner, 1976). *Vert* (37×58 mm)–66p. Space shuttle *Columbia* (first shuttle flight in Space orbit, 1981).

Nos. 1045/50 were each printed in sheets of five with enlarged, illustrated margins.

256 Flag of St.George

257 Big Ben, Swift and Rock of Gibraltar

(Des Christian Hook and Anselmo Torres. Litho Questa)

2003 (23 Apr). 1700th Death Anniv of St. George. T **256** and similar multicoloured designs. P 13½.

1052	30p. Type **256**	1·00	65
1053	40p. Cross of Military Constantinian Order of St. George	1·25	95
1054	£1.20 "St. George and the Dragon" (stained glass window, St. Joseph's Church, Gibraltar) (32×63 mm)	3·50	4·50
1052/4 *Set of 3*		5·25	5·50
MS1055 150×100 mm. Nos. 1052/4		5·25	6·00

(Des Anselmo Torres.) (Eng Geslaw Slania. Recess and photo Stamp Printing Office, Belgium)

2003 (21 June). P 11½.

1056	**257**	(£3) multicoloured†	8·00	8·50

No. 1056 is inscribed "UK express" and was initially sold at £3.

†The Queen's head on this stamp is printed in optically variable ink which changes colour from gold to green when viewed from different angles.

258 Wood Blewit (*Lepista nuda*)

259 Daisy (Latvia), Cornflower (Estonia) and Rue (Lithuania)

(Des Roger Gorringe and Anselmo Torres. Litho D.L.R)

2003 (15 Sept). Mushrooms of Gibraltar. T **258** and similar square designs. Multicoloured. P 14½.

1057	30p. Type **258**	1·00	1·00
1058	30p. Blue-green Funnel-cap (*Clitocybe odora*)	1·00	1·00
1059	30p. Sulphur Tuft (*Hypholoma fasciculare*)	1·00	1·00
1060	£1.20 Field Mushrooms (*Agaricus campestris*)	3·50	4·25
1057/60 *Set of 4*		6·00	6·50
MS1061 105×90 mm. Nos. 1057/60		6·00	7·00

(Des Antonia Eenthoven. Litho D.L.R.)

2003 (15 Sept). Enlargement of the European Union (2004). T **259** and similar square designs showing the national flowers of new member countries. Multicoloured. P 14.

1062	30p. Type **259**	1·25	80
1063	40p. Rose (Cyprus) and Maltese Centaury (Malta)	1·50	1·25
1064	42p. Tulip (Hungary), Carnation (Slovenia) and Dog Rose (Slovakia)	1·50	1·25
1065	54p. Corn Poppy (Poland) and Scented Thyme (Czech Republic)	2·00	3·25
1062/5 *Set of 4*		5·75	6·00

Nos. 1062/5 were each printed in small sheets of ten with enlarged illustrated right-hand margins showing outline maps of new member countries.

260 Baby Jesus Crib Figure, Our Lady of Sorrows Church

261 Street Café

(Des Anselmo Torres. Litho Walsall)

2003 (17 Nov). Christmas. T **260** and similar multicoloured designs. P 14.

1066	5p. Type **260**	20	10
1067	30p. Children making crib	90	65
1068	40p. Three Kings Cavalcade	1·25	1·00
1069	42p. Children's provisions for Santa and reindeer	1·25	1·00
1070	54p. Cathedral of St. Mary the Crowned lit for Christmas Eve Midnight Mass	1·75	3·00
1066/70	*Set of 5*	4·75	5·25
MS1071	100×80 mm. £1 Cartoon characters from Peanuts carol singing around Christmas tree (50×40 mm). P 13	4·25	5·00

(Des Stephen Perera. Litho D.L.R.)

2004 (20 Feb). Europa. Holidays. T **261** and similar vert designs. Multicoloured. P 14×14½.

1072	40p. Type **261**	1·25	1·40
1073	40p. St. Michael's Cave	1·25	1·40
1074	54p. Dolphins	1·75	2·25
1075	54p. Harbourside restaurant	1·75	2·25
1072/5	*Set of 4*	5·50	6·50

Nos. 1072/5 were each printed in sheets of 10 (2×5) with enlarged illustrated right-hand margins.

262 Arms

263 Queen Elizabeth holding Bouquet

(Des Stephen Perera. Litho Cartor)

2004 (24 Apr). 300th Anniv of British Gibraltar. T **262** and similar horiz designs. Multicoloured. P 13×13½.

1076	8p. Type **262**	65	65
MS1077	144×114 mm. 30p. Royal Katarine flying Red Ensign, 1704; 30p. Landing party, 1704; 30p. Soldiers of 1704; 30p. Arms of Gibraltar on military uniform; 30p. Royal Gibraltar police helmet and red phone box; 30p. Post Office arms and red pillar box; 30p. Graduates and University of Cambridge examination certificate; 30p. Crowd waving Union Jacks and Gibraltar flags; £1.20 Union Jack	12·00	13·00

(Des Anselmo Torres. Litho Cartor)

2004 (4 May). 50th Anniv of Visit of Queen Elizabeth II. T **263** and similar square designs. P 12½.

1078	38p. multicoloured	1·10	85
1079	40p. black and yellow	1·10	85
1080	47p. multicoloured	1·25	1·25
1081	£1 black	2·75	4·00
1078/81	*Set of 4*	5·50	6·25
MS1082	95×110 mm. £1.50 black	3·75	4·50

Designs: 38p. Type **263**; 40p. Queen Elizabeth holding out keys; 47p. Queen and Duke of Edinburgh in car; £1 Queen, Prince Charles and Princess Anne with members of British armed forces; £1.50 Queen waving with Duke of Edinburgh.

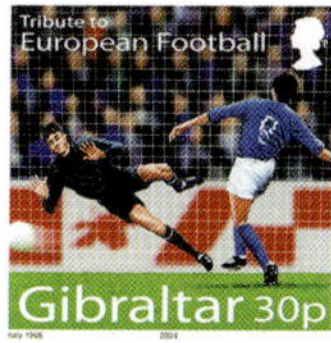

264 Scoring a Goal

265 Landing at St. Aubin, 1944

(Des Lee Montgomery. Litho Cartor)

2004 (6 June). European Football Championship 2004, Portugal. T **264** and similar square designs. Multicoloured. P 12½.

1083	30p. Type **264**	90	65
1084	40p. Two defenders blocking a goal attempt	1·25	1·25
1085	40p. Overhead kick	1·25	1·25
1086	£1 Player performing header	2·75	4·00
1083/6	*Set of 4*	5·50	6·25
MS1087	Two sheets. (a) 102×77 mm. £1.50 Player celebrating with arms in air (51×39 mm) P 13. (b) 105×105 mm (circular). Nos. 1083/6 *Set of 2 sheets*	8·00	8·50

(Des Anselmo Torres. Litho Cartor)

2004 (6 June). 60th Anniv of D-Day Landings. T **265** and similar horiz designs. Each black, brownish-black and red. P 13×13½.

1088	38p. Type **265**	1·25	85
1089	40p. Cruiser tank Mk VIII Cromwell	1·40	1·40
1090	47p. Handley Page Halifax plane	1·60	1·60
1091	£1 H.M.S. *Belfast*	3·00	4·00
1088/91	*Set of 4*	6·50	7·00
MS1092	170×100 mm. Nos. 1088/91	6·00	7·00

266 Union Jack Flag

267 Mallow-leaved Bindweed

(Des Stephen Perera. Litho Cartor)

2004 (10 Sept). 300th Anniv of British Gibraltar (2nd series). Elton John Tercentenary Concert. Circular sheet 105×105 mm. P 13×13½.

MS1093	**266** multicoloured	3·00	3·25

The stamp in No. **MS**1093 is similar in design to the £1.20 stamp in No. **MS**1077.

(Des Stephen Perera (3p., 15p., 53p., £1.60), or Antonia Eenthoven and Anselmo Torres (others). Litho B.D.T.)

2004 (10 Sept)–**06**. Wild Flowers. T **267** and similar vert designs. Multicoloured. P 13½.

1094	1p. Type **267**	15	35
	a. Booklet pane. No. 1094 with margins all round	15	
1095	2p. Gibraltar sea lavender	25	35
	a. Booklet pane. No. 1095 with margins all round	25	
1095*b*	3p. Gibraltar restharrow (20.2.06)	30	40
1096	5p. Gibraltar chickweed	30	30
	a. Booklet pane. No. 1096 with margins all round	30	
1097	(7p.) Romulea	45	20
	a. Booklet pane. No. 1097 with margins all round	45	
1098	10p. Common centaury	60	30
	a. Booklet pane. No. 1098 with margins all round	60	
1099	(12p.) Pyramidal orchid	75	75
	a. Booklet pane. No. 1099 with margins all round	75	
1099*b*	15p. Paper-white narcissus (20.2.06)	75	50
1100	(28p.) Friars cowl	1·25	60
	a. Booklet pane. No. 1100 with margins all round	1·25	
1101	(38p.) Corn poppy	1·40	85
	a. Booklet pane. No. 1101 with margins all round	1·40	
1102	(40p.) Giant Tangier fennel	1·40	65
	a. Booklet pane. No. 1102 with margins all round	1·40	
1103	(47p.) Snapdragon	1·75	1·10
	a. Booklet pane. No. 1103 with margins all round	1·75	
1104	50p. Common gladiolus	1·75	1·50
	a. Booklet pane. No. 1104 with margins all round	1·75	
1104*b*	53p. Gibraltar campion (20.2.06)	2·00	1·60
1105	£1 Yellow horned poppy	3·50	3·50
	a. Booklet pane. No. 1105 with margins all round	3·50	
1105*b*	£1.60 Sea daffodil (20.2.06)	4·75	4·75
1106	£3 Gibraltar candytuft	9·50	10·00
	a. Booklet pane. No. 1106 with margins all round	9·50	
1094/106	*Set of 17*	28·00	25·00

Nos. 1094/5, 1096/9, 1100/4, 1105 and 1106 were available as single stamps and also from £6.40 stamp booklets, No. SB14. Nos. 1095b, 1099b, 1104b and 1105b are sheet stamps.

Nos. 1097 and 1099/103 are inscribed "G", "G1", "S", "UK", "E" and "U" and were initially sold for 7p., 12p., 28p., 38p., 40p. and 47p. respectively.

268 Father Christmas

269 Ferrari F2003 GA

(Des Stephen Perera. Litho Cartor)

2004 (12 Nov). Christmas. Decorations. T **268** and similar square designs. Multicoloured. P 13.

1107	7p. Type **268**	30	20
1108	28p. Cherub	1·25	60
1109	38p. Red star	1·40	80
1110	40p. Gold conical tree	1·40	85
1111	47p. Red bauble	1·60	1·25
1112	53p. Gold star	1·90	3·50
1107/12	*Set of* 6	7·00	6·50

(Des Stephen Perera. Litho B.D.T.)

2004 (12 Nov). Ferrari. T **269** and similar horiz designs. Multicoloured. P 15×14.

1113	5p. Type **269**	35	40
1114	5p. F2004	35	40
1115	30p. F2001	1·00	1·00
1116	30p. F2002	1·00	1·00
1117	75p. F399	2·50	3·00
1118	75p. F1-2000	2·50	3·00
1113/18	*Set of* 6	7·00	8·00
MS1119	161×116 mm. Nos. 1113/18	7·00	7·50

Nos. 1113/18 were each available in sheetlets of 5 with an enlarged, illustrated bottom margin.

273 *Circassia*

(Des Stephen Perera. Litho B.D.T.)

271 Spinach Pie

272 Churchill giving Victory Salute

(Des Stephen Perrera. Litho B.D.T.)

2005 (31 Mar). Europa. Gastronomy. T **271** and similar vert designs. Multicoloured. P 14½×15.

1125	47p. Type **271**	1·75	2·00
1126	47p. Grilled Sea-Bass	1·75	2·00
1127	47p. Veal "Birds"	1·75	2·00
1128	47p. Sherry Trifle	1·75	2·00
1125/8	*Set of* 4	6·25	7·25

Nos. 1125/8 were each printed in sheetlets of ten with enlarged illustrated right margins.

(Des Anselmo Torres. Litho B.D.T)

2005 (8 May). 60th Anniv of VE Day. T **272** and similar vert designs. Multicoloured. P 14×15.

1129	38p. Type **272**	1·40	90
1130	40p. Family with Union Jack flags	1·40	90
1131	47p. VE Day celebrations	1·60	1·50
1132	£1 Returning Gibraltar people on dockside	3·75	4·75
1129/32	*Set of* 4	7·25	7·25
MS1133	150×100 mm. Nos. 1129/32	7·25	7·50

(Des John Batchelor. Litho Cartor)

2005 (31 Jan). Bicentenary of the Battle of Trafalgar. T **270** and similar multicoloured designs. P 13½.

1120	38p. Type **270**	1·75	75
1121	40p. HMS *Entreprenante*	1·75	85
1122	47p. Admiral Nelson (vert)	2·00	1·50
1123	£1.60 HMS *Victory*	5·50	7·50
1120/3	*Set of* 4	10·00	9·50
MS1124	120×80 mm. £2 HMS *Victory* (44×44 mm)	12·00	12·00

Nos. 1120/3 were each printed in sheetlets of six with illustrated margins.

Nos. 1120/4 contain traces of powdered wood from HMS *Victory*.

270 Royal Marine guarding Nelson's Body

(Des Simon Williams and Anselmo Torres. Litho Cartor)

2005 (17 June). Cruise Ships (1st series). T **273** and similar horiz designs. Multicoloured. P 13×13½.

1134	38p. Type **273**	1·40	90
1135	40p. *Nevasa*	1·40	90
1136	47p. *Black Prince*	1·60	1·50
1137	£1 *Arcadia*	3·75	4·75
1134/7	*Set of* 4	7·25	7·25
MS1138	150×85 mm. Nos. 1134/7	7·25	7·50

See also Nos. 1180/4 and 1207/11.

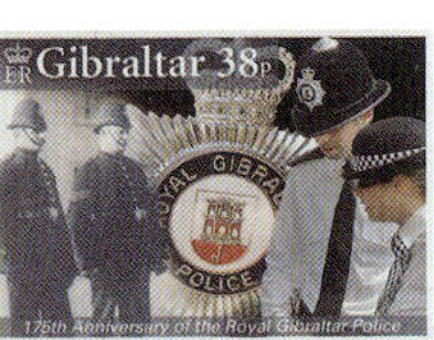

274 Early and Modern Police Officers

275 Pope John Paul II

(Des Stephen Perera. Litho B.D.T.)

2005 (17 June). Anniversaries. T **274** and similar horiz designs. Multicoloured. P 15×14½.

1139	38p. Type **274** (175th anniv of Royal Gibraltar Police)	2·00	1·00
1140	47p. Skull, plate and ceramic horses (75th anniv of Gibraltar Museum)	1·50	1·00
1141	£1 Charter of Justice (175th anniv)	3·75	5·00
1139/41	*Set of* 3	6·50	6·25

The backs of Nos. 1139/41 are printed with a brief description of the subject of the stamp.

(Des Andrew. Robinson. Litho B.D.T.)

2005 (15 July). Pope John Paul II Commemoration. P 14½×15.

1142	**275**	75p. multicoloured	2·50	2·75

No. 1142 was printed in sheetlets of six stamps with an enlarged illustrated left margin.

276 Map of Europe and 1979 Europa 12p. Stamp

(Des Stephen Perera. Litho and die-stamped B.D.T.)

2005 (30 Sept). 50th Anniv of Europa Stamps. P 14½.

1143	**276**	£5 multicoloured	14·00	16·00

277 "Death of Nelson" (William Devis) **278** Two Angels

(Des Anselmo Torres. Litho Cartor)

2005 (21 Oct). Bicentenary of the Battle of Trafalgar and Death of Admiral Lord Nelson. T **277** and similar horiz designs. Multicoloured. P 13½.

MS1144	120×80 mm. £1 Type **277**	3·25	4·00
MS1145	170×75 mm. £1 As Type **277**, but 50×31 mm together with £1 stamp from Isle of Man No. **MS**1264	6·50	7·00

No. **MS**1145 was also issued by Isle of Man.

(Des Stephen Perera. Litho Cartor)

2005 (21 Oct). Christmas. Angels. T **278** and similar vert designs. Multicoloured. P 13½×13.

1146	7p. Type **278**	25	20
1147	38p. Angel with children by Christmas tree	1·25	80
1148	40p. Angel with toys	1·25	80
1149	47p. Angel with hymn book and top of Christmas tree	1·75	1·40
1150	53p. Angel with basket of fruit	2·00	2·75
1146/50	*Set of 5*	6·00	5·50
MS1151	168×86 mm. Nos. 1146/50	6·00	7·00

279 Giant Devil Ray

(Des Anselmo Torres. Litho Cartor)

2006 (20 Feb). Endangered Species. Giant Devil Ray (*Mobula mobular*). T **279** and similar horiz designs. Multicoloured. P 13×13½.

1152	38p. Type **279**	1·25	1·75
	a. Strip of 4. Nos. 1152/5	7·25	8·50
1153	40p. Giant devil ray and trail of bubbles	1·40	1·75
1154	47p. Two giant devil rays	1·75	2·00
1155	£1 Upperside of giant devil ray	3·75	4·00
1152/5	*Set of 4*	7·25	8·50

Nos. 1152/5 were printed together, *se-tenant*, in horizontal and vertical strips of four stamps in sheets of 16.

280 Queen Elizabeth II **281** Uruguay

(Des Stephen Perera. Litho B.D.T.)

2006 (31 Mar). 80th Birthday of Queen Elizabeth II. T **280** and similar horiz designs, each showing 1950s and more recent photograph. Multicoloured. P 15×14.

1156	38p. Type **280**	2·00	2·00
	a. Block of 4. Nos. 1156/9	9·00	9·50
1157	40p. In evening dress, c. 1955 and wearing purple hat	2·00	2·00
1158	47p. Smelling carnation, c. 1955 and wearing yellow hat	2·25	2·25
1159	£1 Princess Elizabeth, c. 1950 and Queen wearing red and black hat	3·75	4·25
1156/9	*Set of 4*	9·00	9·50
MS1160	Two sheets, each 142×82 mm. (a) Nos. 1156 and 1159. (b) Nos. 1157/8 Set of 2 sheets	8·00	9·00

Nos. 1156/9 were printed together, *se-tenant*, in sheetlets of eight stamps with enlarged illustrated left margins.

(Des Stephen Perera. Litho B.D.T.)

2006 (4 May). World Cup Football Championship, Germany. T **281** and similar square designs showing children with flags painted on faces. Multicoloured. P 15.

1161	38p. Type **281**	1·25	1·40
	a. Sheetlet. Nos. 1161/7	8·00	8·75
1162	38p. Italy	1·25	1·40
1163	38p. Germany	1·25	1·40
1164	38p. Brazil	1·25	1·40
1165	38p. England	1·25	1·40
1166	38p. Argentina	1·25	1·40
1167	38p. France	1·25	1·40
1161/7	*Set of 7*	8·00	8·75

Nos. 1161/7 were printed together, *se-tenant*, in sheetlets of seven stamps with enlarged illustrated margins.

282 Children making Model Building

(Des Holli Conger and Stephen Perera. Litho B.D.T.)

2006 (30 June). Europa. Integration. T **282** and similar horiz designs. Multicoloured. P 13×13½.

1168	47p. Type **282**	1·50	1·50
1169	47p. Boy and girl	1·50	1·50
1170	47p. Children playing football	1·50	1·50
1171	47p. Children playing music	1·50	1·50
1168/71	*Set of 4*	5·50	5·50

Nos. 1168/71 were each printed in sheetlets of ten stamps with enlarged illustrated right margins.

283 *Cornwallis*

(Des John Batchelor. Litho B.D.T.)

2006 (15 Sept). Bicentenary of the Gibraltar Packet Agency. T **283** and similar horiz designs showing packet ships of the 1800s. Multicoloured. P 15×14.

1172	8p. Type **283**	60	35
1173	40p. *Meteor*	2·00	1·00
1174	42p. *Carteret*	2·00	1·00
1175	68p. *Prince Regent*	3·00	5·00
1172/5	*Set of 4*	7·00	6·50

284 Saro A21 Windhover Flying Boat, 1931

(Des John Batchelor. Litho B.D.T.)

2006 (15 Sept). 75th Anniv of Gibraltar Airmail Service. T **284** and similar horiz designs. Multicoloured. P 15×14.

1176	8p. Type **284**	60	30
1177	40p. Vickers Vanguard, 1959	2·00	90
1178	49p. Vickers Viscount	2·75	1·50
1179	£1.60 Boeing 737	6·50	8·50
1176/9	*Set of 4*	10·50	10·00

285 *Coral*

286 St. Nicholas and Christmas Tree

(Des Simon Williams. Litho Lowe-Martin, Canada)

2006 (15 Sept). Cruise Ships (2nd series). T **285** and similar horiz designs. Multicoloured. P 13.

1180	40p. Type **285**	1·60	1·25
1181	42p. *Legend of the Seas*	1·75	1·40
1182	66p. *Saga Ruby*	2·75	3·50
1183	78p. *Costa Concordia*	3·25	5·00
1180/3 *Set of 4*		8·50	10·00
MS1184 100×80 mm. Nos. 1180/83		8·50	10·00

(Des Stephen Perera. Litho Lowe-Martin, Canada)

2006 (1 Nov). Christmas. St. Nicholas. T **286** and similar vert designs. Multicoloured. P 13.

1185	8p. Type **286**	40	15
1186	40p. St. Nicholas (in red) carrying presents	1·50	80
1187	42p. St. Nicholas giving present to young girl	1·60	85
1188	49p. St. Nicholas (in green) carrying sack of toys	2·00	1·75
1189	55p. St. Nicholas (in white) carrying sack and small Christmas tree	2·25	3·75
1185/9 *Set of 5*		7·00	6·50
MS1190 165×80 mm. Nos. 1185/9. P 13×12½		7·00	7·50

287 Navigational Instruments

288 Engagement, 1947

(Des Christian Hook and Stephen Perera. Litho Lowe-Martin, Canada)

2006 (1 Nov). 500th Death Anniv of Christopher Columbus. T **287** and similar multicoloured designs. P 13.

1191	40p. Type **287**	1·50	1·25
1192	42p. Columbus writing report of voyage, 1492	1·50	1·25
1193	66p. *Santa Maria*	2·50	3·00
1194	78p. Columbus and Arawak chief	3·00	4·00
1191/4 *Set of 4*		7·75	8·50
MS1195 95×74 mm. £1.60 Columbus' fleet, 1492 (47×47 mm). P 13½		5·75	6·50

Nos. 1191/4 were each printed in separate sheetlets of six stamps with enlarged illustrated margins.

(Des Stephen Perera. Litho Lowe-Martin, Canada)

2007 (28 Feb). Diamond Wedding of Queen Elizabeth II and Prince Philip. T **288** and similar vert designs. Multicoloured. P 13½.

1196	40p. Type **288**	1·50	1·25
1197	42p. Wedding photograph, 1947	1·60	1·40
1198	66p. Silver Wedding anniversary, 1972	2·40	2·75
1199	78p. Ruby Anniversary, 1987	2·75	3·50
1196/9 *Set of 4*		7·50	8·00
MS1200 105×105 mm. £1.60 Wedding photograph with bridesmaids and pageboys, 1947 (diamond shape, 84×83 mm). P 13½×13		5·75	6·50

Nos. 1196/9 were each printed in sheetlets of three stamps with enlarged margins. No. **MS**1200 is perforated 13½ on the two left-hand edges and 13 on the two right edges.

289 Flag of Belgium

(Des Stephen Perera. Litho B.D.T.)

2007 (28 Feb). 50th Anniv of the Treaty of Rome. Sheet 137×100 mm containing T **289** and similar horiz designs showing national flags. Multicoloured. P 15×14.

MS1201 40p.×6 Type **289**; Germany; France; Italy; Luxembourg; Netherlands	6·00	7·00

The stamps within **MS**1201 were arranged in two vertical strips of three separated by a large illustrated gutter.

290 Princess Diana

291 Gibraltar Scout, 1908

(Des Stephen Perera. Litho Lowe-Martin, Canada)

2007 (31 Mar). 10th Death Anniv of Princess Diana. T **290** and similar square designs. Multicoloured. P 13½.

1202	8p. Type **290**	40	25
1203	40p. Seen full-face, eyes looking sideways	1·40	1·40
1204	42p. In half profile, smiling	1·40	1·40
1205	£1.60 Seen full-face, smiling	5·50	7·00
1202/5 *Set of 4*		8·00	9·00
MS1206 165×92 mm. Nos. 1202/4		8·00	9·00

Nos. 1202/5 were each printed in sheetlets of six stamps with enlarged margins.

(Des Simon Williams and Stephen Perera. Litho B.D.T.)

2007 (15 May). Cruise Ships (3rd series). Horiz designs as T **285**. Multicoloured. P 15×14.

1207	40p. *Oriana*	1·50	1·25
1208	42p. *Oceana*	1·60	1·40
1209	66p. *Queen Elizabeth 2*	2·75	3·25
1210	78p. *Queen Mary 2*	3·00	4·75
1207/10 *Set of 4*		8·00	9·50
MS1211 168×67 mm. Nos. 1207/10		8·00	9·50

(Des Christian Hook and Stephen Perera. Litho Lowe-Martin, Canada)

2007 (30 June). Europa. Centenary of World Scouting. T **291** and similar vert designs. Multicoloured. P 13.

1212	8p. Type **291**	40	30
1213	40p. Scout, 1950s	1·40	1·25
1214	42p. Sea scout, 1980s	1·50	1·40
1215	£1 Modern scout	3·50	5·00
1212/15 *Set of 4*		6·25	7·25

292 Postcard from Fez, 1907

(Des Anselmo Torres. Litho B.D.T.)

2007 (26 Sept). Gibraltar Postal Anniversaries. T **292** and similar horiz designs. Multicoloured. P 15×14.

1216	8p. Type **292** (Cent of Gibraltar relinquishing control of British Postal Service in Morocco)	55	30
1217	40p. Gibraltar datestamp of Packet Agency, 1857 (150th anniv of Gibraltar Post Office)	2·00	1·25
1218	42p. Letter with British postage stamps cancelled "G" (150th anniv of the introduction of British postage stamps in Gibraltar)	2·00	1·40
1219	£1 Earliest known letter from Morocco via Gibraltar (150th anniv of first British Postal Agency in Morocco)	4·50	5·50

1216/19	*Set of* 4	8·00	7·75

Nos. 1216/19 have information about the anniversaries commemorated printed on the reverse (gummed) side of the stamps.

293 Bear and Cub feeding on Dolphin

294 Stork ("New baby")

(Des Christian Hook and Stephen Perera. Litho Cartor)

2007 (26 Sept). Prehistoric Wildlife of Gibraltar. T **293** and similar vert designs. Multicoloured. P 13.

1220	8p. Type **293**	40	40
	a. Booklet pane. No. 1220 with margins all round	40	
	b. Booklet pane. Nos. 1220/5	13·00	
1221	40p. Eagle owl	1·50	1·50
	a. Booklet pane. No. 1221 with margins all round	1·50	
1222	42p. Great auk and eagle	1·60	1·60
	a. Booklet pane. No. 1222 with margins all round	1·60	
1223	55p. Red deer and boar	1·75	2·50
	a. Booklet pane. No. 1223 with margins all round	1·75	
1224	78p. Wolf and vulture feeding on wild horse	2·75	4·50
	a. Booklet pane. No. 1224 with margins all round	2·75	
1220/4	*Set of* 5	7·25	9·50
MS1225	154×100 mm. £2 Ibex	7·00	8·50
	a. Booklet pane. As No. **MS**1225, but 150×113 mm	6·50	

Booklet panes Nos. 1220a and 1221a/5a contain a single stamp within a larger illustration.

(Des Holli Conger and Stephen Perera. Litho Lowe-Martin, Canada)

2007 (26 Sept). "YouStamps". T **294** and similar square designs. Multicoloured. P 12½×13.

1226	(8p.)	Type **294**	40	40
1227	(8p.)	Lion, sheep and dog wearing party hats ("Let's celebrate")	40	40
1228	(8p.)	Crab finding heart written in beach sand ("With love")	40	40
1229	(8p.)	Heart enclosed in wedding ring ("Commitment")	40	40
1230	(8p.)	Dolphins and Rock of Gibraltar ("Greetings from Gibraltar")	40	40
1231	(40p.)	As Type **294**	1·40	1·40
1232	(40p.)	As No. 1227	1·40	1·40
1233	(40p.)	As No. 1228	1·40	1·40
1234	(40p.)	As No. 1229	1·40	1·40
1235	(40p.)	As No. 1230	1·40	1·40
1226/35		*Set of* 10	8·00	8·00

Nos. 1226/30 are inscr "G" and sold for 8p. each. Nos. 1231/5 are inscr "E" and sold for 40p. each.

Nos. 1226/35 were each issued in sheets of 20 stamps, each stamp accompanied by a *se-tenant* greetings label. These stamps were also available with blank *se-tenant* labels to which personal photographs could be added.

295 Rock of Gibraltar

(Des Stephen Perera. Litho Cartor)

2007 (1 Oct). Panoramic Views of Gibraltar. T **295** and similar horiz designs. Multicoloured. P 13½.

1236	40p. Type **295**	1·40	1·25
1237	42p. Beach and Rock of Gibraltar	1·60	1·40
1238	55p. Rock of Gibraltar at sunset	2·00	2·50
1239	78p. Town and Rock of Gibraltar	3·25	4·00
1236/9	*Set of* 4	7·50	8·25
MS1240	114×67 mm. £1.70 Gibraltar Trinity Lighthouse (52×20 mm). P 13	6·50	6·50

No. 1236 is inscr "sepac".

296 Joseph

(Des Stephen Perera. Litho Lowe-Martin, Canada)

2007 (2 Nov). Christmas. Porcelain Figurines. T **296** and similar vert designs. Multicoloured. P 13½×13.

1241	8p. Type **296**	25	25
1242	8p. Baby Jesus	25	25
1243	40p. Mary	1·25	80
1244	42p. King Melchoir	1·40	90
1245	49p. King Balthasar	1·60	1·60
1246	55p. King Gaspar	1·75	3·00
1241/6	*Set of* 6	6·00	6·00
MS1247	124×105 mm. Nos. 1241/6	6·50	7·00

Nos. 1241/7 have biblical quotations printed on the reverse (gummed) side of the stamps.

297 Woodchat Shrike

(Des Jonathan Pointer and Stephen Perera. Litho B.D.T. (1252*a*, 1258*a/b*, 1259*a/c*) or Lowe-Martin, Canada (others))

2008 (15 Feb)–**10**. Birds of the Rock. T **297** and similar vert designs. Multicoloured. P 13 (1252*a*, 1258*a/b*, 1259, 1259*b*, 1260), 13×13½ (1259*a*, 1259*c*) or 13×12½ (others).

1248	1p.	Type **297**	10	10
1249	2p.	Balearic shearwater	15	15
1250	5p.	Eagle owl	20	15
1251	(8p.)	Egyptian vulture	40	35
1252	10p.	Razorbill	50	45
1252*a*	10p.	Black stork (16.9.09)	75	80
1253	(30p.)	European bee-eater	90	85
1254	(40p.)	Hoopoe	1·25	1·10
1255	(42p.)	Bonelli's eagle	1·40	1·25
1256	(49p.)	Blue rock thrush	1·50	1·25
1257	50p.	Greater flamingo	1·50	1·25
1258	55p.	Mediterranean shag	1·60	1·50
1258*a*	59p.	Barbary partridge (20.10.10)	2·00	1·90
1258*b*	76p.	Ortolan bunting (20.10.10)	2·50	2·50
1259	£1	Honey buzzard (34×48 mm)	3·00	3·00
1259*a*	£2	Northern gannet (35×48 mm) (16.9.09)	6·00	6·50
1259*b*	£2	Pallid swift (20.10.10)	6·50	7·00
1259*c*	£3	Osprey (35×48 mm) (16.9.09)	9·25	9·50
1260	£5	Lesser kestrel (35×48 mm)	12·00	13·00
1248/60		*Set of* 19	45·00	45·00

Nos. 1251 and 1253/6 are inscribed 'S', 'G', 'E', 'U' and 'UK' and were sold for 8p, 30p, 40p, 42p and 49p respectively.

298 Short 184 and Saro London

(Des John Bachelor or Stephen Perera. Litho B.D.T.)

2008 (15 Mar). 90th Anniv of the Royal Air Force. T **298** and similar vert designs. Multicoloured. P 14×15.

1261	40p. Type **298**	2·00	2·00
1262	40p. Spitfire IV and Hurricane IIc	2·00	2·00
1263	42p. Beaufighter II and Lancaster TS III	2·00	2·00
1264	42p. Hunter Mk.6 and Shackleton MR2	2·00	2·00
1265	49p. Vulcan and Mosquito	2·50	2·50
1266	49p. Tornado GR4 and Jaguar GR3	2·50	2·50
1261/66 *Set of* 6		11·50	11·50
MS1267	107×75 mm. £2 Felixstowe F.3 of No. 265 Squadron on anti-submarine patrol, Gibraltar, 1918	9·50	9·50

299 HMS *Minerve*

(Des John Bachelor and Stephen Perera. Litho B.D.T.)

2008 (15 Mar). 250th Birth Anniv of Admiral Lord Nelson. T **299** and similar multicoloured designs. P 14×15.

1268	40p. Type **299**	2·00	2·00
1269	40p. HMS *Agamemnon*	2·00	2·00
1270	42p. HMS *Vanguard*	2·00	2·00
1271	42p. HMS *Captain*	2·00	2·00
1272	49p. HMS *Victory*	2·50	2·50
1273	49p. HMS *Amphion*	2·50	2·50
1268/73 *Set of* 6		11·50	11·50
MS1274	120×80 mm. £2 Birthplace at Burnham Thorpe, Norfolk (horiz). P 15×14	7·00	8·00

Nos. 1268/73 were each printed in sheetlets of six stamps with enlarged illustrated margins.

300 Sir Winston Churchill

(Des Robert Papp and Stephen Perera. Litho B.D.T.)

2008 (1 June). Europa. Writing Letters. T **300** and similar vert designs. Multicoloured. P 14×14½.

1275	10p. Type **300**	75	50
1276	42p. Lord Nelson	1·75	1·25
1277	44p. President John F. Kennedy	1·75	1·50
1278	£1 Mahatma Ghandi	5·50	6·00
1275/8 *Set of* 4		8·75	8·25

301 Christ the Redeemer Statue, Rio de Janeiro, Brazil

(Des Stephen Perera. Litho B.D.T.)

2008 (1 June). The New Seven Wonders of the World. T **301** and similar vert designs. Multicoloured. P 14×14½.

1279	8p. Type **301**	35	35
1280	8p. Colosseum, Rome, Italy	35	35
1281	38p. Petra, Jordan	1·50	1·50
1282	38p. The Great Wall of China	1·50	1·50
1283	40p. Machu Picchu, Peru	1·50	1·50
1284	40p. Chichen Itza	1·50	1·50
1285	66p. Taj Mahal, India	3·25	3·25
1279/85 *Set of* 7		9·00	9·00

(Des Simon Williams and Stephen Perera. Litho Lowe-Martin)

2008 (15 Sept). Cruise Ships (4th series). Horiz designs as T **285**. Multicoloured. P 13.

1286	40p. *Century*	1·75	1·25
1287	42p. *Grand Princess*	1·75	1·25
1288	66p. *Queen Victoria*	2·75	3·00
1289	78p. *Costa Mediterranea*	3·75	4·50
1286/9 *Set of* 4		9·00	9·00
MS1290	168×66 mm. Nos. 1286/9	9·00	9·00

302 Launch of *Apollo 11*

(Des Stephen Perera. Litho Lowe-Martin, Canada)

2008 (15 Sept). 50th Anniv of NASA (US National Aeronautics and Space Administration). Sheet 144×98 mm containing T **302** and similar square designs. Multicoloured. P 13.

MS1291	10p. Type **302**; 17p. The Earth seen from the Moon; 42p. Lunar module; £2 US flag on the Moon	8·50	8·50

303 Gibraltar Volunteer Corps, World War I

(Des Jonathan Pointer and Stephen Perera. Litho B.D.T.)

2008 (11 Nov). Royal Gibraltar Regiment. T **303** and similar vert designs. Multicoloured. P 14×14½.

1292	10p. Type **303**	45	45
1293	10p. Gibraltar Defence Force, World War II	45	45
1294	10p. Buena Vista Barracks (National Service)	45	45
1295	42p. Thomson's Battery 1958–91 (Gibraltar Regiment)	1·40	1·40
1296	42p. Infantry Company 1958–99 (Gibraltar Regiment)	1·40	1·40
1297	44p. Air Defence Troop 1958–91 (Gibraltar Regiment)	1·40	1·40
1298	44p. 'Guarding the Rock' (Royal Gibraltar Regiment)	1·40	1·40
1299	51p. Training African Peacekeepers (Royal Gibraltar Regiment)	1·90	2·00
1300	51p. Operations in Iraq (Royal Gibraltar Regiment)	1·90	2·00
1301	£2 Operations in Afghanistan (Royal Gibraltar Regiment)	7·00	8·00
1292/301 *Set of* 10		16·00	17·00

304 *When Santa got stuck in a Chimney*

(Des Olympia Reyes and Stephen Perera. Litho Cartor)

2008 (11 Nov). Christmas. Christmas Songs and Carols. T **304** and similar square designs. Multicoloured. P 12½.

1302	10p. Type **304**	45	20
1303	42p. *Rudolph the Red-nosed Reindeer*	1·50	1·25

1304 44p. *Oh Christmas Tree* .... 1·50 1·25
1305 51p. *Away in a Manger* .... 1·90 1·90
1306 59p. *Jingle Bells* .... 2·25 2·75
1302/6 *Set of 5* .... 7·00 6·50

305 Catherine of Aragon

(Des Martin Hargreaves and Stephen Perera. Litho Lowe-Martin, Canada)

2009 (30 Jan). 500th Anniv of the Coronation of King Henry VIII. T **305** and similar square designs. Multicoloured. P 12½.

1307 10p. Type **305** 45 45
1308 10p. Anne Boleyn 45 45
1309 42p. Jane Seymour .... 1·75 1·50
1310 42p. Anne of Cleves .... 1·75 1·50
1311 44p. Catherine Howard .... 1·75 1·50
1312 44p. Katherine Parr .... 1·75 1·50
1313 51p. King Henry VIII .... 2·25 2·75
1314 51p. *Mary Rose* (galleon) .... 2·25 2·75
1307/14 *Set of 8* .... 11·00 11·00
MS1315 120×80 mm. £2 King Henry VIII and Hampton Court Palace .... 7·50 8·00

306 Virgin and Child (shrine of Our Lady of Europe at Europa Point, Gibraltar)

(Des Stephen Perera. Litho B.D.T.)

2009 (10 Feb). 700th Anniv of Our Lady of Europe. P 14×14½.

1316 **306** 61p. multicoloured .... 3·50 3·50

No. 1316 was printed in sheetlets of four stamps with enlarged illustrated right margins.

Stamps of a similar design were issued by Vatican City.

307 Short S27

(Des Jon Bachelor and Stephen Perera. Litho B.D.T.)

2009 (15 Mar). Centenary of Naval Aviation. T **307** and similar vert designs. Multicoloured. P 14×14½.

1317 42p. Type **307** .... 1·90 1·90
1318 42p. Morane-Saulnier Type L and Zeppelin LZ 37 .... 1·90 1·90
1319 42p. Short Type 184 seaplane .... 1·90 1·90
1320 42p. SS Type Non Rigid Airship .... 1·90 1·90
1321 42p. Caudron Gill .... 1·90 1·90
1322 42p. Avro 504 .... 1·90 1·90
1317/22 *Set of 6* .... 10·50 10·50
MS1323 120×80 mm. £2 Short Type 184 seaplane hoisted over stern of First World War seaplane carrier and Hawker Siddeley Sea Harrier on ramp of modern Invincible Class CVS aircraft carrier .... 8·00 8·00

The stamp within No. **MS**1323 has text printed on the back describing the aircraft and ships depicted on the miniature sheet.

308 Peter Phillips

(Des Stephen Perera. Litho Lowe-Martin, Canada)

2009 (1 May). Queen Elizabeth II's Grandchildren. T **308** and similar horiz designs. Multicoloured. P 12½.

1324 42p. Type **308** .... 1·50 1·50
1325 42p. Zara Phillips .... 1·50 1·50
1326 42p. Prince William of Wales .... 1·50 1·50
1327 42p. Prince Henry of Wales .... 1·50 1·50
1328 42p. Princess Beatrice of York .... 1·50 1·50
1329 42p. Princess Eugenie of York .... 1·50 1·50
1330 42p. Lady Louise Windsor .... 1·50 1·50
1331 42p. Viscount Severn .... 1·50 1·50
1324/31 *Set of 8* .... 11·00 11·00

309 Aristotle (early Greek philosopher and scientist)

(Des Robert Papp and Stephen Pereira. Litho Lowe-Martin)

2009 (1 June). Europa. International Year of Astronomy. T **309** and similar vert designs. Multicoloured. P 13×12½.

1332 10p. Type **309** 40 30
1333 42p. Galileo Galilei (astronomer, mathematician and philosopher) .... 1·75 1·25
1334 44p. Nicolaus Copernicus (astronomer) .... 2·25 1·50
1335 £1.50 Sir Isaac Newton (scientist and mathematician) .... 4·50 6·00
1332/5 *Set of 4* .... 8·00 8·00

310 Road to the Frontier

(Des Stephen Perera. Litho B.D.T.)

2009 (16 Sept). Old Views of Gibraltar. T **310** and similar horiz designs showing scenes from postcards. Multicoloured. P 14×15.

1336 10p. Type **310** 40 30
1337 42p. Catalan Bay village .... 1·60 1·25
1338 44p. The Rock of Gibraltar .... 1·60 1·25
1339 51p. The Moorish Castle .... 2·00 1·90
1340 59p. South Barracks .... 2·25 2·75
1336/40 *Set of 5* .... 7·00 6·75
MS1341 163×79 mm. 10p. Garrison Library; 42p. The Piazza; 44p. The Piazza – Casemates; £1 Main Street .... 6·75 7·50

310a Charles Darwin, *Zoology of the Beagle* and *Voyages of the Adventure and Beagle*

(Des Stephen Perera. Litho Lowe-Martin, Canada)

2009 (12 Nov). Birth Bicentenary of Charles Darwin (naturalist and evolutionary theorist). T **310a** and similar vert designs showing portraits of Charles Darwin and extracts from his books. Multicoloured. P 14×14½.

1341*a*	10p. Type **310a**	45	30
1341*b*	42p. Charles Darwin and *The Descent of Man*	1·50	1·25
1341*c*	44p. Charles Darwin and *Animals and Plants under Domestication*	1·50	1·40
1341*d*	£2 Charles Darwin and *On the Origin of Species*	7·00	7·50
1341*a/d*	*Set of 4*	9·50	9·50

MS1341*e* 126×86 mm. £2.42 Charles Darwin, The Mount, Shrewsbury (his birthplace) and *On the Origin of Species* ... 9·50 9·50

311 Santa Tree Decoration

(Des Stephen Perera. Litho Cartor)

2009 (12 Nov). Christmas. T **311** and similar vert designs. Multicoloured. P 13½×13.

1342	10p. Type **311**	45	30
1343	42p. Angel	1·50	1·25
1344	44p. Teddy bear	1·50	1·40
1345	51p. Filigree Christmas tree	1·90	1·60
1346	£2 Bells and baubles	6·75	7·50
1342/6	*Set of 5*	11·00	11·00

312 '100 Ton' Gun, Napier of Magdala Battery, Gibraltar, 1880

(Des John Batchelor. Litho Printex Ltd., Malta)

2010 (19 Feb). '100 Ton' Guns. Sheet 118×102 mm containing T **312** and similar horiz designs. Multicoloured. P 13½.

MS1347 75p.×4 Type **312**; '100 ton' gun, Napier of Magdala Battery, Gibraltar, 1880; '100 ton' gun, Fort Rinella, Malta, 2010; '100 ton' gun, Fort Rinella, Malta, 1882 ... 10·00 11·00

A miniature sheet containing the same designs was issued by Malta.

313 Hawker Hurricane

(Des Westminster Collection. Litho B.D.T.)

2010 (21 Feb). 70th Anniv of the Battle of Britain. T **313** and similar horiz designs. Multicoloured. P 14.

1348	50p. Type **313**	2·00	2·00
1349	50p. Miles Master	2·00	2·00
1350	50p. Bristol Blenheim	2·00	2·00
1351	50p. Boulton Paul Defiant	2·00	2·00
1352	50p. Gloster Gladiator	2·00	2·00
1353	50p. Supermarine Spitfire	2·00	2·00
1348/53	*Set of 6*	11·00	11·00

MS1354 110×70 mm. £2 Douglas Bader (*vert*) ... 7·50 7·50

314 King George V, Queen Mary and Family

(Des Martin Hargreaves and Stephen Perera. Litho Lowe-Martin, Canada)

2010 (26 Mar). Centenary of Accession of King George V. T **314** and similar horiz designs. Multicoloured. P 13.

1355	10p. Type **314**	50	30
1356	42p. King George V with his stamp collection	1·75	1·25
1357	44p. King George V on horseback inspecting soldiers	1·75	1·40
1358	£2 King George V in navy uniform and gun battery	8·00	9·00
1355/8	*Set of 4*	11·00	11·00

315 *Charlie and the Chocolate Factory*

(Des Stephen Perera. Litho Lowe-Martin, Canada)

2010 (4 May). Europa. Children's Books. T **315** and similar horiz designs showing illustrations by Quentin Blake from books by Roald Dahl. Multicoloured. P 13.

1359	10p. Type **315**	45	30
1360	42p. *Matilda*	1·75	1·25
1361	44p. *The Twits*	1·75	1·40
1362	£1.50 *The BFG*	4·75	5·50
1359/62	*Set of 4*	8·00	7·75

316 Emblem

(Des Stephen Perera. Litho and die stamped B.D.T.)

2010 (30 June). 'Miss Gibraltar 2009 (Kaiane Aldorino) is Miss World'. Sheet 140×84 mm. P 14×14½.

MS1363 **316** £2 gold and black ... 6·50 7·50

317 Second Tower, San Marino

(Des B & AR. Litho B.D.T.)

2010 (30 June). Gibraltar and San Marino. Sheet 137×105 mm containing T **317** and similar horiz designs. Multicoloured. P 14½×14.

MS1364 75p.×4 Type **317**; Moorish Castle, Gibraltar; Mount Titano, San Marino; The Rock of Gibraltar ... 10·00 11·00

A miniature sheet containing the same designs was issued by San Marino.

318 Elise Deroche (inscr 'Baroness Raymonde de Laroche') flying Voisin Biplane, 8 March 1910

(Des John Batchelor and Stephen Perera. Litho B.D.T.)

2010 (20 Aug). Aviation Centenaries. T **318** and similar horiz designs. Multicoloured. P 14½×14.

1365	10p. Type **318** (first woman with pilot's licence)	50	30
1366	42p. DELAG's Zeppelin LZ7 (first fare paying passengers), 21 June 1910	1·50	1·25
1367	49p. Hubert Latham sets altitude record at 4,541 ft in *Antoinette VII*, 7 July 1910	2·00	1·75
1368	£2 Clément-Bayard No. 2 (first airship flight across English Channel, 16 October 1910	6·75	7·50
1365/8	*Set of* 4	9·75	9·75
MS1369	163×75 mm. 10p. Henri Fabre flies *Le Canard*, 28 March 1910; 42p. Supermarine S.6B Schneider Trophy winner, 1931; 49p. Short Sunderland, 204 Squadron, Gibraltar, 1941; £2 Saunders-ROE Princess, 22 August 1952 (centenary of seaplanes)	11·00	12·00

319 Rainbow

(Des Stephen Perera. Litho B.D.T.)

2010 (20 Oct). Centenary of Girlguiding. T **319** and similar horiz designs showing uniforms. Multicoloured. P 13½.

1370	10p. Type **319**	50	30
1371	42p. Brownie	1·60	1·25
1372	44p. Guide	1·60	1·40
1373	£2 Senior	6·75	7·50
1370/3	*Set of* 4	9·50	9·50

320 Emblem

(Des Stephen Perera. Litho B.D.T.)

2010 (20 Oct). Commonwealth Games, Delhi. Sheet 90×103 mm. P 14×14½.

MS1374	**320** £2 multicoloured	7·50	7·50

321 Interior of Cathedral of St. Mary the Crowned

(Des Stephen Perera. Litho B.D.T.)

2010 (16 Nov). Centenary of Diocese of Gibraltar. Sheet 114×80 mm. P 14½×14.

MS1375	**321** £2 multicoloured	6·50	7·00

322 Christmas Stocking, Wrapped Presents and Decorations

(Des Stephen Perera. Litho B.D.T.)

2010 (26 Nov). Christmas. T **322** and similar horiz designs. Multicoloured. P 13×13½.

1376	10p. Type **322**	45	30
1377	42p. Christmas stockings hanging from mantelpiece	1·50	1·25
1378	44p. Santa's sleigh flying over snowy landscape	1·60	1·40
1379	51p. Three snowmen as musicians with accordion, fiddle and cymbals	1·75	2·25
1376/9	*Set of* 4	4·75	4·75

323 Prince William and Miss Catherine Middleton

(Des Stephen Pesera. Litho B.D.T.)

2011 (21 Jan). Royal Engagement. Sheet 90×97 mm. P 15×14.

MS1380	**323** £2 multicoloured	6·50	6·50

324 World War I ('Reflection')

(Des Stephen Perera. Litho Lowe-Martin, Canada)

2011 (21 Jan). Royal British Legion. T **324** and similar horiz designs. Multicoloured. P 13×13½ (**MS**1389) or 13 (others).

1381	50p. Type **324**	1·75	1·75
1382	50p. World War II ('Hope')	1·75	1·75
1383	50p. Northern Ireland ('Selflessness')	1·75	1·75
1384	50p. The Falklands ('Comradeship')	1·75	1·75
1385	50p. The Gulf War ('Welfare')	1·75	1·75
1386	50p. The Balkans ('Service')	1·75	1·75
1387	50p. Iraq ('Representation')	1·75	1·75
1388	50p. Afghanistan ('Remembrance')	1·75	1·75
1381/8	*Set of* 8	12·50	12·50
MS1389	120×80 mm. £2 Statue and poppies	6·50	6·50

325 Queen Elizabeth II

(Des Westminster Collection. Litho B.D.T.)

2011 (14 Feb). Queen Elizabeth II and Prince Philip. 'Lifetime of Service'. T **325** and similar diamond-shaped designs. Multicoloured. P 13.

1390	10p. Type **325**	45	30
1391	42p. Queen Elizabeth II and Prince Philip, 1960s	1·50	1·25
1392	44p. Queen Elizabeth II (wearing purple) and Prince Philip, c. 2010	1·60	1·40
1393	51p. Queen Elizabeth II and Prince Philip, c. 1952	1·75	2·25
1394	55p. Queen Elizabeth II (wearing tiara) and Prnce Philip, c. 1965	1·90	2·40
1395	£2 Prince Philip, c. 1970	6·50	6·50
1390/5	*Set of 6*	12·50	13·00
MS1397	110×70 mm. £3 Princess Elizabeth and Duke of Edinburgh on wedding day, 1947	13·50	13·50

STAMP BOOKLETS

1906 (Oct). Black on red cover. Stapled.

SB1 2s.0½d. booklet containing twenty-four ½d. and twelve 1d. (Nos. 56a, 67) in blocks of 6

1912 (17 July). Black on red cover. Stapled.

SB2 2s.0½d. booklet containing twenty-four ½d. and twelve 1d. (Nos. 76/7) in blocks of 6

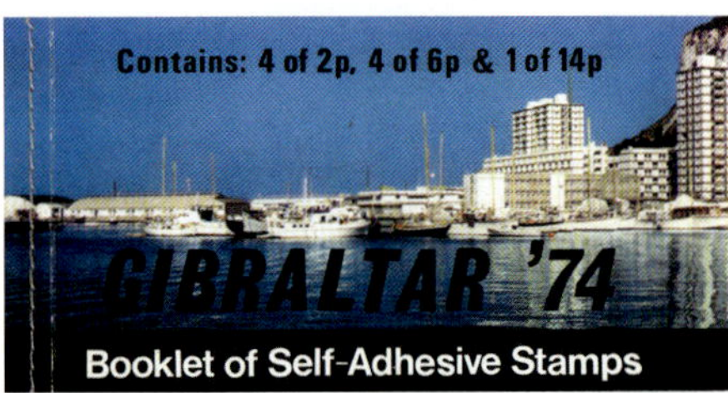

B **1**

1974 (2 May). Centenary of Universal Postal Union. Multicoloured cover, 152×79 mm, as Type B **1**. Stitched.

SB3 46p. booklet containing *se-tenant* panes of 3 (No. 328a) and 6 (No. 328b) 7·50

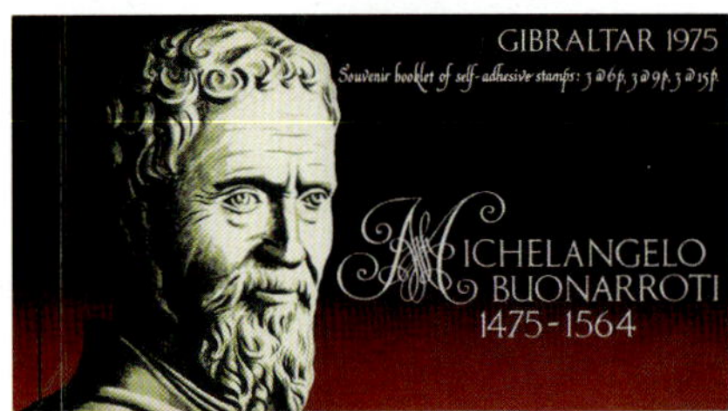

B **1a** Michelangelo

1975 (17 Dec). 500th Birth Anniv of Michelangelo. Multicoloured cover, 165×91 mm, as Type B **1a**, Stitched.

SB4 90p. booklet containing *se-tenant* panes of 3 (No. 358a) and 6 (No. 358b) 4·50

B **1b** Buckingham Palace

1978 (12 June). 25th Anniv of Coronation. Multicoloured cover, 165×92 mm, as Type B **1b**. Stitched.

SB5 £1.15 booklet containing *se-tenant* pane of 6 (No. 404a) and pane of 1 (No. 406a) 2·25

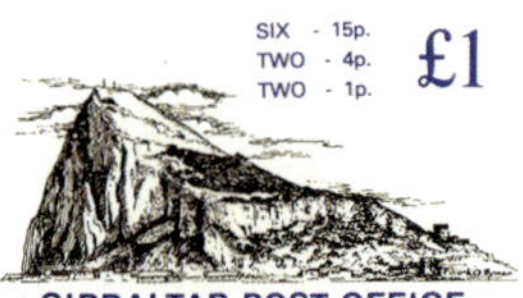

B **2**

1981 (2 Sept). Black and vermilion (No. SB6) and black and ultramarine (No. SB7) covers, 76×51 mm, as Type B **2**. Stamps attached by selvedge.

SB6 50p. booklet containing *se-tenant* pane of 5 and 1 label (No. 451a) 1·75

SB7 £1 booklet containing *se-tenant* pane of 10 and 2 labels (No. 451b) 3·25

B **3** Moorish Castle

1993 (21 Sept). Multicoloured covers, 53×40 mm, as Type B **3**. Stamps affixed by selvedge.

SB8 20p. booklet containing 5p. (No. 699) in strip of 4 2·40

SB9 £1.20 booklet containing 24p. (No. 702) in strip of 5 5·50

B **4** Rock of Gibraltar and Games Events

1995 (8 May). Island Games '95. Multicoloured cover, 175×97 mm, as Type B **4**. Stitched.

SB10 £4.68 booklet containing four panes of 3 (Nos. 745a/b, 746a and 747a) 13·00

B **5** Kitten

1997 (12 Feb). Kittens. Multicoloured cover, 150×80 mm, as Type B **5**. Stitched.

SB11 £5 booklet containing five *se-tenant* panes (Nos. 797a/b, 798a, 799a and **MS**803a) 14·00

B **6** Battle of the Nile

1998 (1 Aug). Bicent of Battle of the Nile. Multicoloured cover, 145×102 mm, as Type B **6**. Stitched.

SB12	£5 booklet containing five panes (Nos. 839a/b and 840a/c)	18·00

B **7**

2000 (9 May). New Millennium. History of Gibraltar. Bright red, yellow-orange and black cover, 144×102 mm, as Type B **7** showing the Gibraltar Coat of Arms. Booklet contains text and illustrations on panes and interleaving pages. Stitched.

SB13	£7.40 booklet containing panes Nos. 916b/31b	22·00

B **8** Flowers on Coastline

2004 (10 Sept). Wild Flowers. Multicoloured cover, 160×98 mm, as Type B **8**. Booklet contains text and illustrations on each pane. Stitched.

SB14	£6.40 booklet containing thirteen panes (Nos. 1094a/1106a)	21·00

B **9** East Side of Rock of Gibraltar

2007 (26 Sept). Prehistoric Wildlife of Gibraltar. Multicoloured cover, 155×114 mm, as Type B **9**. Booklet contains text and illustrations on panes and first page. Stitched.

SB15	£8.46 booklet containing seven panes (Nos. 1220a/b and 1221a/5a)	26·00

POSTAGE DUE STAMPS

D **1**

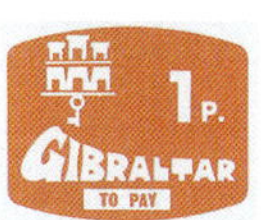

D **2**

D **3** Gibraltar Coat of Arms

Normal

Large "d." (R. 9/6, 10/6)

4d. Ball of "d" broken and serif at top damaged (R. 9/5). Other stamps in 5th vertical row show slight breaks to ball of "d".

(Typo D.L.R.)

1956 (1 Dec). Chalk-surfaced paper. Wmk Mult Script CA. P 14.

D1	D **1**	1d. green	1·50	4·25
D2		2d. sepia	1·50	2·75
		a. Large "d" (R. 9/6, 10/6)	28·00	
D3		4d. blue	1·75	5·00
		a. Broken "d"	40·00	
D1/3 *Set of* 3			4·25	11·00

1971 (15 Feb). As Nos. D 1/3 but inscr in decimal currency. W w **12**. P 17½×18.

D4	D **1**	½p. green	25	80
D5		1p. sepia	25	70
D6		2p. blue	25	1·00
D4/6 *Set of* 3			65	2·25

(Des A. Ryman. Litho Questa)

1976 (13 Oct). W w **14**. P 14×13½.

D7	D **2**	1p. light red-orange	15	60
D8		3p. bright blue	15	75
D9		5p. orange-vermilion	20	75
D10		7p. reddish violet	20	75
D11		10p. greenish slate	25	75
D12		20p. green	45	1·00
D7/12 *Set of* 6			1·25	4·25

(Des A. Ryman. Litho B.D.T.)

1984 (2 July). W w **14** (sideways). P 15×14.

D13	D **3**	1p. black	25	60
D14		3p. vermilion	40	60
D15		5p. ultramarine	45	60
D16		10p. new blue	60	60
D17		25p. deep mauve	1·25	1·00
D18		50p. reddish orange	1·50	1·75
D19		£1 blue-green	2·50	3·25
D13/19 *Set of* 7			6·25	7·75

D **4** Water Port Gates

(Des Olympia Reyes. Litho B.D.T.)

1996 (30 Sept). Gibraltar Landmarks. Type D **4** and similar vert designs. P 14½×14.

D20	1p. black, emerald & bright yellow-green	20	75
D21	10p. black and bluish grey	70	70
D22	25p. black, red-brown and chestnut	1·50	1·25
D23	50p. black and reddish lilac	2·25	2·25
D24	£1 black, olive-brown and chestnut	3·50	3·75
D25	£2 black and light blue	5·50	6·50
D20/5 *Set of* 6		12·00	14·00

Designs:—10p. Naval Dockyard; 25p. Military Hospital; 50p. Governor's Cottage; £l Swans on the Laguna; £2 Catalan Bay.

D **5** Greenfinch

(Des Roger Gorringe and Anselmo Torres. Litho Cartor)

2002 (6 June). Gibraltar Finches. Type D **5** and similar vert designs. Multicoloured. P 13×13½.

D26	5p. Type D **5**	10	10
D27	10p. Seren	20	15
D28	20p. Siskin	40	45
D29	50p. Linnet	1·00	1·10
D30	£1 Chaffinch	2·00	2·10
D31	£2 Goldfinch	4·00	4·25
D26/31	*Set of 6*	7·00	7·25

Heligoland

Stamps of HAMBURG (see Part 7 (Germany) of this catalogue) were used in Heligoland until 16 April 1867. The Free City of Hamburg ran the Heligoland postal service between 1796 and 1 June 1866. Its stamps continued in use on the island until replaced by Heligoland issues.

PRICES FOR STAMPS ON COVER
Nos. 1/19 *from* × 3

PRINTERS. All the stamps of Heligoland were typographed at the Imperial Printing Works, Berlin.

REPRINTS. Many of the stamps of Heligoland were subsequently reprinted at Berlin (between 1875 and 1885), Leipzig (1888) and Hamburg (1892 and 1895). Of these only the Berlin productions are difficult to distinguish from the originals so separate notes are provided for the individual values. Leipzig reprints can be identified by their highly surfaced paper and those from Hamburg by their 14 perforation. All of these reprints are worth much less than the original stamps priced below.

There was, in addition, a small reprinting of Nos. 13/19, made by the German government in 1890 for exchange purposes, but examples of this printing are far scarcer than the original stamps.

Forgeries, printed by lithography instead of typography, also exist for Nos. 1/4, 6 and 8 perforated 12½ or 13. Forged cancellations can also be found on originals and, on occasion, genuine postmarks on reprints.

1

(Currency. 16 schillings = 1 mark)

Three Dies of Embossed Head for Types **1** and **2**:

Die I Die II

Die III

Die I. Blob instead of curl beneath the chignon. Outline of two jewels at top of diadem.
Die II. Curl under chignon. One jewel at top of diadem.
Die III. Shorter curl under chignon. Two jewels at top of diadem.

(Des Wedding. Die eng E. Schilling)

1867 (Mar)–**68**. Head Die I embossed in colourless relief. Roul.

1	**1**	½sch. blue-green and rose	£325	£800
		a. Head Die II (7.68)	£750	£1100
2		1sch. rose and blue-green (21.3.67)	£170	£190
3		2sch. rose and grass-green (21.3.67)	14·00	60·00
4		6sch. green and rose	16·00	£250

For Nos. 1/4 the second colour given is that of the spandrels on the ½ and 1sch., and of the spandrels and central background for the 2 and 6sch.

All four values exist from the Berlin, Leipzig and Hamburg reprintings. The following points are helpful in identifying originals from Berlin reprints; for Leipzig and Hamburg reprints see general note above:

½sch. – Reprints are all in yellowish green and show Head Die II
1sch. – All reprints are Head Die III
2sch. – Berlin reprints are in dull rose with a deeper blue-green
6sch. – Originals show white specks in green. Berlin reprints have a more solid bluish green

1869 (Apr)–**73**. Head embossed in colourless relief. P 13½×14½.

No.	Type	Description	Unused	Used
5	**1**	¼sch. rose and green (background) (I) (*quadrillé paper*) (8.73)	30·00	£1500
		a. Error. Green and rose (background) (9.73)	£150	£3000
		b. Deep rose and pale green (background) (11.73)	90·00	£1500
6		½sch. blue-green and rose (II)	£200	£225
		a. Yellow green and rose (7.71)	£150	£200
		b. Quadrille paper (6.73)	£100	£160
7		¾sch. green and rose (I) (*quadrillé paper*) (12.73)	40·00	£1100
8		1sch. rose and yellow-green (III) (7.71)	£150	£190
		a. Quadrillé paper. *Rose and pale blue-green* (6.73)	£130	£190
9		1½sch. grn & rose (I) (*quadrillé paper*) (9.73)	80·00	£250

For Nos. 5/9 the second colour given is that of the spandrels on the ½ and 1sch., of the central background on the ¼ and 1½sch., and of the central background, side labels and side marginal lines of the ¾sch.

No. 5a was a printing of the ¼sch. made in the colour combination of the 1½sch. by mistake.

A further printing of the ½sch. (Head die I) in deep rose-red and yellowish green (background), on non-*quadrillé* paper, was made in December 1874, but not issued (*Price* £15, *unused*).

All five values exist from the Berlin, Leipzig and Hamburg reprintings. The following points are helpful in identifying originals from Berlin reprints; for Leipzig and Hamburg reprints see general note above:

¼sch. – All Berlin and some Hamburg reprints are Head Die II
½sch. – Berlin reprints on thinner paper with solid colour in the spandrels
¾sch. – Berlin reprints on thinner, non-quadrille paper
1sch. – Berlin reprints are on thinner paper or show many breaks in the rose line beneath "SCHILLING" at the top of the design or in the line above it at the foot
1½sch.– All Berlin and some Hamburg reprints are Head Die II

Berlin, Leipzig and Hamburg reprints also exist of the 2 and 6sch., but these values do not come as perforated originals.

(New Currency. 100 pfennig = 1 mark)

2

3

4

5

(Des H. Gätke. Die eng E. Schilling (T **2**), A. Schiffner (others))

1875 (Feb)–**90**. Head Die II on T **2** embossed in colourless relief. P 13½×14½.

No.	Type	Description	Unused	Used
10	**2**	1pf. (¼d.) deep green and rose	16·00	£500
11		2pf. (½d.) deep rose and deep green	16·00	£600
12	**3**	3pf. (⅝d.) pale green, red and yellow (6.76)	£225	£1100
		a. Green, red and orange (6.77)	£160	£850
13	**2**	5pf. (¾d.) deep yellow-green and rose	19·00	19·00
		a. Deep green and rose (6.90)	23·00	45·00
14		10pf. (1½d.) deep rose and deep green	40·00	22·00
		a. Scarlet and pale blue-green (5.87)	15·00	22·00
15	**3**	20pf. (2½d.) rose, green and yellow (6.76)	£250	£120
		a. Rose-carmine, deep green and orange (4.80)	£170	50·00
		b. Dull red, pale green and lemon (7.88)	21·00	29·00
		c. Aniline verm, brt grn and lemon (6.90)	14·00	50·00
16	**2**	25pf. (3d.) deep green and rose	21·00	28·00
17		50pf. (6d.) rose and green	23·00	40·00
18	**4**	1m. (1s.) deep green, scarlet and black (8.79)	£160	£200
		a. Perf 11½	£1300	
		b. Deep green, aniline rose and black (5.89)	£160	£200
19	**5**	5m. (5s.) deep green, aniline rose, black and yellow (8.79)	£200	£950
		a. Perf 11½	£1300	
		ab. Imperf between (horiz pair)	£5500	

For stamps as Type **2** the first colour is that of the central background and the second that of the frame. On the 3pf. the first colour is of the frame and the top band of the shield, the second is the centre band and the third the shield border. The 20pf. is similar, but has the centre band in the same colour as the frame and the upper band on the shield in the second colour.

The 1, 2 and 3pf. exist from the Berlin, Leipzig and Hamburg reprintings. There were no such reprints for the other values. The following points are helpful in identifying originals from Berlin reprints; for Leipzig and Hamburg reprints see general note above:

1pf. – Berlin printings show a peculiar shade of pink
2pf. – All reprints are much lighter in shade than the deep rose and deep green of the originals
3pf. – Berlin reprints either show the band around the shield in brownish orange, or have this feature in deep yellow with the other two colours lighter

Heligoland was ceded to Germany on 9 August 1890.

Ionian Islands

The British occupation of the Ionian Islands was completed in 1814 and the archipelago was placed under the protection of Great Britain by the Treaty of Paris of 9 November 1815. The United States of the Ionian Islands were given local self-government, which included responsibility for the postal services. Crowned-circle handstamps were, however, supplied in 1844, although it is believed these were intended for use on prepaid mail to foreign destinations.

Examples of the Great Britain 1855 1d. red-brown stamp are known used at Corfu, cancelled as No. CC2, but it is believed that these originate from mail sent by the British garrison.

For illustrations of the handstamp types see BRITISH POST OFFICES ABROAD notes, following GREAT BRITAIN.

CEPHALONIA

CROWNED-CIRCLE HANDSTAMPS

CC1	CC **1**	CEPHALONIA (19.4.1844) ....*Price on cover*	£1700

CORFU

CROWNED-CIRCLE HANDSTAMPS

CC2	CC **1**	CORFU (19.4.1844) ....*Price on cover*	£600
CC3	CC **1**	CORFU (G. or B.) (1844) ....*Price on cover*	—

ZANTE

CROWNED-CIRCLE HANDSTAMPS

CC4	CC **1**	ZANTE (G. or B.) (19.4.1844) ....*Price on cover*	£1300

Nos. CC1/2 were later, circa 1860/1, struck in green (Cephalonia) or red (Corfu).

It is believed that examples of No. CC4 in black are from an unauthorised use of this handstamp which is now on display in the local museum. A similar handstamp, but without "PAID AT" was introduced in 1861.

PRICES FOR STAMPS ON COVER
Nos. 1/3 *from* × 10

PERKINS BACON "CANCELLED". For notes on these handstamps, showing "CANCELLED" between horizontal bars forming an oval, see Catalogue Introduction.

1

(Eng C. Jeens. Recess Perkins, Bacon & Co)

1859 (15 June). Imperf.

1	**1**	(½d.) orange (no wmk) (H/S "CANCELLED" in oval £11000)	£120	£650
2		(1d.) blue (wmk "2") (H/S "CANCELLED" in oval £11000)	30·00	£250
3		(2d.) carmine (wmk "1") (H/S "CANCELLED" in oval £11000)	24·00	£250

On 30 May 1864, the islands were ceded to Greece, and these stamps became obsolete.

Great care should be exercised in buying used stamps, on or off cover, as forged postmarks are plentiful.

Malta

Early records of the postal services under the British Occupation are fragmentary, but it is known that an Island Postmaster was appointed in 1802. A British Packet Agency was established in 1806 and it later became customary for the same individual to hold the two appointments together. The inland posts continued to be the responsibility of the local administration, but the overseas mails formed part of the British G.P.O. system.

The stamps of Great Britain were used on overseas mails from September 1857. Previously during the period of the Crimean War letters franked with Great Britain stamps from the Crimea were cancelled at Malta with a wavy line obliterator. Such postmarks are known between April 1855 and September 1856.

The British G.P.O. relinquished control of the overseas posts on 31 December 1884 when Great Britain stamps were replaced by those of Malta.

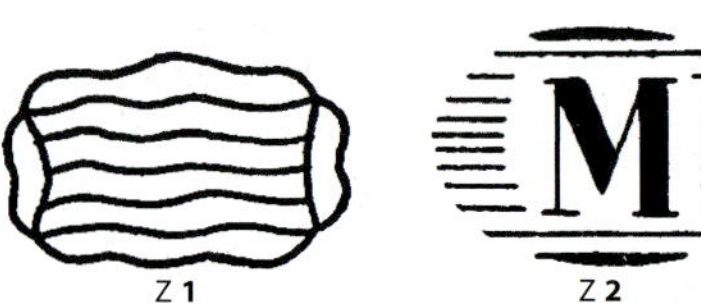

Z **1** Z **2**

1855–56. Stamps of GREAT BRITAIN cancelled with wavy lines obliteration, Type Z **1**.

Z1	1d. red-brown (1854), Die I, wmk Small Crown, perf 16	£900
Z2	1d. red-brown (1855), Die II, wmk Small Crown, perf 14	£900
	a. Very blued paper	
Z3	1d. red-brown (1855), Die II, wmk Large Crown, perf 16	£900
Z3*a*	1d. red-brown (1855), Die II, wmk Large Crown, perf 14	£900
Z4	2d. blue (1855), wmk Large Crown, perf 14 .... Plate No. 5	
Z5	6d. (1854) embossed	£4500
Z6	1s. (1847) embossed	£5000

It is now established that this obliterator was sent to Malta and used on mail in transit emanating from the Crimea.

1857 (18 Aug)–**59**. Stamps of GREAT BRITAIN cancelled "M", Type Z **2**.

Z7	1d. red-brown (1841), imperf	£2500
Z8	1d. red-brown, Die I, wmk Small Crown, perf 16	£160
Z9	1d. red-brown, Die II, wmk Small Crown, perf 16	£950
Z10	1d. red-brown, Die II (1855), wmk Small Crown, perf 14	£250
Z11	1d. red-brown, Die II (1855), wmk Large Crown, perf 14	80·00
Z11*a*	1d. rose-red (1857) wmk Large Crown, perf 16	
Z12	1d. rose-red (1857), wmk Large Crown, perf 14	22·00
Z13	2d. blue (1841), imperf	£3750
Z14	2d. blue (1854) wmk Small Crown, perf 16 .... Plate No. 4	£850
Z15	2d. blue (1855), wmk Large Crown, perf 14 .... *From* Plate Nos. 5, 6	65·00
Z16	2d. blue (1858), wmk Large Crown, perf 16 .... Plate No. 6	£350
Z17	2d. blue (1858) (Plate Nos. 7, 8, 9) .... *From*	45·00
Z18	4d. rose (1857)	40·00
	a. Thick glazed paper	£225
Z19	6d. violet (1854), embossed	£4250
Z20	6d. lilac (1856)	42·00
	a. Thick paper	£250
Z21	6d. lilac (1856) (*blued paper*)	£900
Z22	1s. green (1856)	£130
	a. Thick paper	£200

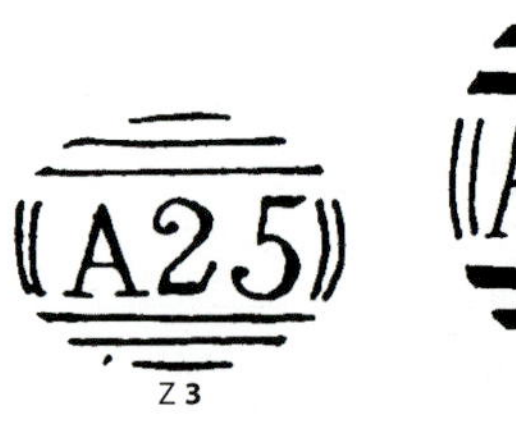

Z **3** Z **6**

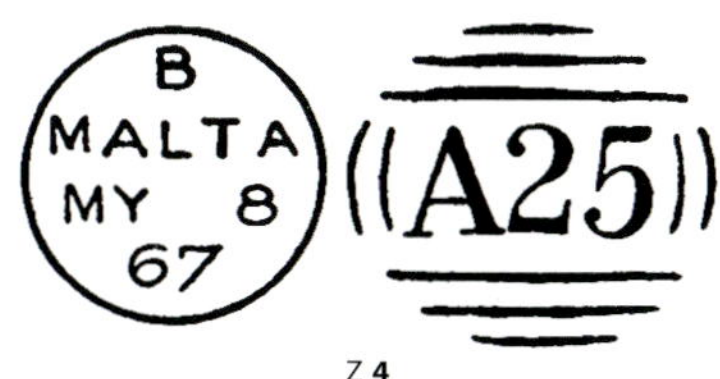

Z 4

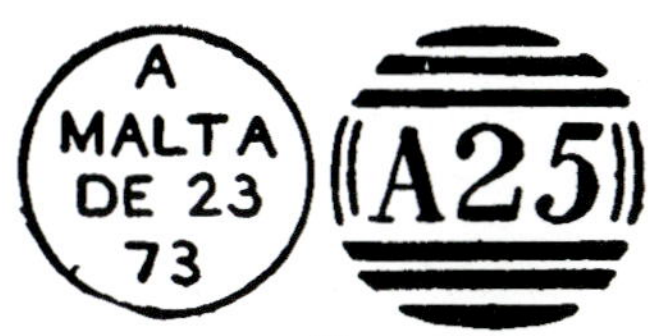

Z 5

Z 7

1859–84. Stamps of GREAT BRITAIN cancelled "A 25" as in Types Z **3**/**7**.

Z23	½d. rose-red (1870–79) *From* Plate Nos. 4, 5, 6, 8, 9, 10, 11, 12, 13, 14, 15, 19, 20.	32·00
Z24	1d. red-brown (1841), *imperf*	£3250
Z25	1d. red-brown (1854), wmk Small Crown, perf 16	£375
Z26	1d. red-brown (1855), wmk Large Crown, perf 14	85·00
Z27	1d. rose-red (1857), wmk Large Crown, perf 14	9·00
Z28	1d. rose-red (1861), Alphabet IV	£475
Z30	1d. rose-red (1864–79) *From* Plate Nos, 71, 72, 73, 74, 76, 78, 79, 80, 81, 82, 83, 84, 85, 86, 87, 88, 89, 90, 91, 92, 93, 94, 95, 96, 97, 98, 99, 100, 101, 102, 103, 104, 105, 106, 107, 108, 109, 110, 111, 112, 113, 114, 115, 116, 117, 118, 119, 120, 121, 122, 123, 124, 125, 127, 129, 130, 131, 132, 133, 134, 135, 136, 137, 138, 139, 140, 141, 142, 143, 144, 145, 146, 147, 148, 149, 150, 151, 152, 153, 154, 155, 156, 157, 158, 159, 160, 161, 162, 163, 164, 165, 166, 167, 168, 169, 170, 171, 172, 173, 174, 175, 176, 177, 178, 179, 180, 181, 182, 183, 184, 185, 186, 187, 188, 189, 190, 191, 192, 193, 194, 195, 196, 197, 198, 199, 200, 201, 202, 203, 204, 205, 206, 207, 208, 209, 210, 211, 212, 213, 214, 215, 216, 217, 218, 219, 220, 221, 222, 223, 224.	19·00
Z31	1½d. lake-red (1870–79) (Plate Nos. 1, 3) *From*	£600
Z32	2d. blue (1841), *imperf*	£4500
Z33	2d. blue (1855) wmk Large Crown perf 14	80·00
Z34	2d. blue (1858–69) *From* Plate Nos. 7, 8, 9, 12, 13, 14, 15.	19·00
Z35	2½d. rosy mauve (1875) (*blued paper*) *From* Plate Nos. 1, 2.	80·00
Z36	2½d. rosy mauve (1875–76) *From* Plate Nos. 1, 2, 3.	35·00
Z37	2½d. rosy mauve (Error of Lettering)	£3500
Z38	2½d. rosy mauve (1876–79) *From* Plate Nos. 3, 4, 5, 6, 7, 8, 9, 10, 11, 12, 13, 14, 15, 16, 17.	17·00
Z39	2½d. blue (1880–81) *From* Plate Nos. 17, 18, 19, 20.	11·00
Z40	2½d. blue (1881) (Plate Nos. 21, 22, 23) *From*	8·00
Z41	3d. carmine-rose (1862)	£130
Z42	3d. rose (1865) (Plate No. 4)	80·00
Z43	3d. rose (1867–73) *From* Plate Nos. 4, 5, 6, 7, 8, 9, 10.	30·00
Z44	3d. rose (1873–76) *From* Plate Nos. 11, 12, 14, 15, 16, 17, 18, 19, 20.	35·00
Z45	3d. rose (1881) (Plate Nos. 20, 21) *From*	£1000
Z46	3d. on 3d. lilac (1883)	£550
Z47	4d. rose (or rose-carmine) (1857)	38·00
	a. Thick glazed paper	£150
Z48	4d. red (1862) (Plate Nos. 3, 4) *From*	32·00
Z49	4d. vermilion (1865–73) *From* Plate Nos. 7, 8, 9, 10, 11, 12, 13, 14.	17·00
Z50	4d. vermilion (1876) (Plate No. 15)	£225
Z51	4d. sage-green (1877) (Plate Nos. 15, 16) *From*	£110
Z52	4d. grey-brown (1880) wmk Large Garter Plate No. 17.	£180
Z53	4d. grey-brown (1880) wmk Crown *From* Plate Nos. 17, 18.	50·00
Z54	6d. violet (1854), embossed	£3750
Z55	6d. lilac (1856)	45·00
	a. Thick paper	
Z56	6d. lilac (1862) (Plate Nos. 3, 4) *From*	38·00
Z57	6d. lilac (1865–67) (Plate Nos. 5, 6) *From*	30·00
Z58	6d. lilac (1865–67) (Wmk error)	£1300
Z59	6d. lilac (1867) (Plate No. 6)	35·00
Z60	6d. violet (1867–70) (Plate Nos. 6, 8, 9) *From*	26·00
Z61	6d. buff (1872–73) (Plate Nos. 11, 12) *From*	£100
Z62	6d. chestnut (1872) (Plate No. 11)	32·00
Z63	6d. grey (1873) (Plate No. 12)	75·00
Z64	6d. grey (1873–80) *From* Plate Nos. 13, 14, 15, 16, 17.	35·00
Z65	6d. grey (1881–82) (Plate Nos. 17, 18) *From*	80·00
Z66	6d. on 6d. lilac (1883)	£150
Z67	8d. orange (1876)	£475
Z68	9d. straw (1862)	£700
Z69	9d. bistre (1862)	£650
Z70	9d. straw (1865)	£650
Z71	9d. straw (1867)	£800
Z72	10d. red-brown (1867)	£130
Z73	1s. (1847), embossed	£4000
Z74	1s. green (1856)	75·00
Z75	1s. green (1856) (*thick paper*)	£275
Z76	1s. green (1862)	65·00
Z77	1s. green ("K" *variety*)	£2250
Z78	1s. green (1865) (Plate No. 4)	45·00
Z79	1s. green (1867–73) (Plate Nos. 4, 5, 6, 7) *From*	30·00
Z80	1s. green (1873–77) *From* Plate Nos. 8, 9, 10, 11, 12, 13.	42·00
Z81	1s. orange-brown (1880) (Plate No. 13)	£300
Z82	1s. orange-brown (1881) *From* Plate Nos. 13, 14.	90·00
Z83	2s. blue (*shades*) (1867) *From*	£160
Z84	2s. brown (1880)	£3250
Z85	5s. rose (1867–74) (Plate Nos. 1, 2) *From*	£425
Z86	5s. rose (1882) (Plate No. 4), *blued paper*	£2500
Z87	5s. rose (1882) (Plate No. 4), *white paper*	£1800
Z88	10s. grey-green (1878)	£3500

1880.

Z89	½d. deep green	16·00
Z90	½d. pale green	16·00
Z91	1d. Venetian red	15·00
Z92	1½d. Venetian red	£500
Z93	2d. pale rose	40·00
Z94	2d. deep rose	42·00
Z95	5d. indigo	75·00

1881.

Z96	1d. lilac (*14 dots*)	35·00
Z97	1d. lilac (*16 dots*)	9·00

1883–84.

Z98	½d. slate-blue	19·00
Z99	1½d. lilac	
Z100	2d. lilac	£110
Z101	2½d. lilac	13·00
Z102	3d. lilac	
Z103	4d. dull green	£180
Z104	5d. dull green	£150
Z105	6d. dull green	£400
Z106	9d. dull green	
Z107	1s. dull green	£400
Z108	5s. rose (*blued paper*)	£2000
Z109	5s. rose (*white paper*)	£1100

POSTAL FISCALS

Z109*a*	1d. reddish lilac (Type F **8**) (1867) wmk Anchor	
Z110	1d. purple (Type F **12**) (1871) wmk Anchor	£850
Z111	1d. purple (Type F **12**) (1881) wmk Orb	£650

PRICES FOR STAMPS ON COVER TO 1945

Nos.	1/3	*from* × 5
Nos.	4/17	*from* × 6
Nos.	18/19	*from* × 12
Nos.	20/9	*from* × 6
No.	30	—
Nos.	31/3	*from* × 4
Nos.	34/7	*from* × 10
Nos.	38/88	*from* × 4
Nos.	92/3	*from* × 5
Nos.	97/103	*from* × 3
Nos.	104/5	—
Nos.	106/20	*from* × 3
No.	121	—
Nos.	122/38	*from* × 3
Nos.	139/40	—
Nos.	141/72	*from* × 4

PRICES FOR STAMPS ON COVER TO 1945		
Nos.	173/209	*from* × 3
Nos.	210/31	*from* × 2
Nos.	D1/10	*from* × 30
Nos.	D11/20	*from* × 15

CROWN COLONY

PRINTERS. Nos. 1/156. Printed by De La Rue; typographed *except where otherwise stated.*

1

Type **1**

The first Government local post was established on 10 June 1853 and, as an experiment, mail was carried free of charge. During 1859 the Council of Government decided that a rate of ½d. per ½ ounce should be charged for this service and stamps in Type I were ordered for this purpose. Both the new rate and the stamps were introduced on 1 December 1860. Until 1 January 1885 the ½d stamps were intended for the local service only; mail for abroad being handled by the British Post Office on Malta, using G.B. stamps.

Specialists now recognise 29 printings in shades of yellow and one in green during the period to 1884. These printings can be linked to the changes in watermark and perforation as follows:

Ptg 1—Blued paper without wmk. P 14.
Ptgs 2 and 3—White paper without wmk. P 14.
Ptgs 4 to 9, 11, 13 to 19, 22 to 24—Crown CC wmk. P 14.
Ptg 10—Crown CC wmk. P 12½ (rough).
Ptg 12—Crown CC wmk. P 12½ (clean-cut).
Ptgs 20 and 21—Crown CC wmk. P 14×12½.
Ptgs 25 to 28, 30—Crown CA wmk. P 14.
Ptg 29—In green (No. 20).

PRICES. The prices quoted for Nos. 1/19 are for examples in very fine condition, with fresh colour. Unused examples should have original gum, used examples should have neat clear cancels. The many surviving stamps which do not meet theses criteria are usually worth only a fraction of the prices quoted, with stamps of poor colour being virtually worthless.

(Des E. Fuchs)

1860 (1 Dec)–**63**. No wmk. P 14.

		(a) Blued paper		
1		½d. buff (1.12.60)	£1300	£650
		(b) Thin, hard white paper		
2		½d. brown-orange (11.61)	£1300	£475
3		½d. buff (1.63)	£850	£400
		a. *Pale buff*	£850	£400

No. 1 is printed in fugitive ink. It is known imperforate but was not issued in that state (*Price* £12000 *unused*).

The printing on No. 2 gives a very blurred and muddy impression; on Nos. 3/3*a* the impression is clear.

Specks of carmine can often be detected with a magnifying glass on Nos. 2/3*a*, and also on No. 4. Examples also exist on which parts of the design are in pure rose, due to defective mixing of the ink.

1863–81. Wmk Crown CC.

		(a) P 14		
4		½d. buff (6.63) (*shades*)	£120	75·00
		w. Wmk inverted	£450	£450
		x. Wmk reversed	£1400	
5		½d. bright orange (11.64)	£800	£200
		w. Wmk inverted	£1300	£1000
6		½d. orange-brown (4.67)	£425	£110
7		½d. dull orange (4.70)	£300	90·00
		w. Wmk inverted	†	£650
		x. Wmk reversed	£1600	
8		½d. orange-buff (5.72)	£180	80·00
9		½d. golden yellow (aniline) (10.74)	£325	£375
10		½d. yellow-buff (9.75) (*shades*)	80·00	60·00
11		½d. pale buff (3.77)	£190	75·00
		w. Wmk inverted	£1100	£600
12		½d. bright orange-yellow (4.80)	£225	£110
13		½d. yellow (4.81)	£130	75·00
		w. Wmk inverted	†	£600
		(b) P 12½ rough (No. 14) or clean-cut (No. 15)		
14		½d. buff-brown (11.68)	£150	£110
15		½d. yellow-orange (5.71)	£375	£180
		(c) P 14×12½		
16		½d. yellow-buff (7.78)	£190	£100
		w. Wmk inverted	†	£1300
17		½d. yellow (2.79)	£225	£110

Examples of No. 4 from the 1863 printing are on thin, surfaced paper; later printings in the same shade were on unsurfaced paper.

The ink used for No. 5 is mineral and, unlike that on No. 9, does not stain the paper.

Some variations of shade on No. 6 may be described as chestnut. The ink of No. 6 is clear and never muddy, although some examples are over-inked. Deeper shades of No. 4, with which examples of No. 6 might be confused, have muddy ink.

Nos. 7/8 and 11 are distinctive shades which should not be confused with variants of No. 10.

It is believed that there are no surviving pairs of the buff-brown imperforate between variety previously listed.

The Royal Collection contains an unused horizontal pair of the yellow-buff perforated 12½×14.

1882 (Mar)–**84**. Wmk Crown CA. P 14.

18		½d. orange-yellow	40·00	35·00
19		½d. red-orange (9.84)	18·00	50·00

2 3 4 5

1885 (1 Jan)–**90**. Wmk Crown CA. P 14.

20	1	½d. green	4·00	50
		w. Wmk inverted	£140	95·00
21	2	1d. rose	85·00	26·00
		w. Wmk inverted	£1800	
22		1d. carmine (*shades*) (1890)	9·00	35
		w. Wmk inverted	†	£1400
23	3	2d. grey	8·00	2·25
24	4	2½d. dull blue	65·00	3·00
25		2½d. bright blue	50·00	1·00
26		2½d. ultramarine	50·00	1·00
27	3	4d. brown	11·00	3·00
		a. Imperf (pair)	£5000	£6000
		w. Wmk inverted	£1800	
28		1s. violet	48·00	12·00
29		1s. pale violet (1890)	60·00	21·00
		w. Wmk inverted	£900	£350
20/8 *Set of* 6			£120	17·00
20s/8s Optd "SPECIMEN" *Set of* 6			£4250	

Although not valid for postage until 1 January 1885 these stamps were available at the G.P.O., Valletta from 27 December 1884.

Three unused examples of the ½d. green, No. 20, are known line perforated 12. These originated from proof books, the stamp not being issued for use with this perforation.

The Royal Collection includes an example of the 1d. carmine printed on the gummed side.

1886 (1 Jan). Wmk Crown CC. P 14.

30	5	5s. rose	£110	80·00
		s. Optd "SPECIMEN"	£700	
		w. Wmk inverted	£160	£130

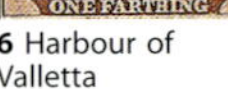

6 Harbour of Valletta

7 Gozo Fishing Boat

8 Galley of Knights of St. John

9 Emblematic figure of Malta

10 Shipwreck of St. Paul

(T **6/10** recess)

1899 (4 Feb)–**1901**. P 14.

(a) Wmk Crown CA (sideways on ¼d)*

No.	Type	Description	Unused	Used
31	**6**	¼d. brown (4.1.01)	8·00	2·75
		a. Red-brown	1·50	40
		b. Wmk upright (reversed)	†	£2000
		w. Wmk Crown to left of CA	2·50	75
		x. Wmk sideways reversed	45·00	24·00
		y. Wmk Crown to left of CA and reversed	65·00	30·00
32	**7**	4½d. sepia	22·00	16·00
		x. Wmk reversed	£750	
33	**8**	5d. vermilion	45·00	19·00
		x. Wmk reversed	£225	£225

(b) Wmk Crown CC

No.	Type	Description	Unused	Used
34	**9**	2s.6d. olive-grey	45·00	14·00
		x. Wmk reversed	£1100	
35	**10**	10s. blue-black	£100	65·00
		x. Wmk reversed	—	£750
		y. Wmk inverted and reversed	£700	£500
31/5 *Set of 5*			£190	£100
31s/5s Optd "SPECIMEN" *Set of 5*			£275	

*The normal sideways watermark shows Crown to right of CA, *as seen from the back of the stamp.*

One Penny
(**11**)

12

1902 (4 July). Nos. 24 and 25 surch locally at Govt Ptg Office with T **11**.

No.	Description	Unused	Used
36	1d. on 2½d. dull blue	1·50	2·00
	a. Surch double	£15000	£3750
	b. "One Pnney" (R. 9/2)	32·00	55·00
	ba. Surch double, with "One Pnney"	£30000	
	s. Optd "SPECIMEN"	70·00	
37	1d. on 2½d. bright blue	1·00	2·00
	a. "One Pnney" (R. 9/2)	32·00	55·00

(Des E. Fuchs)

1903 (12 Mar)–**04**. Wmk Crown CA. P 14.

No.	Type	Description	Unused	Used
38	**12**	½d. green	8·50	85
39		1d. blackish brown and red (7.5.03)	15·00	40
40		2d. purple and grey	29·00	6·00
41		2½d. maroon and blue (1903)	28·00	4·50
42		3d. grey and purple (26.3.03)	1·75	50
43		4d. blackish brown and brown (19.5.04)	26·00	16·00
44		1s. grey and violet (6.4.03)	26·00	7·00
38/44 *Set of 7*			£120	32·00
38s/44s Optd "SPECIMEN" *Set of 7*			£160	

1904–**14**. Wmk Mult Crown CA (sideways* on ¼d.). P 14.

No.	Type	Description	Unused	Used
45	**6**	¼d. red-brown (10.10.05)	8·50	2·25
		a. Deep brown (1910)	6·50	10
		w. Wmk Crown to left of CA	13·00	1·50
		x. Wmk reversed		
		y. Wmk Crown to left of CA and reversed		
47	**12**	½d. green (6.11.04)	5·50	30
		aw. Wmk inverted		
		b. Deep green (1909)	5·50	10
		bw. Wmk inverted		
48		1d. black and red (24.4.05)	22·00	20
49		1d. red (2.4.07)	3·50	10
50		2d. purple and grey (22.2.05)	12·00	3·00
51		2d. grey (4.10.11)	4·25	5·50
52		2½d. maroon and blue (8.10.04)	30·00	60
53		2½d. bright blue (15.1.11)	5·50	4·25
54		4d. black and brown (1.4.06)	11·00	7·50
		w. Wmk inverted		
55		4d. black and red/*yellow* (21.11.11)	4·00	4·50
57	**7**	4½d. brown (27.2.05)	38·00	7·00
		w. Wmk inverted	£425	£300
58		4½d. orange (6.3.12†)	4·75	3·75
59	**8**	5d. vermilion (20.2.05)	35·00	6·50
60		5d. pale sage-green (1910)	4·25	3·50
		a. Deep sage-green (1914)	11·00	14·00
		y. Wmk inverted and reversed	†	£800
61	**12**	1s. grey and violet (14.12.04)	50·00	2·00
62		1s. black/*green* (15.3.11)	7·50	4·25
63		5s. green and red/*yellow* (22.3.11)	65·00	75·00
45/63 *Set of 17*			£275	£110
45*a*s, 47*b*s, 49s, 51s, 53s, 55s, 58s, 60s, 62s/3s Optd "SPECIMEN" *Set of 10*			£450	

*The normal sideways watermark shows Crown to right of CA, *as seen from the back of the stamp.*

†This is the earliest known date of use.

13

14

15

Break in scroll (R. 1/12)

Broken crown and scroll (R. 2/12)

Nick in top right scroll (R. 3/12) (some printings from 1920 onwards show attempts at repair)

Break in lines below left scroll (R. 4/9. Ptgs from May 1920)

Damaged leaf at bottom right (R. 5/6. Ptgs from April 1918)

1914–21. Ordinary paper (¼d. to 2½d., 2s.6d.) or chalk-surfaced paper (others). Wmk Mult Crown CA. P 14.

No.	Type	Description	Unused	Used
69	**13**	¼d. brown (2.1.14)	1·00	10
		a. Deep brown (1919)	2·25	70
		x. Wmk reversed	†	£1000
71		½d. green (20.1.14)	2·50	30
		aa. Wmk sideways	†	£11000
		a. Deep green (1919)	4·75	1·25
		aw. Wmk inverted	†	£375
73		1d. carmine-red (15.4.14)	1·50	10
		a. Scarlet (1915)	1·50	40
		w. Wmk inverted	†	£375
75		2d. grey (12.8.14)	11·00	6·00
		aw. Wmk inverted	†	£1000
		b. Deep slate (1919)	11·00	15·00
77		2½d. bright blue (11.3.14)	2·25	50
		w. Wmk inverted	†	£190
78	**14**	3d. purple/*yellow* (1.5.20)	2·50	16·00
		a. On orange-buff	70·00	48·00
		bs. On yellow, white back (opt. "SPECIMEN")	£300	
79	**6**	4d. black (21.8.15)	15·00	7·00
		a. Grey-black (28.10.16)	35·00	10·00
80	**13**	6d. dull and bright purple (10.3.14)	11·00	21·00
		a. Dull purple and magenta (1918)	15·00	21·00
		w. Wmk inverted		
81	**14**	1s. black/*green* (*white back*) (2.1.14)	15·00	35·00
		a. On green, green back (1915)	12·00	22·00
		ab. Wmk sideways	†	£2250
		as. Optd "SPECIMEN"	60·00	
		b. On blue-green, olive back (1918)	19·00	28·00
		c. On emerald surface (1920)	8·50	32·00
		d. On emerald back (1921)	38·00	85·00
86	**15**	2s. purple and bright blue/*blue* (15.4.14)	50·00	38·00
		a. Break in scroll	£375	
		b. Broken crown and scroll	£400	
		c. Nick in top right scroll	£375	£375
		f. Damaged leaf at bottom right	—	£500
		g. Dull purple and blue/grey-blue (1921)	90·00	65·00
		ga. Break in scroll	£600	
		gb. Broken crown and scroll	£650	
		ge. Break in lines below left scroll	£650	
		gf. Damaged leaf at bottom right	£650	
87	**9**	2s.6d. olive-green (1919)	70·00	80·00
		a. Olive-grey (1920)	80·00	£110
88	**15**	5s. green and red/*yellow* (21.3.17)	£100	£110
		a. Break in scroll	£550	
		b. Broken crown and scroll	£600	
		c. Nick in top right scroll	£600	
		e. Break in lines below left scroll	£650	
		f. Damaged leaf at bottom right	£650	
69/88 *Set of* 12			£250	£275
69s/88s (*ex* 2s.6d.) Optd "SPECIMEN" *Set of* 11			£500	

The design of Nos. 79/*a* differs in various details from that of Type **6**.

We have only seen one example of No. 71aa; it is in used condition.

No. 78bs, the 3d. purple on yellow on white back, was prepared for use in 1914, and "SPECIMEN" examples were distributed to UPU members, but the stamp was never issued.

An example of the 2s.6d. olive-grey with bottom margin attached exists with the "A" omitted from "CA" in the watermark on the margin.

WAR TAX
(**16**)

17

18

1917–18. Optd with T **16** by De La Rue.

No.	Type	Description	Unused	Used
92	**13**	½d. deep green (14.12.17*)	2·00	15
		w. Wmk inverted	£500	
		y. Wmk inverted and reversed	£850	
93	**12**	3d. grey and purple (15.2.18*)	2·00	12·00
92s/3s Optd "SPECIMEN" *Set of* 2			£150	

*These are the earliest known dates of use.

(T **17** recess)

1919 (6 Mar). Wmk Mult Crown CA. P 14.

No.	Type	Description	Unused	Used
96	**17**	10s. black	£3250	£4250
		s. Optd "SPECIMEN"	£950	

Dark flaw on scroll (R. 2/4 1st state)

Lines omitted from scroll (R. 2/4 2nd state)

1921 (16 Feb)–**22**. Chalk-surfaced paper (6d., 2s.) or ordinary paper (others). Wmk Mult Script CA. P 14.

No.	Type	Description	Unused	Used
97	**13**	¼d. brown (12.1.22)	5·50	35·00
98		½d. green (19.1.22)	5·50	30·00
99		1d. scarlet (24.12.21)	5·50	2·25
		w. Wmk inverted	£950	£375
100	**18**	2d. grey	7·50	1·75
101	**13**	2½d. bright blue (15.1.22)	6·50	38·00
102		6d. dull purple and bright purple (19.1.22)	32·00	85·00
103	**15**	2s. purple and blue/*blue* (19.1.22)	70·00	£225
		a. Break in scroll	£350	£750
		b. Broken crown and scroll	£375	
		c. Dark flaw on scroll	£3000	
		d. Lines omitted from scroll	£550	
		e. Break in lines below left scroll	£375	
		f. Damaged leaf at bottom right	£375	
		g. Nick in top right scroll	£375	
104	**17**	10s. black (19.1.22)	£350	£800
97/104 *Set of* 8			£450	£1100
97s/104s Optd "SPECIMEN" *Set of* 8			£450	

For illustrations of other varieties on No. 103 see above No. 69.

Examples of all values are known showing a forged G.P.O. Malta postmark dated "MY 10 22".

(**19**)

(**20**)

1922 (12 Jan–Apr). Optd with T **19** or T **20** (large stamps), at Govt Printing Office, Valletta.

(a) On No. 35. Wmk Crown CC

No.	Type	Description	Unused	Used
105	**10**	10s. blue-black (R.)	£225	£400

(b) On Nos. 71, 77, 78a, 80, 81d, 86c, 87a and 88. Wmk Mult Crown CA

No.	Type	Description	Unused	Used
106	**13**	½d. green	1·00	2·50
		w. Wmk inverted	£150	
107		2½d. bright blue	14·00	42·00
108	**14**	3d. purple/*orange-buff*	4·50	26·00
109	**13**	6d. dull and bright purple	4·25	23·00
		x. Wmk reversed	£1300	£1300
110	**14**	1s. black/*emerald*	4·50	23·00
111	**15**	2s. purple and blue/*blue* (R.)	£250	£500
		a. Break in scroll	£1100	
		b. Broken crown and scroll	£1100	

No.	Type	Description	Unused	Used
		c. Nick in top right scroll	£1300	
		e. Break in lines below left scroll	£1100	
		f. Damaged leaf at bottom right	£1100	
112	**9**	2s.6d. olive-grey	30·00	50·00
		a. "C" of "CA" missing from wmk	£1200	
113	**15**	5s. green and red/*yellow*	55·00	95·00
		a. Break in scroll	£375	
		b. Broken crown and scroll	£375	
		c. Lines omitted from scroll	£375	
		e. Break in lines below left scroll	£450	
		f. Damaged leaf at bottom right	£450	
106/13 *Set of 8*			£325	£700
		(c) On Nos. 97/104. Wmk Mult Script CA		
114	**13**	¼d. brown	30	75
		w. Wmk inverted		
115		½d. green (29.4)	4·00	9·00
116		1d. scarlet	1·00	20
117	**18**	2d. grey	4·00	45
118	**13**	2½d. bright blue (15.1)	1·10	1·75
119		6d. dull and bright purple (19.4)	20·00	50·00
120	**15**	2s. purple and blue/*blue* (R.) (25.1)	50·00	95·00
		a. Break in scroll	£300	
		b. Broken crown and scroll	£300	
		c. Lines omitted from scroll	£425	
		e. Break in lines below left scroll	£375	
		f. Damaged leaf at bottom right	£375	
121	**17**	10s. black (R.) (9.3)	£140	£250
		x. Wmk reversed	£3000	
114/21 *Set of 8*			£200	£375

Examples of all values are known showing a forged G.P.O. Malta postmark dated "MY 10 22".

One Farthing
(21)

22

23

1922 (15 Apr.). No. 100 surch with T **21**, at Govt Printing Office, Valletta.

No.	Type	Description	Unused	Used
122	**18**	¼d. on 2d. grey	85	30
		a. Dot to "i" of "Farthing" omitted	£300	

No. 122a occurred on R. 4/4 of the lower left pane during part of the printing only. Small or faint dots are found on other positions.

(Des C. Dingli (T **22**) and G. Vella (**23**))

1922 (1 Aug)–**26**. Wmk Mult Script CA (sideways* on T **22**, except No. 140). P 14.

No.	Type	Description	Unused	Used
		(a) Typo. Chalk-surfaced paper		
123	**22**	¼d. brown (22.8.22)	2·50	60
		a. Chocolate-brown	5·50	70
		w. Wmk Crown to right of CA	—	£100
124		½d. green	2·50	15
		w. Wmk Crown to right of CA	—	£100
125		1d. orange and purple	4·50	20
		w. Wmk Crown to right of CA	—	80·00
126		1d. bright violet (25.4.24)	4·25	80
127		1½d. brown-red (1.10.23)	5·50	15
128		2d. bistre-brown and turquoise (28.8.22)	3·25	1·25
		w. Wmk Crown to right of CA	—	£140
129		2½d. ultramarine (16.2.26)	4·50	13·00
130		3d. cobalt (28.8.22)	6·00	2·50
		a. Bright ultramarine	5·00	2·00
131		3d. black/*yellow* (16.2.26)	4·25	20·00
132		4d. yellow and bright blue (28.8.22)	3·00	4·25
		w. Wmk Crown to right of CA	£225	
133		6d. olive-green and reddish violet	4·50	3·75
134	**23**	1s. indigo and sepia	10·00	3·50
135		2s. brown and blue	14·00	18·00
136		2s.6d. bright magenta and black (28.8.22)	11·00	15·00
137		5s. orange-yell and brt ultram (28.8.22)	21·00	48·00
138		10s. slate-grey and brown (28.8.22)	65·00	£160
		(b) Recess		
139	**22**	£1 black and carmine-red (wmk sideways) (28.8.22)	£150	£350
140		£1 black and bright carmine (wmk upright) (14.5.25)	£110	£325
123/40 *Set of 17*			£250	£550
123s/39s Optd "SPECIMEN" *Set of 17*			£550	

*The normal sideways watermark shows Crown to left of CA, *as seen from the back of the stamp.*

Two pence halfpenny
(24)

POSTAGE
(25)

1925. Surch with T **24**, at Govt Printing Office, Valletta.

No.	Type	Description	Unused	Used
141	**22**	2½d. on 3d. cobalt (3 Dec)	1·75	5·50
142		2½d. on 3d. bright ultramarine (9 Dec)	1·75	4·50

1926 (1 Apr). Optd with T **25** at Govt Printing Office, Valletta.

No.	Type	Description	Unused	Used
143	**22**	¼d. brown	70	5·50
144		½d. green	70	15
		w. Wmk Crown to right of CA	£110	
145		1d. bright violet	1·00	25
146		1½d. brown-red	1·25	60
147		2d. bistre-brown and turquoise	75	2·00
148		2½d. ultramarine	1·25	1·00
149		3d. black/*yellow*	75	80
		a. Opt inverted	£170	£500
150		4d. yellow and bright blue	17·00	28·00
		w. Wmk Crown to right of CA	£200	
151		6d. olive-green and violet	2·75	5·50
152	**23**	1s. indigo and sepia	5·50	18·00
153		2s. brown and blue	55·00	£150
154		2s.6d. bright magenta and black	17·00	48·00
155		5s. orange-yellow and bright ultramarine	10·00	48·00
156		10s. slate-grey and brown	7·00	20·00
143/56 *Set of 14*			£110	£300

26

27 Valletta Harbour

28 St. Publius

29 Mdina (Notabile)

30 Gozo fishing boat

31 Neptune

32 Neolithic temple, Mnajdra

33 St. Paul

(T **26** typo, others recess Waterlow)

1926 (6 Apr)–**27**. T **26/33**. Inscr "POSTAGE". Wmk Mult Script CA. P 15×14 (T **26**) or 12½ (others).

No.	Type	Description	Unused	Used
157	**26**	¼d. brown	80	15
158		½d. yellow-green (5.8.26)	60	15
		a. Printed on the gummed side	£1400	
		w. Wmk inverted	†	£1100
159		1d. rose-red (1.4.27)	3·00	1·00
160		1½d. chestnut (7.10.26)	2·00	10
161		2d. greenish grey (1.4.27)	4·50	15·00
162		2½d. blue (1.4.27)	4·00	1·50
162*a*		3d. violet (1.4.27)	4·25	4·25
163		4d. black and red	3·25	16·00
164		4½d. lavender and ochre	3·50	4·50
165		6d. violet and scarlet (5.5.26)	4·25	6·00
166	**27**	1s. black	6·50	8·50
167	**28**	1s.6d. black and green	7·50	18·00
168	**29**	2s. black and purple	7·50	23·00
169	**30**	2s.6d. black and vermilion	19·00	55·00
170	**31**	3s. black and blue	19·00	35·00
171	**32**	5s. black and green (5.5.26)	23·00	65·00

172	33	10s. black and carmine (9.2.27)	65·00	£100
157/72 *Set of* 17			£160	£325
157s/72s Optd "SPECIMEN" *Set of* 17			£375	

AIR MAIL	POSTAGE AND REVENUE	POSTAGE AND REVENUE.
(34)	(35)	(36)

1928 (1 Apr). Air. Optd with T **34**.

173	26	6d. violet and scarlet	1·75	1·00

1928 (1 Oct–5 Dec). As Nos. 157/72, optd.

174	35	¼d. brown	1·50	10
175		½d. yellow-green	1·50	10
176		1d. rose-red	1·75	3·25
177		1d. chestnut (5.12.28)	4·50	10
178		1½d. chestnut	2·00	85
179		1½d. rose-red (5.12.28)	4·25	10
180		2d. greenish grey	4·25	9·00
181		2½d. blue	2·00	10
182		3d. violet	2·00	80
183		4d. black and red	2·00	1·75
184		4½d. lavender and ochre	2·25	1·00
185		6d. violet and scarlet	2·25	1·50
186	36	1s. black (R.)	5·50	2·50
187		1s.6d. black and green (R.)	11·00	9·50
188		2s. black and purple (R.)	26·00	70·00
189		2s.6d. black and vermilion (R.)	17·00	21·00
190		3s. black and blue (R.)	21·00	24·00
191		5s. black and green (R.)	38·00	70·00
192		10s. black and carmine (R.)	70·00	£100
174/92 *Set of* 19			£200	£275
174s/92s Optd "SPECIMEN" *Set of* 19			£375	

1930 (20 Oct). As Nos. 157/172, but inscr "POSTAGE (&) REVENUE".

193	¼d. brown	60	10
194	½d. yellow-green	60	10
195	1d. chestnut	60	10
196	1½d. rose-red	70	10
197	2d. greenish grey	1·25	50
198	2½d. blue	2·00	10
199	3d. violet	1·50	20
200	4d. black and red	1·25	5·00
201	4½d. lavender and ochre	3·25	1·25
202	6d. violet and scarlet	2·75	1·25
203	1s. black	10·00	19·00
204	1s.6d. black and green	8·50	25·00
205	2s. black and purple	12·00	27·00
206	2s.6d. black and vermilion	17·00	60·00
207	3s. black and blue	40·00	60·00
208	5s. black and green	48·00	75·00
209	10s. black and carmine	£100	£180
193/209 *Set of* 17		£225	£425
193s/209s Perf "SPECIMEN" *Set of* 17		£375	

1935 (6 May). Silver Jubilee. As Nos. 144/7 of Cyprus, but printed by B.W. P 11×12.

210	½d. black and green	50	70
	a. Extra flagstaff	26·00	42·00
	b. Short extra flagstaff	48·00	
	c. Lightning conductor	35·00	
211	2½d. brown and deep blue	2·50	4·50
	a. Extra flagstaff	£140	£170
	b. Short extra flagstaff	£180	£250
	c. Lightning conductor	£150	£200
212	6d. light blue and olive-green	7·00	9·00
	a. Extra flagstaff	£180	£225
	b. Short extra flagstaff	£325	£350
	c. Lightning conductor	£190	£225
213	1s. slate and purple	17·00	24·00
	a. Extra flagstaff	£425	£500
	b. Short extra flagstaff	£425	£500
	c. Lightning conductor	£350	
210/13 *Set of* 4		24·00	35·00
210s/13s Perf "SPECIMEN" *Set of* 4		£160	

For illustrations of plate varieties see Gibraltar.

Sheets from the second printing of the ½d., 6d. and 1s. in November 1935 had the extra flagstaff partially erased from the stamp with a sharp point.

1937 (12 May). Coronation. As Nos. 148/50 of Cyprus, but printed by D.L.R. P 14.

214	½d. green	10	20
215	1½d. scarlet	1·40	65
	a. Brown-lake	£600	£600
216	2½d. bright blue	1·40	80
214/16 *Set of* 3		2·50	1·50
214s/16s Perf "SPECIMEN" *Set of* 3		£130	

37 Grand Harbour, Valletta

38 H.M.S. *St. Angelo*

39 Verdala Palace

40 Hypogeum, Hal Saflieni

41 Victoria and Citadel, Gozo

42 De L'Isle Adam entering Mdina

43 St. John's Co-Cathedral

44 Ruins at Mnajdra

45 Statue of Manoel de Vilhena

46 Maltese girl wearing faldetta

47 St. Publius

48 Mdina Cathedral

49 Statue of Neptune

50 Palace Square, Valletta

51 St. Paul

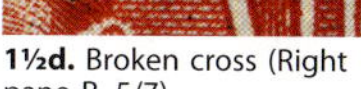

1½d. Broken cross (Right pane R. 5/7)

2d. Extra windows (R. 2/7) (corrected in 1945)

2d. Flag on citadel (R. 5/8)

Damaged value tablet (R. 4/9)

5s. Semaphore flaw (R. 2/7)

(Recess Waterlow)

1938 (17 Feb*)–**43**. T **37/51**. Wmk Mult Script CA (sideways on No. 217). P 12½.

No.	Type	Description	Unused	Used
217	**37**	¼d. brown	10	10
218	**38**	½d. green	4·00	30
218*a*		½d. red-brown (8.3.43)	55	30
219	**39**	1d. red-brown	5·50	40
219*a*		1d. green (8.3.43)	60	10
220	**40**	1½d. scarlet	2·50	30
		a. Broken cross	£225	75·00
220*b*		1½d. slate-black (8.3.43)	30	15
		ba. Broken cross	75·00	60·00
221	**41**	2d. slate-black	2·50	2·00
		a. Extra windows	£110	
221*b*		2d. scarlet (8.3.43)	40	30
		ba. Extra windows	65·00	50·00
		bb. Flag on citadel	75·00	60·00
222	**42**	2½d. greyish blue	5·50	60
222*a*		2½d. dull violet (8.3.43)	60	10
223	**43**	3d. dull violet	3·00	80
223*a*		3d. blue (8.3.43)	30	20
224	**44**	4½d. olive-green and yellow-brown	50	30
225	**45**	6d. olive-green and scarlet	2·50	30
226	**46**	1s. black	2·25	30
227	**47**	1s.6d. black and olive-green	8·00	4·00
228	**48**	2s. green and deep blue	4·50	7·00
229	**49**	2s.6d. black and scarlet	9·00	6·00
		a. Damaged value tablet	£350	£190
230	**50**	5s. black and green	4·75	8·50
		a. Semaphore flaw	80·00	£140
231	**51**	10s. black and carmine	19·00	17·00
217/31 *Set of* 21			65·00	45·00
217s/31s Perf "SPECIMEN" *Set of* 21			£550	

*This is the local date of issue but the stamps were released in London on 15 February.

1946 (3 Dec). Victory. As Nos. 164/5 of Cyprus, but inscr "MALTA" between Maltese Cross and George Cross.

No.	Description	Unused	Used
232	1d. green	15	10
	w. Wmk inverted	£1000	
233	3d. blue	50	2·00
232s/3s Perf "SPECIMEN" *Set of* 2		95·00	

SELF-GOVERNMENT

(**52**)

½d. and **5s.** "NT" joined (R. 4/10)

1½d. "NT" joined (R. 4/6)

2d. Halation flaw (Pl 2 R. 2/5) (ptg of 8 Jan 1953)

2d. Cracked plate (Pl 2 R. 5/1) (ptg of 8 Jan 1953)

(Optd by Waterlow)

1948 (25 Nov)–**53**. New Constitution. As Nos. 217/31 but optd as T **52**; reading up on ½d. and 5s., down on other values, and smaller on ¼d. value.

No.	Type	Description	Unused	Used
234	**37**	¼d. brown	30	20
235	**38**	½d. red-brown	30	10
		a. "NT" joined	19·00	25·00
236	**39**	1d. green	30	10
236*a*		1d. grey (R.) (8.1.53)	75	10
237	**40**	1½d. blue-black (R.)	1·25	10
		a. Broken cross	£110	50·00
		b. "NT" joined		
237*b*		1½d. green (8.1.53)	30	10
		ba. Albino opt	†	£18000
238	**41**	2d. scarlet	1·25	10
		a. Extra windows	£140	85·00
		b. Flag on citadel	£100	75·00
238*c*		2d. yellow-ochre (8.1.53)	30	10
		ca. Halation flaw	£170	£160
		cc. Cracked plate	£160	£150
239	**42**	2½d. dull violet (R.)	80	10
239*a*		2½d. scarlet-vermilion (8.1.53)	75	1·50
240	**43**	3d. blue (R.)	3·00	15
240*a*		3d. dull violet (R.) (8.1.53)	50	15
241	**44**	4½d. olive-green and yellow-brown	2·75	1·50
241*a*		4½d. olive-grn and dp ultram (R.) (8.1.53)	50	90
242	**45**	6d. olive-green and scarlet	3·25	15
243	**46**	1s. black	3·75	40
244	**47**	1s.6d. black and olive-green	2·50	50
245	**48**	2s. green and deep blue (R.)	5·00	2·50
246	**49**	2s.6d. black and scarlet	12·00	2·50
		a. Damaged value tablet	£1400	
247	**50**	5s. black and green (R.)	28·00	3·50
		a. "NT" joined	£275	£130
		b. Semaphore flaw	—	£3250
248	**51**	10s. black and carmine	28·00	23·00
234/48 *Set of* 21			85·00	32·00

1949 (4 Jan). Royal Silver Wedding. As Nos. 166/7 of Cyprus, but inscr "MALTA" between Maltese Cross and George Cross and with £1 ptd in recess.

No.	Description	Unused	Used
249	1d. green	50	10
250	£1 indigo	38·00	45·00

1949 (10 Oct). 75th Anniv of U.P.U. As Nos. 168/71 of Cyprus.

No.	Description	Unused	Used
251	2½d. violet	30	10
252	3d. deep blue	3·00	1·00
253	6d. carmine-red	60	1·00
254	1s. blue-black	60	2·50
251/4 *Set of* 4		4·00	4·25

53 Queen Elizabeth II when Princess

54 "Our Lady of Mount Carmel" (attrib Palladino)

(T **53/4**. Recess B.W.)

1950 (1 Dec). Visit of Princess Elizabeth to Malta. Wmk Mult Script CA. P 12×11½.

255	**53**	1d. green	10	15
256		3d. blue	20	20
257		1s. black	80	2·25
255/7 *Set of 3*			1·00	2·40

1951 (12 July). Seventh Centenary of the Scapular. Wmk Mult Script CA. P 12×11½.

258	**54**	1d. green	20	30
259		3d. violet	50	10
260		1s. black	1·75	1·60
258/60 *Set of 3*			2·25	1·75

1953 (3 June). Coronation. As No. 172 of Cyprus.

261		1½d. black and deep yellow-green	70	10

55 St. John's Co-Cathedral

56 "Immaculate Conception" (Caruana) (altar-piece, Cospicua)

(Recess Waterlow)

1954 (3 May). Royal Visit. Wmk Mult Script CA. P 12½.

262	**55**	3d. violet	45	10

(Photo Harrison)

1954 (8 Sept). Centenary of Dogma of the Immaculate Conception. Wmk Mult Script CA. Chalk-surfaced paper. P 14×14.

263	**56**	1½d. emerald	15	10
264		3d. bright blue	15	10
265		1s. grey-black	35	20
263/5 *Set of 3*			60	35

57 Monument of the Great Siege, 1565

58 Wignacourt aqueduct horse trough

59 Victory Church

60 Second World War Memorial

61 Mosta Church

62 Auberge de Castile

63 The King's Scroll

64 Roosevelt's Scroll

65 Neolithic temples Tarxien

66 Vedette (tower)

67 Mdina gate

68 "Les Gavroches" (statue)

69 Monument of Christ the King

70 Grand Master Cottener's monument

71 Grand Master Perello's monument

72 St. Paul

73 Baptism of Christ

(Recess Waterlow (2s.6d. to £1). B.W.(others))

1956 (23 Jan)–**58**. T **57/73** and similar designs. Wmk Mult Script CA. P 14×13½ (2s.6d. to £1) or 11½ (others).

266	**57**	¼d. violet	20	10
267	**58**	½d. orange	50	10

No.	Type	Description	Unused	Used
268	**59**	1d. black (9.2.56)	1·25	10
269	**60**	1½d. bluish green (9.2.56)	30	10
270	**61**	2d. brown (9.2.56)	1·50	10
		a. Deep brown (26.2.58)	5·00	20
271	**62**	2½d. orange-brown	2·25	30
272	**63**	3d. rose-red (22.3.56)	1·50	10
		w. Wmk inverted	†	£950
273	**64**	4½d. deep blue	2·50	1·00
274	**65**	6d. indigo (9.2.56)	75	10
		w. Wmk inverted	£225	
275	**66**	8d. bistre-brown	4·50	1·00
276	**67**	1s. deep reddish violet	1·75	10
277	**68**	1s.6d. deep turquoise-green	15·00	35
278	**69**	2s. olive-green	13·00	4·50
279	**70**	2s.6d. chestnut (22.3.56)	11·00	2·50
280	**71**	5s. green (11.10.56)	17·00	3·25
281	**72**	10s. carmine-red (19.11.56)	38·00	16·00
282	**73**	£1 yellow-brown (5.1.57)	38·00	35·00
266/82		*Set of 17*	£130	55·00

See also Nos. 314/15.

74 "Defence of Malta"

75 Searchlights over Malta

(Des E. Cremona. Photo Harrison)

1957 (15 Apr). George Cross Commemoration. Cross in silver. T **74/5** and similar design. Wmk Mult Script CA. P 14½×14 (3d.) or P 14×14½ (others).

No.	Description	Unused	Used
283	1½d. deep dull green	15	10
284	3d. vermilion	15	10
285	1s. reddish brown	15	10
283/5	*Set of 3*	40	25

Design: *Vert*—1s. Bombed buildings.

77 "Design"

(Des E. Cremona. Photo Harrison)

1958 (15 Feb). Technical Education in Malta. T **77** and similar designs. W w **12**. P 14×14½ (3d.) or 14½×14 (others).

No.	Description	Unused	Used
286	1½d. black and deep green	15	10
287	3d. black, scarlet and grey	15	10
288	1s. grey, bright purple and black	15	10
286/8	*Set of 3*	40	25

Designs: *Vert*—3d. "Construction". *Horiz*—1s. Technical School, Paola.

80 Bombed-out Family

81 Sea Raid on Grand Harbour, Valletta

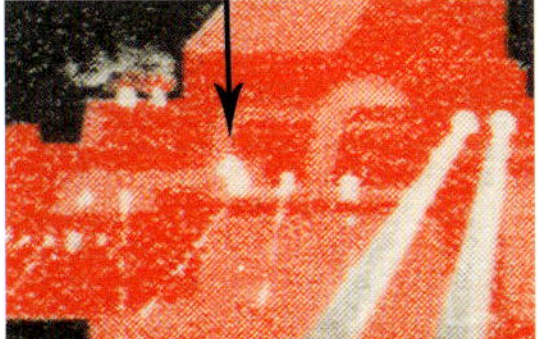

3d. White flaw on third gun from right appearing as larger gunflash (Pl. 1A R. 5/7)

(Des E. Cremona. Photo Harrison)

1958 (15 Apr). George Cross Commemoration. Cross in first colour, outlined in silver. T **80/1** and similar design. W w **12**. P 14×14½ (3d.) or 14½×14 (others).

No.	Description	Unused	Used
289	1½d. blue-green and black	15	10
290	3d. red and black	15	10
	a. "Gunflash" flaw	4·00	
291	1s. reddish violet and black	25	10
	a. Silver (outline) omitted	£600	
289/91	*Set of 3*	50	25

Design: *Horiz*—1s. Searchlight crew.

83 Air Raid Casualties

84 "For Gallantry"

(Des E. Cremona. Photo Harrison)

1959 (15 Apr). George Cross Commemoration. T **83/4** and similar design. W w **12**. P 14½×14 (3d.) or 14×14½ (others).

No.	Description	Unused	Used
292	1½d. grey-green, black and gold	25	10
293	3d. reddish violet, black and gold	25	10
294	1s. blue-grey, black and gold	1·25	1·50
292/4	*Set of 3*	1·60	1·50

Design: *Vert*—1s. Maltese under bombardment.

86 Shipwreck of St. Paul (after Palombi)

87 Statue of St. Paul, Rabat, Malta

8d. Two white flaws in "PAUL" one giving the "P" the appearance of "R" and other a blob over the "L" (Pl. 1A-1A R.5/2).

(Des E. Cremona. Photo Harrison)

1960 (9 Feb). 19th Centenary of the Shipwreck of St. Paul. T **86/7** and similar designs. W w **12**.

No.	Description	Unused	Used
295	1½d. blue, gold and yellow-brown	15	10
	a. Gold (dates and crosses) omitted	75·00	
296	3d. bright purple, gold and blue	15	10
	a. Printed on the gummed side		
297	6d. carmine, gold and pale grey	25	10
298	8d. black and gold	30	60
	a. "RAUL" flaw	4·50	
299	1s. maroon and gold	25	10
300	2s.6d. blue, deep bluish green and gold	1·00	2·50
	a. Gold omitted	£1400	£550
295/300	*Set of 6*	1·90	3·00

Designs: *Vert as T* **86**—3d. Consecration of St. Publius (first Bishop of Malta) (after Palombi); 6d. Departure of St. Paul (after Palombi). *Diamond shaped as T* **87**—1s. Angel with *Acts of the Apostles*; 2s.6d. St. Paul with *Second Epistle to the Corinthians*.

92 Stamp of 1860

(Centre litho; frame recess. Waterlow)

1960 (1 Dec). Stamp Centenary. W w **12**. P 13½.

301	**92**	1½d. buff, pale blue and green	25	10
		a. *Buff, pale bl & myrtle* (white paper)	4·50	2·25
302		3d. buff pale blue and deep carmine	30	10
		a. Blank corner	£400	
303		6d. buff, pale blue and ultramarine	60	1·00
301/3 *Set of 3*			1·00	1·10

Examples of the 1½d. apparently with the blue omitted are from sheets with a very weak printing of this colour.

No. 302a shows the right-hand bottom corner of the 1860 stamp blank. It occurs on R. 4/7 from early trial plates and sheets containing the error should have been destroyed, but some were sorted into good stock and issued at a post office.

93 George Cross

(Photo Harrison)

1961 (15 Apr). George Cross Commemoration. T **93** and similar designs showing medal. W w **12**. P 15×14.

304	1½d. black, cream and bistre	15	10
305	3d. olive-brown and greenish blue	30	10
306	1s. olive-green, lilac and deep reddish violet	1·10	2·25
304/6 *Set of 3*		1·40	2·25

96 "Madonna Damascena"

(Photo Harrison)

1962 (7 Sept). Great Siege Commemoration. T **96** and similar vert designs. W w **12** P 13×12.

307	2d. bright blue	10	10
308	3d. red	10	10
309	6d. bronze-green	30	10
310	1s. brown-purple	30	40
307/10 *Set of 4*		70	60

Designs:—3d. Great Siege Monument; 6d. Grand Master La Valette; 1s. Assault on Fort St. Elmo.

1963 (4 June). Freedom from Hunger. As No. 174 of Gibraltar.

311	1s.6d. sepia	1·75	2·50

1963 (2 Sept). Red Cross Centenary. As Nos. 175/6 of Gibraltar.

312	2d. red and black	25	15
313	1s. 6d. red and blue	1·75	4·50

1963 (15 Oct)–**64**. As Nos. 268 and 270, but wmk. w **12**.

314	**59**	1d. black	50	30
315	**61**	2d. deep brown (11.7.64*)	2·50	4·75

*This is the earliest known date recorded in Malta.

100 Bruce, Zammit and Microscope

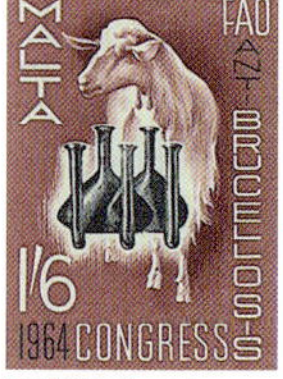
101 Goat and Laboratory Equipment

(Des E. Cremona. Photo Harrison)

1964 (14 April). Anti-Brucellosis Congress. W w **12**. P 14.

316	**100**	2d. light brown, black and bluish green	10	10
		a. Black (microscope, etc) omitted	£425	
317	**101**	1s.6d. black and maroon	90	90

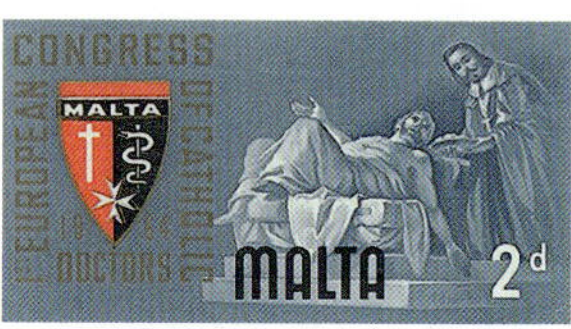
102 "Nicole Cotoner tending Sick Man" (M. Preti)

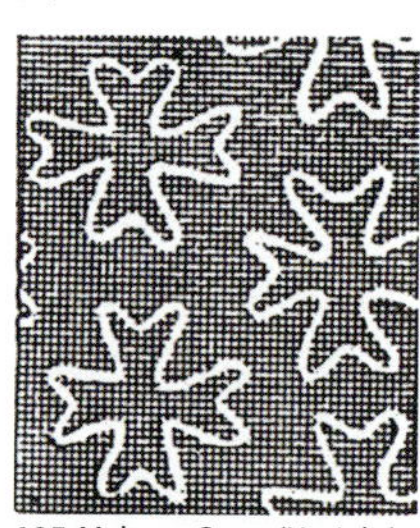
105 Maltese Cross (Upright)

In this illustration the points of the crosses meet in a vertical line. When the watermark is sideways they meet in a horizontal line.

(Des E. Cremona. Photo Harrison)

1964 (5 Sept). First European Catholic Doctors' Congress, Vienna. T **102** and similar horiz designs. (sideways). W **105**. P 13½×11½.

318	2d. red, black, gold and grey-blue	20	10
319	6d. red, black, gold and bistre	50	15
320	1s.6d. red, black, gold and reddish violet	1·10	1·90
318/20 *Set of 3*		1·60	1·90

Designs:—6d. St. Luke and Hospital; 1s.6d. Sacra Infermeria, Valletta.

INDEPENDENT

106 Dove and British Crown

109 "The Nativity"

(Des E. Cremona. Photo Harrison)

1964 (21 Sept). Independence. T **106** and similar vert designs. W **105**. P 14½×13½.

321	2d. olive-brown, red and gold	30	10
	a. Gold omitted	75·00	
322	3d. brown-purple, red and gold	30	10
	a. Gold omitted	75·00	
323	6d. slate, red and gold	70	15
324	1s. blue, red and gold	70	15
325	1s.6d. indigo, red and gold	1·50	1·00
326	2s.6d. deep violet-blue, red and gold	1·50	2·75
321/6 *Set of 6*		4·50	3·75

Designs:—2d, 1s. Type **106**; 3d., 1s.6d. Dove and Pope's Tiara; 6d., 2s.6d. Dove and U.N. emblem.

(Des E. Cremona. Photo D.L.R.)

1964 (3 Nov). Christmas. W **105** (sideways). P 13×13½.

327	**109**	2d. bright purple and gold	10	10
328		4d. bright blue and gold	20	15
329		8d. deep bluish green and gold	45	45
327/9 *Set of 3*			65	60

110 Neolithic Era

117 Galleys of Knights of St. John

119 British Rule

(Des E. Cremona. Photo Harrison)

1965 (7 Jan)–**70**. Chalk-surfaced paper. T **110**, **117**, **119** and similar designs. W **105**. P 14×14½ (vert) or 14½ (horiz).

330	½d. multicoloured	10	10
	a. "½d." (white) printed twice†	10·00	
	ab. ditto, once inverted	†	£2000
	b. Rose-pink ("MALTA") printed twice	10·00	
	c. White (face value) omitted	80·00	
331	1d. multicoloured	10	10
	a. Gold (ancient lettering) omitted	£110	
	b. White (Greek lettering and "PUNIC") omitted	£110	
	c. White ptg double	29·00	
	d. "PUNIC" omitted	£150	
332	1½d. multicoloured	30	10
333	2d. multicoloured	10	10
	a. Gold omitted	26·00	
	b. Imperf (pair)	£275	
334	2½d. multicoloured	1·50	10
	a. Orange omitted*	£100	
	b. Gold ("SARACENIC") omitted	55·00	
	c. Salmon printed twice†	85·00	
335	3d. multicoloured	10	10
	a. Gold (windows) omitted	£100	
	b. "MALTA" (silver) omitted	26·00	
	c. "MALTA" (silver) printed twice	£400	
	d. Bright lilac ("SICULO NORMAN") omitted	£375	
	e. Imperf (pair)	£300	
	f. Value omitted (vert pair with normal)	£850	
336	4d. multicoloured	1·50	10
	a. "KNIGHTS OF MALTA" (silver) omitted	45·00	
	b. "MALTA" (silver) omitted	£110	
	c. Black (shield surround) omitted	70·00	
	d. Imperf (pair)	£170	
	e. Gold omitted	£130	
337	4½d. multicoloured	1·50	75
	a. Silver ("MALTA", etc) omitted	£1700	
337*b*	5d. multicoloured (1.8.70)	30	20
	ba. "FORTIFICATIONS" (gold) omitted	£120	
338	6d. multicoloured	30	10
	a. "MALTA" (silver) omitted	45·00	
	b. Black omitted	£100	
339	8d. multicoloured	70	10
	a. Gold (centre) omitted	42·00	
	b. Gold (frame) omitted	65·00	
339*c*	10d. multicoloured (1.8.70)	50	1·90
	ca. "NAVAL ARSENAL" (gold) omitted	£325	
340	1s. multicoloured	30	10
	a. Gold (centre) omitted	£190	
	b. Gold (framework) omitted	48·00	
341	1s.3d. multicoloured	2·00	1·40
	a. Gold (centre) omitted	65·00	
	b. Gold (framework) omitted	£200	
	c. Imperf (pair)	£375	
342	1s.6d. multicoloured	60	20
	a. Head (black) omitted	£350	
	b. Gold (centre) omitted	55·00	
	c. Gold (frame) omitted	£110	
343	2s. multicoloured	70	10
	a. Gold (centre) omitted	£170	
	b. Gold (framework) omitted	70·00	
344	2s.6d. multicoloured	70	50
345	3s. multicoloured	1·75	75
	a. Gold (framework) omitted	45·00	
	b. Gold ("1964") omitted	£200	
346	5s. multicoloured	6·00	1·00
	a. Gold (HAFMED emblem) omitted	£130	
	b. Gold (framework) omitted	£130	
347	10s. multicoloured	3·00	5·00
	a. Gold (centre) omitted	£300	
348	£1 multicoloured	4·25	5·50
	a. Pink omitted	32·00	
330/48 *Set of 21*		23·00	15·00

Designs: *Vert*—1d. Punic era; 1½d. Roman era; 2d. Proto Christian era; 2½d. Saracenic era; 3d. Siculo Norman era; 4d. Knights of Malta; 5d. Fortifications; 6d. French occupation. *Horiz*—10d. Naval arsenal; 1s. Maltese corps of the British army; 1s.3d. International Eucharistic congress, 1913; 1s.6d. Self-government, 1921; 2s. Gaza civic council; 2s.6d. State of Malta; 3s. Independence, 1964 5s. HAFMED (Allied forces, Mediterranean); 10s. The Maltese Islands (map); £1 Patron saints.

*The effect of this is to leave the Saracenic pattern as a pink colour.

†On the ½d. the second impression is 6½ mm lower or 3 mm to the left, and on the 2½d. 1 mm lower so that it falls partly across "MALTA" and "2½d." Stamps with almost coincidental double impression are common The ½d. and 1d. had white printing plates. Two silver plates were used on the 4d., one for "KNIGHTS OF MALTA" and the other for "MALTA". Two gold plates were used for the 8d. to 10s., one for the framework and the other for the gold in the central part of the designs.

No. 335f comes from a sheet showing a major shift of the grey-black colour, so that stamps in the top horizontal row are without the face value.

No. 337a comes from a sheet on which the silver printing was so misplaced that it missed the top horizontal row entirely.

The ½d. to 4d., 1s. and 1s.6d. to 5s. values exist with PVA gum as well as gum arabic and the 5d. and 10d. have PVA gum only.

129 "Dante" (Raphael)

(Des E. Cremona. Photo Govt Ptg Works, Rome)

1965 (7 July). 700th Birth Anniv of Dante. P 14.

349	**129**	2d. indigo	10	10
350		6d. bronze-green	25	10
351		2s. chocolate	1·10	1·50
349/151 *Set of 3*			1·25	1·50

130 Turkish Camp

131 Turkish Fleet

(Des E. Cremona. Photo Harrison)

1965 (1 Sept). 400th Anniv of Great Siege. T **130/1** and similar designs. W **105** (sideways). P 13 (6d., 1s.) or 14½×14 (others).

352	2d. olive-green, red and black	30	10
	a. Red (flag) omitted	£350	
353	3d. olive-green, red, black and light drab	30	10
354	6d. multicoloured	40	10
	a. Gold (framework and dates) omitted	£350	
	b. Black (on hulls) omitted	£350	
355	8d. red, gold, indigo and blue	80	90
	a. Gold (flag and dates) omitted	£180	
356	1s. red, gold and deep grey-blue	40	10
357	1s.6d. ochre, red and black	80	30
358	2s.6d. sepia, black, red and yellow-olive	1·50	3·25
352/8 *Set of 7*		3·75	4·25

Designs: *Square (as T* **130**)—3d. Battle scene; 8d. Arrival of relief force; 1s.6d. "Allegory of Victory" (from mural by M. Preti); 2s.8d. Victory medal. *Vert (as T* **131**)—1s. Grand Master J. de La Valette's arms.

137 "The Three Kings"

138 Sir Winston Churchill

(Des E. Cremona. Photo Enschedé)

1965 (7 Oct). Christmas. W **105** (sideways). P 11×11½.

359	**137**	1d. slate-purple and red	10	10
360		4d. slate-purple and blue	30	30
361		1s.3d. slate-purple and bright purple	30	30
359/61 *Set of 3*			65	60

(Des E. Cremona. Photo Harrison)

1966 (24 Jan). Churchill Commemoration. T **138** and similar square design. W **105** (sideways). P 14½×14.

362	**138**	2d. black, red and gold	25	10
363	–	3d. bronze-green, yellow-olive and gold	25	10
		a. Gold omitted	£300	
364	**138**	1s. maroon, red and gold	40	10
		a. Gold (shading) omitted	£170	
365	–	1s.6d. chalky blue, violet-blue and gold	50	1·10
362/5 *Set of 4*			1·25	1·25

Design:—3d., 1s.6d. Sir Winston Churchill and George Cross.

140 Grand Master La Valette

145 President Kennedy and Memorial

(Des E. Cremona. Photo State Ptg Works, Vienna)

1966 (28 Mar). 400th Anniv of Valletta. T **140** and similar square designs. Multicoloured. W **105** (sideways). P 12.

366	2d. Type 140	10	10
367	3d. Pope Pius V	15	10
	a. Gold omitted	£600	
368	6d. Map of Valletta	20	10
369	1s. Francesco Laparelli (architect)	20	10
370	2s.6d. Girolamo Cassar (architect)	50	60
366/70 *Set of 5*		1·00	80

(Des E. Cremona. Photo Harrison)

1966 (28 May). President Kennedy Commemoration. W **105** (sideways). P 15×14.

371	**145**	3d. olive, gold and black	10	10
		a. Gold inscr omitted	£300	
372		1s.6d. Prussian blue, gold and black	10	10

146 "Trade"

(Des E. Cremona. Photo D.L.R.)

1966 (16 June). Tenth Malta Trade Fair. W **105** (sideways). P 13½.

373	**146**	2d. multicoloured	10	10
		a. Gold omitted	75·00	
374		8d. multicoloured	30	95
375		2s.6d. multicoloured	30	1·00
		a. Gold omitted	75·00	
373/5 *Set of 3*			65	1·75

147 "The Child in the Manger"

148 George Cross

(Des E. Cremona. Photo D.L.R.)

1966 (7 Oct). Christmas. W **105**. P 13½.

376	**147**	1d. black, gold, turquoise-bl and slate-purple	10	10
377		4d. black, gold, ultramarine and slate-purple	10	10
378		1s.3d. black, gold, bright purple and slate purple	10	10
		a. Gold omitted	70·00	
376/8 *Set of 3*			25	25

(Des E. Cremona. Photo Harrison)

1967 (1 Mar). 25th Anniv of George Cross Award to Malta. W **105** (sideways). P 14½×14.

379	**148**	2d. multicoloured	10	10
380		4d. multicoloured	10	10
381		3s. multicoloured	15	20
379/81 *Set of 3*			30	30

149 Crucifixion of St. Peter

150 Open Bible and Episcopal Emblems

(Des E. Cremona. Photo Harrison)

1967 (28 June). 1900th Anniv of Martyrdom of Saints Peter and Paul. T **149/50** and similar design. W **105** (sideways). P 13½×14½ (8d.) or 14½ (others).

382	2d. chestnut, orange and black	10	10
383	8d. yellow-olive, gold and black	15	10
384	3s. blue, light blue and black	20	20
382/4 *Set of 3*		40	30

Design:—*Square as T* **149**—3s. Beheading of St. Paul.

152 "St. Catherine of Siena"

156 Temple Ruins, Tarxien

(Des E. Cremona. Photo Enschedé)

1967 (1 Aug). 300th Death Anniv of Melchior Gafa (sculptor). T **152** and similar horiz designs. Multicoloured. W **105** (sideways). P 13½×13.

385	2d. Type **152**	10	10
386	4d. Thomas of Villanova"	10	10
387	1s.6d. "Baptism of Christ" (detail)	15	10
388	2s.6d. "St. John the Baptist" (from "Baptism of Christ")	15	20
385/8 *Set of 4*		45	35

(Des E. Cremona. Photo Harrison)

1967 (12 Sept). 15th International Historical Architecture Congress, Valletta. T **156** and similar square designs. Multicoloured. W **105**. P 15×14½.

389		2d. Type **156**	10	10
390		6d. Facade of Palazzo Falzon, Notabile	10	10
391		1s. Parish Church, Birkirkara	10	10
392		3s. Portal, Auberge de Castille	25	25
389/92 *Set of 4*			40	40

160 "Angels" **161** "Crib" **162** "Angels"

(Des E. Cremona. Photo D.L.R.)

1967 (20 Oct). Christmas. W **105** (sideways). P 14.

393	**160**	1d. multicoloured	10	10
		a. Horiz strip of 3. Nos. 393/5	45	25
		b. White stars (red omitted)	£120	
394	**161**	8d. multicoloured	20	10
395	**162**	1s.4d. multicoloured	20	10
393/5 *Set of 3*			45	25

Nos. 393/5 were issued in sheets of 60 of each value (arranged *tête-bêche*), and also in sheets containing the three values *se-tenant*, thus forming a triptych of the Nativity.

163 Queen Elizabeth II and Arms of Malta

(Des E. Cremona. Photo Harrison)

1967 (13 Nov). Royal Visit. T **163** and similar designs. W **105** (sideways on 2d., 3s.). P 14×15 (4d.) or 15×14 (others).

396		2d. multicoloured	10	10
		a. Grey-brown omitted*	£150	
397		4d. black, brown-purple and gold	10	10
398		3s. multicoloured	20	30
396/8 *Set of 3*			35	40

Designs: *Vert*—4d. Queen in Robes of Order of St. Michael and St. George. *Horiz*—3s. Queen and outline of Malta.

*This affects the Queen's face.

166 Human Rights Emblem and People **167**

(Des E. Cremona. Photo Harrison)

1968 (2 May). Human Rights Year. W **105**. P 12½ (6d.) or 14½ (others).

399	**166**	2d. multicoloured	10	10
400	**167**	6d. multicoloured	10	10
401	–	2s. multicoloured	10	15
399/401 *Set of 3*			25	25

The design of the 2s. value is a reverse of Type **166**.

169 Fair "Products"

(Des E. Cremona. Photo Harrison)

1968 (1 June). Malta International Trade Fair. W **105** (sideways). P 14½×14.

402	**169**	4d. multicoloured	10	10
403		8d. multicoloured	10	10
404		3s. multicoloured	15	15
402/4 *Set of 3*			30	25

170 Arms of the Order of St. John and La Valette

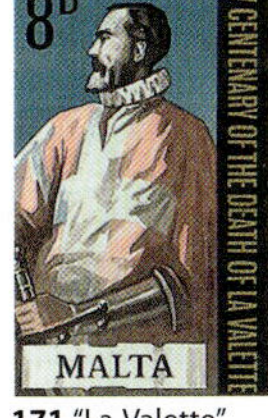

171 "La Valette" (A. de Favray)

172 La Valette's Tomb

173 Angels and Scroll bearing Date of Death

(Des E. Cremona. Photo Govt Printer, Israel)

1968 (1 Aug). Fourth Death Centenary of Grand Master La Valette. W **105** (upright, 1s.6d.; sideways, others). P 13×14 (1d., 1s.6d.) or 14×13 (others).

405	**170**	1d. multicoloured	10	10
406	**171**	8d. multicoloured	15	10
407	**172**	1s.6d. multicoloured	15	10
408	**173**	2s.6d. multicoloured	20	25
405/8 *Set of 4*			55	45

174 Star of Bethlehem and Angel waking Shepherds

177 "Agriculture"

(Des E. Cremona. Photo Harrison)

1968 (3 Oct). Christmas. T **174** and similar shaped designs. Multicoloured. W **105** (sideways). P 14½×14.

409		1d. Type **174**	10	10
410		8d. Mary and Joseph with shepherd watching over cradle	15	10
411		1s.4d. Three Wise Men and Star of Bethlehem.	15	20
409/11 *Set of 3*			35	35

The shortest side at top and the long side at the bottom both gauge 14½, the other three sides are 14. Nos. 409/11 were issued in sheets of 60 arranged in ten strips of six, alternately upright and inverted.

(Des E. Cremona. Photo Enschedé)

1968 (21 Oct). Sixth Food and Agricultural Organization Regional Conference for Europe. T **177** and similar vert designs. Multicoloured. W **105** (sideways). P 12½×12.

412		4d. Type **177**	10	10
413		1s. F.A.O. emblem and coin	10	10
414		2s.6d. "Agriculture" sowing seeds	10	15
412/14 *Set of 3*			25	30

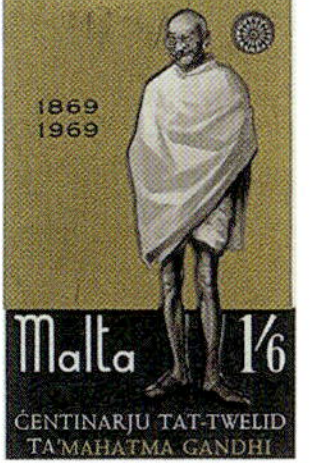

180 Mahatma Gandhi

181 I.L.O. Emblem

(Des E. Cremona. Photo Enschedé)

1969 (24 Mar). Birth Centenary of Mahatma Gandhi. W **105**. P 12×12½.

415 **180** 1s.6d. blackish brown, black and gold 50 10

(Des E. Cremona. Photo Harrison)

1969 (26 May). 50th Anniv of International Labour Organization. W **105** (sideways). P 13½×14½.

416 **181** 2d. indigo, gold and turquoise 10 10
417 6d. sepia gold and chestnut 10 10

182 Robert Samut

(Des E. Cremona. Photo D.L.R.)

1969 (26 July). Birth Centenary of Robert Samut (composer of Maltese National Anthem). W **105** (sideways). P 13.

418 **182** 2d. multicoloured 10 10

183 Dove of Peace, U.N. Emblem and Sea-Bed

(Des E. Cremona. Photo D.L.R.)

1969 (26 July). United Nations Resolution on Oceanic Resources. W **105** (sideways). P 13.

419 **183** 5d. multicoloured 10 10

184 "Swallows" returning to Malta

(Des E. Cremona. Photo D.L.R.)

1969 (26 July). Maltese Migrants' Convention. W **105** (sideways). P 13.

420 **184** 10d. black, gold and yellow-olive 10 10

185 University Arms and Grand Master de Fonseca (founder)

(Des E. Cremona. Photo D.L.R.)

1969 (26 July). Bicentenary of University of Malta. W **105** (sideways). P 13.

421 **185** 2s. multicoloured 15 20

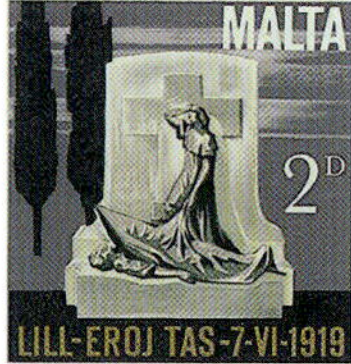

186 1919 Monument

187 Flag of Malta and Birds

(Des E. Cremona. Photo Enschedé)

1969 (20 Sept). Fifth Anniv of Independence. T **186/7** and similar designs. W **105** (upright on 5d., sideways others). P 13½×12½ (2d.), 12×12½ (5d.), or 12½×12 (others).

422 2d. multicoloured 10 10
423 5d. black, red and gold 10 10
424 10d. black, turquoise-blue and gold 10 10
425 1s.6d. multicoloured 20 40
426 2s.6d. black, olive-brown and gold 25 50
422/6 *Set of 5* .... 50 1·00

Designs:—*Vert as T* **187**—10d. "Tourism"; 1s.6d. U.N. and Council of Europe emblems; 2s.6d. "Trade and Industry".

191 Peasants playing Tambourine and Bagpipes

(Des E. Cremona. Litho D.L.R.)

1969 (8 Nov). Christmas. Children's Welfare Fund. T **191** and similar horiz designs. Multicoloured. W **105** (sideways). P 12½.

427 1d. +1d.Type **191** 10 20
a. Gold omitted £170
b. Horiz strip of 3. Nos. 427/9 .... 35 75
428 5d. +1d.Angels playing trumpet and harp ... 15 20
429 1s.6d. +3d.Choirboys singing 15 45
427/9 *Set of 3* 35 75

Nos. 427/9 were issued in sheets of 60 of each value, and also in sheets containing the three values *se-tenant*, thus forming the triptych No. 427b.

194 "The Beheading of St. John" (Caravaggio)

(Des E. Cremona. Photo Enschedé)

1970 (21 Mar). 13th Council of Europe Art Exhibition. T **194** and similar multicoloured designs. W **105** (upright, 10d., 2s.; sideways, others). P 14×13 (1d., 8d.), 12 (10d., 2s.) or 13×13½ (others).

430 1d. Type **194** 10 10
431 2d. "St. John the Baptist" (M. Preti) (45×32 *mm*) 10 10
432 5d. Interior of St. John's Co-Cathedral, Valletta (39×39 *mm*) 10 10
433 6d. "Allegory of the Order" (Neapolitan School) (45×32 *mm*) 15 10
434 8d. "St. Jerome" (Caravaggio) 15 50
435 10d. Articles from the Order of St. John in Malta (63×21 *mm*) 15 10
436 1s.6d. "The Blessed Gerard receiving Godfrey de Bouillon" (A. de Favray) (45×35 *mm*). 25 40
437 2s. Cape and Stolone (16th-century) (63×21 *mm*) 25 55
a. Blue omitted £200
430/37 *Set of 8* .... 1·00 1·50

202 Artist's Impression of Fujiyama

(Des E. Cremona. Photo D.L.R.)

1970 (29 May). World Fair, Osaka. W **105** (sideways). P 15.

438 **202** 2d. multicoloured 10 10
439 5d. multicoloured 10 10
440 3s. multicoloured 15 15
438/40 *Set of 3* 30 30

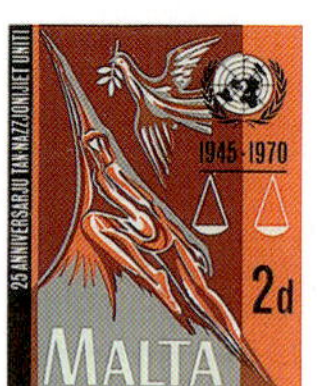

203 "Peace and Justice"

204 Carol-Singers, Church and Star

(Des J. Casha. Litho Harrison)

1970 (30 Sept). 25th Anniv of United Nations. W **105**. P 14×14½.

441 **203** 2d. multicoloured 10 10
442 5d. multicoloured 10 10
443 2s.6d. multicoloured 15 15
441/3 *Set of 3* 30 30

(Des E. Cremona. Photo Govt Printer, Israel)

1970 (7 Nov). Christmas. T **204** and similar vert designs. Multicoloured. W **105** (sideways). P 14×13.

444	1d. +½d.Type **204**	10	10
445	10d. +2d.Church, star and angels with Infant	15	20
446	1s.6d. +3d.Church, star and nativity scene	20	40
444/6 *Set of 3*		40	60

207 Books and Quill

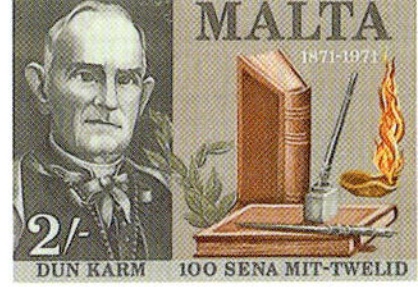

208 Dun Karm, Books, Pens and Lamp

(Des H. Alden (1s.6d.), A. Agius (2s.). Litho D.L.R.)

1971 (20 Mar). Literary Anniversaries. Death Bicentenary (1970) of De Soldanis (historian) (1s.6d.) and Birth Centenary of Dun Karm (poet) (2s.). W **105** (sideways). P 13×13½.

447	**207**	1s.6d. multicoloured	10	10
448	**208**	2s. multicoloured	10	15

209 Europa "Chain"

(Des H. Haflidason; adapted E. Cremona. Litho Harrison)

1971 (3 May). Europa. W **105** (sideways). P 13½×14½.

449	**209**	2d. orange, black and yellow-olive	10	10
450		5d. orange, black and vermilion	10	10
451		1s. 6d. orange, black and slate	60	90
449/51 *Set of 3*			70	90

210 "St. Joseph, Patron of the Universal Church" (G. Cali)

211 *Centaurea spathulata*

(Des E. Cremona. Litho D.L.R.)

1971 (24 July). Centenary of Prodamation of St. Joseph as Patron Saint of Catholic Church, and 50th Anniv of the Coronation of the Statue of "Our Lady of Victories". T **210** and similar horiz design. Multicoloured. W **105** (sideways). P 13×13½.

452	2d. Type **210**	10	10
453	5d. Statue of "Our Lady of Victories" and alley	10	10
454	10d. Type **210**	15	10
455	1s.6d. As 5d.	30	40
452/5 *Set of 4*		45	50

(Des Reno Psaila. Litho Harrison)

1971 (18 Sept). National Plant and Bird of Malta. T **211** and similar horiz design. Multicoloured. W **105** (sideways on 5d. and 10d.). P 14½×14.

456	2d. Type **211**	10	10
457	5d. Blue Rock Thrush	20	10
458	10d. As 5d.	30	15
459	1s.6d. Type **211**	30	1·25
456/9 *Set of 4*		75	1·40

212 Angel

(Des E. Cremona. Litho Format)

1971 (8 Nov). Christmas. T **212** and similar horiz designs. Multicoloured. W **105** (sideways). P 13½×14.

460	1d. +½d. Type **212**	10	10
461	10d. +2d. Mary and the Child Jesus	15	25
462	1s.6d. +3d. Joseph lying awake	20	40
460/2 *Set of 3*		35	55
MS463 131×113 mm. Nos. 460/2. P 15		75	2·50

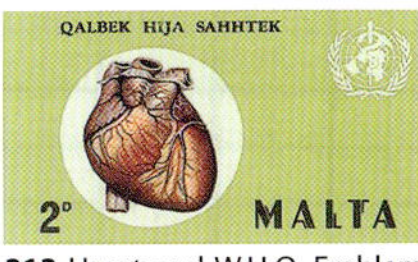

213 Heart and W.H.O. Emblem

214 Maltese Cross

(Des A. Agius. Litho Format)

1972 (20 Mar). World Health Day. W **105**. P 13½×14.

464	**213**	2d. multicoloured	10	10
465		10d. multicoloured	15	10
466		2s.6d. multicoloured	40	80
464/6 *Set of 3*			55	85

(New Currency. 10 mile =1 cent; 100 cents =1 Maltese pound)

(Des G. Pace. Litho Format)

1972 (16 May). Decimal Currency. T **214** and similar vert designs showing decimal coins. Multicoloured. W **105**. P 14 (2m., 3m., 2c.), 14½×14 (5m., 1c., 5c.) or 13½ (10c., 50c.).

467	2m. Type **214**	10	10
468	3m. Bee on honeycomb	10	10
469	5m. Earthen lampstand	10	10
470	1c. George Cross	10	10
471	2c. Classical head	10	10
472	5c. Ritual altar	10	10
473	10c. Grandmaster's galley	20	10
474	50c. Great Siege Monument	1·25	1·25
467/74 *Set of 8*		1·60	1·25

Sizes:—2m., 3m. and 2c. as T **214**; 5m.,1c. and 5c. 22×27 mm; 10c. and 50c. 27×35 mm.

No. 467 exists imperforate from stock dispersed by the liquidator of Format International Security Printers Ltd.

(**215**)

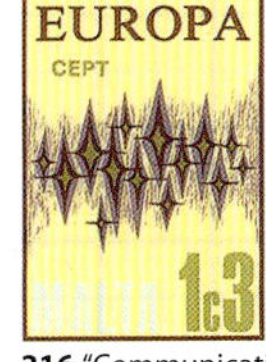

216 "Communications"

1972 (30 Sept). Nos. 337a, 339 and 341 surch as T **215**, by Govt. Printing Works, Valletta.

475	1c.3 on 5d. multicoloured	10	10
	a. Gold ("FORTIFICATIONS") omitted	£150	
476	3c. on 8d. multicoloured	15	10
	a. Surch inverted	65·00	
	b. Gold (frame) omitted	£110	
477	5c. on 1s.3d. multicoloured	15	20
	a. Surch double	£110	
	b. Surch inverted	55·00	
	c. Gold (centre) omitted	£110	
475/7 *Set of 3*		30	35

PRINTERS. All stamps between Nos. 478 and 1093 were printed in lithography by Printex Ltd. Malta.

(Des P. Huovinen; adapted G. Pace)

1972 (11 Nov). Europa. W **105** (sideways). P 13.

478	**216**	1c.3, multicoloured	10	10
479		3c. multicoloured	10	10
480		5c. multicoloured	15	35
481		7c.5, multicoloured	20	75
478/81 *Set of 4*			50	1·10

Nos. 478/81 were each printed in sheets including two *se-tenant* stamp-size labels in the second and third positions of the top row.

217 Angel

(Des E. Cremona)

1972 (9 Dec). Christmas. T **217** and similar horiz designs. W **105** (sideways). P 13½.

482	8m. +2m.dull sepia, brownish grey and gold	10	10
483	3c. +1c. plum, lavender and gold	15	40
484	7c.5 +1c.5, indigo, azure and gold	20	50
482/4 *Set of* 3		35	85
MS485 137×113 mm. Nos. 482/4		1·75	4·25
	a. Imperf horizontally		

Designs:—No. 483, Angel with tambourine; No. 484, Singing angel.
See also Nos. 507/10.

218 Archaeology **219** Europa "Posthorn"

(Des E. Cremona)

1973 (31 Mar)–**76**. T **218** and similar designs. Multicoloured. W **105** (sideways). P 13½×14 (Nos. 500/a) or 13½ (others).

486	2m. Type **218**	10	10
487	4m. History	10	10
	a. Gold (inscr and decoration) omitted	85·00	
	b. Imperf (pair)	£325	
488	5m. Folklore	10	10
489	8m. Industry	10	10
490	1c. Fishing industry	10	10
491	1c. 3, Pottery	10	10
492	2c. Agriculture	10	10
493	3c. Sport	10	10
494	4c. Yacht marina	15	10
495	5c. Fiesta	15	10
496	7c. 5, Regatta	25	10
497	10c. Voluntary service	25	10
498	50c. Education	2·00	50
499	£1 Religion	2·75	2·00
500	£2 Coat of arms (*horiz*)	14·00	19·00
	a. Gold omitted		
500*b*	£2 National Emblem (*horiz*) (28.1.76)	9·00	14·00
486/500b *Set of* 16		26·00	32·00

Nos. 500/b are larger, 32×27 mm.

(Des L. Anisdahl; adapted G. Pace)

1973 (2 June). Europa. W **105**. P 14.

501 **219**	3c. multcoloured	15	10
502	5c. multicoloured	15	35
503	7c. 5, multicoloured	25	65
501/3 *Set of* 3		50	1·00

Nos. 501/3 were each printed in sheets containing two *se-tenant* stamp-size labels.

220 Emblem, and Woman holding Corn

221 Girolamo Cassar (architect)

(Des H. Alden)

1973 (6 Oct). Anniversaries. T **220** and similar vert designs showing emblem and allegorical figures. W **105** (sideways). P 13½.

504	1c.3, multicoloured	10	10
505	7c.5, multicoloured	25	40
506	10c. multicoloured	30	50
504/6 *Set of* 3		55	85

Anniversaries:—1c.3, Tenth Anniv of World Food Programme; 7c.5, 25th Anniv of W.H.O.; 10c. 25th Anniv of Universal Declaration of Human Rights.

(Des E. Cremona)

1973 (10 Nov). Christmas. Horiz designs as T **217**. Multicoloured. W **105** (sideways). P 13½.

507	8m. +2m. Angels and organ pipes	15	10
508	3c. +1c. Madonna and Child	25	60
509	7c.5 +1c.5, Buildings and Star	45	1·50
507/9 *Set of* 3		75	2·00
MS510 137×112 mm. Nos. 507/9		4·75	7·50

(Des E. Cremona)

1974 (12 Jan). Prominent Maltese. T **221** and similar vert designs. W **105**. P 14.

511	1c.3, dull myrtle-green, dull grey-green and gold	10	10
512	3c. deep turquoise, grey-blue and gold	15	10
513	5c. dull sepia, deep slate-green and gold	20	15
514	7c.5, slate-blue, light slate-blue and gold	20	30
515	10c. purple, dull purple and gold	20	40
511/15 *Set of*5		70	85

Designs:—3c. Giuseppe Barth (ophthalmologist); 5c. Nicolo' Isouard (composer); 7c.5, John Borg (botanist); 10c. Antonio Sciortino (sculptor).

222 "Air Malta" Emblem

(Des E. Cremona)

1974 (30 Mar). Air. T **222** and similar horiz design. Multicoloured. W **105** (sideways). P 13½.

516	3c. Type **222**	15	10
517	4c. Boeing 720B	15	10
518	5c. Type **222**	15	10
519	7c.5, As 4c.	20	10
520	20c. Type **222**	35	60
521	25c. As 4c.	35	60
522	35c. Type **222**	45	1·40
516/22 *Set of* 7		1·60	2·75

223 Prehistoric Sculpture

(Des E. Cremona)

1974 (13 July). Europa. T **223** and similar designs. W **105** *(sideways)* on Nos. 523 and 525). P 13½.

523	1c.3c. slate-blue, grey-black and gold	15	10
524	3c. light bistre-brown, grey-black and gold	20	15
525	5c. purple, grey-black and gold	25	50
526	7c.5c. dull green, grey-black and gold	35	1·00
523/6 *Set of* 4		85	1·60

Designs: *Vert*—3c. Old Cathedral Door, Mdina; 7c.5, "Vetlina" (sculpture by A. Sciortino). *Horiz*—5c. Silver Monstrance.

Nos. 523/6 were each printed in sheets including two se-tenant stamp-size labels.

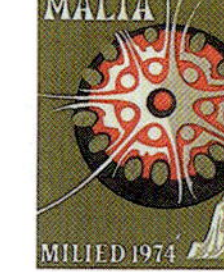

224 Heinrich von Stephan (founder) and Land Transport

225 Decorative Star and Nativity Scene

(Des S. and G. Sullivan)

1974 (20 Sept). Centenary of Universal Postal Union. T **224** and similar horiz designs. W **105**. P 13½×14.

527	1c.3, blue-green, lt violet-blue and yellow and orange	30	10
528	5c. brown, dull vermilion and yellow-green	30	10
529	7c.5, dp dull blue, lt violet-blue and yellow-green	35	20
530	50c. purple, dull vermilion and yellow-orange	1·00	1·25
527/30 *Set of* 4		1·75	1·50
MS531 126×91 mm. Nos. 527/30		4·75	7·50

Designs (each containing portrait as T **224**): 5c. *Washington* (paddle-steamer) and *Royal Viking Star* (liner); 7c.5, Balloon and Boeing 747-100; 50c. U.P.U. Buildings, 1874 and 1974.

(Des E. Cremona)

1974 (22 Nov). Christmas. T **225** and similar vert designs, each with decorative star. Multicoloured. W **105** (sideways). P 14.

532	8m. +2m. Type **225**	10	10
533	3c. +1c. "Shepherds"	15	20
534	5c. +1c. "Shepherds with gifts"	20	35
535	7c.5 +1c.5, "The Magi"	30	45
532/5 *Set of 4*		65	1·00

REPUBLIC

226 Swearing-in of Prime Minister

(Des E. Cremona)

1975 (31 Mar). Inauguration of Republic. T **226** and similar horiz designs. W **105** *(sideways)*. P 14.

536	1c.3, multicoloured	10	10
537	5c. rose-red and grey-black	20	10
538	25c. multicoloured	60	1·00
536/8 *Set of 3*		75	1·10

Designs:—5c. National flag; 25c. Minister of Justice, President and Prime Minister.

227 Mother and Child ("Family Life")

(Des D. Friggieri)

1975 (30 May). International Women's Year. T **227** and similar horiz design. W **105**. P 13½×14.

539	**227**	1c.3, light violet and gold	15	10
540	–	3c. light blue and gold	15	10
541	**227**	5c. dull olive-sepia and gold	25	15
542	–	20c. chestnut and gold	80	2·50
539/42 *Set of 4*			1·25	2·50

Design:—3c., 20c. Office secretary ("Public Life").

228 "Allegory of Malta" (Francesco de Mura)

(Des E. Cremona)

1975 (15 July). Europa. T **228** and similar horiz design. Multicoloured. W **105**. P 14×13½.

543	5c. Type **228**	30	10
544	15c. "Judith and Holofernes" (Valentin de Boulogne)	50	75

The 15c. is a smaller design than the 5c. (47×23 mm), though the perforated area is the same.

Nos. 543/4 were each printed in sheets including two *se-tenant* stamp-size labels.

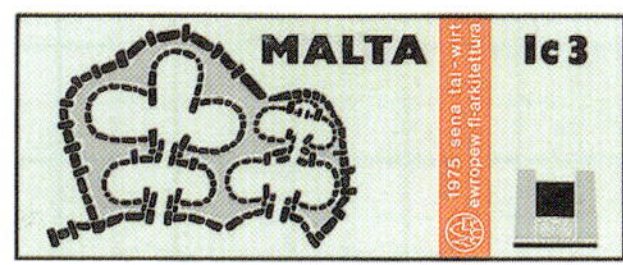

229 Plan of Ggantija Temple

(Des R. England)

1975 (16 Sept). European Architectural Heritage Year. T **229** and similar horiz designs. W **105** (sideways). P 13½.

545	1c.3, brownish black and light orange-red	10	10
546	3c. dull purple, lt orange-red and blackish brown	20	10
547	5c. blackish brown and light orange-red	30	25
548	25c. dull grey-olive, light orange-red and brownish black	1·10	3·00
545/8 *Set of 4*		1·50	3·00

Designs:—3c. Mdina skyline; 5c. View of Victoria, Gozo; 25c. Silhouette of Fort St. Angelo.

230 Farm Animals

231 "The Right to Work"

(Des E. Cremona)

1975 (4 Nov). Christmas. T **230** and similar multicoloured designs. W **105** (sideways). P 13½.

549	8m. +2m. Type **230**	25	25
	a. Horiz strip of 3. Nos. 549/51	1·00	2·25
550	3c. +1c. Nativity scene (50×23 mm)	40	75
551	7c.5, +1c.5 Approach of the Magi	45	1·40
549/51 *Set of 3*		1·00	2·25

Nos. 549/51 were issued in sheets of 50 of each value, and also in sheets containing the three values horizontally *se-tenant*, thus forming the triptych No. 549a which is a composite design of "The Nativity" by Master Alberto.

(Des A. de Giovanni)

1975 (12 Dec). First Anniv of Republic. T **231** and similar vert designs. W **105**. P 14.

552	1c.3c. multicoloured	10	10
553	5c. multicoloured	20	10
554	25c. deep rose, light steel-blue and black	70	1·10
552/4 *Set of 3*		80	1·10

Designs:—5c. "Safeguarding the Environment"; 25c. National Flag.

232 "Festa Tar-Rahal"

233 Water Polo

(Des M. Camilleri)

1976 (26 Feb). Maltese Folklore. T **232** and similar multicoloured designs. W **105** (sideways on 5c. and 7c.5). P 14.

555	1c.3, Type **232**	10	10
556	5c. "L-Imnarja" *(horiz)*	15	10
557	7c.5, "Il-Karnival" *(horiz)*	35	70
558	10c. "Il-Gimgha L-Kbira"	55	1·40
555/8 *Set of 4*		1·00	2·00

(Des H. Alden)

1976 (28 Apr). Olympic Games, Montreal. T **233** and similar horiz designs. Multicoloured. W **105**. P 13½×14.

559	1c.7, Type **233**	10	10
560	5c. Sailing	25	10
561	30c. Athletics	85	1·50
559/61 *Set of 3*		1·10	1·50

234 Lace-making

(Des F. Portelli)

1976 (8 July). Europa. T **234** and similar horiz design. Multicoloured. W **105** (sideways). P 13×14.

562	7c. Type **234**	20	35
563	15c. Stone carving	25	60

Nos. 562/3 were each printed in sheets including two *se-tenant* stamp-size labels.

235 Nicola Cotoner

(Des E. Cremona)

1976 (14 Sept). 300th Anniv of School of Anatomy and Surgery. T **235** and similar horiz designs. Multicoloured. W **105** (sideways). P 13½.

564	2c. Type **235**	10	10
565	5c. Arm	15	10
566	7c. Giuseppe Zammit	20	10
567	11c. Sacra Infermeria	35	65
564/7	*Set of 4*	70	75

236 St. John the Baptist and St. Michael

237 Jean de la Valette's Armour

1c7

(**238**)

(Des E. Cremona)

1976 (23 Nov). Christmas. Designs showing portions of "Madonna and Saints" by Domenico di Michelino. Multicoloured. W **105** (sideways on No. 571). P 13½×14 (No. 571) or 13½ (others).

568	1c. +5m. Type **236**	10	20
569	5c. +1c. Madonna and Child	15	60
570	7c. +1c.5, St. Christopher and St. Nicholas	20	80
571	10c. +2c. Complete painting (32×27 mm)	30	1·25
568/71	*Set of 4*	65	2·50

(Des J. Briffa)

1977 (20 Jan). Suits of Armour. T **237** and similar vert designs. Multicoloured. W **105**. P 13½.

572	2c. Type **237**	10	10
573	7c. Aloph de Wignacourt's armour	20	10
574	11c. Jean Jacques de Verdelin's armour	25	50
572/4	*Set of 3*	45	60

1977 (24 Mar). No. 336 surch with T **238** by Govt Printing Press, Malta.

575	**116**	1c.7 on 4d. multicoloured	25	25
		a. "KNIGHTS OF MALTA" (silver) omitted	£110	

239 "Annunciation"

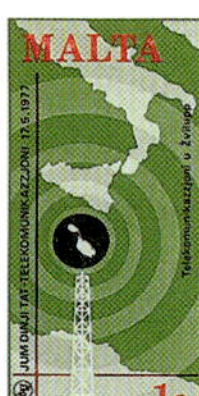

240 Map and Radio Aerial

(Des E. Cremona)

1977 (30 Mar). 400th Birth Anniversary of Rubens. Flemish tapestries (1st series) showing his paintings as T **239**. Multicoloured. W **105** (sideways). P 14.

576	2c. Type **239**	10	10
577	7c. "Four Evangelists"	25	10
578	11c. "Nativity"	45	45
579	20c. "Adoration of the Magi"	80	1·00
576/9	*Set of 4*	1·40	1·50

See also Nos. 592/5. 615/18 and 638/40.

(Des H. Borg)

1977 (17 May). World Telecommunication Day. T **240** and similar design. W **105** (sideways on 1 and 6c.). P 14×13½ (1 and 6c.) or 13½×14 (others).

580	**240**	1c. black, green and vermilion	10	10
581		6c. black, grey-blue and vermilion	20	10
582	–	8c. black, chestnut and vermilion	30	10
583	–	17c. black, dull mauve and vermilion	60	40
580/3		*Set of 4*	1·00	55

Design: *Horiz*—8 and 17c. Map, aerial and aeroplane tail-fin.

241 Ta' L-Isperanza

242 "Aid to Handicapped Workers" (detail from Workers' Monument)

(Des G. French)

1977 (5 July). Europa. T **241** and similar horiz design. Multicoloured. W **105** (sideways). P 13½.

584	7c. Type **241**	30	15
585	20c. Is-Salini	35	1·00

Nos. 584/5 were each printed in sheets including two *se-tenant* stamp-size labels.

(Des A. Agius)

1977 (12 Oct). Maltese Worker Commemoration. T **242** and similar designs. W **105** (sideways on 20c.). P 13½.

586	2c. orange-brown and light brown	10	10
587	7c. chestnut and brown	15	10
588	20c. multicoloured	40	60
586/8	*Set of 3*	55	60

Designs: *Vert*—7c. "Stoneworker, modern industry and ship building" (monument detail). *Horiz*—20c. "Mother with Dead Son" and Service Medal.

243 The Shepherds

244 "Young Lady on Horseback and Trooper"

(Des E. Cremona)

1977 (16 Nov). Christmas. T **243** and similar horiz designs. Multicoloured. W **105** (sideways). P 13½×14.

589	1c. +5m. Type **243**	10	35
	a. Vert strip of 3. Nos. 589/91	40	1·40
590	7c. +1c. The Nativity	15	55
591	11c. +1c.5, Flight into Egypt	20	70
589/91	*Set of 3*	40	1·40

Nos. 589/91 were issued in sheets of 50 of each value, and also in sheets containing the three values *se-tenant*.

(Des E. Cremona)

1978 (26 Jan). Flemish Tapestries (2nd series). Horiz designs similar to T **239**. Multicoloured. W **105** (sideways). P 14.

592	2c. "The Entry into Jerusalem" (artist unknown)	10	10
593	7c. "The Last Supper" (after Poussin)	25	10
594	11c. "The Raising of the Cross" (after Rubens)	30	25
595	25c. "The Resurrection" (after Rubens)	70	80
592/5	*Set of 4*	1·25	1·10

(Des A. Camilleri)

1978 (7 Mar). 450th Death Anniv of Albrecht Dürer. T **244** and similar vert designs. W **105**. P 14.

596	1c.7, black, vermilion and deep blue	10	10
597	8c. black, vermilion and slate	15	10
598	17c. black, vermilion and deep slate	40	45
	a. Vermilion (monogram) omitted	£180	
596/8	Set of 3	55	55

Designs:—8c. "The Bag-piper"; 17c. "The Virgin and Child with a Monkey".

245 Monument to Grand Master Nicola Cotoner (Foggini)

246 Goalkeeper

(Des E. Cremona)

1978 (26 Apr). Europa. Monuments. T **245** and similar vert design. Multicoloured. W **105**. P 14×13½.

599	7c. Type **245**	15	10
600	25c. Monument to Grand Master Racoon Perellos (Mazzuoli)	35	90

Nos. 599/600 were each printed in sheets including two *se-tenant* stamp-size labels.

(Des A. de Giovanni)

1978 (6 June). World Cup Football Championship, Argentina. T **246** and similar vert designs. Multicoloured. W **105** (sideways). P 14×13½.

601	2c. Type **246**	10	10
602	11c. Players heading ball	15	10
603	15c. Tackling	25	35
601/3 *Set of 3*		45	45
MS604 125×90 mm. Nos. 601/3		2·00	3·25

247 Boeing 707 over Megalithic Temple

(Des R. Caruana)

1978 (3 Oct). Air. Horiz designs as T **247**. Multicoloured. W **105** (sideways). P 13½.

605	5c. Type **247**	20	10
606	7c. Air Malta Boeing 720B	20	10
607	11c. Boeing 747 taking off from Luqa Airport	35	10
608	17c. Type **247**	45	30
609	20c. As 7c.	40	40
610	75c. As 11c.	1·25	2·75
605/10 *Set of 6*		2·50	3·25

248 Folk Musicians and Village Church

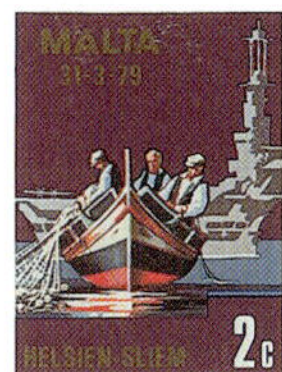

249 Luzzu and Aircraft Carrier

(Des E. Cremona)

1978 (9 Nov). Christmas. T **248** and similar multicoloured designs. W **105** (sideways). P 13½ (11c.) or 14 (others).

611	1c. +5m. Type **248**	10	10
612	5c. +1c. Choir of Angels	15	20
613	7c. +1c.5, Carol singers	20	35
614	11c. +3c. Folk musicians, church, angels and carol singers (58×23 mm)	25	45
611/11 *Set of 4*		60	1·00

The 1, 5 and 7c. values depict details of the complete design shown on the 11c. value.

(Des E. Cremona)

1979 (24 Jan). Flemish Tapestries (3rd series). Horiz designs as T **239** showing paintings by Rubens. Multicoloured. W **105** (sideways). P 14.

615	2c. "The Triumph of the Catholic Church"	10	10
616	7c. "The Triumph of Charity"	20	10
617	11c. "The Triumph of Faith"	30	25
618	25c. "The Triumph of Truth"	95	80
615/18 *Set of 4*		1·40	1·10

(Des E. Cremona)

1979 (31 Mar). End of Military Facilities Agreement. T **249** and similar vert designs. Multicoloured. W **105** (sideways). P 13½.

619	2c. Type **249**	10	10
620	5c. Raising the flag ceremony	10	10
621	7c. Departing soldier and olive sprig	15	10
622	8c. Type 249	30	30
623	17c. As 5c.	40	45
624	20c. As 7c.	40	45
619/24 *Set of 6*		1·25	1·25

250 Speronara (fishing boat) and Tail of Air Malta Airliner

251 Children on Globe

(Des E. Cremona)

1979 (9 May). Europa. Communications. T **250** and similar vert design. Multicoloured. W **105** (sideways). P 14.

625	7c. Type **250**	20	10
626	25c. Coastal watch tower and radio link towers	40	75

Nos. 625/6 were each printed in sheets including two *se-tenant* stamp-size labels.

(Des A. Bonnici (2c.), A. Pisani (7c.), M. French (11c.))

1979 (13 June). International Year of the Child. T **251** and similar multicoloured designs. W **105** (sideways). P 14×13½ (2c.) or 14 (others).

627	2c. Type **251**	10	10
628	7c. Children flying kites (27×33 mm)	15	10
629	11c. Children in circle (27×33 mm)	20	35
627/9 *Set of 3*		35	45

252 Shells (*Gibbula nivosa*)

(Des R. Pitré)

1979 (10 Oct). Marine Life. T **252** and similar horiz designs. Multicoloured. W **105**. P 13½.

630	2c. Type **252**	10	10
631	5c. Loggerhead Turtle (*Garetta garena*)	20	10
632	7c. Dolphin (fish) (*Coryphaena hippurus*)	25	10
633	25c. Noble Pen Shell (*Piano nobilis*)	90	1·25
630/3 *Set of 4*		1·25	1·25

253 "The Nativity" (detail)

(Des E. Cremona)

1979 (14 Nov). Christmas. Paintings by G.Cali. T **253** and similar horiz designs. Multicoloured. W **105**. P 14×13½.

634	1c. +5m. Type **253**	10	10
635	5c. +1c. "The Flight into Egypt" (detail)	15	15
636	7c. +1c. 5, "The Nativity"	20	20
637	11c. +3c. "The Flight into Egypt"	30	50
634/7 *Set of 4*		65	85

(Des E. Cremona)

1980 (30 Jan). Flemish Tapestries (4th series). Horiz designs as T **239** taken from paintings. Multicoloured. W **105** (sideways). P 14.

638	2c. "The Institution of Corpus Domini" (Rubens)	10	10
639	8c. "The Destruction of Idolatry" (Rubens)	20	20

MS640	114×86 mm. 50c. "Grand Master Perellos with St. Jude and St. Simon" (unknown Maltese artist) (*vert*)	80	1·60

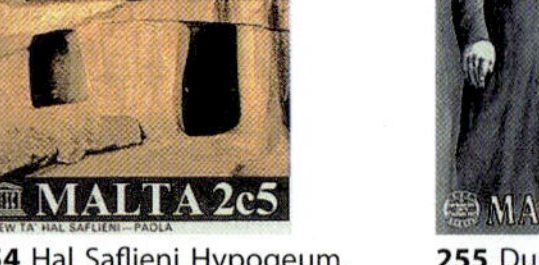

254 Hal Saflieni Hypogeum, Paola

255 Dun Gorg Preca

1980 (15 Feb). International Restoration of Maltese Monuments Campaign. T **254** and similar multicoloured designs. W **106** (sideways on 8 and 12 c.). P 14.

641	2c. 5, Type **254**	10	15
642	6c. Vilhena Palace, Mdina	15	20
643	8c. Victoria Citadel, Gaza (*horiz*)	20	40
644	12c. Fort St. Elmo, Valletta (*horiz*)	30	60
641/4	*Set of* 4	65	1·25

(Des R. Pitré)

1980 (12 Apr). Birth Centenary of Dun Gorg Preca (founder of Society of Christian Doctrine). W **105** (sideways). P 14×13½.

645	**255** 2c.5, black and grey	10	10

256 Ruzar Briffa (poet)

257 "Annunciation"

(Des V. Apap)

1980 (29 Apr). Europa. Personalities. T **256** and similar horiz design. W **105** (sideways). P 13½×14.

646	8c. black, brown-ochre and bronze-green	20	10
647	30c. brown, brown-olive and brown-lake	55	1·25

Design:—30 c. Nikiol Anton Vassalli (scholar and patriot).

Nos. 646/7 were each printed in sheets including two *se-tenant* stamp-size labels.

(Des R. Pitré)

1980 (7 Oct). Christmas. Paintings by A. Inglott. T **257** and similar multicoloured designs. W **105** (sideways on 12c.). P 14 (12 c.) or 13½ (others).

648	2c. +5m. Type 257	10	10
649	6c. +1c. "Conception"	20	20
650	8c. +1c. 5, "Nativity"	25	40
651	12c. +3c. "Annunciation", "Conception" and "Nativity" (47×38 mm)	30	70
648/51	*Set of* 4	75	1·25

The paintings from the 2, 6 and 8c. values are united to form the triptych on the 12c. value.

258 Rook and Pawn

259 Barn Owl (*Tyto alba*)

(Des H. Borg)

1980 (20 Nov). 24th Chess Olympiad and International Chess Federation Congress, Malta. T **258** and similar multicoloured designs. W **105** (sideways on 30c.) P 14×13½ (30c.) or 13½×14 (others).

652	2c. 5, Type **258**	20	20
653	8c. Bishop and Pawn	45	20
654	30c. King, Queen and Pawn (*vert*)	70	1·50
652/4	*Set of* 3	1·25	1·75

(Des M. Burlò)

1981 (20 Jan). Birds. T **259** and similar vert designs. Multicoloured. W **105** (sideways). P 13½.

655	3c. Type **259**	30	25
656	8c. Sardinian Warbler (*Sylvia melanocephala*)	50	25
657	12c. Woodchat Shrike (*Lanius senator*)	60	80
658	23c. British Storm Petrel (*Hydrobates pelagicus*)	1·10	1·75
655/8	*Set of* 4	2·25	2·75

260 Traditional Horse Race

261 Stylised "25"

(Des H. Borg)

1981 (28 Apr). Europa. Folklore. T **260** and similar vert design. Multicoloured. W **105** (sideways). P 14.

659	8c. Type **260**	20	10
660	30c. Attempting to retrieve flag from end of "gostra" (greasy pole)	40	65

The two values were each printed in sheets including two *se-tenant* stamp-size labels.

(Des A. de Giovanni)

1981 (12 June). 25th Maltese International Trade Fair. W **105** (sideways). P 13½.

661	**261** 4c. multicoloured	15	15
662	25c. multicoloured	50	60

262 Disabled Artist at Work

263 Wheat Ear in Conical Flask

(Des A. Camilleri)

1981 (17 July). International Year for Disabled Persons. T **262** and similar vert design. Multicoloured. W **105** (sideways). P 13½.

663	3c. Type **262**	20	10
664	35c. Disabled child playing football	90	75

(Des R. Caruana)

1981 (16 Oct). World Food Day. W **105** (sideways). P 14.

665	**263** 8c. multicoloured	15	15
666	23c. multicoloured	60	50

264 Megalithic Building

265 Children and Nativity Scene

(Des F. Portelli).

1981 (31 Oct). History of Maltese Industry. Horiz designs as T **264**. Multicoloured. W **105**. P 14.

667	5m. Type **264**	10	85

668	1c. Cotton production	10	10
669	2c. Early ship-building	85	10
670	3c. Currency minting	30	10
671	5c. "Art"	30	25
672	6c. Fishing	1·25	25
673	7c. Agriculture	30	1·50
674	8c. Stone quarrying	1·00	35
675	10c. Grape pressing	35	50
676	12c. Modern ship-building	2·00	2·25
677	15c. Energy	70	2·00
678	20c. Telecommunications	70	1·00
679	25c. "Industry"	1·00	2·25
680	50c. Drilling for water	2·50	2·75
681	£1 Sea transport	7·00	7·50
682	£3 Air transport	13·00	18·00
667/82	*Set of* 16	28·00	35·00

(Des A. Bugeja)

1981 (18 Nov). Christmas. T **265** and similar multicoloured designs. W **105** (sideways). P 14.

683	2c. +1c. Type **265**	25	10
684	8c. +2c. Christmas Eve procession (horiz)	35	20
685	20c. +3c. Preaching midnight sermon	50	1·10
683/5	*Set of* 3	1·00	1·25

266 Shipbuilding

267 Elderly Man and Has-Serh (home for elderly)

(Des N. Attard)

1982 (29 Jan). Shipbuilding Industry. T **266** and similar vert designs showing different scenes. W **105** (sideways). P 13½.

686	3c. multicoloured	15	10
687	8c. multicoloured	30	30
688	13c. multicoloured	55	55
689	27c. multicoloured	1·25	1·25
686/9	*Set of* 4	2·00	2·00

(Des R. Pitré)

1982 (16 Mar). Care of Elderly. T **267** and similar horiz design. Multicoloured. W **105**. P 14×13½.

690	8c. Type **267**	30	20
691	30c. Elderly woman and Has-Zmien (hospital for elderly)	1·10	1·40

268 Redemption of Islands by Maltese, 1428

(Des F. Portelli)

1982 (29 Apr). Europa. Historical Events. T **268** and similar horiz design. Multicoloured. W **105**. P 14×13½.

692	8c. Type **268**	40	20
693	30c. Declaration of rights by Maltese, 1802	70	1·40

Nos. 692/3 were each printed in sheets containing 2 *se-tenant* stamp-size labels.

269 Stylised Footballer

(Des R. Caruana)

1982 (11 June). World Cup Football Championship, Spain. T **269** and similar horiz designs showing stylised footballers. W **105**. P 14.

694	3c. multicoloured	20	10
695	12c. multicoloured	60	55
696	15c. multicoloured	70	65
694/6	*Set of* 3	1·40	1·25
MS697	125×90 mm. Nos. 694/6	3·50	4·50

270 Angel appearing to Shepherds

(Des J. Mallia)

1982 (8 Oct). Christmas. T **270** and similar multicoloured designs. W **105** (sideways). P 14 (No. 700) or 13½ (others).

698	2c. +1c. Type **270**	15	20
699	8c. +2c. Nativity and Three Wise Men bearing gifts	40	60
700	20c. +3c. Nativity scene (*larger* 45×37 mm)	80	1·25
698/700	*Set of* 3	1·25	1·90

The designs from the 2 and 8c. values are united to form the design of the 20 c. stamp.

271 *Ta' Salvo Serafino* (oared brigantine), 1531

(Des N. Attard)

1982 (13 Nov). Maltese Ships (1st series). T **271** and similar horiz designs. Multicoloured. W **105**. P 14×13½.

701	3c. Type **271**	25	10
702	8c. *La Madonna del Rosaries* (tartane), 1740	50	30
703	12c. *San Paulo* (xebec), 1743	70	55
704	20c. *Ta' Pietro Saliba* (xprunara), 1798	90	90
701/4	*Set of* 4	2·10	1·60

See also Nos. 725/8, 772/5, 792/5 and 809/12.

272 Locomotive *Manning Wardle*, 1883

(Des R. Caruana)

1983 (21 Jan). Centenary of Malta. Railway. T **272** and similar horiz designs. Multicoloured. W **105**. P 14×13½.

705	3c. Type **272**	45	15
706	13c. Locomotive *Black Hawthorn*, 1884	85	1·00
707	27c. Beyer Peacock locomotive, 1895	1·50	3·25
705/7	*Set of* 3	2·50	4·00

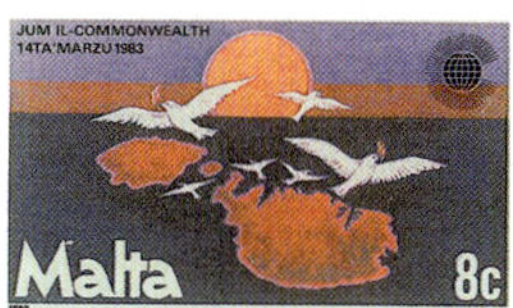

273 Peace Doves leaving Malta

(Des C. Cassar)

1983 (14 Mar). Commonwealth Day. T **273** and similar multicoloured designs. W **105** (sideways on vert designs). P 14×13½. (8, 12c.) or 13½×14 (others).

708	8c. Type **273**	20	30
709	12c. Tourist landmarks	30	60
710	15c. Holiday beach (*vert*)	35	75
711	23c. Ship-building (*vert*)	55	1·00
708/11	*Set of* 4	1·25	2·40

274 Ggantija Megalithic Temples, Gozo

(Des T. Bugeja (8c.), R. Caruana (30c.))

1983 (5 May). Europa. T **274** and similar horiz design. Multicoloured. W **105**. P 14×13½.

712	8c. Type **274**	40	40
713	30c. Fort St. Angelo	70	2·40

Nos. 712/13 were each printed in sheets including two *se-tenant* stamp-size labels.

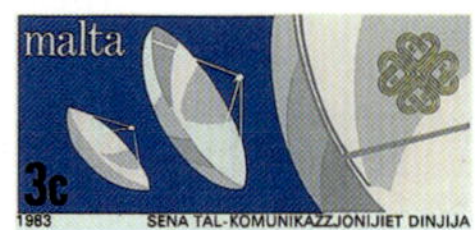

275 Dish Aerials (World Communications Year)

(Des D. Friggieri)

1983 (14 July). Anniversaries and Events. T **275** and similar horiz designs. Multicoloured. W **105** (sideways). P 13½×14.

714	3c. Type **275**	30	15
715	7c. Ships' prows and badge (25th anniv of I.M.O. Convention)	50	55
716	13c. Container lorries and badge (30th anniv of Customs Co-operation Council)	80	90
717	20c. Stadium and emblem (9th Mediterranean Games)	90	2·25
714/17 *Set of 4*		2·25	3·50

276 Monsignor Giuseppe de Piro

277 Annunciation

(Des E. Barthet)

1983 (1 Sept). 50th Death Anniv of Monsignor Giuseppe de Piro. W **105** (sideways). P 14.

718	**276**	3c. multicoloured	15	15

(Des N. Attard)

1983 (6 Sept). Christmas. T **277** and similar vert designs. Multicoloured. W **105** (sideways). P 13½×14.

719	2c. +1c. Type **277**	30	15
720	8c. +2c. The Nativity	70	60
721	20c. +3c. Adoration of the Magi	1·25	2·25
719/21 *Set of 3*		2·00	2·75

278 Workers at Meeting

(Des F. Portelli)

1983 (5 Oct). 40th Anniv of General Workers' Union. T **278** and similar horiz designs. Multicoloured. W **105**. P 14×13½.

722	3c. Type **278**	25	10
723	8c. Worker with family	45	40
724	27c. Union H.Q. Building	1·25	1·75
722/4 *Set of 3*		1·75	2·00

(Des N. Attard)

1983 (17 Nov). Maltese Ships (2nd series). Horiz designs as T **271**. Multicoloured. W **105**. P 14×13½.

725	2c. *Strangier* (full-rigged ship), 1813	30	25
726	12c. *Tigre* (topsail schooner) 1839	80	1·25
727	13c. *La Speranza* (brig), 1844	80	1·25
728	20c. *Wignacourt* (baxque), 1844	1·25	2·75
725/8 *Set of 4*		2·75	5·00

279 Boeing 737

(Des R. Caruana)

1984 (26 Jan). Air. T **279** and similar horiz designs. Multicoloured. W **105**. P 14×13½.

729	7c. Type **279**	50	30
730	8c. Boeing 720B	60	35
731	16c. Vickers 953 Vanguard	1·25	70
732	23c. Vickers Viscount 700	1·50	70
733	27c. Douglas DC-3	1·75	80
734	38c. Armstrong Whitworth A.W.15 Atalanta *Artemis*	2·25	2·75
735	75c. Marina Fiat MF.5 flying boat	3·25	5·00
729/35 *Set of 7*		10·00	9·50

280 C.E.P.T. 25th Anniversary Logo

281 Early Policeman

(Des J. Larrivière and L. Borg)

1984 (27 Apr). Europa. W **105**. P 13½.

736	**280**	8c. green, black and gold	35	35
737		30c. carmine-lake, black and gold	1·00	1·25

Nos. 736/7 were each printed in sheets including two *se-tenant* stamp-size labels.

(Des T. Bugeja)

1984 (14 June). 170th Anniv of Malta Police Force. T **281** and similar vert designs. Multicoloured. W **105**. P 14×13½.

738	3c. Type **281**	65	15
739	8c. Mounted police	1·25	65
	a. Pale Venetian red (background) omitted	£275	
740	11c. Motorcycle policeman	1·50	2·00
741	25c. Policeman and fireman	2·25	3·75
738/41 *Set of 4*		5·00	6·00

282 Running

283 "The Visitation" (Pietru Caruana)

(Des L. Micallef)

1984 (26 July). Olympic Games, Los Angeles. T **282** and similar vert designs. Multicoloured. W **105** (sideways). P 14.

742	7c. Type **282**	25	30
743	12c. Gymnastics	50	70
744	23c. Swimming	85	1·25
742/4 *Set of 3*		1·50	2·00

(Des L. Micallef)

1984 (5 Oct). Christmas. Paintings from Church of Our Lady of Porto Salvo, Valletta. T **283** and similar multicoloured designs. W **105** (sideways on horiz designs). P 14.

745	2c. +1c. Type **283**	55	65
746	8c. +2c. "The Epiphany" (Rafel Caruana) (horiz)	1·00	1·40
747	20c. +3c. "Jesus among the Doctors" (Rafel Caruana) (horiz)	2·00	4·00
745/7 *Set of 3*		3·25	5·50

284 Dove on Map

285 1885 ½d. Green Stamp

(Des L. Micallef)

1984 (12 Dec). 10th Anniv of Republic. T **284** and similar vert designs. Multitoloured. W **105** (sideways). P 14.

748	3c. Type **284**	30	20
749	8c. Fort St. Angelo	60	65
750	30c. Hands	2·10	4·75
748/50 *Set of 3*		2·75	5·00

(Des N. Attard)

1985 (2 Jan). Centenary of Malta Post Office. T **285** and similar vert designs showing stamps of 1885. Multicoloured. W **105**. P 14.

751	3c. Type **285**	45	15
752	8c. 1885 1d. rose	65	45
753	12c. 1885 2½d. dull blue	90	1·40
754	20c. 1885 4d. brown	1·40	3·00
751/4 *Set of 4*		3·00	4·50
MS755 165×90 mm. Nos. 751/4. Wmk sideways		3·75	6·50

286 Boy, and Hands planting Vine

(Des T. Bugeja)

1985 (7 Mar). International Youth Year. T **286** and similar multicoloured designs. W **105** (sideways on 13c.). P 14.

756	2c. Type **286**	15	15
757	13c. Young people and flowers (*vert*)	70	60
758	27c. Girl holding flame in hand	1·40	1·40
756/8 *Set of 3*		2·00	1·90

287 Nicolo Baldacchino (tenor)

288 Guzeppi Bajada and Manwel Attard (victims)

(Des L. Micallef)

1985 (25 Apr). Europa. European Music Year. T **287** and similar vert design. Multicoloured. W **105**. P 14.

759	8c. Type **287**	1·50	50
760	30c. Francesco Azopardi (composer)	2·75	5·00

Nos. 759/60 were each printed in sheets including two *se-tenant* stamp-size labels.

(Des L. Micallef)

1985 (7 June). 66th Anniv of 7 June 1919 Demonstrations. T **288** and similar multicoloured designs. W **105** (sideways on 3c., 7c.). P 14.

761	3c. Type **288**	30	15
762	7c. Karmnu Abela and Wenzu Dyer (victims)	60	40
763	35c. Model of projected Demonstration monument by Anton Agius (*vert*)	1·90	2·75
761/3 *Set of 3*		2·50	3·00

289 Stylized Birds

290 Giorgio Mitrovich (nationalist) (Death Centenary)

(Des D. Friggieri)

1985 (26 July). 40th Anniv of United Nations Organization. T **289** and similar horiz designs. Multicoloured. W **105** (sideways). P 13½×14.

764	4c. Type **289**	25	15
765	11c. Arrow-headed ribbons	60	1·25
766	31c. Stylized figures	1·40	3·25
764/6 *Set of 3*		2·00	4·25

(Des R. Pitre)

1985 (3 Oct). Celebrities Anniversaries. T **290** and similar vert design. Multicoloured. W **105** (sideways). P 14.

767	8c. Type **290**	75	35
768	12c. Pietru Caxaru (poet and administrator) (400th death anniv)	1·25	2·50

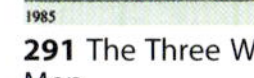

291 The Three Wise Men

292 John XXIII Peace Laboratory and Statue of St. Francis of Assisi

(Des G. Bonnici)

1985 (10 Oct). Christmas. T **291** and similar vert designs showing details of terracotta relief by Ganni Bonnici. Multicoloured. W **105** (sideways). P 14.

769	2c. +1c. Type **291**	45	60
770	8c. +2c. Virgin and Child	1·00	1·50
771	20c. +3c. Angels	2·00	3·50
769/71 *Set of 3*		3·00	5·00

(Des N. Attard)

1985 (27 Nov). Maltese Ships (3rd series). Steamships. Horiz designs as T **271**. Multicoloured. W **105**. P 14.

772	3c. *Scotia* (paddle-steamer), 1844	85	20
773	7c. *Tagliaferro* (screw steamer), 1882	1·25	75
774	15c. *Gleneagles* (screw steamer), 1885	1·75	2·75
775	23c. *L'Isle Adam* (screw steamer), 1886	2·00	3·75
772/5 *Set of 4*		5·25	6·75

(Des A. Agiuus. (8c.). T. Bugeja (11, 27c.))

1986 (28 Jan). International Peace Year. T **292** and, similar horiz designs. Multicoloured. W **105** (sideways). P 14 (8, 27c.) or 13½×14 (11c.).

776	8c. Type **292**	1·25	50
777	11c. Dove and hands holding olive branch 40×19 mm	1·50	2·50
778	27c. Map of Africa, dove and two heads	3·25	4·75
776/8 *Set of 3*		5·50	7·00

293 Symbolic Plant and *Cynthia cardui, Vanessa atalanta* and *Polyommatus icarus* (butterflies)

294 Heading the Ball

(Des M. Burló)

1986 (3 Apr). Europa. Environmental Conservation. T **293** and similar vert design. Multicoloured. W **105**. P 14.

779	8c. Type **293**	1·25	50
780	35c. Island, Neolithic frieze, sea and sun	2·25	6·00

Nos. 779/80 were each printed in sheets including two *se-tenant* stamp-size labels.

(Des T. Bugeja)

1986 (30 May). World Cup Football Championship, Mexico. T **294** and similar horiz designs. Multicoloured. W **106**. P 14.

781	3c. Type **294**	50	20
782	7c. Saving a goal	1·00	1·00
783	23c. Controlling the ball	3·50	6·50
781/3 *Set of 3*		4·50	7·00
MS784 125×90 mm. Nos. 781/3. Wmk sideways		7·00	8·50

295 Father Diegu J4

296 "Nativity"

(Des L. Micallef)

1986 (28 Aug). Maltese Philanthropists. T **295** and similar vert designs. Multicoloured. W **105**. P 14.

785	2c. Type **295**	40	30
786	3c. Adelaide Cini	50	30
787	8c. Alfonso Maria Galea	1·25	60
788	27c. Vincenzo Bugeja	3·25	6·00
785/8 *Set of 4*		5·00	6·50

(Des L. Micallef)

1986 (10 Oct). Christmas. T **296** and similar multicoloured designs showing paintings by Giuseppe D'Arena. W **105** (sideways on horiz designs). P 14.

789	2c. +1c. Type **296**	1·25	1·75
790	8c. +2c. "Nativity" (detail) (vert)	2·75	3·50
791	20c. +3c. "Epiphany"	3·75	7·00
789/91 *Set of 3*		7·00	11·00

(Des N. Attard)

1986 (19 Nov). Maltese Ships (4th series). Horiz designs as T **271**. Multicoloured. W **105**. P 14.

792	7c. *San Paul* (freighter), 1921	1·00	50
793	10c. *Knight of Malta* (mail steamer), 1930	1·25	1·75
794	12c. *Valetta City* (freighter), 1948	1·50	2·75
795	20c. *Saver* (freighter), 1959	2·25	4·50
792/5 *Set of 4*		5·50	8·50

297 European Robin

(Des R. Caruana)

1987 (26 Jan). 25th Anniv of Malta Ornithological Society. T **297** and similar multicoloured designs. W **105** (sideways on 3, 23c.). P 14.

796	3c. Type **297**	1·25	50
797	8c. Peregrine Falcon (*vert*)	2·50	1·00
798	13c. Hoopoe (*vert*)	3·25	4·00
799	23c. Cory's Shearwater	3·75	6·00
796/9 *Set of 4*		9·75	10·50

298 Aquasun Lido

299 16th-century Pikeman

(Des R. England)

1987 (15 Apr). Europa. Modern Architecture. T **298** and similar vert design. Multicoloured. W **105**. P 14.

800	8c. Type **298**	1·00	75
801	35c. Church of St. Joseph, Manikata	2·50	4·75

Nos. 800/1 were each printed in sheets including two *se-tenant* stamp-size labels.

(Des L. Micallef)

1987 (10 June). Maltese Uniforms (1st series). T **299** and similar vert designs. Multicoloured. W **105** (sideways). P 14.

802	3c. Type **299**	85	40
803	7c. 16th-century officer	1·60	90
804	10c. 18th-century standard bearer	1·75	2·25
805	27c. 18th-century General of the Galleys	3·75	4·75
802/5 *Set of 4*		7·25	7·50

See also Nos. 832/5, 851/4, 880/3 and 893/6.

300 Maltese Scenes, Wheat Ears and Sun (European Environment Year)

(Des A. Camilleri)

1987 (18 Aug). Anniversaries and Events. T **300** and similar horiz designs. Multicoloured. W **105** (sideways). P 14.

806	5c. Type **300**	1·25	50
807	8c. Esperanto star as comet (Centenary of Esperanto)	2·00	60
808	23c. Family at house door (International Year of Shelter for the Homeless)	3·00	3·00
806/8 *Set of 3*		5·50	3·75

(Des N. Attard)

1987 (16 Oct). Maltese Ships (5th series). Horiz designs as T **271**. Multicoloured. W **105**. P 14.

809	2c. *Medina* (freighter), 1969	70	60
810	11c. *Rabat* (container ship), 1974	2·50	2·50
811	13c. *Ghawdex* (passenger ferry), 1979	2·75	2·75
812	20c. *Pinto* (car ferry), 1987	3·75	4·00
809/12 *Set of 4*		8·75	9·00

301 "The Visitation"

(Des R. Caruana)

1987 (6 Nov). Christmas. T **301** and similar horiz designs, each showing illuminated illustration, score and text from 16th-century choral manuscript. Multicoloured. W **105** (sideways). P 14.

813	2c. +1c. Type **301**	50	65
814	8c. +2c. "The Nativity"	1·75	2·50
815	20c. +3c. "The Adoration of the Magi"	3·25	4·50
813/15	*Set of* 3	5·00	7·00

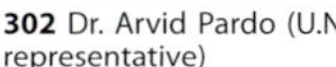

302 Dr. Arvid Pardo (U.N. representative)

303 Ven. Nazju Falzon (Catholic catechist)

(Des S. Mallia)

1987 (18 Dec). 20th Anniv of United Nations Resolution on Peaceful Use of the Seabed. T **302** and similar vert design. Multicoloured. W **105**. P 14.

816	8c. Type **302**	1·00	75
817	12c. U.N. emblem and sea	1·75	3·00
MS818	125×90 mm. Nos. 816/17. Wmk sideways. P 13×13½	3·00	4·50

(Des E. Barthet)

1988 (23 Jan). Maltese Personalities. T **303** and similar vert designs. Multicoloured. W **105**. P 14.

819	2c. Type **303**	30	30
820	3c. Mgr. Sidor Formosa (philanthropist)	30	30
821	4c. Sir Luigi Preziosi (ophthalmologist)	60	30
822	10c. Fr. Anastasju Cuschieri (poet)	80	85
823	25c. Mgr. Pietro Pawl Saydon (Bible translator)	2·00	3·25
819/23	*Set of* 5	3·50	4·50

304 "St. John Bosco with Youth" (statue) (Death Centenary)

305 Bus, Ferry and Airliner

(Des F. Portelli)

1988 (5 Mar). Religious Anniversaries. T **304** and similar vert designs. Multicoloured. W **105** (sideways). P 14.

824	10c. Type **304**	1·00	75
825	12c. "Assumption of Our Lady" (altarpiece by Perugino, Ta' Pinu, Gozo) (Marian Year)	1·25	1·25
826	14c. "Christ the King" (statue by Sciortino) (75th anniv of International Eucharistic Congress, Valletta)	1·50	2·00
824/6	*Set of* 3	3·25	3·50

(Des F. Fenech)

1988 (9 Apr). Europa. Transport and Communications. T **305** and similar vert design. Multicoloured. W **105** (sideways). P 13½.

827	10c. Type **305**	1·25	75
828	35c. Control panel, dish aerial and pylons	2·00	3·75

Nos. 827/8 were each printed in sheets including two *se-tenant* stamp-size labels.

306 Globe and Red Cross Emblems (125th anniv of International Red Cross)

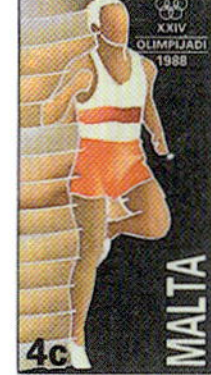

307 Athletics

(Des M. Cremona)

1988 (28 May). Anniversaries and Events. T **306** and similar horiz designs. Multicoloured. W **105**. P 13½.

829	4c. Type **306**	60	50
830	18c. Divided globe (Campaign for North South Interdependence and Solidarity)	1·50	2·50
831	19c. Globe and symbol (40th anniv of World Health Organization)	1·50	2·50
829/31	*Set of* 3	3·25	5·00

(Des L. Micallef)

1988 (23 July). Maltese Uniforms (2nd issue). Vert designs as T **299**. Multicoloured. W **105** (sideways). P 14.

832	3c. Private, Maltese Light Infantry, 1800	50	30
833	4c. Gunner, Malta Coast Artillery, 1802	55	35
834	10c. Field Officer, 1st Maltese Provincial Battalion, 1805	1·40	1·25
835	25c. Subaltern, Royal Malta Regiment, 1809	2·75	4·25
832/5	*Set of* 4	4·75	5·50

(Des R. Gauci)

1988 (17 Sept). Olympic Games, Seoul. T **307** and similar vert designs. Multicoloured. W **105** (sideways). P 14×13½.

836	4c. Type **307**	30	30
837	10c. Diving	70	80
838	35c. Basketball	2·00	3·00
836/8	*Set of* 3	2·75	3·75

308 Shepherd with Flock

309 Commonwealth Emblem

(Des R. Gauci)

1988 (5 Nov). Christmas. T **308** and similar vert designs. Multicoloured. W **105**. P 14.

839	3c. +1c. Type **308**	30	30
840	10c. +2c. The Nativity	75	1·00
841	25c. +3c. Three Wise Men	1·75	2·50
839/41	*Set of* 3	2·50	3·50

(Des F. Portelli)

1989 (28 Jan). 25th Anniv of Independence. T **309** and similar multicoloured designs. W **105** (sideways). P 14 (25c.) or 13½ (others).

842	2c. Type **309**	25	35
843	3c. Council of Europe flag	25	35
844	4c. U.N. flag	30	35
845	10c. Workers hands gripping ring and national flag	75	95
846	12c. Scales and allegorical figure of Justice	90	1·40
847	25c. Prime Minister Borg Olivier with Independence constitution (42×28 mm)	1·90	3·25
842/7	*Set of* 6	4·00	6·00

310 New State Arms

311 Two Boys flying Kite

(Des F. Portelli)

1989 (25 Mar). W **105**. P 14.

848 **310** £1 multicoloured .... 4·00 4·50

(Des R. Gauci)

1989 (6 May). Europa. Children's Games. T **311** and similar vert design. Multicoloured. W **105** (sideways). P 13½.

849 10c. Type **311** .... 1·00 75
850 35c. Two girls with dolls .... 2·50 4·50

Nos. 849/50 were each printed in sheets including two *se-tenant* stamp-size labels.

(Des L. Micallef)

1989 (24 June). Maltese Uniforms (3rd series). Vert designs as T **299**. Multicoloured. W **105** (sideways). P 14.

851 3c. Officer, Maltese Veterans, 1815 .... 45 45
852 4c. Subaltern, Royal Malta Fencibles, 1839 .. 50 50
853 10c. Private, alta Militia, 1856 .... 1·50 1·50
854 25c. Colonel, Royal Malta Fencible Artillery, 1875 .... 2·75 3·75
851/4 *Set of 4* .... 4·75 5·50

312 Human Figures and Buildings

313 Angel and Cherub

(Des L. Casha)

1989 (17 Oct). Anniversaries and Commemorations. T **312** and similar horiz designs showing logo and stylized human figures. Multicoloured. W **105** (sideways). P 14.

855 3c. Type **312** (20th anniv of U.N. Declaration on Social Progress and Development) 30 30
856 4c. Workers and figure in wheelchair (Malta's Ratification of European Social Charter) 35 35
857 10c. Family (40th anniv of Council of Europe) .... 80 1·25
858 14c. Teacher and children (70th anniv of Malta Union of Teachers) .... 1·00 1·75
859 25c. Symbolic knights (Knights of the Sovereign Military Order of Malta Assembly) .... 2·25 3·50
855/9 *Set of 5* .... 4·25 6·50

(Des J. Mallia)

1989 (11 Nov). Christmas. T **313** and similar horiz designs showing vault paintings by Mattia Preti from St. John's Co-Cathedral. Valletta. Multicoloured. W **105**. P 13½.

860 3c. +1c.Type **313** 60 60
861 10c. +2c. Two angels .... 1·40 1·90
862 20c. +3c.Angel blowing trumpet .... 2·00 4·00
860/62 *Set of 3* .... 3·50 6·00

314 Presidents George H. Bush and Mikhail Gorbachev

315 General Post Office, Auberge d'Italie, Valletta

1989 (2 Dec). U.S.A.-U.S.S.R. Summit Meeting, Malta. W **105**. P 14.

863 **314** 10c. multicoloured .... 1·00 1·25

(Des R. Caruana)

1990 (9 Feb). Europa. Post Office Buildings. T **315** and similar multicoloured design. W **105** (sideways on 10c.). P 14.

864 10c. Type **315** .... 1·00 50
865 35c. Branch Post Office, Zebbug (*horiz*) .... 2·00 3·75

Nos. 864/5 were each printed in sheets including two *se-tenant* stamp-size labels.

316 Open Book and Letters from Different Alphabets (International Literacy Year)

317 Samuel Taylor Coleridge (poet) and Government House

(Des T. Bugeja)

1990 (7 Apr). Anniversaries and Events. T **316** and similar multicoloured designs. W **105** (sideways on 4, 19c.). P 14.

866 3c. Type **316** 25 25
867 4c. Count Roger of Sicily and Norman soldiers (900th anniv of Sicilian rule) (*horiz*) 60 30
868 19c. Communications satellite (25th anniv of International Telecommunication Union membership) (*horiz*) .... 2·25 2·50
869 20c. Football and map of Malta (Union of European Football Associations 20th Ordinary Congress, Malta) .... 2·25 2·50
866/9 *Set of 4* .... 4·75 5·00

(Des A. Grech)

1990 (3 May). British Authors. T **317** and similar horiz designs. Multicoloured. W **105** (sideways). P 13½.

870 4c. Type **317** 50 30
871 10c. Lord Byron (poet) and map of Valletta ... 90 70
872 12c. Sir Walter Scott (novelist) and Great Siega .... 1·00 95
873 25c. William Makepeace Thackeray (novelist) and Naval Arsenal .... 2·00 2·25
870/3 *Set of 4* .... 4·00 3·75

318 St. Paul

319 Flags and Football

(Des N. Bason)

1990 (25 May). Visit of Pope John Paul II. T **318** and similar vert design showing bronze bas-reliefs. W **105** (sideways). P 14.

874 4c. brownish black, flesh and carmine .... 50 1·50
a. Pair. Nos. 874/5 .... 2·00 3·25
875 25c. brownish black, flesh and carmine .... 1·50 1·75

Design:—25 c. Pope John Paul II.

Nos. 874/5 were printed together in a sheet of 12 (4×3) containing 10 stamps, *se-tenant* horizontally or vertically, and two stamp-size labels on R. 2/1 and 2/4.

(Des T. Bugeja)

1990 (8 June). World Cup Football Championship, Italy. T **319** and similar horiz designs. Multicoloured. W **105**. P 14.

876 5c. Type **319** 35 30
877 10c. Football in net .... 65 1·00
878 14c. Scoreboard and football .... 1·00 1·75
876/8 *Set of 3* .... 1·75 2·75
MS879 123×90 mm. Nos. 876/8. Wmk sideways .... 3·00 4·25

(Des L. Micallef)

1990 (25 Aug). Maltese Uniforms (4th series). Vert designs as T **299**. Multicoloured. W **105** (sideways). P 14.

880		3c. Captain, Royal Malta Militia, 1889	1·25	55
881		4c. Field officer, Royal Malta Artillery, 1905	1·40	60
882		10c. Labourer, Malta Labour Corps, 1915	2·50	1·50
883		25c. Lieutenant, King's Own Malta Regiment of Militia, 1918	3·75	4·50
880/3		*Set of* 4	8·00	6·50

320 Innkeeper

321 1919 10s. Stamp under Magnifying Glass

(Des J. Smith)

1990 (10 Nov). Christmas. Figures from Crib by Austin Galea, Marco Bartolo and Rosario Zammit. T **320** and similar multicoloured designs. W **105** (sideways). P 14×14½ (10c.) or 13½×14 (others).

884		3c. +1c. Type 320	30	50
885		10c. +2c. Nativity (41×28 mm)	70	1·25
886		25c. +3c. Shepherd with sheep	1·60	2·50
384/6		*Set of* 3	2·40	3·75

(Des J. Mallia)

1991 (6 Mar). 25th Anniv of Philatelic Society of Malta. W **105** (sideways). P 14.

887	**321**	10c. multicoloured	60	70

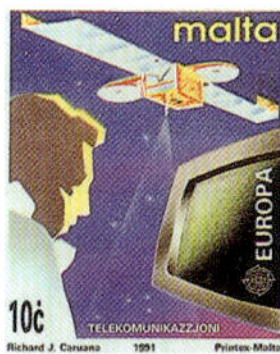

322 "Eurostar" Satellite and V.D.U. Screen

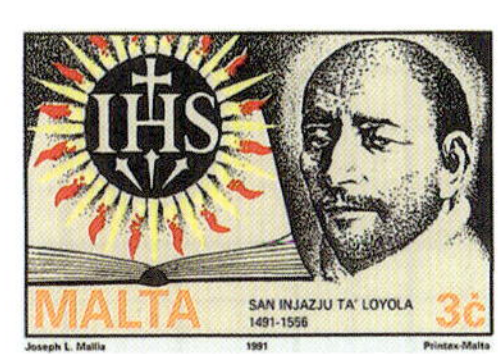

323 St. Ignatius Loyola (founder of Jesuits) (500th birth anniv)

(Des R. Caruana)

1991 (16 Mar). Europa. Europe in Space. T **322** and similar vert design. Multicoloured. W **105** (sideways). P 14.

888		10c. Type **322**	1·00	70
889		35c. "Ariane 4" rocket and projected HOTOL aerospaceplane	1·75	2·75

Nos. 888/9 were each printed in sheets including two *se-tenant* stamp-size labels.

(Des J. Mallia)

1991 (29 Apr). Religious Commemorations. T **323** and similar multicoloured designs. W **105** (sideways on 3,30c.). P 14.

890		3c. Type **323**	30	20
891		4c. Abbess Venerable Maria Adeodata Pisani (185th birth anniv) (*vert*)	35	25
892		30c. St. John of the Cross (400th death anniv)	2·00	2·75
890/2		*Set of* 3	2·40	3·00

(Des L. Micallef)

1991 (13 Aug). Maltese Uniforms (5th series). Vert designs as T **299**. Multicoloured. W **105** (sideways). P 14.

893		3c. Officer with colour, Royal Malta Fencibles, 1860	50	25
894		10c. Officer with colour, Royal Malta Regment of Militia, 1903	1·00	60
895		19c. Officer with Queen's colour, King's Own Malta Regiment, 1968	1·90	1·75
896		25c. Officer with colour, Malta Armed Forces, 1991	2·25	2·00
893/6		*Set of* 4	5·00	4·25

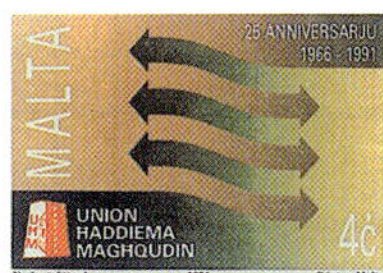

324 Interlocking Arrows

325 Honey Buzzard

(Des N. Attard)

1991 (23 Sept). 25th Anniv of Union Haddiema Maghqudin (public services union). W **105** (sideways). P 13½.

897	**324**	4c. multicoloured	30	30

(Des H. Borg)

1991 (3 Oct). Endangered Species. Birds. T **325** and similar vert designs. Multicoloured. W **105**. P 14.

898		4c. Type **325**	2·50	2·50
		a. Horiz strip of 4. Nos. 898/901	9·00	9·00
899		4c. Marsh Harrier	2·50	2·50
900		10c. Eleonora's Falcon	2·50	2·50
901		10c. Lesser Kestrel	2·50	2·50
898/901		*Set of* 4	9·00	9·00

Nos. 898/901 were printed together, *se-tenant*, in horizontal strips of 4 throughout the sheet.

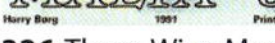

326 Three Wise Men

327 Ta' Hagrat Neolithic Temple

(Des H. Borg)

1991 (6 Nov). Christmas. T **326** and similar vert designs. Multicoloured. W **105**. P 14.

902		3c. +1c. Type 326	55	50
903		10c. +2c. Holy Family	1·25	1·40
904		25c. +3c. Two shepherds	2·25	3·25
902/4		*Set of* 3	3·75	4·75

(Des F. Portelli)

1991 (9 Dec). National Heritage of the Maltese Islands. T **327** and similar multicoloured designs. W **105** (sideways on £2). P 13½.

905		1c. Type **327**	35	50
906		2c. Cottoner Gate	35	50
907		3c. St. Michael's Bastion, Valletta	35	50
908		4c. Spinola Palace, St. Julian's	40	15
909		5c. Birkirkara Church	50	20
910		10c. Mellieha Bay	90	35
911		12c. Wied iz-Zurrieq	1·25	40
912		14c. Mgarr harbour, Gaza	1·50	45
913		20c. Yacht marina	2·00	65
914		50c. Gaza Channel	3·25	1·60
915		£1 "Arab Horses" (sculpture by Antonio Sciortino)	5·50	3·25
916		£2 Independence Monument (Ganni Bonnici) (vert)	10·00	8·00
905/16		*Set of* 12	24·00	15·00

328 Aircraft Tailfins and Terminal

(Des. H. Borg)

1992 (8 Feb). Opening of International Air Terminal. T **328** and similar horiz design. W **105** (sideways). P 14.

917	4c. Type **328**	75	30
918	10c. National flags and terminal	1·25	70

329 Ships of Columbus

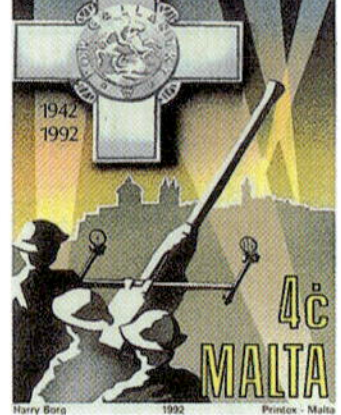

330 George Cross and Anti-aircraft Gun Crew

(Des H. Borg)

1992 (20 Feb). Europa. 500th Anniv of discovery of America by Columbus. T **329** and similar horiz design. W **105** (sideways). P 14.

919	10c. Type **329**	1·25	55
920	35c. Columbus and map of Americas	2·50	2·25

Nos. 919/20 were each printed in sheets including two *se-tenant* stamp-size labels.

(Des H. Borg)

1992 (15 Apr). 50th Anniv of Award of George Cross to Malta. T **330** and similar vert designs. Multicoloured. W **105**. P 14.

921	4c. Type **330**	1·00	30
922	10c. George Cross and memorial bell	1·50	1·00
923	50c. Tanker *Ohio* entering Grand Harbour	7·00	8·50
921/3	*Set of 3*	8·50	9·00

331 Running

332 Church of the Flight into Egypt

(Des H. Borg)

1992 (24 June). Olympic Games, Barcelona. T **331** and similar horiz designs. Multicoloured. W **105** (sideways). P 14.

924	3c. Type **331**	65	20
925	10c. High jumping	1·25	1·00
926	30c. Swimming	2·50	4·50
924/6	*Set of 3*	4·00	5·25

(Des N. Attard)

1992 (5 Aug). Rehabilitation of Historical Buildings. T **332** and similar designs. W **105** (sideways on 4, 25c.). P 14.

927	3c. black, pale stone and bluish grey	55	30
928	4c. black, pale stone and flesh	60	30
929	19c. black, pale stone and pale rose-lilac	2·75	3·75
930	25c. black, pale stone and pale grey-olive	3·00	3·75
927/30	*Set of 4*	6·25	7·25

Designs: *Horiz*—4c. St. John's Co-Cathedral; 25c. Auberge de Provence. *Vert*—19c. Church of Madonna del Pillar.

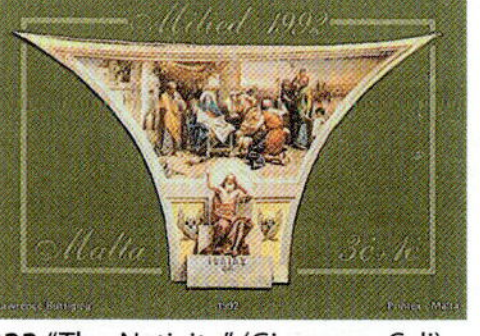

333 "The Nativity" (Giuseppe Cali)

334 Malta College Building, Valletta

(Des L. Buttigieg)

1992 (22 Oct). Christmas. Religious Paintings by Giuseppe Cali from Mosta Church. T **333** and similar horiz designs. Multicoloured. W **105** (sideways). P 14.

931	3c. +1c. Type **333**	1·00	1·10
932	10c. +2c. "Adoration of the Magi"	2·25	2·50
933	25c. +3c. "Christ with the Elders in the Temple"	3·75	4·50
931/3	*Set of 3*	6·25	7·25

(Des L. Buttigieg)

1992 (12 Nov). 400th Anniv of University of Malta. T **334** and similar multicoloured design. W **105** (sideways on 30c.). P 14.

934	4c. Type **334**	75	25
935	30c. Modern University complex,Tal-Qroqq (*horiz*)	2·75	4·25

335 Lions Club Emblem

336 Untitled Painting by Paul Carbonaro

(Des H. Borg)

1993 (4 Feb). 75th Anniv of International Association of Lions Club. T **335** and similar horiz design. Multicoloured. W **105**. P 13½.

936	4c. Type **335**	50	25
937	50c. Eye (Sight First Campaign)	2·75	4·00

1993 (7 Apr). Europa. Contemporary Art. T **336** and similar multicoloured design. W **105** (sideways on 35c.). P 14.

938	10c. Type **336**	1·25	50
939	35c. Untitled painting by Alfred Chircop (*horiz*)	3·00	5·00

Nos. 938/9 were each printed in sheets including two stamp-size labels.

337 Mascot holding Flame

338 Learning First Aid

(Des R. Caruana)

1993 (4 May). 5th Small States of Europe Games. T **337** and similar horiz designs. Multicoloured. W **105**. P 13½×14.

940	3c. Type **337**	20	20
941	4c. Cycling	1·75	30
942	10c. Tennis	1·50	1·00
943	35c. Yachting	2·75	3·50
940/3	*Set of 4*	5·50	4·50
MS944	120×80 mm. Nos. 940/3. Wmk sideways	5·50	5·50

(Des L. Micallef)

1993 (21 July). 50th Anniv of Award of Bronze Cross to Maltese Scouts and Guides. T **338** and similar vert designs. Multicoloured. W **105**. P 14.

945	3c. Type **338**	50	20
946	4c. Bronze Cross	50	20
947	10c. Scout building camp fire	1·10	90
948	35c. Governor Lord Gort presenting Bronze Cross, 1943	2·75	4·00
945/8	*Set of 4*	4·25	4·75

339 *Papilio machaon*

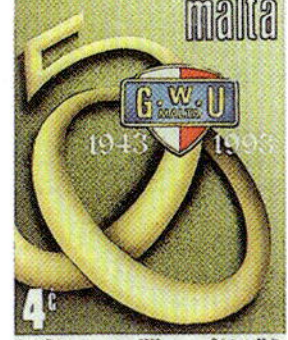

340 G.W.U. Badge and Interlocking "50"

(Des M. Burlo)

1993 (23 Sept). European Year of the Elderly. Butterflies. T **339** and similar vert design. Multicoloured. W **105**. P 14.

949	5c. Type **339**	35	20
950	35c. *Vanessa atalanta*	1·75	2·25

(Des H. Borg)

1993 (5 Oct). 50th Anniv of General Workers Union. W **105** (sideways). P 13½.

951	**340**	4c. multicoloured	35	40

341 Child Jesus and Star

(Des H. Borg)

1993 (5 Nov). Christmas. T **341** and similar vert designs. Multicoloured. W **105**. P 14.

952	3c. +1c. Type **341**	30	35
953	10c. +2c. Christmas tree	85	1·25
954	25c. +3c. Star in traditional window	1·60	2·75
952/4 *Set of 3*		2·50	4·00

342 Council Arms (face value top left)

(Des J. Mizzi)

1993 (20 Nov). Inauguration of Local Community Councils. Sheet 110×93 mm. containing T **342** and similar horiz designs showing different Council Arms. Multicoloured. W **105** (sideways). P 14.

MS955 5c. Type **342** 5c. Face value top right; 5c. Face value bottom left; 5c. Face value bottom right ... 1·50 2·25

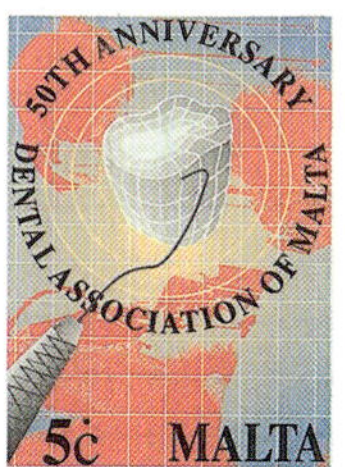

343 Symbolic Tooth and Probe

344 Sir Themistocles Zammit (discoverer of Brucella microbe)

(Des F. Ancilleri)

1994 (12 Feb). 50th Anniv of Maltese Dental Association. T **343** and similar vert design. Multicoloured. W **105**. P 14.

956	5c. Type **343**	35	30
957	44c. Symbolic mouth and dental mirror	3·00	3·00

(Des H. Borg)

1994 (29 Mar). Europa. Discoveries. T **344** and similar vert design. Multicoloured. W **105**. P 14.

958	14c. Type **344**	50	30
959	30c. Bilingually inscribed candelabrum of 2nd century B.C. (deciphering of ancient Phoenician language)	1·90	3·25

Nos. 958/9 were each printed in sheets including two *se-tenant* stamp-size labels.

345 Family in Silhouette (International Year of the Family)

346 Football and Map

(Des F. Ancilleri)

1994 (10 May). Anniversaries and Events. T **345** and similar multicoloured designs. W **105** (sideways on 25c.). P 14.

960	5c. Type **345**	30	20
961	9c. Stylised Red Cross (International Recognition of Malta Red Cross Society)	60	50
962	14c. Animals and crops (150th anniv of Agrarian Society)	90	80
963	20c. Worker in silhouette (75th anniv of International Labour Organization)	1·25	1·60
964	25c. St. Paul's Anglican Cathedral (155th anniv) (*vert*)	1·40	1·75
960/4 *Set of 5*		4·00	4·25

(Des F. Ancilleri)

1994 (9 June). World Cup Football Championship, U.S.A. T **346** and similar horiz designs. Multicoloured. W **105**. P 14.

965	5c. Type **346**	40	20
966	14c. Ball and goal	1·00	80
967	30c. Ball and pitch superimposed on map	2·00	4·25
965/7 *Set of 3*		3·00	4·75
MS968 123×88 mm. Nos. 965/7. Wmk sideways		3·75	4·50

347 Falcon Trophy, Twin Comanche and Auster (25th anniv of Malta International Rally)

348 National Flags and Astronaut on Moon

(Des R. Caruana)

1994 (2 July). Aviation Anniversaries and Events. T **347** and similar horiz designs. Multicoloured. W **105** (sideways). P 14.

969	5c. Type 347	50	20
970	14c. Alouette helicopter, display teams and logo (Malta International Airshow)	1·75	85
971	20c. De Havilland Dove *City of Valetta* and Avro York aircraft with logo (50th anniv of International Civil Aviation Organization)	1·90	1·75
972	25c. Airbus 320 *Nicolas Cottoner* and De Havilland Comet aircraft with logo (50th anniv of I.C.A.O.)	1·90	1·90
969/72 *Set of 4*		5·50	4·25

After printing it was found that all examples of the 20c. were inscribed "Anniverarju" in error. These were withdrawn before issue and replaced by stock showing the word correctly spelt as "Anniversarju". It is reported that all sheets of the incorrect printing were destroyed.

(Des R. Caruana)

1994 (20 July). 25th Anniv of First Moon Landing. W **105**. P 14.

973	**348**	14c. multicoloured	1·10	1·25

349 Virgin Mary and Child with Angels

350 Helmet-shaped Ewer

(Des H. Borg)

1994 (26 Oct). Christmas. T **349** and similar multicoloured designs. W **105** (sideways on 5c.). P 13½ (5c.) or 14 (others).

974	5c. Type **349**	25	10
975	9c. +2c. Angel in pink (*vert*)	65	70
976	14c. +3c. Virgin Mary and Child (*vert*)	90	1·25
977	20c. +3c. Angel in green (*vert*)	1·60	2·50
974/7	*Set of* 4	3·00	4·00

Nos. 975/7 are larger, 28×41 mm, and depict details from Type **349**.

(Des M. Burlo)

1994 (12 Dec). Maltese Antique Silver Exhibition. T **350** and similar vert designs. Multicoloured. W **105**. P 14.

978	5c. Type **350**	50	20
979	14c. Balsamina	1·10	80
980	20c. Coffee pot	1·50	2·00
981	25c. Sugar box	1·75	2·75
978/81	*Set of* 4	4·25	5·25

351 "60 plus" and Hands touching

352 Hand holding Leaf and Rainbow

(Des Anna Grima)

1995 (27 Feb). Anniversaries and Events. T **351** and similar vert designs. Multicoloured. W **105** (sideways). P 14.

982	2c. Type **351** (25th anniv of National Association of Pensioners)	15	15
983	5c. Child's drawing (10th anniv of National Youth Council)	25	20
984	14c. Conference emblem (4th World Conference on Women, Peking, China)	70	80
985	20c. Nurse and thermometer (50th anniv of Malta Memorial District Nursing Association)	1·25	1·40
986	25c. Louis Pasteur (biologist) (death centenary)	1·50	1·75
982/6	*Set of* 5	3·50	3·75

(Des Harry Borg)

1995 (29 Mar). Europa. Peace and Freedom. T **352** and similar multicoloured design. W **105** (sideways on 30c.). P 14.

987	14c. Type **352**	1·00	55
988	30c. Peace doves (*horiz*)	1·50	2·50

Nos. 987/8 were each printed in sheets including two stamp-size labels.

353 Junkers Ju 87B "Stuka" Dive Bombers over Valletta and Anti-aircraft Gun

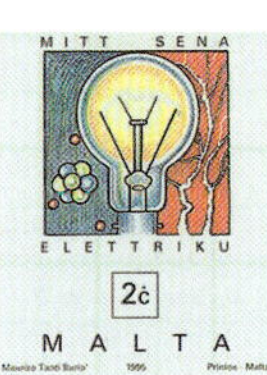

354 Light Bulb

(Des Frank Ancilleri)

1995 (21 Apr). Anniversaries. T **353** and similar multicoloured designs. W **105** (sideways on horiz designs). P 14.

989	5c. Type **353** (50th anniv of end of Second World War)	25	25
990	14c. Silhouetted people holding hands (50th anniv of United Nations)	55	60
991	35c. Hands holding bowl of wheat (50th anniv of Food and Agriculture Organization) (*vert*)	1·60	2·25
989/91	*Set of* 3	2·25	2·75

(Des Maurice Tanti Burlo)

1995 (15 June). Maltese Electricity and Telecommunications. T **354** and similar vert designs. Multicoloured. W **105** (sideways). P 13½.

992	2c. Type **354**	15	15
993	5c. Symbolic owl and binary codes	25	25
994	9c. Dish aerial	45	50
995	14c. Sun and rainbow over trees	70	80
996	20c. Early telephone, satellite and Moon's surface	1·25	1·50
992/6	*Set of* 5	2·50	2·75

355 Rock Wall and Girna

356 Pinto's Turret Clock

(Des Maurice Tanti Burlo)

1995 (26 July). European Nature Conservation Year. T **355** and similar horiz designs. W **105** (sideways). P 14.

997	5c. Type 355	75	25
998	14c. Maltese Wall Lizards	2·25	80
999	44c. Aleppo Pine	3·50	3·00
997/9	*Set of* 3	5·75	3·50

(Des Frank Ancilleri)

1995 (5 Oct). Treasures of Malta. Antique Maltese Clocks. T **356** and similar vert designs. Multicoloured. W **105**. P 14.

1000	1c. Type **356**	15	60
1001	5c. Michelangelo Sapiano (horologist) and clocks	50	25
1002	14c. Arlogg tal-lira clock	1·50	80
1003	25c. Sundials	2·50	3·50
1000/3	*Set of* 4	4·25	4·75

357 Children's Christmas Eve Procession

(Des Harry Borg)

1995 (15 Nov). Christmas. T **357** and simlar multicoloured designs. W **105** (sideways on 5c.). P 14×13½.

1004	5c. Type **357**	25	10
1005	5c. +2c. Children with crib (*vert*)	30	50
1006	14c. +3c. Children with lanterns (*vert*)	1·00	1·25
1007	25c. +3c. Boy with lantern and balus-trade (*vert*)	1·75	2·75
1004/7	*Set of* 4	3·00	4·25

Nos. 1005/7 are 27×32 mm and depict details from Type **357**.

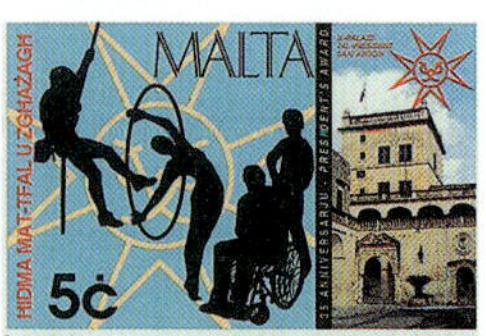

358 Silhouetted Children and President's Palace, San Anton

(Des Frank Ancilleri)

1996 (29 Feb). Anniversaries. T **358** and similar horiz designs. Multicoloured. W **105** (sideways). P 14.

1008	5c. Type **358** (35th anniv of the President's Award)	25	25
1009	14c. Father Nazzareno Camilleri and St. Patrick's Church, Salesjani (90th birth anniv)	65	65
1010	20c. St. Mary Euphrasia and convent (Birth bicentenary)	1·00	1·10
1011	25c. Silhouetted children and fountain (50th anniv of U.N.I.C.E.F.)	1·25	1·40
1008/11	*Set of 4*	2·75	3·00

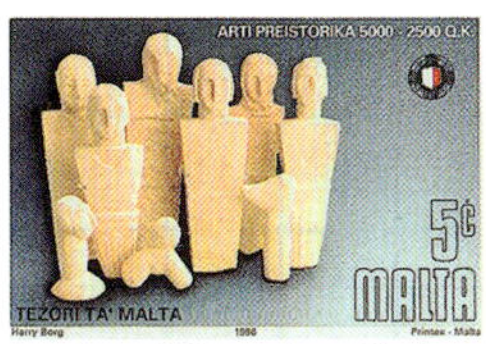

359 Carved Figures from Skorba

360 Mabel Strickland (politician and journalist)

(Des Harry Borg)

1996 (29 Mar). Maltese Prehistoric Art Exhibition. T **359** and similar multicoloured designs. W **105** (sideways on horiz designs). P 14.

1012	5c. Type **359**	30	20
1013	14c. Temple carving, Gozo	80	85
1014	20c. Carved figure of a woman, Skorba (*vert*)	1·10	1·25
1015	35c. Ghar Dalam pot (*vert*)	1·90	2·50
1012/15	*Set of 4*	3·75	4·25

(Des Catherine Cavallo)

1996 (24 Apr). Europa. Famous Women. T **360** and similar vert design. Multicoloured. W **105**. P 14.

1016	14c. Type **360**	75	55
1017	30c. Inez Sole, (artist, musician and writer)	2·00	2·00

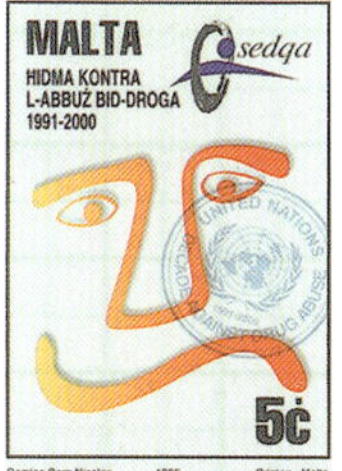

361 Face and Emblem (United Nations Decade against Drug Abuse)

362 Judo

(Des Damian Borg Nicolas)

1996 (5 June). Anniversaries and Events. T **361** and similar vert designs. Multicoloured. W **105**. P 14.

1018	5c. Type **361**	25	25
1019	5c. "Fi" and emblem (50th anniv of Malta Federation of Industry)	25	25
1020	14c. Commemorative plaque and national flag (75th anniv of Self-government)	80	80
1021	44c. Guglielmo Marconi and early radio equipment (Centenary of radio)	2·25	2·50
1018/21	*Set of 4*	3·25	3·50

(Des Luciano Micallef)

1996 (10 July). Olympic Games Atlanta. T **362** and similar horiz designs. Multicoloured. W **105** (sideways). P 14.

1022	2c. Type **362**	10	10
1023	5c. Athletics	30	25
1024	14c. Diving	80	80
1025	25c. Rifle-shooting	1·40	1·60
1022/5	*Set of 4*	2·40	2·50

363 "Harvest Time" (Cali)

(Des Debbie Caruana Dingli)

1996 (22 Aug). 150th Birth Anniv of Guiseppe Cali (painter). T **363** and similar multicoloured designs. W **105** (sideways on 5, 14c.). P 14.

1026	5c. Type **363**	30	25
1027	14c. "Dog" (Cali)	70	70
1028	20c. "Countrywoman in a Field" (Cali) (*vert*)	90	1·10
1029	25c. "Cali at his Easel" (Edward Dingli) (*vert*)	1·00	1·25
1026/9	*Set of 4*	2·50	3·00

364 Bus No. 1990 *Diamond Star*, 1920s

(Des Richard J. Caruana)

1996 (26 Sept). Buses. T **364** and similar horiz designs. Multicoloured. W **105** (sideways). P 14.

1030	2c. Type **364**	40	10
1031	5c. No. 434 *Tom Mix*, 1930s	70	25
1032	14c. No. 1764 *Verdala*, 1940s	1·40	80
1033	30c. No. 3495, 1960s	2·00	2·00
1030/3	*Set of 4*	4·00	2·75

365 Stained Glass Window

(Des Harry Borg)

1996 (17 Nov). Christmas. T **365** and similar multicoloured designs. W **105** (sideways on 5c.). P 14×13½.

1034	5c. Type **365**	35	10
1035	5c. +2c. Madonna and Child (29×35 mm)	40	60
1036	14c. +3c. Angel facing right (29×35 mm)	80	1·40
1037	25c. +3c. Angel facing left (29×35 mm)	1·25	2·50
1034/7	*Set of 4*	2·50	4·25

Nos. 1035/7 show details from Type **365**.

366 Hompesch Arch and Arms, Zabbar

367 Captain-General of the Galleys' Sedan Chair

(Des Richard Caruana)

1997 (20 Feb). Bicentenary of Maltese Cities. T **366** and similar vert designs. Multicoloured. W **105**. P 14.

1038	6c. Type **366**	30	25
1039	16c. Statue, church and arms, Siggiewi	70	70
1040	26c. Seated statue and arms, Zejtun	1·10	1·25
1038/40	*Set of 3*	1·90	3·75
MS1041	125×90 mm. As Nos. 1038/40. Wmk sideways.	5·50	4·50

1997 (11 Apr). Treasures of Malta. Sedan Chairs. T **367** and similar multicoloured designs. W **105** (sideways on horiz designs). P 14.

1042	2c. Type **367**	15	15
1043	6c. Cotoner Grandmasters' chair	30	30
1044	16c. Chair from Cathedral Museum, Mdina (*vert*)	70	70
1045	27c. Chevalier D'Arezzo's chair (*vert*)	1·10	1·10
1042/5	*Set of* 4	2·00	2·00

368 Gahan carrying Door

369 Modern Sculpture (Antonio Sciortino)

(Des J. Mallia)

1997 (5 May). Europa. Tales and Legends. T **368** and similar vert design. Multicoloured. W **105** (sideways). P 14.

1046	16c. Type **368**	1·00	75
1047	35c. St. Dimitrius appearing from painting	1·75	2·50

Nos. 1046/7 were each printed in sheets of 10 and two stamp-size labels.

1997 (10 July). Anniversaries. T **369** and similar multicoloured designs. W **105** (sideways on horiz designs). P 14.

1048	1c. Type 369	10	15
1049	6c. Joseph Calleia and film reel (*horiz*)	40	40
1050	6c. Gozo Cathedral (*horiz*)	40	40
1051	11c. City of Gozo (*horiz*)	60	50
1052	16c. Sculpture of head (Sciortino)	80	70
1053	22c. Joseph Calleia and film camera (*horiz*)	1·00	1·00
1048/53	*Set of* 6	3·00	2·75

Anniversaries; 1c., 16c. 50th death anniv of Antonio Sciortino (sculptor); 6c. (No. 1049), 22c., Birth centenary of Joseph Calleia (actor); 6c. (No. 1050), 11c. 300th anniv of construction of Gozo Cathedral.

370 Dr. Albert Laferla

371 The Nativity

(Des Debbie Caruana Dingli)

1997 (24 Sept). Pioneers of Education. T **370** and similar vert designs. Multicoloured. W **105**. P 14.

1054	6c. Type **370**	30	25
1055	16c. Sister Emilie de Vialar	70	70
1056	19c. Mgr. Paolo Pullicino	80	80
1057	26c. Mgr. Tommaso Gargallo	1·00	1·10
1054/7	*Set of* 4	2·50	2·50

(Des Harry Borg)

1997 (12 Nov). Christmas. T **371** and similar multicoloured designs. W **105** (sideways on 6c.). P 14.

1058	6c. Type **371**	30	10
1059	6c. +2c. Mary and baby Jesus (*vert*)	35	50
1060	16c. +3c. Joseph with donkey (*vert*)	1·00	1·40
1061	26c. +3c. Shepherd with lamb (*vert*)	1·50	2·50
1058/61	*Set of* 4	2·75	4·00

Nos. 1059/61 show details from Type **371**.

372 Plan of Fort and Soldiers in Victoria Lines

373 "Maria Amelia Grognet" (Antoine de Favray)

1997 (5 Dec). Anniversaries. T **372** and similar horiz designs. Multicoloured (except 6c.). W **105** (sideways). P 14.

1062	2c. Type **372**	20	10
1063	6c. Sir Paul Boffa making speech (black and scarlet)	30	25
1064	16c. Plan of fort and gun crew	90	65
1065	37c. Queue of voters	1·50	2·00
1062/5	*Set of* 4	2·50	2·75

Anniversaries; 2c. 16c. Centenary of Victoria Lines; 6c., 37c. 50th anniv of 1947 Self-Government Constitution.

(Des Frank Ancilleri)

1998 (26 Feb). Treasures of Malta. Costumes and Paintings. T **373** and similar vert designs. W **105**. P 14.

1066	6c. Type **373**	80	50
1067	6c. Gentleman's waistcoat, *c.* 1790—1810	80	50
1068	16c. Lady's dinner dress, *c.* 1880	1·10	90
1069	16c. "Veneranda, Baroness Abela, and her Grandson" (De Favray)	1·10	90
1066/9	*Set of* 4	3·50	2·50
MS1070	123×88 mm. 26c. City of Valletta from old print (39×47 mm). Wmk sideways. P 13×13½	1·60	1·60

374 Grand Master Ferdinand yon Hompesch

375 Racing Two-man Luzzus

(Des Joseph Mizzi)

1998 (28 Mar). Bicentenary of Napoleon's Capture of Malta. T **374** and similar horiz designs. Multicoloured. W **51** (sideways). P 14.

1071	6c. Type **374**	60	80
	a. Vert pair. Nos. 1071/2	1·10	1·60
1072	6c. French fleet	60	80
1073	16c. French landing	1·10	1·60
	a. Vert pair. Nos. 1073/4	2·10	3·00
1074	16c. General Napoleon Bonaparte	1·10	1·60
1071/4	*Set of* 4	3·00	4·25

Nos. 1071/2 and 1073/4 were each printed together, *se-tenant*, in horizontal pairs throughout the sheets.

(Des Frank Ancilleri and Richard Caruana)

1998 (22 Apr). Europa. Sailing Regatta, Grand Harbour. T **375** and similar horiz design. Multicoloured. W **51**. P 14.

1075	16c. Type **375**	1·10	55
1076	35c. Racing four-man luzzus	1·50	2·50

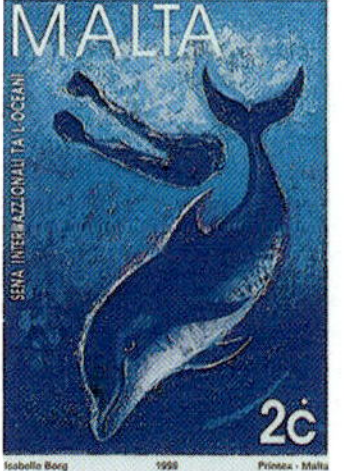

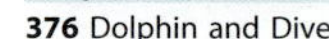

376 Dolphin and Diver

377 Goalkeeper saving Goal

(Des Isabelle Borg)

1998 (27 May). International Year of the Ocean. T **376** and similar multicoloured designs. W **105** (sideways on 16 and 27c.). P 14.

1077	2c. Type **376**	40	25
1078	6c. Diver and sea-urchin	65	25
1079	16c. Jacques Cousteau and diver (*horiz*)	1·60	80
1080	27c. Two divers (*horiz*)	2·00	2·25
1077/80 *Set of 4*		4·25	3·25

(Des Richard Caruana)

1998 (10 June). World Cup Football Championship, France. T **377** and similar horiz designs showing players and flags. Multicoloured. W **105**. P 14.

1081	6c. Type **377**	70	25
1082	16c. Two players and referee	1·40	70
1083	22c. Two footballers	1·60	2·00
1081/3 *Set of 3*		3·25	2·75
MS1084	122×87 mm. Nos. 1081/3. Wmk sideways	3·50	3·25

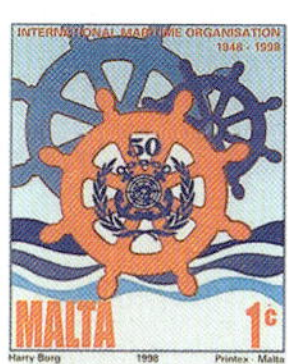

378 Ships' Wheels (50th anniv of Int Maritime Organization)

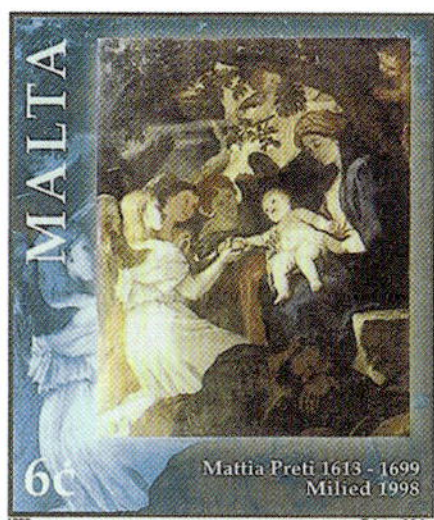

379 "Rest on the Flight to Egypt"

(Des Harry Borg)

1998 (17 Sept). Anniversaries. T **378** and similar horiz designs. Multicoloured. W **105** (sideways). P 14.

1085	1c. Type **378**	10	30
1086	6c. Symbolic family (50th anniv of Universal Declaration of Human Rights)	40	25
1087	11c. "GRTU" and cogwheels (50th anniv of General Retailers and Traders Union)	70	40
1088	19c. Mercury (50th anniv of Chamber of Commerce)	1·10	1·40
1089	26c. Aircraft tailfins (25th anniv of Air Malta)	2·40	2·50
1085/9 *Set of 5*		4·25	4·25

1998 (19 Nov). Christmas. Paintings by Mattia Preti. T **379** and similar vert designs. Multicoloured. W **105**. P 14.

1090	6c. Type **379**	40	10
1091	6c. +2c. "Virgin and Child with Sts. Anthony and John the Baptist"	50	70
1092	16c. +3c. "Virgin and Child with Sts. Raphael, Nicholas and Gregory"	1·25	1·75
1093	26c. +3c. "Virgin and Child with Sts. John the Baptist and Nicholas"	1·75	3·00
1090/3 *Set of 4*		3·50	5·00

PRINTERS. All stamps between Nos. 1094 and 1383 were printed in lithography by German State Printing Works, Berlin.

380 Fort St. Angelo

(Des Frank Ancilleri)

1999 (26 Feb). 900th Anniv of the Sovereign Military Order of Malta. T **380** and similar multicoloured designs. P 14.

1094	2c. Type **380**	50	10
1095	6c. Grand Master De l'Isle Adam (*vert*)	80	25
1096	16c. Grand Master La Valette (*vert*)	1·50	65
1097	27c. Auberge de Castille et Leon	2·50	3·00
1094/7 *Set of 4*		4·75	3·50

381 Little Ringed Plover, Ghadira Nature Reserve

(Des Richard J. Caruana)

1999 (6 Apr). Europa. Parks and Gardens. T **381** and similar horiz design. Multicoloured. P 14.

1098	16c. Type **381**	2·00	55
1099	35c. Common Kingfisher, Simar Nature Reserve	2·50	3·00

382 Council of Europe Assembly

(Des Richard J. Caruana)

1999 (6 Apr). 50th Anniv of the Council of Europe. T **382** and similar horiz design. Multicoloured. P 14.

1100	6c. Type **382**	60	25
1101	16c. Council of Europe Headquarters, Strasbourg	1·00	1·25

383 U.P.U. Emblem and Marsamxett Harbour, Valletta

384 Couple in Luzzu

(Des Ansgar Spratte)

1999 (2 June). 125th Anniv of Universal Postal Union. T **383** and similar horiz designs. Multicoloured. P 13½.

1102	6c. Type **363**	1·25	1·50
	a. Horiz strip of 5. Nos. 1102/6	7·25	8·75
1103	16c. Nuremberg and "iBRA '99" International Stamp Exhibition emblem	1·50	1·75
1104	22c. Paris and "Philexfrance '99" International Stamp Exhibition emblem	1·60	1·90
1105	27c. Peking and "China'99" International Stamp Exhibition emblem	1·75	2·00
1106	37c. Melbourne and "Australia '99" International Stamp Exhibition emblem	1·90	2·50
1102/6 *Set of 5*		7·25	8·75

Nos. 1102/6 were printed together, *se-tenant*, as horizontal strips of 5 in sheets of 10.

(Des Gorg Mallia)

1999 (16 June). Tourism. T **384** and similar multicoloured designs. P 14.

1107	6c. Type **384**	50	25
1108	16c. Tourist taking photograph	95	55
1109	22c. Man sunbathing (*horiz*)	1·25	1·00
1110	27c. Couple with horse-drawn carriage (*horiz*)	1·90	1·40
1111	37c. Caveman at Ta' Hagrat Neolithic temple (*horiz*)	2·50	3·25
1107/11 *Set of 5*		6·25	5·75

385 Common Jellyfish

(Des Andrew Micallef)

1999 (25 Aug). Marine Life of the Mediterranean. T **385** and similar square designs. Multicoloured. P 13½.

1112	6c. Type **385**	70	75
	a. Sheetlet. Nos. 1112/27	10·00	11·00
1113	6c. Peacock Wrasse	70	75
1114	6c. Common Cuttlefish	70	75
1115	6c. Violet Sea-urchin	70	75
1116	6c. Dusky Grouper	70	75
1117	6c. Common Two-banded Seabream	70	75
1118	6c. Star-coral	70	75
1119	6c. Spiny Spider Crab	70	75
1120	6c. Rainbow Wrasse	70	75
1121	6c. Octopus	70	75
1122	6c. Atlantic Trumpet Triton	70	75
1123	6c. Mediterranean Parrotfish	70	75
1124	6c. Long-snouted Seahorse	70	75
1125	6c. Deep-water Hermit Crab	70	75
1126	6c. Mediterranean Moray	70	75
1127	6c. Common Starfish	70	75
1112/27 *Set of 16*		10·00	11·00

Nos. 1112/27 were printed together, *se-tenant*, in sheetlets of 16, forming a composite design.

386 Father Mikiel Scerri

(Des Joseph Mizzi)

1999 (6 Oct). Bicentenary of Maltese Uprising against the French. T **386** and similar horiz designs. Multicoloured. P 14.

1128	6c. Type **386**	90	90
	a. Pair. Nos. 1128/9	1·75	1·75
1129	6c. "L-Eroj Maltin" (statue)	90	90
1130	16c. General Belgrand de Vaubois (French commander)	1·75	1·75
	a. Pair. Nos. 1130/1	3·50	3·50
1131	16c. Captain Alexander Ball R.N.	1·75	1·75
1128/31 *Set of 4*		4·75	4·75

Nos. 1128/9 and 1130/1 were each printed together, *se-tenant*, as horizontal or vertical pairs in sheets of 10.

387 "Wolfgang Philip Guttenberg interceding with The Virgin" (votive painting)

(Des Joseph Mizzi)

1999 (6 Oct). Mellieha Sanctuary Commemoration. T **387** and similar multicoloured design. P 14.

1132	35c. Type **387**	2·25	2·75
MS1133	123×88 mm. 6c. "Mellieha Virgin and Child" (rock painting) (*vert*)	1·00	1·10

388 Sea Daffodil

389 Madonna and Child

(Des Maurice Tanti Burlo)

1999 (20 Oct)–**2003**. Maltese Flowers. T **388** and similar square designs. Multicoloured. P 14.

1134	1c. *Helichrysum melitense* (13.9.2000)	10	10
1135	2c. Type **388**	10	10
1136	3c. *Cistus creticus* (13.9.2000)	10	15
1137	4c. Southern dwarf iris	15	20
1138	5c. *Papaver thoeas* (20.9.01)	30	25
1139	6c. French daffodil	25	25
1139*a*	7c. *Vitex angus-castus* (30.1.03)	50	65
1140	10c. *Rosa sempervirens* (13.9.2000)	40	35
1141	11c. *Silene colorata* (20.9.01)	60	40
1142	12c. *Cynara cardunculus* (13.9.2000)	50	45
1143	16c. Yellow-throated crocus	65	55
1144	19c. *Anthemis arvensis* (20.9.01)	1·00	65
1145	20c. *Anacamptis pyramidalis* (13.9.2000)	1·00	70
1145*a*	22c. *Spartium junceum* (30.1.03)	1·75	75
1146	25c. Large Star of Bethlehem	1·10	85
1147	27c. *Borago officinalis* (20.9.01)	1·75	90
1147*a*	28c. *Crataegus azalorus* (30.1.03)	1·75	95
1147*b*	37c. *Cercis siliquastrum*	2·00	1·40
1147*c*	45c. *Myrtus communis*	2·25	1·75
1148	46c. Wild tulip (30.1.03)	2·25	1·75
1149	50c. *Chrysanthemum coronarium* (20.9.01)	2·00	1·90
1149*a*	76c. *Pistacia lentiscus* (30.1.03)	5·00	3·25
1150	£1 *Malva sylvestris* (20.9.01)	4·50	4·25
1151	£2 *Adonis microcarpa* (13.9.2000)	8·00	8·50
1134/1151 *Set of 24*		35·00	28·00

For Nos. 1139a and 1143 in smaller size and self-adhesive, see Nos. 1335/6.

(Des Harry Borg)

1999 (27 Nov). Christmas. T **389** and similar square designs. Multicoloured. P 14.

1152	6c. Type **389**	60	10
1153	6c. +3c. Carol singers	65	80
1154	16c. +3c. Santa Claus	1·60	2·00
1155	26c. +3c. Christmas decorations	2·00	3·00
1152/5 *Set of 4*		4·25	5·25

390 Parliament Chamber and Symbolic Luzzu

(Des Richard J. Caruana)

1999 (10 Dec). 25th Anniv of Republic. T **390** and similar horiz designs. Multicoloured. P 14.

1156	6c. Type **390**	40	25
1157	11c. Parliament in session and Council of Europe emblem	60	35
1158	16c. Church and Central Bank of Malta building	80	55
1159	19c. Aerial view of Gozo and emblems	1·10	1·00
1160	26c. Computer and shipyard	1·40	1·60
1156/60 *Set of 5*		3·75	3·25

391 Gift and Flowers

(Des Harry Borg)

2000 (9 Feb). Greetings Stamps. T **391** and similar horiz designs. Multicoloured. P 14.

1161	3c. Type **391**	30	15

1162	6c. Photograph envelope and rose	50	25
1163	16c. Flowers and silver heart	1·00	55
1164	20c. Champagne and pocket watch	1·25	1·00
1165	22c. Wedding rings and roses	1·25	1·40
1161/5 *Set of* 5		3·75	3·00

Nos. 1161/5 were printed with greetings labels on the vertical sheet margins.

392 Luzzu and Cruise Liner

(Des Frank X. Ancilleri)

2000 (7 Mar). Malta during the 20th Century. T **392** and similar horiz designs. Multicoloured. P 14.

1166	6c. Type **392**	65	25
1167	16c. Street musicians and modern street carnival	90	65
1168	22c. Family in 1900 and illuminated quayside	1·25	1·25
1169	27c. Rural occupations and Citadel, Victoria	1·75	2·50
1166/9 *Set of* 4		4·00	4·25

393 Footballers and Trophy (Centenary of Malta Football Association)

394 "Building Europe"

(Des Ludwig Flask)

2000 (28 Mar). Sporting Events. T **393** and similar horiz designs. Multicoloured. P 14.

1170	6c. Type **393**	55	25
1171	16c. Swimming and sailing (Olympic Games, Sydney)	85	55
1172	26c. Judo, shooting and running (Olympic Games, Sydney)	1·40	1·10
1173	37c. Football (European Championship)	1·75	2·50
1170/3 *Set of* 4		4·00	4·00

(Des Jean Paul Cousin)

2000 (9 May). Europa. P 14.

1174	**394**	16c. multicoloured	1·25	65
1175		46c. multicoloured	2·75	3·25

395 D.H. 66 Hercules, 1928

(Des Richard J. Caruana)

2000 (28 June). Century of Air Transport, 1900–2000. T **395** and similar horiz designs. Multicoloured. P 14.

1176	6c. Type **395**	85	1·10
	a. Horiz pair. Nos. 1176/7	1·60	2·10
1177	6c. LZ 127 *Graf Zeppelin*, 1933	85	1·10
1178	16c. Douglas DC-3 Dakota of Air Malta Ltd, 1949	1·60	1·90
	a. Horiz pair. Nos. 1178/9	3·00	3·75
1179	16c. Airbus A320 of Air Malta	1·60	1·90
1176/9 *Set of* 4		3·75	3·75
MS1180	122×87 mm. Nos. 1176/9	4·50	5·50

Nos. 1176/7 and 1178/9 were each printed together, *se-tenant*, as horizontal pairs in sheets of 10, with the backgrounds forming composite designs.

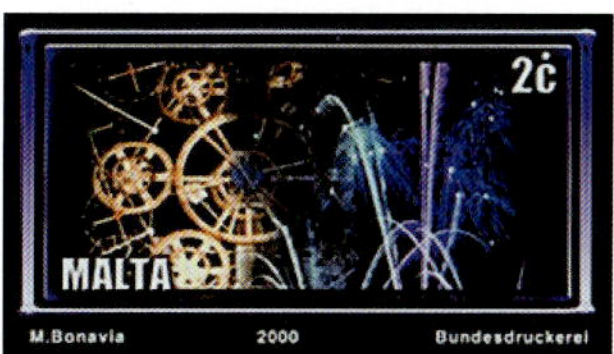

396 Catherine Wheel and Fireworks

(Des Martin Bonavia)

2000 (19 July). Fireworks. T **396** and similar horiz designs. Multicoloured. P 14.

1181	2c. Type **396**	30	10
1182	6c. Exploding multicoloured fireworks	65	25
1183	16c. Catherine wheel	1·25	55
1184	20c. Exploding green fireworks	1·40	1·00
1185	50c. Numbered rockets in rack	3·00	5·00
1181/5 *Set of* 5		6·00	6·25

397 "Boy walking Dog"

(Jean Paul Zammit)

2000 (18 Oct). "Stampin' the Future" (children's stamp design competition winners). T **397** and similar horiz designs. Multicoloured. P 14.

1186	6c. Type **397**	55	65
1187	6c. "Stars and Woman in Megalithic Temple" (Chiara Borg)	55	65
1188	6c. "Sunny Day" (Bettina Paris)	55	65
1189	6c. "Hands holding Heart" (Roxana Caruana)	55	65
1186/9 *Set of* 4		2·00	2·40

398 Boy's Sermon, Nativity Play and Girl with Doll

(Des Gorg Mallia)

2000 (18 Nov). Christmas. T **398** and similar multicoloured designs. P 13½.

1190	6c. Type **398**	65	10
1191	6c. +3c. Three Wise Men (23×27 mm)	75	75
1192	16c. +3c. Family with Father Christmas	1·75	2·00
1193	26c. +3c. Christmas tree, church and family	2·25	3·25
1190/3 *Set of* 4		4·75	5·50
MS1194	174×45 mm. Nos. 1190/3	4·75	6·00

399 Crocodile Float

(Des Francis X. Ancilleri)

2001 (23 Feb). Maltese Carnival. T **399** and similar multicoloured designs. P 14.

1195	6c. Type **399**	50	25
1196	11c. King Karnival in procession (*vert*)	75	40
1197	16c. Woman and children in costumes (*vert*)	90	55
1198	19c. Horseman carnival float (*vert*)	1·10	1·40
1199	27c. Carnival procession	1·50	2·00
1195/9 *Set of* 5		4·25	3·75
MS1200	127×92 mm. 12c. Old-fashioned clowns; 37c. Women dressed as clowns (*both* 32×32 mm) P 13½	2·75	4·00

400 St. Elmo Lighthouse

(Des Richard J. Caruana)

2001 (21 Mar). Maltese Lighthouses. T **400** and similar vert designs. Multicoloured. P 14.

1201	6c. Type **400**	65	25
1202	16c. Gurdan Lighthouse	1·25	70
1203	22c. Delimara Lighthouse	1·75	2·25
1201/3 *Set of* 3		3·25	3·00

401 "The Chicken Seller" (E. Caruana Dingli)

(Des Harry Borg)

2001 (18 Apr). Edward Caruana Dingli (painter) Commemoration. T **401** and similar vert designs. Multicoloured. P 14.

1204	2c. Type **401**	20	30
1205	4c. "The Village Beau"	35	15
1206	6c. "The Faldetta"	50	25
1207	10c. "The Guitar Player"	80	60
1208	26c. "Wayside Orange Seller"	2·00	2·75
1204/8 *Set of* 5		3·50	3·75

402 Nazju Falzon, Gorg Preca and Adeodata Pisani (candidates for Beatification)

(Des Joseph Mizzi)

2001 (4 May). Visit of Pope John Paul II. T **402** and similar horiz designs. Multicoloured. P 14.

1209	6c. Type **402**	1·00	25
1210	16c. Pope John Paul II and statue of St. Paul	1·75	1·50
MS1211	123×87 mm. 75c. Pope John Paul with Nazju Falzon, Gorg Preca and Adeodata Pisani	5·00	5·50

403 Painted Frog

(Des Trevor Zahra)

2001 (23 May). Europa. Pond Life. T **403** and similar horiz design. Multicoloured. P 14.

1212	16c. Type **403**	1·75	65
1213	46c. Red-veined Darter (dragonfly)	3·25	3·75

404 Yellow-legged Gull (*Larus cachinnans*)

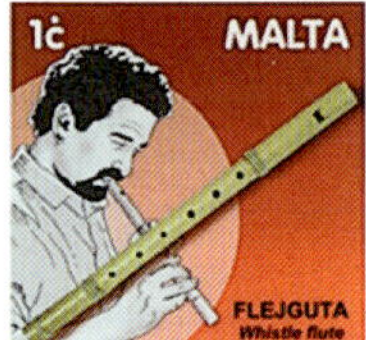

405 Whistle Flute

(Des. Andrew Micallef)

2001 (22 June). Maltese Birds. T **404** and similar square designs. Multicoloured. P 13½.

1214	6c. Type **404**	85	85
	a. Sheetlet. Nos. 1214/29	12·00	12·00
1215	6c. Common Kestrel (*Falco tinnunculus*)	85	85
1216	6c. Golden Oriole (*Oriolus oriolus*)	85	85
1217	6c. Chaffinch (*Fringilla coelebs*) and Eurasian Goldfinch (*Carduelis carduelis*)	85	85
1218	6c. Blue Rock Thrush (*Monticola solitarius*)	85	85
1219	6c. European Bee-Eater (*Merops apiaster*)	85	85
1220	6c. Common House Martin (*Delichon urbica*) and Swallow (*Hirundo rustica*)	85	85
1221	6c. Spanish Sparrow (*Passer hispaniolensis*)	85	85
1222	6c. Spectacled Warbler (*Sylvia conspicillata*)	85	85
1223	6c. Turtle Dove (*Streptopelia turtur*)	85	85
1224	6c. Northern Pintail (*Anas acuta*)	85	85
1225	6c. Little Bittern (*Ixobrychus minutus*)	85	85
1226	6c. Eurasian Woodcock (*Scolopax rusticola*)	85	85
1227	6c. Short-eared Owl (*Asio flammeus*)	85	85
1228	6c. Northern Lapwing (*Vanellus vanellus*)	85	85
1229	6c. Moorhen (*Gallinula chloropus*)	85	85
1214/29 *Set of* 16		12·00	12·00

Nos 1214/29 were printed together, *se-tenant*, in sheetlets of 16 with the backgrounds forming a composite design.

(Des Gorg Mallia)

2001 (22 Aug). Traditional Maltese Musical Instruments. T **405** and similar square designs. Multicoloured. P 13½.

1230	1c. Type **405**	15	50
1231	3c. Reed pipe	30	40
1232	14c. Maltese bagpipe	85	50
1233	20c. Friction drum	1·25	1·50
1234	25c. Frame drum	1·50	2·00
1230/4 *Set of* 5		3·75	4·50

406 Kelb tal-Fenek (Pharaoh Hound)

407 Man with Net chasing Star

(Des Ludwig Flask)

2001 (20 Oct). Maltese Dogs. T **406** and similar horiz designs. Multicoloured. P 14.

1235	6c. Type **406**	75	25
1236	16c. Kelb tal-Kacca	1·50	55
1237	19c. Maltese	1·50	1·25
1238	35c. Kelb tal-But	2·25	3·50
1235/8 *Set of* 4		5·50	5·00

(Des Gattaldo)

2001 (29 Nov). Christmas. T **407** and similar square designs. Multicoloured. P 14.

1239	6c. +2c. Type 407	80	50
1240	15c. +2c. Father and children	1·50	1·75
1241	16c. +2c. Mother and daughter	1·50	1·75
1242	19c. +3c. Young woman with shopping bags	1·75	2·25
1239/42 *Set of* 4		5·00	5·75

The 6c.+2c. incorporates greetings labels into the vertical margins of the sheets.

MACHINE LABELS. From 9 January 2002 gummed 6c. labels in four different designs showing Maltese scenes were available from vending machines, at Malta International Airport.

408 *Hippocampus guttulatus*

409 Sideboard

(Des Martin Bonavia)

2002 (30 Jan). Endangered Species. Mediterranean Seahorses. T **408** and similar vert designs. Multicoloured. P 14.

1243	6c. Type **408**	80	80
1244	6c. *Hippocampus hippocampus*	80	80
1245	16c. Close-up of *Hippocampus guttulatus*	1·60	1·75
1246	16c. *Hippocampus hippocampus* on seabed	1·60	1·75
1243/6 *Set of 4*		4·25	4·50

(Des F. Ancilleri)

2002 (5 Apr). Antique Furniture. T **409** and similar multicoloured designs. P 14.

1247	2c. Type **409**	25	40
1248	4c. Bureau (vert)	45	30
1249	11c. Inlaid table (vert)	85	40
1250	26c. Cabinet (vert)	1·50	85
1251	60c. Carved chest	3·00	5·00
1247/51 *Set of 5*		5·50	6·25

410 Child's Face painted as Clown

411 *Hyles sammuti*

(Des Roberta Zahra)

2002 (9 May). Europa. Circus. P 14.

1252	**410**	16c. multicoloured	1·25	1·00

(Des Maurice Tanti Burlo)

2002 (26 June). Moths and Butterflies. T **411** and similar square designs. Multicoloured. P 13½.

1253	6c. Type **411**	50	55
	a. Sheetlet. Nos. 1253/68	7·25	8·00
1254	6c. *Utetheisa pulchella*	50	55
1255	6c. *Ophiusa tirhaca*	50	55
1256	6c. *Phragmatobia fulginosa melitensis*	50	55
1257	6c. *Vanessa cardui*	50	55
1258	6c. *Polyommatus icarus*	50	55
1259	6c. *Gonepteryx Cleopatra*	50	55
1260	6c. *Vanessa Atlanta*	50	55
1261	6c. *Eucrostes indigenata*	50	55
1262	6c. *Macroglossum stellatarum*	50	55
1263	6c. *Lasiocampa quercus*	50	55
1264	6c. *Catocala electa*	50	55
1265	6c. *Maniola jurtina hyperhispulla*	50	55
1266	6c. *Pieris brassicae*	50	55
1267	6c. *Papilio machaon melitensis*	50	55
1268	6c. *Danaus chrysippus*	50	55
1253/68 *Set of 16*		7·25	8·00

Nos. 1253/68 were printed together, *se-tenant*, in sheetlets of 16.

No. 1260 is inscribed "atalania" and No. 1264 "elocata", both in error.

412 "Kusksu Bil-ful" (bean stew)

413 *Yavia cryptocarpa* (cactus)

(Des J. Smith)

2002 (13 Aug). Maltese Cookery. T **412** and similar horiz designs. Multicoloured. P 14.

1269	7c. Type **412**	70	25
1270	12c. "Qaqocc mimli" (stuffed artichoke)	1·25	50
1271	16c. "Lampuki" (dorada with aubergines)	1·40	75
1272	27c. "Qaghqd Tal-kavatelli" (chestnut dessert)	2·25	2·75
1269/72 *Set of 4*		5·00	3·75
MS1273	125×90 mm. 75c. "Stuffat Tal-fenek" (rabbit stew)	4·50	5·50

(Des A. Micallef)

2002 (25 Sept). Cacti and Succulents. T **413** and similar multicoloured designs. P 14.

1274	1c. Type **413**	15	50
1275	7c. *Aztekium hintonii* (cactus) (vert)	65	25
1276	28c. *Pseudolithos migiurtinus* (succulent)	1·75	70
1277	37c. *Pierrebraunia brauniorum* (cactus) (vert)	2·25	1·50
1278	76c. *Euphorbia turbiniformis* (succulent)	4·00	6·00
1274/8 *Set of 5*		8·00	8·00

414 Chief Justice Adrian Dingli

415 Mary and Joseph in Donkey Cart

(Des H. Borg)

2002 (18 Oct). Personalities. T **414** and similar vert designs. P 14.

1279	3c. bright green and greenish black	30	40
1280	7c. brown-olive and brownish black	80	35
	a. No dot over "c"	1·00	50
1281	15c. reddish brown and agate	1·25	75
	a. No dot over "c"	1·50	90
1282	35c. grey-brown and sepia	2·00	1·75
1283	50c. light blue and deep turquoise-blue	2·50	4·00
1279/83 *Set of 5*		5·75	6·25

Designs:—7c. Oreste Kirkop (opera singer); 15c. Athanasius Kircher (Jesuit scholar); 35c. Archpriest Saverio Cassar; 50c. Emmanuele Vitali (notary).

The "No dot over 'c'" variety occured on R. 2/1-4 on the 7c. and 15c. values.

(Des Debbie Dingli)

2002 (20 Nov). Christmas. T **415** and similar horiz designs. Multicoloured. P 14.

1284	7c. Type **415**	70	25
1285	16c. Shepherds and Kings on a bus	1·25	55
1286	22c. Holy Family and angels in luzzu (boat)	1·60	75
1287	37c. Holy Family in horse-drawn carriage	2·00	1·50
1288	75c. Nativity on Maltese fishing boat	3·75	6·00
1284/8 *Set of 5*		8·25	8·00

416 Vanden Plas Princess Landaulette, 1965

(Des Joe P. Smith)

2003 (26 Feb). Vintage Cars. T **416** and similar horiz designs. Multicoloured. P 14.

1289	2c. Type **416**	25	60
1290	7c. Allard "M" type, 1948	65	25
1291	10c. Cadillac Model "B", 1904	85	35
1292	26c. Fiat Cinquecento Model "A" Topolino, 1936	1·60	1·60
1293	35c. Ford Anglia Super, 1965	2·25	3·00
1289/93 *Set of 5*		5·00	5·25

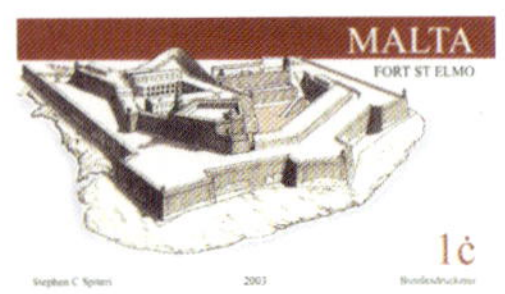

417 Fort St. Elmo

418 St. George on Horseback

(Des S. Spiteri)

2003 (21 Mar)–**03**. Maltese Military Architecture. T **417** and similar horiz designs. Multicoloured. P 14.

1294	1c. Type **417**	15	40
1295	4c. Rinella Battery	40	30
1296	11c. Fort St. Angelo	85	40
1297	16c. Section through Reserve Post R15	1·25	60
	a. Booklet pane. No. 1297×6 (16.4.03)	9·00	
1298	44c. Fort Tigne	2·75	4·25
1294/8 *Set of 5*		4·75	5·50

No. 1297a was available from 96c. stamp booklets, No. SB7.

(Des J. Mizzi)

2003 (23 Apr). Paintings of St. George. T **418** and similar vert designs. P 14.

1299 **418**	3c. multicoloured	30	30
1300 –	7c. multicoloured	60	30
1301 –	14c. multicoloured	95	60
1302 –	19c. multicoloured	1·40	1·40
1303 –	27c. multicoloured	1·75	2·25
1299/303 *Set of 5*		4·50	4·25

419 "CISKBEER"

420 Games Mascot with Javelin

(Des Debbie Dingli)

2003 (9 May). Europa. Poster Art. T **419** and similar vert design. Multicoloured. P 14.

1304	16c. Type **419**	1·10	55
1305	46c. "CARNIVAL 1939"	2·75	3·50

(Des R. Caruana)

2003 (26 May). Games of Small European States, Malta. T **420** and similar horiz designs. Multicoloured. P 14.

1306	25c. Type **420**	1·25	85
1307	50c. Mascot with gun	2·25	1·75
1308	75c. Mascot with ball and net	3·75	2·75
1309	£3 Mascot with rubber ring at poolside	14·00	17·00
1306/9 *Set of 4*		19·00	20·00

421 Princess Elizabeth in Malta, *c.* 1950

422 Valletta Bastions at Night

(Des F. Attard and G. Theuma)

2003 (3 June). 50th Anniv of Coronation. T **421** and similar horiz designs. P 14.

1310	12c. black, brownish grey and cinnamon	70	45
1311	15c. multicoloured	75	50
1312	22c. black, brownish grey and grey	1·00	90
1313	60c. black, olive-grey and deep ultramarine	2·50	3·50
1310/13 *Set of 4*		4·50	4·75
MS1314 100×72 mm. £1 multicoloured		6·50	7·50

Designs:—15c. Princess Elizabeth with crowd of children, Malta, c. 1950; 22c. Queen Elizabeth II in evening dress with Duke of Edinburgh, Malta; 60c. Queen Elizabeth II (receiving book) and Duke of Edinburgh, Malta; £1 Queen on walkabout with crowd.

(Des jp advertising)

2003 (1 July). Elton John, The Granaries, Floriana. Sheet 125×90 mm. P 14.

MS1315 **422**	£1.50 multicoloured	9·00	10·00

No. **MS**1315 also contains four labels showing different portraits of Elton John.

423 *Chlamys pesfelis*

424 Racing Yachts, Malta—Syracuse Race

(Des A. Micallef)

2003 (20 Aug). Sea Shells. T **423** and similar square designs. Multicoloured. P 13½.

1316	7c. Type **423**	50	55
	a. Sheetlet. Nos. 1316/31	7·25	8·00
1317	7c. *Gyroscala lamellose*	50	55
1318	7c. *Phalium granulatum*	50	55
1319	7c. *Fusiturris similes*	50	55
1320	7c. *Luria lurida*	50	55
1321	7c. *Bolinus brandaris*	50	55
1322	7c. *Charonia tritonis variegate*	50	55
1323	7c. *Clanculus corallinus*	50	55
1324	7c. *Fusinus syracusanus*	50	55
1325	7c. *Pinna nobilis*	50	55
1326	7c. *Acanthocardia tuberculata*	50	55
1327	7c. *Aporrhais pespelecani*	50	55
1328	7c. *Haliotis tuberculata lamellose*	50	55
1329	7c. *Tonna galea*	50	55
1330	7c. *Spondylus gaederopus*	50	55
1331	7c. *Mitra zonata*	50	55
1316/31 *Set of 16*		7·25	8·00

Nos. 1316/31 were printed together, se-tenant, in sheetlets of 16.

(Des F. Ancilleri)

2003 (30 Sept). Yachting. T **424** and similar multicoloured designs. P 14.

1332	8c. Type **424**	60	35
1333	22c. Yacht, Middle Sea Race (*vert*)	1·25	1·00
1334	35c. Racing yachts, Royal Malta Yacht Club (*vert*)	2·00	3·00
1332/4 *Set of 3*		3·50	4·00

(Litho Cartor)

2003 (22 Oct). Self-adhesive booklet stamps. As Nos. 1139a and 1143 but smaller, 23×23 mm, printer's imprint omitted and imprint date at right instead of centre. P 12½ die-cut.

1335	7c. Vitex agnus-castus	50	40
	a. Booklet pane. No. 1335×12	5·00	
1336	16c. Crocus longiflorus	1·25	1·25
	a. Booklet pane. No. 1336×6	6·50	

Booklet panes Nos. 1335a and 1336a have imperforate edges, giving stamps imperforate on either two or three sides.

425 Is-Sur ta' San Mikiel, Valletta

426 The Annunciation

(Des M. Vella)

2003 (29 Oct). Windmills. T **425** and similar black designs. P 14.

1337	11c. Type **425**	85	40
1338	27c. Ta' Kola, Xaghra (*vert*)	2·00	1·25
1339	45c. Tax-Xarolla, Zurrieq (*vert*)	2·75	4·50
1337/9 *Set of 3*		5·00	5·50

(Des Harry Borg)

2003 (12 Nov). Christmas. T **426** and similar multicoloured designs. P 14.

1340	7c. Type **426**	70	30
1341	16c. Holy Family	1·00	35
1342	22c. The Shepherds following the Star (*horiz*)	1·40	85
1343	50c. The Three Kings with gifts (*horiz*)	2·75	4·00
1340/3	*Set of* 4	5·25	5·00

427 Pillar Box on Seafront

428 Tortoiseshell Cat

(Des Alfred Caruana Ruggier)

2004 (12 Mar). Letter Boxes. T **427** and similar vert designs. Multicoloured. P 14.

1344	1c. Type **427**	10	30
1345	16c. Pillar box on pavement	1·50	55
1346	22c. Wall pillar boxes	1·75	90
1347	37c. Pillar box inside post office	2·50	1·75
1348	76c. Square pillar box and statue	6·00	8·00
1344/8	*Set of* 5	10·50	10·50

(Des H. Borg)

2004 (26 Mar). Cats. T **428** and similar square designs. Multicoloured. P 13½.

1349	7c. Type **428**	70	30
1350	27c. Tabby	1·90	1·25
1351	28c. Silver tabby	1·90	1·25
1352	50c. Ginger tabby	3·50	4·00
1353	60c. Black and white cat	3·75	4·75
1349/53	*Set of* 5	10·50	10·50

429 St. John Bosco

(Des Paul Camilleri-Cauchi)

2004 (7 Apr). Centenary of Salesians in Malta. Sheet 124×89 mm. P 14.

MS1354 **429** 75c. multicoloured ... 4·25 5·50

430 Pipistrelle (*Pipistrellus pygmaeus*)

431 New Members Flags inside E.U. Stars

(Des Andrew Micallef)

2004 (21 Apr). Mammals and Reptiles. T **430** and similar square designs. Multicoloured. P 14.

1355	16c. Type **430**	85	90
	a. Sheetlet. Nos. 1355/70	12·00	13·00
1356	16c. Lesser Mouse-eared Bat (*Myotis blythi punicus*)	85	90
1357	16c. Weasel (*Mustela nivalis*)	85	90
1358	16c. Algerian Hedgehog (*Atelerix algirus fallax*)	85	90
1359	16c. Mediterranean Chameleon (*Chamaeleo chamaeleon*)	85	90
1360	16c. Sicilian Shrew (*Crocidura sicula*)	85	90
1361	16c. Ocellated Skink (*Chalcides ocellatus*)	85	90
1362	16c. Filfla Maltese Wall Lizard (*Podarcis filfolensis filfolensis*)	85	90
1363	16c. Moorish Gecko (*Tarentola mauritanica*)	85	90
1364	16c. Turkish Gecko (*Hemidactylus turcicus*)	85	90
1365	16c. Leopard Snake (*Elaphe situla*)	85	90
1366	16c. Western Whip Snake (*Coluber viridiflavus*)	85	90
1367	16c. Common Dolphin (*Delphinus delphis*)	85	90
1368	16c. Striped Dolphin (*Stenella coeruleoalba*)	85	90
1369	16c. Mediterranean Monk Seal (*Monachus monachus*)	85	90
1370	16c. Green Turtle (*Chelonia mydas*)	85	90
1355/70	*Set of* 16	12·00	13·00

Nos. 1355/70 were printed together, *se-tenant*, in sheetlets of 16 with the background of each horizontal pair (1355/6, 1357/8, 1359/60, 1361/2, 1363/4, 1365/6, 1367/8, and 1369/70) forming a composite design.

(Des Jean Pierre Mizzi)

2004 (1 May). Accession to European Union. T **431** and similar horiz design. Multicoloured. P 14.

1371	16c. Type **431**	1·00	55
1372	28c. Former Prime Minister Eddie Fenech Adami and former Foreign Minister Joe Borg signing Accession Treaty	1·50	2·00

432 Children Jumping into Water

(Des Joe P. Smith)

2004 (19 May). Europa. Holidays. T **432** and similar horiz design. Multicoloured. P 14.

1373	16c. Type **432**	1·00	55
1374	51c. Hagar Qim prehistoric temples	2·75	3·50

433 Hal Millieri Chapel, Zurrieq

434 Tram

(Des R. Sacco)

2004 (16 June). Chapels. T **433** and similar horiz designs. Multicoloured. P 14×14½.

1375	3c. Type **433**	30	30
1376	7c. San Basilju, Mqabba	60	30
1377	39c. San cir, Rabat	2·25	1·75
1378	48c. Santa LuCija, Mtarfa	2·50	2·75
1379	66c. Ta' Santa Marija, Kemmuna	4·25	6·00
1375/9	*Set of* 5	9·00	10·00

(Des Debbie Caruana Dingli)

2004 (14 July). Trams. T **434** and similar designs. P 13½ (19c, 75c) or 14 (37c, 50c).

1380	19c. bright yellow-green and black	1·25	65
1381	37c. orange and black	2·25	1·40
1382	50c. greenish yellow and black	3·25	3·50
1383	75c. bright new blue and black	4·50	6·00
1380/3	*Set of* 4	10·00	10·50

Designs: (25×42 mm)—37c. Tram driver; 50c. Ticket. (As Type **434**)—75c. Tram under bridge.

PRINTERS. All stamps from No. 1384 onwards were printed in lithography by Printex Ltd., Malta.

435 Discus Thrower

(Des. M. Tanti Burlò)

2004 (13 Aug). Olympic Games, Athens. T **435** and similar square designs. Multicoloured. W **105**. P 14½.

1384	11c. Type **435**	80	40
1385	16c. Greek column and laurel wreath	1·10	55
1386	76c. Javelin thrower	5·00	6·50
1384/6	*Set of* 3	6·25	6·75

436 Children playing on Ascension Day (Luigi Brocktorff painting) (Lapsi)

(Des Francis X. Ancilleri)

2004 (15 Sept). Festivals. T **436** and similar multicoloured designs. W **105**. P 14.

1387	5c. Type **436**	45	30
1388	15c. Votive Penitentiary General Procession, Zejtun (San Girgor)	1·25	50
1389	27c. Pilgrimage in front of the Sanctuary of Our Lady of Graces, Zabbar (painting, Italo Horatio Serge) (Hadd In-Nies)	2·00	1·00
1390	51c. Children with St. Martin's Bags of nuts (Michele Bellanti lithograph) (San Martin) (vert)	3·50	3·75
1391	£1 Peasants in traditional costumes singing and dancing (painting, Antoine Favray) (Mnarja) (vert)	6·50	8·50
1387/91	*Set of* 5	12·00	12·50

437 Church of St. Mary, Attard

(Des Joseph Casha)

2004 (13 Oct). Art. T **437** and similar multicoloured designs. W **105**. P 14.

1392	2c. Type **437**	30	35
1393	20c. Mdina Cathedral organ and music score (vert)	1·40	70
1394	57c. Statue of St. Agatha (vert)	4·25	5·00
1395	62c. Il-Gifen Tork (poem) and books (vert)	4·75	6·00
1392/5	*Set of* 4	9·75	11·00
MS1396	93×100 mm. 72c. Medieval painting of St. Paul (vert)	4·50	6·00

438 Papier mache Bambino on rocks, Lecce

(Des Richard J. Caruana)

2004 (10 Nov). Christmas. Bambino Models. T **438** and similar multicoloured designs. W **105**. P 14.

1397	7c. Type **438**	55	25
1398	16c. Wax Bambino inside glass dome (vert)	1·10	55
1399	22c. Wax Bambino on back, Lija (vert)	1·50	75
1400	50c. Beeswax Bambino under tree (vert)	3·25	4·50
1397/400	*Set of* 4	5·75	5·50

439 Quintinus Map

(Des Alfred Caruana Ruggier)

2005 (19 Jan). Old Maps. T **439** and similar horiz designs. W **105**. P 14×14½.

1401	1c. black and scarlet	15	40
1402	12c. multicoloured	90	50
1403	37c. multicoloured	2·75	2·00
1404	£1 multicoloured	6·50	8·25
1401/4	*Set of* 4	9·25	10·00

Designs:—1c. Type **439**; 12c. Copper-engraved map; 37c. Fresco map; £1 Map of Gozo.

440 Dar il-Kaptan (Respite Home)

(Des Martin Bonavia)

2005 (23 Feb). Centenary of Rotary International (humanitarian organisation). T **440** and similar horiz designs. Multicoloured. W **105**. P 14×14½.

1405	27c. Type **440**	1·50	90
1406	76c. Outline of Malta and Gozo and "CELEBRATE ROTARY"	4·75	6·00

441 Hans Christian Andersen

442 Pope John Paul II

(Des Mette and Eric Mourier del.)

2005 (3 Mar). Birth Bicentenary of Hans Christian Andersen (artist and children's writer). T **441** and similar designs. W **105**. P 14.

1407	7c. black and silver	55	25
1408	22c. multicoloured	1·50	75
1409	60c. multicoloured	3·75	4·50
1410	75c. multicoloured	4·50	6·00
1407/10	*Set of* 4	9·25	10·50

Designs:—7c. Type **441**; 20×38 mm—22c. Scissors and paper cutting; 60c. Ugly Duckling, pen and inkwell; 75c. Moroccan travelling boots and drawing of Villa Borghese, Rome.

2005 (15 Apr). Pope John Paul II Commemoration. W 105. P 14½×14.

1411	**442**	51c. multicoloured	4·25	4·00

443 *Coccinella septempunctata*

444 Cayenne Pepper, Baked, Stuffed Courgettes and Stuffed Eggplant

(Des Andrew Micallef)

2005 (20 Apr). Insects. T **443** and similar square designs. Multicoloured. W **105**. P 14½.

1412	16c. Type **443**	1·10	1·25
	a. Sheetlet. Nos. 1412/27	16·00	18·00
1413	16c. *Chrysoperla carnea*	1·10	1·25
1414	16c. *Apis mellifera*	1·10	1·25
1415	16c. *Crocothemis erythraea*	1·10	1·25
1416	16c. *Anax imperator*	1·10	1·25
1417	16c. *Lampyris pallida*	1·10	1·25
1418	16c. *Henosepilachna elaterii*	1·10	1·25
1419	16c. *Forficula decipiens*	1·10	1·25
1420	16c. *Mantis religiosa*	1·10	1·25
1421	16c. *Eumenes lunulatus*	1·10	1·25
1422	16c. *Cerambyx cerdo*	1·10	1·25
1423	16c. *Gryllus bimaculatus*	1·10	1·25
1424	16c. *Xylocopa violacea*	1·10	1·25
1425	16c. *Cicada orni*	1·10	1·25
1426	16c. *Acrida ungarica*	1·10	1·25
1427	16c. *Oryctes nasicornis*	1·10	1·25
1412/27	*Set of* 16	16·00	18·00

Nos. 1412/27 were printed together, *se-tenant*, in sheetlets of 16 stamps.

(Des Joseph P. Smith)

2005 (9 May). Europa. Gastronomy. T **444** and similar vert design. Multicoloured. W **105**. P 14.

1428	16c. Type **444**	1·00	60
1429	51c. Roast rabbit	3·00	3·75

2005 (24 May). Flowers. Personalised Stamps. Designs as Nos. 1139a and 1143 but printed by Printex and with imprint date "2005". Multicoloured. W **105**. P 14½.

1430	7c. *Vitex agnus-castus*	45	15
1431	16c. Yellow-throated crocus	80	55

Nos. 1430/1 were each printed with a *se-tenant* stamp-size label attached at right advertising the 25th anniversary of Sliema Stamp Shop. These labels could be personalised with the addition of a photograph or, in the case of businesses, advertisments.

446 "The Beheading of St Catherine"

(Des Francis X. Ancilleri)

2005 (8 June). St Catherine in Art. T **446** and similar multicoloured designs. W **105**. P 14×14½ (horiz) or 14½×14 (vert).

1432	28c. Type **446**	1·40	1·40
1433	28c. "Martyrdom of St Catherine" (Mattia Preti) (vert)	1·40	1·40
1434	45c. "Mystic Marriage" (Francesco Zahra) (vert)	2·00	2·75
1435	45c. "St Catherine Disputing the Philosophers" (Francesco Zahra)	2·00	2·75
1432/5	*Set of* 4	6·00	7·50

447 Mons. Mikiel Azzopardi (philanthropist)

(Des Maurice Tanti Burlò)

2005 (13 July). Personalities. T **447** and similar square designs. Multicoloured. W **105**. P 14½.

1436	3c. Type **447**	30	20
1437	19c. Egidio Lapira (professor of dental surgery)	1·25	1·00
1438	20c. Letter and shield of Order of the Knights (Guzeppi Callus, doctor)	1·25	1·00
1439	46c. Hand writing musical score (Geronimo Abos, composer)	2·50	2·75
1440	76c. Gann Frangisk Abela (historian)	4·00	5·50
1436/40	*Set of* 5	8·25	9·50

448 Horse-drawn Hearse

(Des Damian Borg Nicholas)

2005 (19 Aug). Equines in Malta. T **448** and similar horiz designs. Multicoloured. W **105** (sideways). P 14×14½.

1441	11c. Type **448**	1·00	40
1442	15c. Mule pulling traditional wooden plough	1·25	50
1443	62c. Mule on treadmill grinding flour	3·75	4·50
1444	66c. Horse-drawn water sprinkler cart	3·75	4·50
1441/4	*Set of* 4	8·75	9·00

449 Queue outside "Victory Kitchen" and Ruins of Royal Opera House, Valletta

(Des Richard J. Caruana)

2005 (23 Sept). 60th Anniv of End of Second World War. Battle of Malta. T **449** and similar horiz designs, all showing George Cross. Multicoloured. W **105** (sideways). P 14×14½.

1445	2c. Type **449**	50	30
1446	5c. Royal Navy convoy under air attack	75	25
1447	25c. Anti aircraft guns and St. Publius Church, Floriana	2·00	95
1448	51c. Pilots scrambling, Hurricane, Spitfire and Sea Gladiators	3·75	3·75
1449	£1 Tanker Ohio and unloading of supplies at Grand Harbour, August 1943	7·00	8·50
1445/9	*Set of* 5	12·50	12·50

450 "The Nativity"

(Des Paul Camilleri Cauchi)

2005 (12 Oct). Christmas. Paintings by Emvin Cremona from Sanctuary of Our Lady of Ta' Pinu, Gozo. T **450** and similar multicoloured designs. W **105** (sideways on 7, 22, 50c.). P 14×14½ (7, 22c.), 14½×14 (16c.) or 14 (50c.).

1450	7c. Type **450**	60	25
1451	16c. "The Annunciation" (vert)	1·10	55
1452	22c. "The Adoration of the Magi"	1·50	75
1453	50c. "The Flight to Egypt" (69×30 mm)	3·50	4·50
1450/3	*Set of* 4	6·00	5·50

451 Maltese, Commonwealth and CHOGM Flags

(Des Harry Borg)

2005 (23 Nov). Commonwealth Heads of Government Meeting (CHOGM), Valletta. T **451** and similar horiz designs, each showing Maltese and Commonwealth flags. Multicoloured. W **105**. P 14×14½.

MS1454 Four sheets, each 75×63 mm. (a) 14c. Type **451**. (b) 28c. Peace doves. (c) 37c. Maltese cross. (d) 75c. Silhouettes shaking hands *Set of 4 sheets* 7·00 9·50

452 1986 8c. Butterflies Stamp

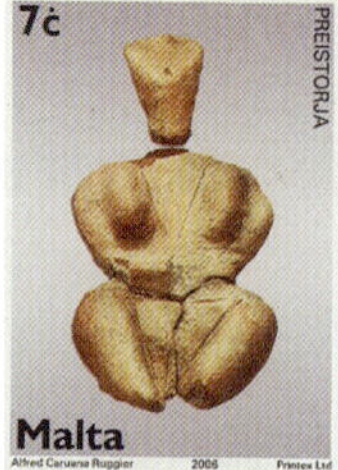

453 Female Terracotta Figurine, c. 4100 B.C.

(Des Martin Bonavia)

2006 (3 Jan). 50th Anniv of Europa Stamps. T **452** and similar horiz designs showing Maltese Europa stamps. W **105** (sideways). P 14.

MS1455	120×85 mm. 5c. Type **452**; 13c. 1983 30c. Fort St. Angelo stamp; 23c. 1977 20c. Is-Salini stamp; 24c. 1989 35c. Girls with dolls stamp	4·00	5·00

No. **MS**1455 has a composite background design.

(Des Alfred Caruana Ruggier)

2006 (25 Feb). Ceramics in Maltese Collections. T **453** and similar horiz designs. Multicoloured. W **105**. P 14½×14.

1456	7c. Type **453**	50	25
1457	16c. Roman terracotta head, c. 1st-3rd century B.C.	1·00	55
1458	28c. Terracotta oil lamp holder, 14th-15th century A.D.	1·25	1·40
1459	37c. Sicilian maiolica display plate, 18th century	2·25	2·40
1460	60c. Modern stylized figure in Maltese costume (Ianni Bonniçi)	3·00	4·25
1456/60	*Set of* 5	7·25	8·00

454 Shetland Pony

455 Penitents carrying Crosses

(Des Andrew Micallef)

2006 (14 Mar). Pets. T **454** and similar square designs. Multicoloured. W **105** (sideways). P 14½.

1461	7c. Type **454**	85	90
	a. Sheetlet. Nos. 1461/76	12·00	13·00
1462	7c. Kelb tal-But (Maltese pocket dog)	85	90
1463	7c. Goldfish	85	90
1464	7c. Siamese cat	85	90
1465	7c. Siamese fighting fish	85	90
1466	7c. Ferret	85	90
1467	7c. Canary	85	90
1468	7c. Terrapin	85	90
1469	22c. Chinchilla	85	90
1470	22c. Budgerigar	85	90
1471	22c. Rabbit	85	90
1472	22c. Zebra finch	85	90
1473	22c. Kelb tal-Kacca (Maltese hunting dog)	85	90
1474	22c. Pigeon	85	90
1475	22c. Guinea pig	85	90
1476	22c. Cat	85	90
1461/76	*Set of* 16	12·00	13·00

Nos. 1461/76 were printed together, *se-tenant*, in sheetlets of 16 stamps.

(Des Joseph P. Smith)

2006 (12 Apr). Holy Week. T **455** and similar vert designs. Multicoloured. W **105**. P 14.

1477	7c. Type **455**	50	15
1478	15c. Crucifixion tableau in procession	1·00	30
1479	22c. Burial of Christ tableau in procession	1·25	75
1480	27c. Statue of the Risen Christ paraded on Easter Sunday	1·50	1·10
1481	82c. Altar of Repose, Collegiate Church of St. Lawrence, Vittoriosa	4·50	6·50
1477/81	*Set of* 5	8·00	8·00

456 Circuit of Linked People

457 Bobby Charlton

(Des Astrid Zammit)

2006 (9 May). Europa. Integration. T **456** and similar multicoloured design. W **105**. P 14½ (16c.) or 14½×14 (51c.).

1482	16c. Type **456**	1·00	50
1483	51c. Four rows of linked people (30×43 mm)	2·50	3·50

(Des Maurice Tanti Burlò)

2006 (2 June). World Cup Football Championship, Germany. T **457** and similar vert designs. Multicoloured. W **105**. P 14.

1484	7c. Type **457**	50	15
1485	16c. Pelè	1·00	30
1486	27c. Franz Beckenbauer	1·60	1·10
1487	76c. Dino Zoff	4·25	6·00
1484/7	*Set of* 4	6·50	6·75
MS1488	160×86 mm. Nos. 1484/7. Wmk sideways	6·50	7·50

(Des 26th Frame)

2006 (5 June). Sting Concert, Luxol Grounds. Sheet 121×86 mm containing design as No. 1188. W **105** (sideways). P 14.

MS1489	£1.50 "Sunny Day" (Bettina Paris)	7·50	8·50

458 *Santa Anna* ("Gran Caracca di Rodi"), 1530

(Des Francis X. Ancilleri)

2006 (18 Aug). Naval Vessels. T **458** and similar horiz designs. Multicoloured. W **105** (sideways). P 14.

1490	8c. Type **458**	80	20
1491	29c. *Guillaume Tell* (French) dismasted by HMS *Penelope*, *Lion* and *Foudroyant*, Malta, 1800 (Edwin Galea)	2·00	1·10
1492	51c. USS *Constitution*, 1837 (J. G. Evans)	3·25	3·00
1493	76c. HMS *Dreadnought* leaving Grand Harbour, November 1913	5·00	6·00
1494	£1 USS *Belknap* (frigate) and *Slava* (Soviet cruiser) providing communications support for Malta Summit, December 1989	6·00	7·50
1490/4	*Set of* 5	15·00	16·00

459 Candles ("Happy Birthday")

(Des Jean Pierre Mizzi)

2006 (18 Sept). Occasions. T **459** and similar square designs. Multicoloured. W **105**. P 14½.

1495	8c. Type **459**	55	15
1496	16c. Heart ("Happy Anniversary")	1·00	35
1497	27c. Stars holding parcel, balloon and candle ("Congratulations")	1·60	1·25
1498	37c. Balloons ("Best Wishes")	2·00	2·75
1495/8	*Set of* 4	4·75	4·00

460 Wignacourt Tower

(Des Anouschka Grech)

2006 (29 Sept). Maltese Castles and Towers. T **460** and similar horiz designs. Multicoloured. W **105** (sideways). P 14×14½.

1499	7c. Type **460**	65	15
1500	16c. Verdala Castle	1·25	35
1501	27c. San Lucjan Tower	1·90	1·10
1502	37c. Kemmuna Tower	2·50	1·75
1503	£1 Selmun Castle	6·00	8·50
1499/503	*Set of* 5	11·00	10·50

2006 (13 Oct). As No. 1134 but W **105** (sideways) and printed in lithography by Printex Ltd. P 14½. Imprint date "2006".

1503*a*	1c. *Helichrysum melitense*	40	50

461 Paolino Vassallo, "Inno per Natale" and Nativity

(Des George Vella)

2006 (5 Nov). Christmas Music. T **461** and similar horiz designs showing composer and score. Multicoloured. W **105** (sideways). P 14×14½.

1504	8c. Type **461**	55	15
1505	16c. Carmelo Pace, "They Heard the Angels" and Three Magi	1·00	30
1506	22c. Paul Nani, "Maltese Christmas" and angels	1·40	1·25
1507	27c. Carlo Diacono, "Notte di Natale", shepherds and angel	1·60	1·60
1504/7	*Set of* 4	3·00	3·50
MS1508	120×86 mm. 50c. Wolfgang Amadeus Mozart (250th birth anniv) and "Alma di Creatoris". P 14	3·00	3·50

(Des Jean Pierre Mizzi)

2006 (22 Dec). Bob Geldof Concert for YMCA, Manoel Island. Sheet 121×86 mm containing design as No. 1189. W **105** (sideways). P 14.

MS1509	£1.50 "Hands holding Heart" (Roxana Caruana)	7·50	8·50

462 Wrought Iron Work

(Des Richard Caruana)

2006 (29 Dec). Crafts. T **462** and similar horiz designs. Multicoloured. W **105** (sideways). P 14×14½.

1510	8c. Type **462**	55	15
1511	16c. Glass making	1·00	35
1512	22c. Filigree work	1·40	70
1513	37c. Pottery	2·00	1·75
1514	60c. Reed basketwork	3·75	5·00
1510/14	*Set of* 5	7·75	7·25

463 Stone Head

464 *Opuntia ficus-indica* (prickly pear)

(Des Josian Bonello)

2007 (28 Feb). Prehistoric Sculptures, c 3000–2500 BC. T **463** and similar multicoloured designs. W **105** (sideways on horiz designs). P 14½×14 (vert) or 14×14½ (horiz).

1515	15c. Type **463**	1·00	30
1516	29c. Stone bas-relief of animals (horiz)	1·75	1·10
1517	60c. Stone-carved spiral pattern (horiz)	3·75	4·25
1518	£1.50 Clay statuette of female figure	7·50	9·00
1515/18	*Set of* 4	12·50	13·00

(Des Andrew Micallef)

2007 (16 Apr). Maltese Fruits. T **464** and similar square designs. Multicoloured. W **105** (sideways). P 14½.

1519	8c. Type **464**	45	50
	a. Sheetlet. Nos. 1519/34	6·50	7·25
1520	8c. *Vitis vinifera* (grapes)	45	50
1521	8c. *Eriobotrya japonica* (loquat)	45	50
1522	8c. *Morus nigra* (black mulberry)	45	50
1523	8c. *Ficus carica* (figs)	45	50
1524	8c. *Citrus limonum* (lemons)	45	50
1525	8c. *Pyrus communis* (pear)	45	50
1526	8c. *Prunus persica* (peaches)	45	50
1527	8c. *Punica granatum* (pomegranate)	45	50
1528	8c. *Prunus salicina* (Japanese plum)	45	50
1529	8c. *Citrullus vulgaris* (watermelon)	45	50
1530	8c. *Citrus sinensis* (orange)	45	50
1531	8c. *Olea europaea* (olives)	45	50
1532	8c. *Lycopersicon esculentum* (tomatoes)	45	50
1533	8c. *Malus domestica* (apples)	45	50
1534	8c. *Cucumis melo* (melon)	45	50
1519/34	*Set of* 16	6·50	7·25

Nos. 1519/34 were printed together, *se-tenant*, in sheetlets of sixteen stamps.

465 Wrought-iron Balcony

466 Lord Baden-Powell (founder) and District Commissioner Capt J. V. Abela, Malta, 1937

(Des Alfred Caruana Ruggier)

2007 (28 Apr). Maltese Balconies. T **465** and similar multicoloured designs. W **105**. P 14.

1535	8c. Type **465**	50	40
1536	22c. Ornate open stone balcony and recessed doorway, Gozo	1·25	1·10
1537	27c. Balustraded balcony, National Library of Malta	1·60	1·40
1538	29c. Carved stone balcony with glazed timber enclosure, Gozo	1·75	1·50
1539	46c. Two balconies on Art Deco 1930's building	2·75	3·50
1535/9	*Set of* 5	7·00	7·00
MS1540	123×86 mm. 51c. Detail of balcony on Hostel de Verdelin, Valletta (horiz). Wmk sideways	2·75	3·25

(Des Mark Anthony Vella)

2007 (9 May). Europa. Centenary of Scouting. T **466** and similar square design. Multicoloured. W **105**. P 14½.

1541	16c. Type **466**	1·00	60
	a. Wmk sideways	1·40	1·40
	ab. Booklet pane. No. 1541a×5	6·00	

1542 51c. Malta scouts marching, Golden Jubilee Jamboree, near Birmingham, 1957 .... 3·00 3·50

No. 1541a was only issued in 80c. booklets, No. SB11.

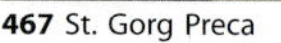

467 St. Gorg Preca

468 Rocking Horse, Tricycle and Car, all Triang (1950s)

(Des Edward Pirotta)

2007 (28 May). Canonization of Dun Gorg Preca. T **467** and similar square design. Multicoloured. W **105**. P 14½.

1543 8c. Type **467** 50 50
1544 £1 As Type **467** but sun rising behind Basilica .... 5·00 6·00

(Des Richard Caruana)

2007 (11 July). Toys from Days Gone By. T **468** and similar vert designs. Multicoloured. W **105**. P 14.

1545 2c. Type **468** 10 10
1546 3c. Pedigree dolls pram (1950s), drums and skipping rope 15 15
1547 16c. Japanese tin cabin cruiser (1960s), sand pails, spade and Triang sailing boat 90 80
1548 22c. Lenci doll, Pedigree doll and 1930s Armand Marseille doll .... 1·25 1·10
1549 50c. Alps clockwork racing car (1950s), P.N. motorcycle (1950s) and Chad Valley delivery van (1930s) .... 3·25 4·00
1545/9 *Set of 5* .... 5·00 5·50

469 "St. Jerome" (Caravaggio)

2007 (20 July). 400th Anniv of the Arrival of Michelangelo Merisi (Caravaggio) in Malta. T **469** and similar multicoloured designs showing his paintings. W **105** (sideways). P 14.

1550 5c. Type **469** 35 35
1551 29c. "The Beheading of St. John the Baptist" (detail) .... 1·75 1·75
MS1552 130×86 mm. £2 "The Beheading of St. John the Baptist" (vert) .... 14·00 16·00

470 Malta GPO Royal Enfield Motorcycle, 1954

(Des Joe P. Smith)

2007 (12 Sept). Motorcycles. T **470** and similar horiz designs. Multicoloured. W **105** (sideways). P 14.

1553 1c. Type **470** 15 30
1554 16c. Malta Garrison Matchless G3/L, 1941 .... 1·25 85
1555 27c. Civilian Minerva, 1903 .... 2·00 1·40
1556 50c. Malta Police Triumph Speed Twin, 1965 .... 4·00 4·50
1553/6 *Set of 4* .... 6·75 6·25

471 Heart and "LOVE"

(Des Harry Borg)

2007 (28 Sept). Occasions Greetings Stamps. T **471** and similar square designs. Multicoloured. W **105** (sideways). P 14½.

1557 8c. Type **471** 55 55
1558 8c. Teddy bears 55 55
1559 8c. Star decorations ("Congratulations!") 55 55
1560 8c. Pink roses ("GREETINGS") 55 55
1561 8c. Balloons 55 55
1562 8c. Champagne glasses 55 55
1557/62 *Set of 6* .... 3·00 3·00

472 Mdina Skyline seen from Mtarfa

(Des John Martin Borg)

2007 (1 Oct). Maltese Scenery. T **472** and similar horiz designs showing watercolours by John Martin Borg. W **105** (sideways). P 14.

1563 11c. Type **472** 90 65
1564 16c. Windmill, farmhouse and church, Qrendi .... 1·25 85
1565 37c. Vittoriosa waterfront .... 2·50 2·25
1566 46c. Mgarr Harbour, Gozo .... 3·00 3·00
1567 76c. Xlendi Bay, Gozo .... 4·75 6·00
1563/7 *Set of 5* .... 11·00 11·50

No. 1564 is inscr "sepac".

2007 (18 Oct). 34U (Tree for You) Campaign. Sheet 100×66 mm containing design as No. 1531. W **105** (sideways). P 14.

MS1568 75c. *Olea europaea* (olives) .... 4·00 5·00

473 Military Band

474 Madonna and Baby Jesus

(Des Joe Mark Micallef)

2007 (13 Nov). Maltese Bands. T **473** and similar square designs. Multicoloured. W **105**. P 14½.

1569 4c. Type **473** 45 40
1570 15c. Police band .... 1·50 85
1571 21c. Band playing at carnival .... 1·75 1·25
1572 22c. Band playing at Christmas .... 1·75 1·25
1573 £1 Band and conductor .... 7·00 8·50
1569/73 *Set of 5* .... 11·00 11·00

2007 (20 Nov). Christmas. T **474** and similar square designs showing details from painting "The Nativity" by Giuseppe Cali in St. Andrew's parish church, Luqa. Multicoloured. W **105**. P 14½.

1574 8c. Type **474** 60 30
1575 16c. Holy Family with two countrywomen and young girl .... 1·25 85
1576 27c. Baby Jesus and young girl .... 2·00 2·25
1574/6 *Set of 3* .... 3·50 3·00

Similar stamps were issued by the Vatican City.

475 Boys playing Football

476 Malta £1 Coin

(Des Harry Borg)

2007 (29 Dec). Anniversaries and Personalities. T **475** and similar multicoloured designs. W **105**. P 14.

1577 4mils Type **475** (25th anniv of Youth Football Association) ... 10 10
1578 9c. Children receiving religious instruction (centenary of Society of Christian Doctrine) ... 65 30
1579 16c. Canon Monsignor Professor Francesco Bonnici (founder of St. Joseph Institute for orphan boys) ... 1·25 85
1580 43c. Father Manwel Magri (ethnographer, archaeologist and educator) ... 3·00 3·00
1581 86c. Carolina Cauchi (founder of Dominican order at Lunzjata Monastery, Gozo) ... 5·50 6·50
1577/81 *Set of 5* ... 9·50 9·50
MS1582 100×70 mm. 76c. Signatories (50th anniv of Treaty of Rome) (horiz). Wmk sideways ... 4·50 5·50

(Des Frank X. Ancilleri)

2007 (31 Dec). Coins of Malta 1972–2007. Sheet 100×66 mm. W **105** (sideways). P 14½.

MS1583 **476** £1 multicoloured ... 6·00 7·00

(New Currency: 100 cents = 1 euro)

(Des Frank X. Ancilleri)

2008 (1 Jan). Adoption of the Euro Currency (1st issue). Sheet 100×66 mm containing square design as T **476**. Multicoloured. W **105** (sideways). P 14½.

MS1584 €1 Obverse and reverse of one euro coin ... 3·50 4·00

477 "Aphrodite" Statue of Cyprus

478 Door Knocker from Ministry of Finance, Valletta

2008 (1 Jan). Adoption of the Euro Currency (2nd issue). Sheet 100×62 mm containing T **477** and similar square design. Multicoloured. W **105** (sideways). P 14½.

MS1585 €1 Type **477**; €1 "Sleeping Lady" statuette, Malta ... 5·50 7·00

A similar miniature sheet was issued by Cyprus.

(Des Frank X. Ancilleri)

2008 (5 Mar). Door Knockers. T **478** and similar vert designs. Multicoloured. W **105**. P 14.

1586 26c. Type **478** ... 1·00 65
1587 51c. Fish door knocker from Museum of Fine Arts, Valletta ... 1·60 1·25
1588 63c. Door knocker from Department of Industrial & Employment Relations, Valletta ... 1·75 2·00
1589 €1.77 Door knocker from Museum of Archaeology, Valletta ... 5·00 6·00
1586/9 *Set of 4* ... 8·50 9·00

479 Shooting

481 Woodcarving by Xandru Farrugia, Conversion of St. Paul Church, Hal Safi

480 Postman and Mail Room (in sepia)

(Des Darren Duncan)

2008 (7 Mar). Olympic Games, Beijing. T **479** and similar horiz designs. Multicoloured. W **105** (sideways). P 14.

1590 5c. Type **479** ... 15 10
1591 12c. Swimming ... 30 20
1592 €1.57 Running ... 4·75 5·50
1590/2 *Set of 3* ... 4·75 5·50

(Des Edward D. Pirotta)

2008 (9 May). Europa. The Letter. Multicoloured. W **105** (sideways). P 14½.

1593 37c. Type **480** ... 1·25 85
a. Booklet pane. No. 1593×5 ... 5·50
1594 €1.19 As Type **480** (in monochrome) ... 4·00 4·25

(Des Paul Psaila)

2008 (28 June). Annus Paulinus 2008–2009 (2000th Birth Anniv of St. Paul). T **481** and similar vert designs showing statues of St. Paul. Multicoloured. W **105**. P 14.

1595 19c. Type **481** ... 70 30
1596 68c. Pápier maché statue by Agostino Camilleri, St. Paul's Shipwreck Church, Munxar, Gozo ... 2·25 2·25
1597 €1.08 Wooden statue by Giovanni Caruana, St. Paul's Shipwreck Church, Rabat ... 3·75 4·25
1595/7 *Set of 3* ... 6·00 6·25
MS1598 120×86 mm. €3 Wooden statue by Melchiorre Gafà, St. Paul's Shipwreck Church, Valletta. Wmk sideways ... 8·50 9·50

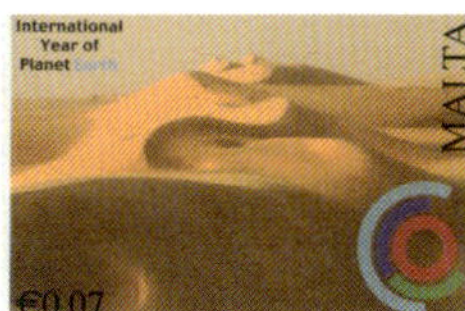

482 Sand Dunes

(Des Paul Psaila)

2008 (11 Aug). International Year of Planet Earth. T **482** and similar horiz designs. Multicoloured. W **105** (sideways). P 14.

1599 7c. Type **482** ... 30 20
1600 86c. Single tree growing in field ... 3·00 3·00
1601 €1 Globe ... 3·50 3·75
1602 €1.77 Rocky coast ... 6·00 7·00
1599/602 *Set of 4* ... 11·50 12·50

483 MSC *Musica*

(Des Daniel Mangini)

2008 (18 Nov). Cruise Liners (1st series). T **483** and similar horiz designs. Multicoloured. W **105** (sideways). P 14.

1603	63c. Type **483**	2·50	1·50
1604	€1.16 M.S. *Voyager of the Seas*	4·00	4·00
1605	€1.40 M.S. *Westerdam*	4·50	4·50
1606	€3 RMS *Queen Elizabeth II*	10·00	12·00
1603/6	*Set of 4*	19·00	20·00

See also Nos. 1627/30.

484 *Madonna and Child with Infant St. John the Baptist* (detail) (Francesco Trevisani)

(Des Daniel Mangini)

2008 (27 Nov). Christmas. Nativity Paintings from the National Museum of Fine Arts, Valletta. T **484** and similar horiz designs. Multicoloured. W **105** (sideways). P 14.

1607	19c. Type **484**	60	30
1608	26c. *Nativity* (detail of Virgin and Christ Child from panel by Maestro Alberto)	90	60
1609	37c. *Virgin and Child with Infant St. John the Baptist* (Carlo Maratta)	1·25	1·25
1607/9	*Set of 3*	2·50	2·00

485 *Laetiorus sulphureus*

(Des Stephen Mifsud)

2009 (27 Mar). Fungi. T **485** and similar square designs. Multicoloured. W **105** (sideways). P 14.

1610	5c. Type **485**	15	15
1611	12c. *Montagnea arenaria*	35	30
1612	19c. *Pleurotus eryngii*	65	40
1613	26c. *Inonotus indicus*	90	70
1614	€1.57 *Suillus collinitus*	5·25	5·75
1610/14	*Set of 4*	6·50	6·50

486 Dornier Wal SANA Seaplane

2009 (28 Apr). Vintage Postal Transport. T **486** and similar square designs. Multicoloured. W **105** (sideways). P 14.

1615	9c. Type **486**	40	25
1616	35c. Postmen on BSA motorcycles	1·75	1·00
1617	€2.50 Postmen with Raleigh bicycles	8·00	9·00
1618	€3 Gozo Mail Boat	9·00	10·00
1615/18	*Set of 4*	17·00	18·00

487 Emblem

(Des Edward Pirotta)

2009 (30 Apr). Tenth Anniv of the Euro. W **105** (sideways). P 14.

1619	**487**	€2 multicoloured	6·00	7·00

488 Galileo Galilei, his Sketch of Moon and Apollo 11 Lunar Module *Eagle*

(Des Alexei Pace and Gordon Caruana Dingli)

2009 (9 May). Europa. Astronomy. T **488** and similar vert design. Multicoloured. W **105**. P 14.

1620	37c. Type **488**	1·50	1·10
1621	€1.19 William Lassell's telescope (set up in Malta 1861–5) and Nebula M42	3·00	3·50

489 Sailing

(Des Daniel Mangani)

2009 (1 June). 13th Games of the Small States of Europe, Nicosia and Limassol, Cyprus. T **489** and similar horiz designs. Multicoloured. W **105** (sideways). P 14.

1622	10c. Type **489**	35	25
1623	19c. Judo	65	40
1624	37c. Shooting	1·40	1·10
1625	67c. Swimming	2·50	2·50
1626	€1.77 Athletics	5·00	6·00
1622/6	*Set of 5*	9·00	9·25

(Des Fabio Agius)

2009 (15 July). Cruise Liners (2nd series). Horiz designs as T **483**. Multicoloured. W **105** (sideways). P 14.

1627	37c. *Seabourn Pride*	1·75	1·10
1628	68c. *Brilliance of the Seas*	2·50	1·90
1629	91c. *Costa Magica* and *Costa Atlantica*	3·25	3·25
1630	€2 MSC *Splendida*	6·00	7·00
1627/30	*Set of 4*	12·00	12·00

490 Headland

(Des Stefan Attard)

2009 (16 Sept). Scenery. T **490** and similar horiz designs. Multicoloured. W **105** (sideways). P 14.

1631	2c. Type **490**	15	25
1632	7c. Watchtower of Knights of the Sovereign Military Order of Malta	35	20

1633	37c. Stone salt pans, Qbajjar, Gozo	1·50	70
1634	€1.02 Segment of the Ggantija Temples, Gozo	3·50	4·50
1631/4	*Set of 4*	5·00	5·00

No. 1633 is inscr 'sepac'.

491 *Mater Admirablis* (in the manner of Botticelli)

2009 (30 Nov). Christmas. T **491** and similar vert designs. Multicoloured. W **105**. P 14.

1635	19c. Type **491**	65	30
1636	37c. *Madonna and Child* (Corrado Giacquinto)	1·25	60
1637	63c. *The Madonna and Child* (follower of Simone Cantarini)	2·00	2·50
1635/7	*Set of 3*	3·50	3·00

492 Skeleton of Prehistoric Animal (Pleistocene Period)

(Des Edward Pirotta and Paul Psaila)

2009 (29 Dec). History of Malta. T **492** and similar multicoloured designs. W **105** (sideways on horiz designs). P 14.

1638	1c. Type **492**	15	30
1639	2c. Ruins of stone temple (Early Temple Period)	20	30
1640	5c. Carved stone pattern (Late Temple Period)	30	25
1641	7c. Pair of pots (Bronze Age)	35	25
1642	9c. Gold statue (Phoenician and Punic Period) (*vert*)	40	40
1643	10c. Mosaic (Roman Period)	40	40
1644	19c. Gold coin (Byzantine Period) (*vert*)	65	30
1645	26c. Fragment of carved stone (Arab Period)	90	60
1646	37c. Painting (Norman and Hohenstaufen Period) (*vert*)	1·25	75
1647	50c. Stone tablet carved with shield (Angevin and Aragonese) (*vert*)	1·75	1·75
1648	51c. Gold pattern with central Maltese Cross (Knights of St. John)	1·75	1·75
1649	63c. Painting of officers and crew disembarking in rowing boats from ships (French Period)	1·75	1·75
1650	68c. George Cross (British Period) (*vert*)	2·00	2·00
1651	86c. Independence (*vert*)	2·75	2·75
1652	€1 Republic (*vert*)	3·50	3·50
1653	€1.08 EU Accession (*vert*)	3·50	3·50
1654	€5 Arms of Malta (*vert*)	16·00	17·00
1638/54	*Set of 17*	35·00	32·00
MS1655	169×263 mm. Nos. 1638/54. Wmk upright		

493 100 Ton Gun, Fort Rinella, Malta, 2010

(Des John Batchelor)

2010 (19 Feb). '100 Ton' Guns. Sheet 118×102 mm containing T **493** and similar horiz designs. Multicoloured. W **105**. P 13½.

MS1656	75c.×4 Type **493**; '100 ton' gun, Fort Rinella, Malta, 1882; '100 ton' gun, Napier of Magdala Battery, Gibraltar, 1880; '100 ton' gun, Napier of Magdala Battery, Gibraltar, 2010	7·00	8·00

A miniature sheet containing the same designs was issued by Gibraltar.

494 Balloons

(Des Sean Cini)

2010 (17 Mar). Occasions Greetings Stamps. T **494** and similar multicoloured designs. W **105** (sideways on horiz designs). P 14.

1657	19c. Type **494**	65	65
1658	19c. Aerial view of coastline and offshore rocks	65	65
1659	19c. Mortarboard and scroll	65	65
1660	19c. Woman greeting man and crowd (painting)	65	65
1661	19c. Two glasses of champagne and bottle in ice bucket (*vert*)	65	65
1662	19c. St. John's Co-Cathedral, Valletta and fireworks (*vert*)	65	65
1663	19c. Hand holding trophy (*vert*)	65	65
1664	37c. Outline map of Malta and Gozo	1·10	1·10
1657/64	*Set of 8*	5·00	5·00

495 Pope Benedict XVI

(Des Sean Cimi. Litho Printex Ltd)

2010 (17 Apr). Visit of Pope Benedict XVI to Malta. Sheet 130×85 mm. W **105** (sideways). P 14.

MS1665	**495** €3 multicoloured	9·75	9·75

496 *Puttinu u Toninu* (Dr. Philip Farrugia Randon)

(Des Edward D. Pirotta. Litho Printex)

2010 (4 May). Europa. Children's Books. T **496** and similar vert design. Multicoloured. W **105**. P 14.

1666	37c. Type **496**	1·50	1·10
	a. Booklet pane. No. 1666×5	6·50	
1667	€1.19 *Meta l-Milied ma giex* (Clare Azzopardi)	3·00	3·25

497 Globe and National Flags

(Des Frank Azzopardi. Litho Printex Ltd)

2010 (11 June). World Cup Football Championship, South Africa. T **497** and similar vert design. Multicoloured. W **106**. P 14.

1668	63c. Type **497**	1·75	1·75
1669	€2.50 Zakumi the leopard mascot	7·00	7·50
MS1669*a*	131×80 mm. As Nos. 1668/9. Wmk sideways.	8·75	9·25

498 Maltese Wall Lizard

(Des Maurice Tanti Burlo. Litho Printex Ltd)

2010 (23 Sept). Biodiversity. T **498** and similar horiz designs. Multicoloured. W **105** (sideways on horiz designs). P 14.

1670	19c. Type **498**	75	40
1671	68c. Storm petrel (*vert*)	2·50	2·00
1672	86c. Maltese pyramidal orchid (*vert*)	3·00	3·00
1673	€1.40 Freshwater crab	3·75	4·50
1670/3	*Set of* 4	9·00	9·00

499 Azure Window, Gozo

(Des Cedric Galea Pirotta. Litho Printex Ltd)

2010 (19 Oct). Natural Treasures. T **499** and similar multicoloured designs. W **105** (sideways on horiz designs). P 14.

1674	37c. Type **499**	1·60	1·10
1675	51c. Blue Grotto, Zurrieq (*vert*)	2·25	2·00
1676	67c. Ta' Cenc, Gozo (*vert*)	2·50	2·50
1677	€1.16 Filfla	3·00	3·75
1674/7	*Set of* 4	8·50	8·50

500 *The Adoration of the Magi* (Valerio Castello)

(Litho Printex Ltd)

2010 (9 Nov). Christmas. T **500** and similar multicoloured designs. W **105** (sideways on horiz designs). P 14.

1678	19c. Type **500**	65	30
1679	37c. *The Flight into Egypt* (Filippo Paladini)	1·50	1·10
1680	63c. *Madonna di Maggio* (Pierre Guillemin) (*vert*)	1·75	2·00
1678/80	*Set of* 3	3·50	3·00

501 Cancelled Malta 1860 ½d. Buff Stamp

(Des Joseph Said. Litho Printex Ltd)

2010 (1 Dec). 150th Anniv of the First Malta Stamp. Sheet 130×85 mm. W **105** (sideways). P 14.

MS1681	**501** €2.80 multicoloured	8·50	9·00

502 *Valletta*

(Des Edward Said. Litho Printex Ltd)

2011 (9 Mar). Treasures of Malta. Landscapes. T **502** and similar horiz designs showing oil paintings by Edward Said. Multicoloured. W **105** (sideways). P 14.

1682	19c. Type **502**	65	30
1683	37c. *Manoel Island*	1·50	1·10
1684	€1.57 *Cittadella* (Gozo)	4·25	4·25
1682/4	*Set of* 3	6·00	5·50

503 *Chimaera monstrosa* (Rabbit fish)

(Litho Printex Ltd)

2011 (29 Apr). 50th Anniv of WWF (Worldwide Fund for Nature). *Chimaera monstrosa* (Rabbit fish). Sheet 130×85 mm containing T **503** and similar horiz designs. Multicoloured. W **105**. P 13½.

MS1685 51c. Type **503**; 63c. Rabbit fish (swimming towards top right; 67c. Rabbit fish (seen from front); 97c. Rabbit fish (with fins outstretched)

504 Trees, Pine Cones, Flowers and Butterfly (Nicole Sciberras)

(Litho Printex Ltd)

2011 (9th–May). Europa. Forests. T **504** and similar vert design. Multicoloured. W **105**. P 14.

1686	37c. Type **504**	1·50	1·10
1687	€1.19 Trees, fallen tree and fungi	3·25	4·00

STAMP BOOKLETS

B **1** General Post Office, Palazzo Parisio, Valletta

1970 (16 May). Brownish black on brownish grey cover, 92×48 mm, as Type B **1**. Stitched.

SB1 2s.6d. booklet containing six 1d. and twelve 2d. (Nos. 331, 333) in blocks of 6 .... 5·50

B **1a** Magisterial Palace, Valletta

1970 (18 May). Black on pink cover 92×48 mm, as Type B **1a**. Stitched.

SB2 2s.6d. booklets containing six 1d. and twelve 2d. (Nos. 331, 333) in blocks of 6 .... 4·00

B **1b** Auberge d'Aragon, Valletta

1971 (29 May). Black on green cover, 92×49 mm, as Type B **1b** depicting Auberge d'Aragon, Valletta. Stitched.

SB3 2s.6d. booklet containing six 1d. and twelve 2d. (Nos. 331, 333) in blocks of 6 .... 11·00

B **1c** Fort St. Angelo

1971 (3 July). Black on white cover, 92×49 mm, as Type B **1c** depicting Fort St. Angelo. Stitched.

SB4 5s. booklet containing twelve 5d. (No. 337*b*) in blocks of 6 .... 9·50

B **2**

1994 (2 Nov). Multicoloured covers, 100×75 mm, as Type B **2**. Stamps attached by selvedge.

SB5 50c. booklet containing 5c. (No. 909) in block of 10, (cover showing Malta 1926 2s. Mdina (Notabile) stamp) .... 4·50

SB6 70c. booklet containing 14c. (No. 912) in strip of 5 with 6 airmail labels (cover showing Malta 1926 1s. Valleta Harbour stamp) .... 6·00

B **3**

2003 (16 Apr). Ultramarine and lemon cover, 55×117 mm, as Type B **3**. Stamps attached by selvedge.

SB7 96c. booklet containing pane No. 1297a .... 9·00

B **4**

2003 (22 Oct). Ultramarine and chrome-yellow covers as Type B **4**. Self-adhesive.

SB8 84c. booklet containing pane No. 1335a (48×80 mm) 5·00

SB9 96c. booklet containing pane No. 1336a (48×73 mm) 6·50

B 5

2006 (9 May). Europa. Integration. Orange-yellow, dull violet-blue and royal blue cover, 50×80 mm, as Type B **5**. Stamps attached by selvedge.

SB10 80c. booklet containing 16c. (No. 1482) in strip of 5... 6·00

B 6

2007 (9 May). Europa. Centenary of Scouting. Chrome-yellow and bright ultramarine cover, 75×79 mm, as Type B **6**. Stamps attached by selvedge.

SB11 80c. booklet containing pane No. 1541ab........................ 6·00

B 7

2008 (9 May). Europa. The Letter. Orange-yellow, bright blue and bright ultramarine cover, 79×86 mm, as Type B **7**. Stamps attached by selvedge.

SB12 €1.85 booklet containing pane No. 1593a .... 5·50

B 8

2010 (4 May). Europa. Children's Books. Ultramarine, bright ultramarine and orange-yellow cover, 77×85 mm, as Type B **8**. Stamps attached by the selvedge.

SB13 €1.85 booklet containing pane No. 1666a .... 6·50

B 9

2011 (9 May). Europa. Forests. Grey, red and black cover, 78×85 mm, as Type B **9** . Stamps attached by selvedge.

SB14 €1.85 booklet containing pane No. 1686a .... 5·50

POSTAGE DUE STAMPS

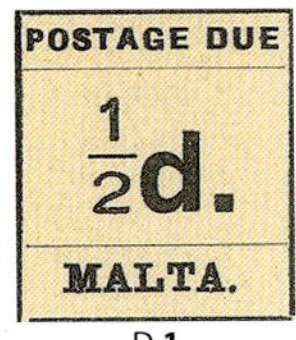

D 1

D 2

1925 (16 Apr). Typeset by Govt Printing Office, Valletta. Imperf.

D1	D **1**	½d. black	1·25	7·50
		a. *Tête-bêche* (horiz pair)	5·00	20·00
D2		1d. black	3·25	3·00
		a. *Tête-bêche* (horiz pair)	10·00	12·00
D3		1½d. black	3·00	3·75
		a. *Tête-bêche* (horiz pair)	10·00	15·00
D4		2d. black	12·00	21·00
		a. *Tête-bêche* (horiz pair)	26·00	55·00
D5		2½d. black	2·75	2·75
		a. "2" of "½" omitted	£900	£1300
		b. *Tête-bêche* (horiz pair)	12·00	15·00
D6		3d. black/*grey*	9·00	15·00
		a. *Tête-bêche* (horiz pair)	30·00	48·00
D7		4d. black/*buff*	5·00	9·50
		a. *Tête-bêche* (horiz pair)	17·00	38·00
D8		6d. black/*buff*	5·00	23·00
		a. *Tête-bêche* (horiz pair)	17·00	60·00
D9		1s. black/*buff*	6·50	23·00
		a. *Tête-bêche* (horiz pair)	25·00	60·00

D10		1s.6d. black/*buff*	16·00	60·00
		a. *Tête-bêche* (horiz pair)	40·00	£140
D1/10 *Set of* 10			55·00	£150

Nos. D1/10 were each issued in sheets containing 4 panes (6×7) printed separately, the impressions in the two right-hand panes being inverted. Fourteen horizontal *tête-bêche* pairs occur from the junction of the left and right-hand panes.

No. D5a occurred on R. 4/4 of the last 2½d. pane position to be printed. Forgeries exist, but can be detected by comparison with a normal example under ultra-violet light. They are often found in pair with normal, showing forged cancellations of "VALLETTA AP 20 25" or "G.P.O. MY 7 25".

(Typo B.W.)

1925 (20 July). Wmk Mult Script CA (sideways). P 12.

D11	D **2**	½d. green	1·25	60
D12		1d. violet	1·25	45
D13		1½d. brown	1·50	80
D14		2d. grey	11·00	1·00
D15		2½d. orange	2·00	1·25
		x. Wmk reversed	£110	
D16		3d. blue	4·25	1·25
D17		4d. olive-green	12·00	16·00
D18		6d. purple	4·00	4·50
D19		1s. black	6·50	13·00
D20		1s.6d. carmine	8·50	42·00
D11/20 *Set of* 10			45·00	70·00
D11s/20s Optd "SPECIMEN." *Set of* 10			£275	

1953–63. Chalk-surfaced paper. Wmk Mult Script CA (sideways). P 12.

D21	D **2**	½d. emerald	70	2·25
D22		1d. purple	70	1·25
		a. *Deep purple* (17.9.63)	75	3·50
D23		1½d. yellow-brown	2·50	13·00
D24		2d. grey-brown (20.3.57)	5·00	9·50
		a. *Blackish brown* (3.4.62)	26·00	13·00
D25		3d. deep slate-blue	1·00	2·00
D26		4d. yellow-olive	3·00	7·00
D21/6 *Set of* 6			11·50	32·00

1966 (1 Oct). As No. D24, but wmk w **12** (sideways).

D27	D **2**	2d. grey-brown	16·00	25·00

1967–70. Ordinary paper. W **105** (sideways).

(a) P 12, line (9.11.67)

D28	D **2**	½d. emerald	4·00	9·00
D29		1d. purple	4·00	9·00
D30		2d. blackish brown	5·50	9·00
D31		4d. yellow-olive	45·00	£100
D28/31 *Set of* 4			50·00	£110

(b) P 12½, comb (30.5.68–70)

D32	D **2**	½d. emerald	35	2·00
D33		1d. purple	30	1·50
D34		1½d. yellow-brown	35	3·25
		a. *Orange-brown* (23.10.70)	1·00	3·00
D35		2d. blackish brown	85	70
		a. *Brownish black* (23.10.70)	2·25	3·00
D36		2½d. yellow-orange	60	70
D37		3d. deep slate-blue	60	60
D38		4d. yellow-olive	1·00	80
D39		6d. purple	75	1·50
D40		1s. black	90	1·50
D41		1s.6d. carmine	2·75	7·00
D32/41 *Set of* 10			7·00	16·00

The above are the local release dates. In the 12½ perforation the London release dates were 21 May for the ½d. to 4d. and 4 June for the 6d. to 1s.6d.

Nos. D34*a* and D35*a* are on glazed paper.

D **3** Maltese Lace

(Des G. Pace. Litho Printex Ltd, Malta)

1973 (28 Apr). W **105**. P 13×13½.

D42	D **3**	2m. grey-brown and reddish brown	10	10
D43		3m. dull orange and Indian red	10	15
D44		5m. rose and bright scarlet	15	20
D45		1c. turquoise and bottle green	30	35
D46		2c. slate and black	40	35
D47		3c. light yellow-brown and red-brown	40	35
D48		5c. dull blue and royal blue	65	70
D49		10c. reddish lilac and plum	85	1·00
D42/9 *Set of* 8			2·50	2·75

D **4**

(Des M. Bonavia. Litho Printex Ltd, Malta)

1993 (4 Jan). W **105** (sideways). P 14.

D50	D **4**	1c. magenta and pale magenta	20	30
D51		2c. new blue and pale blue	25	40
D52		5c. blue-green and pale turquoise-green	35	45
D53		10c. yellow-orange and greenish yellow	55	55
D50/3 *Set of* 4			1·25	1·50

Index

Dear Catalogue User,

As a collector and Stanley Gibbons catalogue user for many years myself, I am only too aware of the need to provide you with the information you seek in an accurate, timely and easily accessible manner. Naturally, I have my own views on where changes could be made, but one thing I learned long ago is that we all have different opinions and requirements.

I would therefore be most grateful if you would complete the form overleaf and return it to me. Please contact Lorraine Holcombe (lholcombe@stanleygibbons.co.uk) if you would like to be emailed the questionnaire.

Very many thanks for your help.

Yours sincerely,

Hugh Jefferies,
Editor.

Questionnaire

2011 Cyprus, Gibraltar & Malta

1. Level of detail
   Do you feel that the level of detail in this catalogue is:
   a. too specialised ○
   b. about right ○
   c. inadequate ○

2. Frequency of issue
   How often would you purchase a new edition of this catalogue?
   a. Annually ○
   b. Every two years ○
   c. Every three to five years ○
   d. Less frequently ○

3. Design and Quality
   How would you describe the layout and appearance of this catalogue?
   a. Excellent ○
   b. Good ○
   c. Adequate ○
   d. Poor ○

4. How important to you are the prices given in the catalogue:
   a. Important ○
   b. Quite important ○
   c. Of little interest ○
   d. Of no interest ○

5. Would you be interested in an online version of this catalogue?
   a. Yes ○
   b. No ○

6. Do you like the new format?
   a. Yes ○
   b. No ○

7. What changes would you suggest to improve the catalogue? E.g. Which other indices would you like to see included?
   ....
   ....
   ....
   ....

8. Would you like to see this catalogue combined with the 'Western Pacific' catalogue?
   a. Yes ○
   b. No ○
   c. Other ○
   ....

9. Would you like us to let you know when the next edition of this catalogue is due to be published?
   a. Yes ○
   b. No ○
   If so please give your contact details below.
   Name: ....
   Address: ....
   ....
   ....
   ....
   Email: ....
   Telephone: ....

10. Which other Stanley Gibbons Catalogues are you interested in?
    a. ....
    b. ....
    c. ....

Many thanks for your comments.

Please complete and return it to: Hugh Jefferies (Catalogue Editor)
Stanley Gibbons Limited, 7 Parkside, Ringwood, Hampshire BH24 3SH, United Kingdom
or email: lholcombe@stanleygibbons.co.uk to request a soft copy

Cyprus, Gibraltar & Malta

From Stanley Gibbons, THE WORLD'S LARGEST STAMP STOCK

Priority order form – Four easy ways to order

Phone: 020 7836 8444 Overseas: +44 (0)20 7836 8444

Fax: 020 7557 4499 Overseas: +44 (0)20 7557 4499

Email: lmourne@stanleygibbons.co.uk

Post: Lesley Mourne, Stamp Mail Order Department, Stanley Gibbons Ltd, 399 Strand, London, WC2R 0LX, England

Customer Details

Account Number ....

Name ....

Address ....

....

Postcode .... Country ....

Email ....

Tel No. .... Fax No. ....

Payment details

Registered Postage & Packing £3.60

○ Please find my cheque/postal order enclosed for £..

Please make cheques payable to Stanley Gibbons Ltd.

Cheques must be in £ sterling and drawn on a UK bank

○ Please debit my credit card for £.. in full payment.

○ Mastercard ○ VISA ○ Diners ○ AMEX ○ Switch

Card Number

CVC Number Issue No (Switch)

Start Date (Switch & Amex) / Expiry Date /

Signature .... Date ....

Cyprus, Gibraltar & Malta

From Stanley Gibbons, THE WORLD'S LARGEST STAMP STOCK

Condition (mint/UM/used)	Country	SG No.	Description	Price	Office use only
			POSTAGE & PACKING	£3.60	
			GRAND TOTAL		

Minimum price. The minimum catalogue price quoted in 10p. For individual stamps, prices between 10p and 95p are provided as a guide for catalogue users. The lowest price charged for individual stamps or sets purchased from Stanley Gibbons Ltd is £1.

Please complete payment, name and address details overleaf